DIARIES

1942–1945

DIARIES

1942–1945

ANCESTRAL VOICES
&
PROPHESYING
PEACE

James Lees-Milne
1908 – 1997

JOHN MURRAY
Albemarle Street, London

First published by Chatto & Windus as
Ancestral Voices (1975) and
Prophesying Peace (1977)

Reprinted in 1995
by John Murray (Publishers) Ltd.,
50 Albemarle Street, London W1X 4BD

A catalogue record for this book is available from the British Library

ISBN 0-7195-5590 6

Typeset in 11½ pt Bembo by Servis Filmsetting Ltd,
Longsight, Manchester

Printed and bound in Great Britain by
The University Press, Cambridge

Contents

Introduction

Ancestral Voices was published twenty years ago, to be followed in quick succession by *Prophesying Peace*. The title of the first volume of diaries was taken from Coleridge's *Kubla Khan*. The well-known phrase related in my mind to the hereditary country-house owners with whom during the middle years of the Second World War I spent much time negotiating. The title of the second volume was a feeble parody of the first's continuance, because the years it covered foresaw the Allies' ultimate victory and the end of the terrible fighting.

Ancestral Voices was very much a trial balloon. I underwent some anguish lest I might be making a fool of myself by recording in print my jejune opinions and, worse still, by exposing the behaviour of certain friends and acquaintances to random obliquy – or even ridicule. For nothing, not charges of murder, theft, fraud, rape or illicit sex, is more wounding of a victim than mockery. Indeed when I began keeping a diary I never for an instant imagined it might one day be printed. I merely thought it might be possible to entertain my grand- or great-grandchildren-to-be with a day-by-day summary of a civilian's circumstances in wartime: how, what and where he ate, how much he paid for his bread and margarine, how he travelled, how he dealt with universal restrictions and how he was affected by bombs, blast and the prevailing beastliness of the whole process.

By 1942, when the diaries began, I was thirty-three, out of the Army and back at work with the National Trust.

Well, I have had no children, grand- or great-, upon whom to inflict my far from extraordinary experiences. But I had a friend in the late Norah Smallwood, in the 1970s joint chairman with Ian Parsons of Chatto & Windus. I submitted to her some extracts of my diaries of thirty years and more ago. She thought fit to publish them.

At the risk of boring the reader I had better explain that in 1936 I had been engaged as secretary to the Country Houses (to become the Historic Buildings) Committee of the National Trust. The preservation of England's historic houses, their architecture, treasures, gardens and parks was a new venture of the Trust. The committee which I served was distinguished and erudite. On the outbreak of war the venture went into cold storage. Country-house owners' minds and energies were absorbed by the war. Their houses, when not requisitioned for troops, schools, emergency hospitals and institutions, were put under dust-sheets. But by 1942 owners had a future of a sort to look to, yet how were they to cope with their massive piles and possessions in the brave new world ahead? They guessed that it would be heavily weighted against the squirearchical system and way of life which, until hostilities broke out, had endured for centuries. Already they were contending with high taxation, lack of domestic staff and the disesteem of the *Zeitgeist*. Several returned and many turned to the National Trust for a discussion, if not a solution, of their problems. This explains how I was largely occupied during the last years of the war and the immediate post-war years.

In 1942 the National Trust office was still installed at West Wycombe Park, Sir John and Lady Dashwood's ancestral seat in Buckinghamshire where it had, by their courtesy, moved shortly after the outbreak of the war. When I rejoined it the entire male staff consisted of the harassed secretary, Donald MacLeod Matheson, an extremely able but delicate man, and Eardley Knollys who had recently been taken on as his helper. Of the female staff two stalwart ladies had remained. The occasional teenage typist came and went. That was all.

My role involved a good deal of travelling, at first solely by train and foot, sometimes by bicycle, and latterly by a ramshackle National Trust motor. Nearly every train journey was fraught with misadventure. All were late; some did not reach their destination, and might come to a dead halt in a siding for the night. If a passenger was lucky he had a seat. If unlucky he squatted in the corridor. It was prudent always to carry a packet of biscuits and a hip flask.

J. L.–M.
1995

1942

West Wycombe Park is a singularly beautiful eighteenth-century house with one shortcoming. Its principal living-rooms face due north. The south front is overshadowed by a long, double colonnade which induces a total eclipse of the sun from January to December. Consequently we are very cold in the winter, for the radiators work fitfully these days. Our offices are in the Brown Drawing Room and Johnny Dashwood's[1] small study beyond it. Matheson, the Secretary, Miss Paterson, Eardley Knollys and I work in the latter room; Miss Ballachey, a typist and the 'junior' (aged 15) in the bigger room with all the filing cabinets. Matheson, Eardley and I are seldom in the office together. Nearly always one and often two of us are away visiting properties.

Monday, 5th January

Early this morning I set out on a short tour in the very old National Trust Austin, which belonged to Hilda Matheson until her recent death. Before I reached Princes Risborough the car practically stopped, and a rather delicious smell of rice pudding, accompanied by a curious knocking sound, came from its inside. I drew up at a garage and asked what could possibly be the matter. The garage man at once, and without any explanations from me, said, 'You've got no water in the radiator.' I was humiliated. I am constantly being humiliated.

I arrived at Althorp [Northamptonshire] more than half an hour late. Lord Spencer was huffy at first because of my lateness, and because of the depreciation of Althorp by the agent whom the Trust had employed to make a report on his property. He understandably associated the Trust with the agent's ignorance and lack of taste. In the end I liked Lord Spencer for not being crosser than he was. He said I was the first National Trust person who had talked sense. Since he is not liberal in compliments I was flattered. Certainly I appreciated Althorp. But the difficulties will be infinite before we get it.

I stayed to luncheon – poached eggs with maize and cabbage – which we ate in a little panelled room to the right of the Wootton Hall. Lady Spencer, like a goddess, distilled charm and gentleness around her.

---

[1] Sir John Dashwood, 10th Bart. (1896–1966), the owner of West Wycombe house and park, created by Sir Francis Dashwood, 2nd Bart. (1708–81).

I continued to Haselbech for the night, where I found Aunt Con [Ismay] in her new cottage, which is too technological for words, being fitted from top to bottom with electrical gadgets. You press one button beside the bed, and a metal arm offers you a cigarette in a cardboard holder; another, and tea spouts from a tap into a cup; yet another and the mattress becomes as hot as St. Lawrence's gridiron. There was an arm-chair in my bedroom which, had I been able to find the lever, would have tossed me into the air like a pancake for the good of my liver. The whole room was a tangle of wires inadequately insulated. I was in terror of being electrocuted.

Tuesday, 6th January

After breakfast I left Aunt Con's loaded with provisions, and motored with the sun in my eyes straight to Finedon Hall. The windscreen was so splashed with thawing slush that I could barely see. At intervals I was obliged to stop and wipe the glass with a rag and spit.

Major Greaves lives alone in a cottage which he thinks wonderfully antique. It was built in 1850. He has two tusks, which I knew to be false because they moved up and down as he spoke, and no other teeth, which is very strange. He is mad about ecclesiology and has photographs of smiling choirboys about the house. He patted little boys on the head in the village. He would not get down to business – with me – in spite of my prompting. Finally I persuaded him to show me round the big house. It is interesting in being the childhood home of Digby Dolben, the poet school-friend of Robert Bridges. Dolben suffered from religious mania, walked about Eton in a monk's habit with a cord round his waist, robbed his schoolfellows of their breakfast rolls in order that they might go to Chapel fasting, and played truant from the Eton and Harrow cricket match by spending his long leave at a nunnery.

The colour of the ironstone of which Finedon Hall is built is the most beautiful imaginable, being a deep orange, sprinkled with a powdery grey film of lichen. The Hall, once Elizabethan, was dreadfully altered about 1850 and is not suitable for the Trust. It is unfurnished and at present houses Free French troops. They were most offhand and rude to the poor Major, who I could see was a great tribulation to them, constantly prowl-ing around and extolling his own property. They kept crabbing it in front of him. In the dining-room was a central stove, gothicky and of the period, connected with a flue under the floor. The grounds sad, the elm avenue disordered. The place neglected and pitiable, like the Major. I was not sorry to leave.

Went on at great speed to Bedford and branched off to look at Willington dovecote, a worth-while property. We must try and acquire the barn opposite, built at the same period as the dovecote, namely, Henry VIII, and also corbie-stepped. Bunyan's name is carved some-where, but I failed to find it. Continued to Potters Bar and Morven Park. Taken round by old Sanderson the donor. A terrible Victorian, yellow brick villa, and the property unworthy of us. We should never have accepted it.

Wednesday, 7th January

It is freezing hard. Filled the radiator with boiling water from a kettle. The car started at once. Motored straight to Hatfield. Stopped to look at the monument by Maximilian Colt of the 1st Lord Salisbury, James I's Lord Treasurer, holding his wand of office, and lying in full regalia on a cold marble slab upheld by four kneeling figures. Mrs. Esdaile[2] says the staff is the actual one he carried in life. Continued to Brocket and stopped opposite the iron gates erected by the present Lord Brocket[3] in memory of his father. Got out and walked across a stile and down a footpath to the James Paine bridge, which the Canadian troops have disfigured by cutting their names, with addresses in Canada, and personal numbers, all complete and inches deep – the vandals. Yet I thought what an interest-ing memorial this will be thought in years to come and quite traditional, like the German mercenaries' names scrawled in 1530 on the Palazzo Ducale in Urbino, and Byron's name on the temple at Sunium. Looked at Hudnall Common and Ivinghoe in dense fog, and saw nothing at all of Mr. Paradine's land that we contemplate purchasing. I might just as well have been blindfolded. Lunched at Tring off sandwiches and beer. Back at West Wycombe I found troops occupying the village and manoeuvres in progress. My bedroom commandeered for a brigadier. The Irish Guards are among the armoured brigade, for Kennedy, once my servant at Dover, saw me cross the road in the village and asked the estate office to ring me up. I went and talked to him and gave him 10/-. Was pleased he should wish to see me.

I forgot to write that yesterday after passing through Hitchin I noticed a little church dominating a hill on my left, and recollected St. Ippollitt's. I turned the car up the hill and got out to search for George Lloyd's[4] grave. On his deathbed he asked to be buried here. I found his grave huddled amongst ordinary parishioners', which I don't suppose he would have liked. There is no stone yet, but the grave is a double one, waiting

[2] Katharine Esdaile (1881–1950), leading authority on English post-Reformation sculpture and author of several books on the subject.
[3] 2nd Lord Brocket (1904–67).
[4] 1st Lord Lloyd of Dolobran (1879–1941), Governor of Bombay, High Commissioner in Egypt and Secretary of State for the Colonies 1940–1. J. L.-M. was his private secretary, 1931–5.

presumably for Blanche. Grass was already growing on it. I knew it to be
his from a card tied to some Christmas holly with 'To George from
Gwen' – his sister – written in fading violet ink. I stood over the grave
thinking of him for a quick moment, and left in a hurry, because it was
bitter cold. He would have done just the same in my place. Then I turned
back for a second and thought, how odd that that body which I had
known so well in its dapper Savile Row suits, that familiar body always
well groomed, was within a few yards of me and rotting below, in this
intense northern cold which he hated. Robert Byron[5] used to say he
never thought of his dead friends in connection with their decomposing
bodies, but I cannot help it. I suppose this signifies that I have too little
faith in the immortality of the spirit.

Saturday, 10th January

Although I had no prearranged plans I went to London this morning,
reaching Brooks's in time to lunch by myself. Keith Miller-Jones had
Claud Berkeley, a secretary in the War Cabinet, lunching with him. He
told Keith that whereas Chamberlain had been a brilliant chairman at
Cabinet meetings, Churchill was a bad one. His Cabinets were a muddle;
solutions to problems were arrived at not through logical discussions but
haphazard, intuitive guesses by Churchill himself. I can imagine the dissatisfaction of his colleagues.

Sunday, 11th January

I am enjoying *Aurora Leigh* as a reflection of mid-Victorian life and
manners, just as *Don Juan* quite apart from Byron's poetry and wit, is a
reflection of Regency manners. I think I may read several long poems as
I would novels.

Found Eddy[6] at tea and Lady Colefax[7] who is staying. Lady Colefax
dressed in thick blue tweed. She must have been pretty once. Her face is
now like an intelligent pug's, or a dolphin's. I felt she might snub me if I
said something ingenuous, whereas she would not snub Eddy, whatever
he might say.

After dinner Lady Colefax talked of Uppark [Sussex] and the wonderful Queen Anne dolls' house there, fitted with every detail. Eddy said
that if sold it would fetch as much as £30,000. Lady Colefax explained
how Lady Meade-Fetherstonhaugh repairs all the original curtains and
hangings, bed covers, etc. at Uppark by a device of her own. She has a

---

[5] Robert Byron (1905–41), traveller, art critic and writer.
[6] Hon. Edward Sackville-West, later 5th Lord Sackville (1901–65), novelist, critic, and musician.
[7] Sibyl, widow of Sir Arthur Colefax, political and literary hostess.

huge rack the size of a billiard table upon which each damask thread is picked off and put on to a new backing. Then she washes the old fabrics in a concoction made from the herb *saponaria*, which grows in the park. It gives renewed life to the fabrics.

Monday, 12th January

It is freezing hard and the park is covered with rime. Helen[8] elects to come to London for the free lift, and plumps herself in the front seat by me so that poor Miss Paterson is obliged to sit in the back seat in the cold. All goes well and the two committees, though dull, pass uneventfully. Lord Zetland,[9] the Trust's chairman, is wry, starchy and pedagogic as usual: Lord Esher,[10] like a dormouse, small, hunched, quizzical, sharp and cynical: Ronnie Norman,[11] the eternal handsome schoolboy, noisily loquacious until he finds the conclusion to an argument, when he stops like an unwound clock: Nigel Bond,[12] dry, earthy, sound, unimaginative: Sir Edgar Bonham-Carter,[13] twisted by arthritis, fair, impartial, but too subdued to be heeded by the others: Mr. Horne, the old, sweet-sour yet genial solicitor, who has sat in attendance these forty-odd years ever since, as an articled clerk, he helped draft the constitution of the National Trust in 1895. But now he is a little beyond his prime, and he havers.

Thursday, 15th January

Eardley said that at dinner the other night in London a mutual friend commented upon Eddy's fondness for Helen. Harold[14] said, 'Yes, but the parasite feels lovingly towards its protector,' or words to that effect. The other replied, 'But the ivy clings rather to the oak than to the holly.'

I go to London after tea in order to start off early on my National Trust expedition the following morning.

At Cheyne Walk Di[15] confides that she may be going to have an infant. Obviously she is pleased by the prospect, and I think it is a very good thing and tell her so, especially now that Patrick is going abroad. She complains that she has not yet felt sick, and lack of this sure sign worries her. She has been looking after old Princess Helena Victoria while

---

[8] Helen, wife of Sir John Dashwood.
[9] 2nd Marquess of Zetland (1876–1961), Secretary of State for India, 1935–40. Chairman of National Trust's Executive Committee, 1931–45.
[10] Oliver, 3rd Viscount Esher (1881–1963), Chairman of National Trust's Finance and Country Houses Committees; and Chairman of the Society for the Protection of Ancient Buildings.
[11] R. C. Norman (1873–1963), Vice-Chairman of National Trust, 1924–48. Chairman of L.C.C. 1918–19.
[12] Nigel Bond (1877–1945), Secretary of National Trust, 1901–11.
[13] Sir Edgar Bonham-Carter (1870–1956), jurist and administrator.
[14] Hon. (later Sir) Harold Nicolson (1886–1968), diplomat, M.P., and well-known author.
[15] Diona (née Stewart-Jones), Mrs. Patrick Murray. J. L.-M. frequently stayed with the Stewart-Jones family in 97 Cheyne Walk, Chelsea.

Catherine Fordham[16] is having a holiday. Di already loves the old lady. When they go out shopping the princess produces a large gold chain-bag full of sixpences. These she doles out to Di in the taxi and works out the day's expenses as they drive along. She will herself hail taxis while Di is endeavouring to look for one so that frequently they have several bespoken at the same time. She does not like shops to be forewarned, yet does not relish no attentions being paid her.

Friday, 16th January

I set off for East Sheen to walk across Sheen Common. This is a worth-while property for it rounds off one corner of Richmond Common. Though the ground is fairly deep under snow I pad across it between birch trees and over heath. I try to find a way into Richmond Park, but the military have commandeered the whole of it, and there is no ingress whatever. So I walk miles round by Mount Clare, which cannot be seen from the road, and across Putney Heath, today quite beautiful and shim-mering under the snow. Before Wimbledon I take a bus into Ewell. There I inspect Hatch Furlong, a wretched property, now a cabbage patch on either side of an arterial road, and surrounded by ribbon development. I lunch with Midi[17] at Ashtead House, the Gascoignes', her in-laws. Lady Gascoigne resembles a cow accustomed to all weathers, with the kindly, rough manners of one.

Before dinner I had a drink with David Lloyd[18] at the Turf. He has the fidgety charm of his father whom he resembles more noticeably now that his father is dead. David adores his memory and regards me, I think, as a small fraction of that memory, as someone who enjoyed his father's con-fidence. He thinks that in some respects I knew his father better than he did and because of this envies me without resentment, for he has a gen-erous nature.

Saturday, 17th January

In the morning to the William Nicholson and Jack Yeats exhibition at the National Gallery. Yeats all purples and yellows, frankly vulgar, but dashing and virile. I cared most for his early pictures in monochrome. William Nicholson is surely a very good English artist, deep-rooted, sure. *The Hundred Jugs* I call a confident, scholarly work.

I lunch alone hurriedly at Brooks's. I have a word with General Pope-Hennessy. From his slowness of speech and the particulars he gives of his last 'turn' I imagine he must have had a stroke.

---

[16] Married November 1942 Major-General Sir John Kennedy (1893–1970).
[17] Hon. Mary O'Neill, wife of Derek Gascoigne, a son of General Sir Frederick Gascoigne.
[18] 2nd Lord Lloyd of Dolobran.

I arrive by bus at Leckhampstead House which Mrs. Stewart-Jones has just bought on the Berkshire downs. It is tea-time. The household is very cheerful, domestic and welcoming after the cold outside. The dove is cooing, the lamps are bright, the toast is thick and the tea steams.

Reginald Blunt[19] is living here. He is a dear old man, courteous and cultivated. He is 85, very independent, and with all his wits about him. I talked to him about the Carlyles. He even remembers Mrs. Carlyle, who died in 1866. He used to take a jug of milk from the rectory cow to them each day, and in the proper season mulberries from the rectory garden. One morning Mrs. Carlyle received the mulberries from him at the door of 24 Cheyne Row and said, 'Wait! Mr. Carlyle has a present for you.' She shouted up the stairs, 'Thomas! Thomas!' Presently Carlyle descended in his long dressing-gown, with a rosy apple on a plate. Reginald Blunt was terribly disappointed that the apple on the plate was made of china; but he has it to this day. He knew Rossetti, who used to play whist at the rectory. His language was appalling. The following day he would write a letter to the rector, Blunt's father, apologizing for his swear words.

Blunt is in favour of absolutely rebuilding Chelsea Old Church,[20] though not of absolutely rebuilding on principle. I agree with him. So apparently do Raby and Walter Godfrey, judging from a letter to Blunt from the latter.

Sunday, 18th January

In the afternoon I bicycle to look at Woolley Park, now taken over by the Admiralty. A terrible house, allegedly built on the site of a shooting box of King John's, with only a vestige of the eighteenth century in the central stairwell, where there is a trace of Wyattesque or Adamesque treatment, a frieze with rams' skulls. The bronze stair balusters are all right. The rest of the house is 1862, haphazard, bulky, inelegant and of no merit. There is a drawing-room with painted plaster wall and ceiling decoration of this date. The family furniture, stacked in the middle of the room under dust sheets, seems indifferent. The house will not do. The park looks derelict, the trees in need of attention.

It had snowed heavily the previous night and my ride without any wind was still and muffled. I got warm bicycling and enjoyed it.

Monday, 19th January

In the morning I bicycled to Farnborough Rectory to see Mr. Puxley, the father of Michael Wroughton, the owner of Woolley. I told him all I

---

[19] Reginald Blunt (1857–1944), Chelsea historian.
[20] Very severely damaged in a blitz.

thought I should but purposely left things vague, for the National Trust can do nothing about the house, although the estate of 4,000 acres covers some very splendid downland. Mr. Puxley sold 6,000 acres for his son before he came of age. The son inherited Woolley from his maternal uncle. In Chaddleworth church are many memorials to the Wroughtons.

Farnborough Rectory is most attractive with its small central gablet, red brick symmetrical façade and sash windows. I don't know what its date is, but suppose mid-seventeenth century, with mid-eighteenth-century alterations. An enchanting little house.

Saturday, 24th January

Nancy[21] [Mitford], who is now living at West Wycombe, is mad about the Antarctic Expedition and has collected every book about it she can lay her hands on.

I went up to London with Helen this morning for David Lloyd's wedding. Met Midi at her new club, a fantastic institution of which all the members are M.F.H.s and their wives. We at once decided we were too poor to eat there and must go to a pub. Could not find one, but instead found Claridge's. Midi directed me to the 'Causerie' where she said there was lovely hors d'oeuvre with wine, as much as you liked thrown in, all for 4/-. There was chicken on the menu too and since it was thrown in with my Madeira, we ate it too. After all that the bill came to 18/-.

Sunday, 25th January

Went to Mass at Cheyne Row held in the vestry for warmth. Afterwards to Carlyle's house and sat in the kitchen talking to the Strongs. The Strong family have now been caretaking for a longer period than Carlyle lived in the house; and Mr. Strong's mother worked for Carlyle. There is nothing Mrs. Strong does not know about the Carlyle ménage, and anyone writing on the subject could not do better than glean from her. When I arrived she was very pleased to see me, but rushed down-stairs to fetch her teeth before she would let me in. I then went to Brooks's. I stood by the fire in the hall talking to Ran Antrim. We over-heard Lord Trenchard saying to Lord Mottistone, 'I don't see how the Japanese can hold out much longer now.' Ran Antrim was appalled, and asked in wonder what could be the mentality of these two old war horses.

After luncheon I bussed to the Brompton Cemetery to look for the grave of Mrs. Duff, a late benefactress of the National Trust. I had

---

[21] Hon. Nancy Mitford (1904–73), married to Hon. Peter Rodd. Novelist and biographer.

discovered that a condition of our receiving a small legacy from her was that we should see her grave was kept in order. It appears that all these years no one of us has ever bothered even to look for it. I could not find it, for the Registry was closed. Returned and read in the club a book of letters edited by Charles Milnes-Gaskell of his great-grandfather while at Eton. The bullying in Dr. Keate's day was horrifying. Also read a short book by Reginald Blunt on the Carlyle household. Eddie Marsh sat reading beside me but did not speak to me. He merely smiled. This is very civilized club behaviour.

Monday, 26th January

Left earlyish for the Brompton Cemetery again. The coldest day I remember being out in. Biting east wind; and I had not got my fur coat on. Was told approximately where the grave was. After a lot of searching I found a double grave to some Duffs which I supposed to be the one, but now doubt if it was the right one. It seemed in fair order although neighbouring graves had been considerably disturbed by a recent bomb. One mausoleum was totally destroyed, and the doors of others were wrenched off so that the coffins on ledges were exposed. When I see such things I am more and more determined to be cremated. The sour look of these coffins and their rusted handles! I must always peer at them, horribly fascinated.

Then off to Leatherhead, reading on the way Cherry-Garrard's *Worst Journey in the World*. I found Fetcham Holt, the villa which belongs to us and is to be sold after the war. Most of the contents have already been disposed of, but I took away with me a framed watercolour of a Rowlandson sort and one sepia wash landscape in a maple frame to show to Paul Oppé.[22] The Merediths who rent the house from the National Trust very cordial and grateful for our £100. I investigated their row of birch trees separating them from the next-door villa and called on the next-door people. The wife was clamorous and vulgar. She demanded the lot to be cut down because they took the sun from their kitchen garden. Talked of digging for victory, etc. All rot I thought, for the birches were planted long before their beastly house was built, and besides I could see no sign of a kitchen garden at all.

Tuesday, 27th January

Nancy at luncheon: 'I said to myself, "in the bloodiest war in all history it's no good being squeamish over one wounded moorhen". So I shut my eyes and twisted its neck.' Spot had mauled it.

---

[22] Paul Oppé (1878–1957), collector, and expert in English water-colours.

Wednesday, 28th January

Went up to London to the dentist. Finished Cherry-Garrard's book in the train. His terrible descriptions of the cold affected me physically. They made me feel far colder than I actually was, so that I shivered all through luncheon at Brooks's, and by the time I arrived at the dentist's, felt sick. After he had finished with me, I was sick. On recovery I walked to Heywood Hill's bookshop. There was a strange bearded man wearing a brown fustian cloak and dictating a letter to Heywood at his typewriter. Anne[23] whispered mysteriously, 'He is the claimant to the throne of Poland.' But there hasn't been a Polish throne since the eighteenth century.

In the club I saw Tom [Mitford],[24] looking extremely wan and absent. He says he may not be going to the East after all; and he much wants to.

Walked across St. James's Park to Westminster and looked at Archer's baroque church in Smith Square. It is completely gutted by fire. Jamesey Pope-Hennessy[25] and I went over it the first winter of the war, and I recollect dragging him reluctantly inside on the plea that it would probably be destroyed. The shell is intact and with a little trained ivy would make a fine Piranesi ruin. Had tea with Lady Colefax in 19 Lord North Street. These are cosy little houses. She was sitting on a stool right in front of the fire so that the room was made distinctly chilly by her acting as a fire screen. There were tea things on a small table beside her. Bogey Harris, whose significance I am unaware of, came in soon after me. Lady Colefax talked of Aunt Jean Hamilton and expressed disappointment with Sir Ian's[26] *Memoir.* It failed to convey the peculiar magic of Jean. We talked of Stratford-on-Avon, led there by mention of Marie Corelli. I said I remembered her well like a plump, superannuated Nell Gwynne, her bosoms lolloping over the plush edge of a box in the old theatre, sparkling with diamonds (or crystals?) and swathed in ivory satin. I remember black curls enveloping a great grinning outline. Lady Colefax is, I should say, not malicious, only extremely curious, with a hunter's instinct for lions. Hers is a scientific sort of snobbery. She is evidently hell-bent on collecting scalps, and impatient with anything that may deflect her from the chase. Although well born she has had to push her way into circles that ordinarily would not have lain open to her. When I left she told me to

---

[23] Lady Anne Gathorne-Hardy, wife of Heywood Hill, owner of the bookshop in Curzon Street which was, and is, a meeting place of writers and friends.
[24] Hon. T. D. Freeman-Mitford (1909–45), only son of 2nd Lord Redesdale. J. L.-M.'s oldest friend. Killed in the Far East on active service.
[25] James Pope-Hennessy (1916–74), biographer. Murdered in 1974.
[26] General Sir Ian Hamilton (1853–1947) of Dardanelles fame. His wife was Jean, daughter of Sir John Muir, 1st Bart. She died 1941.

come again. I said perhaps I would see her at West Wycombe. She said, 'No, here I hope.'

The nice thing about her is that she is totally without ostentation. Because she is quite poor and inhabits a small house this is not allowed to interfere with her mode of living. She gets people just the same, and since she cannot give large parties at her own expense, she now expects people to dine with her at the Dorchester and pay for themselves. In other words it is interesting people she cares about, individuals and not society with a large S. Her friends ring her up about people as one might ring up Selfridges' Information Bureau. Mr. Harris said, 'By the way, Sibyl, I have been meaning to ask you, who is Mrs. Benthall, the mother of Sir Somebody Benthall?' 'Mrs. Benthall, *Mrs.* Benthall,' she repeated with emphasis upon the Mrs. as though that non-title were extraordinary, 'I am afraid I really can't help you there,' in quite an agitated tone. Even Selfridge's can be stumped at times.

Nancy said that Bogey Harris was an old crony of Lady Cunard, noted for his wit, when he deigned to give an exhibition of it.

Sunday, 1st February

After Mass went to Paul Oppé's through deep snow and falling flakes with my two National Trust pictures. He was delighted with them and pronounced the Rowlandsonish one to be charming and interesting. Said it was better than amateurish, but could not tell by whom. As a matter of fact it *is* amateurish when you look carefully at it. He dates it about 1790 by the *vis-à-vis* in the picture, which was first introduced to the smart world in 1783. The scene depicted is obviously not of the smart world but the suburban world. The other he at once recognized as by William Payne. Neither of them the least valuable, the former worth about 8 guineas, the latter 2 or 3. He showed me his book on Rowlandson and told me a lot I did not know. Very friendly and helpful.

After tea went to see the Rosses[27] for a few minutes. They are going to Ireland tonight. I could not get a taxi and so missed my bus to High Wycombe. They let me stay the night at Eaton Terrace after they had gone. Michael looking very well and Anne most affectionate and sweet. They took me to Prince Vsevolode [of Russia] and Mamie's for a drink before they left for Euston. The Prince is very ugly and surely rather dull. She, still beautiful, is called Princess Romanovsky-Pavlovsky, (a stage joke name) because she is a morganatic wife. Had gin and peppermint to drink, not very nice. Mamie does all her own housework.

---

27 The Earl and Countess of Rosse.

He is fifth in succession to the throne of Russia; and his succession is about as unlikely as the uncrowned King of Poland's.

To bed early, worn out, because I sat with Rick[28] [Stewart-Jones] until 2.30 a.m. last night. He suddenly turned up. He is sick of having been drilled and drilled for 2¼ years and believes he really will soon be sent to an Octu. About time too. Although I forget his very existence during prolonged absences, I find after ten minutes talk he is the only person to whom I can say just everything. His advice on all topics is invariably sound. His integrity lies deep down, his humour perpetually bubbles on the surface.

Thursday, 5th February

A horrid day in London. Cold intense, and a bitter wind blowing nasty wet snow – nice snow is dry – in one's face. I was extravagant and to console myself deliberately spent £3. Hailed a taxi at Marylebone, for as usual the train was late on arrival, and drove to *The Times'* Book Club to buy Dudley Ryder's *Diaries 1715–16;* and on to Claridge's 'Causerie'. Waited quite a bit and got a table to myself; had a delicious hors d'oeuvre mountain on one plate and some coffee for 5/-. Then taxied to the S.P.A.B.[29] office in Great Ormond Street. It is almost the only building left standing in this devastated area. All around, where whole squares and streets of houses existed a short time ago, are now empty blankets of snow. The meeting had already begun, with Lord Esher in the chair. They were discussing an invitation, received from I think the Lord Justice Scott Committee, for the S.P.A.B., Georgian Group and London Society to send representatives to list old buildings in London which they consider should not at any cost be sacrificed to post-war improvements: for instance, the Mansion House's future is threatened – George Dance! Our committee struck me after my long absence as a body of serious men facing up to their responsibilities. This is entirely owing to Esher now attending committee meetings as chairman, a thing he used not to do, but left to a vice-chairman.

The chief item on the agenda was Holland House. William Weir has made a detailed report on the condition of the house. He estimates that for £37,000 it can be rebuilt. It appears that the whole interior is gutted, and the staircase is rotting in the rain and snow. Everything else has gone except the walls, which in my opinion are no longer true Jacobean, for the windows, copings etc., were largely Victorianized. Others took the

---

[28] Married 1951 Emma Smith, novelist, and died 1957.
[29] Society for the Protection of Ancient Buildings founded by William Morris, Ruskin and others in the 1870s.

absurd view that this important house is once again pure Jacobean since the Victorianisms have been purged by the fire, which was the best thing that could have happened. I submitted that the chief point about Holland House was its historical associations, which have now gone for ever. Only Esher, Hiorns and I voted against its retention. Anyway the Ilchesters will never live in it again, if built up, and I feel sure the £37,000 will not be forthcoming after the war. The prospect of a twentieth-century Jacobean fake is worse than a Victorian Jacobean fake.

Friday, 6th February

Still perishingly cold and freezing hard. The drive coated with slippery ice. Dirty frozen snow is lying and even more snow falling today. We have had snow for a month now and since the New Year the weather has been most severe. Mercifully West Wycombe is a bit warmer and my new room, the Adam Room at the top of the stairs on the first floor, one of the warmest in the house. It faces south on to the colonnade. I am very pleased with it. It is an elegant room, the walls papered with a stiff olive green and hung with picturesque oils of the house and surrounding views by Daniell I think, done just after the building of the house. It is luxurious and comfortable. Judged strictly as a work of art this house is indifferent; all the interior painted ceilings and the *grisaille* work on the walls are frankly bad. Yet the quality of the joinery is good. The general effect is charming.

Thank goodness I have at last finished Scott's lengthy journals of the polar expedition. There is no question that the man could write. I did not skip, not even the details of horse and dog management. Scott was a little bit of a poet and contriver. Nevertheless, instead of wanting to weep, I was irritated by his dramatization of the end of the story. His letters are too carefully heroic. What an unattractive, schoolmastery fellow. His sense of decency and duty hideous, and almost embarrassing. He was not at all unlike his successor Lord Kennet, who is smug, superior and conde-scending. I don't believe Kathleen Kennet[30] was ever much in love with Scott. I finished Leigh Hunt's autobiography tonight in bed. Hunt is a boring writer, though a nice man. He admits he was a vulgar snob when a young man. Endearing. He was unheroic.

I see that Beaverbrook is the new Minister of Production. Lady Lindsell[31] was saying in London on Sunday how much her husband, Sir Wilfred the General, loathed the Beaver, and loathed working with him.

---

[30] Kathleen (*d.* 1947), wife of 1st Lord Kennet and widow of Captain R. F. Scott (*d.* 1912) of the Antarctic. Sculptor.
[31] She was an aunt of the Stewart-Jones brothers and sisters.

He would override the generals, give way to passions of temper and neglect detail, thus incurring a multitude of small mistakes. Not unlike Churchill in these respects. But these men are dictators and we are becoming rapidly nazified, let us face it.

Sunday, 8th February

Still freezing hard and the drive desperately dangerous and slippery. Eddy is here again, and Cecil Beaton came last night. He is quite grey, and darts like a bird. He is flagrantly twentyish. He must be very successful if money-making is an indication. I do not mean to be critical for he is an artist. Jamesey likes him and I find him very sympathetic though a little alarming. This morning on my return from Mass at High Wycombe I gave him an hour's typewriting lesson; and made him use all his fingers too. He showed promise. Towards the end we started gossiping, and then I saw how entertaining and sharp he is.

I much dislike the High Wycombe church. It is ugly and always so full I have difficulty in squeezing a way in; but this morning for the first time I warmed up to something approaching devoutness. That was because I took my missal, followed the Latin and pondered over the beautiful succinctness of each word, so carefullly, blessedly placed. In spite of the recollection of Nancy's blasphemous witticisms about 'munching' and 'munchers' nothing disturbed my devotions. I have not been to confession since the cave days under the Dover cliffs with my regiment. Bad.

Yesterday's luncheon revealed Helen in a new light, for the curate and his old mother came. H. said to us just before they arrived that there must be no witticisms and no house-party talk. I took this well from her for it is the sort of thing Mama would say. They were indeed an eminently 'bedint'[32] couple, and H. said so poor that they undoubtedly hadn't enough to eat. The mother was sadly dressed for the terrible cold, was most humble and pathetic. Yet the two were proud in their reciprocal love. He was a facetious young man, with black, dusty hair badly cut, and a blue blotchy face. He wore a long, black cutaway coat. Eddy disliked him intensely and said he had aspirations to muscular Christianity, and with little encouragement would have been coarse, if thereby he could have impressed a sophisticated house-party with his broadmindedness; that he was the very worst type of C. of E. clergyman. But he was far too pathetic to be dislikeable. Helen made great efforts to entertain them, and induce them to have a square meal. Alas, they were far too genteel to be pressed to second helpings.

---

[32] A Sackville-Nicolson expression, meaning 'second-rate'.

During a walk I asked Eddy if he would marry. He said that he never could, for how was he to find a woman prepared to undertake the role of nanny, housekeeper and hospital-nurse combined; that he [heir to Knole] had nothing to offer in return. He started denigrating himself in all sincerity. When I expostulated he replied naively, 'It's true of course that I am a very clever man.'

After dinner I took up my knitting – 'the true sock' Clementine [Beit] calls it, which on St. Milne's Day, instead of liquefying, will unravel if there is to be a good harvest. Cecil had hiccoughs he laughed so much. Eddy took up his knitting, an endless khaki scarf. We were sitting side by side on a pair of upright Chinese Chippendale chairs before the fire, Eddy wearing his blue cloak with silver buckles, and his red velvet waist-coat with the Sackville coachman's gold livery buttons. I suppose we were an odd spectacle. Still, I wish Helen would not call us the two old bombed houses.

We talked about beautiful women, and it was interesting to listen to Cecil on the subject. He depreciated Tilly Losch, and said Diana Cooper was probably the most beautiful woman he had photographed. Lady Goonie Churchill, that divine, mysterious, sphinx-like creature looked, he said, like a cream bun. Of Sarah Churchill, Vic Oliver's wife, 'Perhaps I should not tell tales out of school, but if her nose were only her own.' 'Well, whose is it?' Nancy asked. 'Gillies's,'[33] he said.

Monday, 9th February

The thaw has at last set in. Eddy and Cecil sat in the back of the National Trust car with a cabin trunk between them and a magnolia tree Cecil had been given. I dropped them in Chester Square. Cecil was telling Eddy that he did not touch up his photographs himself, but directed how each should be done. Special experts with very fine pencils spend hours on the negatives. No wonder he charges £50 for a sitting. He asked Eddy to sit for him with a walking stick.

After the Finance Committee Mr. Bond invited me to lunch with him at the Travellers'. We walked there. He was extremely friendly but upset me by saying that Esher was writing to poor Eardley that the Trust could not employ him any longer. When I remarked that I sometimes won-dered whether there would be a niche for me in the National Trust after the war he said, 'You do not know the nice things they always say about you.' We ate gnocchi and mashed potatoes, sultana roll and coffee. Nigel Bond is a dear old boy. He was the first secretary of the National Trust, in the last century I think.

---

[33] The eminent surgeon.

Friday, 13th February

Today is Friday 13th and we hear the news of the three German battleships escaping from Brest and, worse still, from our fleet by slinking up
the Channel and through the Straits. It is the greatest sea disaster in some
ways since the Dutch sailed up the Medway; and I hope to God there is
no more glossing over it, but that enquiries are made and pursued. The
English are sick of bad news being twisted to resemble good.

Saturday, 14th February

Wickhamford. Walk with Deenie [Doreen Cuninghame, my mother's
widowed sister] in the afternoon to the Sandys Arms and talk with
Maggie in her back room which smells of dusty plush and stale cheese,
little Maggie with cheeks like the shiny crust of a cottage loaf, and a knot
of hair on the top of her head like the twist of a loaf. She is big with the
child to be born in April and heartily disgruntled by the prospect. 'Oh,
Master Jim, I could kill that there Bert [husband] for what he's done to
me – and at such a time too [the escape of the 3 German battleships].' I
could also readily kill Bert for having taken away Maggie from us in the
first place.

Sunday, 15th February

This morning after breakfast Haines and I took ten minutes thawing with
a warm sponge the film of ice upon the Austin's windscreen. There were
15 degrees of frost last night and almost as many the night before.

    After Mass in Broadway, during which I made plans instead of listen-
ing to the Archbishop's pastoral letter, which read like a legal document
without punctuation, I motored to Hayles Abbey. Looked inside the tiny
parish church. It is a gem, utterly unspoilt. Paved floor with medieval tiles
from the abbey, un-stripped plaster walls with a deal of stencil work. Oak
pews and oak Jacobean pulpit. Minute chancel with benches facing
inwards. In this space there must once have stood an altar table, east to
westwards. Some fifteenth-century glass panels in the east window
placed there by old Andrews of Toddington, having formerly been taken
to Toddington by a Lord Sudeley from the abbey. They are now home
again.

    I walked round the abbey. How I wish we could dispense with the
museum like a hideous yellow squash court. It needs brushing out and
there are flies under the glass cases. The paths need weeding and the grass
cutting back. The restoration by the Office of Works of part of the cloisters is quite disgusting, all cement with carefully interspaced stone
coping like a suburban rockery. Nevertheless there is still an atmosphere

of sanctity about the abbey, and it is moving to read the lead plaque on the ground, 'Here Richard Earl of Cornwall lies buried.' I wonder where they chucked the Holy Blood of Hayles, so deeply venerated by generations of pilgrims. Did some rare and celestial flower grow upon the spot? And does it still?

I stopped at Didbrook and found the old priest Allen at home – after many years. In 1929 Johnnie Churchill and I were here. He has not altered a bit, is just as vague and forgetful of all names. He laughs and sucks through his false teeth a spate of saliva as of old. I returned by Stanway. Stopped the car just to gloat upon the gatehouse and the gabled front of the house. With the yellow church this group is the most romantic, most moving thing I know. It stirs within me my deep, deep love, stiffly coagulated at times, for England. Nothing whatever inside the church.

Monday, 16th February

Off at at 10 o'clock on a sort of tour, taking Deenie and Mama with me.

Went straight to Bewdley, to Dowles Manor, where I went in and talked to Mr. Elliott. Very frail and ill with rheumatism, he spoke of dying shortly and wants the National Trust to have the house and twenty acres of the valley as soon as he can get the consent of his elder daughter now in Ceylon. This may take six months or more. A complete picture postcard house, olde worlde black and white, the outside almost ridiculous. Mama at once said, 'What a dream! What a heavenly little house!' Certainly the stencilling inside is remarkable. It is of the date of the house, *circa* 1570 and covers both beams and plaster panels. On this account alone the building is important. So too is the mouth of this valley and the fact of its practically adjoining our Knowles Mill property. Walked by the trout brook to the mill and talked to the woodman's wife. Lovely rustling walk beside the water under trees.

Mr. Elliott said he was almost sure one room's panelling came out of Ribbesford [House]. Another room's panelling he bought for a song from the old Angel Inn, Bewdley. He has a fireback of the Herbert of Cherbury arms and coronet which is a cast from the one we have in the hall at Wickhamford. Papa allowed him to have the cast made many years ago. He asked why on earth we left the overmantel and other oak panelling at Ribbesford, which Grandfather brought from Crompton Hall. Why indeed? The overmantel was part of a superb four-poster at Crompton.

On to Harvington Hall where a garrulous caretaker took us round. Mama and Deenie delighted with this house too, and the secret hiding holes. Bad restoration work here, and the National Trust furniture very indifferent.

Tuesday, 17th February

Dined with Harold Nicolson and Jamesey at Rule's. Harold talked much about Byron. The conversation arose from the present Jamesey brought Harold of a posthumous print of the boy Byron (bald at the temples!) reclining on a tomb in Harrow churchyard. Jamesey is always bringing suitable offerings like this, and H. was delighted. We discussed Byron's sex life of course. Lady Byron is said to have recorded in her diary that when she once told Byron he could not share her bed because she had the 'curse', Byron replied, 'Oh, that's all right! I can now sleep with Augusta.' Sounds improbable to me – I mean Lady Byron recording it. In Hobhouse's copy of Moore's *Life of Byron,* which Harold possesses, Hobhouse has pencilled in the margin that Lord Holland told him the reason why Lady Byron left her husband was that Byron attempted to bugger her; that Augusta was not the cause. Harold attributes the incest boasting to one of Byron's subconscious getting-his-own-backs on Augusta, who when he was a boy was much his senior in social sophistication. For it was Augusta who schooled Byron how to speak of 'Lady Jersey', not 'the Countess of Jersey', etc., and how to behave in London drawing-rooms – indeed who taught him correct manners which Byron was supremely backward in acquiring, if he ever properly acquired them, owing to Mrs. Byron's slipshod and provincial upbringing of her son. As late as 1823 Lady Blessington laughed at Byron's antiquated dandy airs and graces, and the pretentious bed he slept in under the Byron coronet, crest and motto.

Again in Hobhouse's copy, where Moore gives a highfalutin poetical reason for Byron's desire to be left alone in Greece, without Hobhouse's presence, a caustic marginal note gives the true reason. It was quite simply that Byron did not want another English gentleman, even his best friend, to witness his sexual aberrations, which were – in Hobhouse's words – a disgrace to his class and country. Harold has read a letter from Pietro Gamba, written in Italian after Byron's death, to Hobhouse as one of the executors, explaining the disappearance of some £300 from Byron's bedside at Missolonghi. Byron instructed Gamba to give it all to Luca Kalandrinos, the boy peasant with whom he was much in love at the time. This peasant, when an old man, used to meet once a year a Miss Hancock, the young niece of Charles Hancock an attorney, or banker, who became a friend of Byron in Greece and advanced him money. The old peasant had a fantastic suit of clothes which he claimed had belonged to Byron and of which he was inordinately proud. He used to wear it only on this anniversary. Years later Harold sent a drawing of the suit Byron was known to have worn at the very end of his life to Miss

Hancock, then a very old lady. This was in the 1920s when Harold was writing his Byron book. She replied that the clothes in the drawing exactly resembled the clothes she remembered Kalandrinos wearing. Harold immediately wrote again from England begging her to go to Kalandrinos's village, to try and find the cherished suit. Unfortunately his letter was returned undelivered for Miss Hancock had died in the meanwhile.

Harold spoke of Byron's lasting love for his school-friend, Lord Clare, and their dramatic meeting in Italy; of Shelley's reference to the concubines and catamites in the Palazzo Lanfranchi in Pisa. After the failure of Harold's delegation in 1924 to persuade the Dean and Chapter of Westminster Abbey to allow a bust of Byron to be erected in Poets' Corner, owing to Byron's flouting the marital rules of the Church, Harold walked away from the abbey and across the park with Lord Ernle. Harold said, 'I suppose the Dean and Chapter were, according to their rights, justified in refusing?' Lord Ernle who always denied in print the Augusta scandal, replied, 'Of course they were right, but they might have overlooked it.'

Sir Edmund Gosse told Harold that the Dorchester papers were destroyed on his recommendation. Gosse said to him, 'If I had been a little older at the time, I would have had copies kept.' Harold disliked Gosse very much.

It was my fault that we got on to politics. Jamesey and I always find ourselves in disagreement with Harold. H. upheld Churchill's speech in which he twisted the escape of the German battleships to our advantage. We walked in the pitch dark to have a glass of beer at the Charing Cross station bar. Then we parted.

Thursday, 19th February

Up to London again by the morning train. Found myself at a table next to Mr. Winant lunching with Lord Reith. I watched the American Ambassador closely. He is very dark, luminously so, very like portraits of Lincoln, and not untidily dressed as he is supposed always to be. Limpid black eyes, burning like coals, with black dashes of eyebrows beetling over them. Nervously passing his hand across his eyes and through his lanky hair. Smiling perpetually and knowingly. I liked the honest look of him but could not decide whether he were a stupid man or shrewd in spite of his gauche manners.

To my surprise Ralph Jarvis[34] walked into the dining-room. He drank coffee with me afterwards. He arrived from Portugal yesterday by air,

---

[34] Ralph Jarvis (1907–73), of Doddington Hall, Lincs. Merchant banker.

having had breakfast at Cintra only yesterday morning. He has been away a year, secretary in the Lisbon Embassy, having been extracted from the army for the purpose. He encouraged me to come out. Said he was sure there was lots to be done. You have to flatter, he says, the Portuguese vanity and indulge their sentimentality to get on with them. They are very friendly though some are pro-German through fear of communism, and because of German propaganda which is subtler than ours. There are two German professors at Coimbra University. The British Council representative, who is non-public school, suffers from an inferiority complex. He is engaged on the compilation of a history of pornography at this particular juncture of our affairs! Ralph says the British Council is not to be despised. It is the only place where the young Portuguese of both sexes may meet and the boys take out their girls. Very oriental in their treatment of women in their own orbit.

Walked to the Epstein exhibition at the Leicester Galleries. Jacob and the Angel in alabaster. Strong, ugly and vastly arresting. One is awed and repelled by the Jew. I was struck by the number and variety of people wrapt in contemplation. There is undoubtedly a growing interest in works of art among all sections. Other virile busts and flower paintings, always chrysanthemums. I would give my soul to be busted by Epstein, and then would probably be sick at the sight of the thing. Some Dod Procters in the other room – insipid breakfast trays and still lifes. Almost old-fashioned because so comprehensible.

I took the 4.10 from Euston to Manchester and arrived at 10, worn out by the journey. At the Midland Hotel ordered supper, very expensive, about 10/-, of chill soup, golden plover with wet swimmy veg. presented on one plate, and coffee. Extraordinary people in the hotel, peroxide blondes decked with false gems, and middle-aged men with their ears sunk into the fat of their necks and the wire bridges of their specs into their noses. Rolls of skin over their collars.

Friday, 20th February

Telephoned to the District Bank to fix my appointment with them. Paid my hotel bill and went to the bank at 10.15. Motored with one of the sub-managers to Ashton-under-Lyne and picked up a surveyor, a solicitor, another bank manager, and off we went to inspect Hen Cote cottage and Daisy Nook. Had been considerably put off by the names, but lo! the property was immensely worth while. Surrounded by Manchester, Oldham, Ashton, it is a blessed oasis. A deep gulley of some thirteen acres with a rushing yellow-backed burn through it. Much frequented by the inhabitants of these towns. There are wildish moors near by, and I decide it is just the sort of land the Trust should hold. My companions charming. Lancashire people are like children, friendly and warm, but inferiority-complexy about people from the south, which is so strange. They are always talking of Lancashire qualities, and seemed pleased when I told them that I derived from Lancashire, from these parts indeed. Worcestershire people never go on about Worcestershire qualities, I notice. We all drank tea in Hen Cote cottage, which is half-timbered, one-storeyed and peasanty. Our taxi driver came with us as a matter of course; was very communicative and kept spitting into the fire between his gulps of tea. I said, 'Don't put it out, chum. We need it.' Bitterly cold day, and a film of ice practically covering the burn.

Took only four hours in an express train back to London in order to dine with Jamesey. Had I not made this arrangement, I would have gone to see the cathedral in Manchester. Waited in Brooks's till 9, too late to get dinner there, and when Jamesey came he had no money. I was extremely tired by then, and cross. Walked to the Barcelona restaurant where we had to wait half an hour before we were served. A disappointing evening. Testily I tell J. he is becoming spoilt and too reliant upon his youthful charm. At once realize I make the mistake of admitting that he still has these qualities, not that he isn't perfectly well aware of them.

Saturday, 21st February

To Moss Bros. in the morning where I bought a maroon velvet smoking jacket for 8½ guineas and thirteen coupons. I still have a few coupons left till June.

Saw the Margaretha Trip portrait exhibited at the National Gallery, by Rembrandt, bought recently from Lord Crawford's collection. Looked at it a long while. The old lady reminds me of someone, I think old Mrs. Burgess of Farncombe, near Broadway. How ashamed I would be were Ben Nicolson to know that this is all I find to say about one of the world's great masterpieces.

At West Wycombe Sarah [Dashwood] had an 18th birthday weekend. After dinner we played telegrams. I could have been funny if I dared be vulgar, which one daren't be with the young. They of course allow themselves every licence.

Sunday, 22nd February

I cannot concentrate on sermons, however good. A kind young woman in front of me in church entertained a bored child by showing her pretty pictures of the Pope, Our Lord in colour from her missal, while the mother attended to her devotions. This unsolicited attention is the very height of saintliness. From High Wycombe I bussed to Bray Wick. Walked from there to Ockwells Manor.

I was last here in 1936. My host, Sir Edward Barry, now eighty-four, is as lively as ever. He has one servant. Sir Edward stokes the boiler himself each morning. The house is sadly dusty. We had a delicious English roast beef luncheon with Yorkshire pudding, not hard or spongey, but soft and melting. Rhubarb tart to follow. A gin and vermouth warmed me first of all. Today it is still bitterly cold and the ground frozen hard.

Sir Edward wants to sell. He owns 600 acres with a rental of £1,200 p.a. and is asking £75,000 because of the Ockwells glass and because an American millionaire offered him that figure ten years or more ago. He spurned Hill's offer from Mr. Cook[35] of £40,000. I fear I cannot help him unless he changes his tune. He took me round the house again. Although it is most important, it yet does not please. The herringbone nogging was taken out and replaced before he bought forty years ago. The hall is undoubtedly fine and just as when Nash drew it in the 1830s. The long oak table of two planks is longer than the Baddesley Clinton table Baron Ash has at Packwood. He showed me an early fourteenth-century chest with English Gothic carving on the front. Several Elizabethan portraits of the Scotts who formerly lived here. Much good oak furniture. Sir E. is 2nd baronet and Baron de Barry in Portugal, which is strange.

At tea at West Wycombe the Eshers present with Dick Girouard who is staying with them. Esher talked about Tuesday's meeting and I told him I had for the past five years thought, as he at last is coming to think, the Trust must not expect mighty high endowments from country house donors. We talked about colour blindness at tea. Lady Esher stated that every man who *was* a man was partially colour blind. We disputed this, and so it was put to the test. Lord Esher failed lamentably, so did Dick. I fear I didn't, for I pronounced the table-cloth to be egg blue. Whereupon Lady E. gave me a searching look. Helen, as though to affirm my virility in her guests' eyes, very kindly suggested that the cloth was sky blue.

Tuesday, 24th February

Packed all the relevant papers into my old black bag and caught the 9.06 from West Wycombe station to London for the Country Houses Committee meeting which I had to take by myself since Matheson is away ill, with a temperature of 104. Rather nervous how I was going to acquit myself this first time I have ever taken a meeting alone. But as a matter of fact all went fairly well. The old gentlemen are so fearfully ignorant of the intricacies of most items on the agenda that one need have little fear of them. Besides they one and all are *so* nice.

---

[35] Ernest Cook, a rich, eccentric recluse and great benefactor of the National Trust, to which he gave Montacute House and the Bath Assembly Rooms.

I had luncheon with old Mr. Horne at Stewart's afterwards. I suspect from things he let fall that he does not care for Matheson. He is in awe of him and M. snubs him, shouts at him and makes him feel dense. Now no one likes that sort of treatment, even when he is dense.

Went to see the income tax authorities. My hatred of them is so intense that I cannot be polite, which is unwise and stands me in no good stead. Then to the Leger Galleries to look at Dunlop's pictures. Several land-scapes like water-colour, but in fact tempera smeared on to the canvas with a palette knife. The still-lifes have more life in them than the land-scapes. I do not think he is an inspiring artist. In the next room were the works of a Welsh surrealist, C. Richards. He is a superb, confident drafts-man with keen sense of composition. I enjoyed several of his fantastic designs in the way that I enjoy Chelsea china cabbages and cauliflowers.

Already there is a wooden gate at the end of the drive at West Wycombe. The iron gates were requisitioned for scrap about a fortnight ago, two days only after Helen had the notice served on her. They were very indifferent ironwork, about fifty years old, and are no loss. Rather the contrary.

Saturday, 28th February

In considerable discomfort this week in the lumbar region as well as the leg. Today was the worst day so far, owing to a two-mile walk with Miss Paterson last night to the farm.

The weather is still bitterly cold, with a biting east wind. Snow lying on the slope by the north front. We haven't been without it or frosts since Christmas. One of the severest winters, apart from that of 1939–40, I can remember.

Eddy for the weekend, and not very well; and a certain Christopher Bramwell from the Foreign Office, about forty, hugely tall, shaped like a pear, and ungainly, but affable. Rebecca West and her husband came to luncheon. Rebecca West speaks in a high, rolling, not unaffected voice which somehow does not become her, and does not give a right indica-tion of her essentially masculine mind. She is handsome-plain, of big build, with uncouth legs and hands. And she is big enough to brush aside and defy all conventions that are a hindrance. Yet I get the impression that she has reached that comfortable stage of her career when few conven-tions are a hindrance. On the contrary she allows most conventions to enhance her established position. Nancy has arrived at this same stage, which is why she so often shocks me, accustomed as I still am to think of her running contrary to conventions in her old girlish, mocking manner. For example she said today, looking at me very seriously in the way people do when they know what they are about to say will meet

ANCESTRAL VOICES

26

with disagreement, 'It is clearly our duty to remain in England after the war, whatever the temptations to get out. The upper classes have derived more fun from living in this country since the last war than any other stratum of society in any other country in the world. No more foreign parts for *us*,' with a hiss on the last sibilant. Rebecca West seemed bewildered that we should all have been steeping ourselves in Antarctica, and when she rose to leave said she would write a short story about it.

The Beits[36] have got, in their newly rented house at Holmer Rise, a small portrait by Gainsborough of Madame Bacelli, dancing and holding with one hand a gauzy, flowered skirt with blue ribbons. She is an ugly horse-faced woman, who was the mistress of a Duke of Dorset. Nancy observed that her eyes were the same as Eddy's. Another picture is a striking oil by Jacques de Lajoue of a fantastic, rococo pillared building in process of construction, furnished with incongruous scientific instruments, magnifying glasses, cranes, pulleys – a kind of eighteenth-century *surréaliste* picture, very attractive.

Sunday, 1st March

I find May the kitchen maid on the bus and accompany her to Mass. She is very Irish, blarney, at ease and amusing. Like a perfect guest I keep her off gossip – which I long to hear – about the household. Waiting for the return bus I stand hunched against the bitter cold in a shop entrance. Suddenly a group of Salvationists march past and strike up a hymn with portentous solemnity and discipline, two stalwart matrons in blue bonnets goose-stepping at the fore. As they disappear round a corner an old beggar with crutches and a real wooden leg (which these days is a rarity) hobbles across my vision, briskly in step. I think what a Rowlandish scene this is in its English, laughable, humourless way. The strains of 'God Our Help' were stifled by a gust of piercing wind and a swirl of old bus tickets and dust.

May and I were both given a lift back to West Wycombe by a seedy, sandy, red-bearded, arty-crafty fellow and an Eskimo wife in a red riding-hood. They were both wearing sandals. I asked them how they could bear it in this weather ! 'You get used to it,' was the reply. But why have to get used to it?

I have finished Siever's life of Dr. Bill Wilson, that goody-goody prig of the Wykehamist stamp. Doubtless he had charm for those other tough Antarctic creatures. He hated coarseness of speech and profanity, and must have been intolerable. There is a gulf between his generation and ours which is unbridgeable. I sometimes fear that I have drifted so far

---

[36] Sir Alfred Beit, Bart., M.P. Married 1939 Clementine Mitford

from the concept of a gentleman that I can no longer appreciate the genuine article when I read about it.

Before luncheon Nancy said, 'I must just dash to the Beardmore. I won't be a minute, you bet.' 'The what?' Helen asked. 'Don't you know,' we said, 'that the upstairs lavatory is called after the Beardmore Glacier. It faces due north, the window is permanently propped open so that it can't be shut, and the floor is under a drift of snow.' Helen doesn't find this a funny joke. After luncheon Eddy, Nancy and I must huddle over a few green logs in the fireplace, Eddy trying to read *The Mill on the Floss*, I Jane Carlyle's letters. We turn to discussing H. and her extraordinary unadult character, her terror of being left out of anything that may be going on, her pique over preconceived plans going wrong, and a certain resentment over others enjoying something she fears she may be missing.

The guardian of the Wallace Collection (its pictures are stored in the house for the war) got out some of the Watteaus and Fragonards for us to look at. He arranged them in a row in the saloon. We had a perfect view of the lady incising a large S on a tree and the *scènes champêtres*, all of which suit the particular elegance of this house and park.

I motored to Eton in time to take Francis out to tea in the Cock Pit where we ate the familiar bap rolls with jelly jam, whipped cream, and Austrian chocolate cake. Only the cream was ersatz, made from soya beans, and the cake tasted of straw rolled in dung. Then to evensong in College Chapel where the traditional ceremonial is invariable. The 'ram'[37] marches in the same deliberate, self-conscious manner. The same scrubby little boys sit demurely on the knife boards. In how short a time is contact with a younger generation completely lost. How can I be sure of what I believe these boys to be thinking about the service and each other, for I could never ask one, and no one would venture to tell me? Yet there they are, very well mannered it is true, but flashing across the nave confidential smiles that mean so much, ogling and making assignations without a word being spoken. Oh the squalid thoughts and the romance of it all at the time, I remember!

At dinner this evening Helen remarked on the beauty of a ring Eddy always wears. E. said, 'Yes, I have several spare stones for it which can be changed from day to day.' 'How many?' I asked. 'Forty-five,' E. said with a sigh. The ring belonged to Lady Betty Germaine. Nancy told a story of an American millionaire's wife who on meeting a parson's daughter wearing a small necklace of lapis lazuli remarked, 'I have a staircase made of those.'

---

[37] The 'ram' is the procession of Sixth Form boys, led by the head of the school up the nave before services begin.

Monday, 2nd March

Eardley and I motored to Princes Risborough to look at a wall at the bottom of the manor garden which is falling down. Afterwards Mrs. Vaughan, our tenant, showed us over the house. She is the widow of Dr. Vaughan, late headmaster of Rugby, a distinguished lady who has 'let herself go'. She is a mixture of Vita – perhaps the dark down on her upper lip suggested this resemblance, as well as her tallness and thinness – and Mrs. Ponsonby-Fane, the *châteleine* of Brympton D'Evercy. Very countrified, untidy and dressed in subfusc. She has the thinnest nose bridge I ever did see. It was like the edge of a pocket-knife blade. I could not take my eyes off it.

On the way home we saw Nancy sitting on a horse trough by the bus stop in the village, waiting for the Oxford bus. She is leaving after nearly three months and will be a great loss. I shall miss her terribly.

Wednesday, 4th March

After work this evening to London by train. Went straight to St. James's Court and there dined with Kathleen Kennet from whom I got a long letter on Tuesday. Lord Kennet was luckily in bed with bronchitis so we were alone. K. as outgiving as ever. The first glimpse of her showed how she is ageing. Her figure is noticeably spread, and not mitigated by the shapeless, sacklike garments she always wears. She is the worst dressed woman I know; and rejoices in a sort of aggressive no-taste in clothes and house.

For the first time I talked to her about the Antarctic expedition. She said Cherry-Garrard was a poor creature, an ugly youth of twenty-three who was only accepted because his family advanced £1,000 towards the expedition. If this is so and Scott truly addressed only two words to him throughout, then so much the less credit to Scott. But I don't altogether believe this. It appears that Cherry-Garrard submitted the first draft of his book to K., which she approved. One day while staying at his lovely Adam house in Hertfordshire, which she habitually did, she introduced him to Bernard Shaw. Shaw looked through the manuscript, and persuaded C.-G. that in a book about a great hero human interest was forfeited unless the biographer was candid about his subject's failings. C.-G. subsequently rewrote a great part of the book in which he dwelt upon Scott's deficiency in humour and so forth. He did not submit the redraft to K. She maintains that Scott did have a sense of humour. I said, 'I suppose he was a difficult man to live with, moody and hard to understand.' She said, 'Yes, he was rather moody. In this respect Peter[38] is superior to him.' Then in her gay manner, 'But I knew him.'

Shackleton, she said, was rotten; bad blood and no good at all. He had promised Scott, who for a long time could not get released by the Admiralty to go south, that he would not use his base; then straight away went and did so, leaving the hut in an appalling mess, 'but a disgusting mess in every respect', K. added with a meaning look which didn't mean anything to me. The two men never spoke to one another again. Scott when pressed to appear on the same Albert Hall platform once gave a pretty-pretty speech on Shackleton's behalf, yet without exchanging a word with him in private.

Wilson, K. said, was a prig, just like a private school boy with no humour whatever. He was a good-looking, honest fellow whom the simple sailors could not see through. Mrs. Wilson is still alive, and K. described her as a drab female. Ponting was an artist who was all out for money; and somehow Alfred Bossom got mixed up in the purchase of the Antarctic film. K. cannot find bad enough words for him.

She said it is true that the whole lot of them never snapped, or nagged at each other. In this respect they were splendidly controlled. The only one of the party Scott disliked was Evans ('Ted). He said so in no measured terms in his journals. However, K. thought it better to cut out the references.

Scott hated the cold, she said.

Amundsen was unscrupulous, and his going to the South Pole at all was a dirty trick. He borrowed the *Fram* from Nansen, thus depriving him of the means of making an expedition elsewhere, on the grounds of taking it to the North Pole. When at sea he turned round without a word to anyone, and sailed straight for the south. Nansen in a letter to K. wrote that the King and Queen of Norway on learning that Amundsen had reached the South Pole first, said how sorry they were, both wishing it had been Scott.

Birdie Bowers, a tiny man, with no legs to speak of, was wonderful. 6,000 applicants wrote for interviews, and K. was present at all the interviews held in a small, hired office in Victoria Street. Bowers's chits were so good and he himself so ugly and unprepossessing that K. persuaded Scott he should be accepted. A man with such physical disabilities and yet such testimonials, must be first-rate at the job.

She says that Peter is so exactly like Scott (although not so good-looking) that in her mind they are one and the same person. 'Peter

---

[38] Later Sir Peter Scott, her son, artist and naturalist. Founder of the Wildfowl Trust; *d.* 1989.

inherits Con's uncontrollable urge for adventure.' She has just done a bust of Peter which she is sending to the Academy.

Thursday, 5th March

The reason for my coming up in the middle of the week was to attend General Pope-Hennessy's Requiem Mass this morning. Beforehand I tried seven shops for razor blades, and not one blade was obtainable. Damn it!

The Requiem was at the Chapel of Sts. John and Elizabeth Hospital, Grove End Road. In front of me a youthful figure was sitting, judging from its back view. When it turned its head I was surprised to notice Harold. He, Clarissa Churchill and I met at the church door. Jamesey conducted the three of us through an ante-chapel and got us a taxi. Harold was impressed by the service and interested in the ritual. 'All those bells,' he kept saying. 'I could not follow it through,' in an aggrieved tone.

Saturday, 7th March

There is a great stir in Brooks's about the member who has been asked to resign, and won't go. He doggedly makes use of the library every day and even insists upon privileges which the most hardened old members would not dare demand after half a century's membership. He has been so rude to the servants that in a body they informed the secretary they would leave unless he did. Now there is to be an extraordinary meeting in order formally to expel him. Such a thing has never been known to happen in the whole history of Brooks's. The offender is a vulgar, sinister-looking figure, who prowls round the club. When he leaves a room the other old gentlemen break into muffled whispers. They follow his retreating figure with their swivelling bald heads, and give vent to loud sneers.

I went to tea at the Kinnairds' house in Lennox Gardens. Tea was on a table in front of the fire and Lady Kinnaird on her knees with the toasting fork. Very friendly, but offered the butter half-heartedly, and when I said, 'I don't eat butter,' also half-heartedly, she did not press. I refused the sugar offered, taking out my saccharine, and again was not pressed. I was asked to take the honey from the comb with my kuife to save dirtying a spoon. Lord K. wanted to know all about the National Trust and the country houses scheme. He lamented the servant scarcity and said it was a scandal elderly people should not be allowed a full quota of servants. Lamented education of the lower orders. I was a good deal entertained, and couldn't help liking them. All so unrealistic and old fashioned.

Sunday, 8th March

In the afternoon Rick [Stewart-Jones] and I walked in the sun. He wanted to look at the slum parts of Chelsea around Lot's power station. It is remarkable what vast areas there have been destroyed, and yet the power station is unharmed. R. is fascinated by the problems of reconstructing these devastated areas when the war is over. It is slums in which he is really most interested. I am not at all. We looked at the Moravian Cemetery at the back of Lindsey Palace. There is a nice little cottage, and an old chapel, now a studio. Half-hidden by the long grass of a lawn are round and square stones on the ground, with inscriptions on them. The Moravians were buried standing up, the easier to scamper away at the sounding of the last trump.

Monday, 9th March

The sun was shining and the air almost balmy as I walked through Belgravia. For the first time this year I inhaled that familiar scent of London, which ought to be so full of promise and happy days. But alas, now it augurs despair, inevitable misery, and destruction. For the spring is a season one has come to dread. Yet the birds in the Green Park were singing oblivious of the future; and in spite of my awareness of it I found my feet skimming over the grass.

I once firmly believed in the permanency of human relationships. I suppose I read about their impermanency in books, but could not bring myself to acknowledge it. Now I know it to be a fact, just as every physical creation is transitory. The realization ought doubtless to strengthen my divine love, but I do not think it does.

Saturday, 14th March

I had a charming letter from Professor Trevelyan,[39] quite unsolicited, in which he said he did not know what the Trust would have done without me and how glad he was I had been invalided out of the army. Gratifying, but guilt-inducing. Matheson's illness continues. He is now removed to a nursing home for his temperature refuses to go down. I chose a delicious tweed at John Walls for a new suit. But I only have fourteen coupons left till next June. A suit requires twenty-six, although without a waistcoat I can manage with twenty-one.

I went to Heywood Hill's shop. Both he and Anne were away. Mrs. Willie King was taking charge for them. I enquired after her husband. She says he is the oldest subaltern in the British Army, a gunner stationed on Hadrian's Wall. He asked to join MI.5 so they put him into the R.A.

---

[39] G. M. Trevelyan, O.M. (1876–1962), historian.

He is delighted with the mistake, if it is one. She says he revels in army life and is blissfully happy. Certainly one would never expect this flimsy, weak creature, like the Chelsea porcelain of whith he is such a connoisseur, actually to like the rough and tumble. But then I am constantly surprised by the attitude of friends to their wartime occupations.

I walked round St. Paul's Cathedral. It was full of little brown men, Burmese or Siamese, herded by kind English drago-ladies. The ambulatory and the transepts are closed to the public, and there is a great chasm where the bomb fell in the north transept. The inner screen whereon used to be the 'Si monumentum requiris circumspice' is totally destroyed. The Duke of Wellington's ornate monument is bricked up with iron stays from one side to the other. All the sculpture covered with dust and dirt.

I walked through the devastated area to the north of the cathedral. It was like wandering in Pompeii. The sun was shining warm and bright. There was not a breath stirring, only the seagulls wheeling and skirling over the ruins. Not a sound of traffic when I was in the midst of the isolation. From one spot there is waste land visible as far as the eye can roam. It was most moving. Unfortunately the ruins are not beautiful, too like scarred flesh, and as yet untoned by time. I do pray they will at all costs keep the Wren spires, even if they must clear away the shells of the naves. I walked past the ruins of Christchurch Newgate, St. Giles's Cripplegate, St. Vedast, St. Lawrence Jewry, St. Benet's, St. Mary-le-Bow (when I last saw this church about a year ago it still had its roof on though badly damaged. A subsequent raid has evidently finished it off) and so on. Walked to Finsbury Circus via the Guildhall. Noticed for the first time a good classical buildmg, called Armourers' Hall I think. Past Liverpool Street, back via St. Botolph, little St. Ethelburga the Virgin, St. Helen's (these three unharmed), up Queen Victoria Street and back to St. Paul's where I took a bus to Brooks's. Exhaustion and tea.

Sunday, 15th March

Lunching at the old Gascoignes at Ashtead, Aunt Puss[40] politely praised the (rather dry) currant-cakey pudding. With considerable satisfaction Sir Frederick replied, 'Yes, we have had that pudding every Sunday since we were married.' That must be forty years ago.

Wednesday, 18th March

The weather is mild, though rainy. The birds are very busy and singing their throats out as if in relief that at last the winter is over. There is no

---

[40] Lady Constance Milnes-Gaskell, mother of Charles Milnes-Gaskell. Lady-in-Waiting to Queen Mary.

green on the trees, which are still winter bare, but the snowdrops have sprung up inches high in vast carpeted circles round the big trees on the drive. I do not recollect such a thickness of snowdrops before.

I went straight to the National Gallery and met Clarissa Churchill walking down the steps. She said she had failed to get in, having been told that only ticket holders would be admitted. I thought there must be some mistake. She had in fact gone to the wrong door. We bought tickets (1/- each) and just squeezed in. We had very bad seats right at the back behind the performers. Elena Gerhardt sang Schubert and Brahms songs, and Myra Hess played Schumann. No wonder it was a popular day. Elena Gerhardt came out close to where we were sitting. She is an enormous woman with so dropsical a belly that it looks like a pillow tied to her front not belonging to her person at all. She wore a black velvet dress like a monk's habit, tied with a black cord round her middle. She must be about sixty but still has a voice. When she walked in she was beautifully powdered, her grey hair teed up, immaculate. When she came out all the powder was gone, her face shining with sweat. She was mopping her forehead with a handkerchief. Yet she looked happy, fulfilled. Where we sat it was difficult to hear her clearly, and her low notes not at all. We ate sandwiches and drank cups of coffee in the canteen.

Clarissa walked with me as far as Brooks's. She told me that Randolph's wife had no intention of sticking to him; and that Mr. Churchill would be very sad if their marriage broke up. She said that General Pope-Hennessy's death was brought about by a stroke. A Colonel Someone was having tea with him and put him into a rage by remarking that Russian tanks were bad. When the visitor left the General went to Dame Una's[41] room, very upset, had a seizure and died four hours later. Cecil Beaton observed, 'Careless talk costs lives.'

A special meeting of members was held at Brooks's this afternoon formally to expel the member who has been rude to the servants and used bad language. The chairman announced that he had just received a letter from the member announcing his resignation after all, and promising never to cross the threshold of the club again. Great relief was expressed by everybody at this end to their embarrassment. Later in the day, I passed the man, looking unconcerned and truculent under the arcade of the Ritz. Instantly I felt sorry for him and wondered why he had behaved like this. I can quite understand how, if one senses that one is disliked, one is impelled to make oneself detested.

---

[41] Dame Una Pope-Hennessy (d. 1949), wife of General Richard Pope-Hennessy, author, and mother of John and James.

Fairly warm and heavy showers with gleams of muslin sunshine inter-mittently. Today I start on my Lincolnshire tour.

I take two hours in starting, for that damned car refuses to work and Helen's, which she most generously offered to lend me, also refuses. In the end the National Trust car gets going and I leave at 11.45. On the way I look at the privet hedge at Whiteleaf Field which has been decently layered. I pass Ivinghoe Windmill, and walk across plough to inspect it. It stands in the middle of a flat waste silhouetted against the grey sky, with its black spectral arms now pinioned down its body. The Swan at Leighton Buzzard has no room for me, but the landlady is civil and indi-cates a tea shop a few doors off. I lunch there for 2/7 surprisingly well. There is a medieval cross in the centre of the street. Instinct told me to stop at the church in Lowick. Or was it the stone Gothic lantern on the tower? I was well rewarded, for in the north aisle every window was filled with medieval glass of kings, etc. The alabaster tomb of Ralph Greene (*d.* 1419) and wife most lovely. He is holding her hand in his and she is wearing the crespine headdress, netted stiffly and sticking out from both sides of the head. Also there is a table tomb to the Earl of Wiltshire (1498), again of alabaster, his bare head resting upon a heaume. There is a mon-ument in the north aisle of a Lady Germaine, formerly Duchess of Norfolk, lying sideways, head on elbow, uncomfortable and Kneller-like. Her husband, also in marble, ostracized behind the organ case. Altogether a most rewarding church. This chance discovery brings a brimful cup of joy.

I arrive at Hambleton Hall late for tea. Old Mrs. Astley Cooper, now eighty-eight, the same as ever, rolling about in a huge bed like a stranded whale. Rather pathetic and lonely and so pleased to see me. We talked of Father Francis [Moncrieff] who has been made Prior and may become Provincial of the Dominican Order. Mrs. C. said that his pleasure at being made Prior slightly disappointed her. I liked this touch of her old acer-bity. But she loves him. I put up at the George in Grantham. Good fare and comfortable, but uncivil people.

A goddamn awful day, cold and leaden. After breakfast I walked to the parish church. The blackout arrangements have made the inside dingy and dark. I was arrested by one large Georgian mural monument, and crossed over to look at it, and lo! it was Sir Dudley Ryder's, the Dudley Ryder whose diaries I have just enjoyed so immensely. I had no idea he was buried here. There was a Lenten service in progress in the choir; one curate with a cultured, gentlemanly voice reading from the New Testament, and one elderly devout lady in the congregation. I sat and listened to the lesson. I said to myself, this woman must be Miss Sedgwick. I followed her to the back door of Grantham House, where she entered. So I caught her up and asked if she were Miss Sedgwick. She took me into the garden and all round the house which she is leaving to the National Trust.[42] It occupies a large green area in the middle of the old town, adjoining the parish church – a strategic position.

In Tattershall I lunched at the Fortescue Arms. The host a very surly fellow who kept ejaculating 'Christ!' in an offensive manner.

Tattershall church may be the most beautiful I have ever seen. Perpendicular, it was built by the Lord Cromwell who built the castle. The nave windows are vast, and so are the clerestory windows, *and* there is no stained glass at all; just white translucent diamond panes. No pews either over the undulating flagged floors. The emptiness is Catholic and ancient. The castle is now filled with stacks of Natural History Museum fossils, neatly packed. The whole place reeks of mothballs.

Saturday, 21st March

Norton Place and Gainsborough Old Hall. The first an elegant seat built by Carr of York for Mr. Harrison, out of the prize money he received for making the best chronometer for the Admiralty, in 1770. A fitting and just reward for merit. The latter house is stacked, literally stacked, one on top of the other, with treasures belonging to Sir Hickman Bacon. They are not even covered with dust sheets; and are gathering dust and filth from the pigeons which scramble through the roof and roost in the great hall. There is a device in one bedroom, a hammer attached to the wall under the ceiling over the bed, which when pulled knocks loudly against the beam under the floor of the housemaid's room in order to wake her up.

Finding Lincoln Cathedral shut at 5 o'clock I walked disconsolately through the close. Met a canon's wife coming out of her house to post a letter. She was perfectly charming, took me into her house, gave me tea and lent me a book about the minster, and introduced me to her husband. They showed me their garden. I thought she was the perfect example of a Christian clergywife.

At Doddington I found Mrs. Jarvis picking snowdrops in the garden, and helped her. She is an old woman, witchlike in appearance, with a quiet, dry sense of humour. When she retired upstairs to rest I wandered round the house in the dusk. Doddington is one of the most appealing houses I know, Jacobean outside and Georgian inside. But the most

---

[42] Actually given by the Misses M. and W. Sedgwick to the National Trust in 1944–50.

sympathetic sort of Jacobean, plain, clean-cut surfaces and skyline only broken by cosy pin-cushion towers. And the deep rosy brick walls, the four great cedars, the detached gatehouse. What more could one demand of romance and seclusion? The rooms inside are very plain. Furniture walnut and mahogany, and lots of tapestry and needlework fabrics. The house smells of sweet log fires and of Knellers and Lelys. Coney[43] cooked a delicious dinner of beetroot soup with cream, duck, raspberries from a bottle and cream again, burgundy and port. The top floor is full of children and so far the house has escaped requisitioning. It seems an isolated, far-away family home, struggling happily and comfortably.

Monday, 23rd March

Last Thursday, the very day I meant to call on Diana Worthington[44] on my way to Lincolnshire, it appears that Greville Worthington was killed by a sentry who fired at his car because he failed to stop when challenged to halt. Greville never heard the sentry and the bullet hit him in the back. He pulled up the car, collapsed and died. The girl with him was unhurt. He was to have married her, his divorce from Diana having just come through. Diana is very upset and miserable, for she never meant or wished to lose Greville.

Wilson Steer is dead.[45] I passed him in Cheyne Walk only the other Sunday. He was a big, burly, gruff man, always wearing a wide, black, untidy stock or scarf, walking painfully, grimly and determinedly, very much preoccupied by inner thoughts.

Tuesday, 24th March

Eardley and I hose and wash the National Trust car, each doing a side thoroughly we think, with sponge and leather. When the car has dried I am horrified to find streaks of mud still on my side. I look shyly at Eardley's side. It is just as bad. I am pleased.

Chichester Cathedral is chiefly Norman, clean and spacious, yet inexplicably lacking sanctity. It is full of monuments, none interesting. There is a life-size figure of Huskisson, who was killed by a train in 1830. He is wearing a toga. What an extraordinary fashion that was. Considered ridiculously archaic no doubt at the time, it is in our eyes symptomatic of the early nineteenth century. In other words artists should never be afraid of their work appearing derivative and unoriginal. For whatever they produce inevitably retains the flavour of their epoch.

---

[43] Wife of Ralph Jarvis, and daughter-in-law of old Mrs. Jarvis.
[44] Lady Diana Worthington (*d.* 1943), daughter of 2nd Earl of Feversham.
[45] Philip Wilson Steer (1860–1942), Post-Impressionist artist.

I arrived at Brede at 7.30 in time for dinner with Clare Sheridan.[46] A very pretty girl of twenty, Maxime Birley, was staying. I had not seen Clare for years. She looks a little older, is stout but magnificent. She was wearing corduroy trousers which did not suit her, but the next morning she wore a terracotta skirt with flowing shawl to match. She kept flinging the shawl about her person in an Isadora Duncan fashion. Clare is a pacifist, and we spoke of the war, and of spiritual values. I found that I agreed with her almost fundamentally. She is a big woman and she has the bigness to remain detached from the war. I remember once thinking that in the event of another war most of my friends would have the bigness to be so detached, but no, none of them seems to be, not even myself. Clare is. It is true that now Dick [her son] is dead, she can afford to be. Clare has woven a spiritual seclusion and wrapped herself in it like a cocoon. She is often a little silly, but she can be impartial and wise.

She thinks her cousin Winston ought to go. She praises the contrasting virtues of Stafford Cripps, who neither smokes nor drinks, and is impressed by the love of the people in his own village for him.

I slept in Clare's studio, surrounded by uncarved tree trunks and busts of Red Indians. Her shelves were groaning with her own books, translated into German, French, Danish and even Russian.

Thursday, 26th March

After breakfast, at which I was offered a goose's egg and, like an ass, refused it for fear of appearing greedy, we went down the park to look at Brede Place, now occupied by soldiers. It is a wonderful house and to my surprise not large. Nothing, save Dick Sheridan's five bathrooms and heating plant, has been added to the house since Henry VIII's reign, so Clare says. It is a very perfect late medieval house, with a wide view, yet remote. It has several panelled rooms. One small room over the porch has masks, somewhat negroid, in the cornice. Clare would sell Brede for £7,000, but there is little land – sixty acres at most – and no other form of endowment. Yet it would let if the Trust held it, I feel sure.

Left for Smallhythe. Miss Edith Craig[47] was in bed, but the two other odd old ladies were about, Christopher St. John and Tony (really Clare) Atwood. They were dressed in corduroy trousers and men's jackets, one homespun, the other curry tweed. Their grey locks were hacked short and both wore tam-o'shanters. They were charming to me and gave me a huge two-handled mug of coffee. In Ellen Terry's little house one feels

---

[46] Sculptor, died 1970. Her mother, Winston Churchill's mother and Shane Leslie's mother were the Jerome sisters.
[47] Daughter of Ellen Terry. She gave Smallhythe Place near Tenterden, her mother's home, to the National Trust in 1939.

that she might walk past one at any minute, and in her bedroom that she might appear sitting before her dressing-table brushing her hair.

At Bodiam Castle I walked on the leads of the gatehouse. At Batemans[48] the tenants were away. Rudyard Kipling's study has atmosphere. It is filled with his books, the sort of books you would expect him to have, histories of the British Empire, Meredith's poems. The house of grey Burwash stone and a great cluster of chimney stacks was evidently larger, and has been truncated.

Saturday, 28th March

The coffee-room at Brooks's was full. I was just going to withdraw when the Professor [Richardson][49] hailed me and told me to sit with him. He is a dear man, and a little dotty. I don't always understand his esoteric jokes, and insinuations. Besides he laughs so much at his own jokes that one can barely hear what he says. Yet he halts, peers at one and demands an understanding. He is always punning. He spoke disparagingly of Groping Ass and Meddlesome, his two *bêtes-noires*. He says all great architecture is derivative when it is not deliberately imitative. He claims to have discovered Wren's own working notebooks, but will not reveal or publish them, for there is no one alive worthy to profit from them. He only reads eighteenth-century newspapers, of which he has an enormous stock, for he says the news in them is just the same as it is today. You merely have to substitute the names of countries occasionally, and not invariably. He read me some passages from Swift. Wants me to join the Council for the Preservation of City Churches. He asked who he could find to fill the chair of the Royal Fine Art Commission. Ronnie Norman has declined because he will not take a peerage which is essential to the office. Esher is not serious enough, he maintains.

At 2.15 I straightway joined the Hills at Miss Jourdain[50] and Miss Compton-Burnett's[51] where they were lunching. I arrived for coffee. This is a great occasion. Margaret Jourdain is patently jealous of Ivy Compton-Burnett, whom she keeps unapproachable except through herself, and even when approached, guards with anxious care. This is evident from the way in which the former diverts one's attention if she thinks one is talking too much to the latter. It is a selfish kind of affection, to say the least. The two have lived together for years and are never parted. They are an Edwardian and remarkably acidulated pair. The coiffures of both look

---

[48] Rudyard Kipling's home, acquired by the National Trust in 1940.
[49] Professor, later Sir Albert E. Richardson, P.R.A. (1880–1964).
[50] Margaret Jourdain (*d.* 1951), connoisseur and author of books on furniture and decoration.
[51] Miss, later Dame Ivy Compton-Burnett (1884–1969), novelist. The two ladies lived in Braemar Mansions, Cornwall Gardens, S.W.7.

like wigs. The hair is bound with a thin fillet across the forehead and over a bun at the back. Thin pads of hair hang down their foreheads unconvincingly. Miss C.-B., whom I consider to be the greatest living novelist, is upright, starchy, forthright and about fifty-seven to sixty. There is a bubbling undercurrent of humour in every observation she makes, and she makes a good many, apparently hackneyed and usually sharp, in a rapid, choppy, rather old-fashioned upper-middle-class manner, clipping her breathless words. She enunciates clearly and faultlessly, saying slightly shocking things in a matter-of-fact tone, following up her sentences with a lot of 'dontcherknows', and then smiling perceptibly. She has a low, breasty chuckle. She has not unpleasing, sharp features, and her profile is almost beautiful. But she is not the kind of woman who cares tuppence for appearances, and wears a simple, unrememberable black dress (I guess all her clothes are unrememberable), which she smoothes down with long fingers.

The two were very entertaining about their refugeeing with the niece of an old friend near Chedworth. They hated the niece, who tactlessly referred to her aunt's impending demise from senility, and let them know what she would then do with the aunt's furniture and belongings. We talked chiefly of country houses. Miss Jourdain looks rather wicked and frightening, when she peers through her quizzing glass. Miss C.-B. says that Miss J. has too little occasion to use it these days, now that there are so few houses available with furniture to be debunked; that she lost a lens in the train, and it has hardly mattered.

Sunday, 29th March

I walked in the sun down the Long Walk from Windsor, past the Copper Horse to Cumberland Lodge for tea. Lord FitzAlan[52] very charming. He drank a large glass of sherry at tea-time. He is eighty-seven. He spoke with profound affection of Lord Lloyd's memory, and said he never knew a greater patriot or more honourable man.

Thursday, 2nd April

At breakfast this morning, just as I was in a hurry to be off, I cut the index finger of my left hand with the bread knife, rather deep. I drove with Eardley straight to Avebury. He took me round the Circle. He is madly keen on Avebury and rather peevish about my lack of enthusiasm and disrespect for the ugly stones which Keiller has dragged from the ground into the light of day. I cannot approve of the proposal to destroy the old

---

[52] Lord Edmund Howard (later Talbot), 1st Viscount FitzAlan of Derwent (1855–1947), Lord Lieutenant of Ireland 1921–2.

village inside the Circle. I admit that the empty sections of the Circle are impressive where the terraces have been cleaned of scrub and are neatly cropped by sheep; but to remove medieval cottages and clear away all traces of habitation subsequent to the Iron Age seems to me pedantic and a distortion of historical perspective. We walked round the Manor garden. Eardley was bored by the house because it is not classical and is romantic. Today's fashionable distaste for the romantic in English country houses is as overemphasized as was the Edwardians' for the classical and regular.

We lunched at the inn off cold beef and potatoes in skins, and a trifle (the very word makes me retch) which was surprisingly sweet and good. At Tilshead we walked to the Long Barrow. I agreed with Eardley that the scrub and untidy spruce trees ought to be eradicated in order to reveal the simple contours of the Barrow. The undulations of these tumuli along the backs of the downs against the sky are their only point and beauty. To hell with archaeology! Although the White Barrow is right off the road and miles from Tilshead a party of children was playing round a little russet tent they had pitched here.

At Stonehenge we looked at our land, part of which on the north side of the Amesbury road has been ploughed. I cannot see that this matters in the present circumstances, although the archaeologists make a clamour. Having bought tickets at the turnstile we walked up to and round the monument. Both of us in agreement that the wire fencing is most unsightly; its criss-cross pattern suggests an internment camp. If there were more of Stonehenge left it would lose its awe.

What a contrast with the finished refinement of Dinton House where we had tea with the old Philippses.[53] How splendidly proportioned, clean-limbed and precise this great house is, springing straight out of the rough grass and silhouetted against a crescent belt of beech trees. The stair hall with its trim brass balusters, dividing flights, yellow scagliola columns and circular top lantern makes me gasp with admiration. All my cravings for proportion, propriety and architectural solution of problems are satisfied.

Friday, 3rd April

Good Friday at Westwood. Ted[54] has given me the North Room next to the parlour, the room with a double bed and original blue-green and white crewel-work William and Mary hangings. The ceiling is divided

---

[53] Mr. and Mrs. Bertram Philipps who gave Dinton Park and Hyde's House, Wiltshire, to the Trust in 1943.
[54] E. G. Lister, under whose will Westwood Manor, Wiltshire, came to the Trust in 1960.

into four compartments by two beams, the whole stuccoed about 1610 with pendants. The walls retain their plain plaster surface but the chimneypiece is stuccoed with floral designs. There are three little children's masks over the fire, which was lit for me last night. I lay in bed with one candle guttering behind a glass hurricane globe (for there is no electric light in the house) and the logs flickering thin flames, seen rather than felt through the half-drawn bed curtains.

We strolled down the lane to Farleigh Castle. It is very tidily kept by the Office of Works, but the gatehouse and scanty remains have been thickly pointed with a black cement made of Brighton pebbles. I cannot approve of this pointing which the Office of Works use all over the country regardless of regional customs. It is certainly enduring, but unnatural and ugly and prevents wild flowers growing in the crevices. The chapel is hung with armour, for the cleaning of which the owner, Lord Cairns, recently paid an expert in advance. The best pieces mysteriously disappeared. There is Flemish glass in the windows. A panel depicts St. Colette doing penance for having prayed successfully to be changed from a squat, plain lady into a comely, tall abbess. The iron grille, dating from 1411, round the early Hungerford monument has at the four corners finials frizzled to resemble black hearse plumes.

Ted has received a photograph from Tom Goff who is A.D.C. to the Athlones in Ottawa of the whole Government House party including Princess Alice and himself knitting, and Lord Galway crocheting. When Tom went to Buckingham Palace the other day to attend to Handel's harpsichord the two princesses were playing to the Queen a duet they had learnt by heart. The Queen said to Tom, 'You are a lucky man to be able to do what you like.'

Saturday, 4th April

I have finished Froude's three volumes of Mrs. Carlyle's letters. I am struck by the Victorians' apparent concern for the health and well-being of their relations and friends, whereas we are really indifferent to the tribulations of our nearest and dearest, unless they are very dear indeed. Deathbed scenes bore us to tears.

Two young men to luncheon, one called Eric Knight who is half German, having a German mother and a German wife, the other in the air force and reeking of cheap scent. Knight with long, golden hair, a large nose and thick, ugly Yiddish lips, was unprepossessing but interesting when he talked of Russia which he visited in 1935. His impressions in that year were that the Soviet system was a laughable, and total failure. Nothing worked. Everything was tawdry and drab. The people were corrupt and ready to commit any treason for money which all lacked.

He spoke to many beggars, some of them educated old ladies who complained to him of their miseries in frightened undertones.

I must say my convictions regarding the Russian campaign are that the Germans are not yet in earnest. Although they miscalculated in assuming that the campaign would be over before last winter, they have been treading water since then, and merely keeping up their line. The Russian advance has been inappreciable. I foresee a renewal of the German onslaught when the mud has gone, and a terrible Russian defeat.

Tuesday, 7th April

Talked with Mama in her bedroom this morning.[55] She is full of complaints as usual. Papa has let the large cottage for only £2 although it is fully furnished; there are endless parties of people in the house; the garden boy is leaving, and the gardener, who is only forty-three, may be called up; and Gertrude is to be married in a fortnight. She is the only servant in the house now, and Colonel Riley, who is billeted on them, has to be waited upon, hand and foot. Mama is very distressed because Gertrude is due to have the curse the very day of her wedding, which could not be arranged otherwise because her young man has to take his leave when he is given it. Mama says the curse will come precisely at 11.55 a.m. that day, that it always comes regular as clockwork with strong, healthy girls, a thing I never knew before and can scarcely credit.

Wednesday, 8th April

This afternoon Sarah [Dashwood] ran into the office at West Wycombe calling for Miss Paterson. The tapestry room chimney was on fire. They rely on Miss P. for everything. I dashed upstairs and with Helen went on to the flat roof. Smoke was pouring from the chimneystack. I got a stirrup pump and soaked the stack with water. Within five minutes of the fire being extinguished the fire brigade arrived. They swarmed all over the house. I secretly enjoyed the incident. Helen was very scared, which was only natural, looked very white and issued and counter-issued orders snappishly in a confused way.

Thursday, 9th April

After lunching by myself in a tiny, stuffy, Italian-serviced café near Covent Garden off sausages and golden roll, I went to the S.P.A.B. meeting. Very annoyed to find that it had been put off and I had come all this way to no purpose. But Mrs. Esdaile and Maresco Pearse were also there on the same misunderstanding. So we talked of the scheme to house all the

---

[55] This was at Wickhamford Manor, Worcestersbire, where J. L-M. was born and brought up.

amenity societies in Holland House. Mrs. Esdaile was pleased that I too was in favour, and particularly favoured the two advantages I put forward, that there should be a central library and a communal solicitor in the building. Rick and I have long advocated this and we go further in advocating amalgamation of the societies under one name as well as under one roof

Thursday, 16th April

A tedious 2½-hour journey by a series of buses to Englefield Green. Mediterranean sky, and the chestnuts having burst their buds are in the fan-unfolding stage. All the trees along the Thames valley are shooting buds noisily. The green is almost too shiny, too polished.

I walked through Bishop's Gate into Windsor Park and was overtaken by Alathea FitzAlan-Howard on her bicycle. She is the FitzAlan's pretty granddaughter aged eighteen, frail and freckled. I arrived just in time for dinner for which there is no changing these days. Lord FitzAlan's son staying. It is the first time I have seen him, a tiny, rather wizened, insignificant man with a wooden leg. Magdalen[56] sad as ever, with heavy folds of tumbling, wispy hair parted in the middle of her head and looped behind anyhow. Two Grenadier officers came to dinner. They are guarding the King and Queen who are at present in Royal Lodge next door. One is called Lascelles and is, I believe, Blanche Lloyd's nephew, very good-looking and fair-haired, tall and the 'flower of English youth', a plant that always makes me stare and rub my eyes in admiration and envy. Both are on guard for a week, may not leave the locality, and sleep only half-undressed in the royal stables. Yet they look uncrumpled, immaculate. They seldom see the King. They had just been in a new stratosphere Wellington bomber. These bombers are being turned out at a small factory near by at the rate of two a week. They hope to reach 43,000 feet. This is highly confidential. When over a certain height the crew collect in one confined cabin, where no oxygen apparatus is required, and a switch from the engine supplies them with what they need in the cabin. These machines fly blind by radar. The boys said the beauty and finish of the instrument boards were wonderful beyond words. Every convenience of the crew was studied and brought to perfection.

Lord FitzAlan is delighted with the Cripps breakdown in India and does not think it presages any immediate ill-consequences, but in the long run good results. He fears Cripps intends to be next viceroy. He talked to me after dinner in his study about the Stanley Baldwins. S.B. is by no means a fool; is on the contrary extremely astute, and far from

---

[56] Hon. Magdalen FitzAlan-Howard, unmarried daughter of Lord FitzAlan, *d.* 1974.

obstinate as is generally supposed. His besetting fault is indolence. He confided in Lord F. that his reason for not rearming was that the country would not stand for it at the time.

Friday, 17th April

I was given the Chapel Room, a stuffy, old-fashioned bedroom, with a huge made-up, oak bed, very comfortable with two fat rich linen pillows.

Mass in the chapel at 9. One of the Jesuits from Beaumont comes three times a week to say Mass. The Blessed Sacrament is kept in this chapel which is well arranged and well furnished. It is not the usual makeshift type found in most country houses, like for instance poor Mrs. Cooper's at Hambleton. The floor is covered with a red plush carpet up to the walls which are simply panelled. The prie-dieux are well padded and heavy with plush. Rare vestments are kept in the sacristy. Alathea came in late and bare-headed. She hastily snatched a black veil from her prie-dieu and adjusted it as she knelt.

The ceremony was somehow extraordinary. There were Magdalen, Alathea, a lady's maid and one old woman from I don't know where, all under veils. Lord FitzAlan served in spite of his eighty-seven years, shuffling about and genuflecting like a two-year-old. The priest, Father Day, a son of the judge in the Parnell case, is a cripple with arthritis and can barely move with a stick. He crawls at a snail's pace, leaning heavily on the stick. I was in agonies lest he or Lord F. should collapse and have to be propped up. As it was each supported himself upon the other. Yet the scene was impressive and the recollection of it fills me with pleasure. I went to Confession and as usual had to rack my brains to extract the worst sins since I last confessed, which was at Dover I believe. I find it hard to decide what are my sins. I was given 3 Paters, 3 Aves and 3 Reginas. Only Lord F. and I communicated. Lord F. handed me a clean napkin and I trembled lest the priest, who was creaking and groaning, should drop the wafer. The wafer dissolves so foamlike in the mouth, always adhering to the roof of the mouth first of all.

I drove to Egham station with Father Day, who is an inquisitive old man, wanting to be told everything, who I am (who am I?), how I spell my name, how long I have known Cumberland Lodge and what is my age. Not an agreeable priest, and his false teeth do not fit.

Saturday, 18th April

The Wintertons are here for the weekend. I met them with Helen in the village, and we walked back to the house for luncheon. Lady Winterton is a curious stick, frumpish, contradictory, prudish you will think. She makes surprisingly outspoken remarks which are quite uncompromising and often unconsciously funny. Lord W.,[57] who at twenty-one was the promising young man in the House of Commons, has at sixty not progressed beyond this unfulfilled stage of adolescence. He is tall, gaunt, willowy. He talks a great deal, has attentive manners of the old school, and indeed a schoolboy's charm. He is particularly sweet with children. At times he gets angry, for he is very retentive of anciently formed opinions. Apparently he senses every fluctuation of the moods of the House of Commons, and has known every politician and every great house in London since Gladstone's day. He has trustful, open blue eyes that rove around. You can tell by the movement of his mouth and his giggles that he is not a clever man. He sits bent over himself at table, and in his enthusiasms rubs his long hands together and shoots out an arm ahead of him in gesticulation and sheer joy of expression. When he laughs, which he often does over his own stories, he jumps up and down in his chair like some elongated doll on a spring.

Sunday, 19th April

Francis has been mowing the lawns round the house with the motor tractor, leaving the dead grass lying, so that there is a heavenly amber-sweet smell of hay, as in midsummer. I wish there were more wild flowers here besides the dandelions, which I love and others disdain. I lay on the grass and peered closely into the head of one. It was like looking into the inmost recesses of the sun, aswirl with petal flames alive and licking each other. To think that each of the million dandelions in Buckinghamshire, which are taken for granted or ignored, is in fact a marvellous star of golden beauty. How blind human beings are to the best around them, and perceptive of the worst! I must admit that the dandelion's leaves are coarse and common, unworthy of the resplendent head.

After dinner Eddie Winterton poured out stories of the last war, the dance he gave in Cairo, and Lord Allenby's outbursts of temper over small matters, *viz.* with his A.D.C.s because they could not find his Easter eggs. They called him the Bull. E.W. thinks he was a great soldier. He said that Churchill had quarrelled with Roger Keyes and Lord Trenchard so that they could no longer meet; that recently Trenchard left Downing Street in the middle of dinner after Winston called him a liar, and that Mrs. Winston followed Trenchard down the pavement and begged him to return. Lord W. says that as a young man Winston's manners were worse than Randolph's, which seems to me incredible. He thinks Randolph will not achieve anything because he lacks the industry and application

---

[57] 6th Earl Winterton (1883–1962), an Irish peer. Conservative M.P. for nearly 50 years. Lady Winterton *d.* 1974.

of his father. Lord W.'s aunt was Lady Blandford, sister-inlaw of Lord Randolph. She told him that all Churchills were undoubtedly eccentric even when brilliant. Her husband, who died young, was more brilliant than Lord Randolph. Lord W. told how each of two women guests at a Hackwood house-party confided in him separately that Curzon loved only her. All sorts of gossip he reeled off.

Wednesday, 22nd April

Motored to London after work and gave a lift to a man from the Pedestal to High Wycombe. He told me he was a milkman and was only allowed five gallons of petrol a month to do his rounds. When the allowance ran out, he delivered on foot. At Brooks's Eddy S.-W. dined with me. He warned me not to make marriage an objective, declaring that the only successful marriages were chance ones.

Poor Rick [Stewart-Jones] told me that his mother has had a tumour as large as her fist cut out, besides other smaller ones. The ovaries too have been removed, but nothing else vital. Unfortunately some smaller tumours have had to be left and are to be treated with radium. All were malignant. Di [Murray] rather to my surprise has found faith in some prayer centre people, always a desperate sign with intelligent people.

Thursday, 23rd April

Today at Bradbourne [Kent] that once most romantic, untouched, primitive Queen Anne home of the Twisdens, I was reminded of a meeting in a House of Commons committee room just before the war. A few of us were assembled to discuss how the East Malling Horticultural Research station could buy and establish itself in the place. For some reason Lloyd George joined us. He swept into the room like a whirlwind. When he settled down I observed him. He resembled a red turkey cock with a crest of white feathers. He gobbled and spluttered, was opinionated and rude. When this plethoric old bird announced that he did not care a damn about the beautiful Bradbourne, or for any country house for that matter, I hated him. Of course I was too insignificant for him to address a word to me. But I cast such intensive looks of hatred and indignation at him that he was obliged to notice them. He merely gave me a frown of irritation as though I were a tiresome fly. I was glad that I had at least caused him a fly's irritation.

My reception at the Wool House in Loose was just as Eardley foretold. The house has been divided into two since the war. Miss Hunt lives in one part; some people called Beeson in the other. The house is a hideous, pretentious, genteel over-restored fake, just like its inhabitants. A horrible property. I hope it gets bombed. Miss Hunt shouted a catalogue of grievances against the Trust for not carrying out repairs to the bogus half-timber which she had been obliged to attend to at her expense. It is true that plaster is falling off the panels, and you can see daylight between plaster and beams, most of which should never have been exposed. The Beesons came out of their part and shouted abuse at Miss Hunt, and then at me. I could not bear it and fled, without seeing the museum of African flints and trophies.

Drove down Watling Street, by Gravesend and Deptford. This unconfined, Thames estuary is rather exciting, sprinkled as it is with drifting pylons, factory chimneys and distant gasometers gleaming in the sunshine across the river, with squadrons of bombers flying overhead.

Saturday, 25th April

Wickhamford. Up at 7.10 with Deenie to prepare breakfast. This early hour is quite unnecessary, but Deenie fusses inordinately and is in deadly terror of my father. We made porridge, coffee and toast. Papa came down at 8.45 to ask why breakfast wasn't ready – why indeed? – and at that moment the toast, which we had forgotten, burst into flame and, when I had blown it out, emitted black smoke and a stink. The vicar, who had had communion in the church all by himself, came in to talk while we cooked; then Mrs. Haines, then Mrs. Mansfield for a gossip before starting housework; then Haines carrying tins of evil-smelling paraffin. While we were seated round the kitchen table the milkman's wife ambled in to fill the jugs and pass the time of day. Papa took all this informality quite well, though looking very stiff and starch as my grandmother used to look at her croquet parties.

Tuesday, 28th April

Miss P. told me in the office that the Bath Assembly Rooms had been gutted by fire in the Bath raid on Sunday night. It has upset me dreadfully that so beautiful a building, hallowed by Jane Austen and Dickens, should disappear like this in a single night. Eardley, who was staying the weekend with his mother, came in for the full brunt. He says the Circus has a crater in the middle of the grass, and all its windows are blown out. Two houses in Royal Crescent are burned out, the abbey windows are gone, and the fires and destruction have been devastating. There were no defences, no A.A. guns were heard, and the Germans dived low and machine-gunned the wardens and A.R.P. workers in the streets. This is a reprisal raid for ours over Lübeck. Both raids are sheer barbaric bloody-mindedness, anti-culture and anti-all that life stands for. I positively want not to survive the war when things like this can happen.

At 11 Ted Lister called for me and I took him to Holland House. We walked in at the gates and right up to the house where we talked to the caretaker, who had been on the spot when the house was burnt about a year ago. It is a shell. The only apartment remaining, though badly damaged, is oddly enough the Jacobean staircase, with one of the Jacobean doorways leading to it. The Spanish leather under the stairs is still hanging in festoons from the walls. A sedan chair and a small lacquer chest, half-burnt, are left. The painted panelled room for Charles I which I remembered Lord Ilchester once showing me is gone. We could just distinguish where it had been, and I saw traces of one painted pilaster. The library and everything else irretrievably gone. I am glad I once visited the house, and danced in it, in its heyday. Ted and I walked along the terraces, through the old walled garden and northwards through the park, and down a long lime avenue. The grass was long and unmown, but the trees were fresh and re-budding, quite indifferent to the terrible indignities of last year. The tranquillity made it difficult for us to realize we were in the centre of London. How important it is to preserve what remains of this sanctuary.

I was an usher at Peter Scott's wedding but did precious little work. Kissed K. [Kennet] at the reception but had only a quick word with her. Peter shook hands warmly, and thanked, and God blessed, which I thought nice of him, considering that I have not given him a present – yet.

At tea on the train a small boy without his mother sat at my table and ordered and ate five chocolate cakes. I wondered if I ought to stop him ordering a sixth, and didn't. I spent twenty minutes with Mrs. S.-J. in her Reading nursing home. She is a pathetic little spectacle, shifting about on the bed from side to side, looking white and ghastly ill. She said that she longed to leave her body. 'I am just about to be sixty, and the children say I am still needed. But I don't know.'

Thursday, 30th April

I sent Lord Esher a cutting from *The Times* of today quoting a Wilhelmstrasse statement that they will make a point of bombing English country houses, those haunts of bloated plutocrats and aristocrats, especially the famous 'Tudor' ones. I think the Germans have now plumbed the depths of human degradation by a positive intention to destroy monuments of art.

In King's Bench Walk I was joined at 10.30 by Harold and Jamesey who had been dining together. Jamesey was bright, affectionate and entertaining. He was ebullient and furious about our senseless destruction of the old town of Lübeck, where he said there were no military or factory objectives of any kind.[58] The 'Baedeker' reprisal bombing was consequently brought about by our foolish philistinism. Even Harold did not deny that this Lübeck raid was a mistake on our part. I had no idea of this which puts an entirely different complexion on the whole business. Jamesey said we were worse philistines than the Germans, who do at least care for their own monuments whereas the British are bored to tears by theirs. Harold agreed. Then J. and I became provocative. Harold remonstrated with us in an aggrieved, shocked tone once or twice. He says that when we are with him, it is like a sunny day until a magnifying glass (James, I suppose) is applied to shavings. Jamesey asserted that all civilized people desired a compromise peace. Harold hastened to contradict him with a vehemence which suggested to me that he was in secret agreement. I backed Jamesey up. Harold admitted to me later that Singapore was a bad business; also Hong Kong; that our people were demoralized, and did not fight.

Friday, 1st May

In bed during the night I thought – for I could not get to sleep – I am mentally deficient in some respects. My mind is like a ravine with dense patches of fog. I get along all right until suddenly – blank! I become muddled, fuddled, at a loss for words, even thoughts, and quite inconsistent and irrational; often silly and sometimes hysterical.

At breakfast Harold said, 'Jamesey asks me at times, "Did you not realize in September 1939 that this war would mean the end of the world?" Of course I realized that it meant the end of it for us, but not for the vast majority.' I replied that since I did not belong to the vast majority his argument had no appeal for me.

Caught the 10 o'clock from Liverpool Street to Cromer. Met Harry Strauss[59] on the train. I told him what I thought about the bombing of Lübeck. He answered that the Baedeker bombing would have happened anyway, sooner or later – an inept reply. He seemed distraught and although polite in rising from his seat to shake hands, he was not listening to much I said. He is a worthy man, and earnestly loves the country*side* (I find myself writing this awful word, although 'country' is what I mean). Strauss is small and dark, with straight hair in a line across the forehead as though it were a wig.

I waited half an hour or so in Norwich. Walked from the station to the cathedral, but saw no signs at all of bomb damage, and none to the cathedral and close.

---

[58] James's statement was in fact totally incorrect. Lübeck-Blankensee was a legitimate military target.
[59] Later Lord Conesford, died 1974.

I was met at West Runton by the local committee, headed by the rector, on the station platform. I jumped down hatless and unimpressive. We discussed on the site of the Roman camp (in reality a Napoleonic beacon) with a representative of the Ministry of Supply, the erection of a saw mill on our property. I capitulated, with the committee's concurrence I think. The rector motored me part of the way to Felbrigg. I walked down a lane and along the drive carrying my bag.

It is frightfully cold in Norfolk. There is a bitter wind. The trees are still in bud and hardly green. Ketton-Cremer[60] was not in when I arrived but his manservant, Ward, gave me tea. I learned later that only Ward and his wife 'do'. K.-C. spends most nights at his mother's house, and the daytime here. Then Ketton-Cremer came in. He is big and shapeless, ugly, mild and podgy. He carries his head on one side, and is wan and delicate. He is donnish, extremely cultivated and an urbane and polished writer. He is a trifle ill at ease rather than shy, yet punctilious, methodical and determined. If one let fall ill-considered opinions, he would not leave them unpicked-over, I feel sure. Toryish, if not prejudiced in his views of conduct. Yet open-minded and friendly in a cautious way. Very courteous too. His conversation, though measured and correct, is informative and agreeable. Oh, a most sympathetic man! No wonder Christopher Hobhouse was fond of him.

Saturday, 2nd May

After inspecting our mill at Burnham Staithe I walked to Burnham Market. No food at the Hoste Arms, but at the Nelson I got beer, sausage rolls and hot meat rolls. There were evacuees toping at the bar and recounting their bomb experiences in London. 'The wife said to me, she said, did you ever? Me and my kiddies,' etc. Slightly drunk on a pint of bitter, after my walk, I joined in the conversation and found myself recounting my experiences (they were non-existent) of the Germans and their atrocities. 'Would you believe it,' I said, 'they cut out the heart and began . . . ?' 'Well, I never,' they said in a chorus of delight. Cockneys are good-hearted people. These particularly deplored warfare against women and children. Yes, I said, and put in a plea against the deliberate bombing of our cathedrals and churches, to test their reaction. Reaction: 'One in a hundred may care for such old fashioned places. They are all right to see now and then. It's flesh and blood what matters. For myself, the whole lot can go. Hear! Hear!' All most good-natured and honestly meant. Philistines !

---

[60] R. Wyndham Ketton-Cremer (1906–69), man of letters and biographer. He bequeathed Felbrigg Hall and estate to the National Trust.

The old cottages in this part of the world are faced with smooth flints, or large pebbles picked from the shore, and washed smooth by the sea. They give a cream to the strawberry brick walls. Sometimes they look like Easter eggs stacked in a pile by children. All along the coast to Cromer there is a great structure of iron barricading, covered with barbed wire in defence against the invaders, if they should come this way. The bus with a trailer containing gas kept breaking down, which delayed my return to Runton, whence I had to walk four miles back to Felbrigg.

Sunday, 3rd May

After luncheon walked with Ketton-Cremer round Felbrigg park, now mostly under plough. By the lake we were joined by Rick who is posted at Sheringham for a month's course of gunnery. He was very dirty in his battledress, but bronzed and shiny with health. Also rather smelly – tommy-gun oil and sweat – I could not help noticing. He stayed to tea and departed on his borrowed bicycle. He told us how the A.T.S. all swore, and that now he did not discriminate between a gunner and an A.T. in daily intercourse and speech. When Rick had gone Ketton-Cremer read me his will from beginning to end, asking for comments. Since the will covered foolscap sheet after sheet, and like all legal documents had no punctuation whatever, and the fire in the hall where we sat was hot, I kept dropping off. Politely K.-C. would throw me a deprecatory glance, and continue: 'And such Trust moneys may be invested in or laid out or applied in the subscription or purchase of or at interest upon the security of such stocks funds shares securities or other properties holdings or investments of whatsoever nature and wheresoever as my Trustees shall in their absolute discretion . . .' Pause, and another interrogative glance. 'That sounds perfectly satisfactory,' I would say with too little conviction before nodding off again.

Saturday, 9th May

Over a cup of tea in Brooks's I opened the *New Statesman* and began an artide by Raymond Mortimer on the Royal Academy exhibition. I read that there was one gallery devoted entirely to pictures by Wilson Steer and Sickert, that there was a Vanessa Bell of the Queen and princesses, someone else of the Prime Minister and a Moynihan of Eddy Sackville-West. I was so excited that I did not even finish the article or my tea, and rushed to the Academy before it shut, bought a catalogue and went the rounds. Nowhere could I find any of the sixty or so pictures by the most eminent contemporary artists mentioned by Raymond. The beast had, by way of skit, written a mock review of all those artists' works which he would have liked to see exhibited. I was furious with him.

Monday, 11th May

I went to see Miss Davy, Lord Astor's private secretary at the back of St. James's Square. She is a dear lady, dressed in a well-tailored coat and skirt. Lord Astor has decided to make over to the National Trust, with as little delay as possible, Cliveden House, contents and grounds with an endowment of £200,000, and a hospital in the park, providing another £3,000 to £4,000 p.a.

Churchill's broadcast last night, in which he announced that the Germans had already lost more men on the Russian front than they lost in the whole of the last war, and that the Russians had evidence that the Germans might use gas, gave my stomach a twist, and made me think rapidly and desperately all last night.

Thursday, 14th May

Mr. Forsyth the architect met me at Marylebone station at 10.05 and drove me in a respectable Austin saloon up the Great North Road to Norfolk. Mr. Forsyth is so scrupulously polite, correct, pudic and imperturbable that I feel ill at ease. He listens deferentially and nods his head to every inanity that I utter. He clears his throat continuously and speaks in a low voice for fear of being assertive. Conversation in the car is constrained, and dull. He has a queer straight profile with returning Roman nose, like a face cut out of cardboard. No flicker of changing mood alters his dead-pan expression. Never looking to left or right he drives straight ahead hour after hour. I shift uneasily in my seat. I long to let out an expletive like 'Fuck!' just to see how, or even whether Mr. Forsyth would react. Instead I say timidly, 'Mr. Forsyth!' He inclines his granite profile one inch, and says, 'Yes, Mr. Lees-Milne,' with Uriah Heep-like humility. I say, 'If you don't stop this instant and let me get out, I shall burst my bladder.' He is absolutely appalled. I look him full in the profile. I detect a grey flush on the one cheek visible, and a bead of sweat on the brow. He stops the car in silence. As I get out I say in a jolly way, 'Don't you want to pee too?' He actually scowls, and replies, 'Well, I wouldn't put it quite like that,' yet gets out himself. Long after I am relieved, and back in my seat, I see him through the mirror still at it at the rear wheel of the car. Quite clearly he was in just the same straits as I was. Silly ass. I fear I have so shocked him that he will never think the same of me again.

At Attleborough we look at the magnificent fifteenth-century screen in the church. Later we lunch by the roadside on ham sandwiches, national loaf and chocolate.

On arrival at Blickling we are greeted by a sea of Nissen huts in the park in front of the Orangery, and a brick Naafi construction opposite the entrance to the house. The sudden view of the south front takes the breath away. The front is undeniably noble and impressive. We walk round the outside. Then Lord Lothian's secretary, now our housekeeper-caretaker, conducts me round those staterooms on the first floor that are not occupied by the R.A.F. The furniture, which has not been removed to Henley Hall for safety, is under dust sheets. All the best pictures have been removed too. The R.A.F. are in Miss O'Sullivan's bad books for they have needlessly broken several window casements, and smashed the old crown glass. They have forced the locks of the doors into the state-rooms, out of devilry. This sort of thing is inevitable.

We stay the night at Rippon Hall with the Birkbecks. He[61] was Lothian's and is now our agent, a genial, simple, woolly bear type, very friendly and co-operative. Over coffee I was handed a vinaigrette of saccharine, early nineteenth century, on the lid of which I noticed Newstead Abbey engraved. 'Oh,' said my hostess, 'that was given by Byron to Mary Chaworth. I thought the engraving was Westminster Abbey or something.'

Friday, 15th May

At Melton Constable we were welcomed most kindly by Lord Hastings,[62] who is living in the stable wing, lateral to the main block. He is a sort of Edwardian stage peer with a purple visage. He wears his hat at a roué's angle. He is vastly proud of the place and has recently celebrated his family's 700th anniversary of their lordship of Melton Constable, unbroken from father to son, which is remarkable. He prefaced his reception of us with a resumé of his family honours and connections. His ignorance of the house's architecture was however startling. He kept dogmatizing pompously, and wrongly, about this and that feature. The house is ruined to my mind by the 1880 additions. They could easily be pulled down so as to leave the lovely 'Wren' block intact. But Lord Hastings prefers them to the original house. A pity that it has lost its roof balustrade and cupola. We looked at the church in the park. It contains a Caroline family pew hugely out of proportion to the nave, and an ugly war memorial to the men of Melton Constable. It is headed by the name in large letters of The Hon. – Astley, followed underneath by the names in smaller lettering of the humble privates and gunners of the village.

Sunday, 17th May

Sir Courtauld Thomson's[63] proposition is an extraordinary one. He wants to make over Dorney Wood and the 250 acres in which it stands to the

[61] Christopher Birkbeck (1889–1973).
[62] 21st Lord Hastings (1882–1956).
[63] Sir Courtauld Thomson (1865–1954) was created Lord Courtauld-Thomson, 1944.

National Trust now, reserving a life interest to himself, aged seventy-seven, and his sister, aged seventy-nine, with an endowment of £30,000, and on his death to leave a further endowment of £170,000, a preposterously large sum. The house is to be used as a small Chequers either by the Prime Minister or a Cabinet Minister recommended by the reigning Prime Minister. Mrs. Churchill is lunching with Courtauld Thomson on Monday to look at the place and report to her husband. If the Prime Minister approves, the National Trust and the Government must fight out the problem of holding and administering the endowment. The house is not up to our standard, although a fairly pleasant red brick building, now swathed in, rather dribbling with, great bunches of wonderful wisteria. The central part is possibly of Queen Anne time. Lorimer's additions are indifferent in C. T.'s opinion which I felt free to corroborate. The out-buildings, motor-house, etc. have been faked about in half-timbering to look olde-worlde. The green fields close to Burnham Beeches, in which the house stands, should be preserved. There are several good contents, a large collection of mezzotints and engravings, much late eighteenth century imitation bamboo furniture (beech really), very pretty.

Sir Courtauld is a weird person. I do not quite understand him. Matheson thinks he is after a peerage, and I think he may be disingenuous. He appears to be a very kind old man and devoted to his faithful retainers, whom he pats on the shoulder and orders about gruffly with a twinkle (to the gallery) in his eye to fetch and carry – for their own use and recreation. For instance he sternly ordered his man, who had been unwell, to fetch a chair from the garden house, place it on a certain spot on the lawn and there sit himself down and rest, without moving until he was told.

Eddy said this evening that I was very bad in keeping my friends apart, that I did not like them meeting, and that this was 'one of my small perversities'.

Friday, 22nd May

I was the last to leave the office for the Whitsun holiday, and motored to Wickhamford. Immediately outside the West Wycombe gates a young hitch-hiker hailed me. He told me he had walked throughout the previous night from Oxford to Marlow solely to buy some books, which I thought most laudable. Outside Halls, the shirt shop in Oxford High Street, Auberon Herbert was standing on the pavement. He dragged me off to tea in his rooms in Oriel Street. He said Gabriel [Herbert] was coming to stay the night with him, so I said I would stay too. He had just been staying with the Zogs at Parmoor. He said Queen Geraldine was a real beauty and the little Crown Prince, already a prodigy of learning at the age of four, knew four languages. The Queen's grandmother, a dreadful old American matron, lives with them, and never draws breath for speaking. King Zog is frankly a cad. He wants to buy *The Times* newspaper and told Auberon, 'And I won't give a penny more than ten million for it.' The princesses were present and he overheard them openly speculating on his sexual potentialities. Auberon, who speaks Albanian, understood every word. Champagne flowed before and during every meal. The King enjoys diplomatic status, does nothing but nurse his majesty and take tiny Parisian walks.

Auberon, long, lanky, pale, with his square, low-eyebrowed little face, has much charm. He burbles rather than speaks words, which proceed from his mouth like water from an airlocked pipe.

Wednesday, 27th May

Mrs. Stewart-Jones has been brought back from the nursing home. They found she could not stand the radium treatment and since her chances of recovery are now nil, they have chosen the melancholy course of making her as comfortable as possible in her own room at Cheyne Walk surrounded by the family. She has two nurses and is not expected to live more than three weeks at most. Rick said goodbye to his mother yesterday morning while she was well enough to talk to him, and both were happy. He and I dined together and talked of everything except her condition. I slept in my old room on a lilo, R. in the bed, and was reminded of that evening in September 1938 when we expected war, and the situation was reversed, I in the bed and R. on the lilo. How intense was the agony of unhappiness then.

Thursday, 28th May

Lord Lytton talked about transferring Knebworth to the Trust, as I expected. He betrayed no misgivings about Knebworth being unacceptable on historic or architectural grounds. Since one cannot turn down a man's offer without first seeing the place, I persuaded him to let me go over the property with him in order to report to the committee. Graciously he consented. He is tall, immaculately dressed in a black suit with a long, thin gold chain round his neck, the end of the chain hidden in a waistcoat pocket. He has silvery hair, curling at the back, handsome regular features and a stick-like manner. He is rather pompous, dry, fussy and I should guess, difficult.

I lunched in Cornwall Gardens with Margaret Jourdain and Ivy Compton-Burnett. Ernest Thesiger[64] was the fourth person. He is an old

---

[64] Ernest Thesiger (1879–1961), actor.

pansy, affected, meticulous, garrulous and entertaining. I had not met him
before. We were introduced in the dark hall. M.J. 'So you have met on
the way up?' E.T. 'I knew at once he was the sort of young man you
would rope in.' M.J. 'He is quite a new acquisition.' We sat in a high-
ceilinged, pitch-dark dining-room, with one window opening upon
blank walls and a fire escape. We ate lentil soup, white fish with sauce and
steamed potatoes, a rhubarb and ginger tart, Morecambe shrimps and biscuits. Margaret Jourdain opened a large bottle of Cidrax, poured out
Thesiger's and my glasses and was about to pour her own when Miss C.-
B. shouted, 'Margaret! Remember at breakfast it was decided that you
were to finish the opened bottle of flat Cidrax.'

She makes very acid comments in a prim, clipped manner, enunciat-
ing sharply and clearly every syllable, while casting at one a sidelong
glance full of mischief. We talked about servants. She agreed that today
fewer servants managed to get through double the work, doubly effi-
ciently, to what a greater number did a generation ago. They are better
fed and housed, she said. Her parents took care to have excellent food
themselves, whereas their children were thrown the scraps. While today
children are given pheasant and all that goes with it, in her day they were
given the chips and bread sauce, but no pheasant. For supper she used to
be given the crusts cut from her parents' toast. She has an insatiable
appetite for chocolates, and Ernest Thesiger told her she was intemper-
ate in some of her habits. Miss Jourdain gave us cherry brandy, but did
not offer any to Miss C.-B., who took some for herself. She swigged it
all in one gulp instead of sipping, declaring that it was excellent and she
would have some more. Miss J. intervened and would not allow it.

Talking of sham marbling as a form of wall decoration, Miss C.-B. said,
'I'm all for shams. So long as they are good ones, what do they matter?'
Miss Jourdain said of Freya Stark, who is at present broadcasting from
Cairo under the direction of the Foreign Secretary, that hers 'is the voice
that breathed o'er Eden'.

Saturday, 30th May

I picked flowers to take to Mrs. Stewart-Jones in London. When I
reached Cheyne Walk after tea, I learned that she was dying and not
expected to last many hours. All the family were wonderfully calm and
resigned. Di took in my flowers and about 7.30 came to tell me I could
now go in to see her, for she was having a lucid moment. I went in. She
lay in a bed by the window at the far corner of the room. Rick was at
one side of the bed, offering her a drink of water from a spoon, Edward[65]

---

[65] Edward Stewart-Jones (*d.* 1972), brother of Richard and Diona Murray.

holding her hand at the other side, and Di sitting by the window smiling at me. I went to the end of the bed and blew her a kiss, to which she replied by raising her hand to her lips very feebly. I was struck by the change in her appearance, particularly by her sunken eyes and the sharp, thin line of her jaw. She was propped against raised pillows. Di said to her, 'Jim has brought you these flowers,' and to me, 'Tell her you have brought them for her.' So I said rather foolishly, 'I hope you like them. They came from the garden today.' Edward raised the bowl of roses and honeysuckle and handed her a rose to smell. She understood perfectly and looking at it, said, 'Lovely' in a slow, painful way. This was, I believe, the last word she spoke. She looked at me a little and smiled, then closed her eyes and remained so quiet for a few seconds that I thought she must have died. I saw Rick glance at Edward who did not move a feature. Then she took a deep breath and held her hand to her breast. I noticed how swollen her hands were, and blue. Rick gave me a chair to sit on, but I felt embarrassed by seeming to be curious in just watching her die; and wondered if she were aware of us all listening to her awkward breathing. So I quietly slipped away.

I slept that night in my old room, Edward on the lilo on the floor, R. in the next-door room where Di and Eff were also sleeping. At about 1.30 I heard R. leaning over Edward and whisper something like, 'She is unconscious.' Then I went to sleep again.

Sunday, 31st May

I am only glad to be here at this particular moment because for once in my life I am able to help others. I can wash up – for we eat upstairs by ourselves – run messages and I hope, cheer at times. Nanny brought me a cup of tea at 8 and when I asked how Mrs. S.-J. had passed the night, she answered, 'She left at 1.30 in her sleep quite peacefully and looks happy and beautiful.' People always say these words, and I wonder if they are ever true. At breakfast there was no reference to what had happened so that I wondered if indeed it had.

Rick was particularly anxious for me to go and see her, so I did. When I opened the door the wind through the wide open window blew the bed clothes about gently. Mrs. S.-J. lay on her back as though asleep, with her head visible on the pillow. The room was unnaturally quiet. A screen had been put round the head of the bed, my lupins on the side table, and photographs of all the children, including my Peter Scott drawing, around her. Her handbag by the bed and a handkerchief on the top sheet. It was difficult to believe she was not just asleep as I tiptoed up as though not to wake her. Her grey hair had been plaited and the wind was fanning the loose wisps very gently which gave a further impression of life and only sleep. I looked very closely at her dear little head. The colour was fairly natural, but the features were very sharp and the eye sockets sadly deepened. R. had also said how young and beautiful she was looking; but somehow I did not like the hard line of her tight shut mouth which was not at all characteristic, for in life she had the sweetest, most innocent face conceivable. The outline of her tiny body under the thin covering of the sheet was pathetic.

Monday, 1st June

Matheson met me at Brooks's. He prefaced the interview with the remark, 'If I may say so I think you have done extremely well in my absence.' I replied, 'Well, that remains for you to find out when you return to the office.' How can he have the slightest indication whether I have done well or ill, yet?

Today Rick went to a memorial service for his mother at Leckhampstead, which the villagers had organized on their own. The church was packed with the inhabitants of Leckhampstead and the neighbouring villages. On the way down R. bought sixty cream buns at Newbury, and after the service entertained all the schoolchildren and their parents in his mother's house. He said it was one of the most satisfactory days of his life and just what his mother would have liked.

Saturday, 6th June

A cloudless, grilling day, wonderful to live through. Miss Compton-Burnett and Miss Jourdain came down from London to lunch. I met them at High Wycombe station where they inadvertently left the return halves of their tickets. Away from her own house Miss C.-B. is not quite herself, but at luncheon when we were discussing what we ought to do with the Germans at the end of the war, she came out with a startling, 'I am actuated by a healthy spirit of revenge.' She was wearing a beige governessy dress, beige stockings and a beige straw hat to match. She was very spruce and upright. After luncheon I conducted Miss Jourdain round the house. Miss C.-B. sat all the time on the edge of a Windsor chair, wearing her hat and clutching her parasol as though just about to leave. Walking up the drive they both carried their parasols open although under the trees. Eddy said they looked the epitome of late Victorian, middle-class respectability. Helen noticed how nothing escaped them, how their beady eyes looked through her, up and down, through her, letting nothing slip, quietly curious, missing nothing.

Miss C.-B. remarked to Eddy (apropos her greed), 'I like Manchester. One gets such good teas there.'

I asked her at luncheon to which county she belonged. She said, 'Wiltsheer', for her father had a house there when she was a child. I think the Hills told me she had a brother, whom she adored, killed in the last war, and two sisters, each of whom committed suicide in the same room within an interval of some three years.

Her opening remark to Eddy was, 'We are such cowards. We both hate air-raids and are frightened to death of bombs.' To me she said, 'We could never possibly win a George Cross.' 'You never know,' I answered, 'the most unlikely people have done so.' She said, 'We might be the cause of someone else getting it through our being in the way for them to save.'

Sunday, 7th June

Eddy was staying last weekend at Victor Cazalet's, where King Peter and the Queen of Yugoslavia were guests. They brought no retinue, no valet or maid, only one lady-in-waiting. The King had an enormous Cadillac in which they drove to the cinema in Cranbrook. The King washed up after dinner, or rather carried some glasses into the pantry and made a gesture of washing up, *'pour rire'*. Eddy liked the Queen, who is stout and simple, and intelligent. He did not much care for the King, whom she addressed as 'Son'.

Wednesday, 10th June

After dinner I went down to Miss Millbourne's cottage in the village where Captain Hill and William Weir were dining. I guessed that Miss Millbourne had been sitting on the empty chair because it felt warm when my bottom touched it. Weir is a splendid old man, and so Scotch that often I cannot understand what he is saying. Now that Troup is dead he is the father of the S.P.A.B. committee. He is the foremost expert at repairing old buildings alive today. He told us he knew William Morris intimately, and in Morris's lifetime looked after Kelmscott for him. He also worked under Philip Webb whom he considers the greatest architect of his time. Weir helped Webb build Clouds for the Wyndhams. Mr. Wyndham wanted Morris to do the interior decorations and Weir was present when Morris visited Clouds during a weekend while the guests were lounging about the hall in armchairs. Morris was provoked to say: 'I see this is already a home for incurables.' Weir said there was no one quite like A. R. Powys[66] for distinction of manner, appearance and scholarship.

Weir is always eager to impart the knowledge he has gained throughout a full working lifetime. He gave Hill and me several hints which we

---

[66] Brother of T. F., John Cowper, and Llewelyn Powys. He was for many years Secretary of the S.P.A.B. He died in 1937.

put down on paper. For re-leading roofs he advised the use of 'cast' rather than 'milled' lead, in sheets no larger than 7 ft. by 3 ft., in order to avoid excessive expansion and contraction; and the use always of old lead for re-casting. He said lead will perish if laid on oak, owing to some form of acid in oak. Even the lead casings of electric light wires will so perish, whereas they will not if laid on pine. With regard to beetle, he said the bugs begin eating the damp parts of wood where there is sap, which is usually on the ends of timber resting in the walls. The bugs then work their way to the dry wood in the centre. Beetle won't attack pine, and never pitch pine where there is resin. The time to de-beetle is in May and June when the creatures fly out to mate, returning to lay eggs at the end of their three years' existence. He considered Heppels Fluid far the best antidote for beetle, although too strong for furniture. It is apt to take away varnish and polish.

Saturday, 13th June

I took a bus to Knebworth where I was met by the agent and motored to Knebworth Manor. Lord Lytton pompous, courteous in a keep-your-distance manner, patrician and vice-regal. He was wearing rather precious country clothes, a too immaculate tweed suit, a yellow-green shirt of large checks loose at the collar, and that gold chain round the neck again. He has truly beautiful blue eyes. If one did not know otherwise one would suppose him to be what my father calls 'effeminate' by the well cut, yet long silver hair deliberately curled over the nape of his neck.

We walked through the gardens to Knebworth House. It is undeniably hideous. The old house was rebuilt by Bulwer Lytton in 1847 and if only Lord Lytton had not recently removed the gargoyles from the absurd turrets and the heraldic animals from the terrace, it would be a perfect specimen of a Disraelian patrician's Gothic mansion. The whole outside is stuccoed in a base way. The Jacobean grand staircase and the Presence Chamber upstairs are terribly shoddy. The only room that I liked was the Palladianized great hall. Lord Lytton has had the paint stripped off the wainscote. He said it was the first stripping to be undertaken in England. At present the Froebel Girls' College is installed in the house, which becomes them. Lord Lytton is determined to return to the house after the war. I insisted on going round the estate for he offers the whole 3,000 acres in endowment. My view is that the estate is more worth holding, because of its nearness to London, than the house, for all its historic associations.

We had tea with Lady Lytton who is still a beautiful woman. The tragedy of Antony Knebworth[67] hangs heavily upon her.

---

[67] Antony, Viscount Knebworth (1903–33), was a paragon about whom a memoir, *Antony*, was published in 1935.

I got back to London late for dinner to find Jamesey waiting. We dined at Brooks's over claret and returned to his flat in Chester Square where I stayed the night. We talked of Bulwer Lytton and he lent me a book about him.

Jamesey said he wanted to sleep with a woman, and expressed misgivings. I said it was as easy as falling off a log. The moment these words were out of my mouth I realized how discouraging the simile must have sounded.

Sunday, 14th June

I went to Dorney Wood to tea with Sir Courtauld Thomson who wanted to tell me all about his luncheon with the Prime Minister yesterday at Chequers. To his delight Churchill insisted upon motoring to Dorney Wood there and then in spite of the fact that he habitually rests every afternoon. Mrs. Churchill and Miss Thomson motored in the Thomsons' car, Sir Courtauld with Churchill in his. The car is armour-plated and the windows are bullet-proofed, an inch thick. Churchill had a tommy gun beside him which he played with throughout the journey. He was wearing his siren suit and smoking endless cigars. Sir C. said he was in the best of form; and Sir C. was flattered to death at engaging the Prime Minister's attention from 1 till 7 p.m. Churchill has evidently approved the scheme and told Lord Portal he must accept the offer without to-do. Sir C. expressed some anxiety over the endowment and death duties, and Churchill said quite calmly but firmly, 'Then I shall have an Act of Parliament passed.' Although a quondam Chancellor of the Exchequer Winston showed childlike ignorance about death duties.

Saturday, 20th June

At the White Hart in Lincoln I met Lord Brocket who motored over from Burghley. He drove me in his blue two-seater Rolls-Bentley up the Roman road to Norton Place. Here we met Major Hoult, his agent, and his nephew, a Colonel Trevor (younger than me), in the Commandos. We motored round the whole property. Lord Brocket went conscientiously into every cottage and over every farm building. We spent two hours doing this. The outcome was that he did not agree with Captain Hill that the estate is 'derelict'.

At 5.30 we left for Culverthorpe, giving lifts on our way to R.A.F.s and W.A.A.F.s. Brocket is breezy and good-natured although he does 'buck' a bit. He has a slightly tiresome seeing-the-sunny-side-of-every-thing manner. He is amusingly conscious of his nobility, and explained at great length his Irish descent from the O'Cains, whoever they may be. His crest of a cat rampant figures prominently on the radiator of his car.

However, he is condescending enough to include me among the well-bred. He did not care much for Culverthorpe. I think it is lovely although in a deplorable condition owing to the troops stationed in the house all the war. The splendid hall has been partitioned into an orderly room and officers' mess with passage in between. The capitals of the columns have been boarded up, and the Wootton panels shrouded under canvas. I noticed a great crack in the Hauderoy painted ceiling over the stairs. Many glass panes are broken and the surrounds of one window are blackened by a projecting stove pipe.

We reached Ayot St. Lawrence at 11 p.m. The whole village, olde worlde and rather horrifying, particularly the Brocket Arms, belongs to him. Much to my surprise he banged on the inn door. I saw he had been leading up to something. It was to be a pretty piece of patronage. The publican opened the door and there was a great deal of, 'Oh, your lord-shape! You must come in. My friends would be honoured to see your lord-shape,' for it was after closing time. We were ushered into the saloon bar, I keeping well to the rear like a bad smell. The publican clapped his hands, and announced in an awful voice, 'This is Lord Brocket.' B., still wearing his cap at a jaunty angle, beamed, bowed and received the homage of a dozen demi-mondaines and flash-alfs during an impressive hush. Trying to be inconspicuous I was pushed forward. I must say B.'s friendliness is unfeigned. He introduced me to all and sundry, and shook hands with them in a hearty fashion. The peer charmingly condescending. We were supplied with 'gin and It' and cheese rolls. There was much forced hilarity, B. nudging me and laughing a bit too much. With more ushering, the other way round, and 'Good night, Lord Brocket! Good night your lord-shape,' we swept out, having caused a stir, and left them all astounded.

We got to Brocket at midnight. The big house is filled with expectant and parturiating mothers from the East End, so Brocket keeps a room at Warren House across the lake, a little seventeenth-century bailiff's house. Here we drank tea and ate sausage rolls. I asked him outright how closely associated he really had been with Hitler. He said he had only met Hitler three times through H . . . (whose name I forget), his link with the Nazis. He knew Ribbentrop quite well, and liked Goering, who was 'the only gent of the party'. In fact Brocket has faint hopes even now that at some future date terms might be reached through Goering. I asked him if he had believed Hitler to be honest. He said, 'No, not exactly.' From the first he thought him repellent and abnormal. For instance, in 1938 Hitler foretold that something dramatic must happen on 1st October that year. H . . . told Brocket that to make sure the Führer's presentiment was fulfilled the leading Nazis felt obliged to arrange that something – no matter what –

should take place for face-saving reasons. The democratic press had infuriated Hitler by saying the Germans were massing along the Czech frontier, whereas they were not doing so. The democratic press was Hitler's bugbear, and he told Brocket that Chamberlain ought to put the English press lords in a concentration camp. Brocket replied, 'I agree. Only you will have to put your press controllers in camps likewise, and we shall all be happier.' And Hitler added, 'I will put them in the same camp.'

Brocket greatly admired and liked Chamberlain. The truth is that although Brocket is a fundamentally nice man, he is stupid. Chamberlain ought not to have been so intimate with a man of his calibre. One infers that the fleshpots of Brocket and Bramshill were a bait. At any rate Chamberlain made a confidant of Brocket who found himself in an exalted position undeservedly. Then he was made a scapegoat. B. told me that because he was so frequently in Germany and was so closely connected with the leading Nazis Halifax used him as a channel through which to communicate to Hitler and Ribbentrop the views of the Government. He assured me that he constantly warned the Nazi leaders that Britain would fight, if only with her fists, were the Germans to march into Poland. The Nazis just would not believe this threat. Hitler never relinquished his belief that Chamberlain had bluffed him at Munich by pretending that Britain was in a position to fight, if sufficiently provoked, nor his subsequent conviction that such action was quite impossible. Hitler harboured a grievance against Chamberlain ever after.

Brocket's nervous breakdown at the beginning of the war was brought about by the aspersions thrown at him from all quarters. He confesses that he has not yet recovered, and cannot walk any distance, and is suffering from a weak heart. At all events he was graded Class 4 and rejected for military service. At the end of these confidences he said we must be on christian name terms; but I don't for the life of me know what his name is. I feel rather sorry for him. He is by no means dislikeable.

Sunday, 21st June

I sat reading all morning while Brocket interviewed his men of various kinds. He is a very keen and enthusiastic landowner, and flits from one country seat to another. We motored across the park to the pub for luncheon, and ate cold but excellent lamb sandwiches and drank shandy. He is too breezy with yokels in the bar. It don't quite ring true, embarrasses me a lot and them a little, I dare say.

Brocket told me that the ironwork clairvoyée, gates and railings, came from the Grove, Chiswick, and are a pair to and contemporary with the Devonshire House gates now in the Green Park. They certainly are fine, in spite of the addition of the Brocket cat rampant, an excusable vanity, and quite in the tradition of the new nobility.

I returned to West Wycombe while the 9 o'clock news was blaring. Helen and Gerry Villiers, listening-in in the dining-room, were very depressed about the fall of Tobruk. It is a great disaster and seems unaccountable. It has been a terribly hot day. Lovely days will always be associated by me with international crises, like the ghastly fall of France, and indeed the outbreak of the war, and then the Battle of Britain.

Thursday, 25th June

I attended an interview with the Chief Medical Officer of Health at the Ministry about the Cliveden hospital problem: whether or not the Government will give an assurance that they will rent the hospital after the war, if it is made over to the Trust as endowment. Both Sir Wilson Jameson, the Chief Medical Officer, and Sir John Maude, who is Secretary to the Minister, gave an assurance that the hospital *would* be used right enough, although they could not provide a rental figure, or affirm whether one would be forthcoming. This is not altogether satisfactory. When I saw Miss Davy afterwards, she said that Lord Astor was adopting the attitude of 'take it or leave it' (Cliveden). We must make up our minds at once. This is hardly fair, for the Trust cannot commit itself to accepting a property of such size without carefully weighing income and expenditure.

Friday, 26th June

I found a mural tablet in Oxford Cathedral which fascinated me. I looked at it a long time, and it gave me a strange aesthetic kick. It is quite small, of a Viscount Brounker and his lady, *circa* 1645, in relief. The two of them are reclining, he with his head on his hand, a bland, round, moustachioed head, like that of any bluff, extrovert Brigade officer today, caught in a quick moment of questioning the vanities of his profession. His wife has the seraphic, resigned look of the wise little woman who already knows the answer.

I sat in the shade of St. Mary's looking across at the Radcliffe Camera, meaning to wait until my appointment at 11.45 in New College. Evidently my watch had stopped, for I suddenly awoke to the fact that it was 12.15. I ran to the Warden's House. Mrs. H. A. L. Fisher was quite unconcerned about my lateness. She is a hirsute, plain, very untidy elderly lady, wearing no stockings (at her age!) and showing black, wiry legs emerging from shabby, down-at-heel slippers. She was packing to leave, and was very abrupt, efficient and self-assured. Not at all my sort of woman. The house not my sort of house either. Only the small panelled

room over the porter's lodge was worth a glance, apart from the
Restoration stairway with continuous newel posts. Though coarse, this is
the outstanding feature.

I dined at Braemar Mansions, where there was a lot of plain cooking
to be got down. Basil Marsden-Smedley the other guest, a very loosely
knit man with one withered arm. Miss Compton-Burnett was so
defeatist about the news that Miss Jourdain rebuked her. Miss C.-B. complained that Miss J. on the other hand always thinks the war will be over
in three days' time. Miss J. hotly denied this, and the two contradicted
one another. Miss C.-B. said of Tobruk, 'If *she* is of no use strategically,
why do we endeavour to hold *her*?' She told another story against their
friend at Chedworth, laughing so much that she could barely get the
words out. The friend is so unpopular in the neighbourhood that her
only social intercourse with the local colonels, vicars and doctors is
achieved through blood transfusion parties. She goes to one after
another, where they all lie prone on sofas and the floor in most intimate
positions, and are publicly 'cupped' in turn, and refreshed with tea afterwards.

Speaking of Dorothy Wordsworth Miss C.-B. said she was 'sadly' in
love with William, who reciprocated the passion. It was definitely inces-
tuous, she affirmed. Miss J. denied this. Miss C.-B. said that she knew
Virginia Woolf to speak to when they met, but that was all. She thinks
she was not a great novelist, but a great writer in other respects. She did
not enjoy *Between the Acts*, which betrayed muddled thinking, and was
'too flimsy'. We talked of diaries like Pepys's which had been expurgated
in the nineteenth century. When unexpurgated editions came out these
days, she was invariably disappointed. There was never much revealed
after all. She said that Charlotte M. Yonge was 'a potential strayer'. It
amused her that in *Cranford*, when Lady X after her mésalliance with the
doctor, explained that the two of them had long had an 'understanding',
the ladies of Cranford found the word coarse. The Duke of Windsor had
had an 'understanding' with Mrs. Simpson right enough.

Saturday, 27th June

I drop a pound of truffles on Miss C.-B. first thing, to assuage her passion
for chocolate.

I look at the picture of the week on show in the National Gallery. It
would be an excellent plan never to show more than one picture at a
time. I look greedily, intimately into the Pieter de Hooch courtyard,
examining the details of the pump, the Flemish bond of the brick walls,
the plaster flaking away, the worn steps. The scene might be any old
woman's backyard today.

I dine with Johnnie Churchill[68] and his new little wife. Pam[69] and Derek Jackson join us in the neat little flat. Derek is positively pro-Nazi. What a catching disease Mitfordism is! There is Derek, a gallant man older than me, a rear-gunner in air-force blue, awarded a D.F.C., in private life a brilliant scientist, saying that we can't win the war, that he loathes the British lower classes who have forced us into this unnecessary war (absolute tosh!), and that the Germans know the best way of treating them, which is to crush them under heel. We argued. I think he cannot be absolutely in earnest, but is probably more so than a stranger might suppose possible.

Before the Jacksons came Johnnie told me about his experiences at Dunkirk. He said it was hell, but not such hell as an ordinary air-raid on London. He did not see many of our people die, but he did see Belgian civilians cutting off the heads of German parachutists, and he watched unmoved German airmen burning to death in their planes. He felt very savage, yet exalted. Although only a camouflage major he was put in charge of a whole company of men whose captain, a Highland officer, had been removed for cutting off the fingers of German prisoners for their rings.

Sunday, 28th June

I walked from the station to Clandon where Noel and Giana Blakiston are living among the stored documents from Noel's Record Office. Otherwise they and the two children have this enormous house to themselves. They live in the small room on the right of the hall, and dine in the servants' quarters in the basement. The house is dirty and in decay. We went on to the roof. One chimney stack had a name and the date 1790 carved on the brick. The lead on the roof is thin in places and needs recasting, and relaying. The hall and most of the downstairs rooms are stuffed with records. After tea Noel and the children gave a play in a toy theatre, with scenery of Clandon made by themselves. The words were written by Noel in Pope couplets, very cleverly. The Blakistons are sweet people.

There is a kind of grotto at Clandon, the roof picked out in hewn flint and brick, interspersed with the bottoms and necks of wine bottles.

Wednesday, 1st July

To London for an S.P.A.B. meeting to discuss the society's policy about the rebuilding of churches and other monuments after the war. Esher was

---

[68] John George Spencer-Churchill, artist and old friend.
[69] Hon. Pamela Mitford, married 1936 Professor Derek Jackson.

in the chair. There was, as I expected, considerable difference of opinion, and some members like Mr. Hiorns bored us very much with long, irrelevant dissertations. Lord Esher was clearly not in favour of any form of rebuilding, it seemed to me. I do not go as far as this myself and think that each case must be judged according to its own merits and the state of its damage; that certain churches like St. James's, Piccadilly, where more than the outside walls have survived and where detailed and measured drawings exist, should be rebuilt as they were. Finally a sub-committee was appointed to elaborate the memorandum drafted by John Macgregor.[70]

Macgregor said that the original moulds for the plaster cornices at the Assembly Rooms, Bath, were known to exist, which favours the argument of those wishing to rebuild the Rooms.

Friday, 3rd July

At the Jardin des Gourmets we had a modest dinner, with only lager to drink, and the bill was £1.11s. 6d. for two. It is monstrous! You pay 7/6 table cover, for the mere privilege of sitting down. In fact the new limit of 5/- for every meal seems to be evaded and the price of meals to be increased if anything.

Monday, 6th July

After cashing a cheque at the club and buying Turkish cigarettes at Benson & Hedges I went straight to Miss Davy, whom I now treat like a beloved, old-fashioned aunt. I showed her the figures of our estimates for running the Cliveden property. She believes that what is worrying Lord Astor most is the question how much rental the hospital may command, for if it yields £3,000 p.a. endowment, why should he hand over unnecessary capital to produce that amount. She said to me, as aunt to nephew confidentially, 'As a matter of fact Lord Astor in giving away £200,000 is actually losing only £150 a year.' It is fantastic how high taxation is.

I went straight to the Georgian Group meeting and sat next to Dame Una. Professor Richardson made her and me into a sub-committee to deal with the affiliation of schools, which Mrs. Esdaile's son, a schoolmaster at Stowe, is sponsoring. Dame Una is very much *en deuil* like a French war widow. I put her into a taxi and went to Horne & Birkett.[71]

Mr. Horne took me to lunch at the Law Society, a kind of club. We

---

[70] A pupil of William Weir and leading architect-restorer of ancient buildings.
[71] Messrs. Horne & Birkett, Lincoln's Inn Fields, the National Trust's solicitors. Mr. Horne was the operative figure in the firm.

had a perfectly horrid luncheon, and the cabinet pudding with sweet custard nearly made me sick. Had I only not taken the custard I could have put the pudding into my handkerchief while Horne was not looking. We then walked across Fleet Street to Withers & Co., solicitors to Major Fuller of Great Chalfield. On the way Horne, to my surprise, pointed with his stick and said: 'That is where Clifford's Inn was, and where I used regularly to have tea with my old friend, Samuel Butler.' I asked him what he was like. He said he was a little shrivelled man with a scrubby beard and eyes that twinkled mischievously. He had been at school with Horne's uncle and was an old Salopian. He lived with an odd sort of servant. Butler and Horne watched the Coronation (King Edward's) together, so the latter told me.

The Withers' solicitor was stout and pompous. Afterwards Mr. Horne said, 'That man would have browbeaten me if I had been just an insignificant little attorney instead of a solicitor of standing.' I was impressed.

From 4 till 6 we were closeted with the Brettingham agent, a fairly handsome bounder. This man cast glad eyes at me. He did this once before. He is very genteel and familiar in an uncertain sort of way.

Old Ted Lister took me to *Iolanthe* which began at 6.45. We sat in the front row of the stalls. Ted adored it and chortled so loudly that I was embarrassed. 'We couldn't help ourselves,' they sang. And the Fairy Queen commented, 'But you seem to have helped yourselves liberally.' In the interval I rang up Cheyne Walk and was told that Q. had been trying to get hold of me. I had a sharp pang, for this information made me wish I were with Q., drinking wine and flirting with her in some expensive restaurant instead of with old Ted in Schmidt's (whither we went to drink dark beer and eat Frankfurter sausages).

Ted gave me this example of how women stink and men do not. Mrs. Jenkins was playing the harp one hot afternoon at Westwood, and smelt horribly. Then her daughter sang and she stank so much that Ted had to put his handkerchief to his nose and rush to the window to avoid being sick. Then the son played the harp and the nostrils could detect nothing amiss. However, Ted would not risk a repetition of mother and daughter's performances, and moved the whole party on to the lawn.

Thursday, 9th July

I met Sir Courtauld Thomson by appointment. He is going to see Lord Portal[72] tomorrow about Dorney Wood, having asked Sir John Anderson, who is a member of Brooks's, what sort of a man Portal is. The reply was

---

[72] 1st Viscount Portal (1885–1949), industrialist. Minister of Works 1940–42.

that he is a very cautious man who before making a decision endeavours to fathom peoples' motives.

I stepped out of Trumper's straight into Heywood Hill's shop, and the horrid, pungent Brilliantine which they put on my hair nearly asphyxiated everybody. Nancy said that if there had been a window that opened, she would open it. She told me she had refused to go to Deborah Cavendish's[73] ball or to any party because the news was so bad, and this attitude had annoyed Helen who is staying with her. Tom [Mitford] is in Libya and may at this moment be fighting for his life. He is in the armoured division, she thinks diverted there from India in order to reinforce our troops. She also refuses to use her electricity for hot water, and this too annoys Helen quite a bit. The public, she says piously, have been asked to save electricity.

Friday, 10th July

Matheson, Eardley and I attended an absurd Trust meeting at Watlington [Park], absurd because there was not a single committee member apart from the chairman. When it was over Esher sent Eardley and me out of the room in order to discuss with Matheson the staff reorganization. Eardley and I stood in the hall straining our ears to catch what Matheson was shouting to Esher, who is a little deaf. I crept down the passage as far as I dared. I nearly reached the keyhole but Eardley made me giggle so much that I had to come away for fear of betraying myself.

Saturday, 11th July

On my way to stay with Midi in her cottage on the Buscot estate I had an hour between buses to spend in Oxford. I wandered into the Sheldonian Theatre. An old, bent woman sold me an admission ticket and would follow me, sitting and breathing heavily whenever I stopped to look at the ceiling. This irritated me profoundly and I asked acidly if visitors were never left alone. She said No, they weren't. Thereupon I lost my temper, and walked straight out. In one way and another the Sheldonian leaves something to be desired.

After luncheon Midi and I bicycled to see Margaret Douglas-Home, living in another cottage, but in Buscot village. It is a single sitting-roomed workman's cottage, and her children play in the street with the other village children. Margaret got the George Medal a year ago for saving two children, one after the other, from a blazing house in the East End during a blitz. She told Midi she did not do it out of courage but

---

[73] Lady Andrew Cavendish, now Duchess of Devonshire. She is the youngest daughter of the 2nd Lord Redesdale.

anger with the children's mother for making a scene in the street. She had to break one child's leg to release it from a fallen beam. She gave her name as Mrs. Hume and walked away. But her identity was discovered. After tea we bicycled over the fields and across the river to Kelmscott [Manor].

The old, grey stone, pointed gables are first seen through the trees. The house is surrounded by a dovecote and farm buildings which are still used by a farmer. The romantic group must look exactly as it did when William Morris found it lying in the low water meadows, quiet and dreaming. It is like an etching by F. L. Griggs. The garden is divine, crammed with flowers wild and tangled, an enchanted orchard garden for there are fruit trees and a mulberry planted by Morris. All the flowers are as Pre-Raphaelite as the house, being rosemary, orange-smelling lilies, lemon-smelling verbena. The windows outside have small pediments over them. Inside there are Charles II chimneypieces, countrified by rude Renaissance scrolls at the base of the jambs. The interior is redolent of Morris and Rossetti, yet not the least nineteenth century, which speaks loudly for their taste. Most of the rooms have Morris wallpapers, and contain many framed drawings by them both, of Mrs. Morris and the children. The room in which Morris worked has a great four-poster. Rossetti's room is lined with the tapestries which, when the wind blew them about, worried him and induced nightmares. I like bad old tapestries to be chopped about and treated as wallpaper. They make a superb background to pictures. I leant out of the casement window, unlike the Lady of Shalott, and gazed across the flat, meadowy landscape and the winding river which looked so comfortable and serene. I do not remember experiencing such sweet peace and happiness as during these two hours.

Old Miss May Morris stupidly left the house and contents to Miss Lobb, the woman she lived with. On the latter's death six months afterwards everything was sold. Interested friends bought back what they could. All Mrs. Morris's clothes went and were last seen tossed about by farmers' wives. We saw the room where Miss Lobb died, while eating veal pie and shouting at the top of her voice.

Sunday, 12th July

Midi and I went for a long walk through hayfields, talking chiefly about her circle of women friends. She says there is nothing they will not discuss with her and each other unashamedly. They tell her how often they sleep with their husbands, what they do in bed, and whether it brings on palpitations. One of them says her husband, although little over forty, cannot sleep with her more than once a month because all his life he has had too much sex. I just don't believe this reason is the true one. There can't be any man of that age incapable of sex at least once every night in the year. What I do know is that husbands do not talk together about their wives in this fashion.

Wednesday, 15th July

Sir Courtauld Thomson told me he had seen Lord Portal who was courteous and business-like, that six architects from the Ministry of Works have thoroughly surveyed Dorney Wood, and that he still wants the National Trust to accept the property and the £30,000 endowment now in his lifetime. He will leave by will two separate funds amounting to £200,000 in all, one for Government expenditure on the Minister of the Crown who is to enjoy the house, and the other for the Trust to buy additional land round about, as it comes into the market.

At Brooks's I ran into Eddy [Sackville-West], Raymond [Mortimer] and Roger Senhouse,[74] who on seeing me said, 'What a svelte figure he still has!' Eddy said, 'I should think so too at his age. But I must tell you he's blind as a bat and out of vanity won't wear his spectacles.'

Q. dined with me at the Mirabelle in Curzon Street. Together we drank a couple of bottles of *vin rosé* at 18/6 the bottle, the whole dinner costing £4. It was an absurd evening. We both got rather tipsy. On leaving the restaurant at midnight we had to walk down Curzon Street to sober ourselves. Linked arms we swayed. I told her Brocket had written me a letter saying, 'Stop brocketting me.' And Q. said 'And don't start brocketting me either.' In the taxi I thought what is happening now must have happened a hundred, no a thousand, no a million times. How bored taxi drivers must get at nights. Or are they merely revolted? And I also thought, women have legs, and tongues like conger eels.

Thursday, 16th July

I got to Lapworth station in the evening and was met by Baron Ash[75] in a smart trap drawn by a small grey pony. I was very tired but could not sleep for thinking of dear Hamish[76] reported missing in Libya last month. I read the news in an evening paper while sitting on the platform of Wolverhampton station. It seems a short time ago that I spent his last weekend with him before he sailed away. We motored to stay a night with Diana Worthington and Dig Yorke[77] at Weston. We sat on the terrace

---

[74] Roger Pocklington-Senhouse (1899-1970), bibliophile, translator, and co-founder of the publishers, Secker & Warburg.
[75] Donor of Packwood House, Warwickshire, to the National Trust, 1941.
[76] Hon. Hamish St. Clair-Erskine, M.C. (1909-74).
[77] Wife of Henry Green (Yorke), the novelist.

beneath a wall covered with pears. I remarked upon the pears. The two girls sighed, and said how sad it was there was no one left now to pick them.

Friday, 17th July

After luncheon Baron and I drove in the pony cart to Earlswood Moat House[78] in pouring rain, he holding the reins, I an enormous carriage umbrella over our heads. It was an old-fashioned sort of outing. Baron would hold the reins very high, flourish a whip and cry appealingly, 'Now then, laddie! Whoa, little laddie!' nervously, without admitting it. He continually expressed the hope that I was not nervous. I wasn't in the very least.

The Moat House is a yeoman's house built in 1480 and altered in 1550. It has been owned by the Misses Smythe's family since 1743. It is an archaeologists' gem because of its high rich roof and ceiling timbers. It is wonderfully uncomfortable. There is no telephone, no water – but a pump in the garden – no heating, no light, no bath, and no water closet – but an outdoor twin earth closet also in the garden. The two old Smythe sisters gave us tea, stone cold, and delicious rye bread and butter, in a cosy, pitch-dark parlour with a bright fire in an open grate. Grate and fireback depict the fable of the fox and the grapes. I noticed a small oak chest and some rude country oak chairs at the top of the newel staircase. The two sisters must be unique, for they are absolutely of yeoman stock, certainly not gentry, although educated. They spoke slight Warwickshire dialect. Both were dressed in subfusc, buttoned up to the chin. One had a patch over her eye. They were very sweet, and very old-world. They own a house in Wimbledon, which is strange, and said they both haunted the British Museum reading room. The intellectual one is reading the eighth volume out of nine on the *History of the Crimean War*. She was very solemn about this. Their garden is a wilderness, and shrubs are growing over the windows, which are festooned inside with the thickest blackout curtains of flannel.

Saturday, 18th July

From Warwick station I was driven to Charlecote Park. It is the second time that I have been here; the first was in 1936, which shows how long negotiations have been dragging on. On that occasion I was sent to consider and report upon the merits of the house. Sir Henry Fairfax-Lucy, military, dapper and arrogant walked me quickly round the park and garden. It was a rainy day I remember. On returning to the porch,

---

[78] A small house given to the Trust by the Misses J. and M. Smythe, 1929–40.

whence we had set out immediately on my arrival, Sir Henry stretched out his hand and bade me good-bye. In those days I was shy. Nervously I asked if I might see inside. The reply was, 'There is absolutely no need. Charlecote is known to be one of the great, *the* greatest houses of England. Good morning.' So without disputing I went off with my tail between my legs. On my return to the office I was told I had been a fool.

Now as for Sir Henry Fairfax-Lucy, I have today found out about him. He may be a pompous ass like Justice Shallow (who was supposed to be Sir Thomas Lucy), but underneath the strutting, the peppery, the arrogant, surface a kindly old man lurks. In fact I am rather sorry for him, because I think he is a little odd. He is obstinate and muddle-headed because of his oddness. I believe he struggles to be reasonable, and just cannot manage to be. His ideas do not co-ordinate. His lisp is like that of a peevish child eating pap.

We went inside the house this time; and then round the park, again in the rain. He showed me the complicated boundaries of the land he proposes to make over. But he kept contradicting himself so that neither he nor I knew at the end of my visit what his intentions were. Although most indefinite he was most exacting. He was also very cheese-paring, reducing the total income the Trust should receive to shillings and pence as well as pounds. I thought he was rather touching when he urged haste – how is this to be achieved with him? – if we wanted the transaction to go through. 'I don't want to say anything unseemly, but Lady Lucy is very seriously ill.' The place is of course hers, not his.

Sunday, 19th July

I read in the paper that the new Lord Knebworth has been killed in Libya. This will be a devastating blow to the Lyttons, and I dare say will dish the scheme for Knebworth after all.

Monday, 20th July

I stayed the night with the Price Woods at Henley Hall outside Ludlow. Mrs. Wood and her head housemaid helped me go through the Blickling tapestries in search of moth. I unrolled them on trestle tables out of doors and brushed them with hard bristle brushes. Then spread them loosely on the lawn and yew hedge in the sunlight. Then spread them flat and sprinkled them with napthaline flakes, rolling them up with wax paper, and tying them round with newspaper outside. This operation took all afternoon.

I was struck again by the selfishness of the Woods. They have eight servants in the house, wearing uniforms as in pre-war days. When Colonel Wood suggested having someone to stay, mentioning a name, his wife retorted, 'We can't have sick people to stay here.' She said to me, 'If there is any threat of evacuees I shall spread out the art treasures and furniture into more rooms.' And she added, 'We are keeping it very dark. We do not want them to take away our cars. We have two Rolls Royces and one Rolls-Bentley laid up.'

Wednesday, 22nd July

To my surprise the dentist did not pull any teeth out, but said the cause of the trouble was an old stopping. This he removed and replaced. As I write the toothache is as bad as ever.

Nancy lunched with me at Fleming's Hotel. It was a mingy meal for which I paid 18/-. To my joy she said that Hamish was a prisoner of war, slightly wounded.

At luncheon the waiter asked, 'Will you have cream with your gooseberries, m'm?' 'Yes, rather,' said Nancy. 'Delicious chalk.'

By the evening my toothache began again, and was far worse than before. I had a terrible night without any sleep at all. Each time I nodded from utter exhaustion, I was woken by the pain. It kept recurring in spasms with such acuteness that I had to get out of bed and walk up and down the room, holding my head. The only relief was sipping cold water and rinsing it round the bad tooth.

Friday, 24th July

After another terrible night, during which I kept sponging my face with cold water, for rinsing the mouth ceased to be effectual, I went to London again. The dentist took out the temporary stopping of Wednesday which was pressing on the nerve, and substituted gutta-percha. Now there is no pain at all. An extraordinary thing is how quickly humans like animals forget that only hours ago they were in agony. When free of pain one cannot sympathize with the pain of others. The person in pain becomes a bore, and the painfree person hates him.

Monday, 27th July

The committee today raised my salary from £400 to £500 p.a. Eardley's to his, and my disgust, was raised a mere £25 p.a. He is going to write to the committee refusing it.

Wednesday, 29th July

When the others had left the office this evening Matheson became confidential. He told me the committee had agreed to engage a head agent to be paid £1,200 to £1,500 a year. This man would gradually replace our local agents and local committees. Meanwhile he must visit all the properties and formulate plans for their management. He went on to say he wished to see the Trust's organization put on a new footing before he left when the war was over. To my great surprise he thought I should take his place, and the committee thought so too. It is surely gratifying to be told this, but honestly I do not know that I should care for the responsibility of secretaryship: and certainly not if it meant relinquishing my country houses.

Friday, 31st July

Another breeze with Helen thus morning. She was very annoyed that the National Trust would not consent to register as a householder in order to acquire twenty-five hens, in other words to keep her twenty-five hens (already acquired) for her. We cannot because it is illegal. So she said, 'Then you National Trusts will have to go without and watch us eat eggs, that's all.' I replied, 'Rather than do that, we will go elsewhere where we shall get eggs.'

Saturday, 1st August

I saw Robert Donat in *The Young Mr. Pitt*, and was moved to tears. I feel very ashamed when cheap patriotism makes me weep. It is not a true emotion. The most casual sights make me weep, Queen Mary with her parasol, a military band playing, and even a kitten being removed by a kind policeman from the middle of a road.

At 6.30 Jamesey and I met at the New Theatre for the last performance of *Othello*. Our seats were at the back of the dress circle, with no more than an inch above our heads. The heat was stifling, our neighbours smelt. We left after the second act through sheer exhaustion. Shakespeare is like *The Times*. One must feel strong before plunging into either. Noël Coward and *The Daily Express* require less effort. We dined at a Turkish restaurant in Frith Street off vine leaves cooked in rice, sour milk and sugar.

Sunday, 2nd August

Jamesey says that if knowing famous men and keeping diaries is all that is necessary to acquire fame, he wonders more people do not keep them. Cecil Beaton, he says, writes such a diary, and J. has read parts of it. I didn't ask if he had cribbed it, as he cribbed Harold's, or if he was shown it.

I lunched with James and Dame Una in her new house in Ladbroke Grove.

After luncheon she and I went by bus to visit Clarissa Churchill who is living in a gardener's bothy in Regent's Park. We found Clarissa alone in this tiny bothy, very pale and white, and listless. The Dame and I walked round the garden of Hanover Lodge along the bank of the Paddington Canal. She told me how depressed she was about the conduct of the war. She believed that people were beginning to lose faith in their leaders. She experienced a sense of frustration in all people she met on committees. She said it was a positive fact that our leaders were muddling along, without policy or plan. She is amazed at the Government's decision to evacuate large towns like Brighton in order to bring people back to London. She only hopes the reason may be to provide billeting space for American troops who will lead the second front. In fact the news is so depressing that one can only dismiss it from one's mind, and not read newspapers or listen to the wireless.

Monday, 3rd August

I have finished Mrs. Gaskell's *Life of Charlotte Brontë*. It leaves out a lot one would like to know; yet the picture she paints of that churchyard at Haworth and the moors behind the rectory is a superb drop-scene to the lives of those queer sisters.

I had tea at Dorney Wood. Sir Courtauld wished to tell me of his interview with Lord Zetland. No very fresh particulars except that he has made up his mind to give Dorney Wood and the preliminary £30,000 endowment without conditions of any sort, reserving no life interest, but taking a lease at a peppercorn rent from us as soon as the deed of gift is signed.

Wednesday, 5th August

I wanted to see the mausoleum at Blickling, so Forsyth and I walked across the park to it. It is a squat pyramid designed by Joseph Bonomi in 1793. Very solid and well constructed with openings on four sides, and an escutcheon and coronet over the entrance. The whole is surrounded by thin iron railings. We found that the padlock had been forced and the gate opened. Also the extremely heavy and large door of the mausoleum was ajar. It too had been forced and even bent. Considerable strength must have been required to do this, and possibly the use of one of several tree trunks lying in the bracken. The floor inside is paved. The interior is, somewhat surprisingly, circular with a domed ceiling which reverberates. Within three deeply splayed recesses are sarcophagi of marble, the central one the 2nd Earl of Buckinghamshire's, the side ones his two countesses'. The left sarcophagus had been hacked with a blunt instrument, and the marble coating prised off the side. Evidently the culprits are the R.A.F. boys who have tried to break open this sarcophagus, believing they would find inside the body of the second countess, who is reputed to have been buried wearing all her jewellery.

Thursday, 6th August

My birthday. I am thirty-four, though I pretend to be thirty-three.

It is wonderful being, if not totally, then chiefly responsible to the committee for Blickling. I am in love with the house, garden, park and estate. Birkbeck takes me round the woods all the afternoon, showing me his new plantations. In spite of the R.A.F. station, Blickling seems to be at the furthermost extremity of East Anglia, even of England.

Friday, 7th August

Spent the morning in the attics with Miss O'Sullivan[79] looking at the portraits which belong to the Peter the Great Room. She showed me the tower and described the route which the black dog takes across the staterooms. Miss O'Sullivan, the most matter-of-fact of ladies, has seen this ghostly creature once. I had a long talk with Miss James the housekeeper, and decided to keep her. She seems a friendly woman in spite of her grand talk of the responsible jobs she has had in the past, at Blenheim, Clandeboye, etc. She told Miss O'Sullivan that at Blenheim she over-ate to the tune of putting on two stone.

I took a bus from Aylsham to Norwich. An old man with a nose the size of his hand and covered with blistered bubbles of skin, got in. A revolting sight. I changed in Norwich for Haddiscoe, where I arrived at the wrong time. There was no one to meet me but the stationmaster, who was most helpful. I had a late tea with Kathleen [Kennet] at Fritton, for I am to stay with the Kennets for the weekend. Lord Kennet arrived shortly after me. We dined off rabbit, claret, nectarines and raspberries. I am already getting a few spots from all this fruit. Lord K. showed me his books. Evidently I said something disparaging. His old bound editions are as great treasures to him as houses are to me. I must concede this. But I do resent Lord Kennet's superciliousness. He is so morose too.

Saturday, 8th August

I stroll about with K. in the morning after being given breakfast in bed. I find myself strangely tired and long to be left alone with the book I have picked up here, Geikie Cobb's on the Ductless Glands, instead of embarking upon intense conversations with K. so early in the day. I give up, for one must pull one's weight a bit in other people's houses when one has been such a fool as to visit them. So I pick raspberries with K. and converse. A Major Jack Abbey comes to luncheon. He is gossipy and wet. In the afternoon I feel really ill and heavy, owing to my epanutin, I

[79] She had been private secretary to Philip Kerr, 11th Marquess of Lothian, who bequeathed the Blickling estate to the National Trust, 1940.

suppose. I sleep hard until tea-time. Peter Scott and his new wife, Jane, come unexpectedly after tea for two nights' leave. At dinner I feel horribly shy with them and hardly speak. This family makes one feel inferior and excluded. I have an admiration for their prowess, and at the same time despise their intellects. They are more intelligent, less intellectual than I am. In fact they are thorough middle-brows. K.'s great failing is to blow the trumpets of her family until one is deafened and wants to run away from the din. It's true they always do the decent, and the right thing. But they appear priggish and self righteous.

We drank champagne for dinner to celebrate Peter's arrival, so surreptitiously, so ostentatiously unostentatiously produced by Lord K. Peter showed us his latest drawings of Jane, also some photographs of earlier drawings of his, including the one of me, which I must say looks better in photograph than in the original. Kathleen was enraptured with the drawings, and cried, 'Look, [Augustus] John could not produce anything finer than these!' None of them has any understanding of art whatever. Then Peter talked of his sea exploits; and I marvelled. He explained how bomb effects are greater on sea than on land. He has certainly done gallant things. His adoring wife is only nineteen. She is a little too skinny and lank to be really beautiful yet. Beauty may come. I am not surprised that she worships Pete who must be romantic in her eyes. For this philistines' ideal of manhood, no, this god, is of course attractive. He is stocky, sturdy and square to be sure with a small bright face and a turned-up nose. There is something great about the sweep of his brow. He is untidy in his dress. His blue eyes twinkle and when he smiles he can be fascinating; and his short, deep laugh is unforced.

Sunday, 9th August

The others sail spasmodically on the lake in their beastly boats, but the water bores me and I don't go near it. When we all meet the fun is not furious and the conversation not sparkling. I feel discontented and unwell. Indeed I wonder why on earth I ever came. With K. alone it would have been fun. Wayland[80] I find no more sympathetic than his father. When at last I can leave for my train I am relieved and happy. Dear K. accompanies me to the station in the Austin 7 and kisses me fondly when the train steams out. She herself said it was a pity my visit coincided with Peter's.

I was very touched to fimd on my return a cable of birthday greetings from my dear brother Dick in Egypt. To think of his bothering to remember while on active service!

---

[80] The present Lord Kennet.

Tuesday, 11th August

While I was walking through the Ritz an umbrella hooked my arm from behind, and there was Peter Derwent.[81] This was my first sight of him since the war. He was looking far thinner, younger and more handsome than formerly. I commented on his thinness and he replied, 'It would be difficult to be otherwise these days.' He has returned from Berne once and for all and hopes to join the R.A.F. He said how sorry he was about Robert's [Byron] death, adding, 'But then we have all had our private troubles,' his only reference to his wife's death in Switzerland. He said what a long time ago it seemed when we four – the other two being Robert and Michael [Rosse] – founded the Georgian Group. Yet it was only five years ago. He seemed unhappy, lost and hopeless.

Wednesday, 12th August

I caught the 8.45 from Waterloo for the Isle of Wight. From the train window Portsmouth looked devastated, with hardly a house intact, yet all the buses and trams were running. The sergeant examining credentials allowed me on board, having looked cursorily at Matheson's letter and my identity card. All harbours are beautiful. Here the width of water, the great chimneys, the cranes and dock buildings, camouflaged in a slipshod, garish way, were no exception. There was much activity of speedboats with barrage balloons floating above them on strings; much leisureliness of warships, grey or camouflaged in sea colours. There were spiky things sticking out of the water along the shores to prevent landings, I suppose. It was a fine and wet day in fits and starts. I noticed some huge floating fortresses out to sea. The docks and harbours looked the only part of Portsmouth not destroyed.

At Newport I was met by Sir Vere Hobart who peered closely at me and said, 'Brigade tie?' It was not, because I never wear one. *Ergo,* he must be rather blind. But he was wearing one. He is a small old man who can't pronounce his 'r's or 'th's. He started off with a long exposition on the pronunciation of surnames, *vide* Hobart, which is always Hubbard, except in Tasmania. Hobart was founded by his relation, Lord *Hubbard.* Did I know this? No, but I might have guessed, had I thought. 'Where that fellow Sir George Arthur left his name, Port Arthur. Did I know?' Yes, I actually did because he was my relation. This retort took him aback, and rather annoyed him. Was I going to like Sir Vere Hobart? And how was I going to stick two nights at Gatcombe House? I wasn't at all sure.

Sir Vere bought this property some six years ago. I cancel my erstwhile

---

[81] 3rd Lord Derwent (1899–1949), diplomat and man of letters.

unfavourable opinion of the Isle of Wight, for the landscape here is beautiful, not flat and uneventful. From all sides of the house spread steep downland hills with distant prospects, and afar off is visible the white crest of a sea cliff near Ventnor. The property extends to 800 acres.

Gatcombe is in good condition, it is built of ashlar; a large square box of 1751 to be exact, with regularly spaced windows. At the back of the house is a huge double chimney for the contending winds. Otherwise only two top-heavy chimneys remain, since Sir Vere has had all the fireplaces blocked up and the chimney-stacks removed.

The inside of the house is ghastly for Sir Vere has painted the woodwork burnt sienna. There is a very nice oak staircase with moulded handrail, continuous to the top of the house. The handrail ends on the ground floor with an abnormal clenched fist over the newel. The dining-room has an ornate rococo chimney-piece, with central carved basket of flowers, also painted burnt sienna. The breakfast-room stucco ceiling is like its walls, salmon pink.

Sir Vere is a genealogist and archaeologist (below ground), two things I detest; also a big bit of a bore. But he is kind to his old grey-haired wife, who is surprisingly commonplace. They seem devoted. They are loquacious on the subject of the parson, with whom they have quarrelled in the true squirearchical tradition. In consequence they patronize the church in Newport, and have constructed their own vault in the garden, out of reach of the Gatcombe graveyard.

After tea the Deputy Mayor – of Newport I suppose – came to drink sherry and meet me!

Thursday, 13th August

Breakfast at 9 and Sir Vere luckily not down until 10.30 so I had some peace. Lady Hobart met me in the hall and told me how delicate Sir V. was. She is obviously anxious about his state of health. She launched into a long, sad story of his first wife's death from a sudden accident while he was ill in a nursing home after a serious operation. This was only seven years ago. I suspect it was suicide on the first wife's part by the way she spoke, but I didn't like to ask outright. She told me how from that day she took him in hand and looked after him. 'Poppy, he said to me,' etc. A touching old thing, shining clean with her white hair, domesticated and shuffling around like a dear old cat. She is very pussylike and motherly.

After luncheon we motored to Newport to see Sir Vere's solicitor. I was made to read the relevant codicil to his will which contains his wishes for the future of Gatcombe. Meanwhile covenants.

I think Sir Vere is a nice old boy really, though a little pigheaded and full of his own importance. His interminable narratives about the Hobart lineage are enough to drive one to drink.

Friday, 14th August

I met John Summerson in Warwick Street and we lunched at the Majorca restaurant. He is with Walter Godfrey running the National Buildings Record. All their photographs are stored in the Bodleian and All Souls, Oxford. After the war John expects the Record will take over the Royal Commission survey. It appears that the Courtauld Institute have given it all their architectural papers.

At 3 the dentist. My old tooth extremely tender when he removed the temporary filling. I always sweat the moment the drill touches my teeth, if not before. I caught the 4.15 to Bradford-on-Avon, changing twice and arriving at Ted's at 8.20, worn out. Yet we sat knitting until long after midnight.

Saturday, 15th August

At 8.30 Christo [Ted Lister's Bulgarian servant] brought me a pot of tea and two thin slices of bread and butter. Otherwise nothing to eat until 1 when Ted got down to breakfast, which he calls brunch. I was ravenous by then. The purpose of this visit was to settle the restrictive covenants which I have persuaded him to give over the house and property of some sixty acres. Ted is considering leaving Westwood to the Trust in his will, if it can be arranged for his cousin to live here. His chief consideration is undoubtedly the house, for I don't think he much cares about his cousin or any relation. The truth is he cannot bear to dwell on the likelihood of his ever dying.

We went conscientiously round the house, and I made copious notes of each feature in each room, which he particularly wants mentioned in the deed, plaster ceilings, plaster friezes, plaster overmantels, stone fireplaces and doorways, panelling, notably the portrait panels of the Kings of England in the Kings' Room, and so on. Each time I come here I am overwhelmed by the perfection of this house. Everything Ted has done to it is in the best possible taste and proves his astonishing, instinctive understanding of the late medieval and Jacobean periods. He has restored the interior porches, the late Gothic mullions and glazing bars, the stucco and stonework, with a restraint and sensitivity which I have never experienced in any English country house of these early dates. Even the patchy rendering of the outside walls, washed over with a primrose to russet harl, rough and broken, with an occasional rambler rose lolloping over the upper windows, is contrived to perfection.

I left on Sunday under something like a cloud. He is a very touchy

old man and was cross with me for venturing to question his allegation
that Helen Dashwood had allowed some myrtle trees at West Wycombe
to die. He claimed that they derived from a myrtle wreath brought
to England from Catherine the Great's floral tiara by Sir Francis
Dashwood, who was an envoy to Russia in her time. He sulked and left
the dining-room, and there was a noticeable coolness right up to my
departure.

Di [Murray] tells me that every preparation is being made for the
evacuation at twenty-four hours' notice of the south coast towns to
London, presumably to make room for troops with which to invade the
Continent. She is on an Evacuation Committee to receive the unhoused.
She also says that convoys of barges are to be seen taken down the roads
to the south coast.

During the last few days I have been reading Byron's *Don Juan* for the
third time. I remember the first was in 1927 during Mama's and my
voyage to Genoa, when I was confined to my cabin in the Bay of Biscay,
feeling wretched. Even then I was able to perceive the wit of it. Now I
still find myself gasping aloud in admiration. There is nothing like it. I am
also in the middle of Symons's Life of Baron Corvo, a most nauseating
figure. Even reading this book makes my flesh creep. It is the aroma of
the soiled priestly habit that makes me feel sick, the very vicious creature
masquerading as deeply devout. I must take warning. I met Symons at
Lady Cranbrook's in the thirties. He was a horrid, sinister character too.

Wednesday, 19th August

As I left the drive in making for the bus stop this morning, a khaki car
hooted at me. Helen was in the company of her American beau, Colonel
Jingle Bubb (this is his real name), being motored to London. They
offered me a lift which I accepted.

At luncheon Esher sat himself down at the table next to mine and
began talking about the country houses scheme. He was disappointed
that so few houses were coming to the Trust. I said I thought they would
come with a rush once the war seemed to owners to be nearing an end.
He asked how the new office arrangements were working out. I said I
was sorry I had decided to take a fortnight's holiday at a stretch lest, on
my return, I found all my jobs filched by the secretary. Esher said the only
way was to be quite determined, and take them back again. This is all very
fine for a chairman, but not so easy for a subordinate.

Helen's second American beau, General Acres, nearly died as the result
of standing in a wasps' nest while shooting at West Wycombe last Sunday.
He was stung in fifty-two places and his heart all but stopped beating. I
don't believe Helen minds a bit.

Friday, 21st August

This afternoon I came upon Rick talking to a lodger who is a Commando and was in the Dieppe raid this week. He is young, bronzed and incredibly tough. When introduced he shook my hand in a vicelike grip. I felt so shy in his presence, and humble, and inferior, that I could find nothing to say. Nor did I much care for him. He casually remarked that a man in his troop had shot two of his officers for cowardice, one at Dunkirk and the other during a recent cross-Channel raid.

Sunday, 23rd August

John Russell wants to write a biography of Henry James. He showed me a suitcase of his letters which he had been lent by Philip Morrell's sister. After a time I get used to John's stammer and hesitations. I do not look at him while he is speaking and try to appear unconcerned. I took him to Old Battersea House. Mrs. Stirling[82] was bedecked in jewels and gems. When she walks across the room it is like a chandelier which has been let down from the ceiling and, without collapsing, mysteriously manages to move. I like the old lady, but John was rather bored. She told me that her brother-in-law, William de Morgan,[83] used as a boy to spend his holidays with Lady Byron, who was a friend of his parents. I find Mrs. de Morgan's pictures infinitely more sympathetic than most of the well-known Pre-Raphaelites. Hers of the five mermaids rising from the sea, their tails visible through the green waves, lacks the nauseating sentiment of Burne-Jones, and is arcane in subject, as well as opulent in treatment. Her use of gold is more lavish than Botticelli's.

Jamesey urged me to return to London and live with him. Very sweet of him, but he knows, and I know, that it would not work. We walked across St. James's Park in the moonlight. He accompanied me as far as Chelsea Hospital, remarking on the beauty of the Belgravia houses, their flat unfussy façades so placid in the moonlight which tonight was soft and misty.

Monday, 24th August

The National Gallery picture now on show is Turner's *Frosty Morning,* an early work *circa* 1813 between his frankly Claude Lorraine and later rainbowy periods. This is a Wordsworthian interpretation of dull, cold, still nature, with the rising sun's glow just beginning to steal over the hard fields.

---

[82] A. M. W. Stirling, author of *Thomas Coke and the Building of Holkham,* 1908.
[83] William de Morgan (1839–1917), artist and potter.

Wickhamford. In the morning I clip the yew hedge by the lawn, destroying the silvery spiders' webs as I advance like Atropos with my shears from end to end. I think 'Who the hell am I, wilfully, mercilessly to wipe out a whole world of insects? I am as bad as Genghis Khan, as bad as Hitler.'

Mama told me that Lord FitzAlan and Magdalen came to tea here, and were a great success with Papa. The Horsfield children were in the garden for the afternoon and told their mother when they got home that there was a real lord at the manor, so old that he should never have been allowed out: and that Magdalen looked like a fish with a red neck.

This morning while shaving and listening to the news I heard the announcement of the Duke of Kent's death. I felt a sharp shock and could think of nothing else for some time. I only once saw him in the flesh, when he made a nervous speech at an S.P.A.B. dinner. He was sitting next to May Morris, an upright, smiling old dame very self possessed, with a small, curly head. The Duke had a boyish figure and complexion.

Lily Horsfield complained that people in the Evesham streets would stop to condole with her over her son Hugh's death. If only they wouldn't, she said pathetically.

A grilling hot day. I work in the garden all morning, sweating into my blue aertex shirt. While plum-picking in the evening, Deenie said, 'My dear child, I believe you stink.' I laughed and said I was sure I did, for I knew I did, yet the fact that I had been detected worried me a little. Even when the circumstances may be excusable, one does not relish this particular charge.

Mama and I have been sorting out old trunks in the loft above the motor-house. We came across some of my drawings done at the Ashmolean where Albert Rutherston was teaching. To my surprise a few of them were not too bad. The discovery has inspired me to sketch again. This evening I drew the house across the pond, and recaptured the immense joy of using my eyes as hard as I could. Eyes get wasted, like muscles, for lack of intensive exercise.

I had a row with Papa after dinner. He expressed idiotic views about the Duke of Kent. Said that he was a worthless fellow and 'no better than a pansy', a phrase I abominate. I could not tolerate this silly imputation by someone who knew nothing whatever about the prince. I blew up. Words flew, as of old, as of old. I cannot, alas, stay here more than two nights without allowing myself to be provoked beyond endurance.

Tuesday, 1st September

Today Helen's mother, Mrs. Eaton, and her aunt, Miss FitzRandolph and young John Dashwood, arrived back from Canada. It has taken them over three months to work their passage. Helen had moved all hell and pulled all strings. She was determined to get little John back so that he might go to Eton. He is a funny little boy, plain and perky like his father, hunched like a flea, and with a large load of fun. The two old sisters are typical transatlantic matrons, *soignées,* white faced with mauve hair, who talk in unison. They are kind old things, in awe of Helen who snubs them mercilessly. They flew in the clipper from New York, after waiting there for weeks with very little money allowance and being sent back to Canada once. At Lisbon they stopped only two days, whence they proceeded to Ireland. They are delighted to be back. Helen has engaged an old, old maid called Clara to look after them. She wanders about the large house like a lost sheep and is so pitiful to watch that she wrings my heart.

Thursday, 3rd September

Lady Hermione Cobbold rang me up, and I went to meet her and her husband at their farm near Stokenchurch. She is Lord Lytton's eldest daughter and has inherited Knebworth's part of the estate at Knebworth. Both expressed themselves averse to the idea of the Trust, saying they could never live in a place made over to the Trust. He is a landowner as well as someone important in the Bank of England.[84] They want to keep the estate to farm, and asked if we would accept the house and gardens only, if he found endowment funds from his own resources. I told them straight what I had not dared tell Lord Lytton, that I thought it doubtful whether the committee would accept the house on its own merits without the estate. She quite understood, and said Lord Lytton was surprised that the Trust was even interested in the house. Lady Hermione has beautiful deep, violet eyes, is shy, proud and farouche, and I think means to be friendlier than her manner allows her to appear.

Friday, 4th September

Jamesey arrives at Brooks's like a whirlwind and whisks me off to dine with Dame Una. He has come from Cecil Beaton, full of gin and

---

[84] Later 1st Lord Cobbold, Governor of the Bank of England 1949–61; *d.* 1987.

excitement, for he has just been paid by Batsford's £300 in arrears for his book, and another sum in advance for his next book, having been £200 in debt when I last saw him. Says he had a wonderful 'grouse' luncheon with Charles Fry who complained that it is more profitable for publishers to give away money to authors than to keep it, because it is all taxed.

John Pope-Hennessy is at Dame Una's too. He is less forbidding – though God knows still frightening enough – and has grown very distinguished. He has a bull terrier puppy called Jason, which is boisterous and delicious. Dame Una talked against John's gramophone about Lady Blessington. She was Dickens's first friend, and a real charmer. No woman would go to her house because of the Count D'Orsay scandal, but the Dame thinks her feelings for D'Orsay were purely maternal. He was her stepson-in-law, and she mothered him. At least there is no evidence whatever to the contrary. She talked also of Letitia Landon,[85] about whom I know nothing except that she died of an overdose of prussic acid, six months after her marriage, against which all her friends had warned her. Dame Una has been to Canonbury, which she found fascinating, and quite unaltered since the early nineteenth century. I asked if it had been bombed much. 'Not at all,' she said in that concise way of hers.

Sunday, 6th September

Miss O'Sullivan and I walked to the Blickling mausoleum through the park this morning. She is a weird, embittered woman, whom life has obviously treated unkindly. It is sad how many people there are whose natural goodness can only be brought to light by persistent delving beneath an unpromising surface. So often one has not the time, or energy, or circumstance for the operation, and consequently a false impression of a person may remain with one for a lifetime. During our walk we talked about the war. Miss O'S., who is a regular churchwoman and churchwarden at Blickling, said that the English did not deserve to win, for it was idle to presume we were fighting for the Christian ideal, and that the young, having been brought up without any religious instruction to fend for themselves, which meant to make money, were spiritually barren. These sentiments are, I dare say (although I am not absolutely sure), irrefutable. I told her that I was still fundamentally a pacifist, and only decided to join the army and fight when I realized – not till six months after war had broken out – that no amount of pacifism would stop the war, and the only way to stop it was to win it, which involved the killing of as many Germans as possible. She replied that my decision showed lack of principle.

---

[85] Letitia Elizabeth Landon (1802–38), poet under initials L. E. L.

Tuesday, 8th September

At 2 o'clock I left my attaché case at Etchingham station and walked to Hurst Green village, where I telephoned Lady Milner.[86] She pressed me to come and see her, saying she remembered me and knew how fond of me Lord Lloyd was. Fortified by these kind words and two apples which I bought at the village shop, I continued my four-mile walk to Great Wigsell where she lives. A glorious early autumn day, the sun shining bright as I tramped, stick in hand, across fields and through woods. The country is remote, unspoilt, rich Sussex landscape.

Great Wigsell is similar in size, date and type to Bateman's. Both were built in the early seventeenth century of hard ironstone, and fittingly commemorate the solid integrity of the prosperous, non-armigerous stock who lived in them. Great Wigsell is more regular than Bateman's, and has pointed gables and tall chimneys. It is surrounded by barns and outbuildings, and has several forecourts enclosed by old stone walls, so that the garden is divided into separate compartments. It is a very rural and tranquil place. I found Lady Milner talking to her gardener by the front door. She is oldish, over seventy I would guess, with a broad, lined face and a robust and spread figure. She is very sharp. She reminded me that ten years ago I lunched with her and Sir Edward Grigg[87] in Manchester Square. I remember the house best.

Lady Milner is a sister of Leo Maxse and editor of the *National Review*. She was married first to Lord Edward Cecil, and secondly to Lord Milner. We talked of George Lloyd to whom she was absolutely devoted. She told me that a day or so ago three of the most distinguished journalists were in her house. They all agreed that the worst turning points of this war had been Munich, the fall of France, and the death of Lloyd. She thought G. Ll. would not have died if Lady Lloyd had not let Clouds Hill, so that during the severest blitzes, when he was overworked, there was no retreat for him to go to. She last saw him two days before Christmas 1940, when he already looked desperately ill. At that time I was in hospital after Dover. She then asked him what he honestly thought of Churchill after sitting with him in the Cabinet. G. Ll. said he had come to think more highly of his brain, but less of his character. She believed that Churchill was jealous of Lloyd, because he does not like having able men about him; that he was never loyal to Lloyd, even during the thirties when Winston was flirting with the Navy League yet refusing to

---

[86] Viscountess Milner (1872–1958). Violet, daughter of Admiral F. A. Maxse, married firstly, 1894, Lord Edward Cecil, and secondly, 1902, Alfred (Viscount) Milner. Editor of *National Review*, 1932–48.
[87] Sir Edward Grigg, 1st Lord Altrincham (1879–1955), administrator and politician.

commit himself to rearmament; and that in earlier days still, when Chancellor of the Exchequer, he had positively discouraged rearmament. This I cannot dispute, for I do not remember.

She said Pétain had always been bad, and the last volume of Poincaré's *Memoirs* bears this out. He was always terrified of communists (ever since his experiences with the Communard in 1871), and shot his officers and men whom he suspected of communism in the last war. I said I liked to think that Weygand was not sitting on the fence so much as biding his time when he could most usefully throw in his weight with the Allies. Lady Milner said No, he too had become quite rotten. She instanced Lloyd's experience with Weygand, who was with the French Government when Lloyd was sent by Churchill to Bordeaux in June 1940. Weygand was insolent and forgot his manners. By then he was firmly convinced that England was also beaten, and when contradicted by G. Ll. became angry and offensive. He was reproachful and accused England of having let France down. Yet he contradicted himself by asserting that it was necessary for France to go through a cleansing process, and suffer for her sins. Lady Milner said that when in 1936 she was with Weygand in Paris, she asked him what he would want of England if France were again involved in war with Germany. His answer was: 'Only six divisions.' She was astonished, and made him repeat this.

She said that G. Ll. gave her a full account of his visit to Bordeaux immediately after his return (as indeed he did to me), and she published it, without mentioning his name, in the *National Review.*

As for G. Ll.'s biography, she thinks Lady Lloyd will do nothing until the end of the war, and that Colin Forbes-Adam[88] may be the right person for it. Lady Ll. asked Thomas Cadett to edit his speeches (at the time she was asking me for my advice), and horrified him by suggesting that he should rewrite the unrecorded ones in the way she believed G. Ll. must have delivered them! Cadett declined. Blanche Lloyd was hurt and withdrew the offer. Lady Milner said one should beware of wives dictating their husbands' biographies. When Alfred Milner died she consulted F. S. Oliver[89] whose advice was, 'Do not write his biography yourself, but collect his papers, and edit, and publish these.' She did so.

She said G. Ll. was the only person she respected so much that she would have gone to him from wherever she happened to be, at a whistle. One day the two of them agreed that they had consistently upheld the same policy and had never been wrong. She said too that there was

---

[88] Colin Forbes-Adam published *Life of Lord Lloyd,* 1948.
[89] Author of *Alexander Hamilton,* 1906, and *The Endless Adventure,* 1930–5.

absolutely *no* able man in England today. This convinced me that, clever as she is, she lives in the past and is out of date.

Hugh Whistler rang up during our talk. She said he was a great ornithologist, and they discussed birds for hours on end. During Dunkirk the rooks would never settle in her trees, and strange birds, never seen by her before, flew from France across the Channel. When the *Gneisenau* and the *Prinz Eugen* were chased down the Channel last year, the gulls flew over Great Wigsell at a great height all that day.

We barely had time to talk about Bateman's, and the local committee of which she is chairman. She thinks Mr. Parish[90] a most unsuitable tenant, with no respect for the Kipling association. She was an intimate friend of the Kiplings, and bought Great Wigsell to be near them. I had tea with her and her sister, and walked back to Etchingham.

I met Mr. Parish at the station, pretending I had come down from London on his train. I purposely disclosed nothing about my Great Wigsell visit. Mr. Parish, though of good family – his great-grandfather Parish having been at Eton, and his mother a Cotterell-Dormer of Rousham, he was at pains to tell me – is a curiously brash man. His neon light smiles, switched on and off like the illuminated advertisements in Piccadilly Circus during peacetime, are calculated to assure one of his good intentions. But since they are accompanied by a staccato clicking of his too regular, too snow-white dentures, the effect is on the contrary, predatory. They, the teeth, strike fear in the beholder (and auditor). Yet I found him extremely friendly, if a trifle sinister: Lady Milner said he exactly resembled the butler in *Dear Brutus,* who is sinister indeed. Mrs. Parish, slightly 'bedint', is a sister of Lord Luke and Lady Laurie – 'my sister, the Lady Mayoress, you know.' I didn't.

Before dinner Parish took me all round the Bateman's property; which to my eyes looks in apple-pie order. He refers to the local committee as 'those old bitches'. He has the grace to admit to having made a few mistakes. He has spent a lot of money on Bateman's, and positively enjoys showing the house to visitors at all hours, even on Saturdays and Sundays. I think we should be grateful to him.

He gave me a delicious dinner of partridge and Chateau Haut-Brion claret, 1920, with brandy afterwards. I slept in the oak four-poster, too short for my legs, in the little room at the top of the stairs.

Wednesday, 9th September

Read in the train a fascinating diary written by Myles Hildyard, a friend of one of Parish's sons, both of whom escaped from the Germans in Crete

---

[90] Clement Woodbine Parish (1888–1966).

last summer. It is written in a straightforward, not unpoetic way, and is thrilling and charming. I would love to meet Hildyard who seems an angelic person, sensitive, sympathetic and of lion courage.

My plans went wrong today for I was to have gone to Gravesend. This fell through. At Brooks's I read Churchill's speech in *The Times* verbatim; then went to the London Library where Mr. Cox[91] told me it was a fact that Rommel had been killed in an aeroplane and the Foreign Office would not release the news, for some unspecified reason.

Went to the National Gallery where Mrs. Heath at the canteen would shake hands and talk while endeavouring to serve others. I saw this would lead to awkwardnesses, and slunk away. Looked at Bellini's *Agony in the Garden*. The boy angel holding a chalice in the sky has a pot belly and heavy shape for a cloud to bear. The sunlight is wrong and illuminates the side of the castle which is away from the sunset. The other picture on view is a recently acquired Giotto, the *Gift of Tongues* on a small panel. For a picture painted *circa* 1300 or earlier it is remarkable how the figures are in the round, how three-dimensional they are made to appear by the scantiest of curves.

I met Harold walking outside the Gallery, looking vague and a little wan. When he noticed me he at once became his jaunty self. He said Lady Milner was terrifying to meet, and absolutely wrong-headed. I went to the Leicester Galleries. I admire Paul Methuen's[92] pictures more and more. There was a line wash by him of St. Paul's which I coveted.

Friday, 11th September

Mr. Fortescue and his wife came to luncheon at West Wycombe. He is an Eton master and I was up to him for German during one half. He is now Francis's classical tutor. He is a tall, dirty, uncouth creature, very intelligent and a good linguist. He visits Iceland for the Government because he speaks Icelandic. He surprised us by saying he hoped that after the war the custom of wearing Eton clothes and top hats would be discontinued. It is curious how today people want to abolish uniforms as though they are something to be ashamed of, or are emblematic of servility. But we are all servants, whether we are generals, bishops, cooks or Etonians. Helen and all of us, Francis included, fell upon Mr. Fortescue at once. Francis claimed that it was more economic to wear Eton clothes for, being black, they don't show the spots, and last longer. The seats of the trousers can be patched *ad nauseam,* since they are concealed by the tails.

---

[91] Frederick James Cox, on the staff of the London Library, 1882–1952. He remembered Disraeli taking out books.
[92] 4th Lord Methuen, R.A. (1886–1974), artist and owner of Corsham Court.

Tuesday, 15th September

Mr. Brown, Lord Hesketh's solicitor, summoned me in a peremptory fashion to his office. He wished to inform me of Lord Hesketh's irritation with the Trust for taking so long a time in making up its mind to accept his lordship's generous offers. He demanded the appointment of a special committee on which he, Mr. Brown, would be pleased to serve, in order to deal immediately with these pressing matters. I had business with Mr. Brown when Rufford Old Hall first came the Trust's way, and recall the spirited manner in which he would button-hole Lord Crewe, who performed the opening ceremony in 1936, and who ignored Mr. Brown as he would have ignored a distant buzzing midge. Mr. Brown is a subservient attorney with a high opinion of himself for being on close terms with his client, to whose colossal wealth he much likes to refer. He intimated that Lord Hesketh, if not irritated further, might make more munificent donations to Rufford; but that he was leaving Easton Neston and several other important houses, of which I know Gayhurst to be one, not to the National Trust, but to some family trust. He confided in me that Lord Hesketh has lately had a stroke and may not live long, and that Lady Hesketh now leads 'a cotton-wool existence'.

Lady Throckmorton[93] asked me to Coughton [Court] for the night, to go through the list of family heirlooms with her. She is living in the south wing only. The rest of the house is empty, in expectation of American officers, or nuns.

Lady Throckmorton is delightful: plain, unfashionable, intelligent and downright. *Très grande dame.* She has worked in Coughton's interests for thirty years, upholding its Catholic tradition, without becoming a Catholic herself. It is entirely owing to her that Coughton is to become Trust property, in the face of seemingly insuperable obstacles raised by the entail and the hostility of the Throckmorton family.

Coughton is a thoroughly romantic house, but I must say the late Georgian front is gloomy. There is something unconvincing and drab about thin rendering which peels. The central Perpendicular tower and the half-timbered wings are beautiful, as well as picturesque. The family associations – the papistry, recusancy, Gunpowder Plot, and intermarriages with other ancient Catholic families – are thrilling.

Wednesday, 16th September

All morning Lady Throckmorton and I went round the house, she dictating to me notes on the contents which she considered ought to remain

---

[93] Lilian, mother of the present baronet, was granted by Royal Warrant, 1927, the title of Lady Throckmorton, her husband having been killed fighting in World War I.

in the house, on loan by her son Robert to the Trust, under a form of covenant. In fact her one idea is to push the deal through now, while Robert is abroad and before he returns to alter his mind. She has been given absolute power of attorney, and she means to exercise it.

In spite of her dowagerial correctness Lady T. is amusingly mischievous about people. She said that when Madame de Navarro[94] died, Toty her son wrote that he was sending her some jade earrings which his mother had often worn and cherished. Later there arrived the cheapest pair of jet earrings which the housemaid might have bought to wear at the funeral. Either Toty knows no difference between jade and jet, which is quite probable, or somebody else substituted the jet for the jade. The daughter, whom Madame detested, went to her mother's funeral dressed in Madame's own black hat and dress, which Lady T. easily recognised.

On my way home I went into Birmingham Cathedral, by Archer. The roof has been quite burnt away, and is replaced with temporary corrugated iron.

Friday, 18th September

While I was sitting at breakfast in the coffee-room at Brooks's Lord Spencer entered in evident ill-humour, and grunted a good-morning. I spoke not a word until he remarked, 'I see the National Trust has come into another property.' 'Oh, which one?' I asked. 'Polesden Lacey,' he said. One of Mrs. Ronnie Greville's[95] executors had told him. I was not surprised and had wondered since her death if this would be the case.

Rick and I walked for hours round and round Chelsea in the moonlight. In the course of a rather distracted conversation he told me that while dying, his mother, whom they thought asleep, overheard their despairing talk, and surprised them by asking in a frightened little voice, 'What are you going to do with me?' This haunts him. Clearly one should never speak confidentially to others before the dying.

Sunday, 20th September

Sat with Henry Andrews at luncheon. He is Rebecca West's husband. He says his wife does not take naturally to housework, but is conscientious and slow. He and she make their bed every morning.

I walked to the Temple. It is curious to see cabbages growing round the empty plinth of King William's equestrian statue in St. James's Square. Found John Summerson in the Temple directing a number of pupils

---

[94] Mary Anderson, American Shakespearean actress, married Antonio de Navarro, and lived in Broadway, Worcestershire.
[95] Margaret, daughter of Rt. Hon. William M'Ewan, brewer, who married 1891 Hon. Ronald Greville. She was a rich hostess.

who are making measured drawings. Since more than three-quarters of the old buildings are already destroyed it seems a little late in the day.

Monday, 21st September

At Sheffield I walked from the station to the Grand Hotel for an expensive, indifferent businessman's luncheon. There has been much destruction of the town, large stores burnt out and great untidy open spaces, which at first I took to be the usual Midlands squalor, then realized to be caused by bombing. The executors to the late Miss Watt told me the trustees definitely offer Speke Hall [Lancashire] to us straight away, with an endowment of not more than £10,000, either in land or cash. In waiting for my train on Sheffield platform I went to the Gents'. I could not believe my eyes in reading the graffiti on the walls. Invitations to buggery, and long accounts of what boys like done to them, completely illustrated, dates asked and answered, names and addresses given, etc. Are they just bad jokes? Are they serious? Or the repressed fantasy longings of respectable clergymen? And are similar graffiti to be found in the Ladies'?

The train to York was so crowded that I was obliged to stand on the concertina part connecting one coach with another. The floor beneath me twisted and swayed like water skis.

Tuesday, 22nd September

After a visit to the Treasurer's House I caught a bus to Wetherby, crossing Marston Moor. Mr. Foster met me and took me to lunch at the small priest's house at Stockeld, where he is living at present. His agent and accountant were present. Stockeld Park is now a maternity home. The place was bought by Mr. Foster's father in the nineties from the Middletons, a Catholic family. The chapel is by Detmar Blow. The house is eighteenth century and was greatly added to *circa* 1900 and decorated by Gillow. But the central elliptical staircase with iron, crinoline balusters and apsidal recesses leading to various rooms on each storey, is striking. A beautiful walled garden, woods and estate of 1,700 acres of fine, spreading country. I stayed to tea and the agent after many questionings motored me to Farnley, of which estate he is also agent.

Farnley Hall near Otley is on a splendid site above Wharfedale. Both the Horton-Fawkeses very friendly, and absolutely easy. Until recently he was an Eton master. Farnley is an enormous house. On arrival we found husband and wife cooking the dinner for they have no servants at all. One part of the house is early seventeenth century, wainscoted with chopped-up panelling, mostly taken from old beds. The dining-room panelling is painted with minute hunting scenes of horsemen and hounds, about 1820, by one George Woods. Tacked on to this house is a large block by John Carr. The furniture made for the Carr block is stacked away, for until a month ago Farnley was also a maternity home. Chippendale came from Otley, so I wish I could have seen the furniture. Turner in his early years was patronized by a Fawkes, and his room is shown. There are still some forty of his water-colours of the park, lodges, and even of the interior of the house. Most of them are put away but I saw one of the present Mrs. Horton-Fawkes's room, wherein nearly all the furniture is discernible. I helped clear away after dinner, and dried to my hosts' washing up. I wish all my visits were as fun and as carefree as this one.

Wednesday, 23rd September

Bussed to East Riddlesden Hall. The house is perched above the Aire with a romantic view across the river to the hills in the west, but hugged by beastly development on the Keighley side.

Lunched late at the Victoria Hotel, Keighley. Yorkshire people are all friendly, unlike the gruff Lincolnshire folk. I went to Haworth Parsonage on pilgrimage. The bus climbs an interminable hill all the way from Keighley. The village street is still cobbled, and excessively steep. The women wear clogs. The church has been rebuilt, but the pathetic Brontë mural tablet has been preserved. In the churchyard is an impenetrable forest of tombstones. The Parsonage lies on higher ground overlooking the forest, not below grave level as I had supposed, but seemingly healthily if coldly situated. The moors stretch away from the very back door. Alas, the house was given an annexe round about 1880, also plate glass for square panes. The rooms, though small, are airy. The contents now exiguous. I walked on the moors which are windy, weird and inhospitable, and saw the heather and the black crags. It is surprising how many habitations up here are perched on the highest skylines. A pity, for they rob the contours of much of their weirdness. However every untouched contour, and some of the built-up ones, and every rock, almost every tuft of blasted heath I saw must have been known by the Brontës like the backs of their hands. The museum should be better arranged. Yet one is allowed freedom to roam in it, which is something.

Thursday, 24th September

In my York hotel I heard a siren in the night. At 9 in the morning I climbed to the top of the Minster tower. It was a fine autumn morning but too misty to see far. I was entirely alone up there, and free, my pleasure spiced with that persistent fear of heights. I get a crinkling of the toes, a tingling of the instep. When I descended a verger said I ought not to have gone up. 'There was no notice to that effect,' I said. 'No,' he said, 'but a live bomb was dropped close to the tower during the night, and has not been de-fused yet.'

I reached Catterick Bridge hotel at midday. After luncheon bussed and walked to Moulton Hall. Always the best way to approach a house is on foot. It is a beautiful, compact little house, built in 1654, with curved and pedimented gables in the Kew Palace style. There is plate glass in the windows. A peculiarity is the rusticated ashlar bands, each alternate one being fish-scaled. Nothing left inside beyond a superb Charles II stair-case, pierced and scrolled with baskets of flowers and fruits on the newels, and carved pendants from the soffits. Pretty little garden with yew and beech hedges.

Mrs. Pease kept me waiting, and appeared a little sombre. She is an elderly, grey, good-looking widow, dressed in black. She soon melted. She thinks she may leave the house in her will.

I walked back to Catterick, five miles. I stopped to look at Moulton Manor from the gate. The owner appeared and showed me round. The house was built by the same family a little earlier than the Hall, and is only a few hundred yards from it.

Friday, 25th September

I took a bus from Newcastle, standing all the way, and arrived at Wallington at 7.30 in the rain and dark. Matheson and John Dower met me by the stables and carried my bag. I was tired and depressed all day, and found the Trevelyan[96] family overpowering in spite of the kind welcome they gave me. Lady Trevelyan came out of the drawing-room in a sweeping, stately rush, shaking my hands warmly and exuding cor-diality. When I went into the dining-room Sir Charles rose and shook hands in the same hospitable way. I don't quite know why, because they are dyed in the wool socialists, this should have surprised me. A newly married daughter Patricia, big with child, is living here; so is another daughter Pauline (Mrs. Dower). Her husband, the aforementioned John Dower, is working on post-war National Park schemes, is very left-wing, and from his connections and position is, according to Matheson, impor-tant.

Lady Trevelyan speaks succinctly, carefully and measuredly, using the north country clipped 'a', and is distinctly 'clever'. Gertrude Bell was her sister. Lady T. is handsome in a 'no nonsense about appearances' manner, and looks as though she may have been the first woman chairman of the

---

[96] Rt. Hon. Sir Charles Trevelyan, 3rd Bart. (1870–1958), President of the Board of Education 1924, and 1929–31. Lady Trevelyan was a daughter of Sir Hugh Bell, 2nd Bart.

L.C.C. I don't know if she ever was this. She is authoritarian, slightly deaf, and wears pince-nez. The two daughters are abrupt and rather terrifying. Mrs. Dower paints water-colours, competently. After dinner I am worn out, and long for bed. But no. We have general knowledge questions. Lady T. puts the questions one after the other with lightning rapidity. I am amazed and impressed by her mental agility, and indeed by that of the daughters, who with pursed lips shoot forth unhesitating answers like a spray of machine-gun bullets. All most alarming to a tired stranger. At the end of the 'game', for that is what they call this preparatory school examination, they allot marks. Every single member of the family gets 100 out of 100. The son-in-law gets 80, Matheson (who is also a clever man) gets 30. I get 0. But then I am a half-wit. Deeply humiliated I receive condolences from the Trevelyans and assurances that I shall no doubt do better next time. I make an inward vow that there never will be a next time.

Saturday, 26th September

A beautiful sunny but frosty morning. Breakfast at 8. Having slept well and eaten well, I felt fit for anything. In fact having girded my loins I was prepared for the worst. As it turned out I enjoyed the day. Matheson and I spent morning and afternoon tramping, map in hand, round the entire estate, to Chesters Farm and the distant moorland in the north; and to Scots Gap in the opposite direction.

After tea Sir Charles took me round the house. He is seventy-one, rather old and slow, white-haired and bent, with a large nose. He is very like Professor Trevelyan, but less grim. Although an advanced socialist, he has lost his old fanaticism, is courteous, and not absolutely humourless. I quite like him.

The saloon is one of the loveliest rooms I have seen. It has a high coved ceiling, of which the ground colour is the original egg blue, with rococo plaster motifs in white. Under the cornice the walls are painted a Naples yellow, verging on terracotta.

Friday, 2nd October

I have again developed a streaming cold. Since doctors have done nothing to alleviate or cure, far less prevent the common cold, how can one have faith in them when one suffers from more serious complaints? Surgery has of course progressed, but medicine is pure quackery. When I think of the contradictory way in which doctors have treated my complaint over the past two years, the agonizing lumbar punctures, the torture chamber wracks, the psychoanalysis, the conflicting drugs, how can I have the least confidence in their ridiculous profession? The best one can say for doctors is that they are not all rogues, like all lawyers.

Feeling wretchedly ill and not knowing whether I am treading on air or land, I enter the London Library. I tease Mr. Cox over his misinformation about Rommel being killed in an air crash. 'Ah!' he says, 'but now we read what applause he received at Hitler's meeting in Berlin, he will surely be bumped off.'

While I was having tea in Brooks's Ben Nicolson[97] walked in. He looks older, more poised, more aware of the world around him. He said he was going to the Middle East immediately. He was to have flown this morning in a stratosphere bomber which to his delight was cancelled at the last moment, for he was not looking forward to this mode of transport. He felt sure he would feel ill, sick and frightened. Nigel[98] is also leaving shortly with his battalion, and Harold is very sad at losing them both.

A. H. said this afternoon that Charles Fry[99] swore to her he had slept, at different times, with three of her cousins, two sisters and a brother – a good record. This reminds me that Randolph [Churchill] once told me O. M. boasted to him of having what he called 'stretched the cock over three generations,' i.e. slept over an interval of years with a grandmother, her daughter, and her granddaughter. I don't know who they were. Jan, Angela Kinross's mother, came to tea with the Hills, where I am staying. It appears that Angela has had her illegitimate child, a son, before her divorce from Patrick is through. She has entered his birth under the father's name, although he is still married. Legally speaking however, the child could be the Hon. Something Balfour, and if Patrick were killed he might have a claim to be Lord Kinross unless the Balfour family disputed the title.[100]

Monday, 5th October

At Englefield Green I called on Mrs. Whitbread about her house, Burford, in Shropshire. She was unnecessarily modest about it, trying to rake up some Norman associations, whereas from the photographs it appears a decent George I house. It is extraordinary how quite intelligent people think that a house's site mentioned in Domesday is a better qualification than its architecture by Wren.

In pouring rain I walked to Cumberland Lodge. Soaked to the skin and my feet squelching in my shoes I sat talking for half an hour with Lord FitzAlan, who was lying in a vast four-post bed, gazing straight ahead, not at me, but the chimneypiece.

---

[97] Harold Nicolson's elder son. Later editor of the *Burlington Magazine*.
[98] Harold Nicolson's younger son, writer and biographer.
[99] Partner of B. T. Batsford, publishers.
[100] In fact in an exchange of letters between lawyets, both Lord Kinross and his former wife established the fact that the child was not his.

Tuesday, 6th October

Standing with Alathea on Egham platform this morning, I was greeted, coldly enough, by the awful adjutant of my old regiment. The sight of this man, who can now do me no possible harm, made my knees quake. I could hardly pull myself into the train. Strange how such encounters can affect one physically. I would sooner 'go over the top' any day than meet him again.

Michael Peto who lunched with me said I had the most enviable life of anybody he knew. It is true and in the circumstances I do not deserve it. He is still absurdly optimistic, and assured me that the Germans would crack and the war would be over by the next Armistice Day. How can he be so foolish? I reminded him that in 1939 he assured me it would be over by March 1940.

Friday, 9th October

Helen gave me a lift into High Wycombe in her taxi. At the traffic lights she leapt out, and into a green bus bound for Windsor, as it was waiting to cross, leaving me aghast at her promptness and agility, and under the obligation to pay the taxi fare. She is a woman of resources.

I went to Farrer & Co. who told me that Lord Mount Edgcumbe was toying with the idea of leaving Mount Edgcumbe and Cotehele to the Trust. Mount Edgcumbe house has been burnt out and all its contents destroyed during a raid on Plymouth. There is a lot of land which is of great importance to Plymouth. Lord Mt. E., over seventy, has a poor life; his successor is another old man whose only son has just been killed in this war, and the ultimate heir is a New Zealander whom he cares nothing for and who won't come to England. Farrer, in showing me over 66 Lincoln's Inn Fields, said the house has been the Farrer family office for 150 years, which is surely remarkable.

At 2.30 I attended a meeting of Mrs. Ronnie Greville's executors – Lords Ilchester, Bruntisfield and Dundonald, and Terence Maxwell. Lord D. asked me what relation I was to Aunt Dorothy. He said she was a real eccentric. The meeting lasted till 5. A most interesting and complex subject, involving an estate of some £2 million. Mrs. Greville has left Marie Antoinette's necklace to the Queen, £20,000 to Princess Margaret Rose, and £25,000 to the Queen of Spain. Everyone in London is agog to learn the terms of Mrs. G.'s will. She was a lady who loved the great because they were great, and apparently had a tongue dipped in gall. I remember old Lady Leslie once exclaiming, when her name was mentioned, 'Maggie Greville! I would sooner have an open sewer in my drawing-room.'

At Brooks's I had tea with Lord Ilchester who wanted to talk more about Polesden. He said John Fox-Strangways [his son] is expected home any day. He is among the first six officer prisoners to be exchanged for Germans. He is now in New York where he has had an operation and a plate inserted in his thigh, which was shot through. Lord Ilchester was alarmed last week by finding Ministry officials walking round Melbury Park measuring it up for a possible hospital. He had had no warning of their visit.

Saturday, 10th October

Eddy and I went to the Arts Theatre Club to see *The House of Regrets* by a very young Russian, Peter Ustinov, son of Nadia Benois. It is a brilliant play about a White Russian family in some North London suburb before and during the war; quite in the *Cherry Orchard* tradition. There is too little drama, but it shows acute observation, exact feeling, humour and pathos. I was very much moved by it.

Monday, 12th October

In Salisbury I had a quick snack and walked to the cathedral. The setting of this and the setting of Durham Cathedral, which I saw last month, make them far and away my two favourite English cathedrals. The aspirant verticality of this spire literally takes the breath away. On entering the close, I gasped. But I was also transfixed by what I saw happening on the spire. Two boy steeplejacks were suspended from the very apex in cradles on ropes. I suppose they had been doing repairs to the stonework. Now they were playing the fool in swinging across one another, so that their ropes crossed and became entangled. With hoots of laughter they pressed their feet against the spire and swung themselves back again. An old man on the grass below shouted to them to stop. He clapped his hands, which made the pigeons fly off the clerestory. I felt so apprehensive that I rushed inside the cathedral in order not to witness the ropes break and the boys crash to the ground. Then I talked to a workman painting the jambs of the great west doorway. He said he was applying linseed oil to the Devonshire marble shafts, the pale greeny-yellow outdoor shafts, as a weather protective; and he pointed out the surface of the marble he had not yet painted, which was pitted all over. This treatment had been neglected, he said, for twenty years, at least.

By appointment with Sir Henry Hoare[101] I was at the County Hotel by 2 o'clock. I gave my name to the porter and sat in the dreary lounge to wait. A young R.A.F. sergeant came in and sat down. I looked up and

---

[101] Sir Henry Hoare, 6th Bart. (1865–1947). Gave Stourhead to the National Trust, 1946–7. He and Lady Hoare died on the same day, 25th March 1947.

saw a face of ineffable beauty which smiled in a most beseeching manner. The sergeant took out a cigarette, offered me one and was about to introduce himself when, damn it! Sir Henry Hoare was announced.

Sir Henry is an astonishing nineteenth-century John Bull, hobbling on two sticks. He was wearing a pepper and salt suit and a frayed grey billycock over his purple face. He had a very bronchial cough and kept hoiking and spitting into an enormous carrot-coloured handkerchief. En route for Stourhead I sat in the back of the car beside him and behind an old chauffeur of immense, overlapping fatness who had an asthmatic wheeze, like a blacksmith's bellows. Sir Henry talked about his bad knee, and told me he had lost a knee-cap. I found myself shouting, for he is rather deaf, 'Do you find it much of a handicap having no knee-cap?' After the third repetition I decided that my remark was inept.

Lady Hoare is an absolute treasure, and unique. She is tall, ugly and eighty-two; dressed in a long black skirt, belled from a wasp waist and trailing over her ankles. She has a thick net blouse over a rigidly upholstered bosom, complete with stiff, whaleboned high collar round the throat. Over this a black and white check jacket, evidently reinforced with stays, for it ends in tight points over her thighs. The sleeves are exaggeratedly mutton-chop. She has a protruding square coif of frizzly grey hair in the style of the late nineties, black eyebrows and the thickest spectacle lenses I have ever seen. She is nearly blind in one eye. She is humorous and enchanting. She adores the memory of George Lloyd and is quite convinced that he was the greatest Englishman of this century.

The Hoares took me round the house, which is packed to the brim with good things, and some ghastly things like cheap bamboo cake stands and thin silver vases filled with peacocks' feathers. On the grand piano an impenetrable forest of silver photograph frames. The house was gutted by fire in 1902 and rebuilt by Sir Aston Webb from old photographs and records. There are some rococo chimneypieces brought after the fire from another Hoare house in Northamptonshire. Only the Regency picture gallery and library in the projecting wings were spared. All the contents however were saved, including the wonderful suite of furniture by the younger Chippendale. I was given to read his bills from 1795 to 1812, and the *Stourhead Annals,* kept fairly regularly from 1792 to the present day.

For dinner we had soup, whiting, pheasant, apple pie, dessert, a white Rhine wine and port. Lady Hoare has no housemaid, and only a cook and butler. But she said with satisfaction, 'The Duchess of Somerset at Maiden Bradley has to do all her own cooking.'

We ate in the little dining-room at a long table, Sir Henry with his back to a colonnaded screen, Lady Hoare with hers to the window. He spoke very little, and that little addressed to himself. She kept up a lively, not entirely coherent prattle. She said to me, 'Don't you find the food better in this war than in the last?' I replied that I was rather young during the last war, but I certainly remembered the rancid margarine we were given at my preparatory school when I was eight. 'Oh!' she said. 'You were lucky. We were reduced to eating rats.' I was a little surprised, until Sir Henry looked up and said, 'No, no Alda. You keep getting your wars wrong. That was when you were in Paris during the Commune.'

The purpose of my visit was to talk over Sir Henry's offer to leave with the estate the live and dead stock of the Home Farm, valued at £15,000. He told me that Rennie Hoare, his heir, would almost certainly not live at Stourhead, and this saddened him. The Hoares have reigned fifty years here. Their only son was killed in the last war, and both of them live on his memory.

They are the dearest old couple. I am quite in love with her outspoken ways and funny old-fashioned dress. She is humorous in the gentlest, kindest manner conceivable. They have had soldiers in the basement of the house, and their present unit is leaving tomorrow.

Tuesday, 13th October

During breakfast the officers of the departing unit come in one by one and fervently thank the Hoares for their kindness, and express genuine sorrow to be going. Lady Hoare is much affected.

It is a beautiful morning and Sir Henry gets into his electric chair, and I accompany him to the lakes and the temples; or rather, I gallop at breakneck speed behind him. He is quite unaware that his chair goes the devil of a pace and I have the utmost difficulty in keeping up. As he presses the accelerator he asks me questions which demand answers and intelligent comments. He keeps saying 'Where are you? Why don't you say something?' When I do catch up I am so out of breath I can't get the words out. All he says (to himself) is, 'I don't understand what's come over the boy.' Mercifully when I was on the verge of total collapse we met Michael Rosse on the far side of the large lake. He had come from the Guards Brigade H.Q. near by. I am glad to have introduced him to the Hoares who will undoubtedly ask him to Stourhead again. Somehow I can't see Michael running after that chair.

Wednesday, 14th October

I motored with Captain Hill[102] to Polesden Lacey. The house was built by Cubitt in 1818 and looks from a distance across the valley much as it

---

[102] John Hill, agent to Sir John Dashwood at West Wycombe. He made many reports of prospective properties for the National Trust.

did in Neale's view of that date. The interior was, I imagine, entirely refitted by Mrs. Greville, in the expensive taste of an Edwardian millionairess. But it is not vulgar. It is filled with good things, and several museum pieces. The upstairs rooms are well appointed, in six or seven self-contained suites with bathrooms attached. There is a grass courtyard in the middle of the house.

Mrs. Greville has been buried in the rose garden to the west of the house, next to the dog cemetery in accordance with female country house owner tradition. The gardens are unostentatious and rather beautiful: the grounds very beautiful, with a splendid view across the vale from the south front to a wooded hill beyond. Queen Mary's Walk is a straight grass ride bordered with yew.

Sunday, 18th October

Last night I caught the 10.55 for Scotland. I did not sleep much because of the heat of my third-class carriage. It was not over-crowded. There were only two other bunks occupied. The train was an hour late reaching Stirling this morning. I made friends with a commercial traveller in my carriage by giving him some chocolate. In return I borrowed his soap. Then he managed to bribe a cup of tea for each of us in a first-class coach. There was no restaurant car. At Stirling I bought some bannocks and jam buns at a service canteen by buttoning up my old army mackintosh. Between Stirling and Oban I watched the brown burns dashing down the hill-sides; and from the train window inhaled the strong heathery, peaty smell. Of course it is pouring with rain. Aunt Dorothy met me at Connel Ferry. She is thinner since I last saw her in 1938, and she wheezes more, presumably because of her pipe. She smokes a ghastly tobacco called Afrikander Flake, which rasps the skin off one's throat. Ardachy, or Straw Castle as she calls it, was built by her before the war, literally out of deal lathes and cardboard. It is ugly outside and comfortable inside, for she has a cook, kitchen maid and parlourmaid (three sisters), a housekeeper and a housemaid, besides a chauffeur-handyman-gardener, and a farm worker, who is brother to the three sisters.

Tuesday, 20th October

This morning we motor over the mountains to a village by the sea. Aunt D. and Joan Hewitt[103] interview a land girl. I walk down the village street of single storey hovels, with one window on either side of a doorway. Very clean they look through the windows, but the accommodation must be very restricted, and the services presumably nil. Yet the

---

[103] Dorothy Lees-Milne's friend who lived with her for over thirty years of her widowhood.

inhabitants look well and robust. Aunt D., who defends everything Highland, says these hovels are surprisingly spacious, comfortable and warm inside. They are exactly what Walter Scott described in the Waverley novels, no more no less. I walk along the road and sit on a rock, the sun full out, with my feet just above the breakers. The gulls are screaming, and there are clearly defined views of distant islands and a jagged coastline. There is a delicious smell of salty, antiseptic seaweed. The place is remote and romantic, and melancholy. On the way back we have glimpses of mountain tops across fertile valleys, with corn and hay as yet unstooked.

In the afternoon Aunt D. sits on a panel in Oban judging 'call-up' cases, and listening to the pleas of her friends and neighbours to keep their servants. Meanwhile I walk round, or rather along the town, for it has no breadth and only has length, looking at the sea-planes land and rise, and the camouflaged boats bob up and down in the harbour. I approach the new Roman Catholic cathedral, of which only the east end is completed, the walls of the nave and west tower still standing roofless. The church is of granite and I pronounce it horrid, until I see on a notice board that Sir Giles Scott is the architect. Whereupon my interest is aroused. I look again, and find some merits in the design. I believe the thing may eventually have style, although the Gothic lancet windows are weak and conventional.

Friday, 23rd October

Today I climbed the highest of the two peaks overlooking Loch Etive from behind the house. It was a stormy day with only fair visibility yet I could see the Firth of Lorne beyond Oban, the isle of Lismore to the west, Ben More on Mull, the mountains of Morvern, and to the east Ben Cruachan and Loch Awe. I must actually have reached the summit, a thing one too seldom achieves. To the north there was nothing but desolate heathery bog, bare shoulders of rock and a purple sky curtain of storm and anger. Below me I saw distant deer, and above me a buzzard or two. Around me I heard the cackle of grouse. I was absolutely alone, enjoying uninterrupted views in every direction. There was not a human being within miles and miles and miles.

Sunday, 25th October

I went to see Jamesey who is ill in bed. We both agreed it was high time we got married. Jamesey has in mind a really rustic 'yeowoman'. But how, he asked plaintively, does one set about finding one? I could only think of the old spinster with a patch over one eye at Earlswood Moat House. Dame Una interrupted our conversation by carrying into the room a silver crucifix given her by Lady Gregory.[104] Very ancient it was, and hollowed for the purpose of containing green leaves, arranged to sprout from the head, arms and feet of the cross, and represent the living Christ. She said it was Spanish.

Eddy was in Brooks's and I had tea with him. I congratulated him for having produced the reading of *Maud* by Laurence Olivier the other evening on the wireless, surely the best way, I said, of reviving interest in poetry. He said many such perforrnances went on weekly, if only I took the trouble to listen-in.

Tuesday, 27th October

Lord Ilchester told me he was very cross with Esher and the S.P.A.B. for worrying him about making Holland House into an amenity centre after the war, and then never till this day telling him whether or not they wanted it. He complained that the S.P.A.B. in stating that £40,000 would suffice for rebuilding the house had badly queered his pitch with the War Damage people, for it was quite obvious to him that the actual figure ought to be in the region of £100,000. Now that the War Damage people knew about the lesser figure, he stood no chance of getting from them the full compensation.

Sir Courtauld Thomson caught me again and made me have tea with him to tell me he had seen Lord Portal this afternoon. Lord Portal was more determined than ever to get Dorney Wood for the Cabinet's use. The Ministry of Works however want the full endowment of £200,000 now, and will not agree to the Trust having the £70,000 for the purchase of additional land. Matheson says this will make us review the whole proposition, which is accordingly less attractive to us than before.

Thursday, 29th October

I met Goodhart-Rendel[105] at his office in Crawford Street. The very next house to his has been bombed, and is sliced off. He is a captain in the Grenadiers, although over fifty, working at the Caterham depot, and simply loves it. He told me the order of his chief interests in life is: 1. the Roman Catholic Church, 2. the Brigade of Guards, and 3. Architecture. He walked restlessly up and down the room, talking about his men. He claimed that the type enlisting today is superior than ever before in physique and morale. He is anxious for the Trust to work out a modified

[104] Isabella Augusta Gregory (1852–1932). Irish playwright, literary hostess and patron, and friend of W. B. Yeats.
[105] Harry Goodhart-Rendel (1887–1959), architect. Gave Hatchlands, Surrey, to the National Trust, 1945.

scheme for taking over Hatchlands. The Trust must be satisfied with less endowment than they are asking for.

Mr. Frank Green's agent, James, has an office in John Street, Bedford Row. Its immediate neighbour has likewise been bombed to atoms. Without its support Mr. James fears his house may collapse without warning. He says Frank Green[106] changes his mind every day, but believes he really wishes to give us Culverthorpe, but not one square inch of garden; merely covenants and £10,000. I said firmly that these silly conditions were not acceptable.

I met Rick on the 3.40 for Aylsham as the train was leaving Liverpool Street Station. He had jumped through one door, I through another of the same corridor while the train was gathering speed. We collapsed in a heap of breathlessness, relief and helpless laughter. He was wearing a smart, rather flashy new suit that had belonged to a friend killed in the war. I was wearing for the first time Desmond Parsons's Irish suit, which Anne Rosse gave me. Both of us in dead men's clothes. From Aylsham station we walked to Blickling, he carrying my heavy bag. We stayed the night in Miss O'Sullivan's flat.

Friday, 30th October

We walked round the gardens and the lake, R. making countless good and not so good suggestions. We met the R.A.F. officer in charge, a Wing-Commander Fry, who is very proud of living in so great a house. He asked to be allowed to use the front door, but Birkbeck the agent and I refused, because it would necessitate the men using the hall and grand staircase. R. disagreed with us, saying that if we let him he would then be under an obligation and would co-operate with us in stopping R.A.F. vandalism m the house.

Miss James the housekeeper is in a woeful state because her dog was stolen on Monday by the R.A.F. and has not been seen since. In between her tears she told me he was the sweetest and cleverest being imaginable, and she loved him more than anyone in the world. To comfort and distract her I led her on to her favourite subject, Blenheim. She told me how Gladys Duchess of Marlborough would have her spaniels in the staterooms in order to annoy the duke who was inconceivably fussy. He would spend hours examining the curtains looking for stains made by the dogs, and was very disappointed if he failed to find any. He would indicate to Miss James the exact spots on the carpet on which the front or back legs of certain tables were to stand. The duchess took drugs, and swore at the odd man for wheeling the coal into the cellar beneath her

---

[106] Donor of Treasurer's House, York, to the Trust, 1930.

bedroom and waking her up with the noise. In her dressing-gown at the window she called him dreadful names. After an hour of these and similar tales, none of which I believe to be true, Miss James dried her tears and recovered her composure.

Willey the gardener explained to me how to cut back yews to make them 'break', which means allowing the green to sprout low down on the boles. He said, 'The crueller you are the better, so long as you give them air and light.'

Sunday, 1st November

I called for Anne Rosse at her uncle's house in Stafford Terrace, a house bought by her grandfather, Linley Sambourne, the *Punch* cartoonist of the 1880s. It is a period piece, untouched. It is choc-a-bloc with *art nouveau*. The Morris-papered walls are plastered with old photographic groups and Sambourne drawings, the frames touching each other, weird clocks galore, stained-glass windows, Victorian walking-sticks and parasols. Anne and I walked round the pretty back streets by Holland Park, and took a bus to the Ritz, where Michael joined us at 1 o'clock, and Oliver [Messel][107] at 2 o'clock. We talked over the luncheon table till 4. Oliver is a camouflage major in Norwich. He has discovered Ivory's[108] disused Assembly Rooms, made them into his headquarters, and is redecorating them.

Tuesday, 3rd November

Was met at Farnham [Surrey] by Mr. W. L. Wood, a newspaper proprietor, and wife, who motored me to their house. It was built by Wood in the colonial style, neo-Georgian with a portico of slender columns. Unfortunately in every room one hears what is going on in the next. When Mr. W. went to the loo I heard everything, but everything. We lunched at 12.30 off cold partridge, which I could not get off the bone, and tinned sausage. Mr. W. is a tough businessman sprung from I don't know where. He speaks softly and burrs his 'r's. He mounted me on a small black horse, I changing into my plus-fours brought for the purpose, and we rode to Frensham Common. It was a sunny, crisp, invigorating afternoon. He conducted me round the boundaries of the common to inspect a lot of 140 acres which the Robertson trustees have agreed to purchase for us. The lot covers a wide space of sandy heath and small Scotch firs, a natural lung in this horrid part of Surrey so near accursed Aldershot. We cantered along the grass. The Great and Little Ponds are

---

[107] Oliver Messel, artist and stage designer. A brother of Lady Rosse.
[108] Thomas Ivory (1709–79), leading Norwich architect.

drained of water so as not to make landmarks from the air. In the Great Pond thousands of birches have seeded themselves, and are already too tall to be uprooted. Mr. Wood knew Christopher Hobhouse[109] who wrote for his paper, the *Builder,* and had a great admiration for him. He thought Christopher the most brilliant writer of my generation.

Wednesday, 4th November

At 2.30 the Eshers, accompanied by Lady Eliot,[110] and I went round 16 Charles Street W.1. It is a palace. We all agreed it was unsuitable for offices, being far too rich and big. We saw the furniture stacked in the drawing-room, which I have got to sort through. Mrs. Greville's house steward had come from Polesden to be our guide. He was very drunk and lachry-mose. Esher did not like this at all. I heard the man sobbing behind us as we went round, and felt sorry for him. He had been forty-two years with Mrs. Greville, to whom he was genuinely devoted. He was constantly intoxicated during her grand dinner parties. Once she scribbled him a note from her silver pad, 'You are drunk. Leave the room immediately.' He swayed down the table, and handed the note to Sir John Simon.

Saturday, 7th November

The servant situation at West Wycombe is becoming more and more impossible. All this week Helen has been hysterical, staying in bed, saying she is ill, but going out mysteriously to dine with the Americans and returning worse than before. The new butler has been frightfully rude to us National Trusts, and I was driven to call him an insolent scoundrel. Since then he has behaved himself better, but it is uncomfortable. He will not speak to me, and I feel the waves of his hatred.

Y. has been graded Class 4 by the army. He told them he was a homo-sexual and on that account they graded him so low. I was shocked because the reason seems a frivolous one. He might as well have said he preferred peppermints to chocolate biscuits. When Y. said, 'What earthly use would I be in the army?' I did think perhaps he would be no use. But what earthly use is he out of it?

In the dense blackout I walked, torchless, to dine with Margaret Jourdain and Ivy Compton-Burnett, who had also invited their great friend Soame Jenyns.[111] He is heavy, Jewish-looking (though he isn't a Jew), dark, sallow, has a seat in Cambridgeshire called Bottisham, and in peacetime works in the British Museum. We had an enjoyable evening.

---

[109] Christopher Hobhouse, author of a life of Charles James Fox. He was killed while serving in the Marines, 1941.
[110] Nellie, wife of Hon. Sir Montague Eliot, who succeeded in November 1942 as 8th Earl of St. Germans.
[111] Deputy Keeper of the Department of Oriental Antiquities at the British Museum.

Miss C.-B. is not as good a conversationalist as Miss J., and is always listening to what the other is saying to her neighbour. It is very difficult to get them to talk together. Miss C.-B. says she cannot get on with her book; the war is drying her up. We agree that this war has produced no poetry or works of art. But she says perhaps it is too soon to judge; we must wait for the war to be over for the slow inspiration to eke its way out.

At Cheyne Walk I found Rick drinking tea and claret alternately out of tumblers. He gets very sleepy, he says, after one glass of the last since the crack on his head from a girder, and has to turn to tea to counteract the effects of the wine. I began the night on a small sofa. R. was in the big bed. I could not sleep a wink. First my toes were out at the end; then my head and chest out at the top, freezing. At 3 a.m. R. allowed me to join him in the big bed, and we talked. He said something; I said something; he said something; I was saying something, when all of a sudden I heard him snoring. I cannot for the life of me do this. I am a hopeless getter-to-sleep.

Sunday, 8th November

I took a 10 o'clock train to Luton, where a taxi met me and drove me to the agent's office at Luton Hoo, where I found Sir Harold and Lady Zia Wernher. They showed me maps of the estate and talked generally of their intentions to give the house, contents and some 1,000 acres. The National Trust must run the house as a museum, and they must be allowed to live in a part of it. The collections, most from the house and some from Bath House, Piccadilly, belonging to his mother, Lady Ludlow, are reputedly very fine indeed. Since they were stacked away in the chapel I was unable to see them.

The Wernhers are charming people. He is simple and forthcoming; she is pretty and sweet. She is a daughter of the Grand Duke Michael of Russia by his morganatic wife, Countess de Torby.

We got into a small car and were motored round the estate to Someries Farm and the old brick castle, a fifteenth-century ruin. We came back and walked through the walled garden, which is immense and contains an ocean of hothouses. We lunched in the agent's house where the Wernhers are living. We listened to the 1 o'clock news and were thrilled to hear that the Americans had invaded North Africa and Giraud had declared for the Allies in Algeria. Perhaps this is the turning point of the war in our favour, if only the campaign goes happily. Lady Zia said that although she was a Russian, she had never been in Russia. She speaks with a faint accent which is seductive. She said her father and mother had taken Kenwood, where she lived in the last war. The Wernhers bought some of the Chippendale furniture from Kenwood, and it is now at

Luton Hoo. Lady Ludlow is still the actual tenant for life of Luton Hoo.

After luncheon he changed into uniform and I saw that he was a general, a staff officer with red tabs and a red band round his cap. We walked through the pleasure gardens, quite gone to seed, and over the house, which is now the Eastern Command headquarters. The house is terrible, outside as well as in. Built by Adam in the 1760s for Lord Bute, it was burnt down in 1840 and rebuilt by Smirke. It was deliberately gutted in 1903 and reconstituted for the Wernhers by Mewes & Davis, architects of the Ritz Hotel. The outside walls are still more or less Adam, but in 1903 a top storey with mansard roof was added. The roof line is very untidy, with odd chimneys and unsightly skylights. The interior, or as much as I could see of it, for it is boarded up to eye level, is opulent Edwardian and Frenchified. Walking down the cavernous basement passages is like being in a tube station. In one room below stairs I came upon my cousin, Joe Napier, now a colonel, billeted here.

After an early tea the three of us went to Luton station where we had to wait fifty minutes for the train to London. When the train came in it was crowded with people standing on top of each other in the corridors. Advised by a porter we all went to the rear of the train. Having boarded it we were greeted by a guard who conducted us into an empty, first-class Pullman saloon, with detached armchairs. We sat there like royalty, which one of us partly was.

Monday, 9th November

Esher met Miss Paterson and me at the drive gates punctually at 10. We had a slow drive to London because of the fog. Several times I nearly drove into the back of cars ahead of me. Finally Esher said, 'Now having averted three major catastrophes, we may arrive safely.' We discussed whether the Trust office and staff, including the typists, should move to Polesden Lacey. He said the English race would never reconcile itself to communal living. He thought this war had had a salutary effect in proving how odious communism would be to the English. Socialism had also been proved odious through the number of documents and forms we have had to sign in war-time. The English were all grumblers whatever people might say about Julius Caesar, 'and in any case he was nothing but an ice-creamer'. He had received a letter from the Margeries excusing themselves for working in Shanghai after the fall of France. The reason they gave was that unless they had done so, reprisals would have been taken against their relations. 'Now no Englishman,' Esher said, 'would have been actuated by that motive. On the contrary, an Englishman would take every opportunity to ensure that reprisals *were* taken against his relations.'

The General Purposes Committee considered at length whether the office should move to Polesden, or not. Finally it was decided that we should return to London. I like to think I was partly responsible for this decision, in stressing the disadvantages of communal living in the country and the difficulties of getting to and from the station. Esher, who was in the chair, winked at me.

Tuesday, 10th November

I met Benton Fletcher[112] at 3 Cheyne Walk. He thinks this house is a suitable one for the Trust to buy with the War Damage monies in compensation for Old Devonshire House, which was destroyed by bombs last year. The house was last lived in by Prothero, Lord Ernle. The trustees are asking £5,000 for the freehold. Rick, who knows his Chelsea, says we should offer £3,000.

Mr. Russell, Mrs. Greville's solicitor, said that when he visited Buckingham Palace and handed his client's necklace to the Queen, she asked, 'Why do I have to pretend I know nothing about Mrs. Greville's will, when everyone I meet informs me that she has left her property to the National Trust?' Indeed the Queen spent her honeymoon at Polesden. I think this weighed with the executors, who have decided to make a public announcement straightaway.

Sir Courtauld took me aside to say he had received a letter from the Prime Minister, congratulating him on his gift of Dorney Wood, and intimating his great pleasure. I suppose Sir C. is now awaiting a further honour for his unparalleled munificence.

Thursday, 12th November

Helen has taken the news of our departure manfully. I feel sorry for her, as she will have to look for other lodgers. She knows she may do worse than have us. Yesterday the odious butler walked out of the house at 9.30 without a word of warning because Helen asked him, quite nicely, to fetch her some marmalade for breakfast.

Because of a slight fog the train chose to be three-quarters of an hour late on arrival at Paddington. This put me in a furious temper, and I rang up Sir Courtauld's secretary to say I could not keep my appointment. I had a snack at the station buffet and took a seat in the train for Newton Abbot.

I stay the night at Bradley Manor with Mrs. Woolner.[113] Her mother-

---

[112] Major Benton Fletcher gave to the National Trust Old Devonshire House, W.C.1, and a collection of old musical instruments. The house was totally destroyed in the war. Today the instruments are installed in Fenton House, Hampstead.

[113] Who as Miss Diana Firth gave Bradley Manor and 68 acres to the National Trust in 1938.

in-law is living with her. Her husband in the R.N.V.R. is a grandson of Thomas Woolner the sculptor. At dinner I drank beer from a silver tankard inscribed 'To Thomas Woolner from Alfred and Emily Tennyson 1864.' Old Mrs. Woolner said her mother-in-law's sister married Holman Hunt, whose first wife was another sister. This Mrs. Woolner was so shocked over the deceased wife's sister business that she refused ever to speak to her sister again. Mrs. Woolner also told me that Tennyson used to ask her husband when he was a boy, 'Why is your nose not as straight as your sister's?' He hated Tennyson in consequence ever after.

Diana Woolner's husband has been to Murmansk. Indeed to Russia on several convoys. He says the Russians shoot their own officers for the slightest breach of discipline, frequently unjustly and always without trial. He made friends with one naval officer who was to be shot at dawn for a most venial misdemeanour. He spent the previous evening with Woolner on board his destroyer, happily playing chess as though nothing were the matter. Next morning he was shot.

Friday, 13th November

A bomb falling near the house [Bradley Manor] this spring broke a number of windows, drawing out the leads, damaging the Blue Room ceiling, and dislodging many stone mullions and transoms. I had forgotten all the history of this house until I was reminded by reading the guide-book, every word of which I had written as recently as 1939. From time to time I discover total blanks in my memory since my accident in 1940.

In between changing trains in Exeter I walk to the cathedral. The west end is unharmed and the nave roof line is unbroken, but every window is blown out. This probably doesn't matter, but it gives the building a dead, skeletal look. A vast area to the west of the cathedral has been completely laid waste. I arrive at Montacute station at 9.15. Carrying a knapsack and two cumbersome files I walk to the King's Arms. I stay the night in this friendly, clean little inn. Mr. Yates,[114] the welcoming host, sits and talks to me over the fire, while I drink tea and munch a sandwich. This is the kind of rustic hospitality I like.

Saturday, 14th November

A cold white frost, and a most beautiful autumn morning. I am very content to be here. To warm myself I walk up the *Mons Acutus,* which is slippery with greasy mud. It is an ancient British earthwork with spiral terraces up it, and a 1760 tower at the top. The village below is wreathed

---

[114] Arthur Yates and Mrs. Yates subsequently became custodians of Montacute House for many years.

in silver mist, and blue smoke from the chimneys is twirled straight in the crisp air. Then I meet Rawlence the agent and his absurd Sancho Panza, a risible, strutting sparrow, throwing a chest and exclaiming, 'I, I, I have done so and so.' This is a warning how careful I must be not to become too proprietary in talking about the National Trust properties which I look after. The house [Montacute] is lovely, with the low sunlight on the orange Ham-stone walls and the crinkly glass windows. It is in very fair condition, thanks to Shoemark the village mason whose family has tended it for generations.

Sunday, 15th November

In Brooks's Lord Ilchester hailed me and we breakfasted together at the big table in front of the fire. He has a slow gurgling voice which rises into a whine. He is asking in the Lords whether the military should be allowed to walk into people's property and take over without previously serving requisition orders. I mentioned the case of the black unit doing this at Montacute. Lord Ilchester said that he had removed most of the good furniture from Holland House before it was destroyed and only lost a few pictures which he valued. He had also moved the most valuable books from the library.

I had an impulse to telephone Mama this morning. I told her how much I had enjoyed my visit to Montacute, which was the most beautiful Elizabethan house in England. 'No,' she said, 'it is a perfectly beastly house. You can't see out of a single window.' 'But,' I said, 'I didn't know that you had ever been there.' 'On the contrary,' she said, 'I stayed there in 1892 with Robert who was a school friend of the Phelips boy. And I hated it.' I calculate that she must have been eight years old, when of course a small child would not be able to look out of those high windows.

The church bells have been ordered to ring this morning to celebrate the victory in Egypt, rather prematurely I think. However in Piccadilly I heard not a sound. After Mass Rick took me over 104 Cheyne Walk having climbed a drainpipe and swung from a window ledge before my horrified eyes to break a way in as usual. He is determined that I shall live in it when we come back to London. After luncheon he and I talked to the Strongs in Mrs. Carlyle's kitchen. Mr. and Mrs. Strong were engaged in a hot discussion about the merits of J. S. Mill's correspondence.

I walked to 1 Hyde Park Gardens to tea with Sir Ian Hamilton. This house, which in 1910 was decorated by Roger Fry in sombre black and green for Aunt Jean, is redolent of memories of her and her lovely great luncheon parties. There used to be a perpetual smell of joss-sticks burning in the hall. Sir Ian was in the dining-room which he now uses as a living-room. It is panelled and has Scotch ancestors on the walls above. He was lying on a sofa with a rug over his knees. Mrs. Leeper at the tea-table. He will be ninety in February, and is thinner and less frisky than formerly. In fact when I arrived he was quiet and listless. He appears to be asleep until something rouses his interest. Then he is full of fire. Mrs. Leeper talked to me about the Royal Academy plans for the rebuilding of London, and the war in North Africa. Suddenly Sir Ian woke up, and launched into a long, irrelevant story about his talking very confidentially in fluent but execrable French with Marshal Lyautey, who was stone deaf, at a Foreign Office reception, and realizing that the other guests were drinking in every word. He said he was in this house last year when a bomb destroyed the house opposite. He swears his house moved a foot out of place, hesitated for an awful second, and fell back into place. He can prove the truth of the statement by some marks made by a supporting girder in the basement. Sir Ian is always courteous and cheerful. He said that we were third cousins, once or twice, or thrice removed – I forget which – through the Menteiths of Cranley. I have always liked this old warrior, and I dearly loved Aunt Jean. When on leaving I shook his hand, with its bony protuberance from the wrist, he said, with much earnestness, 'Thank you, my dear boy.'

Monday, 16th November

Rick and John Russell organized a concert tonight at Whistler's House, 96 [Cheyne Walk], in which Eddy and young Benjamin Britten played on two pianos Schubert and Chopin, and a tenor, Peter Pears, sang extremely competently the Dichterliebe of Schumann as well as Seven Sonnets of Michelangelo, composed by Britten himself. Everyone said what a good concert this was. I am so ignorant I can only judge music emotionally, not intellectually. Ivy C.-B., who with M. Jourdain and John Pope-Hennessy dined with me beforehand at the Good Intent – Jamesey chucked this morning in favour of Lady Crewe[115] – said that at best music induces in her a nice, comfortable dreamy feeling. I said it is also conducive to thought. Jamesey is just frankly bored by it.

The concert was to raise funds to procure railings for the protection of Chelsea Old Church. Rick in his usual generous way had paid for them in advance. Cecil Beaton on leaving thanked me profusely for the lovely party. I did not disabuse him by saying it was nothing to do with me. Actually I was in such pain with my leg during the concert that I

---

[115] Lady Margaret Primrose, a daughter of 5th Earl of Rosebery K.G., Prime Minister, and widow of 1st and last Marquess of Crewe (*d.* 1945).

could not sit. I stood outside the door of the ballroom with K. Clark, who I could see was cold and bored.

Wednesday, 18th November

At the S.P.A.B. meeting we discussed the Bath Assembly Rooms. The committee agreed, quite rightly in the circumstances, that the surviving walls, outside and within, should be preserved, that where partial interior decoration was left it should be repaired and reproduced, but that those rooms totally gutted without trace of decoration should be rebuilt with no attempt to replace original decorative treatment. I have a renewed respect for the S.P.A.B. They are a responsible body of, for the most part, experts, unlike the Georgians who are nearly all amateurs. Mrs. Esdaile, Marshall Sisson and Fyfe are intelligent and useful members. Esher was in good form. Miss Soppit said, 'We have not prepared the 1941 Report yet. Shall we print it with the 1942 one?' 'And publish both in 1945? I think that would be an excellent plan,' said Esher laconically.

Saturday, 21st November

I have got through a lot of difficult work this week and should be feeling pleased with myself. Instead I have such a consuming sense of guilt, about nothing particular that I can recall, accompanied by an uneasy queasiness in the stomach, that I can only attribute it to mental instability.

Sunday, 22nd November

Immediately after breakfast in Cheyne Walk, which was horrid, cold weak coffee as usual, and cold meat which I can't face at this hour of day, Rick and I went once more to 104. The owner has taken every stick of furniture out of it, leaving nothing but the curtains in what will be my bedroom. This means that, if I take it, I shall have to furnish it entirely. As I have no capital at all, I cannot raise £20, far less £50 to buy equipment. This saddens me for I do believe the house is just what I want. From the sitting-room window I watched the low orange sun make through the fog a bleeding daub on the river.

Jamesey and I walked through Camden Hill to his new flat. We looked at some fascinating and some extraordinary houses, notably Aubrey House, a Queen Anne country house stranded in this nineteenth-century urban area, and next door to it, 'Tower Crecy', the most astonishing, thin, gaunt monster of a house imaginable. It is thoroughly Pre-Raphaelite, all turrets, like the late lamented Lululaund of Herkomer. Jamesey's flat is rich and rare, spotlessly new and clean, but I do not covet it.

Had tea with Catherine Fordham – now Kennedy – in 98 Cheyne

Walk. She said that if she had had to wait another two days she would never have married at all. Now it is over she is pleased. He is older than her, with five wild children, is a general, the D.M.O., in fact a very important soldier who planned the North African campaign. I said to Catherine surely it was surprising that at such a time he could have thoughts of matrimony. She said that, although the campaign had not come off, all the planning was over and done with weeks ago. He had nothing else to do but wait, and propose to her. He was so relieved by the campaign's success, that he instantly became ten years younger.

Wednesday, 25th November

In the Travellers' Club Harold was dressed in tails and white waistcoat, the first time I had seen anyone so dressed since the war began. He said he had been told to put on these clothes by the Camroses, with whom he was to dine, and suspected the presence of royalty, the King of Greece most probably. Harold was looking sleek, smarmed and bald; and was in fact feeling very shaken and stiff, poor thing, having been run down by a taxi on his way to Buckingham Palace to see a diary of Nigel's in the hands of a brother Grenadier officer on guard there. Another taxi driver picked him up, put him into his cab and asked where he should take him. Harold said, determinedly but rather unconvincingly, 'Buckingham Palace.' 'No, no, sir! Come, come! St. George's Hospital or the Westminster?' was the reply. But Harold insisted, not however without being taken to St. George's first.

Harold talked of Mrs. Greville, a common, waspish woman who got where she did through persistence and money. She was her father's illegitimate child, her mother being unknown. She married the reputable, dull Captain Ronnie Greville, and jumped off from this safe springboard. She built herself a fictitious reputation for cleverness, and was not even witty. But she had the ambition to cultivate ambassadors and entertain them at Polesden Lacey, so that in her constant travels she could demand return favours in special trains and red carpets, much to the chagrin of foreign officials.

Jamesey said he would dine with me at Brooks's, for he had no money at all. Actually he is far richer than I am. I told him I had already invited John Gielgud to supper, if he were free. Nevertheless Jamesey insisted on eating immediately for he was ravenous. So I ordered dinner and we began on pheasant. Then a message came that John Gielgud would have supper with me at 9.15 at the Ivy. It was then 8.15 and we were already surfeited. But we finished our dinner, and James decided he would come to the Ivy too. I made him promise me he would behave, even if he disliked John. We walked to the Ivy in the blackout and James told me

Harold had come upon a passage in *Thraliana* in which Mrs. Thrale lamented the fashionable vice among young men, especially prevalent in Scotland. This she attributed to the kilt. She said Sir Horace Mann and Mrs. Damer were her informants. Raymond Mortimer said afterwards that Signor Piozzi may have been the root of Mrs. Thrale's suspicions.

Jamesey immensely liked John Gielgud who is charming, but inattentive. In conversation sophisticated remarks patter off him like undirected raindrops. He kept nodding to left and right to his friends coming and going. He is about to fly in a bomber to Gibraltar for a four weeks' performance of sketches. He says if there is no rival show of legs, the troops will come. He was very scandalous about M.B., who decoyed a young man into his Eaton Square house, and made him strip M.B. and beat him. The young man laid on with such violence that M.B. screamed in agony, and the butler appeared. When confronted with the scene all the butler remarked was, 'I thought you rang, sir.'

John said that in pre-war days he was able to keep all the suits ordered for him on the stage, and so had a large, free wardrobe. Nowadays the suits are severely rationed.

When I entered Brooks's for the night I thought there was a piece of the railings missing in front of the club.

Thursday, 26th November

On leaving the club at 8.45 I saw workmen tearing out a large chunk of the William IV railings which flank the doorway. I was livid with rage, and told the porter to allow no more to go. At Waterloo Station I sent the club secretary a furious telegram: another to Lord Ilchester, and another to the Professor [Richardson].

I walked from Dinton station to Little Clarendon. This dear little Tudor house was given to the Trust in 1940. Mrs. Engleheart the donor, opened the door. She was dressed in a mauve moreen conventual habit down to the ankles. On her feet were black sand-shoes. A silver girdle round her waist. On her head a mauve bonnet with pearl beads on the crown. She is eighty-seven and lives with her gentle, down-trodden spinster daughter. I like her, although she cannot be described as a dear old lady. She has imposed in the deed of gift stringent conditions that we shall never put in electric light, radiators or the telephone. She is a fanatical Papist, and has a chapel in the garden made of bits and pieces of rubbishy antiques including, as a facing to the altar, the cantilever springs from the Penruddock family coach.

Mrs. Engleheart told me that her great-grandmother, who lived to be ninety-seven, brought her up as a little girl near Birmingham. I think the name may have been Viscountess Southwell. This great-grandmother had been a friend of Dr. Johnson, and Mrs. E. showed me a Chinese porcelain teapot with a silver spout which had belonged to him. In fact these particulars tumbled out because in looking at her china cupboard I admired this piece. She remarked, 'That is the doctor's teapot which he gave to Granny.' So I asked, 'Which doctor?'

These poor old people have no indoor or outdoor servant.

Friday, 27th November

I walked from Sole Street station to Owletts [Cobham, Kent]. Daphne Humphreys welcomed me. She is now married to Sir Herbert Baker's third son. We strolled round the chalk pit, looking at the spindleberries. One forsythia was actually in bloom. Sir Herbert,[116] who has had a stroke, is eighty, kind, Christian-like, and cultivated. He was reading French poetry when I arrived. He insists on accompanying one, dragging his legs in a manner which pains one as it must pain him. But he will not give in. We lunched and discussed which pieces of furniture ought to stay permanently in the house. Lady Baker is no less delightful than her husband, who is also her cousin. She was an Edmeades of Nurstead Court, two miles away. They call themselves with justifiable pride, yeomen of Kent; but they are more than that. The Bakers have lived at Owletts since 1780. Both are of stalwart stock, and their integrity is written in their faces. We talked of Christopher Wren, and Lady Baker said to her husband, 'I wonder if future generations will attribute all decent buildings of these times to Lutyens or Baker?' Daphne, who accompanied me back to the station, said that Sir Herbert bore no resentment against Lutyens, and even gave the casting vote in favour of his election to the presidency of the Royal Academy.

Sir Herbert is devoted to South Africa and told me he wanted all the contents in the house associated with that dominion to be regarded as his memorial. Among them are the Dutch chests with brass hinges and the oriental porcelain he bought out there. But the whole of Owletts indeed is as much a memorial to him as it is of its seventeeth-century builders. Besides, he has contributed several additions, like the clock in the drawing-room. Baker was Cecil Rhodes's specially chosen architect. I feel that in spite of his detractors – and he is not popular today – there is something great about him when he is creative, and not being simply imitative. I admire his South Africa House. I prefer it to most of the trash around it.

---

[116] Sir Herbert Baker (1862–1946), architect. Joined Milner's 'Kindergarten', 1902. Collaborated with Sir Edwin Lutyens as architect for New Delhi from 1912.

I went to Cumberland Lodge for the night. Lady Shaftesbury, belonging to the 'sweet' type of patrician, and a clipper of 'g's, is staying. Magdalen too is all 'sweetness', combined with real goodness. Boydie is sour, and I feel sure dislikes his father. Lord FitzAlan was in bed, having had a fall. He was cross because the doctors had forbidden him going to London more than twice a week. He complained that he was more busy than ever with his House of Lords committees. I said, 'I believe, sir, that you just go to bed whenever you hear I am coming to stay.' He said, 'It is you who keep away when you hear that I am up and about.' He told me that Smuts's presence in Westminster Hall was impressive, though he, Lord F., heard not a word he said. But he fails to umderstand why Smuts talks about the great fight continuing into 1944, for he believes that, if we drive Rommel out of North Africa, Hitler is already beat. He regards the turn of the tide in Russia as a major defeat of the Germans. Boydie said over port that his father was habitually optimistic owing to his great age; and that all old people underestimated Hitler's reserves.

Alathea came for dinner. Yesterday she was at the Buckingham Palace party given for the Americans. She had to stand for two hours for there was nowhere to sit. Princess Elizabeth complained to her that she hadn't a minute to spare for her real friends. Alathea says she is good at trying to find words for strangers, but it is a great strain for her. Not so for Princess Margaret Rose who burbles away naturally and easily.

Wednesday, 2nd December

I met the builder at 104 Cheyne Walk who thinks he may be able to do the necessary work in time, i.e. by mid-January, but I am still rather worried by having no furniture, not to mention no money for the expense of moving in.

This morning I had a letter from Lord Ilchester thanking me for having drawn his attention to the railings at Brooks's. He at once took the matter up with Lord Portal at the Ministry of Works. Apparently it was just a stupid mistake, and the club secretary, poor old fool, and the Ministry appeal panel were to blame. Ilchester assured me that the pieces of railing taken away would be replaced. Professor Richardson also wrote to me to the same effect. If these railings really are saved it will be owing to one of those rare chance interventions, my happening to stay the night at Brooks's while the demolition men were beginning their beastly work. I met Sir Courtauld Thomson in Jermyn Street. He took me aside into a hat shop to tell me he is lunching tomorrow with the Prime Minister, and is presenting him with a copy of the deed of transfer of Dorney Wood. I can scarcely believe the Prime Minister will be very thrilled by this token. I am sure Sir C. is hoping for a peerage. We shall see.

Thursday, 3rd December

A cold, raw, grey December day on Frensham Common. I was begged to forestall the felling of some scruffy Scots firs on a little property which does not even adjoin ours, by accepting covenants over the land they stand on. Urged, cajoled, threatened, bullied, I was inconclusive and, weak ass that I am, failed to tell these people outright that their covenants were not acceptable. Oh, to be like a sledgehammer instead of a wet dish cloth!

Friday, 4th December

Helen had General Acres to dinner tonight. He has been promoted from the American Bomber Command to what amounts to being Commander-in-Chief of the whole American Air Force in Britain and Europe. It is hard to understand, for he is quite dumb in company and, Helen says, scarcely more talkative when alone with her. Yet on looking at him closely tonight I thought, 'You are cleverer than you seem. You put women on pedestals, and humble yourself in their eyes.' He thinks Helen the most brilliant conversationalist he has ever met. His father was a rancher in the West, and he had to educate himself. He has piloted every American machine that has been produced, and the other day returned from the U.S.A. in a new machine which goes 700 miles an hour. It is scarcely credible. It is a secret that the U.S. are producing these machines in large numbers. No wonder the runways are being lengthened so that England is becoming one mass of concrete.

Sunday, 6th December

Helen entertained to luncheon ten shooting guests, including Prince Radziwill who sat next to me. She thinks he is divine, but in reality he is a very ordinary man with a moustache. Eddy and I slunk off to walk in the woods and talk. Half-way up the lane his nose bled, and he had to sit on the bank while it poured like a fountain. He was quite unconcerned for it does this daily, and spoke about Paul Latham[117] all the while. He nourishes a sort of masochistic affection for Paul, who treats him as a fractious child treats an over-loving, over-solicitous great aunt. Talking of age Eddy said that old women were pleasanter than old men because they resigned themselves more readily to their condition, and were, on the whole, content to enjoy vicariously the happiness and success of their children; whereas old men tended to remain competitive long after they could be of any use to the community. They would not resign themselves to the shelf, but must always be interfering in concerns for which they were no longer qualified. Lytton Strachey was the first person to point

---

[117] Sir Paul Latham, 2nd Bart (1905–55), M.P. 1931–41.

this out to Eddy. I think it is true. In any case men are naturally jealous of other men, particularly old men of young men.

Mama wrote yesterday that Simon [Lees-Milne], my nephew, is desperately ill with meningitis in a London hospital. Only last weekend he was at Wickhamford in the best of health. On Thursday he was stricken. Helen and Eddy say there is never a chance of a child recovering from meningitis without being mentally defective. I wonder if this is so.[118] The news has depressed me greatly, more so than I would have thought possible, for I hardly know the child. I conclude that perhaps blood is thicker than water, notwithstanding all my protestations to the contrary.

Tuesday, 8th December

I walked to West Wycombe station to catch the early train. The mornings now are pitch dark at 8 and barely light at 9. I find it impossible to wake without a knock at the door. How dependent one's body is upon the course of the sun. I watched it rise over High Wycombe. Like a magician's wand, the rays roused the houses from decent, grey, shrouded haystacks into what they really are, hideous, pretentious little dwellings of the most commonplace architecture.

In London my first appointment was in Garrard's St. James's Street office, with Horne and Sir John Oakley to discuss the report they have made on Knole, before typing it out for the Trust and Lord Sackville. Sir John Oakley is considered the cream of the estate agent's profession. He is a highly respectable old gentleman of about seventy, very clean-shaven, beautifully trimmed moustache, snow-white starched collar and cuffs, pin-stripe suit without a rumple, and, over highly polished black shoes, brown spats. His rôle is that of confidential grandfather to every member of the nobility and gentry who owns more than 5,000 acres in Kent and Surrey, and more than 25,000 acres in Northumberland and the Welsh Marches.

I walked to the Cumberland Hotel at Marble Arch to meet one of the Trust's tenants. The Cumberland is just the sort of place she would choose. She was looking particularly common in an enormous shovel hat, erect from her neck like a Queen Anne lady's headdress. She had come to London to tell me she wished to break her lease. From a very dirty metal pot she poured out pitch black Indian tea, and from somewhere under that ghastly hat and a peroxide wig a catalogue of domestic woes. When she confided in me her dislike of her husband I became wary, and switched off my moderate allowance of sympathy.

---

[118] Fortunately it was not so in this case.

In Heywood's shop Anne [Hill] promised me the loan of a sofa and Nancy [Rodd] of two chairs for my house.

In the Hyde Park Hotel Elaine [L.-M.] told me that the L.C.C. hospital will only vouchsafe her the minimum information about Simon's condition. They treat her as though she were an imbecile, instead of the child's mother. She is not allowed to see him because when she leaves he cries for hours, and this is the worst possible thing for someone suffering from cerebral disturbance. She only knows that he has not got meningitis, but is half-paralysed. I counselled her to get our doctor to inform Simon's hospital of the family trouble. I told her that our cousin Billy Northey drove his car into a tree and killed himself, supposedly because of a fit.

Tuesday, 15th December

Benton Fletcher wishes himself and me to be co-trustees of a fund, deriving from rents of two houses in which he has a life interest, for the benefit of the new Cheyne Walk house we are buying. As soon as the war is over his collection of musical instruments from bombed Old Devonshire House will be installed in this house.

Tancred Borenius[119] told me he knew Polesden Lacey very well and would give any advice or help I might need. He said some of the pictures were good, the china was first-rate, and the whole collection a most interesting one.

I dined at the Ritz with Geoffrey Houghton-Brown[120] and Morogh Bernard. Morogh told a true story about a Belgian friend of his who with a rich aunt escaped in a closed car when the Germans invaded Belgium. The aunt, who was very delicate, died in the car. The niece could not stop to bury her for obvious reasons. For three days she continued driving with the aunt's body propped in the back seat. On the fourth day this state of things became insupportable, because it was hot summer weather. So the niece put her aunt on the roof of the car wrapped in some valuable rugs. At last she was able to stop at a café, and get out for a meal. When she returned to the car the rugs had been stolen, together with the aunt, whose remains she never saw again. Now it appears that, since the aunt's death cannot be legally certified, the niece must wait thirty years before she can inherit her money.

I stayed the night in Geoffrey's flat in Pall Mall on a sheetless bed, surrounded by pots, pans, and stacks of furniture waiting for the removal men to call the following morning at 8.30.

---

[119] Tancred Borenius (1885–1948), lecturer and writer on art. Editor, *Burlington Magazine,* 1940–45.
[120] Connoisseur and old friend of J. L-M.

Wednesday, 16th December

All the servants have gone from Polesden Lacey except the housemaid, whom I have re-engaged. I met there Mr. Abbey of Christie's who has completed the inventories of all the contents save the pictures, which Sir Alec Martin[121] is listing tomorrow. I went round the rooms with Abbey who pronounced that there is hardly a piece of furniture of museum worth, the bulk of it being made up, or deliberate copies. We ate sandwiches and drank tea in the servants' hall after this depressing perambulation. I am disappointed by his verdict.

I found Di [Murray] in Cheyne Walk in deep gloom of spirit. When people are mentally ill for no apparent cause, I find it difficult to sympathize and impossible not to be irritated.

Thursday, 17th December

I went very early to Heywood Hill's shop to buy Christmas cards; and happened to arrive just as poor Heywood was about to go off to the army, for he has at last been called up. Anne very miserable and unnaturally cheerful. She is to have a baby in May. Heywood slunk off sadly and infinitely quietly, as is his wont, Anne trying to be brave. I meant to appear unconscious of the true situation, and chatted away brutally; then left as soon as possible.

Wednesday, 23rd December

I met Mr. Abbey from Christie's and his secretary at 16 Charles Street. He galloped round this house less thoroughly than Polesden for the simple reason that he thinks there is nothing in the furniture line worth keeping for show purposes. On the other hand he thinks some of the silver is valuable, notably a few James II porringers, Queen Anne salvers and Georgian teapots. He classifies a piece with lightning rapidity. He picks up a salver, blows on its underneath, rubs the moisture off the hall mark, and makes a pronouncement immediately. He has discovered a number of distinct forgeries among the silver. There were two large porcelain jars he had not seen before. He gave a quick glance at one, tapped it, and without hesitation dictated to his secretary, 'Nankin, blue, lambrequin border at base, date so-and-so value £40 each.' He valued a dinner service without looking at more than one plate, without investigating whether the service was complete, or even counting the number of pieces.

---

[121] Sir Alec Martin (1884–1972), Managing Director of Christie's and Hon. Sec. of National Art Collections Fund.

Sir Roy Robinson[122] sat himself down next to me at luncheon. He is a large, blustering, cruel-looking, unsure-of-himself man. He complained that people when making their wills and intending to leave woodlands to the Forestry Commission would not consult him. He wanted to know what we were going to do with the Blickling and Polesden woods. Bearing in mind our recent differences with the Forestry Commission I was as non-committal as could be termed polite.

Thursday, 24th December

I went home for Christmas, or rather I stayed with Midi in the village having half my meals with her and half with the family. Midi's younger child Veronica is undeniably beautiful with copper-coloured hair and a fair skin, but she tries to be funny, and is strikingly unfunny. Bamber[123] is a sensitive, delicate and adventuresome little boy.

Deenie has come down from Stowe for Christmas. She is very miserable because one of her two great friends is dying, and she regrettably made a deathbed promise that she would have the surviving friend to live with her for the rest of her days, a rash thing to do. And so I told her.

Mama told me how last week she was in the room while Papa and Colonel Riley were planning a Home Guard exercise to take place the following day. Rather brutally they intended to humiliate another officer for stupidity, saying to each other, 'William, the damned fool will never be able to capture the aerodrome. If he were the slightest use, of course he would, etc.' They then discussed how it ought to be done, tracing on a map the complicated route he should take, mentioning the names of bridges, roads, villages and the map numbers. Mama all the while was pretending to read *The Times,* but was actually jotting down on a pad all they said. When they left the house she rang up the damned fool William, and reported to him word for word what they had said, giving the exact map references. The result was that much to their surprise and disgust William captured the aerodrome with flying colours. When I told Midi this she said, 'Your mother told me in confidence that whenever she wants to get out of the Red Cross functions she puts her thermometer on the hot-water bottle, and shows it to your father, who positively forbids her to leave her bed. Your mother, to make her feigned illness more convincing expostulates with your father just a little, but not too much, knowing that he will not give his consent.'

---

[122] Afterwards Lord Robinson (1883–1952), forester from Australia, chairman of Forestry commission, 1932–52.
[123] Bamber Gascoigne, television star and author.

Tuesday, 29th December

I went to Boarstall Tower which 'the anonymous benefactor', Mr. Cook, is presenting to the Trust. It is the Tudor gatehouse to a large house of the Aubrey-Fletcher family, which was destroyed at the end of the eighteenth century after the owner's son and heir met a premature death there. [A. D.] Peters the literary agent is the tenant. On the second floor is one superb room, the length and breadth of the building with, at either end, huge bay windows from floor to ceiling. You freeze in it in winter, and boil in it in summer. I shall recommend it.

Wednesday, 30th December

In the office this afternoon the telephone bell rang, and Eardley said to me, 'You are wanted. The name is Stuart Preston[124] or something like that.' I was amazed. Stuart flew from America yesterday. He is a G.I. The last time I saw him was at dinner with Harold in the House of Commons in the summer of 1938. I remember Harold saying, 'The next time we see Stuart over here, he will be in uniform.'

Thursday, 31st December

I was sent to Harrods agency to try and reduce the price the vendor is asking for 3 Cheyne Walk. I am a perfectly hopeless bargainer. The agents held out for £4,000. Tentatively and apologetically I asked whether they would not reduce it to £3,500. No, they said, of course they wouldn't. I gave in without a struggle and agreed to their £4,000, which I consider a reasonable figure. I would rather go without a thing than haggle over it. But the National Trust will not be of this opinion, and I shall be in disgrace. However I feel sure Benton Fletcher, who is mad keen for us to buy the house, and who quite likes me, will forgive me.

I 'saw' or rather 'slept' – and not alone – the New Year in. Could there possibly be a happier augury for 1943? I think not.

---

[124] Stuart Preston came to England in the van of the American troops. His military duties were at the U.S.A. headquarters in London. In 1944 he went overseas with the invasion forces. Meanwhile he was much fêted in London social and literary circles owing to his charm and intelligence.

1943

Friday, 1st January

I walked to Brooks's and had breakfast with Simon Harcourt-Smith. The War Office had told him that the Germans stood to lose 1,000,000 men by the time Rostov was reached, that is to say in total since the Russian offensive began last November. He took me to look at 3 Tenterden Street off Hanover Square, now divided into several apartments for Jewish costumiers and tailors. It is a wonderful eighteenth-century house with a perfect façade and thick, contemporary iron railings along the pavement. It has a mitred stair rail of mahogany over twisted iron balusters, rococo plaster ceilings, good wainscoting and arcaded doorways. It is remarkably unspoilt, not even damaged by raids and retains several original glass panes in the windows. Simon claims that it is the old town house of the Harcourt family.[125]

I left him for 16 Charles Street, where I went over the house inventory in hand, marking what to keep and what not. Stuart called for me at 1.30 and took me to lunch at the Berkeley. Luncheon cost 17/- for two, without drinks. It consisted of indifferent thick soup made of God knows what, minced chicken hash and no pudding. Really scandalous. I returned to Charles Street and was joined by Miss Paterson, who found all sorts of valuable household things like soap, mops, brooms, etc., impossible to buy nowadays even at exorbitant prices. We put these aside with a view to buying them for the new house if allowed to do so. I dined at Brooks's with Nigel Birch[126] who talked affectionately of Tom Mitford, and Randolph whose marriage is, he says, breaking up. But then Randolph only married to have a son. And the young Winston is now born.

Saturday, 2nd January

Trenchard Cox[127] lunched at Brooks's. A very affable man whose chief purpose in life seems to be charity to his neighbours. He has just been appointed private secretary to Sir A. Maxwell, the Permanent Secretary at the Home Office. It is a good appointment but involves work from 9 till 8 every day, including Saturdays. We walked to Charles Street. He looked over the furniture and agreed with Mr. Abbey that it was not of

---

[125] Needless to say it was demolished after the war.
[126] Later Lord Rhyl, Conservative politician, who held several ministerial posts.
[127] Later Sir Trenchard Cox. Director of Victoria and Albert Museum 1956–66.

very high standard. In normal times Trenchard Cox is custodian of the French furniture at the Wallace Collection. Stuart joined us at 2.45. He and I left to catch a train to High Wycombe. We chased it down the platform and the guard allowed us to jump into the van just in time. In the train he talked with rapture and awe of his dinner last night with the Duff Coopers. He finds her wondrous, incredibly flippant, brilliant and witty, but cruel and un-middle-class. He kept on repeating the last phrase, with wide open eyes. 'But of course,' was all I could find to say, 'what else do you expect?' He says that in his billets in North Audley Street he sleeps on straw with one blanket.

Tuesday, 5th January

Woke up to find snow and a tightening of the chest, the beginning of a cold. Breakfasted early and caught a bus to Cookham, and on to Netley Park. This is a Surrey property of which I expected greater things than were apparent under the snow. A bad 1840 house with great plate-glass windows and ugly grey stucco front. I looked at the downstairs rooms, of which the licentious soldiery have made an awful mess, smashing the pair of gilt looking-glasses in the drawing-room. But then they should have been boarded up with the chimney-pieces over which they hang. They are Louis Philippe, I guess, with oval medallions containing portraits of a lady in the crests.

I got back to West Wycombe at 8 feeling tired. Yet I sat up in the office till 11 waiting for Q. who never telephoned. Went to bed torturing myself unnecessarily.

Friday, 8th January

My temperature being sub-normal I decided to risk pleurisy, pneumonia, death, and go to London to catch a glimpse of Q. even if I had to come straight back again. Waiting for the bus in the half light and the frost my body felt sweaty hot, and my hands and feet like icicles. The extremes of temperature simultaneously in one body seem to me most unnatural and odd. In Charles Street I gave the old caretaker, Mrs. Reid, a pork pie as a present. It was by way of throwing a sop to Cerberus. For when Q. breezed in she was quite polite to her. I find the attitude of humble women to well-dressed women invariably the same, suspicious and resentful. And when Q. breezed out after five minutes of ecstasy, Mrs. Reid, though cordial, looked triumphant. Then Harold [Nicolson] called to leave a note for Stuart. He was bright and shabby, so Mrs. Reid beamed upon him. Harold strode up and down the stone hall nostalgically but unregretfully recalling the awful parties he had attended in this house. In between the interruptions I managed to work away at my listing. Again the doorbell rang. Mrs. Reid bustled eagerly from basement to ground floor. Stuart walked in, and because he is under thirty Mrs. Reid beamed upon him. Over a huge fire in the dining-room Stuart and I crouched under the steel scaffolding and between the stacks of French furniture. I ate sandwiches and Stuart a plateful of ready-cooked American field rations of meat minced up with beans from a tin which Mrs. Reid heated for him. Disgusting it looked too. Both of us drank whisky from a flask. I continued to work alone in this eerie house, and left after dark, purloining like a thief in the night a broom, a brush and a cake of scrubbing soap.

I dined with Q. at Prunier's off homard à l'americaine and a glass of champagne each. I was obliged to stay at Duke's Hotel, St. James's Street.

Saturday, 9th January

Cough very thick in the morning, otherwise surprisingly well. Health is largely determined by one's state of happiness or the reverse.

Frank Partridge [the dealer], whom I called on, told me the collections at Luton Hoo and in Bath House were incomparable, notably the French furniture, the pictures and the English porcelain.

At 104 Cheyne Walk I found Miss Paterson and the new char, Mrs. Beckwith, a dear, gentle little mouse from Battersea, sweeping and washing floors busily. Jamesey called and took me to lunch at the Good Intent. He is very happy at the moment. He talked of Stuart whom he had met last night dining with Harold. He thinks him personable, but in that Pope-Hennessy way is terrifyingly analytical. Asks me if he is sincere. Suspects insincerity. I don't yet know, I tell him. We return to the house and this time I really get down to sweeping and clearing away the mess of two years' accumulation of air-raid detritus. Jamesey very immaculate with a calf-bound book under one arm follows me around, asking querulously if it is really necessary for me to sweep. He says other peoples' ploys of this kind are a great bore. This makes me laugh at him. He soon slopes off to call on Logan Pearsall Smith.[128] When he has gone Miss P., Mrs. Beckwith and I drink tea in front of a huge fire in my room, sitting on the bed, the only piece of furniture that has yet arrived.

After dinner I went to 4 King's Bench Walk to stay the night at Harold's. Jamesey was going to warn him to expect me there. He and Harold went to an American party tonight. Harold came in at 10.30 and we talked till after midnight. He makes me talk freely as though I am cleverer than I am, and feel happier than I am. He is still optimistic about the outcome of the war. He said the Poles' estimate of losses was

---

[128] Logan Pearsall Smith (1865–1946), man of letters. Of American Quaker origin.

considered the most accurate. They declare that the Russians, whom of course they hate, have lost 4,000,000 men and the Germans 2,500,000. The Czechoslovakian Prime Minister, with whom Harold lunched yesterday, had that morning been interviewing two Czech youths just arrived in England after walking across Germany. They reported that every German they met spoke of defeat as the inevitable outcome for them.

Monday, 11th January

Miss Paterson and I motored up to London for the meetings. The Polesden Lacey reports were considered at great length by the General Purposes Committee. They said the combination of reports on agriculture and art by [Hubert] Smith, the new Chief Agent, and myself, with a foreword by the Secretary, was just what they had hoped for. They agreed to let me do what I thought best with the contents subject to Clifford Smith[129] and Kenneth Clark endorsing my opinion. Sir Edgar Bonham-Carter urged, sensibly I thought, that we keep Polesden looking like an Edwardian lady's country house, and not a museum.

Tuesday, 12th January

By the early train to London again in order to meet Kenneth Clark at Charles Street. Found Stuart there for he had rung me up the previous evening after dining with Jamesey. Together we sorted out the pictures for K. Clark to look at. Stuart left and K. Clark arrived. He was extremely helpful and took much trouble examining all the pictures, of which he was to my contentment even more critical than Christie's and recommended keeping even less than they did. Moreover he offered to motor down to Polesden with me one day and look through the pictures there.

I joined Stuart at the Connaught Hotel but since we could not get a table we lunched at Brooks's. Stuart had spent the weekend at Panshanger. The only other guest was Lord Hugh Cecil.[130] He and the Desboroughs spoke about Lord Rosebery and Queen Victoria not as legendary figures, but as friends whom they had all known. Lady Desborough is in fact a step-granddaughter of Lord Palmerston and a great-granddaughter of Byron's Lady Melbourne. Stuart slept in a room the walls of which were hung with the heraldic achievements of a Lord Cowper, an eighteenth-century ancestor who was a Prince of the Roman Empire.

---

[129] H. Clifford Smith (1876–1960), Keeper of Department of Woodwork at the Victoria and Albert Museum before the war.
[130] Later Lord Quickswood (1869–1956), fifth son of 3rd Marquess of Salisbury, the Prime Minister. Provost of Eton 1936.

Thursday, 14th January

Today we leave West Wycombe for good, to return to our London office and life. Whiteley's only sent one van, and that an hour and a half late, instead of the two ordered. I drove Miss Paterson and Miss Ballachey in the National Trust car stacked with our own belongings. On the way we picked up my dachshund Pompey. He was sick, once over Miss Paterson's second-best coat and again out of the open window into a London street. Dreadful confusion on arrival at the office, but worse when Miss Paterson and I reached 104 Cheyne Walk after dark. The charwoman had not even lit a fire for us. There was no electric light because the company said the house was too damp to test the wiring. No stick of furniture yet save one bed each. The Ascot heater not working, and so no hot water. We had an uncomfortable night, Pompey sleeping and falling off a chair beside me.

Saturday, 16th January

Some furniture arrived this morning. Miss P. and I worked like Trojans. I had to help haul my large sofa through the window on the first floor, since it had stuck on the staircase. After tea I changed and went to Ian Hamilton's ninetieth birthday party. He had invited ninety friends, mostly relations, and all the children from the neighbouring streets. He gave them a conjuring entertainment and a Punch and Judy show, with one marionette arrayed as Hitler. Mrs. Churchill was leaving the door as I arrived. I talked to Shane Leslie about his boy Jack, now a prisoner of war since Boulogne. He often hears from him and says Jack laughed when the Germans manacled him. Dined with the Pope-Hennessys, Dame Una talking of Shane Leslie's new edition of Cardinal Wiseman's love letters to Lady Herbert of Lea.

Sunday, 17th January

Rick turned up last night a Coldstream guardsman, looking the picture of health, but in actual fact depressed and overcome by the whole experience. He said he could not cope and was so dispirited with so little to say, and that said so haltingly that I, friend as I am, was really bored. For the first time since I have known him I made an excuse to leave, and slunk home to bed.

The siren went during dinner at Brooks's, and the noise of our gunfire was worse than I have ever known it. During the night there was a second raid. Miss P. was rather frightened by the din, so we sat under the stairs in our dressing-gowns. Pompey was quite unmoved. I did not like to ask Miss P. if she regretted our having left the country for this sort of thing.

Monday, 18th January

Horne and I, and the clerk to Mrs. Greville's solicitors went to consult counsel, a Mr. Raymond Needham, at his chambers in the Temple about a financial point to be forwarded to the Capital Issues Committee, relating to some £500,000 stock. It was interesting how very lucidly and confidently the clerk unravelled and presented the complicated story. I mentioned this afterwards to Horne, who said this is what often happens: intelligent solicitors' clerks become first-class at their jobs, yet because of their cockney voices get no further up the scale and never become attorneys. It seems all wrong to me. Needham was like a wise old owl listening behind thick horn-rimmed spectacles, interjecting a word only occasionally, yet grasping the issues quietly and faultlessly, and finally pronouncing a definite opinion.

Tuesday, 19th January

Lunched at the Ivy with W. L. Wood to discuss Frensham Common. I could barely hear a word he mumbled through his closed yellow teeth. He gave me a delicious meal of braised beef and French salad, coffee mousse and a sweet white liqueur. I then went for an interview with Sir William Leitch at the Ministry of Works, and Usher of the Treasury, about the large legacy of £200,000 which Sir Courtauld is leaving for Dorney Wood.

Wednesday, 20th January

In the morning I met Clifford Smith at Charles Street. I am hoping he will confirm the decisions I have come to in the choice of contents to be retained. At 2.30 to Miss Davy to discuss Cliveden accounts. It appears Lord Astor is so ill that he cannot attend to details. And because he is a Christian Scientist no one may refer to his bad health.

Went to tea with Jamesey in his flat to meet Rose Macaulay and Lady Crewe. Lady C. was there when I arrived, wrapped in expensive furs and wearing black gloves. She talked spicily to Jamesey in whispered asides, and they giggled a lot. This behaviour did not make a comfortable trio. Then she talked to us both about Polesden Lacey. 'Whatever you do, you will have to rip off the yellow buttons in the drawing-rooms,' she counselled me. She told how Mrs. Greville's mother was the wife of the day-porter at Mr. M'Ewan's brewery. M'Ewan 'for convenience' put him on night duty. I brought some of my photographs of Manoeline architecture to show Rose Macaulay, who is shortly going to Portugal to write a book for the Ministry of Information. My first impression was of a very thin, desiccated figure in a masculine tam-o'-shanter, briskly entering the room. James says she is like Voltaire to look at. Actually her profile is less sharp than her full face, and is handsome. She talks too fast and too much.

Saturday, 23rd January

Lunched with Margaret Jourdain and Ivy Compton-Burnett to meet Elizabeth Bowen. When she first came into the room I thought she was ugly with a prominent nose and a drop on the end of it. Then I decided she was handsome, but not beautiful. She has a long face. A forward tuft of hair dances above a bandana tied round the forehead. When she smiles her charm is apparent. She speaks well and rapidly but speech is suddenly interrupted by an occasional stammer, not enough to embarrass one because she has the mastery of it. I liked her. We talked of the recent bombing. The two 'brown girls' as Helen calls them, admitted that they were terrified last Sunday night. Indeed the four of us confessed we were. I. C.-B. is apt to be shy during a meal. During coffee she expands.

My house is settling down. The room with three large and long windows on the front faces the river and the big barge moored along-side. A fourth window at the west end faces Lots power station and the bend in the river opposite Battersea and the next bridge upstream. The windows being so very dirty, since the cleaners have not yet come, make it all but impossible to see the views, but I know they are there. My glazed curtains have white sheaves of flowers on a cherry ground, and are torn and shabby. The floor is parquet. In one corner beside an Adam hob-grate is the Empire bureau with fall flap on which I write this diary. Other pieces are my unsightly bed with hideous servants' pink cover; an upright winged armchair in crimson damask; a silk covered sofa of a different crimson; a mahogany half-circular fronted commode; an anthracite stove always burning in the other fireplace; Persian rugs; a large painted tin tray of Margate, *circa* 1850 over one chimneypiece. The room is thoroughly unpretentious and on the whole pretty.

Sunday, 24th January

Breakfasting at Brooks's I sat with Lord Spencer who told me with disgust that during a seven-day absence from London 'they' took away the contemporary gates from Spencer House for scrap. Attended High Mass at the little Sardinian chapel in Warwick Street. It is far and away my favourite worshipping place in London. The candlelight flickered across the silver hearts which line the walls of the presbytery while the transalpine chants made me long for Italy and for peace and goodwill among nations.

Monday, 25th January

Went to Warfield House, Sir George Leon's near Bracknell, for luncheon, and stayed till 4. He considers making over his house and 400 acres, consisting of four small farms with pedigree herds. Rather an absurd, opinionated little man, but public-spirited and pathetically patriotic like many rich Jews on this side of the Channel. We parted fast friends. The red brick house is Queen Anne. He has had it colour-washed, and the thin window sashes and even the reveals painted dark blue. The interior was decorated sumptuously by Lenygons before the war. There are fawn pile carpets in every room and passage. All the wainscoting and the grand stair flight have been pickled. His furniture is first-rate, chiefly late seventeenth- and early eighteenth-century walnut. He showed me a suite of Charles II armchairs from Holme Lacey with particularly delicate stretchers. His pictures are immaculately cleaned and varnished, and include Poussins, Richard Wilsons, Cuyps. A typical, safe, rich, decent man's collection.

Met Jamesey at Brooks's and he conducted me to Argyll House. Lady Crewe was curtseying to Hapsburg Archdukes. Straightaway Jamesey got off with Lady Cunard,[131] and was delighted with her and the party. I disliked her and it as I knew I should. Stuart drank too much and we had great difficulty in getting him to leave. James and I had some anxious moments with him in the bus. In the restaurant he ate no dinner and talked of lords and ladies in a loud American voice.

Wednesday, 27th January

Went by train to Farningham Road where I was met by Sir Stephen Tallents[132] in tweed breeches, a blue polo sweater and no hat. A jolly, extrovert, pipe-sucking man, clever, well-read yet uncultivated. He accompanied me on foot to his house, St. John's Jerusalem, which is a pretty place, with an early monastic chapel attached to an early eighteenth-century house. It is surrounded by watercress beds and willow plantations. Lady Tallents is big, handsome, outspoken and rather eccentric. She is very musical and sings. I liked this place and considered it worthy.

Thursday, 28th January

Dined with Oliver Hill the architect, at his house in Cliveden Place. It is at the west end of the row, an eighteenth-century house near Sloane

---

[131] Emerald, widow of Sir Bache Cunard, 3rd Bart., whom she married 1895. Well known hostess. She died 1948.
[132] Sir Stephen Tallents (1884–1958), civil servant and writer.

Square. One end is cut back at an acute angle to allow a stream to flow beside it. Oliver Hill has decorated the rooms in his own inimitable, modernistic way which I admire. His eating-room walls are lined with a kind of grey granite, incised with life-size graffiti of nudes by Eric Gill. With a strong light thrown across the walls the graffiti stand out impressively. Hill has just bought from a house in Shropshire some English seventeenth-century tapestries, probably Mortlake, of idyllic Hampton Court scenes. He much admires our Mortlake tapestry which he borrowed from Wickhamford for the exhibition in Whistler's House in 1940. He is a tall, shaggy, rough, ruthless creature, very deaf and untidy. He usually has saliva dribble on his chin, and he wears dark blue woollen shirts with frayed collars, and a flopping, striped knitted tie. He told the other guests that Mama has a most uncanny power over birds; that during her three days' stay in Cheyne Walk for the exhibition the Chelsea birds found her out, and flocked to her bedroom window.

Saturday, 30th January

Stuart's portable alarm clock went off at 6.30 a.m. with the most tremendous din. This dreadful clock has for him some esoteric significance. Whenever he comes to stay the first thing he does is to produce it from a voluminous pocket and place it carefully on a table, like setting up a tent. The last move is to pick it up, fold it away, like drawing up the tent pegs. There is something atavistic in the procedure. Perhaps he had Bedouin forebears.

Margaret Jourdain and Ivy C.-B. came to tea. I had forgotten at what time to expect them or if I had even specified a time. To my surprise and concern they arrived on the dot of 4. They are slightly prim and correct, and it evidently distressed them that I had to descend to the kitchen, make and fetch the tea, and lay the table in their presence. I was made to feel that I was not behaving quite as I should. As it was, I did not like to spend time making toast. It was a horrid tea in consequence, and this they clearly minded, without saying so. To make matters worse John Russell, whom I had bidden to meet them, did not turn up till after 5, having been to a concert. However they stayed till after 6. Ivy C.-B., talking of the ineffectual results of the Germans' last raid on London when they hit a school and killed thirty children, observed, 'It isn't as though they were even impeding our war effort. On the contrary, they are really helping it by making the milk ration go further.'

Jamesey took me to dine at the Royal Court hotel, where we drank sweet Sauternes. He stayed the night on my lilo, but slept very little on account of the loud ticking and striking of my clock, he maintained. I maintained that had he not spurned the spare bed he would have slept soundly.

Took the 1.30 to Cullompton in Devon to stay two nights at Bradfield with Mrs. Adams, who was Lottie Coats, sister of the present Glentanar and the Duchess of Wellington. She was formerly Mrs. Walrond and her son is Lord Waleran. The Walronds have owned Bradfield since 1100. Her father bought it from this impoverished family and put it in trust. She is the present life tenant, the next her son and then the children of the duchess. I find country peoples' houses bitterly cold. Here one green log faintly glimmers in a small coal grate. Adams, the present husband, is a jovial retired naval commander who cracks bawdy jests and whose every adjective is 'bloody'. Yet he is a decent country gent, like my father. He listens to every news bulletin on the wireless right to the end of the postscript.

Mrs. Adams talked a great deal about her family; how her younger son died a few months ago of drink, aged thirty-four, and his wife two months before him, of dropsy. Commander Adams told me she too drank. Mrs. Adams worries about her sister at Stratfield Saye, where there is no electric light and no central heating. The little duchess, Maudie, lives in her bedroom, and freezes. The Queen rang up the duchess a year ago to ask if it were true that the treasures in Apsley House had not been evacuated. The duchess admitted that it was true. 'Well then, I am coming round at 11 with a van to take them to Frogmore,' the Queen said. And punctually she arrived with the King. With pencil and paper she made lists and decided what should be moved and what left behind. 'You mustn't be sentimental, Duchess. Only the valuable pictures can go,' she said. Mrs. Adams who is simple and sweet, said to me in her broad Scotch (or is it Glasgow?) accent, 'I quite realized when I married into the Walrond family that they were the squirearchy, whereas I was only a tradesman's daughter. Our ethical standards were entirely dissimilar. I had to adapt myself to the family I had married into.'

Spent the day walking round the estate, the garden and the house, now a military convalescent home. The outside of Bradfield was almost totally rebuilt in 1854. A coarse local stone was substituted for cob in reconstructing the mullioned windows and gables. The inside has likewise suffered, though not so generally. The restorer had the wit not to tamper unduly with the remarkably fine great hall with its Henry VIII medallion busts in the panelling, the Gothic foliage frieze, Jacobean screen, and the tempera painting of Gog and Magog. The Spanish Room with grotesque interior porch and painted overmantel is equally remarkable, all in a barbaric way. I do not however much like the house, or property as a whole.

Wednesday, 3rd February

I had a horrible day with Colonel Pemberton at Pyrland Hall near Taunton. He is a fiendish old imbecile with a grotesque white moustache. When I first saw him he was pirouetting on his toes in the road. He has an inordinate opinion of himself and his own judgment. He is absolutely convinced that Pyrland is the finest house in Somerset and he is doing the Trust a great service in bequeathing it. The truth is the property does not comprise land of outstanding natural beauty and is of insignificant size; moreover the house, though large, and basically eighteenth century, has been thoroughly Victorianized as to windows and rendering. The army occupies it at present. It has a nice Georgian staircase and some plaster cornices and mahogany doors on the curve. I was drawn into several acrimonious arguments with the old man, whom I cordially disliked, for he insisted upon contradicting whatever I said. He gave me an exiguous lunch of bread and cheese, both hard as wood, a baked potato in its skin, dry as sawdust, and watery apple pie with Bird's custard. Ugh! He expected me to return and waste the following day in discussion. But I had already made up my mind after the first half-hour of the visit. I could not have borne him or Pyrland an hour longer. Having hated me like poison he was nevertheless furious when I left at 4. I conclude that he has to have a victim on whom he can vent his spleen. I got back to London in time to have a late supper of oysters and stout with Gabriel Herbert.

Friday, 5th February

Lady Colefax's luncheon party; but she had bronchitis and stayed in bed. Norah Lindsay acted hostess in her place. She was wearing a flat, black hat like a pancake on the side of her head, pulled down over one eye. It was adorned with cherry-coloured buttons. Her white frilled blouse had more cherry buttons. She is kittenish, stupid-clever, and an amusing talker. On her left was Osbert Peake, now a Minister of some sort, a boring, stuffy man. Jamesey was on my right and in the circumstances we had nothing, but nothing to say to one another. On my left was Laurie Johnston,[133] who had just seen my father at Hidcote. A man called Palewski,[134] who is General de Gaulle's *chef du cabinet*, and rather spotty,

---

[133] Major Lawrence Johnston, creator of Hidcote Manor garden, Glos., which he gave in 1948 to the National Trust largely through the persuasion of Lady Colefax.
[134] Later President of the Constitutional Council of France.

talked about North Africa. He has just returned from Casablanca where he attended the Churchill-Roosevelt meeting. He said Roosevelt was in high spirits; he had to be carried in a chair from the aeroplane for he cannot walk at all and can barely stand unaided. After luncheon, which was delicious, Laurie Johnston took me aside to ask if the National Trust would take over Hidcote garden without endowment after the war, when he intended to live in the South of France for good. He is a dull little man, and just as I remember him when I was a child. Mother-ridden. Mrs. Winthrop, swathed in grey satin from neck to ankle, would never let him out of her sight. Jamesey calls him a Henry Sturgis American.

Sunday, 7th February

Midi, Stuart and I went to Windsor by train. We walked to Eton and looked for our various boys in their houses. Then Stuart and I lunched with the Provost, Lord Quickswood. There were just the three of us. I was surprised to find Lord Q. such an old man. He was shy at first, though full of solicitude for Stuart, the American soldier ally, who seems to be treated by all society as a lion. But then Stuart is attentive to the old and throws off anecdotes and literary quotations like pearls before swine. Lord Q. warmed after a time, but has little charm, and is impersonal. An old-fashioned luncheon of roast turkey, brown potatoes and sprouts, 'shape', that ghastly wobbly pudding and bottled blackberries, accompanied by beer followed by sherry. Lord Q. showed us all the portraits in the Provost's Lodge from the Gheeraerts of Lord Essex to the Romneys and Beecheys of old boys. He also took us over Lower School, and Upper School, showing us the bombed bit. The Headmaster's room has quite gone, all but the roadside wall. There is a deep crater where it was. Stuart fascinated by it all, and particularly by Lord Quickswood's use of 'ain't', his top hat and white bands. Stuart asked if we might see the College Library. Lord Q. thought for a moment, and said apologetically, 'I much fear I cannot do that. My man is out this afternoon, and I do not know where to switch on the lights.'

Tea at the Cockpit. Stuart took out Lady Desborough's grandson, and I Francis Dashwood who is in Pop. After College Chapel Stuart and I called on Mrs. Montgomery[135] who lives in a hideous corner house facing the entrance to Windsor Castle. She is the eighty-year-old daughter of Sir Henry Ponsonby. She has evidently had a stroke and it is not easy to understand what she says. She is wizened, sharp and brimful of

---

[135] Alberta Victoria Ponsonby, married 1891 Major-Gen. W. E. Montgomery who died 1927. She died 1945.

talk. She repeated to Stuart the most flattering things told her about him by Logan Pearsall Smith, who is a close friend. She spoke of Queen Victoria who was her godmother and whom she disliked. She said that during dinners at the castle no one was allowed to speak, and if they had to ask for something, not above a whisper. Dinners were interminable and dreadful. The Queen would address her family in German. The familiar phrase, '*Das ist schrecklich!*' haunts her. She once witnessed the Queen greeting Mr. Gladstone, who had been summoned to dine. Gladstone was nervous about what his reception would be, and fumbled with his walking-stick. He was then over eighty. But contrary to expectation, when the Queen appeared she went straight up to him, leaning on a stick herself, and said, 'Mr. Gladstone, you and I have known days when neither of us was lame,' and laughed very sympathetically.

Monday, 8th February

I sat down on a sofa in Brooks's to read the evening paper. A form next to me leant over from the shadow and said, 'I was right. The man simply loathes comfort, or any semblance of it.' It was Esher. 'Who? When?' I asked. He was referring to Matheson who, he said, deliberately selected the most uncomfortable chair in a room, and perched on it in the most uncomfortable way. We talked about the Country Houses Committee, and I asked if Michael Rosse might be elected to it. He agreed.

I dined at the Travellers' with Harold, James and Stuart. Harold pulled me up for using the word 'relative', which he said was bedint. Jamesey agreed. Now I come to think of it, it is. Harold and Stuart talked of North Africa and the war, which made Jamesey sulk. He complained he could not bear any mention of the war, and 'wanted literature from Harold only'. After dinner over port Jamesey said to me that Stuart irritated him with his permanent smile of appreciation. Stuart, with whom I walked away at 9.30, said that Jamesey irritated him with his *'petit maître'* manner, his finickiness, his Miss Mitford, tidy little appearance. Of course they will be dining together tomorrow night, and were probably dining last night, and making similar criticisms of me.

Thursday, 11th February

Matheson and I had an interview with Sir Robert Wood, Secretary to the Board of Education, to discuss the Board's co-operation with the Trust in the use of country houses after the war. He was fairly helpful and promised to put me in touch with various educational departments.

I arrived in the full swing of Cecil Beaton's party in Pelham Place. Cecil's house is sophistically decorated. It is nineties-ish, with red flock walls and varnished aspidistras in tall pots, and tight, little smart leather chairs. He was saying about his secretary 'When I go away I leave her, not on heat, but on board wages, I mean.' While talking to Alice Harding I felt something boring, boring into my spine, which means that one is being talked about maliciously. True enough, on turning round I saw Eddy and Nancy sitting on a low sofa dissecting each guest one by one and hooting with laughter. I joined them. Nancy was telling how Lady Leconfield[136] had been certified for descending in the lift at Claridge's stark naked. The little lift boy was sharply reprimanded by the hall porter. In self-defence he protested that he could not see above the lady's knees, she was so tall.

Friday, 12th February

I had an interview with Sir John Maude at the Ministry of Health. It was unprofitable. He bluntly said that old houses were totally unfitted for medical purposes.

Saturday, 13th February

Did not go to the office this morning but at midday met Gerry Villiers at 16 Charles Street, and tried in vain to find a stair carpet for him to buy. All we did find were some candle bulbs which he took away without buying. He begged me to get Professor Richardson the job of designing and making Mrs. Greville's tombstone, for he is the contractor who provides Portland stone for all the professor's works of this kind. He was almost appealing. I said it was not within my power to commission the professor to do anything of the sort, although I guessed the executors would commission him.

Anne Hill came to tea. We were alone and ate toast and golden syrup. She is to have a baby in May and is now bigger than Midi. She says the child already jumps about in her womb so that the bedclothes literally heave at nights. Nancy is the greatest help to her in the bookshop. As we talked I finished scraping off the anti-bomb stuff from my west window. Now I can enjoy the full view up the river of Lots power station. Everyone says it is the best view in London.

Mrs. Montgomery told James she supposed I was too young to be in the army. 'On the contrary,' said James, 'he is too old.'

Monday, 15th February

All day at Polesden going round the house with Christie's inventory. It is strange how happy I am at Polesden. Chips Channon[137] asked me to look

---

[136] Violet, wife of 3rd Lord Leconfield, who d.s.p. 1952.
[137] Sir Henry Channon (1897–1958), M.P. and diarist.

for and bring back to him a blood-stone, which was his last present to Mrs. Greville. But I can't, I can't, even if I find it.

Wednesday, 17th February

A tiresome and unprofitable meeting about the English Town Exhibition all morning. At 12.45 I lunched with Michael Peto at the Guards Club. He was amused and amazed that I had never been inside the building before, and kept repeating breezily, 'It is very brave of you to admit it openly,' as though I had something to conceal and be ashamed of. He is liaison officer between the American H.Q. and the War Office. He said the Americans in Tunisia could not encounter a more terrifying baptism of fire than Rommel's Panzer divisions were giving them.

Thursday, 18th February

Today I bought a new eye-glass on a black string. It is the greatest help in reading menus and bus numbers, instead of fumbling for spectacles.

At 6 o'clock I went to St. George's Hospital where Stuart has been removed, for he is suffering from jaundice. He is happy there because he is in the centre of London and can see Apsley House from his window. He is quite a different colour, no longer grey, but saffron. He pulled up the bedclothes and showed me his stomach which is bright lemon. I delivered chocolates, stamps and writing paper.

Jamesey talked about his rich, eccentric, plethoric admirer with whom he stays in Scotland. He assures me no demands whatever are made; but active adoration from a respectful distance keeps him warm, and is what he likes.

Friday, 19th February

Puss Milnes-Gaskell rang me up at breakfast and I lunched with her in the Ladies' Carlton Club. How tiny she is! She has come out of waiting at Badminton. I said I was reading the Henry Ponsonby book and enjoying it. She said, 'They', meaning Queen Mary *en principe*, did not like it at all. Their indignation was aroused against Sir Henry for having betrayed a private secretary's confidence in recording in letters to his wife matters of such a personal nature; not so much against Lady Ponsonby who after all is responsible for publication of these documents. Stuart says he regards the book as a last fling of the old-fashioned Whiggery against the Monarchy.

Saturday, 20th February

Went to see the Sergeant[138] [Stuart] in St. George's Hospital at 3 o'clock. Found there Stephen Spender who stayed talking for some time. He was in London fireman's uniform, wearing a blue fireman's overcoat. He is extremely handsome still, with an open radiant face framed in fuzzy, wind-blown yet close-cut hair which in its stellar way reminds me of Einstein's. In fact his looks are Teutonic and his mother was a German. Is he as innocent and guileless as he appears? He is very polite, with a schoolboy's awkward good manners. I hardly know him. I suppose Stuart murmured something, for he rose from a chair, shook hands nervously and said, 'Oh, yes, Jim.' He is shy and childlike which is endearing. Eddy says he can be a great bore for he is unrealistic and often silly, like most idealists. This I can well believe. I asked him if he saw anything of Henry Yorke,[139] who is also a fireman. He said Yes. Henry has written a new novel attacking the lower orders which Spender of course finds shocking. Yet as Eddy again says, Henry at least knows them, having lived among them; whereas Stephen has merely slept with them, which is not the same as knowing them uncarnally, and so romanticizes them. Indeed he got on to the sex lives of the lower orders this afternoon. He says they are on the whole remarkably strait-laced and puritanical, except the taxi drivers, who are the bohemians of the lower classes. Being constantly on the move, roaming around, they are on the fringe of the lives of poor and rich alike, especially of the Ritz rich. Their lives are so full of the promise of romance and actually so frustrated. After he left, Stuart said how successful the encounter had been. He immensely admires Spender. Funny creature Stuart, with his boundless capacity for admiration, his extravagant interest in people, his keen awareness of environment and absorption in class distinctions, at least in the multivariant intellectual and social distinctions of English life. He is as sensitive to our traditions as Henry James. Then I watched him eat his tea, so grossly, or do I mean youthfully? He consumed during this meal the whole of a pound pot of jam someone brought him yesterday. I was aghast and wondered whether in pre-war days I was ever so lavish.

Midi, Keith and Eddy came to tea. Eddy said, 'You do *not* take sugar with your tea. You take medicine.' And I said, 'You take liberties.' But unfortunately this retort was not my own.

---

[138] Stuart Preston was known to his English friends as the Sergeant, because he was a sergeant in the U.S. army. But woe betide the friend whom Stuart overheard using this term of endearment.
[139] Henry Yorke (1905–74), wrote novels under the pen name Henry Green.

Jamesey on the telephone tonight said he did not admire Stephen Spender. He contradicted his first observation that Stephen was disingenuous, saying that perhaps he was ingenuous; and if so, then he was stupid. That he wrote silly prose and his poetry was incomprehensible. He was like Wordsworth whom James detests. This resemblance I do not see.

Sunday, 21st February

I walked with Pompey from Chelsea, across the park to Paddington. From Windsor station we walked, Pompey off his lead, good as gold, down the Long Walk, past the Copper Horse to Cumberland Lodge; (and in the afternoon back to Windsor). I was five minutes late for luncheon and they had begun eating. They being only Lord FitzAlan, Magdalen and Mrs. Wyndham[140] (Methuselah's wife), sweet, fragile and shaky. Lord FitzAlan was worried by the rumour that the Pope might be leaving Rome for Brazil. I said it was the cheap Protestant press that was fabricating the rumour. We looked through the Catholic papers and, sure enough, they made no reference to it at all. It is sad how the Protestant papers must invent the most ridiculous canards to discredit the Pope these days. Lord F. was also worried about Tunisia. He thinks our delay in attacking will enable the Germans to muster reinforcements to outnumber us. Stuart expressed unfeigned delight in the American reverses, thinking them the best thing that could happen, 'for we are a conceited, self-satisfied race,' he said humbly.

I had tea with Mrs. Montgomery in Windsor. It was, I believe, a success. We found we liked and disliked the same people and the same books. She was thrilled that I knew Ivy Compton-Burnett, whom she considers our greatest novelist. She has lent me one of her books that I have not yet read, as a hostage she explained, so that I should have to come back and return it to her. Alan Pryce-Jones is her cousin. She loves Jamesey very much and the Sergeant [Stuart Preston] not so very much. She absolutely loathes Queen Victoria and Evelyn Waugh. She cannot feel dispassionately about anyone. We touched on Raymond, Eddy, Basil Dufferin. As their names cropped up, 'Now we have another,' she cried eagerly. 'We will put him *here*,' indicating a place at the large empty tea-table, 'and will come back to him when we have disposed of X. We will give him ten minutes,' or 'quite twenty minutes' as the case might be. When I left she referred to me as being 'quite one of us'. 'I loathe lowbrows,' were her parting words. What will she think of me when she finds me out?

---

[140] Gladys, later Lady Leconfield, wife of 5th Lord Leconfield.

Monday, 22nd February

Cecil [Beaton] dined with me. I was rather alarmed having him alone. For
one so sophisticated he is shy. And his polished courtesy makes me shy at
first. He is very observant, misses nothing, the speck of potato on one's
chin, the veins in one's nose, the unplucked hair sprouting from the ear.
Yet how sensitive and understanding he is! After ten minutes I succumb
to his charm, and am at ease. For there is nothing one cannot say to him.
At least I think there is nothing. Talking of the Kents whom he knew well,
he said the Duke refused to take the war more seriously than a tiresome
interruption of his life, and was never moved with compassion for the
R.A.F. This irritated Cecil. So did the Duke's pernicketiness and perpetual grumbling. But he had innate good taste, without knowledge of the
arts. We talked till 11.20 and went our several ways. I drank too much this
evening. Pompey was sick on my bed during the night.

Tuesday, 23rd February

At 2.30 a Colonel Adams, solicitor to John Christie, called to discuss the
possibility of Glyndebourne being handed over.

In Heywood's shop I asked Anne to lunch with me on Friday, in order
to plead with her that they raise Nancy's salary. They only give her
£3.10s.0d. a week.

Was miserable all night trying to make up my mind whether to break
with Q. or not, having received a letter from her this afternoon ending,
'I see a gulf yawning between us.' Now the dreadful thing is that it will
continue to yawn, and I shall not make up my mind.

Wednesday, 24th February

Had an interview with the Royal Society and Professor Richardson
about Newton's birthplace [Woolsthorpe Manor] in Lincolnshire. The
Royal Society regards the little house as of the very highest importance
from the historical point of view, the formative years, the vision of the
falling apple, etc. To them Newton is what Shakespeare is 'to us', as Mrs.
Montgomery would say.

Friday, 26th February

Called at the bedside at 6. Stephen Spender came with some books but
did not stop longer than to say that he had dined with the Princesse de
Polignac[141] last night. James, who was present, asked Stephen if it were
true that she was the origin of Proust's Madame Verdurin. Stephen did

---

[141] Princesse Edmond de Polignac, born Winifred Singer. Friend and patron of artists, musicians and
writers. Died 1943.

not seem to think so, but said she knew Proust very well and her stories about him were fascinating. Proust used to take a taxi for a hundred yards and tip the cabman 100 francs for the pleasure of feeling himself a '*grand seigneur*'. This practice got him into trouble.

Saturday, 27th February

Walked to tea with Anne Hill in Little Venice. She is truly one of the world's worth-while women, so intelligent, male-minded, and deliciously humorous. She is "a dark mare" and worth a million more than the glittering women, such as Nancy. I tackled her about their underpaying Nancy, which she admitted. She did not resent my interference but explained laughingly that whereas Nancy got paid £3 10s. od. she only got £2 10s. od.; that the shop barely paid its way. She accompanied me on foot across the Park, and left me at Hyde Park Corner.

Stuart was sitting in bed eating a lobster. No wonder he was in bad form, and feeling languid. He complained that Stephen Spender had stayed too long and tired him out with talking, talking. He believed he came so often, sometimes twice a day, in order to talk about himself, his poetic perplexities, his wish to write better, his teeming ideas and inability to express them right (so unlike Tennyson and Swinburne, he said), the usual anxieties of a poet. But I am sure Stuart is very proud of being the recipient of these confidences.

He told me, also with pride, that Mrs. Corrigan has sent him eggs and provisions. Referring to Raymond's *Channel Packet* she asked Chips, 'What is this book everyone is talking about, called *Chanel Jacket?*' She spoke quite seriously about Richard Gare de Lyon. Chips told Stuart this morning that there are two things the Englishman doesn't forgive – ill manners, and a person striving to move in a class to which he does not properly belong. Rather acidly I told Stuart of Robert Byron's remark to Chips at the time of Munich, 'The trouble with you, Chips, is that you put your adopted class before your adopted country.' Robert was proud of this remark and repeated it to me.

Dined with Catherine Fordham and her new husband, General Kennedy, a nice, quiet man with no humour whatever. Catherine supplies these deficiencies. After dinner he expanded and talked about the war. He is sure the British soldier is not made of the same mettle as the German. He spoke of the Russians as our enemy no. 1 and said that we must hope for their utter exhaustion; and that they were hoping the same of us. I told him Tony Beaumont's story of the German prisoner whom he recently interrogated. When asked, 'What do the Germans truly think of your Italian allies?' he replied, 'The same as the Russians think of the English.' Kennedy was at Casablanca with the Prime Minister and had many stories about him. Mr. Churchill was found by his valet sitting on his hot-water bottle in the aeroplane. The valet said, 'This is not a good idea, sir.' 'It is not an idea. It is a coincidence,' was the reply. To get to Casablanca they left secretly at 2 a.m., arriving at 10 a.m. for a late breakfast. Randolph greeted his father on the tarmac. 'Well, this is a surprise for you, Randolph.' 'Not at all,' said Randolph, 'a woman in Algiers told me a week ago.'

Monday, 1st March

On the train from Waterloo Clifford Smith kept reiterating how he did not wish to ask the Trust for too high a fee for his advice, yet could not afford to accept too low a fee – the same old story and very tiresome. I could not listen and just said, 'Yes, yes,' hoping thereby that he would take the hint, and shut up. We went slowly round Polesden Lacey together. The old boy is going to be quite a help in the selecting and discarding of contents. He is really very sweet and kind, though the most crashing bore. After a picnic in the servants' hall I gave him the slip, and wandered round the garden in the glorious sunshine, and picked violets out of the frames for Q. After delivering these on my return to London, I went to the hospital.

The whole of London congregates round the Sergeant's bed. Like Louis XIV he holds levées. Instead of meeting now in Heywood Hill's shop, the intelligentsia and society congregate in public ward no. 3 of St. George's Hospital. When I arrived Stephen Spender, looking worn out by his fireman's duties, was sprawled on the end of the bed. Raymond came for a brief visit. Lady Cunard called at the moment when the entire ward were stripped to the waist and washing. She pronounced the procedure barbaric. Then a member of Stuart's unit came to announce baldly that he must expect to be in the front line when the invasion starts. S., quite unconcerned, said he could not possibly be killed. I wonder, does every soldier feel as confident?

By dint of bussing, walking and bussing again miles in the blackout, I finally reached Osbert Lancaster's flat. Only myself for dinner, deliciously cooked by Karen – chicken and rum jelly. Karen very affectionate and sweet. I admire her total indifference to the world's opinion. Whereas Osbert is incorrigibly social, she is a natural recluse. On my return I found a charming note from Q. thanking me for the violets and foreseeing the gulf narrowing.

Tuesday, 2nd March

Caught the 9.47 with Clifford Smith and Kenneth Clark for Polesden again. The former is at his worst on occasions such as this, when he has to hold his own. It was quite obviously K. Clark's day, but old Cliffy bundled me into a carriage corner, wedged me there and aired his views upon irrelevant matters in Christies' inventory. K. retired disdainfully to a distant corner, declined to speak and read Maurice Bowra's book.

We only had one hour at Polesden but K. was the greatest help. He looked at all the pictures and his general opinion of them was favourable. He pronounced a few small Germans to be trash and recommended selling two van der Vliet portraits, and a bad Cuyp. He said the David was a fake. On Bookham platform he told me that to accomplish anything today a man must be resolute and ruthless, and must act and think afterwards. He impresses me as being extremely intelligent and capable, very ambitious and energetic. He has the missionary drive, just as he has the tight, resilient build and physique of George Lloyd. He dresses like a dapper footman on his half day off. He is immaculate, spruce and correct in blue topcoat, gloves and blue Homburg hat. He talked about the National Trust and dis-approved of 'your Mr. Matheson' for not having sufficient 'standing'. He offers personally to hang the pictures for me at Polesden.

After luncheon at Brooks's I drank coffee with John Christie who talked about Glyndebourne. He seemed rather mad and was very excitable. He was so angry with the Government for their lack of enthu-siasm over his plans to promote opera that he was barely articulate. After 6 I called at the hospital. While Harold was talking to Stuart, Eddy com-mented on the latter's hands. He asked, could I not tell by his hands how ill he was? Honestly I could not.

Eddy gave me a drink in Chester Square and lent me three pictures for my house, a large Graham Sutherland, a smaller Samuel Prout and a Bonington drawing. These I took away.

Wednesday, 3rd March

An air-raid this evening in retaliation for our having bombed Berlin. The guns made a terrible noise. Miss Paterson and I crouched together, she knitting furiously, I reading with grim concentration. We were both so horribly frightened that we drank glasses of neat whisky.

Thursday, 4th March

Got through a hard day's work at Polesden with Clifford. We decided finally what to keep and what to dispose of. We also moved all the pic-tures up from the cellar and stacked them in the blue cloakroom.

Friday, 5th March

I rose very early and boiled myself an egg. Then caught the 8.20 from Liverpool Street to Cambridge. Professor Richardson drove me, the

Secretary of the Royal Society and a builder, in his old-fashioned motor
into Lincolnshire. I felt very tired all day and dozed in the car, ruminat-
ing upon Q.'s remark last night, 'I want to hold you for ever', but read in
the train Cecil Beaton's 'Libyan Diary' in *Horizon* and finished *Wives and
Men*. Thought I must be beginning influenza. A cold day, so I wore my
fur-lined coat, but the sun shining brightly at Woolsthorpe I took it off
while we lunched under a haystack.

Newton's house[142] in which he was born in 1642 is about twenty years
older. It is Cotswoldy, with good steep pitched roof, stone corniced
chimneys and mullioned windows. It has four large bedrooms, one of
which was partitioned off about 1666 with panelling of that date so as to
form a study for Newton. Upstairs the L-shaped room is said to be the
one whence Newton watched the apple fall. The original tree's descendant, now very aged, stands on the site of its forebear in the little apple
orchard in front of the house. The secretary is going to find out what
species of apple it is.[143] Tenant farmers have lived for 200 years in the
house. The present ones are only leaving because all the surrounding land
has been exploited commercially for the limestone, and is now arid,
blasted heath and hummocks of infertile slack. It is a scandal that good
agricultural land is allowed to be so treated by commercial firms and left
thoroughly wasted and useless. The little manor house has light, but no
sanitation. There are earth closets in the garden.

Saturday, 6th March

I lunched with the Kennedys, whose bed arrived yesterday for my spare
room. It is of inordinate length.

I went to St. George's at 3 and found Stephen Spender talking to
Stuart. He rose and left as I approached. After a few minutes Lady Cunard
came with Lord Queensberry who is a Governor of the hospital. He is
the boxer marquess, a youngish forty-five, with a deep resonant voice.
Lady Cunard wore a pale fur toque to match her fur coat. She is small
and incredibly vivacious and about seventy. She has a white powdered,
twisted little face and deeply mascaraed eyes. She frolicked in like a gusty
breeze, talking volubly, and quite unconscious of the impression she was
making upon the other patients, who being rankers must be astounded
by the Sergeant's host of society friends. She kissed Stuart in an animated
and natural manner. She pressed Lord Queensberry into reciting two
Shakespeare sonnets, which he did in a low and rich tone, but with

---

[142] Woolsthorpe Manor, Lincs., was given to the Trust in 1943 through the Royal Society and the Pilgrim
Trust.
[143] The authorities at Kew Gardens disclosed that it was a very old, if not otherwise extinct species, called
the *Flower of Kent*.

bitterness and hatred in his voice, which was not becoming. Lady Cunard applauded each sonnet too loudly. She was polite and attentive to me, and wanted to have the National Trust explained to her. Before she left she invited me to luncheon tomorrow, which I declined, and to dinner on Monday before a concert, which I accepted. I doubted whether at heart Stuart approved, and I feel sure Jamesey, who is at present in bed with a high temperature, will not.

Monday, 8th March

I arrived at the Dorchester at 8 and was wafted in the lift to an upper floor, then directed down airless, daylightless passages to Emerald Cunard's apartments. Her sitting-room is sympathetically furnished with French things. Already assembled were Lady Moore,[144] Garrett Moore's lovely wife, and Lady Lamington,[145] a pretty woman. Garrett Moore[146] followed me. I have known him more or less, less rather than more since Eton days. He is tall, thin, willowy, sharp-featured, distinguished and patrician. A poetic and romantic looking man if ever there was one. Lady Cunard darted like a bird of paradise into the room at 8.25; and we dined off expensive, pretentious food which lacked the necessary refinements of good cooking. Our hostess kept complaining how bad the Dorchester food was, and how at this stage of the war the country should have learnt to have adequate butter and milk distribution. I sat on her left, Lady Moore on my left. The latter is animated and bewitching. Her coif à la Queen Alexandra was most becoming. Lady C. was a little *distraite* throughout, I thought; and conversation was not sparkling in spite of a promising beginning.

At 10 we went below to a concert given for Sibyl Colefax's benefit by the Griller Quartet and Denis Matthews at the piano. Unmusical though I am, I enjoyed it immensely. Lady Cunard introduced me to all and sundry, some of them my friends of a lifetime, as though I were a visitor from Mars. And so l suppose I am to her. I walked all the way home from the Dorchester, cogitating the evening's experience, and thinking myself a fool for being so buttoned up, and suspicious – of what? Some friendly and decorative and sophisticated people in a circle to which I do not belong.

Tuesday, 9th March

At 6 to St. George's, arriving simultaneously with Logan Pearsall Smith. I wanted to retire but Stuart earnestly begged me to stay. Pearsall Smith

---

[144] Joan Moore, the pianist, later Countess of Drogheda.
[145] Riette, wife of 3rd Lord Lamington. She died 1968.
[146] 11th Earl of Drogheda, K.G. He died 1989.

is an old, frail man, of heavy, ungainly build. He may be a bore for he tells long stories 'at' one, in a laborious, monotonous tone, laughing all the while and salivating a good deal. But he was quite funny with his story of a practical joke he played on Virginia Woolf in pretending to be the outraged person whose name she had in *Jacob's Room* 'taken in vain' from a tombstone in Scarborough churchyard. This delightful blackmailing story was interrupted by tiresome Lady H-[147] arriving. Again Stuart implored me not to leave, so l did my best by talking to her in order to allow him to have some conversation with the old man. When he had left I helped get rid of Lady H-. Stuart got back into bed, looking tired indeed. He promptly began eating a lobster. Whereupon Harold arrived. I got up to go, not without promising to return tomorrow, for there was apparently something very important S. had to tell me alone. But S. never is alone; and doubtless won't be tomorrow.

Wednesday, 10th March

I picked up the Eshers in the National Trust car and motored them from the Lansdowne Club to Polesden Lacey. Lady E. sat in front with me, Lord E. behind. He behaved like a schoolboy, calling out for me to stop at intervals, so that he could buy cakes, she rebuking him. Referring to the appalling cold of West Wycombe in winter and Helen's apparent indifference to it he remarked 'People are never cold in their own houses. They derive warmth from satisfaction with the economies they are making.'

At Polesden they went round every room, and looked into every corner, cupboard and drawer. They commented on every object, liked the outside of the house and the grounds, and distant view. Esher said he had no quarrel to make with my plans and schemes. Yet he teased me unmercifully; also joked about Matheson's dislike of comfort and terror of beauty.

I dropped the Eshers at Paddington station, and went to see Jamesey. He was lying in bed with the curtains drawn. Under the shaded lamp his pallid face looked like old ivory. With his glowing coal eyes and glossy hair he resembles a Florentine prince. Then I called on the Sergeant and gave him Lady Esher's violets with her love. He was better, but there was no opportunity to hear those important words, whatever they may be. I give up. Dined at the Travellers' with Harold. Raymond [Mortimer] and Roger Senhouse present. Since Harold and Raymond talked politics together throughout the meal I was entertained by Roger. He has a moth-eaten, shabby appearance. He is, I fancy, a virtuous man with only

---

[147] Name forgotten before it could be recorded.

a light regard for the truth. When the two R.'s left, Harold assured me how responsibly he took his onerous duties as a governor of the B.B.C. He feared he was losing Jamesey's confidence. I reassured him on this point.

Thursday, 11th March

A gruesome luncheon at the Bagatelle with Mrs. Bruce Ismay[148] and three other old hens, one of whom has some needlework she wants to lend to the Trust. It comes from Stoke Edith in Herefordshire.

Went to St. George's for the last time because Stuart leaves tomorrow. Lady Desborough[149] had just paid him a visit like a queen, a chauffeur following her with a shawl. Mrs. Montgomery had written to her about me and described me as an Eton boy. She honestly believes I am still there!

Friday, 12th March

Was unwell during the night, so had breakfast in bed where I remained all morning. Anne Rosse telephoned and came to see me for ten minutes. It was a lovely morning with the sun streaming through my windows. She was enchanted with the view of the river and the mud flats, for the tide was low. Miss P., like the saint she is, came back at midday to give me some soup. Pompey is ill too, and shows no sign of improvement, which is a worry.

Saturday, 13th March

I lunched with Anne Rosse and Bridget Parsons.[150] Afterwards we taxied to the Dorchester and waited in Lady Cunard's suite. She waltzed in on her small, beautiful little legs (the Sergeant says I must notice her feet, the most beautiful in the world), looking frail and ill as the old do who are made up to the eyes. Hers had mysterious drops exuding from the corners. She pulled down all the blinds, saying, 'I hate the sun. I hate the elements. We must get away from nature, or we shall get nowhere.' We drove to see Carlyle's House in Cheyne Row. I was rather embarrassed by Anne saying, 'Only you would bring her to see a catacomb with nothing in it.' Indeed I had forgotten how little there was to see nowadays, everything of interest being packed away, and the windows of the

---

[148] Widow of the chairman of the White Star Line. Bruce Ismay (1862–1937) was on board the *Titanic*, but did not 'go down' with her in 1912 as some ill disposed people at the time thought he should have done.
[149] E. A. P. Fane ('Etty') married 1887 1st and last Lord Desborough. One of the Souls and mother of Julian Grenfell, the soldier poet, killed 1915.
[150] Lady Bridget Parsons (1907–72), sister of Lord Rosse.

principal downstairs rooms boarded up. The visit was not a success, and Lady C. returned to the Dorchester almost at once. Anne and Bridget and I walked here for tea.

Monday, 15th March

After breakfast I carried out what I had resolved. That is to say I took Pompey's basket, hid it away, burned his two bones, his cotton reel, his blanket and cushion in the incinerator in the yard. I threw his chain as far as I could into the river. I got a taxi, and told the driver to take me to the vet. I held the little dog on my knees without looking at him, without thank God, seeing his eyes. I told the vet to destroy him, and walked out, and away. All this I did without a qualm, for his cough was getting worse, and his fits persisted. For five or ten minutes I felt almost jubilant. Had I not done the right thing? Would someone ever do the same service to me? In walking rapidly along the embankment I felt, at first with surprise, then shame, the tears coursing down my cheeks. By the time I reached the door I felt nothing but unmitigated grief. I had been no better than a murderer.

Miss Paterson was terribly upset when she came back from the weekend. I know she holds me responsible for the dastardly deed. But she is so good, she does not say so.

I dined with Puss Gaskell at the Berkeley. Douglas Woodruff[151] and his wife, formerly an Acton, to both of whom I felt antagonistic and was provocative, Carmen Wiggin and Hubert Howard, were there. Mrs. Woodruff told me that Alec Dru and Evelyn Waugh were her two best men friends. The first I could accept. The second finished me. I said that Evelyn represented the English Catholicism which was anathema to me. It was the very reverse of Roman Catholicism. It was sectarian, superior, exclusive and smug. Besides, Evelyn was the nastiest tempered man in England, Catholic or Protestant, and not an acceptable advertisement of the Christian faith. I said his review of Raymond's book was personal vituperation. Having delivered myself of these ill-mannered phrases, I felt better and enjoyed the dinner party. I talked to Puss about Queen Mary's gifts to Mrs. Greville. She promised to find out from Queen Mary which they exactly were. I shall thus be able to identify them. She said there was nothing the Queen would like more than to visit Polesden and 'play around'. Thank God, she can't.

Tuesday, 16th March

I took two of the Polesden pictures to Drown's, one to have the fungus which has assaulted it cleaned off, the other, the David, to be examined

---

[151] Editor *The Tablet* 1936–67. Married 1933 Hon. M. I. Acton.

by him. Drown positively declares that it is genuine, contrary to K. Clark's opinion. I lunched at the Travellers' with Johnny Dashwood, who grumbled a good deal about Helen and her desire for a house in London, which he says he cannot possibly afford. Instead he wishes she would take a small flat and a job in London, and leave him to live at West Wycombe with a housekeeper, the prettier the better. He said that to raise the necessary endowment for West Wycombe the Trust could sell thirty acres of outlying parkland at £800 per acre.

Dined with Sibyl Colefax (we are on Christian name terms now) at the Allies Club. Roger Senhouse and an American woman, a Mrs. Stephens from the embassy, were the other guests. Sibyl read us Nigel Nicolson's last letter to her from Tunisia. I am bound to admit it certainly was a good letter. When I told Jamesey afterwards, he said Nigel is sure to be killed so that we must endure the chagrin of hearing him described as a Julian Grenfell. We had the best dinner at this club in years, real pot au feu, ragoût and a lowly Algerian wine, which nevertheless had that heavenly, nostalgic twang of the Mediterranean.

Thursday, 18th March

Wrote my name in the Cardinal's book at Archbishop's House as Dame Una enjoined me to do at yesterday's S.P.A.B. meeting. Very few names seemed to be written, and mine was the third today. I noticed Dame Una's and John's, and General de Gaulle's.

At 2 o'clock to Martin's Bank at which were present Colonel Robin Buxton, Lord Sackville,[152] his solicitor, and Lord Willingdon[153] – the first and last Knole trustees. They had been lunching well, and I was given a glass of port. We discussed Knole. Lord Sackville could not have been more friendly or anxious to co-operate. I can't think why Eddy does not like him more. He is gentle and sympathetic and always treats me with paternal affection because I am a friend of Eddy. We left it that I was to send him Garrard the estate agent's figures for his comments, whereafter the trustees would decide how much endowment they could and would provide – the capital suggested is enough to yield £3,000 p.a. I am not sure how pleased the Trust will be with me for disclosing these figures, but I believe we must always be absolutely frank with decent donors like Lord Sackville. My sympathies are always with them. In fact my loyalties are first to the houses, second to the donors, and third to the National Trust. I put the Trust last because it is neither a work of art nor a human being but an abstract thing, a convenience.

---

[152] Major-Gen. 4th Lord Sackville (1870–1962).
[153] Later Marquess of Willingdon.

Gordon Russell[154] called on me in the office. He began talking about alabaster, saying he knew I was interested in it. Surprised I said, 'Yes, and why?' He had visited the monuments in Wickhamford church and enquired why they were so clean. 'Because,' the answer came, 'Master Jim washes them.' The object of his visit was to express a fear lest the National Trust, in becoming a very large landowner, might dwell too much on preservation, and sterilize too much of the country. The Trust ought to become more positive in its outlook, ought to develop along contemporary lines. It ought not to employ exclusively archaic-minded architects, but avant-garde architects. Above all, it must not conceal, say, modern necessary things like petrol pumps under olde-worlde thatched roofs, etc. I said I agreed with much of this, but pleaded that we were solely a preservation body and had to care for our own properties, which did not for the most part comprise petrol stations and gasometers. The C.P.R.E. was the body which he should stimulate. He said no one knew anything about the C.P.R.E. I begged him to stimulate it. He is a shy craftsman, and as such has my sympathies. He has been made chairman of the Committee of Craftsmen and Designers of the new Utility Committee.

This afternoon I took the tube to Richmond, and thence a bus to Petersham. I walked down the long drive to Ham House. The grounds are indescribably overgrown and unkempt. I passed long ranges of semi-derelict outhouses. The garden is pitted with bomb craters around the house, from which a few windows have been blown out and the busts from the niches torn away. I walked round the house, which appeared thoroughly deserted, searching for an entrance. The garden and front doors looked as though they had not been used for decades. So I returned to a side door and pulled a bell. Several seconds later a feeble rusty tinkling echoed from distant subterranean regions. While waiting I recalled the grand ball given for Nefertiti Bethell which I attended in this house some ten years or more ago. The door was roughly jerked open, the bottom grating against the stone floor. The noise was accompanied by heavy breathing from within. An elderly man of sixty stood before me. He had copper hair and a red face, carrot and port wine. He wore a long coat and a starched shirt front which had come adrift from the waistcoat. 'The old alcoholic family butler', I said to myself. He was not affable at first. Without asking my name, or business, he said, 'Follow me.' Slowly he led me down a dark passage. His legs must be webbed

---

[154] Later Sir Gordon Russell, then member of the Board of Trade Design Panel.

for he moved in painful jerks. At last he stopped outside a door, and knocked nervously. An ancient voice cried, 'Come in!' The seedy butler then said to me, 'Father is expecting you,' and left me. I realized that he was the bachelor son of Sir Lyonel Tollemache,[155] aged eighty-nine. As I entered the ancient voice said, 'You can leave us alone, Boy!' For a moment I did not understand that Sir Lyonel was addressing his already departed son.

Sir Lyonel was sitting in an upright chair. He was dressed, unlike his son, immaculately in a grey suit, beautifully pressed, and wore a stock tie with large pearl pin. I think he had spats over black polished shoes. A very decorative figure, and very courteous. He asked me several questions about the National Trust's scheme for preserving country houses, adding that he had not made up his mind what he ought to do. After several minutes, he rang the bell and handed me over to the son who answered it.

The son showed me hurriedly, I mean as hurriedly as he could walk, round the house, which is melancholy in the extreme. All the rooms are dirty and dusty. The furniture and pictures have been moved to the country for safety. There is no doubt whatever that even without the contents this house is worthy of acceptance because of the superlative interior treatment, the panelling, the exquisite parquetry floors, the extraordinary chimneypieces, the great staircase of pierced balusters, the velvet hangings, etc. It is a wonderful seventeenth-century house, and from the south windows the garden layout of symmetrical beds, stone gate plinths and ironwork is superb.

The son was full of complaints. Once we were away from the father, he said the family were worth £2,000,000 and did not receive as much as 6d. from each £; that they had two gardeners instead of twelve, no indoor servants except a cook (and himself). He told me he was distracted by looking after the Ham property and the Lincolnshire estate. At times he felt suicidal. I looked straight at him, and knew that the poor man meant it. When I waved goodbye the faintest flicker of a smile crossed his bucolic face, and a tiny tear was on his cheek.

Slept in the office on a camp bed, Eardley on another. We gossiped ourselves to sleep.

Saturday, 20th March

Went to Windsor in the afternoon to see Mrs. Montgomery, 'Mrs. Betty' I am now to call her. Met her on the doorstep, and we pottered across to St. George's Chapel. She is very bent and walks with difficulty. It was

---

[155] Sir Lyonel Tollemache, 4th Bart. (1854–1952).

impossible to ask her questions about the chapel because she talked cease-lessly of other things. She said she was one of the original 'Souls'. Jean Hamilton was a great friend and so brave about her cancer which she referred to by the dreaded name. Mrs. Betty wanted me to bring Raymond to see her, but I don't think he would come. I like her coined words, 'pointful' and 'dank' being most frequently used. 'Carp' is another. And her proverb, 'A bird in the hand is worth a feather in the cap.'

Dined with Q. at the Mirabelle. She offered me a £1 towards the evening expenses, which I accepted without demur. I do hope and believe she meant me to. I told her I hated the Mirabelle. Got home at 11.30 and sat over the fire for hours. Felt overcome with loneliness. It was too late to ring up Q. I have nothing to reproach her for, yet I keep think-ing, 'Would I, if I were she, gratuitously go off to . . . for ten days leaving Jim behind in London?' Obviously, yes, I ought to in the circumstances. But would I, that's the point? I am such a fool in these respects. She is obviously right. She has duties. Every day I have a letter, sometimes a postcard too. There can be no mistaking their underlying meaning – which is now, and not for ever.

Monday, 22nd March

At home after work I sat reading *Asylum Pieces* by one, Anna Kavan – experiences of a woman about to become mad and finally shut up in an asylum. I became hideously and terrifyingly depressed by these stories and was obliged to drink neat whisky. At the Dorchester Eddy Sackville-West told me he felt horribly unwell and did not know how he was going to get through dinner. He sat on Emerald Cunard's left, and was brilliant and amusing. On his left Stephen Spender's wife, with ringlets down her neck. Me so wedged between her and Stephen Spender that I could only raise my fork to my mouth when neither of them was doing the same thing. Conversation is always general at this table. Lady C. gets cross if two guests try to talk to each other. She is a watchful hostess, and when-ever there is a pause in the scrum throws in a ball, usually of a most unex-pected sort. I stayed till 11.

Chips [Channon] walked with me across the park. He tried to pump me about the Sergeant, so that I wondered at first whether he were in love with him. He asked me whether Stuart was really rich, or really very poor. Everyone was asking, for S. is extremely mean with money if he is not poor. I honestly did not know. Was S. an imposter, he wondered? I said such an idea had not occurred to me. I thought an imposter was a person masquerading as someone who he wasn't. But I volunteered to observe it was rather a pity that S. was undiscriminating in his choice of friends. Chips did not agree, and asked me to explain what friends I had in mind. I could not do so for fear of being rude. He said, No, in that respect S. had not erred. He cared for distinguished people like Lady Desborough and myself. I could not help laughing. Then he said I looked years younger and handsomer than Stephen. I said Stephen was a very handsome man. I had never been that. More awkward laughter. When we parted in Pont Street, he said, 'Do not worry yourself about the Sergeant. He is being well looked after by X.B. He won't come to any harm.' I said, 'I don't believe it. Besides, I am not his keeper.'

Tuesday, 23rd March

This conclusion was confirmed by what Stuart told me at dinner tonight. He said it took him some time to realize that X.B. was madly in love with him in the same teasing sort of way that Robert Byron once was with me. When he was obliged to tell X.B., who is one of Chips's best friends, that he could not return his affection, he received, much to his astonishment, a tremendous scolding from Chips. Chips was plaintive. He had meant to do S. a good turn by introducing him to a rich man who would ply him with champagne and load him with jewels. But, said S., 'I can buy my own champagne, and I don't like jewels. Thank you all the same.' Oh, the cynicism, the worldliness of these people!

Wednesday, 24th March

I go to Polesden with Margaret Jourdain who thinks but little of the contents, apart from the pictures. Mrs. Bruce Ismay and Mrs. Foley came over for the day. Boring old women. I am sure M.J. bothers with them only because they are rich, for she is far too intelligent for them. They are sugar, and she is salt. I picked violets and daffodils and dropped them on Emerald Cunard at the Dorchester. Then to see Jamesey, who was sitting up in bed correcting proofs. Jamesey said Emerald Cunard does not know me yet. This is true. She thinks I am very fond of him, Jamesey. Yes, but how fond does she think I am, I asked? Little escapes her, he says, but sometimes she gets hold of the wrong end of the stick. Logan Pearsall Smith has written to him: 'Who is this Jimmy L.-M.? Mrs. Betty writes that he is delightful, although Master P.-H. comes first.'

Thursday, 25th March

When I told Eddy today that I was going this afternoon to stay at Gunby Hall, in Lincolnshire, with Field-Marshal Sir Archibald Montgomery-Massingberd,[156] he could not believe his ears. Could there possibly be

---

[156] The Field-Marshal (1871–1947) was C.I.G.S. 1933–36. Lady (Diana) Montgomery-Massingberd died 1963.

such a man? Indeed the Field-Marshal received me in his study. He is tall, large, a little ponderous, handsome and impressive; yet very gentle and kind. Lady Massingberd is slim, grey, jolly and also kind. They are Peter Montgomery's uncle and aunt on both his father and mother's sides of the family and are very fond of him. But because he has not yet married they are leaving him out of any subsequent settlement of Gunby which they may make. The house is 1700, symmetrical, of secondary size, and of deep-plum brick with stone dressings. Every room and passage within has simple contemporary panelling. It was built by the Massingberds and is full of their portraits, including two Reynoldses. Now the Air Ministry is threatening to fell all the trees in the park and demolish the house, both in direct line of a runway which they have constructed without previously ascertaining the proximity of these obstacles. If the threats can be averted with our help, the Montgomery-Massingberds are ready to make the property over to the Trust straight away. They are such dear people that even if the house were worthless I would walk to the ends of the earth to help them.

A plain dinner with only water to drink. Wine and spirits are put away for patriotic motives. Hot water cut off for the same reason. Otherwise the house full of servants, including a butler and pantry boy and four gardeners. Of course they revel in their imposed suffering. I wish I did.

Friday, 26th March

The Field-Marshal was incapacitated by sciatica this morning so Lady Massingberd took me round the house and gardens, both of which I pronounced to be of national importance. Then I wandered round the grounds by myself. It is curious how the moment I leave London I feel ill and dispirited.

The Field-Marshal told me last night that of all the politicians he had dealings with Neville Chamberlain was the most abjectly ignorant of military matters. He smiled sweetly when Sir Archibald as G.O.C. endeavoured to explain some simple manoeuvre, but did not know the difference between a division and a company, and made no effort to learn.

Saturday, 27th March

Nancy came round at 3.30 and found me painting the stairs. I took her to Carlyle's House, after which we returned here and made toast. Eddy and Dame Una Pope-Hennessy joined us – a most enjoyable tea. The Dame looking like a priestess, sat on an upright chair so as to see out of the window. She said the Cardinal's Requiem Mass was wonderfully moving. It went like clockwork as though it had been rehearsed. All the bishops and abbots in the kingdom were present; also the Papal Delegate and the Archbishop of New York. She said I was a fool not to have asked for a ticket. She feels sure Bishop Mathew will be the next Archbishop of Westminster. I do hope so, for he is a brilliant and witty, if worldly man, and has been courageous in the air-raids.

John Russell came and talked after dinner. He has a new job in the Admiralty and is well paid. He left his article on Henry James's house at Rye for me to read. He is ambitious to become a recognized man of letters. At 2 o'clock in the morning I was woken by the telephone. It was Stuart to tell me he had been dining with Emerald Cunard, Rex Whistler and Duff Cooper, and they had talked of love and kissing on the mouth, one of Emerald's new pet subjects. He was in ecstasy over the evening. Petulantly I asked why this astounding piece of information could not have been withheld until later in the morning.

Monday, 29th March

Was called by telephone at 5.30, cooked my breakfast and by 6.15 was off. Met Hubert Smith at Watford and drove with him straight to Burton Agnes in the East Riding. Here we were taken round by young [Marcus] Wickham-Boynton on leave from the army. He and his mother are undecided what to do. He struck me as obstinate, if not owlishly stupid. Burton Agnes is still well kept up and not requisitioned. It is superbly beautiful. Walls of rose red brick. The hall screen and chimneypiece are stupendous. So are the painted panelling of the drawing-room, the japanned room and the staircase with arcading. When I was here in 1936 the house was dilapidated and spooky. Mrs. Wickham-Boynton, before showing me round, said one room was haunted, and it was not a room you would expect to be haunted. I was asked to guess which it was. When we came back to our starting point I told her which I thought the haunted room to be. I was right. There is a screaming skull immured in this house. When it was removed ghostly noises and manifestations of a terrifying kind took place. But with the recent tarting up of this house I suspect that the spirits have been driven away.

When I stayed – also in 1936 – at Bradshaw Hall near Bolton there were two skulls mounted on silver seventeenth-century stems. They were religiously kept upon a Family Bible. Col. Hardcastle, the owner, told me that one day his housemaid in dusting broke a skull off its stem. He took both skull and stem to the local jewellers to be mended. But that night and the following such a caterwauling ensued from the skull left behind in the house that he and the servants were terrified. Col. Hardcastle had to retrieve the broken skull and stem, and beg the jeweller to come and

mend them in the room to which they belonged. He never had any
further trouble. One of the skulls was supposed to be Bradshaw the regi-
cide's, and the other his wife's.

I have little hope of negotiations over Burton Agnes coming to a conclusion. The owners are at least candid about their motives. Smith and I
stayed at a squalid local inn, with filthy food. I could hardly bring myself
to get into bed lest the blankets touched my face.

Tuesday, 30th March

Very cold up here and windy. A grey, melancholy day. We drove by Goole
and south of the Humber through stark fenland and potato-growing
fields that stretch wearily into infinity. At Norton Place we motored
round the boundaries of the estate. Smith's opinion was that this was
good second-class agricultural land, and the farm buildings were in no
bad state of repair. I find it very tiresome that acceptance of a beautiful
house by Carr of York has to depend upon such irrelevancies. We continued to Stragglethorpe Hall, now a nursery school. We were conducted
round by the owners, Colonel and Mrs. Jack Leslie. It is a mid-sixteenth-
century half-timbered house on a stone base. A misleading, fakey sort of
house, yet not unpleasing. The owners want it to be used after the war
by disabled servicemen.

Wednesday, 31st March

Went to see Jamesey who is better. He said Clarissa was enchanted with
her tea with me on Sunday. I was naturally pleased but said that I never
would have guessed it at the time. We asked each other: why does one
see in every affair a picture of oneself enjoying the same ecstasy, the same
unalterable relationship right into old age? For one knows perfectly well
that such a state of things cannot last longer than a matter of months, possibly only weeks.

Thursday, 1st April

To Knole in the afternoon, where I talked to Lord Sackville and his agent
for one hour and a half. Discussions began stickily but ended hopefully.
I stayed to tea, Lady Sackville[157] dispensing. She is a singularly brash and
ignorant woman, whereas he is the exact opposite, well-bred and educated. He told me Eddy's mother[158] and grandfather were both bleeders
like Eddy.

---

[157] Anne, widow of Stephen S. Bigelow of Boston, married 1924 4th Lord Sackville as his second
wife.
[158] The first Lady Sackville was Maude Cecila Bell (d.1920).

Johnny Dashwood lunched with me at Brooks's. An expensive guest for he had a gin and tonic, a whisky and soda and a bumper brandy. We talked of West Wycombe affairs. At 2.30 the town clerk of Liverpool and two other worthies came to see me about Speke Hall. They are resentful of the Trust having been left the Hall and consider Liverpool corporation the proper body to hold it, since they are older than the National Trust by 700 years. It seems to me a curious reason to put forward.

I took the 4 o'clock train to Preston. Stuart came with me to Euston, the faithful creature, and walked up and down the platform until the train left. At the Park Hotel, Preston, they would not give me dinner because I arrived after 9 o'clock, and only some dry cheese sandwiches, without margarine, and tea to drink, for 4/6.

Saturday, 3rd April

At 9.30 Bruce Thompson[159] arrived, then Sir William Ashcroft who motored us to Rufford Old Hall. There we were met by Mr. Brown, Lord Hesketh's know-all solicitor, the Treasurer of the Local Committee and Philip Ashcroft, who has arranged the rural implements in the small museum. All such meetings are most formal in the north, I notice. We went round house and garden, both of which I know well, on a conducted tour, headed by Sir William. The sole outcome of this visit was that my recommendation to remove the ivy from the red brick 1660 wing was adopted.

Sir William, who is Sheriff-elect, entertained Bruce and me to luncheon in the County Hall; then took us to see a ghastly exhibition of local artists' pictures in the Town Hall. Bruce and I took a taxi to Samlesbury Hall to meet its trustees, an astonishing bunch of Lancashire businessmen with red faces, protuberant paunches, execrable taste and strong accents. They conducted us round with much solemnity. They are contemplating handing the place over to us. The Hall has been gravely tampered with, externally and internally. Its 'speres' and movable screen have been cut up to make a bogus minstrels' gallery. There is much mock magpie work. House and ugly outbuildings are crammed with a vast collection, formed by the late Mr. Lewis, chief of the trustees, of Italian and Continental cabinets, some perhaps good, and the majority devastatingly ornate. All unsuitable in this black-and-white setting. The trustees entertained us to a vast, substantial but delicious tea at 3.30. I caught the 5.25

---

[159] Then the National Trust's representative in the Lake District, having been on the head office staff until shortly before the war.

from Preston, reaching Euston at midnight tired and hungry, having eaten a few sandwiches on the train.

Sunday, 4th April

Robert Lutyens told me that the quality of the Adam furniture at Osterley was indifferent – a surprising statement. In rebuilding Middleton [Park, Oxon] for Grandy Jersey[160] before the war he found him an obstinate client. Virginia too was difficult because she insisted on having a cocktail bar and other Hollywood features introduced. The house was built to hold forty people, including servants, at weekends. He said the old Middleton house was of no interest. Nevertheless he preserved the portico. He said the new Waterloo Bridge was bad because it looked as though it could not stand up to the weight of present-day traffic. An engineer's ingenuity did not necessarily make good architecture.

Monday, 5th April

The Sergeant must be a very simple man. He said he had been obliged to tell X.B. that he could not see him again. His conduct was spoiling a beautiful friendship, etc. X.B. was suicidal, and quivered so on receiving this broadside that he could not hold his glass, and had to put it on a table. S. has come to hate him as far as he can hate anybody. He said 'Do you know, he tried to embrace me in Chips's house, and Rex Whistler walked into the room.' He was very indignant at being exposed to such a false situation. I said, 'Couldn't you have laughed it off without being unkind?' 'Laugh?' he said, 'Laugh? But it is no laughing matter.' I said, 'But it seems to me it is.' Then he said a Cabinet Minister was mad about X.B. 'Marvellous!' I said. 'Not at all. X.B. won't look at him.' I see no way out of the tangle.

Tuesday, 6th April

Went this evening with Q. to the ballet – *Sylphide*, *Quest* and *Façade*. *Quest* a new ballet, with music by William Walton and décor by John Piper. Interesting and colourful, but I shall have to see it several times before I understand it.

Thursday, 8th April

Yesterday I was quite ill, and had to stay in bed. Terrible headache, and turned my head first to one side of the pillow, then the other, like the pendulum of a clock, seeking and never finding relief. Not since my

---

[160] The present Earl of Jersey.

hospital days have I been unable to read, when ill. And what did I think about? Nothing whatever. The mind can be a total blank and blackness, conscious only of that relentless, regular throb.

This evening I dragged myself out of bed, bathed, shaved, and took a taxi to dine with the Osbert Lancasters. Contrary to expectation I enjoyed myself. So often when one has a temperature and is feeling like death, one can be gay, and scintillate, knowing that when the festivity is over, one will collapse again.

Friday, 9th April

Although on fire-watching duty I dined at the Dorchester, prepared to dash off if the siren went. I sat on Emerald's left, Cecil [Beaton] on my left, Lady Pamela Berry, Peter Quennell, Garrett [Moore]. I drank everything offered me to keep myself going. Emerald said Stuart was in love with Alice Harding, that he was a virgin, that he told Duff Cooper and Rex Whistler he understood kissing on the cheek to be more passionate than on the mouth. All sorts of nonsense sparkled off her like miniature fireworks. Emerald gets gay on one sip of cherry brandy and pours forth stories helter-skelter, wholly unpremeditated, in an abandoned, halting, enquiring manner that appears to be ingenuous, and is deliberate. Her charm can be devastating. Left for the office just before midnight.

Saturday, 10th April

Unless I write in my diary the events of the past day that evening, or at latest the next morning, there is little point in keeping one. Is there anyway? A catalogue of names, places and engagements is stale and unprofitable. That is what a diary tends to become after a time. And I cannot stop. I would like this diary to entertain two or three generations ahead when I am under the sod. I cannot really believe that I ever shall be dead. The prospect is too squalid to dwell upon. It is impossible to think that I and those I love, and our loves can be snuffed out like a streak of wind over a wave. Surely some lingering vibration must be left behind, for ever?

The Sergeant said I credited no one with sensibility but myself – quite true; that I believed the world to revolve round me – quite true (who doesn't?); that I supposed only *I* understood the meaning of love, and the mysteries of the universe, etc. – quite true. What about him, for instance? Well, the truth certainly is that he does lack sensibility, and has no inkling of the meaning of love or the mysteries. He is a feather on the stream of life. Feathers can be decorative but they are easily blown about. But he is a very clever feather all the same. He also quivers with sensitivity, if not sensibility.

Poor thing, he has had a row this morning with Chips, who advised him to get a transfer out of London, anywhere so long as he leaves the capital. And the reason? He is unwittingly destroying X.B. who is suffering from a breakdown, being odious to his old mother, cruel to his young wife, and about to commit suicide or else murder the Sergeant. It makes me indignant with the egoism of these people. How dare they behave like this? I told S. he had made a mistake in seeing X.B. again. He admits it, but says his intentions were strictly 'honourable'. They were idiotic. At all events he is moving his belongings from Chips's house and will not see him again.

Nancy came to tea. Quite alone with her I am not at ease, and never have been. I think she recognizes this, for just as she was standing on the doorstep about to leave Cecil [Beaton] turned up. She stayed for another hour and left ultimately with him. I was not in good form, and feared I was going to have jaundice. I went up to a glass and said, 'My God, how yellow I look!' Nancy said Nonsense, so did Cecil, so did Anne Rosse whom I saw later. I felt almost disappointed.

Sunday, 11th April

I was about to enter my bath when Emerald telephoned. She talked for thirty-five minutes while I was in a state of semi-nudity, about books, French politics in the thirties and forties of the last century, about Guizot and Madame de Lieven, about Whig hostesses and there being no great ladies today. 'What about Lady Desborough?' I asked, shivering. Emerald said her food was too bad for her to qualify, and she was too little of a snob. In her day, Emerald went on — while my right foot which had touched the water, dripped — every country house had powdered footmen. Even so, such an establishment was cheaper to run than two rooms at the Dorchester today. She talked of Jean Hamilton. Her two best friends were Lady Desborough and Norah Lindsay — 'Are you sneezing, dear?' — Her house was hideous. She herself was sweet, but her skin was too delicate. Had I read Santayana? 'Yes, I thought him a worse charlatan than Charles Morgan.' At last she rang off. I got to Mass in Cheyne Row, and was absolutely sure I was going to have a severe chill.

I decided during Mass that I really must not saddle myself with the nicest people who bore me. I promptly invited one to lunch with me at the Queen's Restaurant. She insisted upon coming back to 104 and staying to tea. She complained about her horrid daughter who, to spite her, had married a Hungarian-Jew refugee, who is a communist, and not even a gentleman, my dear.

At 11, Stuart telephoned from the Savoy where he was having supper, to tell me he had walked today from Fairlawne to Sissinghurst, and there met Vita for the first time. He thought her beautiful, but was disappointed that she was not as Spanish, masculine and hirsute as he had pictured her.

Tuesday, 13th April

I left the office early to greet Magdalen FitzAlan-Howard who came to tea. I don't suppose an uncharitable or horrid thought has ever passed through her head. Sitting close beside her over the 'Earl Grey' I wondered whether all that goodness was aware of the badness inside my head, only three feet from hers. I hoped not – any more than a soul is aware of the guts, intestine, viscera (or whatever the disgusting things are called) inside the most beautiful body of the twin soul held within its arms. Lord FitzAlan called for Magdalen and insisted upon climbing my narrow stairs which, now painted, are pitch black and dark for a blind nonagenarian, and admired my room and view.

James dined with me at the Café Royal, having come from Lady Crewe's literary party. He said she was unusually gauche and awkward. Chips was there, asking, 'Where are the poets? Is Lady Colefax a poet?' James was horrified by the X.B. story and the cynical rôle played by Chips. When I wanted to confide in him some of my problems he instantly became bored and inattentive. I ought to have learnt by now never to ask for sympathy from a friend. James rapidly changed the subject and once again said, with sparkling eyes, how much he was longing to sleep with a woman, and Cecil [Beaton] told him how easy it was. If Stuart thinks I am egocentric, James is far worse. He not only knows, but proclaims that he is the centre of the universe.

Wednesday, 14th April

At 1.30 I take a train for Dulverton [in Somerset]. I still feel ill, and my cold will not go. My nose blows catarrhal gobs like leather oysters. I am feverish, and can neither smell nor taste. Cigarettes disgust me; and yet I am in a smoking carriage. The day is sunny and warm, and the railway cuttings are a mass of primroses. The leaves of the trees are yellow-green and turn upwards. Summer is here.

At Dulverton I prepare to walk to Pixton [Park], but Mary Herbert[161] meets me down the road in an old car. Pixton is like an Irish house, large, shabby, chaotic and comfortable. Laura Waugh[162] and Bridget Grant[163] come in late for supper from farming. They are both cold and distant. Mary, a magnificent, imperious stag by Landseer, perhaps an

---

[161] Widow of Hon. Aubrey Herbert (*d.* 1923) and daughter of 4th Viscount de Vesci. She died 1972.
[162] Her daughter (*d.*1973), wife of Evelyn Waugh
[163] Another daughter, wife of Major E. Grant who died 1947.

eagle, is masterful and very clever. She is full of opinions and Catholic prejudices. She said Lady Salisbury told her that Lord FitzAlan had risen to his great heights of wisdom and saintliness through conscientious persistence. As a young colonel of a regiment he was ordinary, and not particularly saintly. His brother, the Duke of Norfolk, made him go into the House of Commons. From that moment he cultivated his natural intelligence. Aubrey Herbert valued his counsel highly. Mary thinks the Vatican has consulted him on the appointment of the new Archbishop of Westminster. For he is the leading lay Catholic in this country. She thinks Magdalen ran away with somebody before the last war, was hauled back by the family and held in disgrace for ages. I question the truth of this.

Thursday, 15th April

I took a taxi to Ashwick to see Mr. Frank Green about Culverthorpe which belongs to him. Nothing much came of the interview beyond threats. The old tyrant lay in a large four-poster, wearing a striped dressing-gown and a woollen nightcap with a bobble on the end of a string. The bobble bounced up and down his nose as he spoke. His face is that of a rugged, wicked John Bull. It is an eighteenth-century, Rowlandsonish face. He dismissed the subject of Culverthorpe, which was the purpose of my visit, and concentrated on the Treasurer's House, York. Was he to understand that someone had dared, had dared to shift the furniture in one of the rooms? Did I not realize that he had put little studs in the floors to mark the precise spot on which every single piece of furniture in the house was to stand? I did. Then no piece of furniture was ever to be shifted therefrom. He looked me full between the eyes in an accusatory manner. I flinched under the awful gaze. 'There!' he cried out, '*you* are guilty. I knew it,' and the bobble on the string flew around his cheeks and on to his mouth. In a rage he blew it up again. In actual fact I was not guilty. I hadn't been to the house for ages. 'Mark my words,' he went on, 'I am an old man. I may not have very long to live. But I warn you that, if ever you so much as move one chair leg again, I will haunt you till your dying day.' And he wagged a skinny finger under my face. I slunk off, chastened, with my tail between my legs.

The taxi driver who was waiting for me said, 'You look as though you had seen a ghost, sir.' 'I have,' I said. I dismissed the taxi and walked back the remaining miles. A hot, Mediterranean day. I was struck by the beauty of the deep wooded valleys, each with a rushing stream at its foot. The cherry blossom was full out. The magnolia tree at Pixton looked like a giant Christmas cake, covered with solid pink and white icing sugar.

Friday, 16th April

Back in London I lunched with John Russell at the Russell Hotel to meet Professor Geoffrey and Mrs. Webb.[164] He is a bearded figure in a black suit, she, plain, unwomanly, bespectacled, blue-stocking. Both so earnest and middle-class in their humourless outlook. Ten years ago I should have wanted to make fast friends with them. Today I cannot be bothered because I am just a little too much of a snob.

Saturday, 17th April

Joined the Sergeant at his American canteen where I sat with him while he ate his final luncheon. Such a good meal it was, too, for one shilling. I remarked how tidy and clean these G.I.s looked compared to British rankers. S. said the regulars were fed and looked after better than our regulars. I took some of his clothes and books to keep at Cheyne Walk while he is away.

Jamesey came for the night, arriving at 11.45 when I was asleep on the sofa with the *Guermantes Way* open on my lap. He was in a state of hysterical bewilderment. He had been dining with M.A.B. who told him he was 'beautiful as the dawn', and gave him a strong drug. He suspected she wanted to seduce him, and was repelled but fascinated. He fears the next time he will be lured into her bed. 'But isn't that just what you are wanting?' I asked. 'Don't be so disgusting,' was the retort. M.A.B. told him some terrifying things: how Lady Crewe in spite of her indolence intrigues like a mole; by sheer determination she undermined the Alington marriage because Napier Alington, a hundred years her junior, with whom she was madly in love, married without telling her.

Sunday, 18th April

James and I breakfasted at Brooks's, then went to Warwick Street where I wanted to get a palm. But they only had one communal bit of box for all to kiss. We walked to Waterloo Station, met John Pope-Hennessy and took a train for Polesden Lacey. John spent the afternoon assiduously viewing the pictures while James and I ran around the bedrooms gossiping and giggling, he purloining a black coal-scuttle glove and some india rubbers. Then we lay on the grass in the sun, he imparting further astonishing things which M.A.B. had regaled him with as they went over Argyll House by candlelight. Lady Crewe believes no relationship, no emotion, no motive to be straightforward, and suspects everything and everyone. This is truly Proustian. She is very attached to, and attracted by

---

[164] Geoffrey Webb was secretary of the Historic Monuments Commission. M. I. Webb was author of *Michael Rysbrack, Sculptor*, 1954.

Jamesey. I looked at him carefully this afternoon, and I see that he is beautiful with his amber complexion, coal-scuttle eyes and black wavy hair, even if one discounts his fascinating mind.

To Lady Cunard's box at the Phoenix. After the concert Bridget [Parsons] dined with me at the Turkish restaurant. She is ravishingly beautiful with her long, arrogant neck, golden hair, fair complexion and sulky mouth. This evening she was pathetically sweet, I say 'pathetically' because her nature is not sweet but sour. And there is poignancy in watching her trying to overcome her nature.

Tuesday, 20th April

A letter from Stuart, saying that all his letters will be censored. This puts a restraint upon correspondence. What hell life is today! There is Stuart, intellectual and sensitive, treated like a Spartan slave, and made to undergo a Commando course, for which he is totally unfitted, among plebeian thugs, yet submissive, uncomplaining.

This evening I had a talk with Harold while he was bathing and changing. He said we must bear in mind that the values and standards of Chips and his world were not ours, and we must not be shocked by them, or corrupted by them, but outwardly amused, if inwardly censorious. Chips was not a bad man, but his loyalties were often mistaken. He would go to any lengths in the interests of his chosen friends, even to that of absolutely doing down some innocent individual. In other words, I said, he would commit evil for the betterment of evil. Harold said, 'Well, you could put it like that if you were the headmaster of a boys' preparatory school.'

I took him to dine at Brooks's. He purred with approval of the silver plate and the excellent service; and our bottle of Burgundy. He complained that his enemies criticized him for being National Labour when they saw how much he enjoyed the delicacies of life. They called him inconsistent. He said, 'True, I do not care for the society of the lower classes. I have no desire to live with them, or be like them. I hate them. I do want them to become like me.' He said Lady Gerald Wellesley[165] was determined to sue somebody for saying she was drunk during the Poetry Reading at the Aeolian Hall, and preventing her from reciting on the platform. Indeed Vita [Sackville-West] to prevent this contingency accompanied her to the Hall, and like a saint never let her out of her sight, except when she went to the loo. This however she did five times within three-quarters of an hour, coming out each time less sober than when she went in. At last Vita said, 'But, Dotty, you can't possibly want to

---

[165] Dorothy Wellesley, later Duchess of Wellington and poet, died 1956.

go again!' She sat down on the Bond Street pavement screaming, and tapping with her stick, because by herculean methods they had mercifully prevented her from being presented to the Queen. She threw Harold's arm off her shoulder, shouting, 'Take your bloody arm away!' Harold fears she may decide to sue him. 'You see,' he said ruefully, 'it is always the innocent who get punished.'

Good Friday, 23rd April

I worked in the office all morning. In the afternoon took the train to Yarmouth, to stay over Easter with the Kennets. Kathleen and Lord K. alone. He was more agreeable and attentive than I have ever known him, so that I liked him more than I had previously thought possible. He showed me his precious books – *The Book of Hours*, medieval, with brilliant hand-coloured miniatures – and read Tennyson and Traherne to us in a toneless, melancholy and low voice. Throughout this visit I felt distinctly unwell, with intolerable toothache. Desperately kind Kathleen tried to find a dentist for me, without avail. Is this general unwellness and tiredness (I went to bed at 9.30 and had breakfast in bed every day) due to the sudden onslaught of vigorous eastern air after the quiet, insalubrious air of London? A hurricane was blowing every day. One afternoon Kathleen and I punted on the lake. On Sunday we motored to tea at Somerleyton, a hideous red brick edifice of 1860. Hideous indeed, but fascinating and more than just a Jacobean pastiche. Well-kept garden, and well-ordered estate. Somerleyton now a naval hospital, but the Somerleytons living in a part of it. Lord Somerleyton rugged, and at first surly, but in conducting me through the Maze, warmed. He suffers from that typical English public schoolboy affliction – shyness. She kindly gave me Veganin to alleviate my toothache. On Sunday night Peter Scott broadcast the postscript to the 9 o'clock news, to which we listened reverently. It was good – how splendid of him to be able to do it! – and Kathleen of course delighted and proud.

Monday, 26th April

I left Fritton for Blickling. On the way lunched with Oliver Messel in Norwich. Oliver as a Captain in khaki seems a contradiction of nature. He took me to the Assembly Rooms. He has made his men repair ravages and paint the walls of the rooms an appropriate Messelish pink. The 1750 interior decoration of panelled swags and plaster ceilings is very elegant. The proportions of the rooms are finer than those of the Bath Assembly Rooms. It is splendid what Oliver has done.

At Blickling after tea I walked through the park, map in hand, past the folly tower to Itteringham, which is at the far end of the estate. I fought my way against, or was driven by, a tearing, blinding, deafening hurricane. I hardly knew where I was going until I found myself deposited beside the lake at Wolterton, in full view of the imposing red brick house. The park is flat and meagre. Lady Walpole lives with a brigade of Guards in the house. On my return through the park I came upon a wretched rabbit in a snare, and could not kill it. I walked past feeling ashamed, sad and physically sick.

Miss James the housekeeper told me over a cup of tea that at Blenheim up to 1939 precedence in the servants' hall was rigidly observed. The visiting valets and maids were, as I already knew, called after their masters and mistresses, viz. Mr. Marlborough and Mrs. Bibesco; and, which I did not know, the valet of the eldest son of the house always sat on the housekeeper's right, taking precedence even over the valet of the most distinguished guest, whether Archbishop, Prime Minister or Prince of Wales.

Tuesday, 27th April

Birkbeck and two architects from the Ministry of Works and I examined the condition of the house. After tea in the officers' mess Birkbeck and I looked at the recently burnt-out part of Hercules Plantation. We found another fire burning and put it out by stamping, beating. I was sadly deficient in this respect, alas, Birkbeck doing most of the work effectively. The exertion gave me sciatica. When the fire was put out I came upon a scorched wooden board on the ground, raised it and lo! it was a trap-door over a Home Guard bomb dump, from which smoke was pouring. I looked down into the pit bravely, but refused to descend to see what the smoke issued from. Stayed this night with the Birkbecks, nice, cosy, easy people.

Wednesday, 28th April

In an ambling country train from Aylsham to Dereham [in Norfolk] I did not read, and sat looking out of the window. First, I counted the telegraph posts. When I got to ninety-nine I thought this was a silly waste of time. I looked at the wild flowers on the embankments. The physical effort of pinning the eye on an object from the moving carriage, and swivelling the body round soon made me giddy. I desisted. Instead I looked at the faded photograph under the luggage rack of children paddling on Yarmouth sands. The vision palled. My thoughts turned to love. It seemed to me incredible that any human being could not fall in love with woman and man, and, furthermore be in love with both simultaneously. It was just not true that one could not be in love with more than one person at a time. To go further, there was absolutely no reason why one could not be in love with a horse or a dog. If one were – and I never have been – should one be ashamed? In other words, was I wicked to allow such thoughts and questionings to pass through my mind? The Church would say Yes. Then the Church ought to revise its precepts. All I do know is that 'in love' is damned and devilish, can only bring unhappiness and must be eradicated root and branch. Therefore one is left with unadulterated jolly old lust exclusively. And a good thing it is too. If only, however, one had complete mastery of one's emotions! At this moment there was a jolt, the train which had stopped, started, gathered speed, and flashed past the noticeboard with Dereham written in large letters. I had failed to get out. Oh Lord! No doubt the Church would say this was a judgment for harbouring impure thoughts.

At the next station I descended, telephoned to the previous station to apologize for not having got out, and for a taxi. I motored miles, and at great expense, instead of motoring a short distance for nothing. Arrived at Elsing Hall late. It is a 1470 house built in square knapped flints; and has square gables typical of these parts with heraldic finials and twisted chimney-stacks. It has been unfortunately restored in the 1850s. Nearly all the mullion windows have been repaned with plate glass. A moat completely surrounds the house. There is an open roofed hall, and an intact 1470 chapel. Mrs. Thackeray and her sister Miss Clarendon Hyde are the owners, and the last of their line since the reign of Egbert. The line was Browne, their mother being the Browne heiress. The Brownes held the place for two hundred years, inheriting from the Hastings, through the de Warennes, the first of whom married a daughter of William the Conqueror. At any rate their neighbour Lord Hastings, having lately celebrated on a grand scale the Astleys' ownership of Melton Constable in direct descent of eight hundred years, was very put out when the Browne representatives, not to be outdone, followed suit by celebrating their inheritance of humble Elsing in direct descent of one thousand years.

The present owners are impoverished. They have one indoor servant only. The house is incredibly shabby, dirty and primitive. The porch room ceiling fell when Norwich was bombed and the debris has been left on the tables and chairs. I noticed an early Georgian dolls' house, complete with contemporary furniture, and suggested to the old ladies that they should cherish it. They were amazed by the suggestion. The walled garden is an absolute wilderness. It is pathetic how within three years country people, who are unable to travel, become blind to the squalor to which they have been reduced. In spite of the terrible *délabrement* among which they live, these ladies with their long Plantagenet pedigree, their courtesy and ease of manner, were enchanting.

On my return to London I dined with Geoffrey Houghton-Brown to meet Colin Agnew. He bought three-quarters of Mrs. Greville's pictures for Polesden. He said she was a true friend, but a terrible enemy (like others in her world I can think of).

Lunched with Lady Harris, who is very amusing, and very deaf. She speaks in a honeyed voice, slowly and distinctly, with raised eyebrows, and makes outrageous remarks with no emphasis. Osbert [Lancaster] was bright gold like a guinea with jaundice, but feeling well, which annoyed Eddy who was present and bright green, and feeling ill as usual. Osbert turned to his mother-in-law and shouted in her ear, 'My pee was paler this morning.' In the evening I went with Johnny Churchill to Auberon Herbert's coming-of-age party. I drank rum and ate mincepies with the Herbert girls.

Eardley and I motored to Betchworth [Surrey] to see Broome Park. The house is not important, being a muddle of Georgian periods over-Victorianized. The grey drawing-room alone is unspoilt. It has a 1750 rococo ceiling and walls with plaster swags in panels, retaining the original paint. But the gardens are like Stourhead in miniature and were laid out about the same date. There are three lakes, a sun temple, and a Gothic hermitage, both *circa* 1750 and exceedingly good. The lakes are bordered with primulas.

I went from Westwood where I stayed last night to Kingston House, Bradford-on-Avon, was shown round by the agent, and talked with young Mr. Moulton who with his brother and sister owns the place. It is a textbook example of the Jacobean style, yet with a somewhat tight, fussy Victorian air about it. Ted told me it was refaced from top to bottom in 1850 or thereabouts. A full-scale replica of it was exhibited at the Paris Exhibition of 1900 as an example at that date of the ideal English country house. Inside it is rather over-restored, although there are some fine panelled rooms and several interesting contemporary fireplaces on a monstrous scale. Undoubtedly it is an important house, and with its lantern windows and terrace balustrading of intricate carved stone, recalls Montacute.

I left Westwood early and got to Swindon at 10.30 where to my surprise I found Stuart at the station before I expected him. On stepping out of the carriage, I saw a tall, smiling figure wearing a long gas cape on the platform. We took a taxi bound for Marlborough and were put out two miles this side of that town because we had reached the ten-mile radius limit from Swindon allowed the taxi driver. We walked the rest of the distance and lunched in Marlborough. Stuart is still distressed about the X.B. incident and worried about what Chips might yet do to him. He is over-sensitive and hates making enemies. Having a very charitable and sunny disposition he is hurt and surprised when he meets evil in others. After lunching at a Polly's Pantry we walked two miles down the Bath road to visit Miss Ethel Sands[166] and Miss Hudson who are living in a small, late Georgian rectory at Fyfield. Miss Sands opened the door. She looks like the typical American spinster one meets in a seedy *pensione* in Florence. She has a round smiling face and a gash of prominent teeth. She is rather like an ugly horse, yet her mother was a famous beauty, as indeed we witnessed from the drawings of her by Sargent. Miss Hudson is older and resembles old Lady FitzAlan. We did not like her so much. Stuart said they belonged to the '*haute Lesbie*', and theirs was a romance of years. They looked to him like two old men wearing wigs. Stuart began by talking to Miss Sands, so I had Miss Hudson. My attention was distracted from her by what the other two were saying. Miss Hudson is a Catholic but passionately anti-clerical and anti-Vatican. She attributes blame to the Church in Spain, Ireland, Poland and in fact everywhere, notwithstanding she is most devout. Ethel Sands showed us her modern pictures, includung Sargents and Sickerts of herself and Nan Hudson. They gave us toasted buns and chocolate cakes for tea. After tea I talked to Ethel Sands, and Stuart to Miss Hudson, to whom he paid not the slightest attention, while politely answering Yes and No, and listening to our conversation about Proust and Lady Bessborough. In talking to Miss Sands you realize how very astute she is behind her simple manner and nervous giggle.

Wednesday, 5th May

Lunched at Sibyl Colefax's canteen with Nancy [Mitford] and Bridget [Parsons]. Nancy brought me Edith Sitwell's *Poet's Notebook*. Bridget rather catty about her nearest and dearest. Nancy whispered that she believed Peter Derwent had proposed to Bridget and had been rejected. Instead of being flattered Bridget seems to be affronted by each proposal of marriage she receives. Strange.

James, who was to stay with me after M.A.B.'s party, never arrived or telephoned; so by 1 a.m. I presumed he was not coming and went to bed. At 3.15 I was awakened by a violent pealing of bells. I was angry and

---

[166] An intellectual, Europeanized American artist.

disagreeable. Jamesey pretended to be aggrieved, which made me angrier. He said his behaviour was turning the other cheek. I said it was cheek all right.

Thursday, 6th May

At 5 o'clock I was given gas and had a molar tooth extracted. I was quite frightened beforehand. I did not like the preliminaries, although the anaesthetist was kind and gentle. The gas did not smell disagreeable, and within a minute I was off. There was no escape, yet I sought it. I gasped for fresh air and had to take deep breaths; and they involved more gas. The battle was fruitless. I imagine drowning is like this: a terrible stifling, but soon over. I woke up abruptly with a tug. I suppose the tug was the tooth coming out. Time becomes quite mad in the circumstances. I thought, 'Now I have to face my tooth coming out,' and was worried. It had already come out. I looked at my watch. It was only ten minutes past five. Ten minutes only, which had seemed an age of unconsciousness. The gap in my mouth bled but I did not feel too unwell. I asked the dentist what he did to bring me round. He said he merely took away the mask and within 1½ minutes I was round. I did not realize that all this time of the operation I was inhaling the gas. My jaw may ache, they say, for ten days. Stuart says he loves gas. It is a vice with him and he welcomes any opportunity to have it. The experience makes one understand how close life is to death, and indeed wonder which is the more real, consciousness or unconsciousness.

Friday, 7th May

Accompanied Johnnie and Mary Churchill to Congreve's *Love for Love* with John Gielgud and Yvonne Arnaud; superbly done and the scenery by Rex Whistler. Johnnie is not the least grown up, and lives in a delightful fantasy nonsense world. He talks *eggy-peggy*[167] as we used to do when we were at the Priest's together, aged eighteen.

Sunday, 9th May

In a bitter cold, piercing wind I walked round the Manor garden at Wickhamford. The lawns are now unmown and the grass is a foot high. The beds are overgrown. Yet the garden is surprisingly beautiful still. Midi thinks more beautiful than when it was kept up. Before catching my train I went to Benediction in Evesham. I was unaccountably moved by the procession of the children, all so clean and *endimanche's*, little girls in

---

[167] A child's language which consists of putting *egg* after the first letter of every syllable. Invented to confuse and annoy grown-ups.

white veils, little boys with Mary blue sashes, all singing lustily without a trace of self-consciousness. Would I like to be the father of the little dears? The answer is an emphatic No.

Monday, 10th May

To Mark Watson's[168] new flat in Park Lane looking down upon the green bosom of the park trees. He has an orange tree in a tub, bearing fruit and blossom. The strong, exotic smell made me long for Spain or Portugal. Old Tancred Borenius rushed up to me, saying breathlessly, 'You are the one person I wanted to see about an article I am writing for the *Burlington* on historic houses.' Raby of the Ministry of Works had told him he must consult me on several points. He did not put a single point to me; but talked volubly of Mrs. Greville's shortcomings. I am heartily tired of that deceased lady.

Tuesday, 11th May

Had several drinks of very neat whisky with Jamesey in his dolls' house flat. Then the objective of the visit, M.A.B. arrived. She is dark, thin, with most beautiful legs; and has a dead white, slightly horsey face. She was dressed in black, very smart; had exotic scent, plenty of gold bangles and bracelets, and a suspicion of a blue bow somewhere at the back of her hair. She moved delicately as though she might dope, with the dope fiend's caution. She drank a lot, and seemed to admire James a lot. She was very entertaining in a dead-pan way which was disarming. Talked of Welbeck, Wilton and other habitual haunts, her relations, friends, enemies, anything that came into her head, without forethought. She was good company, and very sophisticated. I liked her up to a point.

Thursday, 13th May

Philip Farrer lunched with me at Brooks's. He is a mystery man. I cannot make out what the purpose of his life is. He must be verging on sixty and is handsome in a military way. He was an intimate friend of and admired above all men, George Lloyd, whose political opinions he shared to the full. I first met him in my Lloyd days when he was Lord Salisbury's secretary. He admitted today that in the Spanish Civil War he went to Spain as a spy. He reveres the Duke of Alba, and cordially dislikes Lord Cherwell,[169] the 'Prof'.

---

[168] Hon. Mark Watson, 4th son of 1st Lord Manton. R.A.F.V.R 1940–5.
[169] Professor F.A. Lindemann, 1st and last Lord Cherwell (1886–1957). Physical scientist. Personal Assistant to the Prime Minister.

I went to a party at Sibyl Colefax's. Harold and Desmond [Shawe-Taylor][170] were elated by the African victory. I sat for a long time on a sofa with old Princesse Edmond de Polignac. She had ensconced herself for the evening in one place, spread and immobile, with a hat on, rather like a large Buddha. There is something godlike about her, and she is very Faubourg Saint-Germain. I wanted but did not like to talk to her about Proust. Her sentences are interspersed with French expressions. She seemed not particularly interested in her surroundings. She kept asking me in an indifferent manner who so-and-so was who had come up to talk to her; and when I replied that I had absolutely no idea, chortled as though taking me into her confidence. But this illusion was spoilt somewhat by her asking me my name (and not registering when I gave it, for it conveyed nothing to her) on the plea that if she wrote to the Chavchavadzes she would want to say she had met me. Then she said she never wrote to the Chavchavadzes.

Friday, 14th May

Lunched today with Captain Berington of Little Malvern Court, a pathetic little dark man who has recently inherited the property. For centuries it has been in his family and the Blessed Sacrament has been in the house since the Reformation without a break.

Saturday, 15th May

While lunching in Rick's café next door Ethel Walker sat herself down at my table. For months I have watched her pass my windows in a lost, painful stagger, with her fat old dog on a chain. She is an ancient woman with a face striated like the valleys of the moon, a face balanced on an overweighted sack. Her voice is like the thunder of waters from a subterranean cavern. She told me she had just completed her masterpiece of two small children, very naughty, bad sitters. Miss Walker grumbled at the food and ate the lot.

I took the train to Windsor to have tea with Mrs. Betty [Montgomery]. I enjoyed the visit. She lent me several books, including *Au Bal avec Marcel Proust* by Marthe Bibesco. Mrs. Montgomery never met Proust. But he sent her his photograph which she showed me. It is of a sleek young waiter wearing a gardenia. Mrs. Betty is irritated that Proust has 'come into fashion'. Even this fact 'can't make me drop him'. We 'put him on the block' for quite twenty minutes, and we pinned beside him Lord Alfred Douglas, who as a young man, Mrs. Betty said, was no Adonis but spotty and without colour. She once met Oscar Wilde who afterwards

---

[170] Desmond Shawe-Taylor, musical critic.

said of her to Lady Oxford, 'She is so deliciously morbid.' She claims that she is a 'Catholic atheist', and that Jamesey and I are the only other members of this sect. She said to me without forethought, 'Just hand me my spectacles, dear James ll,' and when I left, 'Tell Jamesey he is still James I.'

Monday, 17th May

I lunched with Sibyl alone at her canteen in Belgrave Square. On this sort of occasion she is simple and totally unpretentious. She never tries to be the great lady. She told me how poor she had been all her life. It had not mattered because, apart from entertaining her friends, all her recreations and tastes had been inexpensive ones, like bicycling in her early days, and reading. She said that I must go and see Logan Pearsall Smith who wished to meet me; and that with Mrs. Betty I was rapidly becoming James I. I said that if I told Jamesey this he would pay her a flying visit, and I would be James II again in a flash. I went to Jamesey at 6 o'clock and nobly pressed him to go to Windsor. Clarissa and Harold were present. Harold said the description he gives in his new book[171] of the meeting with James Joyce in Paris was the occasion when I accompanied him.

Tuesday, 18th May

As Dame Una's guest I heard Father D'Arcy address the Wiseman Society on Portugal and Spain where he has just been. Before the lecture I had a long talk with Rose Macaulay, back from Portugal collecting material for her book on Anglo-Portuguese relations. James and I agreed afterwards that she must be an unhappy woman. She has that dried-up look of the unenjoyed. Father D'Arcy told me that Georges Cattaui has become a priest in Switzerland.

After dinner I went, at Jamesey's request, to M.A.B.'s flat. Although it was a hot night, the curtains were drawn, and the two were crouching before a red anthracite fire. M.A.B., tiny, and huddled up, much the worse for whiskies, mumbling in her attractive, but incoherent manner, and hiccoughing. She intersperses every sentence with 'darling' and 'sweetheart'. Her language is stagey and twentyish. Speaking of some family she said, 'They're nuts like us', and to Jamesey, 'I can't read a book with woodcuts in it. Woodcuts are such a bore. Wouf!' James, with whom I walked to Sloane Square, told me he was encouraging her to write her experiences. 'Tales of an old world mistress,' was her reply to this suggestion. She said she had been the Prince of Wales's mistress. His hair, she said, was the

---

[171] *The Desire to Please.*

most attractive part of him. She also had an affair with Lord Dudley[172] at the same time. Once she was flown in the Prince's aeroplane to stay with Lord Dudley on the Riviera. She was given a bedroom sandwiched between Lord Dudley's and the Prince's. Both kept wandering into hers all night so that there was a great mix-up. 'Finally the woman with molars came along.' When Jamesey confided in her that some of his friends were homosexual she replied, 'Darling, now I'm going to say something that will make you cross. I never felt that way when I was young.' When he told her that his dislike of Sibyl was inexplicable, she said, 'It's chemistry, my dear.'

Wednesday, 19th May

A very hot day at Cliveden. The site over the river is, as John Evelyn observed in the seventeenth century, superb. The house too is well worthy of the Trust. It illustrates the very end of the Palladian tradition. Barry conceived it with a real regard for architectural principles. It is heavy and majestical outside. The interior, altered by the architect J. L. Pearson in the nineties, has very little distinction. The Astors were away and I went inside. The famous Orkney tapestries have been taken down. The pictures, including the Reynoldses are hanging, for the greater part of the house is still in use by the family. The splendid gardens are unkempt.

Anne Rosse dined with me. Having seen her home I walked to the Dorchester to get a taxi. After waiting an age I saw Lady Crewe and Lady Victor Paget get into one, so I asked if I might accompany them, and take the taxi on. They said yes, but the cab driver was furious because I had not asked him. We mollified him. In the taxi we talked of happiness, and Lady Victor said she had not had fifty-two days' happiness in her life. Lady Crewe said she knew at the time when she was happy. Lady Victor said to her, 'That is because you have been loved.' Lady Crewe retorted partly under her breath, for she did not want me to hear, 'It's not true. I've *not* been loved.' Her tone was one of indignant rebuttal.

Thursday, 20th May

I left the house at 7.30 and took the tube to Hendon station where Forsyth picked me up. We motored to Six Mile Bottom station where we met Professor Trevelyan who had come by train from Cambridge. We motored him to Blickling. I felt tired and needlessly depressed. Forsyth is a good old man but so respectable, so conventional and so dull. Goodness is by no means enough. G. M. Trevelyan, that distinguished

---

[172] 3rd Earl of Dudley (1894–1969).

historian and Master of Trinity, is dry as a stick and totally lacking gaiety and humour. He is very uncouth in his dress and person, and has long, untrimmed hair down the back of his neck. I was sitting behind him and as we approached Blickling he took out his false teeth and cleaned them with his handkerchief. I remember watching old Lord Dysart do this in the lavatory at Brooks's. He was very blind and was scrubbing his set with one of the hairbrushes.

Trevelyan enjoyed the day and adjudicated upon the colour with which to paint the cottages on the estate to, I believe, everyone's satisfaction. Miss James was delighted to see me and, when we left, Willey the gardener handed me some flowers. 'You seem very popular here,' the professor barked. I think he said it approvingly, but he is dour.

Saturday, 22nd May

In the morning I saw Lady Berwick who talked about the future of Attingham and asked me to stay. Then I passed Q. in St. James's Street. She was accompanied by a friend. With the touch of her hand all my misgivings evaporated and I was happy.

I had tea with Y. who is hoping for another child having averted a miscarriage. She was lying on a sofa after injections. I stayed with her till after 7. She told me how before she was married she had to have an abortion. She went early one morning to a squalid villa in the suburbs of London dressed in her drabbest clothes. She had the operation on an old deal kitchen table, and was sure the instruments were not properly sterilized. She was determined not to give her name for fear of blackmail. She paid £75 in banknotes and walked away, bleeding profusely and feeling wretchedly ill and absolutely unfit for any effort. There were no taxis in that part of London and she had to take a tram and then a bus. Her loneliness and misery were worse than her physical suffering. Women's tribulations could not be borne by most men.

I dined with Marie Belloc Lowndes in her charming small house in Barton Street. Just ourselves. She gave me an orange cocktail, iced, from a jug, and quaffed her glass like a medicine. She was wearing a flowing, flowered dress over her enormous wide frame down to her ankles. Her dinner was the best I have had since the war began – gulls' eggs (two each), fried salmon with rich sauce, poussin with red wine, a pudding, coffee, African brandy. How does she manage it? She talks volubly with a French intonation, rolls her 'r's, is excellent company, extremely knowledgeable on most subjects and very gossipy. There is no writer on the Continent whom she does not seem to know. She is certain that the Prince Consort was a Jew. She said Magdalen FitzAlan-Howard was shrewd and her stupidity assumed, the better to sweeten relations with her mother; that Lady FitzAlan was a clever, though difficult mother. This is a sad thing to have heard.

Mrs. Belloc Lowndes has insatiable curiosity about people. She began dinner with, 'I am told there is a most charming, handsome and clever American over here, a Mr. Sergeant. I am sure you must know him. Do tell me all about him.' Oh Lord, I thought, the same old subject. 'To begin with,' I said, 'he is called Mr. Preston. He happens to be a sergeant in the American forces. So his friends refer to him as *The* Sergeant. It is true he is everything you say.' 'Oh, I would so much like to meet him. Will you introduce him to me.' 'Of course,' I said. 'That is easily arranged. He would simply love to know you. You will like each other immensely.' At that moment the telephone rang. To my intense surprise Chips Channon (how does he know the engagements of his acquaintances?) was on the line to tell me that Stuart's young brother, a G.I. was in London at a loose end, looking for Stuart. Where was Stuart? I said I thought he was staying the night in the country. What was to be done with the brother? He was now at Chips's house. Chips could not possibly give him a bed for the night. Not in that enormous house in Belgrave Square? I thought that strange. So I said I would willingly put him up. I would call for him at 10.30. 'No, no,' said my hostess, 'send him r'round here at once. What is he like?' 'What is he like?' I asked Chips. 'Fascinating. The living spit of Stuart,' Chips said.

Marie Belloc Lowndes was full of excitement. She is always eager to make new friends, to be kind to the young and to show goodwill towards our American allies. In ten minutes time the doorbell rang. I opened the door. Without saying a word a short, sallow, oleaginous youth, wearing large square spectacles, stood on the mat, shaking my hand like a pump handle. He was surprisingly uncouth, answered 'yah' to our enquiries whether he had got the right number of the street door, and whistled when he was not grunting. My hostess's face fell a foot, and she threw me a beseeching glance which clearly meant, 'Surely there must be some mistake.'

Sunday, 23rd May

I took the young yahoo – who turned out to be a gentle, diffident, rather pathetic yahoo – to the station, and spent the rest of the morning reading Gerard Manley Hopkins. I lunched at the Ritz with Diana Worthington and Sir Timothy Eden. Diana and I walked all the way to Cheyne Walk, she flitting like a will o'-the-wisp beside me, and laughing. She is either down in the dumps or pie in the sky. Today she was in the sky. Quite a jolly tea party assembled, some by invitation. Some were just strays. Besides Diana there were Ivy Compton-Burnett, Margaret Jourdain,

Dame Una, Roger Senhouse, Mark Watson. Roger, thinking to flatter Miss C.-B., endorsed Raymond's tribute to her in *Horizon*, wherein he says she is the nearest approach to Henry James among novelists of our generation. Miss C.-B. said sharply that she could not read Henry James. Roger said afterwards that no one talked more tattling nonsense, but he succeeded in getting her down to bedrock. I didn't hear how he succeeded, for she hates talking about literature and wards off any reference to her own novels, parrying it by referring to Margaret Jourdain's books. At times when she goes on and on like a clockwork toy about nothing in particular I do wonder if she could be a bore. But her own starchiness is so like that of most of her characters that I am always fascinated listening to and watching her.

Mark Watson brought a drawing of himself by Augustus John. He had fetched it this afternoon. Though a good likeness it was not a good drawing. He said John had been drawing him for over a year and was not yet satisfied with the result.

Wednesday, 26th May

I spent all yesterday in the train from Euston to Windermere. This morning Bruce Thompson motored me through heavy rain across the moors, to Kendal and Appleby. The intermittent sun and great plumes of black cloud made a sublime scene sweeping and chasing each other across the moors. Yet, cockney that I have become, I find the mountains lonely and depressing. We stopped on the side of the road before Appleby at a wood where Mary Thompson [Bruce's wife] and some land girls were measuring trees for the Ministry of Supply. All the trees are being taken from this part of the world. We lit a bonfire and ate luncheon. We moved on to Temple Sowerby, the McGrigor-Philips's house. Mrs. McGrigor-Philips is a tall, ungainly, exceedingly coy woman, and a low-brow writer under the pen-name of Dorothy Una Ratcliffe. He a grubby, red-visaged, hirsute old teddy bear. They laid down a lot of nonsensical conditions in making over the house, intending to provide the minimum endowment although she is a millionairess, having inherited an enormous fortune from her uncle, Lord Brotherton. Bruce Thompson was infinitely patient and polite, and only occasionally betrayed what he was thinking by pursing his lips. The house, which I once saw in 1938, is of tawny orange sandstone, a beautiful texture, yet in photographs looks dull. Although the core of the house is Jacobean, what one now sees is eighteenth century: Venetian windows and a staircase ceiling, *circa* 1740 of rich Italian plasterwork. Temple Sowerby is at present occupied by the Railway Wagon Repairers and their families. The Philipses retain one small wing and a caravan for a bedroom. The walk above the flowing burn at the rear

of the house is very romantic. From the front are distant views across
green pastures of the mountains in the Lake District. It is a lovely setting.

Friday, 28th May

Dined at Dame Una's house with her and James. She said Mrs. Belloc
Lowndes was by far the most mischievous woman she knew. She, the
Dame, was devoted to her but since her rule in life was never to be indiscreet, a restriction was thereby put upon their confidences. James and I,
after draining the whisky in his flat, began walking to Chelsea. After
nearly an hour we realized we had been walking in the opposite direction and were quite lost. This was brought about by earnest talk of our
various perplexities. I had warned James that he ought to be more reti-
cent with his women friends who were incorrigible gossips; that by con-
fiding everything in them he risked betraying his men friends, and there
was a freemasonry among men friends which he ought not to abuse. He
said I was Machiavellian. I said tartly that I hoped my character might
improve with age. He doubted it. He assured me he could not possibly
have a friend without being honest to him or her. I could not agree with
this policy and said surely it was better to withhold the truth, and not to
spill it before everyone who took one's fancy. One must have loyalties,
and they necessitated reticence. But no. He immediately disclosed how
M.A.B. had passionately kissed him in a taxi yesterday, but he was warding
off the affair by pointing out the ludicrousness of it in view of the dis-
parity of their ages. Coward! Her passion was truly terrifying. Jamesey is
so engaging that maddened as I am by him at times, I forgive him all his
trespasses.

Saturday, 29th May

Poor Professor Richardson created an adverse impression at the
Georgian Group meeting – I learned later that he was feeling ill and
taking M & B – by implying that the Group's primary objective was to
encourage the design of modern architecture on Georgian lines. John
Summerson strongly dissented, and so did I. I scribbled a note, which I
passed to the professor in the chair, begging that the committee should
be given the opportunity to discuss this contentious question of policy
before a pronouncement was made at the annual meeting. Dame Una
complained that he was irresponsible.

I went as Dame Una's guest to Harold's lecture on Byron at the
Alliance Hall. In looking for the Hall I met Harold and accompanied him
to a pub for a drink. The pub had nothing but beer, so we left. I was
immensely impressed by Harold's fluency and attractive fireside manner
of delivery. As a rule I cannot listen to lectures. My attention wanders.

But listening to this one was just like reading a book of Harold's. I was not distracted once, and was riveted by the case he made for Byron's poetry. When he read stanzas from *Childe Harold* I was almost moved to tears. Desmond MacCarthy in the chair was mealy and mouthy. Emerald Cunard was there. When the lecture was over Harold ran after me down the street, asking me to find a cab for her. I put her and Dame Una into one. As it left Emerald called out, 'Tomorrow at 8.30. What *do* you think? Wavell is coming.'

Off I went to Herstmonceux to stay with Paul Latham. This was an act of charity because I have never known him well. To my surprise Eddy had told me he would be glad to see me, whereas he declined to see most of his closer friends. I got muddled with my trains and was 1½ hours late. Paul was sitting at the window of the bothy where he lives. He left prison in January having been there 1½ years. He was very thin but healthier and handsomer than I remember him. He still has a frightening look of craziness in the crimped gold hair, anthropoidal head, albino eyebrows and cold blue eyes. He talked incessantly of himself and prison. He is touched that everyone on the estate is nice to him. Indeed the lady taxi driver went out of her way to extol his popularity because of his open-handedness and generosity to all his tenants. Paul has become incredibly sentimental, yet his conversation is more depraved than anyone's I have ever heard. He kept reading aloud poems from the *Spirit of Man* and extracts from the letters written in a garbled fashion from the friends he has left behind in prison. He is obsessed by sex and already haunts the most dangerous places, he told me. He also enjoys repeating disobliging things said about one. How much is true, and how much invented it is hard to say. He is a sadistic man.

He had the grace to acknowledge Eddy's great kindness in helping him. He won't move from the estate or see any close friends from his old world, except Eddy; yet he is irritated by Eddy's devotion. We walked round the grounds and the outside of this fairy-tale castle. The Hearts of Oak Benefit Society have done great damage to the contents, which Paul foolishly left in the building. By the end of the visit I was worn out by listening to so much about Paul by Paul, although some of his experiences were interesting. I am terribly sorry for him but would pity him far more if he were less wayward and less egocentric.

I got back only just in time to dine with Emerald Cunard. Even so I was still wearing my brown country suit. Jamesey took me to task about it next morning. Dinner was at 8.30 yet the blinds were all drawn, the windows firmly shut, and the room was stifling. I was in a muck sweat. There were Field-Marshal Wavell, Sir D'Arcy Osborne, our Minister at the Vatican, a nineteen-year-old Paget girl, Bridget Parsons, Chips

Channon, Jamesey and myself. I sat next to Jamesey and Chips, who is bear-leading Wavell, and indeed treating him as a considerate owner would a performing bear before an audience, sitting in the background with a proud expression on his face and flipping the whip gently from time to time. Wavell is stocky, with a smiling rugged face and a wall eye. He is slow, distracted and shy. Emerald's prattle, sometimes very funny nonsense, flowed like a river. I think this embarrassed him at times, as it did the other guests. It was too much of an exhibition contrived by her and Chips in advance. D'Arcy Osborne did not speak once throughout the evening, and looked cross. Lord Queensberry came in at 10.30 and recited Shakespeare sonnets in a torrent of venom. Wavell was coaxed by Chips into reciting Browning and Ernest Dowson, which he did in a muffled, inarticulate voice incredibly badly. Much too much applause from Emerald and his prompter. It seems extraordinary that a man in his position should be staying with a flibbertigibbet like Chips. I found him cosy and cultivated. The other guests were disappointed with him. He is certainly an old man who seems finished. I had not realized this before I met him, and was inclined to wonder why the Government was not making more use of so eminent a soldier.

Tuesday, 1st June

Feeling singularly unwell today I went to Holt Court near Lacock [Wiltshire] for the night. This house belongs to the Goffs. The main front is a rich, provincial piece of stage scenery in Bath stone. Major Goff is the great-grandson of William IV and Mrs. Jordan. Lady Cecilie told me he had been brought up by his grandmother, Lady Augustus Fitz-Clarence, a great favourite of Queen Adelaide. This accounts for the Goffs having so many portraits and so much furniture from Windsor Castle, in spite of Lord Augustus being the youngest of the King's sons.

Wednesday, 2nd June

On my return I was very ill, and crawled to see my doctor, Pierre Lansel. A recurrence of the old trouble and change of drugs, leading to shingles, retention of urine, catheters, germs in the bladder, high temperatures, agonies, despair, and bed for over four weeks. The worst affliction of the lot was a nurse who positively revelled in philistinism. One day she glee-fully smashed the lid of my Worcester sugar bowl. When I remonstrated she got cross, and said it was ugly. 'Ugly?' I screamed at her. 'Ugly! Even if it were, it is old and precious. But it's beautiful. Surely you can see that.' 'I can't,' was the reply. And she added with a shrug, 'Oh, well!' 'It isn't well,' I said. 'It's bad, very bad.'

Next morning she remarked through pursed lips, 'Any-wan mate sue-pose [this is how she spoke] yew pre-furred old ob-jects tew persons,' as though this were the most heinous charge she could bring against my morals. 'Anyone would be supposing perfectly correctly,' I snapped back. She was so flabbergasted by the barefaced admission that she left almost immediately. I got better.

Thursday, 1st July

I went to Wickhamford and was restored to health by Mama, who was angelic to me. Only Mrs. Haines helps her in the mornings. Otherwise Mama does everything – housework, cooking, washing up, to which, because she is hopelessly disorganized, there is absolutely no end. She spends as much time in either complaining or congratulating herself as in actually working. And what she does, she does indifferently. I am reminded of Dr. Johnson's remark to Boswell. 'Sir, a woman's preaching is like a dog's walking on his hind legs. It is not done well; but you are surprised to find it done at all.'

Tuesday, 6th July

Papa drove me to Hidcote to tea with Laurie Johnston who took us round his famous garden. No reference was made by him to the National Trust. The garden is not only beautiful but remarkable in that it is full of surprises. You are constantly led from one scene to another, into long vistas and little enclosures, which seem infinite. Moreover the total area of this garden does not cover many acres. Surely the twentieth century has produced some remarkable gardens on a small scale. This one is also full of rare plants brought from the most outlandish places in India and Asia. When my father and Laurie Johnston were absorbed in talk I was tremendously impressed by their profound knowledge of a subject which is closed to me. It was like hearing two people speaking fluently a lan-guage of which I am totally ignorant.

Wednesday, 7th July

From Evesham to Shrewsbury by train, changing at Hartlebury on to the Severn Valley line. What a beautiful valley it is, with gently sloping wooded banks and miniature scenery, even on a grey day with occasional rain. I stayed two nights with the Berwicks at Attingham [Park]. They inhabit a fraction of the east wing. The W.A.A.F.s occupy the rest of the house. The Ministry of Works has at my instigation protected the prin-cipal rooms by boarding up fireplaces and even dadoes. The uniform Pompeian red of the walls is I presume contemporary, that is to say late eighteenth-century. In my bathroom the walls were papered with Captain Cook scenery just like the upstairs bedroom at Laxton [Hall,

Northants]. The first night we had champagne to celebrate our and Attingham's survival up to date. After dinner I read through the 1827 Sale Catalogue of contents, many of which the 3rd Lord Berwick, then Minister to the Court at Naples, bought in from his elder brother the 2nd Lord.

Thursday, 8th July

Lady Berwick and I went to tea at Cronkhill, one of the houses on the estate. It was built by John Nash about 1810 and is interesting on that account. It was designed in the romantic style of an Italian villa, with one round tower, a colonnade and overhanging eaves, and is the precursor of many similar Victorian villas. Lady Berwick behaves towards her neighbours with a studied affability, a queenly graciousness which must be a trifle intimidating to those upon whom it is dispensed.

After tea I walked with Lord Berwick in the deer park, having been enjoined by her to talk seriously about Attingham's future, and press him for a decision on various points. I did not make much progress in this respect. On the other hand he expanded in a strangely endearing way. When alone he loosens up and is quite communicative. All the seeming silliness and nervousness vanish. He talked to me earnestly, in his shy, diffident manner it is true, of the ghosts that have been seen at Attingham by the W.A.A.F.s. Lady Berwick would not, I know (and he also knew full well), have tolerated this nonsense, if she had been present. He kept stopping and anxiously looking over his shoulder lest she might be overhearing him, but he did not stand stock still and revolve, which he does in the drawing-room whenever she starts talking business. He told me that Lady Sybil Grant, his neighbour at Pitchford, constantly writes to him on the forbidden subject, passing on advice as to his health which she has been given by her spiritual guides. She no longer dares telephone this information for fear, so Lord Berwick asserted, of the spirits overhearing and taking offence, but I suspect it is more likely for fear of Lady Berwick overhearing and strongly disapproving. He is not the least boring about his psychical beliefs but is perplexed by the strange habits of ghosts. He asked me, did I think it possible that one could have been locked in the housemaid's cupboard? And why should another want to disguise itself as a vacuum cleaner? Really he is a delicious man.

Friday, 9th July

On my way back to Evesham I stopped at Bewdley. I walked to Wynterdine just outside the town and was given luncheon by Kathleen Sturt, with whom I was in love at the age of six. She was then a sprightly spinster in her thirties. She gave me a little box with an onyx lid which

I treasured as my most precious possession for several weeks. I then lost it and never gave it or the donor another thought. She is now a jovial, good-natured, grey-haired, tub with a veined face. She could not have been kinder or nicer. After luncheon I was taken upstairs to see Mrs. Sturt, aged ninety-three, in bed. A toothless, clean-looking, smiling old dame, she was an intimate friend of my grandmother in Ribbesford days. Kathleen walked me round the Wynterdine fields and through the shrubberies to the red cliffs with the grottoes above the Severn. I remember these romantic Germanic walks so well. She and her mother are anxious to do what Mrs. Lloyd has done at Areley Kings down the river, namely give covenants.[173] It would be splendid because the Wynterdine land goes right into the heart of Bewdley.

Tuesday, 13th July

I went by myself to Ibsen's *Master Builder*, with Donald Wolfit in the chief rôle. This play is a little too melodramatic and of course damned depressing. I returned to Cheyne Walk thoroughly out of sorts and unhappy.

Thursday, 15th July

Went to see the Picasso of *La Hollandaise*, naked and wearing a Dutch cap, painted about 1903. It was exhibited at the gallery of a character called Bilbo, a German Jew of enormous girth and paunch. He was in corduroy trousers and short shirt sleeves, and was smoking a pipe through meshes of black, wiry beard. Bilbo is asking £6,000 for the Picasso and the Tate is appealing for funds for its purchase. Stuart dined with me at Brooks's very exhausted after a night out yesterday. He left early in order to get to bed at Alice Harding's, where he is staying, before she should come in. Oh the subterfuges and tergiversations of this sublunary life!

Friday, 16th July

My luncheon with Eddy at Brooks's was not altogether a success for we had little to say. This is often the case after absences. The more one sees of intimate friends the more one has to say to them, and the less one sees them the less one has to say. I went to Dr. Simpson this morning and endured every sort of indignity, too squalid to relate. He considers me well which is nice of him; and is recommending to Lansel yet another drug.

Saturday, 17th July

I went to the Ritz at 3 to take Emerald Cunard to Keats's House, Hampstead. Everything went wrong. I should have had a cab waiting for

---

[173] These unfortunately came to nothing.

her, and not one could be found. It took me half an hour running up and down Piccadilly in the sun. Diane Abdy who was to have accompanied us, failed to turn up, so we were alone. This put Emerald out. When we got there I thought the little white villa looked fresh and pretty through the nightingale mulberry tree branches. Emerald thought it undistinguished. I suppose she imagined that because Keats was a great poet he ought to have lived in a great baroque palace. She thought the inside lacking in character and associative interest. It is in a sense, for there is hardly a stick of furniture or even an internal feature which Keats knew. Emerald was very silly in her remarks about Shelley's immorality in front of the custodian. On the return journey she had an altercation with the nice cab driver about the route. And she was in the wrong. We reached the Dorchester at 4 and although she had bidden me to tea, it was too early, so I took my leave. Her last words were to remind me of the Rutland ball tonight.

Now all today I have been in a maddening, filthy mood. When I told Q. that I could not face tagging on to Emerald's party after dinner and going to the Rutland ball with them, she asked me to 'dine with us', meaning herself and spouse. This infuriated me. I said I would think about it. When she said on the telephone this morning, 'I am not pressing you. I don't want to hear one word from you now, but if you want to come, there is a place for you, and dinner is at 8,' I still said nothing. She rang me up again at 7.15. I said I would not go. And I didn't. Miserably I dined by myself, and gratuitously chucked the only privately given ball since the war began. In fact I deliberately cut off my nose to spite my face, and derived only the tiniest bit of satisfaction thereby.

Sunday, 18th July

Today I felt happy because I was alone, and working like a black at Polesden Lacey. I had a sandwich luncheon in the garden, did not lie in the sun, and checked various inventories. Having collected the pictures for K. Clark's exhibition I motored to Clandon to dine with Giana Blakiston. Noel was away. She is so easy that I can chatter with her unreservedly, a thing I can do with very few. The Blakistons seem perfectly content to live in this vast, dust-filmed house, in a makeshift manner. They are not the least deterred by lack of domestic comforts and what are termed the minimal amenities. Giana walked with me down to the lake and back before dinner. I was depressed by the soullessness of this house and the hideousness of the surrounding grounds, for there is no garden. The Onslows can have no taste whatever. Trees have been allowed to grow right up to the front door so that the main elevation (which faces the wrong way and gets no sun) cannot be seen from a distance. A screen of revolting conifers has been planted as a windbreak against the only elevation that could otherwise have been seen.

Monday, 19th July

In the afternoon I took the Polesden pictures to the National Gallery. Kenneth Clark met me in the vestibule to discuss their arrangement. Before I left he showed me a Rothschild collection of French pictures which he is housing. I urged him to exhibit them, but he said he couldn't.

On returning in the bus I was put into a paroxysm of rage by reading in the evening paper that Rome had been bombed. I was to have seen Harold tonight. I did not dare go for I should have been hysterical and abused the Government. Instead I drank three Pimm's No. 1 with Jamesey at the Carlton Hotel. Together we vented our rage over the bombing. He said Churchill had sanctioned it, with 'I don't care a damn what buildings they destroy.' Then I dined with Johnny Dashwood at the Travellers' and drank a whisky and soda, a bottle of Burgundy and a glass of port – and came home sober.

Tuesday, 20th July

John Pope-Hennessy, the Dame and Anthony Blunt are, according to Jamesey, working up a protest against the Rome bombing. And Lord FitzAlan has put down a question in the House of Lords.

In the afternoon I went to see Lord Astor in St. James's Square. Matheson said he wished to see me. But when I was ushered into his room he asked very politely, 'What can I do for you?' So at random I said I hoped he would give me some particulars of Cliveden history for the guide-book I was preparing. I couldn't very well have asked him what he wanted of me. As it happened he seemed pleased and began to rattle off facts and dates, but I had nothing to write them down in. He did not strike me as delicate and tubercular. He is tall and florid, and what the eighteenth century called a black man. Indeed there is a touch of the coal black mammie in his appearance. Lady Astor swept in and began rather offensively with, 'Whatever you people do, I cannot have the public near the place,' and before I had time to expostulate, corrected herself to the extent of adding, 'At any rate their hours will have to be clearly defined.' There is an insolence and silliness about her. But how young and handsome and well dressed she is.

Wednesday, 21st July

I looked at a portrait of Violet Hunt in red crayon that Geoffrey Mander wants the Trust to buy for the Wightwick collection. A pretty thing but I consider the Pre-Raphaelite association too remote. Then to the Steer exhibition at the National Gallery. K. Clark said he had been severely criticized for holding so large an exhibition of a *pasticheur*. It certainly is remarkable how Steer never seemed to develop a recognizable style of his own. But how good he can be. His landscape oils can be like Gainsborough, Constable, even Turner. His early water-colours of Boulogne beaches are as charming as Tissots.

Thursday, 22nd July

I went to Slough in the afternoon to see Sir Wyndham Dunstan.[174] He is a nice old man who is Secretary of the Sudeley Committee.[175] He said no one holding a paid official post could be a member, not even K. Clark. He took me in his car round the confines of Burnham Beeches, for he wants the Trust to induce the L.C.C. to expostulate with the army for the mess of it they are making. A difficult thing for us to do, I tried to explain. He showed me his collection of water-colours. He told me he used frequently to stay with Rossetti at the Queen's House, in Cheyne Walk, acting as a kind of secretary to him for a time. His grandfather received the Rossetti family when they first came to England.

On my return to London I called on Harold in King's Bench Walk. A young man was painting his portrait, which was atrocious, and made him look like Gerald Berners. Harold said people were gossiping about Stuart's relations with Alice Harding, and asked, 'What are his conjugal chances there?' Then Victor Cunard[176] walked in. We talked of the Rome bombing, and I was pleased that Victor condemned it strongly. To my surprise Harold deplored it, admitting that so long as it was not repeated he would be satisfied with this one gesture. Anthony Eden had however given him no assurance that it would not happen a second time. Victor said Eden always makes a mess of our relations with Italy. This bombing will have stiffened Italian resistance and will make the Italians hate us for a long time. Harold rushed off to dine with Sibyl and meet Wavell.

I dined with the Princess de Polignac. Clarissa, John Pope-Hennessy and David Horner were present. The last was invited because apparently the princess thought he was E. M. Forster. He is a slightly epicene, elderly young man who lives with Osbert Sitwell. He has a soothing, low voice, but his manner is embarrassingly affected. After dinner we talked of the Rome bombing. John, who is cautious and sensible, advised that we must collate our facts before launching into protests. Then we talked about English novelists. This led to Proust. Our hostess evidently disliked him.

---

[174] Sir Wyndham Dunstan (1861–1949), chemist and director of the Imperial Institute, F.R.S. 1893.
[175] Advisory body on museums.
[176] Victor Cunard (1898–1960), *The Times* correspondent, diplomat and connoisseur.

She had known him since he was a handsome young man with melting brown eyes, until his death. It was impossible to endure his company for long at a time. He was touchy and took umbrage at every supposed slight. In fact he detected slights where they never were intended – in a tone of voice or a look. As a result he would fire off thirty letters to you in rapid succession. In France before the first war none but the Saint-Germain set recognized his gifts. When the princess found that there was already a Proust Society in England, only *Chez Swann* having been published, she was amazed. Proust was either in the depths or the heights, when he would toss money to servants as though it were chicken food. His life was studded with unfulfilled romantic attachments. He never ceased to correspond with the princess, although their periods of intimacy were fitful. She supposes he enjoyed quarrelling with his friends. She dispelled the rumour I had heard that she was the origin of Madame Verdurin by telling us that when she entertained Proust lovers in her King's Road house before 1914 they called themselves for fun by the names of characters in *Chez Swann*. One was Cottard, another Brichot, and she was Madame Verdurin.

Friday, 23rd July

Nancy and I lunched at Sibyl's canteen. Nancy said, 'If Henry Yorke had called his novel *Court* instead of *Caught* and written about dukes instead of firemen we would all have acclaimed it.' A woman has written asking her which are the better dinner parties, Emerald's or Sibyl's. Nancy has replied, Emerald's without a doubt, because they are smaller, the food is better, and they are free. Stuart, who had joined us by this time, was shocked by the pleasantry, and began to explain that poor Sibyl could not afford to pay for her parties. 'Yes, I know that, Sarge,' Nancy interrupted him with her mischievous laugh. Stuart, who loves Nancy, criticized her hardness of heart, which only made her laugh more.

This evening I walked home – about three miles – across Hyde Park and down Exhibition Road, listening to the voices of Czech, Polish and French soldiers. I love the present cosmopolitanism of London. Summer nights in London are soft and velvety even if the previous day has been grey. At nights the colourlessness disappears, and the savage emptiness of the black-out is filled with pools of violet, blue and yellow light. I am at last feeling well again and have a zest for living. Harold said yesterday from the bath tub, 'How nice to hear Jim laughing again.' I asked Stuart if I had been gloomy lately. He said, 'Yes, even before you were ill you had become very depressing.' 'Or depressed?' I asked. 'You had become very glum. Certainly you *never* laughed,' he said, as though I must have been aware of the fact.

I had tea with Logan Pearsall Smith at 5 and left at 7. I enjoyed my visit. The old man coughs and spits incessantly. He is vastly entertaining. I certainly should have visited him before. He has a splendid capacity for mockery and fun. And of course he has literary refinement; perhaps no other sort. Stuart seems to be his present preoccupation. He admitted that at first he thought Stuart too good to be true, endeavoured to catch him out, and failed. Having checked him up through mutual friends he pronounced him to be aristocratic (according to American social rules), rich and popular. He queried whether his success had been achieved through art or nature. At all events it was success. And at all events Logan has succumbed, for Stuart has flattered him by not merely congratulating him on his books (which is easy), but by quoting long passages from them (which is clever). He read me his poem to be published in next month's *Horizon*. But he slushed so that I could not hear a word of it. He knew Henry James intimately, but could only guess at James's sex proclivities. He certainly did not dare discuss them with him. He thought Shane Leslie's disclosures in *Horizon* horrifying. James's letters were written to a young soldier in World War I and were unmistakable love letters. Shane was given 300 of them by the man's widow early this year. Cyril Connolly had evidently not cottoned on to the indiscretion of publishing them. Logan P. S. said there was much that was lovable in Cyril. He instanced the dinner Cyril gave for Ethel Sands's seventieth birthday. We discussed whether one should tell one's friends their faults. He was once told by Ethel Sands that he nearly drove his friends to distraction by criticizing their friends who were not his. At the same time she made him promise he would point out to her any fault she had. He now longs to tell her that she spoils his stories by her own interpretations of them. But he dares not do so because she is bound to take offence. Jean Hamilton was a 'dove'. No one spoke ill of her, but she lacked discrimination, and was taken in by frauds. Some frauds he mentioned were: Sir Ronald Storrs, Professor Joad and Humbert Wolfe. He was pleased when I said I was merely on the fringe of the Mayfair Jezebel world. He feared it might be Stuart's undoing for he too lacked discrimination.

We talked about many things, rapidly, disjointedly, leaping from one topic to another. He recounted one 'awway'[177] after another. Finally he expressed the hope that Stuart was not a 'marrano', i.e. a Jew in Spain who adopts Christian methods, and later relapses into what he was originally.

---

[177] One of many words and phrases invented by Logan Pearsall Smith and in current use by his circle. He described 'awways' as stories that in one's dotage one tells more than once.

When I told James and Stuart all Pearsall Smith had said, they laughed. They knew all the topics, all the 'awways' by heart. I was disconcerted. In fact Jamesey says he is a poor, senile old man, who repeats himself over and over again.

Sunday, 25th July

Motored to Polesden in a hired car to fetch the two remaining pictures, the Ter Borch *Introduction* and the lovely Jacob Ruysdael. I went early and spent the day there till 8.30, working very hard, going through every cupboard, turning out and throwing away rubbish. A wonderful day. Smith told me that Hilda, the housemaid, who professes to be so fond of me, cursed like a trooper when I insisted on coming down last Sunday; that she bites and bullies everyone, abuses her trust and has her friends to stay all the week. He advised me to watch her carefully. I never expect gratitude, loyalty, affection, etc. from servants. They don't know the meaning of these qualities. From the uneducated one must expect self-interest, meanness, mendacity and guile. Of such is the kingdom of the proletariat.

Monday, 26th July

Today was the Trust's annual meeting; so dull and turgid that I cannot dwell upon it. Stuart dined with me in Soho, and was tired and hot. We are now in the depths of summer. It is like being at the bottom of a well, enclosed on all sides with only a glimmer of relief somewhere miles above one's head. Nevertheless I was in a jolly, carefree mood. I angered Stuart again by repeating, with absolutely no malice prepense, James's complaint made half in jest, of Stuart's approbation of the bombing of Cologne. He denied it, took the charge seriously and was deeply worried. Oh why do people take anything seriously these days? He is too sensitive; and says that my tongue wounds, and I repeat inaccurate gossip; that I am alarmingly bitter about people; and that at times he is genuinely worried about my – sanity! I admitted my insanity, and said he should remember that fundamentally I disliked the human race; that if I were happily married to some retiring woman I would never, never go near society. This was the truth. He was shocked. So I thought I would shock him further. I said I not only hated people, I sought to do them down on every possible occasion by whatever devious means came to hand. He was sorry to learn this. I said I knew my character was a great disillusion to him, who had once thought it fairly commendable. He said this was true. I said I was really a fiend incarnate. I said it, not in anger, not in bitterness, but softly, dulcetly. He was perplexed, and saddened.

Tuesday, 27th July

I dined with Dame Una. Only Rose Macaulay there. She was dry and twitchy. Stuart cannot bear her. She said some silly things about the Germans having been highly civilized in the past when they formed the core of the Holy Roman Empire. Dame Una and I both disputed this fallacy. She talked of her book on the English in Portugal. She has got as far as John of Gaunt.

Dame Una complained that a miller, called Rank, has bought up all the cinemas so that every one shows the same film at the same time. A good plan, I think, for it makes fewer to see. Dame Una can be a little sour.

Wednesday, 28th July

At 10 a.m. to the Travellers' to talk to Major Algar Howard about the chance of the National Trust acquiring the College of Heralds – this will come to nothing – and of his own house, Thornbury Castle [Gloucestershire].

I asked Mrs. Belloc Lowndes and John Pope-Hennessy to lunch at Wilton's to meet Joan Moore. Joan looked as pretty and cool as a porcelain shepherdess on this hot day. The luncheon was, I think, a success. Mrs. Belloc Lowndes fell for Joan, who was sweet and attentive to her. Marie B. L. had two glasses of port wine. Talk was of Violet Hunt and Marie Corelli. Marie B. L. is pessimistic about the outcome of the Italian affair. She says there will be revolution, the Germans will occupy the peninsula and we will make of it a battleground.

I had tea with Stuart – he is no longer to be called the Sergeant and gets fretful when addressed by that term of endearment – at the Travellers'. I can't understand why, since he has so low an opinion of my character, he bothers to see so much of me. Talk was too much of personalities. His social activities make me acid. They arouse the worst instincts in me. While we walked afterwards across the Green Park in the sun he said he had asked Lady Islington why her husband had chosen that particular title. I laughed, and remarked in a bantering way that only an American would ask that question. He was hurt. I should not say such things. I was constantly saying such things, whereas he refrained from saying similar things to me that would be intensely wounding. Now this retort distressed me as much as my remark had distressed him. Neither of us has half a grain of humour between us.

Thursday, 29th July

I took a morning train to Bath. The platform at Paddington was crowded when the train sidled in. Before it stopped I leapt into a first-class compartment and took a corner seat. We took precisely two hours to reach Bath. I was met at the station by Mr. [Robert] Henshaw, an estate agent, and taken to Forts where Major Strutt gave us luncheon. Strutt is a very decent fellow, in the Home Guard. He made me feel too sophisticated, and shallow. We motored to his house, St. Catherine's Court, five miles from Bath. I was sent to see this house in 1936 but Major Strutt had forgotten the occasion. I cannot be a very memorable person. The situation on the western slope of a narrow valley is picturesque. The peace was disturbed by fleets of noisy aeroplanes, a reminder to the poor Strutts that their younger son in the R.A.F. was killed three weeks ago. It was a sunny, boiling afternoon and the dry earth crackled with heat and the valley crinkled with haze. The gabled house with old church in the garden is typically English. The best things about it are the half-octagonal porch with balustraded sides, and the terraced garden, also balustraded. There is a good stone chimneypiece in the hall and a Jacobean screen. Otherwise not much. Strutt's father added to the house not too badly. It is strange how little owners know about their own houses. This family have owned St. Catherine's Court for over 100 years.

Friday, 30th July

One of the hottest days in England that I have lived through. I took Anne Rosse, back from Ireland, to lunch at the Turkish restaurant. We both strove not to break into a sweat. Anne kept stopping in the street, standing immobile and saying, 'Keep quite still. Don't laugh. Don't speak. I may be all right.'

At 5.30 I went to tea with Emerald. She was charming and solicitous about my health. I sat next to Lady Lamington, who is beautiful, stately, stiff and a little prim. She said how much it horrified her to see girls drink. I was far too hot to argue, so hypocritically I agreed by a slight inclination of the head. The Princesse de Polignac came in and said to Emerald, 'This charming young man came to dinner with me, and wrote me a beautiful letter. Then, if you please, he sent me *Tom Jones* – but in a rare edition of two volumes of priceless value.' This frightened me stiff, for I asked myself how much that villainous Nancy would charge me for this book. Anne [Rosse] came in. We talked of 'the situation'. I was much impressed by Anne's intelligence and use of words. She was totally unaffected. Emerald said she was sure great movements were on foot for the Cabinet met last night at 11. She said that the Russians were proposing peace terms to Germany.

I joined Jamesey at Rule's restaurant. We drank quantities of Pimm's and enjoyed ourselves hugely. There is no one with whom I can be happier. We can be as one. I say 'can be'. We were tonight. Unlike Stuart he is far from being seduced by society. He told me Lady Lamington was charming and very intelligent, although she was a little precious. As we talked and laughed in an animated way two very tough-looking men at a neighbouring table were staring at us critically and discussing us. I then realized how we must have struck them, both youngish and out of uniform, both enjoying ourselves, which in their eyes we had no right to do. In truth they had no right to judge us, for James is in the army, and I was.

We walked out of the restaurant into the heat, and down the embankment. We crossed London Bridge to the south side of the river, and ambled along Cardinal's Wharf. Jamesey was extolling in the most candid and engaging manner his age – he is twenty-six – his good looks and his successes, saying he did not believe he could ever die. He said, 'Our relationship is such a one that can never have existed in the past. I don't think anything marks the progress of civilization so vividly as improved personal relations.' I said, yes, I felt certain that before our time personal relations could never have been so intimate, though of course we could never tell what, for instance, Byron and Hobhouse talked about at nights in a tent during their travels in the Morea. I said that more people ought to keep diaries, but the trouble was that the most unscrupulous diarists were too scrupulous when it came to putting personal truths on paper. James said that Cecil [Beaton's] diary would be the chronicle of our age, that we would only live through it. I said Eddy Sackville West kept one. James said, 'We could not be hoisted to posterity on two spikier spikes.' We looked at bombed churches and sat in churchyards, and drank shandies in City pubs.

Saturday, 31st July

At Boodle's I ran into Professor Richardson and together we did a tour of the club. He took a print of Brooks's façade to the window opposite Brooks's, and demonstrated how he hoped after the war to take down the roof balustrade, which should never have been added. He would put back the first floor balcony and the projecting piers on which it rested, as indicated in the print.

I had tea at Windsor with Mrs. Betty who looked older and frailer. She was very stiff with rheumatism. I learned several of her expressions: 'carp' and 'carping' for scandalizing about friends; 'carpet atmosphere' to describe bores, a mild bore being an 'Aubusson', a real bore a 'Kidderminster', and a cracking bore a 'velvet pile'. She said that Stuart, whom she does not like and refers to as 'that Mr. Stuart', forced his way into 'dear Etty's' room when she was at her worst, lying on her front with her face on the pillow, and read poetry to her. Her comment was,

'Have you ever heard of such a cruel thing? It is like the worst Polish atrocity.' I feared that this might mean Lady Desborough had taken against Stuart, but was glad when Mrs. Betty admitted that she still liked him. Mrs. Betty is very penetrating for her years. She alarms me at times by ranking me with her as someone of impeccable taste, culture and judgment.

I walked from her house leisurely down the Long Walk, to Cumberland Lodge. How regal and serene the view is from the Copper Horse. At the end of the drive I sat on a bench to cool and watch the thunder clouds gather. I was surprised to see a stocky figure with stick in hand and coatless in braces, approach me rapidly. It was Lord FitzAlan, very sprightly and fit, come to meet me. Boydie and Magdalen and Alathea were there. I enjoyed this short visit. I pretend to see in this household a Compton-Burnett family. Lord F. is 88, Boydie 58, Magdalen 60, and Alathea 20. It is a pity Alathea is not older and there are no great-grandchildren. Lord F. gave me iced cider to drink. I had a long talk with him about the Italian news. He knows nothing whatever of [Marshal] Badoglio, and could not even pronounce his name. I asked about the new Archbishop [of Westminster]. He said the procedure was for the Westminster canons to elect three names. These were submitted to the hierarchy. The bishops usually reduced them to one name, or else added a fourth of their own choice to be submitted to the Vatican. It was customary for the Pope to consult ecclesiastical and lay opinion in England before deciding upon the candidate. It was apparent that Lord FitzAlan had been consulted. I stayed to supper and talked to Magdalen after Lord FitzAlan went to bed. I left by cab for Egham at 9.20. Lord F. was quite of my mind about the bombing of Rome.

Sunday, 1st August

In spite of the thunder and rain it has been an insufferably stuffy day. I lunched with Clarissa [Churchill] at her flat in the Rossmore Court block. I found her extremely white and pale, wearing a brocade dress down to her ankles, and lying on a Récamier sofa under a long window, the blind partially down but not so as to obscure the views over Regent's Park to Highgate and St. Paul's. She gave me an excellent luncheon. Yet it was not a very vital meal, for Clarissa is languid. She is certainly clever, and might be exasperating. I am bewildered by her present Elizabeth Barrett invalidism. I had invited her to lunch with me but she preferred not to stir in the heat.

Lady Lamington had asked me to dine with her tonight to meet Mrs. [Gilbert] Russell. Was rather annoyed when at 7.30 she rang up to say we were to go to a party instead. So I met her at Mrs. Russell's flat and we walked down South Audley Street to Lady Queensberry's[178] studio at 9. We had no dinner; only a few dry sausages and bits of cheese on sticks. There was dancing and much noise. I knew no one and we left at 10.30. I excused myself from returning to the flat on the plea of firewatching, which was untrue. Instead I telephoned Stuart and arranged to call on him. I walked across Hyde Park, and there he was on the pavement waiting. We walked down a pitch dark passage, I clinging to his coat tails. He lay on his bed. I sat on a chair. He talked about his weekend at Faringdon in a sort of ecstasy which blinded me with its fatuity. I felt overwhelmed with depression and buttoning up my coat, rose to go. Is this all life has to offer, I asked myself? In a moment the onslaught of truth dissolved. I was back in the happier world of total unreality, as it were under the influence of the opiate of our being. I sat down again on the end of the bed. I stayed. It was cool and wonderful, but unreal. It took me nearly an hour to walk home after midnight.

Monday, 2nd August

The 'Brown girls' and Janet Leeper came to tea with me. Ivy Compton-Burnett ate half a pot of raspberry jam, and I was shocked to see her surreptitiously wipe her sticky fingers upon the cover of my sofa. Both she and Margaret ate like horses. This time Miss C.-B. talked a great deal more than Margaret. Her description of the Poetry Reading and Lady Gerald Wellesley's antics was very funny. They are a wicked pair.

Wednesday, 4th August

I took an early train to Birmingham and was met by Lord Doverdale's agent. He gave me luncheon at the Grand Hotel and the low-down about his client's situation. I have known this man for some time. He will take my arm and gaze retriever-like into my eyes. I remember once before thinking this odd, but now I believe it is his idea of being pally. It goes with his constant interrogation, 'Pardon me?' – which I don't want to do – and his ingratiating approval of whatever I say as 'topping'.

We drove to Westwood Park, outside Droitwich. Lord Doverdale met us at the door. For an instant I thought he was an ostler out of livery, for he wore a dark blue double-breasted jacket, striped tie with a thin gold chain to keep it in place, stained lavender flannel trousers and mole-coloured suede shoes. A suspicion of straw in the hair too. He was also slightly deformed about the shoulders. Delicate undoubtedly, and from what he said about his lungs, consumptive I guess.

---

[178] Cathleen Mann (1896–1959), official war artist. Daughter of Harrington Mann, portrait painter.

He took us round the boundaries of the whole estate of some 5,000 acres. It covers unexciting Worcestershire landscape. The park is not of outstanding beauty, but spread and spacious with a sixty-acre lake. The house however, planned like a star-fish, is eccentric, interesting and splendid. Years ago Desmond Parsons and I trespassed and photographed it from the gatehouse, which with two out of several original garden houses remains. Sir Reginald Blomfield[179] restored the four towers to their present ogee shape to match the authentic caps of the gatehouse and garden houses. In nineteenth-century illustrations the dunce caps of the towers on the house looked more stately. The interior is very fine indeed. The entrance hall has a mock Jacobean ceiling and beautiful Jacobean panelling brought from a house in Newent. The curious ball-topped finials of the great staircase are most unusual. The best rooms are the splendid saloon, white drawing-room and the Japanese room. The last has a flowered paper on a buff ground. The cornice and ceiling of the saloon are in stucco, dated 1660; and the Flemish tapestries were bought when the room was built. Doverdale has put a Rembrandt self-portrait in the rich oak overmantel. The carpet of the room is Axminster, *circa* 1740, and many of the Chippendale chairs have always been here. In fact the 1st Lord Doverdale, a paper manufacturer with the name of Partington, bought most of the contents of the Pakington family who previously owned the place. Uncharitable people say he bought several Pakington ancestors and dexterously altered the 'k' on the picture labels into 'rt'. The house is well furnished and in excellent condition. It is a weird house inside and one has difficulty in keeping one's bearings. Lord Doverdale, who speaks with that rather common Prince of Wales accent, is interested in motor-racing. He was very friendly and frank, easy and agreeable to discuss business with. I liked him.

Thursday, 5th August

The agent came back at 9.30 and we finished our discussions. Lord Doverdale intends to leave Westwood at the end of the war. Under his father's will the house and park, with an endowment of £1,500 p.a. comes to the National Trust on his death. He wants to hand over now with capital to yield this income. It should be a most satisfactory arrangement. I think this visit has been a success. Doverdale is very lavish with his drinks, and the establishment is un-warlike. All but the state-rooms and principal bedrooms are in use, and there is a grand butler waiting.

---

[179] Sir Reginald Blomfield (1856–1942), architect of the new Regent Street. Author of *Renaissance Architecture* in England, etc.

My birthday. I am thirty-five! The horror of it! Except for my incipient baldness, fortunately on the crown of my head and on account of my height not always noticeable, I do not think I have changed much. My figure is the same as it was fifteen years ago.

At 7 o'clock I went to Jamesey's flat. The gay little creature was splashing about in the bath. He gave me two stiff whiskies to keep up my spirits, which were actually quite high. He made me change out of my nice blue shirt and put on a white shirt of his and a blue tie with large, white round spots, which he said looked more festive. He admired the transformation, explaining that it was like seeing part of himself in me. He gave me as a birthday present a little water-colour sketch of the interior of a church by Pugin. Thus fortified and encouraged I set out with him for Boulestin, where at luncheon time I had ordered a table and food for eight guests. We drank again in the bar where Harold and Stuart joined us. Then Dig and Henry Yorke came. I had not seen Henry since the war. He was absolutely charming and rather reserved; Dig her usual sweet self. Harold gave me a book of Freya Stark's (and later a tooth-brush!). Then Joan Moore came but without Emerald, whom she had said she would bring. Emerald arrived at 8.40 just as we were about to begin dinner. Harold said in front of everybody, 'What worries me about this party is how Jim will afford to pay for it.'

I had Joan on my left and Emerald on my right. The dinner passed with perfect ease. Never was there less need for anxiety. Excellent food – fish in shells, partridge and plenty of Algerian wine; brandy afterwards. Joan was divine. I was so absorbed with her and James with Emerald that I hardly spoke to Emerald. As it happens I prefer listening to her than talking with her; just as I prefer watching a canary flit from perch to perch and scattering feathers and shrill cries, to trying to pick up its song. I enjoyed my party immensely. As we sat on, and the waiters longed for us to leave, Emerald arranged marriages for James, Stuart and myself.

When at last the party ended I walked away with Harold to stay the night at King's Bench Walk because I could not have got home so late. Harold began by saying, 'The worst of women is their selfishness. They must make slaves of men.' He extolled the advantages of homosexuality and relationships between men, who allowed individual independence. Then he praised Vita as an exceptional wife. He said that he and Vita had pledged to tell each other the moment one of them fell in love, but not to confess to casual affairs because that was rather squalid. Their marriage began badly because Vita immediately fell in love with a married woman – Violet Trefusis I presume. He said that in his whole life he had only been in love three times, and these times were before his marriage, with two subsequent ambassadors, and a 'bedint' young man of no consequence, called Eric Upton, whose only recommendation was extreme beauty. 'Oh, I may have once fallen a fourth time, with R.' He told Vita about this fall, and she was wonderful. But then Vita truly is exceptional.

Saturday, 7th August

I bought a life of Harriet Martineau from Nancy in Heywood's shop, and there saw Stuart. He said he refused to discuss the war with me any further, my views were too silly.

I went to tea with Ivy Compton-Burnett and Margaret Jourdain. Anne Hill was there; also Dame Una and Rose Macaulay. Again I was the only man among blue-stockings. Rose Macaulay said the Portuguese were having bread riots. Ivy C.-B., I noticed, when she did condescend to speak, shouted everyone else down. The tea was a sit-down spread of breads of different hue, jam, potted meat, biscuits, shortbread and cake, delightful but curiously middle-class and such a contrast to Emerald Cunard's weak China and a thumb-nail of chocolate cake. Ivy, who now addresses me by my christian name, said it took Harriet Martineau[180] forty years to discover what it had taken her eighteen, namely that there was no God.

I joined Rick at 7.30 and we dined together at 97 [Cheyne Walk]. He said I was moving in a set to which I did not properly belong, that since I was far from gregarious by nature, I was behaving foolishly. I admitted that in a sense he was right, but protested that instead of acting foolishly I was acting out of curiosity, if by 'set' he was referring to those people who congregated round the Dorchester. Then we drank coffee with the Robin Darwins.[181] Robin refuted my opinion that Wilson Steer forfeited greatness because he worked in too many styles. He said that because he assimilated so many styles, he was great.

Sunday, 8th August

Today London was peaceful and happy. I sat on my window seat in the sun reading. Nancy telephoned and asked me to lunch with her alone in her little house in Blomfield Road. She was in high spirits and full of stories about Eddy's anxieties – 'Chalky water is so binding,' and so forth. She told me she had begun her autobiography but would not be able to publish it until her parents were dead, for it would wound them. She said the mistake the Redesdales had made was to refuse to educate a clutch

---

[180] Harriet Martineau (1802–76), miscellaneous writer.
[181] Sir Robin Darwin (1910–73) artist. Rector and Vice-Provost, Royal College of Art 1967–71.

of intelligent daughters. I walked home, and continued reading until the late evening. I packed my haversack for firewatching in the office. Stuart, having returned from the weekend, telephoned and asked me to call on him. So I walked to Lancaster Terrace. He had left the front door unlatched. I entered and saw the light through his open door at the end of the long passage. He was in blue pyjamas applying lotion to his hair about which he is very particular. He got into bed and read to me today's parable of the unjust steward which I had failed to understand at Mass this morning. His interpretation of the story did nothing to disabuse me of the belief that it is unfortunate and wicked doctrine. I walked away through Hyde Park to Buckingham Palace Gardens for night duty. It was so dark that I lost my way and ran into a barbed wire entanglement. I was challenged by a sentry, 'Who goes there?' I could not remember the proper reply, and answered after a pause rather feebly, 'Jim Lees-Milne.'

Monday, 9th August

The Astronomer Royal came to see me this morning to ask if the Trust could provide a country house for him. After 300 years the Observatory is leaving Greenwich because of the smoky atmosphere and the glare from the lights at night. I suggested Herstmonceux Castle but he did not seem taken with the idea.

Tuesday, 10th August

I lunched with Emerald Cunard at the Dorchester. It was a match-making party. I sat next to the girl I am to marry. She had a brown, greasy face with a down-covered, slip-away chin. I was not at all attracted. 'But she is very, very rich,' Emerald expostulated. On my other side was an amiable girl who laughed a great deal, and was plain as a pike staff. She is a contemporary of Anne, who tells me she once had great allure and for years was the mistress of Lord somebody or other. Other guests were the Greek Ambassador, Nancy, Louis Golding and Alastair Forbes.[182] The last is a deb's delight of classic beauty, with fair, unblemished skin. Very young and a little portentous. He is diplomatic correspondent of the *Sunday Times*, ambitious for a parliamentary career, witty, mischievous, censorious and bright. Emerald began abusing the waiters, calling them Bolsheviks and Nazis, and telling them they deserved to be killed in Sicily. I was deeply shocked. When the waiters left the room conversation began. The Greek Minister spoke of the 'rottenness' of the French. Nancy, who is Francophile, retorted that their government could have done no good by retiring to Africa in 1940. I told the story of George

---

[182] Freelance journalist.

Lloyd flying to Bordeaux in a desperate attempt to persuade Weygand not to give in. The Greek Ambassador confirmed it. He had been Secretary-General at Geneva at the time and remembered the incident. Conversation turned to Spain and Franco. I shocked everyone by saying I had been pro-Franco during the Civil War. Nancy called me a fascist. Such rot, for one does not have to be a Fascist, Nazi or Falangist to fight the world's common enemy, Marxism.

Wednesday, 11th August

Bruce Thompson is in a great state because he left behind at Temple Sowerby [Manor] during our visit his file containing letters and copies of letters between him and me, criticizing Mrs. McGrigor-Philips. Some of mine were strongly worded and I remember saying she was an impossible woman to do business with. Mrs. McGrigor-Philips read all the correspondence and has written to the secretary and the chairman complaining about our misconduct. She said to Bruce on the telephone, 'I thought you were both gentlemen,' which much upset Bruce who is 100 per cent a gentleman to my 25 per cent. I told him he ought to have retorted, 'And I thought you were a lady.' For ladies do not read other people's letters.

Matheson and I lunched with the Eshers at Watlington to discuss West Wycombe Park negotiations. Both Esher and Matheson were ready to reject the offer altogether. I dare to think I saved the situation by suggesting that as a compromise we ask Johnny Dashwood to allow us to hold thirty acres of the far end of the park as endowment land for us to sell for building, if at some future date after the Dashwoods' time the Trust is obliged to raise funds for maintenance of the house and garden.

Got back just in time to join Janet Leeper's party at the Playhouse for *Blow your own Trumpet*, the second play by Peter Ustinov. Janet's nephew Michael Warre had a prominent part in it and acted well. The play was too ambitious and lacked movement and action; and not as good as the first, *House of Regrets*, but the characterization very brilliant.

Thursday, 12th August

Johnny Dashwood rang me up first thing and I lunched with him. He agreed to our proposal about the thirty acres. Today I have felt curiously unwell and tired.

Friday, 13th August

Rick, who is on a week's leave, insisted on taking me to lunch at Claridge's with two of his Brigade friends from the Octu. They were both absolute boys just left Eton, aged eighteen and nineteen, in fact almost a generation younger than me, who could actually be their father. They were touchingly naive in trying to appear grown-up.

At 5.15 I went to 33 Portman Square to hear Jamesey deliver a paper on Monckton-Milnes[183] to the Poetry Society. The front row was packed with his friends. I sat between Clarissa and M.A.B. who in the daylight and at close quarters looked raddled and whose breath was distinctly unpleasant. I was nervous at first on James's account, but quite needlessly. He started off with self-confidence and throughout was in absolute control. Even so I refrained from looking at him for fear he might want to giggle. Our front row must have appeared comical to him, composed as it was almost exclusively of old women, such as Lady Crewe, Dame Una and Rose Macaulay. He read from his typed pages and quoted extracts of Lord Houghton's poems very beautifully indeed. The lecture was a great success, the only pity being the smallness of the audience.

Some of us went to James's flat where we drank gin. Cecil [Beaton] had the previous night been at a bomber command station from which the raiders over Germany and Italy set forth. In the control room he followed the full course of the raids. The planes were absent eight hours and all returned safely. Cecil heard the orders given to each crew before they flew off. In talking to him many of the men expressed sympathy with the 'poor I-ties' because their ack-ack defences were so very inadequate. Cecil said it was useless to appeal to their sentiment where historical monuments were concerned. Such things meant nothing to them at all. On the other hand their distaste for taking life unnecessarily was genuine. He said that unlike soldiers and sailors the airmen harboured no feelings of hatred or revenge against the Germans.

They were totally objective in their work. He said, 'You simply have to be tough in speaking with them,' referring, I suppose, to the orders and the manner in which their officers issued them. Dame Una said that Badoglio was doing excellently by gradually replacing key posts in Italy with non-fascists, but gradually in order to prevent economic collapse. She maintained that the present economic stability in Italy was entirely due to the fascist efficiency, and the Bank of England recognized this. In fact a banker told her that the Bank of England had full control of British/Italian relations and was even 'running' Sicily, whatever that may mean.

Lady Victor Paget, Jamesey and I drove to Argyll House where Lady Crewe gave us iced cocktails. We took her to dine at the Speranza restaurant. I cannot say that I find her very fascinating. She is devious without

---

[183] In 1950 he published *Monckton Milnes, The Years of Promise*; and in 1952 *Monckton Milnes, The Flight of Youth*.

being clever, and vain. For her age she is remarkably well preserved. Stuart calls her a great lady, and admires the manner in which she, like Lady Desborough and other great ladies, walks up steps and enters a room or a cab in that confident, blind, unseeing way. Lady Victor is an eccentric. She sat hunched up, her face in her hands, saying how miserable she was and always had been. She told me she had had shingles, once across the forehead, and once round the middle, which was 'like nurturing a hedge-hog'.

Tuesday, 17th August

It is half past six. I have been sitting for an hour on my window seat looking at the cheerful river, with the evening sunlight dancing upon the wavelets, and at the gay motor boats, painted black and yellow, dashing down the river and growling busily. There are water boys on them. There are old men with sticks and pipes just below my window and across the road. They are squatting on the embankment wall, smoking and gossiping. 'Are these young men,' I ask myself, 'and these old men wracked by hopeless love, a prey to their miserable natures, slaves to their emotions, and irredeemably wretched?' I think not. They may wish the war was over. They don't want to lose their lives or the lives of their sons. But this is negative wishing. On the other hand they are positively living, with a zest for being alive which they do not stop to question or understand. How sensible they are. Whereas I seldom live carelessly, with abandon. Most of the year I mope, moan, resent other people's happiness, lament my own unhappiness, and waste this precious living. And what is it all about now? Neither last night nor the night before has the voice spoken to me. In the office today I hardly dared leave the room in case the telephone should ring. Whenever it did my heart jumped. And when the voice at the other end was not the right voice I was in despair. I became edgy, bad-tempered. I could hardly bear it when my colleagues were using the line in case my voice was trying to get through to me. And what am I doing now? Waiting again for the telephone to ring. This is preposterous, infantile and reprehensible. I must snap out of it.

Audrey[184] came. I watched her tittuping along the pavement in the highest of high-heeled shoes, like some funny little bird. She looked pretty but her hair was brushed off her nuque into a bob on the crown of her head. She is too small and featureless for this to suit her. Now she really has troubles enough to daunt the stoutest soul, and yet she rides above them; and she never, never mopes or moans. We drank tea. She was enraptured with the view.

---

[184] The diarist's sister, then Hon. Mrs. Matthew Arthur, later Mrs. Tony Stevens.

Wednesday, 18th August

I went to Dinton, the other side of Salisbury, for the day and met the *Country Life* photographer at Dinton station. We pushed his heavy plates, camera and paraphernalia in a handcart uphill to the village.

Thursday, 19th August

I went to the laboratory in the morning, and until luncheon time had blood tests taken every forty minutes. They bled me and gave me sugared water to drink in pintfuls. By the end I felt faint.

Friday, 20th August

This morning a man came here at 9.30 with a great bag. A clip was put on my nose, a mask over my face and for five minutes on end I breathed into the bag. I was then made to eat three eggs. Mrs. Beckwith my little charwoman did not know how to cook powdered eggs, neither did I, so to my distress I was obliged to take out three crock eggs. These she fried for she had never scrambled in her life.

This evening after dinner I went to Jamesey's flat. He had a bad attack of hiccoughs. We strolled into Kensington Gardens where he left me to walk home. James said that that ridiculous Lady Crewe thought I was in love with him. She told Bridget Paget it was obvious I suffered tortures when James left the room the other night, and I was longing to go after him. Lady Victor replied, 'He suffered tortures because he has shingles.' James also surprised me a little by repeating a conversation he had had this evening with his mother. He explained to her that the nettle rash on his behind was diagnosed by his doctor as the effect of nervous disorder. This was brought about by his being semi- in love with M.A.B. and Enid Paget and yet physically desiring boys. Dame Una expressed disapproval of his going to a psychoanalyst. 'What, darling,' said James, 'would you rather that I never learnt to get an erection with women?' 'No,' said Dame Una.

Saturday, 21st August

Caught a morning train to High Wycombe and walked up the drive at West Wycombe just as the Eshers arrived for luncheon with Johnny and Helen. Esher was in splendid form, teasing the Dashwoods about their progeny. After luncheon we drove to the far end of the park and inspected the temples, follies and cottages on the property to be transferred; also all that distant part of the park to be held alienably. Esher has a genius for persuading people to act sensibly against their deep-rooted inclinations by his jocular manner and sheer fun. I really believe we may acquire this beautiful house and park in the end. After tea I caught a train which was so slow and late that I missed my train from Waterloo to Woking. I did not reach Send Grove till nearly 9.

Spent the weekend at Loelia Westminster's. Only Emerald and a dull but affable young man called Sharman, staying. Send is an enchanting small Jane Austen house, symmetrical, stuccoed and washed pink. The front is covered by an enormous wistaria. It dates from the end of the eighteenth century. The prospect from the house covers a long expanse of grass, with curving boundary to the left, and to the right open views across a river bordered with pollarded willows in the direction of Clandon. Stuart calls this neighbourhood the New Dukeries, for in addition to Loelia Westminster, the Dukes of Sutherland, Northumberland and Alba live within a few miles.

My hostess has impeccable taste. She bought this house a year after the war when it was not too late to buy French wall papers. As you enter there is a charming little stairwell with a balustered staircase corkscrewing steeply upwards towards a domed ceiling. To the right and left are projecting bays forming a small dining-room and boudoir. Beyond the boudoir is a library with coffered ceiling. The bookcases in this room appear to be late eighteenth century. I arrived late and rather flummoxed. The duchess greeted me at the dining-room door, napkin in hand. I washed and joined the party straight away. A delicious dinner at a small round table. After dinner we talked in the library about Keats and Shelley. Emerald said Shelley had had a child by Claire Clairmont and that Mary Shelley had adopted it as her own. We then talked of eccentric people living in country houses. I told them of my experience with the Dymokes of Scrivelsby.

In 1938 the committee of the Society for the Protection of Ancient Buildings was very concerned about the fate of a cruck cottage in Lincolnshire called Teapot Hall. It was shaped like a tent and the two end walls were of half timber construction. This unique, textbook house was falling into disrepair and all letters written by the Society to the owner, Mr. Dymoke[185] of Scrivelsby were unanswered. So Rick Stewart-Jones and I, who were on the committee, volunteered to call on the owner. We motored to Lincolnshire, and arrived at the lodge of Scrivelsby Court on the main road. The lodge-keeper was friendly but said that Mr. Dymoke (who was the King's hereditary Champion and Standard Bearer of England) was living in the Court but had not been seen for years. It was not even known whether Mrs. Dymoke[186] were still alive. He, the

---

[185] F. S. Dymoke (1862–1946), 32nd of Scrivelsby, the Honourable the King's Champion and Standard Bearer for England.
[186] His second wife (*m.* 1907).

lodge-keeper, delivered parcels and food to the man who lived in the gatehouse, and he in turn put them into a basket which was let down from a first floor window of the big house. He said the man in the gatehouse over the moat would certainly not let us through. However we walked to the gatehouse. We were denied entry. Not to be outdone we walked away from the gatehouse round the moat, and clambered over a part of it that was dry. The garden up to the house was waist high in grass and weeds. All the ground floor windows of the melancholy house were either boarded up or sandbagged. The place seemed dead. We walked round the house. I happened to look up, and there at a window above us was an ashen face with a snow-white beard, completely expressionless, pressed against the glass pane. As we continued round the outside of the house the same face appeared at every window, gazing down upon us vacuously. Not a word was spoken; not a gesture of annoyance was made. It was an eerie experience. We came away, and both of us have been haunted by that face ever since.

Emerald told us how when she was first married and lived in the English country, she went to call on the Mexboroughs. She was shown into the drawing-room, and waited. Presently Lord Mexborough[187] was wheeled into the room. He had a long white beard down to his knees and was wearing a top hat. As soon as he saw Emerald he let out a piercing scream, 'Take her away! Take her away!'

Sunday, 22nd August

Emerald did not appear till 1.35 for luncheon. In the afternoon we sat in the garden. The others depressed me by dwelling upon the bad state of affairs at present. It appears from what Sir Paul Dukes told Loelia last weekend, that our relations with Russia are strained, and she may make a separate peace. If she does, I at least shall not be astonished. My view also is that we have badly bungled the Italian situation, which at the time of Mussolini's downfall was favourable to us, by insisting upon unconditional surrender, and so forth. All we have done is to stiffen Italian resistance. Had we been conciliatory but firm, we would have had Italy out by now, and with us. Mr. Churchill is a disastrous man. I hate him more and more.

Tuesday, 24th August

The M.P. for Northampton, one Summers, came to talk about Thenford, the house he has rented for several years and contemplates buying. At 6 I joined Lord Spencer at Brooks's and he took me to Spencer House

---

[187] Presumably 4th Earl of Mexborough (1810–99).

overlooking the Green Park. He brought torches because it is quite dark inside. All the windows have of course been blown out. The house suffered most severely from the bad raid in April 1941 when I watched the corner house, which also belonged to Lord Spencer, burn to the ground. Incendiary bombs have destroyed parts of the top floor, and blast has torn away the stucco from many ceilings. It is a wonderful house. Lord Spencer lived in it during the 1920s, then let it to a women's club till two years ago. He removed the best mahogany doors and marble chimney-pieces to Althorp, where I saw them last year. The rooms facing the park on the ground and first floors are very fine, notably the rooms at the south-west corner, one over the other. The lower room has spreading palm tree leaves from the capitals of the columns – a trick of Vardy the architect, Lord Spencer told me – and the upper room, now alas badly damaged, was painted by Athenian Stuart. The ceiling of this room is almost totally down. The staircase balusters are of tawdry beaten metal work, painted red and gold to resemble drapery and tassels. There are seventy bedrooms, some very small and poky.

Jamesey, with whom I dined, is so disgusted by the attitude of the press that he thinks this country deserves reverses.

Wednesday, 25th August

I went to Knole for luncheon. Just Lord Sackville and me. We ate in the large oak-panelled dining-room. He has a butler, a cook and one house-maid who has 250 bedrooms to keep clean. He was as courteous and charming as ever. We had venison liver from deer killed in the park. In the afternoon we and the agent toured the house very rapidly in order for me to get some idea of the parts which the Trust would lease back to him. Most large houses upon acquaintance look smaller than at first they appeared. Not so Knole. It is a veritable rabbit warren. It turned out today that in our recent discussions we had all three overlooked the north wing, which consists of fifteen bedrooms as well as reception rooms.

On my return to the office I felt a little squeamish about the stomach. Nevertheless I dined late with Cecil Beaton, and like a fool ate lobster and pigeon.

I parted from James at South Kensington station and proceeded to walk home. In the street I was seized with violent attacks of diarrhoea. I was in agony and thought I should never get home. Did so with difficulty and had a terrible night.

Thursday, 26th August

I attribute it to the Knole venison liver. I stayed in bed, reading, all day and ate nothing.

Friday, 27th August

Better again. Drs. Simpson and Lansel's diagnosis of the tests is that I lack sugar content, and do not retain sugar in the system, and am anaemic. Lansel injected me with a needle the size of a dagger, pumping some ghastly mixture into my behind.

After Malcolm Sargent's concert in the Churchill Club I dined with Emerald and Joan Moore. Diana Sandys mistook me for Garrett. We have not met for years. She is very pop-eyed and her figure has lost its shape. Malcolm Sargent told me that the other day old Mrs. Astley Cooper sent for her amorous butler, Fred. She asked him if he knew his Bible and the parable why you cannot serve two masters. Fred all this while was standing stiffly at attention, answering, 'Yes, m'm. Yes, m'm.' 'Then how on earth, Fred,' she went on, 'do you suppose you can serve three mistresses?' Although Malcolm Sargent's figure is still young, and he is brimful of vitality, his little monkey face is sallow.

Emerald grumbled a good deal about war-time conditions when I called for her this evening. She said that she was wretched at the Dorchester; she had no real friends left; was tired, and too old to cope with life. Yet she does and will cope until she drops. I thought she was going to faint in climbing the steep stairs in the Central Hall.

Sunday, 29th August

Having stayed last night with Miss O'Sullivan in her wing at Blickling I spent the morning going round the house with her. We decided to remove a number of good eighteenth-century bedroom pieces of furniture which [11th] Lord Lothian had lent to the R.A.F. Many of them had been badly spoilt. Miss O'Sullivan agrees that Blickling, though melancholy, has a very strong hold upon one. It is a sad, lonely, unloved house with a reproachful air. I dare say it will be burnt down before long.

Tuesday, 31st August

I got up at 7 and went to Polesden Lacey so as to be there when Druce's vans arrived. At last they are moving out the secondary furniture. I got back at 1 and went straight to the Ritz where I met Loelia Westminster. She was dressed in red, and limping from a sprained ankle. We went to the Dorchester in a taxi. She said that Lord Rothermere, with whom she had been staying, told her this morning that the troops had just invaded the mainland of Italy. Churchill would announce the fact in his broadcast tonight. As it happened Churchill made no mention of it, and his broadcast was empty verbiage and kowtowing to the Russians.

At Emerald's luncheon were Billy McCann, Mrs. Reggie Fellowes and Duff Cooper, who sloped in late. It was not a sparkling meal. Duff

Cooper hardly spoke. He was probably thinking of more important things. He did say that Brendan Bracken had made a mistake in revealing the story of Hess's flight at all, and particularly in giving it to the American press. I said it seemed so innocuous I wondered why we could not have been told as soon as it had happened. He said there was much more that Bracken had not revealed. He has a slightly foxy face. Emerald addresses him as 'Duffy darling.' She said to Mrs. Fellowes, 'Oh dear, no. He has no temper. I ought to know since I have lived with him intimately for so many months now.' Today Mrs. Fellowes was wearing a wide-brimmed black hat and did look handsome. She was very friendly, and said she too had been quite ill after Cecil's dinner. Was this meant to please? For it was Lord Sackville's venison liver, not Cecil's lobster and pigeon which made me ill.

I thought what a contrast my luncheon with Emerald at the Dorchester to my elevenses three hours previously with Hilda and Doris, the two maids, round the kitchen table at Polesden. I enjoyed the elevenses as much as the luncheon party.

Wednesday, 1st September

At an S.P.A.B. meeting I found a small attendance considering a matter of the first importance, whether or not to protest in the press against the night bombing of historic German cities. Maresco Pearse and Marshall Sisson were uncompromisingly in favour of protesting. Esher took the view that to do so would have no effect whatever; that the Government would not be the least deterred and many members of the public would be antagonized. I dare say he is right in saying that protest would be fruitless, nevertheless I am in favour of our making some gesture of disapproval of the indiscriminate bombing. I had come unprepared for such a discussion and thought the committee should have been warned in advance. After much talk it was decided that no letter of protest should be sent by the Society to the press, but that Esher should submit to the Secretary for Air a list to be prepared by Sisson of historic German towns with the recommendation that the Air Ministry might spare them as far as possible.

Thursday, 2nd September

Had a talk with Blaise Gillie and Anthony Wagner[188] at the Ministry of Planning. They warned me that the Trust must soon inform the Ministry before accepting restrictive covenants over land.

I met Eddy to discuss the Knole developments up to date. Eddy very

---

[188] Later Sir Anthony Wagner, Principal Garter King of Arms.

defeatist and suspicious of his father's motives. He left to dine with Sibyl Colefax.

Friday, 3rd September

Eddy told me that at Sibyl's dinner there were T. S. Eliot, Prof. Joad, Arthur Waley, Edith Sitwell, and Cyril Connolly. The pack of lions were so disconcerted by each other's presence that none of them spoke at all.

Tancred Borenius told me that Lydiard Tregoze, the Bolingbroke house, had been bought by the town of Swindon, which proposed to gut it, after removing all the contents; and that the Ministry of Works was unaware of what was afoot. Such things can still happen in England. Gerry Wellesley went many years ago to see this house, which was built by Colen Campbell. Getting no reply from the front door he went to the back. There at a large kitchen table presided over by the Dowager Lady Bolingbroke sat several strapping farm labourers. Amongst them was a youth, the present peer. The others were his elder brothers, born before his mother married their very old father, and so out of wedlock. They were all happily working on the estate in the employment of their youngest brother.

Saturday, 4th September

Bridget Parsons lunched with me. She was very sweet and disarming. She talked about the war, her hopes in 1939, her disillusionment today. She believed the Germans were happier under their regime than the British were under theirs. I agreed, because whereas the Germans were fighting to establish a creed, we were merely fighting to preserve the status quo.

Sunday, 5th September

I went to tea with old Logan Pearsall Smith whom I found in a black overcoat and black hat, sitting on a bench in the public garden opposite 11 St. Leonard's Terrace. As usual he talked a lot about Stuart, but said he could do without the brother, and next time he would tell Stuart frankly he would prefer him to come alone. He said 'doves' were beautiful, gentle and guileless people, inclined perhaps just a little to silliness. Lady Berwick was one. The last time she was in London he made a mistake in asking her to meet Raymond and Cyril, 'serpents' he called them, corrected himself and asked me what they were. 'Rattlesnakes,' I suggested, 'which are quite harmless creatures.'

He read me a letter from Shane Leslie describing Lady Leslie's death and funeral. We agreed there was something distasteful in Shane's account of the thousands of telegrams he had received from crowned heads, etc., of his placing his brother's grave cross from France in her coffin with a poem of his own addressed to her on her deathbed, and of his carrying his brother's sword instead of the crucifix at the head of the bier. There was something distasteful not so much in the actions as in the satisfaction he so evidently derived from dramatizing the funeral. Logan repeated the story of his practical joke played on Virginia Woolf, adding the sequel that he pretended to demand money from her. And he told how he wrote amorous letters to Lady Leslie in Lord Beaverbrook's name. He calls Stuart's social success a 'swimgloat', and a bore who comes to stay and won't leave, a 'gluebottom'. His last word of advice was, 'You may quote any of the scandalous things I have told you, but do not quote me as the author of them.'

Monday, 6th September

Went to Highfield, near Otford, Kent, at midday. This property of 250 acres belongs to Sir Herbert and Lady Cohen,[189] rich and very gentle Jews. They were very pathetic, for they have lost their two sons in the war and have no one to leave the property to. Unfortunately the house is an ugly villa built in 1885. I do not know how to help them.

After dinner I walked in the twilight to have a drink and chat with Geoffrey Houghton Brown. An armada of our bombers, bound on a Continental raid, passed overhead. It took three-quarters of an hour for them to pass. The roar they made was terrifying. People came out of their houses on to the pavement to gaze skywards. They were pleased and jubilant. As I watched the green lights in the sky twinkling the V signal I felt sad for the thousands of innocent lives the bombers were about to destroy. In Geoffrey's drawing-room the windows rattled with the vibration.

Wednesday, 8th September

Eardley and I went to the George, Southwark,[190] meaning to lunch, but the inn was so full and dirty that we came away after walking round it. Its general condition is poor indeed. It has suffered from raids and badly needs painting. Forsyth wants to paint it yellow, but I favour the dull chocolate which the Dickensian galleries always have been painted.

I went to Enfield to see Mr. Leggatt, the last of five brothers of the St. James's Street Leggatts. He was a courteous old gentleman of the old school. The object of my visit was to look at the room bought by him from Enfield Palace when the rest of the building was destroyed in the

---

[189] Sir Herbert Cohen, 2nd Bart. (1874–1968) married 1907 Hannah Mildred, daughter of Henry Behrens.
[190] Acquired by the National Trust 1937, it is the only galleried inn remaining in London.

1920s, and re-erected by him at his villa. The panelling is very rich and intricate. There is a large Elizabethan chimneypiece in one piece of stone. The ceiling is not the original one, for I compared it with the print of the room in C. J. Richardson's book.[191] I returned in the train with the nephew, a charming man. The Leggatts belong to a definable caste of Englishman: the highly respectable, highly respected gentleman dealer.

At 5.20 Raymond rang up Eardley in the office to report that Italy had surrendered unconditionally. At Brooks's it was on the tape and members were talking about it with great excitement. My first reaction was one of relief; my second one of anxiety lest worse fighting than ever against the Germans might take place in Italy. When I spoke to Harold Nicolson on the telephone he said what a relief it was that henceforth we, Britain, would no longer be under the sad necessity of destroying further Italian towns, whereas whatever future destruction there might be we could comfortably attribute to the Germans. I said this reflection was no comfort to me. I should feel no happier if the world's greatest architecture was wiped out by Germans, and not by Englishmen.

Friday, 10th September

Took the 9.10 from Liverpool Street to Cambridge, stopping at every station on the way. Was met at Cambridge and driven by the agent to Anglesey Abbey. On our arrival Lord Fairhaven was strutting in front of his porch, in too immaculate a blue suit, and watch in hand. He is a slightly absurd, vain man, egocentric, pontifical, and too much blessed with this world's goods. He is an enthusiastic amateur, yet ignorant of the arts he patronizes. Without waiting we drove straight off to Kirtling Tower, the far side of Newmarket. Lord Fairhaven and I were teed up in the back seat, he looking at his fair, plump hands, picking at his finger-nails and flicking invisible specks of fluff off his suit – on to mine. Having begun by adopting the grand manner, he gradually thawed, and by the end of the visit was friendly and communicative. But he speaks as one accustomed to exercising authority and receiving flattery, which I am constitutionally incapable of delivering.

Kirtling is beautiful and English. A wide moat encloses a large terraced layout, part of a larger garden now disappeared. A Perpendicular church like a cosy old hen peacefully nestles under trees, having hatched a clutch of grey tombstones. The North Chapel contains one particularly rich monument to an Elizabethan North: a heavy elaborate canopy carried by six columns entwined with vine leaves. We walked along the moat through an attractive wilderness under trees to the tower. It is a 1530 tall,

---

[191] *Studies from Old English Mansions*, 4 vols., 1841.

red brick gatehouse with four angle turrets. The great house to which it led was destroyed in 1801 and a lump of a house was tacked on to the gatehouse in 1872. It is of the wrong brick and has plate-glass windows. There is a vast copper beech just in front of the tower which should never have been planted there. Lord Fairhaven offers covenants over the tower and some 400 acres of surrounding land.

We returned to Anglesey for a late luncheon, I ravenous by then, having breakfasted at 7.30. Even so I did not eat as much as my host, who at forty-seven has a large paunch, a heavy jowl, pugnacious chin and a mottled complexion. He lives too well and smokes endless cigars. The nice agent, a gentleman from these parts (Lord Fairhaven is not from these parts) only spoke when spoken to. Relations between the two are very much those of gracious employer and subservient employee. After luncheon the agent was dismissed and we strolled down the Lode bank into the garden. The day was sweltering with sticky heat as though a storm were imminent. Lord Fairhaven kept wiping his brow surreptitiously as though greatly afraid to be seen sweating. I mopped unashamedly. The garden is well kept up in spite of the war. It has been laid out on eighteenth-century lines. Just before the war Fairhaven planted a long, straight avenue of limes, chestnuts and planes in four rows with caryatid statues by Coade of Lambeth at the far end. Unfortunately the vista does not begin from and so cannot be enjoyed from the house. In the garden are several urns signed by Scheemakers and L. Delvaux.

Anglesey Abbey is, like Packwood [House, Warwickshire], more a fake than not. The only genuine remains are the calefactorium, or crypt (used as the dining-room) dating from 1236, with thick, quadripartite ceiling of clunch, some medieval buttressed walls and the greatly restored 1600 south front. Lord Fairhaven put back the pointed gables and added the cresting to the porch. The interior is entirely his, opulent and pile-carpeted. But his new library with high coved ceiling, lined with books (first editions and un-cut) is fine. He has a desultory collection of good things that do not amount to a great collection. There is a corridor of Etty nudes in his private bedroom wing.

Exhausted, I had a bath and changed into a dark suit. Lord Fairhaven wore a dinner jacket. We had a four-course dinner of soup, lobster, chicken and savoury, and were waited upon by a butler. Lord Fairhaven is served first, before his guests, in the feudal manner which only the son of an oil magnate would adopt. Presumably the idea is that in the event of the food being poisoned the host will gallantly succumb and his instant death will be a warning to the rest of the table to abstain. Port and brandy followed.

Saturday, 11th September

We motored after breakfast to the north of the county to see Thorney. Lord Fairhaven is driven everywhere in a high-powered khaki Buick by a soldier, for he has something to do with the Red Cross. Thorney Abbey House is a sort of miniature Coleshill, but without a parapet. It is enchanting but now reduced to the status of a farmhouse. The magnificent staircase and most of the panelled rooms survive. At present the wainscote is all painted a uniform mustard. Lord Fairhaven offers covenants over this superb little house which stands opposite the two towers of the Abbey church.

Monday, 13th September

Last night, returning from Ashtead by train, there were, counting two babies, twenty-one souls (would indeed there had only been souls and no bodies) in my compartment.

Tuesday, 14th September

I lunched with poor Lady Cohen at the Greek restaurant run by the British Council at the corner of Grosvenor Square. She talked of Dr. Weizmann whom she admired, although she said neither she and her husband, nor the d'Avigdor-Goldsmids, nor the Rothschilds were Zionists. They regarded Zionism as quite impracticable. Tonight I went to Nancy Rodd's party at Boulestin's. All the old gang – Raymond Mortimer, Clarissa Churchill, Alice Harding, Gerald Berners, Stuart. I piloted Nancy to the tube station and left her, as it were, at the jaws of hell. I watched her slim, brisk figure descend into the bowels of darkness, and walked home to Chelsea. It took me well over an hour.

Wednesday, 15th September

Clare Sheridan dined with me at La Belle Meunière. Clare is older, but still beautiful in her big, rumbustious way. She is affectionate and sympathetic. But she has become very spooky and talks a great deal about her psychic experiences. She says she lives more in the 'other world' now than in this. She told me that the whole of her youth had been in pursuit of adventure, or rather pursuit of love. She had had affairs with [1st] Lord Birkenhead, who notwithstanding his intellect and beauty was fundamentally coarse, with Lenin, with Mustapha Kemal and with Mussolini. Throughout the last affair Mussolini behaved like a musical comedy joke figure. He was so portentous and self-opinionated that she could not prevent herself laughing at him out loud. Mussolini was a bounder as well as a cad. Clare said she had come to realize that breeding was what mattered ultimately in men and women. Yet she is still red at heart. She disapproves of her cousin Winston in spite of her admiration for him. Earlier this year she spent fifteen hours sculpturing his head while he lay in bed in the mornings as he does till midday, surrounded by telephones. She was surprised how off-hand Anthony Eden appeared to be with the Premier, in making lame excuses not to lunch or dine with him. One day an admiral was bidden to lunch with Mr. and Mrs. Churchill and [Sir] Stafford Cripps. The admiral sent a message that he had forgotten, when accepting the invitation, that he had an official luncheon elsewhere which he could not get out of. Churchill sent him back a message that unless his engagement was with the King, no other took precedence over his invitation. The admiral came to luncheon. Clare heard Churchill refer to Aneurin Bevan over the telephone to Eden as 'that son of a bitch'.

Friday, 17th September

Geoffrey Houghton Brown and I went to Glasgow by the day train. Only by jumping on to the in-coming train before it stopped on the platform was I able to get two seats in a first-class compartment. During the journey I read this month's *Horizon*, Elizabeth Bowen's *Dublin Childhood* and finished Turgenev's *House of Gentlefolk*. For luncheon Geoffrey provided a bottle of Algerian wine. Opposite us was a most beautiful woman with whom we made friends. She had a peach and white complexion, liquid grey-blue eyes, corn ripe hair and a Grecian nose. Geoffrey said it was a Roman nose, and then advised me to stop staring. We stayed the night at the Station Hotel.

Saturday, 18th September

We caught the 8.45 bus to Inverary. In Glasgow the weather was appropriately grey and misty with that familiar peaty smell wafted down from the hills. Loch Lomond was glassy calm and the water blue-grey like my lady's eyes of yesterday. This is my great-grandmother McFarlane's country and the beginning of the Highlands. When we reached the Pass the sun came out fitfully and spread a gold and purple patchwork on the hills. At Loch Fyne sun and sky and water were Mediterranean. As the bus turned a corner I had my first view of Inverary, a wide bay in the loch with little boats and large ships in the harbour, and a minute classical town in the background. Then I saw the gaunt, grey block of the castle, the two classical bridges and the romantic peaked hill with watch tower upon it. A man from the castle met us on the quay and wheeled our luggage on a trolley. We followed him through a gate, and to avoid the soldiery whose huts are in the park, along the drive and among the shrubs, we took a path through the desolate garden, and crossed a bridge over the moat straight into the great saloon.

The castle is built of an ugly stone, which turns grey in the sunlight and black in the rain. This is a pity, for all the old houses in the town are of a lighter, kindlier stone. The castle has been greatly spoilt by peaked dormer windows added in 1880, and unsightly chimneys stuck on turrets and steeples. Outside it is grim and forbidding like some hydropathic hotel. The bridge to the front door had a sloping shelter erected over it for the benefit of Queen Victoria. Geoffrey led me through the saloon into a library where the Duke of Argyll was writing. He was seated at a large table in the middle of the room, with a bronze replica of a Celtic cross and one lighted candle on it. He rose and was very welcoming. He is obviously fond of Geoffrey.

He is a short old man with white hair and a smooth white face, for he seldom if ever has to shave. He has handsome blue eyes. He has a woman's voice, very eunuchy. Lady Victor Paget described him to Jamesey as an elderly hermaphrodite. He was wearing an old Harris tweed, deer-red jacket, with wide buttoned revers up the sleeves, an immensely old tartan kilt, old blue woollen stockings (revealing white knobbly knees), dirk, sporran, and most surprising of all, shoes à l'espadrille. He conducted us up a long, stone staircase with plain iron balusters curved for crinolines, and threadbare carpet. The central hall, exceedingly high, reaches to the roof of the central tower. High though it is, it always retains a strong smell of lodging-house cooking. Windows are never opened, and no wonder, for the castle is bitterly cold in September without fires. My small bedroom is just over the front door. It has double doors, with a moth-eaten, red rep curtain over the inner one. On the blue and white wall-paper hang a large framed photograph of the widowed Queen Victoria (looking like Robert Byron) at the time of the first Jubilee, a large oil of an eighteenth-century duke in a beautiful rococo frame, and a foxed print of the Porteous Riots. The Victorian iron bedstead has a red plush covered canopy. The wash-stand, dressing-table and clothes cupboard are solid Victorian mahogany pieces. A fire is actually burning in the grate – rather feebly. There is a lovely view from my window (which has not been cleaned for years) of the watch tower hill and a corner of the loch.

We had a delicious luncheon of mackerel, and grouse, helping ourselves from the sideboard. The duke is very voluble and has an insatiable appetite for gossip, as well as food. Conversation revolves round people and their relationships. After luncheon he put on a Glengarry green with age, and set off to the hospital in the park with some French newspapers for wounded French Canadian troops. A soldier on guard stopped us going up the long ride. 'What's this? I can go where I like. I am the duke,' came from a high-pitched, slightly hysterical voice. From the hospital Geoffrey and I went on to the little eighteenth-century fishing lodge by the first fall, looking for salmon. I saw one leaping, but the wrong way, not upstream but down. We continued up the burn, the Aray I presume, crossed over a bridge where I pointed out a rock in midstream, like a surrealist sculpture of a torso with one buttock incomplete, and bitten away. We tested each other on the trees we passed. I failed over a sycamore and a rowan. We found the eighteenth-century pigeon house which is at the end of the vista.

Meals here are excellent in that solid Scotch way I love – porridge, bannocks, scones, plum cakes and game. The duke prattles as ceaselessly as the Aray flows over the stones. Sometimes he is very entertaining; sometimes he is boring, and one does not listen. It makes no difference to him. He is a recognized authority on all church ritual, and a scholar of medieval liturgy, hagiology and Saxon coins. He is eccentric. He will rush without warning out of the room to play a bar or two of a Gregorian chant on a harmonium, or to play on a gong, or a French horn. He also has a cuckoo whistle which he likes to blow in the woods in order to bewilder the soldiers. He takes the keenest interest in the soldiers, both officers and men, learns their names and where they come from, and the names of their diocese and bishop. The great advantage of this place is that after meals the duke disappears, and we are left to read, write, walk out of doors, or roam round the house.

After tea we looked at the rooms on the ground floor. Great bushes of laurel and ungainly spruce trees have been allowed to grow close to the house, with the result that the magnificent views from all sides are shut out. Geoffrey once suggested their being felled, but the duke would not hear of it. It is true that today they serve as screens against the myriad Nissen huts. In the lower part of the hall are two ugly fireplaces. Over them and indeed all the way up the walls practically to the roof are ranged archaic weapons, guns, rifles, pistols, spears and daggers, in giant Catherine wheel patterns. Elks' horns are interspersed. In the blank spaces are numerous family portraits. On one chimneypiece stands a bronze equestrian effigy of Richard Coeur de Lion by Princess Louise, 'my aunt'.[192] The staterooms on this floor contain some splendid eighteenth-century furniture and on the rose damask walls of the saloon portraits by Gainsborough, Cotes and Batoni, hung higgledy-piggledy. Amongst these things is the most astonishing bric-à-brac, including a forest of framed photographs collected by 'my aunt'.

Sunday, 19th September

The duke trotted off to the Anglo-Catholic church which he has built at enormous expense in the town. We were left with a fine choice of

---

[192] H.R.H. Princess Louise, 4th daughter of Queen Victoria, married 1871 9th Duke of Argyll.

breakfast food, porridge, boiled eggs, sausages, oatcakes and honey. I ate everything. Then spent the morning looking through the books in the library in which we eat. The library is very pretty, and the ironwork gallery was designed by Uncle Lorne, the princess's husband. The design incorporates a galleon, the chequer arms of the Campbells and ducal coronet over all. Among the innumerable books in the library and throughout the house, even piled up in heaps on chairs, I have found none that I want to read. There are books on Celtic brasses and crosses, on lepidoptera, on ecclesiology, on Campbells, on numismatism, but nothing on art, and nothing on literature.

Geoffrey and I walked down the road after luncheon, along the Loch and back through the woods. It was a grey day. He does not think much of the scenery. I think Inverary one of the loveliest places in the United Kingdom.

Monday, 20th September

The first thing I was aware of this morning was the sound of bagpipes. At first I thought they were being played out of doors. But no, the sound came closer and soon reached my bedroom door. It was the duke's piper in the gallery. He does this every morning except Sunday at 8.30 to wake the duke up. I went down the passage and talked to him. He said it was a dirty day. At 9.15 there was a different sound: this time the duke playing a French horn very badly. After breakfast I worked at an article and Geoffrey at the prophecies of Nostradamus. We were interrupted by the duke skipping in and out of the room to fetch and show us Victorian photograph albums of the royal families of Europe, including several of the Queen and her children in deep mourning clustered round a white pedestalled bust of the Prince Consort, whose neck was garlanded with a wreath.

After luncheon – I am eating far too much here – Geoffrey and I walked to the top of the watch tower hill. It was a desperately showery day with deep blue skies between the clouds. There is a cold east wind which makes sitting indoors without a fire uncomfortable. We set forth with sticks, crossing the bridge over the Aray. This is Frew's bridge. The duke told us that when he stayed here as a boy the strangest procession used to take place from the house to the bridge every morning after breakfast. There might be twenty male guests. Over each a footman carried an umbrella. They marched to a spacious privy under the bridge, where they sat facing each other ten in a row. When the last man had finished the platoon marched back two by two to the house, each with his footman and umbrella.

We tried to follow the track which the Queen took in her pony carriage, but lost it. The view from the watch tower is very fine. The great castle thrusts shadows like bulwarks towards us. Boats are dotting the loch for miles, invasion barges, and gondola-shaped vessels with odd prows. The town is tiny from here and I wondered how any enemy aeroplanes could possibly aim at so pin-head a target.

Conversation about people is endless, and at times exhausting. 'Who was his mother? Let me see. He married one of those Rutland women. She capered about with that apish fellow – you know quite well who I mean – that fellow Taplow. That's it. She was quite mad, Beatrice Taplow. She used to climb trees like a baboon, and one day she dropped a coconut on Peter Coats.' 'Peter Coats?' I asked incredulously. 'Yes, he was the brother of old Podgy Glentanar. I'm talking of an earlier generation,' he said snappishly, and on he went. Intelligent conversation is consequently quite impossible. Geoffrey says it is worse than he ever remembers; and besides, the duke gets everything wrong.

Tuesday, 21st September

A beautiful blue and purple day. This afternoon Geoffrey and I walked up the loch, along the road we came by in the bus, to Dundarave Castle, four miles away. There was much army traffic on the road which was a disturbance. It was otherwise a tranquil walk through the chequered shade of trees. Having reached the castle we sat on a rock over a smelly beach looking towards Inverary. Dundarave Castle is compact, medieval and very faithfully restored, so faithfully that the old window openings have been retained; and they are minute and must be disagreeable to live behind. The granite of which it is built is brown, unlike the horrid black stone of our castle. Here the grass grows right up to the walls and there are no flower beds. There is no isolation of dwelling from the wild country, no timid, artificial barrier. The castle is rented by Lord Weir.[193]

At tea the duke talked of fairies, in whom he implicitly believes, as do all the people here. He described them as the spirits of a race of men who ages ago lived in earth mounds, which are what they frequent. They are usually little green things that peer at you from behind trees, as squirrels do, and disappear into the earth. The duke has visited numerous fairy haunts in Argyll. So has his sister, Lady Elspeth [Campbell], who at dinner one night announced with solemnity, 'The fairies are out in their sieves tonight.' 'Crossing over to Ireland no doubt,' her brother replied. 'We are not good enough for them in Scotland. Why! last year at Tipperary there were so many of them that they caused a traffic block.' In the middle of tea a young man, son of one of the duke's crofters on Iona, and now a lieutenant in the navy, called, uninvited. The duke gave him tea and with

---

[193] 1st Viscount Weir (1877–1959), industrialist and civil servant. Descended from Robert Burns.

the greatest friendliness and interest asked after him, his family and relations, remembering each one by name and occupation. There is no doubt the old feudal, clan feeling is still very strong.

Wednesday, 22nd September

It is impossible to judge how many servants there are in this house. Certainly the moment one leaves one's room, the ashtrays have been emptied and one's things straightened. Yet the house is a shambles, and extremely dusty. Although one's shoes are taken away they are never cleaned properly. It is far colder here than in the south, although less raw. I am always sleepy. Breakfast is not till 9.30, yet by 9.30 p.m. I am so tired and yawning that I can barely keep awake till 10.30 when punctually we go to bed.

I was so exhausted by my walk yesterday that today the fronts of my legs ached. Geoffrey and I ambled painfully to the town to post letters. There have been grand military exercises and just as we had settled in the saloon the duke announced that Sir Bernard Paget, Commander-in-Chief, General MacNaughton, the Canadian G.O.C., and his cousin Sir Ralph Glyn, were about to call. Presently they did so, and Geoffrey and I fled upstairs. At 5 we thought they had gone, and slipped into the library for some tea. The duke came in to find us eating, disappeared to look for more cups and saucers, so Geoffrey and I fled again. Afterwards I was sorry not to have seen MacNaughton, who told the duke that his grandfather came from Argyllshire in the 1850s and had been a crofter of his.

Geoffrey and I looked through two heavy volumes of plans and elevations midway on the staircase, hoping to find the name of the original architect of the castle. We discovered plans dated 1746 signed by Roger Morris, and another of the 1770s signed by William Mylne.

Friday, 24th September

Geoffrey and I walked along the Lochgilphead road, sat on a bridge and talked. On our return the sun burst upon a field of golden stooks right in front of us, swept across the indigo loch, and ran up a gentle mountain the other side, leaving wide footsteps of light and shade.

Reading *The Times* today I told the duke that a Nicolaes Maes portrait of the 9th Earl of Argyll was on exhibition at the Guildhall among the late Lord Wakefield's collection. He expressed surprise because, he said, he had got it. He told me to go into the turret room next to the library we were then in, and look at it. What I saw was a Dirk Maes of the 1st Duke over the fireplace. It is a small picture with glowing colours in the drapery, and the face very clearly drawn. There are two other Dirk Maeses here, both of early dukes I think, one in the saloon, the other in the great hall. This duke knows absolutely nothing about his pictures or indeed what he has got. He has a superb collection of family portraits. The full-length Cotes of the Gunning Duchess in a green dress is stupendous; the beauty of her Irish complexion and white bosom was renowned. The Gainsborough of Marshal Wade has at some time been enlarged to make it fit the huge frame.

Saturday, 25th September

Geoffrey and I left Inverary by the 10.15 bus for Glasgow. After luncheon we walked from the station to the Art Gallery through several delightful early nineteenth-century squares and crescents in the one-time residential area. What are now offices and lodgings were once the town houses of the rich merchants, like my forebears the White-Thomsons. Perhaps I passed their town house. There are a number of fine churches in the neo-Greek, and neo-Egyptian styles. The 'gloomth' of the blackened freestone is not without its charm. In fact I learnt for the first time that architecturally Glasgow is by no means to be despised. There is a distinctive character in the uniformity of the streets which has not been tampered with. The art gallery is early twentieth century. I find it hideous. All the pictures are now put away.

Sunday, 26th September

I left Glasgow this morning for Euston, parting with Geoffrey who went through to Edinburgh. He is a kind, patient and humorous travelling companion, easy-going and always good tempered. Just what one, who lacks all these qualities, most needs.

Wednesday, 29th September

The solicitor to the Wingfield-Digby family came to see Matheson and me about the future of Sherborne Castle in Dorset. Matheson suggested that I should visit Sherborne. He warned me that Colonel Wingfield-Digby detested the arts and despised everyone who did not kill foxes and pheasants to the exclusion of all other recreations. His advice that I should have to control my enthusiasms was not lost on me.

I went to tea with Emerald Cunard before she left for Victor Cazalet's[194] memorial concert. She had a bad cold, and was wearing a black velvet dress which swathed her throat. It was very becoming. Emerald said Mrs. Wellington Koo had complained to her that she did

[194]Victor Cazalet (1896–1943), M.P. Killed with General Sikorsky, Prime Minister of Polish Government and Commander-in-Chief of Polish Army, in a mysterious aeroplane crash.

not like London because the English men were all so ugly. I asked, 'What did you reply to that?' 'I said, "Well, that is strange, Mrs. Koo, for to me all Chinamen look exactly the same. They all have flat faces, no noses, and wear round horn-rimmed spectacles."' Emerald complained that Lady Wavell never speaks at meals to anyone. She says not one word. Emerald asked me where on earth I had been all these past weeks. When I told her I had been staying at Inverary, she said she had no idea I was a relation of the duke. I said I wasn't. She said there could be no other possible reason for staying with him.

Friday, 1st October

On stepping out of the train on Dorking platform I saw a couple descend from the next compartment. He was an officer, rather round-shouldered, his face covered with hard pustules. She was wearing an untidy black coat and skirt, covered with hairs and dandruff, her sharp face badly rouged. I passed by them, and the man said, 'Hullo, Jim!' He was Basil Dufferin.[195] I was appalled by the change in his appearance. After two minutes conversation the endearing gentleness of his character was again apparent to me.

A taxi motored me to Wotton House where I lunched and spent the afternoon. Today it belongs to a John Evelyn just as it belonged to the diarist John Evelyn in the seventeenth century. It is a long, rambling, untidy house. The nucleus of it is Jacobean, and a few rich doorways of that period survive upstairs. But the present Evelyn's grandfather spoilt the house in every conceivable way in the 1870s. In the hideous, Ruskin-style library are many rare books, including some 200 of Evelyn's own; also royal seals, miniatures and nineteenth-century busts. There are innumerable family portraits, including three of John Evelyn, of which the Kneller is the most remarkable. There is a table carved by Grinling Gibbons, whom Evelyn discovered, and an Italian ebony cabinet in which Evelyn's manuscript diaries were found. The army have occupied most of the house during the war. They allowed a fire to blacken the classical doorcases, walls and ceiling of the dining-room. Could Evelyn have called in Wren to design this room? The garden, now a wilderness, has a mound cut into terraces by Evelyn, and below it a temple on Doric columns, which he built. All the trees are magnificent, and the beeches are said to have been planted by him.

The present Evelyn is an odd fish. He is only a little older than me, stoops and is quite bald. He seems permanently distracted, does not look

---

[195] 4th Marquess of Dufferin and Ava (1909–45), a contemporary at preparatory school, Eton and Oxford. Killed on active service in Burma.

you in the face, but looks at nothing in particular over his shoulder. He is an eccentric, shy, clever and presumably unhappy man.

Saturday, 2nd October

Geoffrey and I went to the Guildhall to see Lord Wakefield's pictures, and in particular the Nicolaes Maes of the 9th Earl of Argyll. It closely resembled the three Dirk Maeses at Inverary, being of the same size. The face is carefully drawn and the clothes are painted in the same gorgeous crimsons and greens. We agreed that the Guildhall is vastly improved by having lost its roof. The fakery that remains looks more convincing, blackened as it is with smoke. We agreed too that the setting for the statues was totally wrong, for they need sharp lighting which they don't get here. We walked to St. Mary Lothbury. Why did Wren not bother to make the inside east end wall straight? A disappointing church. We tried to enter St. Stephen Walbrook, and could not. St. Augustine Watling Street is burnt out but the pretty tower is left. I hope the ugly building to the west of it will disappear with the remains of the church. The Perpendicular ceiling and pendentives of St. Mary Aldermary are of plaster. It has a crooked east end wall likewise. We gave first prize for spires to St. Mary-le-Bow, second to St. Stephen, and third to St. Vedast Foster Lane.

In St. Paul's Geoffrey pointed out what I had not noticed before, that the heavy iron railings on the nave cornice over-accentuate the depth of the cornice out of all proportion to the nave it serves. It thus seemingly narrows the nave to the detriment of the whole interior. From below the rails look well wrought, but I suppose Wren never intended them to be there. Whereas the Thornhill dome is delightful, the spandrel paintings are atrocious. Who on earth allowed them to be done, and when?

Sunday, 3rd October

I lunched with Dame Una. She said Jamesey was over-sensitive about his new book, *West Indian Summer*. He dreaded lest the reviews might not be favourable enough. He has just sent me an inscribed copy. Rose Macaulay thinks it brilliant. I hope it is. The Pope-Hennessy family are very self-protective, and each exalts the work of the other. The Dame read me extracts from a Penguin book, just out, by H. G. Wells, in which he says this war is waged between democrats and the Catholic Church; that no Englishman who is a true Papist can be in favour of the Allies, but must be a quisling in disguise; and that the Pope, who is an ignoramus and other pejorative things besides, is in league with the Nazis. The man must be a lunatic.

I met Geoffrey at the gate of Chiswick House. To our surprise we found the place in better shape than we had expected. The garden, though overrun with children, is quite well kept up. True, the roof of the temple, 'the first essay of his lordship's happy invention', is in a bad state. The house requires repointing, replastering and repainting. A great temporary garage for the firemen's engine has been erected in front of the main portico which is supported by iron girders. We could not get inside. I think the chimneys on the Palladian core spoil the house and must have looked worse before the Wyatt wings were added.

I dined at Emerald's. I appreciate her more and more. Bridget [Lady Victor] Paget was sitting next to me. She kept smiling in her gracious, disarming, sphinx-like way, and remaining silent. She drank tumblers of neat whisky when the red wine gave out, and relapsed into a controlled stupor. Emerald complained how the Duchess of Portland has been left a mere £2,500 a year to spend after being accustomed to £150,000 a year. She said it was scandalous of the late duke, and appealed to Bridget, who mumbled that she found it very difficult and tiring to express her feelings on the subject. Lady Juliet Duff told a story about her grandmother Lady Herbert of Lea, whose impassioned correspondence with Cardinal Vaughan has been published by Shane Leslie. Lady Herbert went to confess to her favourite priest. There was a queue waiting on its knees at the confessional. She spied a friend at the head of the queue, went up to her and said, 'I can't wait. Just tell Father X that it was the same as last time.' When the party broke up, Jamesey and I stayed behind to talk to Emerald. She spoke of love and read a passage on the non-reciprocity of it by E. M. Forster. She expressed horror at the soldiers having girls against walls in the dark streets. 'I am told they do these things. Whatever for?' she asked.

Monday, 4th October

At luncheon at the Churchill Club canteen I sat with Nancy, Sibyl Colefax and Mrs. Gladwyn Jebb. They were all full of the news of Gerry Wellesley having succeeded to the dukedom of Wellington. Sibyl asked should she congratulate him. 'Gracious no,' Nancy shrieked, 'you should condole.' 'What! for becoming a duke?' 'For the death of his nephew,' we suggested.

Tuesday, 5th October

At Liverpool I booked a room at the Adelphi, a mammoth, modern hotel entirely lit by artificial light. An old gentleman, Mr. George Leather, one of the Speke Hall trustees, gave me luncheon. He spoke in glowing terms of Lord Woolton, whose business is in Liverpool. From the town hall we were motored by the City Engineer's representative and several other gentlemen of that ilk to Speke.

The object of this visit was for me to see the heirlooms which the trustees offer to make over to us with the house. I made a note of every piece; and a gruesome lot they were, mostly consisting of made-up Charles II chairs with cut velvet stuffed seats and backs, and four-poster beds made out of chests and any bit of oak, ancient or mid-nineteenth century. As for the great embattled chimneypiece in the great hall, I am inclined, in spite of *Country Life*, to date it from the early 1800s, since it is made of plaster. I cannot believe it to be Jacobean.

A neighbouring aerodrome has made the trustees fell the trees on the garden side. The result is a magnificent open view of the Mersey and the Welsh mountains beyond.

Before dark I walked to the Protestant cathedral. It was shut. The outline of the great tower is from a distance impressive. On close inspection the detail of the carving is unconvincing, and repetitive. It is too much a reproduction of the medieval. The nave has yet to be built. The site is very well chosen. The Woolton stone of the tower, being still clean, has a fresh butter surface, whereas on older buildings this stone has become blackened and harsh.

Wednesday, 6th October

I had a great shock at breakfast in reading that poor Diana Worthington, having walked out of Weston [Underwood, Olney] early yesterday morning, is assumed to have drowned herself in the Ouse. She left letters to the effect that she was going on a long journey. Her coat was found on the river bank, and her handkerchief in the river. They have dragged the river, so far without success. She wrote so sweetly asking me to stay with her and recuperate after my illness, and I nearly went. Now I wish I had. When she last came here in May she struck me as almost manic, and not quite rational. How I wish I had talked to her then about what I knew was on her mind, namely Greville having left her. But I thought I did not know her well enough, and refrained. One should never refrain from anything. How this sort of thing hurts!

I came back from Liverpool particularly early to dine with the Princesse de Polignac. But she had rung up, putting off the dinner because Clarissa Churchill was ill.

Friday, 8th October

I went to see Anne in the evening. When I arrived at her flat she was alone, running about in her chemise, pretending as she skipped about to be coy and hiding herself behind an old towel. She can be funnier than anybody I know, and she made me laugh so much that I nearly 'did myself a mischief', as my Aunt Dorothy puts it.

Saturday, 9th October

Stuart dined with me at Brooks's. It was a disastrous evening. The moral of it is that there are no limits beyond which the idiocy of adults will not go. At dinner we argued, I cannot even remember over what. I was certainly difficult and disagreeable about some friends of his. He contradicted me. I contradicted him. He said I always snubbed him, and was ruder to him than anyone he knew; and I said outrageous and insulting things to him, just for fun. I said, 'If they are funny, why don't you laugh?' He said, 'They're not funny. They make me want to cry they're so un-funny.' 'But you never do cry,' I said, 'so they must be funny.' 'They're *not* funny,' he almost shouted. 'Remember where you are,' I said. 'We are in the coffee-room.' 'There you go again – correcting, finding fault, patronising.' There was a seething silence of several minutes duration. He looked very put out, and ate nothing. Then he said, 'I am too tired to argue any more.' (How often have I not heard my parents say this?) And he added, 'You had better go.' '*I* had better go?' I asked. 'But it's my club we're in.' 'Oh, so it is,' he said, rising from his chair. 'No, no,' I said, 'I will go all the same.' I paid the bill and went to fetch my coat and umbrella. I said, 'I am off now, and I do not intend that we shall meet again. We have nothing in common'. He said, 'Good night!' I said, 'It's goodbye,' and left. I walked home.

Monday, 11th October

I lunched with Clifford Smith at the Athenaeum. I guessed the poor old man really wanted to find out whether, as the result of the announcement in the press of Knole coming to the Trust, there would be any inventory-making for him. He kept nosing around the subject without getting to the point. So to put him out of his misery I had to tell him – no. I was sorry, and felt I had had no right to take a meal off him, without any return. Anyway I gave him a lift in the National Trust car on my way to a job. Coping with the traffic I paid little attention to what he was saying in his hesitant, halting speech. When we were approaching Hyde Park Corner I heard him mumble, 'Jim, will you, um, er, drop the Smith.' So I drew up along the pavement, leant across and opened the far side door for him. But instead of getting out he said, 'What, um, er, has happened?' I said, 'I thought you wanted to get out here, Mr. Clifford Smith.' He said rather sadly, 'I wanted you to drop the Mr. and to call me Clifford.' We proceeded to Kensington High Street.

This evening I received a most grateful and charming letter from Vita, thanking me for having warned her in advance of the impending Knole announcement. I know how miserable she must be feeling about it. I also had a letter from Eddy, who clearly does not mind.

Q. and I sat on her sofa. She began: 'Now you are unhappy. What is it? You have quarrelled with Stuart, and it is your fault, I know.' How did she know? She has never met him. Really the intuition of women is uncanny. She gave me much advice, telling me quite severely that I must make it up with him. 'You simply can't lose a good friend for an idiotic reason,' and so forth. We found a cab and she insisted on coming with me to Cheyne Walk. In the cab she took my hands and kissed me over and over again. I lit a fire in my room. We turned the lights out, and sat on the window seat looking at the moon on the river.

Tuesday, 12th October

At 8.20 I telephoned Q., who I knew would still be in bed. She answered the telephone. I said, 'It's me, Q.' 'Is it you, Terry?' she said in a voice of unconcealed excitement. 'No,' I answered, and put the receiver down gently.

I dined with Patrick Kinross at his house, the first time for over three years, since I used to come up from Hobbs Barracks in the summer evenings of 1940. Lady Kinross [his mother] was with him, looking silvery and radiantly good. Yes, Patrick has changed a little, and not only physically. He is bigger than heretofore, and he speaks with a sort of new found inner conviction. He is philosophic about life, holds definite views, is confident and sure of himself. We argued long about war and peace, he disagreeing with my pacific views, and adopting the realistic and conservative attitude on post-war policy and the ultimate treatment of Germany, the squeeze-her-till-the-pips-squeak attitude.

Thursday, 14th October

Went to Koestner's to look at the Nicolaes Maes there of a young prince – of Orange I think. Wrote and told the Duke of Argyll that his Dirk Maeses were probably Nicolaes Maeses.

In the afternoon to Ashford, Middlesex. I was met at the station by a young man in corduroys, with a flaming shock of hair and a red beard. He told me he was an artist and chief of the Echelford Society for protecting amenities in this rather dank part of the world. He took me to Ashford Lodge, over which he wants the Trust to hold a covenant. I had to tell him it was no good. The house has a late Georgian aspect but is of very little merit. He took it so well and was not at all hurt. 'Righty-ho!' he said bravely. We parted friends.

Friday, 15th October

The wretched National Trust car would not start again. The battery was dead. So I took a train to Tunbridge Wells, and a bus to Wadhurst. I was

not feeling very grand because last night Pierre gave me my last whop-
ping injection. Hot and cold by turns I walked, wearing my black overcoat down the long, straggly, dull village street to The Gatehouse. For
some reason I expected the owner to be a man, having addressed it as
such. It was on the contrary an old woman in a mackintosh. I have never
been more astonished by such squalid living. The house is a genuine early
Tudor – say late fifteenth-century – yeoman's dwelling, typical of this
region. It is of half-timber, with sloping roof, over-hanging eaves and a
central brick chimney stack. There is nothing fake about it. But the condition! It has no services, no water, no drains, no light. The old creature
has no domestic help, and obviously no money. For these deprivations I
am indeed sorry for her. But the dust, dirt and junk littering every square
inch of space inside were indescribable. Filthy saucepans, opened and
half-emptied tins of sardines, jam and baked beans, and worse still, piles
of snotty grey handkerchiefs and other unmentionable rags littered the
tables and chairs of the living-room. The garden shrubs have got so out
of control that they obliterate the little light which lattice panes allow at
the best of times. None of the windows open. The stench was asphyxi-
ating. The old dame gave me a cold luncheon of salmon, lettuce and
cheese, not off plates, but out of tins. I hardly dared swallow a mouthfill,
and when her back was turned, shoved what I could out of my tin into
a handkerchief, which I stuffed into my trouser pocket. Had I seen the
kitchen before luncheon I would not even have eaten one mouthful.
After this terrible meal she insisted upon my looking at the kingpost
upstairs. Now if there is one thing which bores me it is a kingpost.
However, obediently I trudged up the creaking staircase. But when I
reached the top landing I dared not proceed for fear of putting a foot
through the crazy floor boards and the ceiling of the downstairs sitting-
room. When I turned back she knew that I hadn't seen the damned kingpost, and was very hoity-toity. She then told me that she wished the Trust
after her death to allow the Women Farmers and Gardeners Association
to have the use of the house as their rest home. By which time the whole
rickety old dump will have collapsed in a heap. I could not be encouraging, and I suppose I showed my boredom with her ceaseless rattle about
the importance and antiquity and rarity of the house. I was not well, and
I did not respond as dutifully and enthusiastically as is my wont to offers
which I know from the first glance are unacceptable.

When I left her on the high road she said, 'I don't think much of the
National Trust.' 'You mean', I replied, 'that you don't think much of me,
I'm afraid.' 'You have done nothing but sniff and crab the place,' she said,
giving me a stiff handshake, holding her arm high up in that injured
manner peculiar to the very sensitive poor. I felt a little abashed, a little

ashamed and sorry that I had not been more forthcoming. But I did not feel guilty of her accusation. It was just not true that I had crabbed. I may have sniffed, for I am beginning a cold. I had merely tried, possibly a little too forcefully, to check her extravagant enthusiasms with which she relentlessly bombarded me. With the exception of that odious old gentleman, Colonel Pemberton of Pyrland Hall, she is, I think, the first owner with whom I have failed to make friends.

Saturday, 16th October

A Georgian Group committee meeting this morning. I sat next to Dame Una and Trystan Edwards,[196] who fascinated me with the number of objects tied to his person by black strings; fountain-pens, spectacles, magnifying glasses, etc. It was a good meeting and the professor in the chair dealt well with the items. I brought up several: Claremont – the park advertised for building plots: Chiswick – Lord Burlington's little temple in poor condition: 37 Portland Place – the beautiful central façade of the last intact terrace being demolished now: Dropmore – the estate bought by speculative builders. When I got home for tea Jamesey telephoned proposing a night of adventure. I was thrilled and for once our enthusiasms coincided. We drank first at the Ritz, then the Gargoyle, dined at the White Tower and visited disreputable pubs in that area. The only person we met was Guy Burgess, drunk and truculent, and we soon shook him off. We both agreed that depravity was a bore, and that on this account alone the evening would have been worth while as a gentle reminder – in the hideous sweaty faces, the human stench, the risk of beer being spilt upon one's best suit, of one's pocket being picked, and ten to one the likelihood of meeting no one rewarding. We returned to the Gargoyle and joined a table of Brian Howard,[197] that affected, paradoxical figure of the twenties, and two other dreary queens. As I walked home about midnight from South Kensington station I ruminated upon the loneliness of my lot.

Sunday, 17th October

I walked to the Ladies' Carlton Club, met Puss Milnes-Gaskell and taxied to the Ritz with her. We were joined by Douglas Woodruff and Blanche Lloyd. While we were ordering luncheon Stuart and Lady Islington sat down at the table next to ours, Stuart with his back to mine, our chairs practically touching. Electric sparks of indignation must have been visible to others in the space of inches between us. Neither of us made the

---

[196] Trystan Edwards (1884–1973), architect, planner and writer.
[197] Well-known aesthete at Eton and Oxford in the twenties.

slightest sign of recognition. Blanche Lloyd is no longer handsome, is thinner and older. Today she had an unscrubbed look. She was affectionate but distrait. She wanted me to go to Clouds Hill for a weekend. But without George Lloyd I don't think I could face it. Douglas Woodruff was far more genial than last time, but still wore that expression of intellectual complacency. He was cross with the Vatican for not giving us an archbishop; and said the usual policy was to hold a successor up the sleeve when the actual holder of that dignity was an old man. There should not be a long interregnum. We went on to the Coliseum for a variety show in aid of the Lord Lloyd Memorial Prize for the Navy League. Anything less suitable for this particular purpose could hardly be conceived. The jokes were bawdy beyond words. Sandwiched as I was between the two po-faced ladies-in-waiting I did not dare laugh when a joke was funny, which was seldom.

To my surprise Stuart telephoned, proffering an olive branch. So we dined at Brooks's. He made absolutely no reference to our last meeting and behaved as though there had been no row. In fact we behaved like two old club members finding themselves next to each other at the same table. We were both bored. He said he might soon be going abroad. I said what a good idea that was. I said I might be going to Italy (there is little likelihood, worst luck). He said what a good idea that was. By 9.15 we could bear the cold and gloom of the club no longer. Outside it was pouring with rain. We put scarves and handkerchiefs on our heads and ran to the Green Park tube station. There I said 'Would you like to come home for a drink?' He said, 'How can I in this rain?' So I said not a word and dived into my train.

Monday, 18th October

All today I walked about with a hollow in my chest where my heart once was. I kept singing sadly to myself, 'I cares for nobody, no, not I, and nobody cares for me.'

But I had a busy, not unsuccessful day. I had asked Paul Methuen and Colin Agnew to lunch. Both accepted but only Paul came. He was very charming and we talked about Corsham's future. We have done this for years now ever since I first worked for the Trust. He says his brother is at last coming round to the idea. Talking of Lydiard Tregoze, he said none of us must upset the hyper-socially sensitive Mayor of Swindon, who is an excellent fellow and an engine driver. Professor Richardson and Sir Charles Peers[198] joined us over coffee. Paul was vastly entertained by the

---

[198] Sir Charles Peers (1868–1952), antiquary and editor of *Victoria County Histories 1903* and Inspector of Ancient Monuments.

professor. Peers told me that the neo-Greek, unlike the neo-Roman style, was not suited to this climate for it depended essentially upon a clear atmosphere, sharp light and shadow. He said Nash would always hold his own in the hierarchy of British architects, although he borrowed designs for façades from other architects, stuck the façades up anyhow and used the shoddiest lath and plaster and patent cements.

Eardley and I went to Mr. Lloyd-Johnes (who gave us Dolaucothi) at his flat in Holland Park, to see his pictures and furniture. They include much fine stuff, notably interesting family portraits, and some Chippendale chairs with original tapestried seats. I made a list of what he stipulates shall return to Dolaucothi after his time. He is a wicked old fox determined to diddle his family at all costs, and is a de-frocked clergyman on what accoumt I do not know.

Saturday, 23rd October

Patrick Kinross lunched. He was much more like his old self. He admitted that at first he found it difficult to reconcile himself to the un-war minded lives of his friends in London. They seemed unaware of and unconcerned with what was happening overseas. Furthermore, having accustomed himself to leading a picnic sort of life for so long he slightly disapproved of the conventional, pre-war way of living here. But he is already getting over these inhibitions. They are quite understandable. He still misses the mixture of seriousness and fun of his friends in the desert. He says that in spite of their deprivations they are happier than people here who have their comforts; and that in the 8th Army there is much wholesome buggery.

I slipped away from a tea party at the Kennets when charades started, and went to Mérode Guevara's flat in Athenaeum Court. She talked a lot about Russia and communism. She shouts one down like everyone else these days. She said she was trying to like England and Englishmen again without succeeding. Stuart says she is stupid and dull. James says, 'Let's face it, she's a moron.' Emerald says she is brilliant. I don't know what to think.

I called for Emerald and escorted her to dinner at the Argentine Embassy. I like the tall, dark and cultivated ambassador. There were only four of us, the fourth being his younger daughter, who has fair hair scooped up in a frizz on top as they all have it now, and a pretty pouting mouth. Emerald talked of the Duke of Alba's love affairs that last long and always come to nought. I said but all love affairs come to nought, and not all last long. She then described her recent visit to 10 Downing Street. Mr. Churchill candidly admitted that he was enjoying the conduct of the war, and so did Randolph. Mrs. Churchill has become so pious about the war that she will not even allow her daughter Mary to go to a dance. Odious family! By 10.30 the ambassador was longing for us to leave. Whereupon Emerald, who hates leaving, began her maddening telephoning for cars. Eventually one came at midnight and I accompanied her to the Dorchester. As the car would not take me to Chelsea and it was too late for a bus I was obliged to walk.

Monday, 25th October

Passing St. James's Palace on my way to the London Museum I came upon Blanche Lloyd, a stick-like figure in black, scuttling along and carrying bags. She looked pathetically humble and poor (I hope she is neither of these things). How unlike the high and mighty ex-Governor's lady of Portman Square days, only a decade ago. She said she was off to wait upon the Princess Royal. I longed but did not like to tell her that she had a preposterous black smudge on her nose.

Drown gave me back the little David from Polesden most beautifully cleaned and restored.

Tuesday, 26th October

I motored Lord Ilchester and Professor Richardson to Polesden and back within the morning. We just had time to study Richardson's design for Mrs. Greville's monument *in situ*. I am pleased with the result. I had my way in persuading both that the yew hedge which the professor proposed should be done away with altogether. We got back to Brooks's just too late for Anthony Blunt whom I had asked to luncheon. He came in however for coffee, and I asked him how best I could get sent to Italy under Amgot. He said he would see what he could do, but advised that the right plan was to approach Lord Rennell[199] direct. Nancy also advised this, and I have now approached him.

The fog was so bad tonight that no buses were running. Consequently I missed the 9.50 train I was to have taken for Truro. However I caught the 11.30. There was no sleeper and I had to sit up all night. A terrible train for stopping. It did not reach Truro until 11 a.m. Having had no breakfast I was famished.

Wednesday, 27th October

The [Trevor] Holmans met me at Truro. Unfortunately no time to see the cathedral. They motored me to Chyverton and gave me coffee, toast and marmalade. This is an attractive 1730 brick house with a pair of wings

---

[199] Major-Gen. Lord Rennell of Rodd, Nancy Mitford's brother-in-law, then Civil Affairs Administrator in the Middle East, East Africa and Italy.

oddly enough in stone. They were originally connected to the main block by retaining walls. All the interior decoration dates from the early nineteenth century. The grounds are especially beautiful. There is a wooded valley filled with rhododendrons and maples. I left Chyverton in the afternoon, and took a train to Ivybridge where Eardley met me. We motored to Salcombe, having lost our way down lanes – all the sign-posts having been removed so that the German parachutists shall not know where they are – in the dark.

Thursday, 28th October

Woke to find the sun shining upon the sea. Salcombe is as mild as the Mediterranean. At ten we went to Lady Clementine Waring's[200] house, a cheerful, Gothic villa in which Froude wrote his history, and to which he added a wing. Lawns slope down to the sea. Lady Clementine looks at one with the intensity of a psychoanalyst. And the expression on her face says, 'I have seen the inmost recesses of your squalid little mind. You are a worm only fit to be trampled underfoot.' She is a handsome and forbidding woman, who is chairman of the small local committee which runs the Sharpitor property. This contains a perfectly hideous villa called after its donor, the late Mr. Overbeck, a mysterious German quack doctor whose interests embraced stuffed birds, oriental brass, Wedgwood cameos, every conceivable form of bric-à-brac, and small boys. The garden is famed for its rare shrubs, and is as unappetizing as the house. It has no layout. It is crisscrossed with serpentine paths of yellow flags and tarmac, and is adorned with pergolas fashioned out of drainpipes, handrails made of tube pipes, terracotta urns on concrete piers, and the soppiest sculpture of simpering little children. The eucalyptus trees, which really must have been attractive features, were all killed by the frosts of recent winters.

Having inspected this unprepossessing property we lunched under the eagle eye of Lady Clementine and motored to Dartmouth. After cross-ing the ferry we continued to Brixham. I don't like Devon in spite of the beautiful coastline and cliffs. There is a littleness about its valleys and lanes, a meanness in the cramped views, an oppression in the claustro-phobic, dinky little towns. Besides it is being overbuilt, spoilt by rashes of Tudor bungalows with miniature drives of grey granite pebbles and white-washed boulders at the gates. And, oh the gates! Either made of old wagon wheels, painted orange, or the rising (or is it setting?) sun in cheap metalwork. Devon is too much beloved by too many of the wrong people.

---

[200] Lady Clementine Hay, married 1901 Captain Walter Waring, M.P.

Brixham is like a foreign fishing village; and is indeed filled with Flemish fisherfolk, who escaped here with their craft from the Netherlands. We watched the fishing smacks sail in and unload, while we had tea. We reached Torquay in the dark and stayed in tremendous luxury in the most expensive hotel in England, the Imperial. It has been decorated and furnished by Betty Joel.

Friday, 29th October

The bay reminds me of Nice. And the sea this morning was as blue as it is at Nice. Sitting on the terrace after breakfast, it being 9 o'clock by Greenwich, but not by Mr. Churchill, we got quite hot in the sun. After browsing in antique shops we proceeded to a property which must be nameless. I had warned Eardley that the owner might be just a little bit smelly. But I did not expect that she would on this occasion, when she was expecting us, stink worse than a badger. Indoors the stench was fit to kill. Indeed I nearly died of it, in spite of the fact that the leads of most of the windows have been torn out by bomb blast. We made every excuse to walk in the garden. Even so, when sitting on a bench Eardley in leaning backwards was practically supine. I was obliged to light a cigarette.

Saturday, 30th October

Professor Richardson button-holed me in Brooks's and asked if I would consider the post of secretary to the Fine Art Commission. I said I was only an architectural amateur, and suggested Anthony Blunt. He thought Blunt was too much of a dilettante. I said he was a scholar, and besides had a good manner. He does not think Summerson would be interested.

After tea I took a train to Woking. There I waited an hour for a taxi which never came. Eventually I took a bus to Send, and walked to Send Grove, carrying my bags. I arrived just in time to change for dinner at 8.30. A house party staying. Conversation at dinner was of rape and unnatural vice, the women, Loelia Westminster, Georgia Sitwell[201] and Joan Duff having some odd notions of both. After dinner we played until midnight a paper game of Loelia's invention – of the 'Truth' variety. It was great fun, and very scandalous. The party was divided into two schools of thought over one question: 'Would you sooner steal the affections of your best friend's husband or wife, *or* commit a fraudulent act, involving the penury of widows and children?' I said that of course I would have less compunction in doing the latter – so did Georgia and Loelia. The others said the opposite, and were as shocked by us as we were by them. Another question – 'Who do you consider the most sexually desirable woman?' I answered, 'Bridget Parsons or Evelyn Laye.'

---

201 Wife of Sir Sacheverell Sitwell.

Sunday, 31st October

A drizzly, muggy, drab day. I had breakfast downstairs with Charles
Ritchie and Philippe de Rothschild, the latter in his dressing-gown. He
looks like Johnny Churchill and is 'galant'. Takes the women's arms and
paws them. He escaped from unoccupied France only this year and said
that the English here have no idea of conditions on the Continent. He
was pained by the bland way in which the English criticize the behaviour of various French men and women in France. They do not realize
the pressures put upon them, or the motives behind their behaviour. They
may be perfectly honourable ones. We discussed our different ideas for
the preservation of peace in the post-war world. The two men favoured
the creation of a federal bloc in Western Europe for practical purposes.
By this means future war might be averted for longer than the interval
between Wars I and II. (So far so good.) By the end of that period the
weapons of war would be so devastating that with the growth of arma-
ments in the opposing blocks, the likelihood of an outbreak would surely
be nil. I disagreed with this notion, although I felt bound to admit the
interesting fact that in this war gas has not so far been used simply because
both sides realize the deadliness of a weapon which would rebound on
the side which first used it. We all agreed that meanwhile the peoples of
the whole world must be indoctrinated against the war spirit, and its
futility.

Wednesday, 3rd November

Margaret Jourdain, who lunched with me at the Istanbul restaurant,
amazed me by saying that she and Ivy, in order to effect economies when
they needed a change in the country, used to stay in convents. Their only
embarrassment was caused by meeting the Host carried through the
cloisters when they were in their Jaeger dressing-gowns, spongebags in
hand, on the way to the bathroom. Should they then kneel, or merely
genuflect as a matter of politeness? They are of course avowed agnostics,
not to say scoffers. When I told Geoffrey this he said it was no bad thing,
for it would convert them in the end.

I dined with the Princesse de Polignac, arriving with David Horner
whom I met bound for the same destination on a bus, just as the all
clear went. The princess's flat is in a block next door to the Dorchester.
You pass down long passages behind the doors of which similar people
are giving similar parties with similar smells of food issuing therefrom.
The princess, being very frightened of air-raids, sits in the passage
outside her flat on a milking stool until they end. Tonight there were
Mrs. Anthony Chaplin, who cooked a delicious dinner; Sir Paul Dukes,

a curious, slim, dandyish man, a great authority on Russia; a Mrs. Peto Benet (?), a Norwegian who had been having tea today with King Haakon. She was expressing fear lest the Russians would after the war seize the top of Norway so as to gain access to the North Sea. The king however feels quite sure Russia has no expansionist ambitions and is confident of her integrity (which strikes me as naive). There were also Mrs. Taffy Rodd, a pretty, jolly girl; the aforementioned David Horner, croaking like a cheap gramophone; and a young Frenchman, the Prince de Beauvau.

I sat on the princess's left. She wore a Juliet cap on the back of her head. She spoke seldom and always to the point, in a deep voice and a trenchant manner, ending each sentence with a French epithet which I often could not understand. The hero of the evening was the young Frenchman just escaped from France. He had been in Paris only in August. He said there were no cars of any kind there, no taxis, no buses, and the metro was running at most three times a day. People have to walk, and the rich hire pedal bicycles with wicker-work sidecars. The opera takes place every night, but only German officers and their wives attend. A meal at Maxime's costs 1,000 francs per person. Today all French people listen-in to the B.B.C. and you hear the British news blaring from every house. This is quite a new development. The prince says the French are united in a way they have never been before. The underground movement is organized to the nth degree. We are dropping arms and ammunition all over France where it is instantly collected. The French are living for the day when they can drive the Germans out, and they will not relish anyone else doing it for them. Whereas until lately there were many collaborationists, today the French are as one people revolting against the Germans, who like locusts have fleeced them of everything. At first the Germans were polite and conciliatory. Now the Gestapo is well established and thoroughly organized. But it does not co-operate with the Wehrmacht. Neither knows what the other is doing. Each distrusts the other. German troops in France already talk of Germany having lost the war. Prince Beauvau laughed as he told us that the Germans had cut down the legs of every chair in his *château* for fun. For no apparent reason they move furniture from one *château* to another. He witnessed with his own eyes Germans destroying the Rubenses and Van Dycks of his cousin, simply because he refused to collaborate. As against this Jamesey tells me that at Benghazi the Germans removed an ancient Greek statue out of the danger zone, admittedly with the intention of taking it back to Germany as loot. But when the Australians came in they destroyed the statue as junk.

Thursday, 4th November

At 3 o'clock an appointment with Sir Leonard Woolley,[202] an old gentleman with courtly manners, now a colonel in charge of the monuments
section of Amgot. As I entered the room he rose and said, 'Lord Esher
told me you would be coming to see me.' Now how could Esher have
known, for I had told no one at the National Trust? Woolley burbled in
an undertone so that I could barely hear, about the little damage to works
of art in Sicily, apart from a few baroque buildings, which, he said, nobody
could regret! In fine I gathered that at present no more volunteers for
Italy were wanted. Nevertheless he took down my name and asked me
to send him particulars of myself. If Amgot should extend to other countries, then they would want more volunteers with experience.
Unfortunately this would entail joining the army; it would be difficult
for me.

Friday, 5th November

Jamesey telephoned to say that he stayed at Bridget Paget's party last night
till 4.30 this morning, and made great friends with Noel Coward.[203] He
loved it all. There must be something very much the matter with me, for
I hated every moment, and slipped away at 11.

Saturday, 6th November

Emerald lunched with me at the Ritz. I called for her at the Dorchester
and walked straight into her sitting-room. Whereupon I heard a very
scared, 'Mercy! Shut the door!' shouted at her maid from the bedroom.
When our taxi reached the lights by the Green Park station Emerald leapt
like a gazelle on to the road regardless of passing traffic. At luncheon
she complained about the steak in her pie, the Brussels sprouts and the
rice pudding. She said there was grave dissatisfaction in high places
with the present Government, and there were to be changes, because 'the
food situation is so very bad,' which is of course quite untrue. She said
that at tea yesterday Jamesey was much impressed by Hore-Belisha's
happy flow of words and wit. She has the highest opinion of James's intelligence. The 'Bibelot' she calls him affectionately. Most of our conversation was about the derivation of words, and the exact meaning of
'meiosis', 'litotes' and 'euphemism'. I love her interest in etymology and
literature.

I bought in Chelsea for 7/6 a small white marble bust of, I think, the
Empress Eugénie. It is very pretty. Elizabeth Stewart-Jones saw me with

---

[202] Sir Leonard Woolley (1880–1960), archaeologist and author.
[203] Whose biography he was beginning to write just before his own death in 1974.

it, and said, 'What on earth did you buy that thing for?' I washed it under the tap and it is as white as snow.

Monday, 8th November

Meeting day. Esher asked me to lunch with him at the Grosvenor Hotel. It was to tell me that Anthony Martineau was to be appointed to the staff with a view to becomung the National Trust's solicitor exclusively; but that I was to remain assistant-secretary. I said I hoped old Mr. Horne[204] would not be affronted, or upset. Esher agreed that the staff was under-paid, and asked me what I thought I should be receiving. I did not know how to answer because there is no other comparable profession. He inti-mated that Bruce's, Eardley's and my salaries would be raised next Wednesday. He is so kind, friendly and funny that I love him dearly. He almost begged me not to go to Italy under Amgot, even if I got the chance – 'which you won't get of course,' he added.

On looking through old letters this evening I came across this one from Jamesey, written to me in July 1940: 'Your collapse from pacifism into the class convention of the Guards[205] worries me, but then everyone who began the war with one viewpoint has now got some other. Harold defending Chamberlain is the best example. My own detestation of the war, which I do not much attempt to rationalize, has on the other hand increased; I had a few months of thinking it was a just war, but now I see it as the destruction of everything that could even now be saved, a destruction planned by the Germans but made possible by us, and to which there is no alternative; we have become a purely *Daily Mirror* nation, and our vulgarity seems to me little better than Nazi injustice. And I have always preferred evil to stupidity – haven't you? My patrio-tism wanes; it is anyway largely a literary and architectural one, and I have to think very hard of the Brontës and Castle Howard when I want to remember that we represent something I like. How I envy you your age. At least you have enjoyed the twenties, and I was beginning to so much. I wish I felt inspired by something to do with the war – but to be living at the moment of modern history bores me merely, and I feel no inter-est in a future generation or a better world, because I believe in neither. Christianity is of course still there, but it seems a clear and tranquil stream running parallel to but utterly detached from the turgid river of the war, and as I said the other day too unapropos for words. There is a compla-cency about Christ that begins to irritate me; nailed on to that cross through all the churches of the world, and making the sort of no-effort

---

[204] Whose firm, Messrs. Horne & Birkett, had acted as the Trust's solicitors since its foundation in 1895.
[205] J. L.-M. joined the Irish Guards in 1940.

Heywood Hill does at Doreen's lunch-parties.[206] And as for that Pope on a board bed . . . The war seems to me to have made idealism impossible and sterile; only Edwardian liberals like Harold, or *New Statesman* fanatics can believe in any future for mankind or in perpetual peace or in democracy. Personally I foresee a general fascism in which one's moral duty will be limited to hacking out a niche for oneself and trying to keep in touch with the few people one does feel attached to. Don't you agree? It annoys me to have seen so little of the old Europe and to realise that I must now rely on reading in lieu of direct experience . . . Your point of view about the war amuses me, it is exactly between mine and Mummy's; but I have before noticed this about your points of view. They form a bridge from the pre-1914 to the pre-1940. Which is natural.'

I don't prefer evil to stupidity, and alas, I did not enjoy my twenties as much as I should have done. As for the rest of Jamesey's letter I am at one with all his sentiments. And some of the things he wrote then are a reproach to me now.

Wednesday, 10th November

As the result presumably of my talk with Lord Esher, my salary has been raised to £600 a year.

I left at 4 for Lincolnshire, arriving at Gunby Hall at 7.45 in time for dinner. The old Field-Marshal [Montgomery-Massingberd] in his dark velvet jacket and expanse of dazzling evening shirt looked inconceivably white in the face. At first glance he appears the epitome of blimpishness. In fact he is benign, simple-hearted and understanding. Lady Massingberd is vivacious, a little bit arch, and very godly and kind, not to say motherly. After dinner we talked exclusively of Gunby's future. They both adore this place.

Thursday, 11th November

Today was bright, sunny and very cold. Yet after breakfast the Field-Marshal took me walking to the chalk pits and the northern part of the estate. He moves very slowly, muffled up in a rain coat, and voluminous scarf, and wearing enormous gumboots. Every six yards he stands stock still to emphasize a point, while I freeze. He seems impervious to the cold. Whenever he meets someone he stops again. He is charming too, almost humble with his employees and tenants, and especially the ordinary soldiers. After luncheon we walked over the other part of the estate, across the railway line to Bratoft, where we looked at the square moat of the Massingberds' old castle, destroyed when Gunby was built. Nothing

---

[206] Doreen Colston-Baynes (Dormer Creston the biographer), a great mutual friend. Died 1973.

else remains. After dinner he showed me books of letters of Bennet Langton,[207] scrupulously copied and edited by Bennet's son Peregrine, who became a Massingberd by marriage. I exhorted him to have them published, they seemed so full of interest, and Bennet Langton was after all an intimate of Doctor Johnson and Boswell, a delightful sketch of whom by another son still hangs at Gunby. A huge steel structure like the Eiffel Tower with a beacon on the top has been erected on the tennis court, close to the house, as a guide to pilots and a safeguard of the house. I am overjoyed that the Trust has been largely instrumental in preventing this dear old place from being razed to the ground in order to extend the runway.

I was distressed to see in *The Times* today an announcement of George Lennox-Boyd's sudden death from pneumonia in Edinburgh. Poor George, I was distressed, but not rendered inconsolable. I had not seen him for a year or more. The sad truth is that prolonged absence does not make the heart grow fonder.

Friday, 12th November

After a visit to the doctor I dined with Stuart at the Travellers'. When dinner was over he announced that he must go to Michael Duff's to say goodbye. He added that he had already said goodbye to him three times. I said that seemed a pretty generous quota. I returned to Cheyne Walk on foot in the moonlight. There was no raid. The Germans do not seem to favour a full moon without clouds.

Saturday, 13th November

Lord Newton came to see me about Lyme Park (Cheshire). I have seldom met a man more beset by domestic tribulations and worries over what to do with a vast house. He looks and behaves like a dazed, elderly hare watching the pack of beagles close in. We fixed a date for me to go to Lyme.

Monday, 15th November

I had written to Alan Lennox-Boyd[208] condoling with him over George's death. When I got back to London I found that Alan had been telephoning me. He asked me to meet him urgently. This I did today at the Travellers'. He, poor man, has just been made Parliamentary Secretary to the Ministry of Aircraft Production. He looked grey and very tired. He asked me to write a tribute to George for *The Times,* which I did this

---

[207] Bennet Langton (1737–1801), Greek scholar and friend of Dr. Johnson.
[208] Later Viscount Boyd of Merton, 1951–2 Minister of State for Colonial Affairs.

evening. He told me George was delirious for twenty-four hours before
his death, during which time he never ceased talking and begging Alan
and their mother to take him out of a lunatic asylum. The irony is that
the military hospital they took him to was in fact an asylum, and on
arrival he saw the lunatics at large. This preyed on his mind.

Tuesday, 16th November

Joan Moore, Mérode Guevara (whom Clarissa calls the 'black crocus')
and Colin Agnew lunched with me at the Ritz. In the afternoon I went
to Hampstead to see Grove Lodge where Galsworthy lived. It is a low,
rambling, attractive house, Queen Anne-ish but not of architectural distinction. It has a spacious garden at the rear. Mrs. Galsworthy is selling it,
and her furniture and his books were still there. Furniture and decoration had a greenery-yallery flavour. Galsworthy's study where he wrote
was at the top of the house, approached by a separate staircase from the
garden.

Thursday, 18th November

I attended Kenneth Clark's lecture at Greek House, the Greek
Ambassador in the chair. The subject of the lecture was the influence of
Greek art upon British art, in particular architecture. K. must be the most
brilliant of lecturers – superhuman learning worn with ease, diction
perfect – because he makes me concentrate as though I were immersed
in a book. I can say this about no other lecturer, except Harold. He sat
beside me for a few moments before the lecture, talking most graciously.
Gracious is the word. He makes me feel like a nurserymaid addressed by
royalty. He makes me feel a snob because I record that he spoke three
words to me. Is he a very great man, and am I a very small one? The
answer to both questions must be Yes.

Friday, 10th November

I went to Wisbech and met Alec Penrose[209] on the train. I had not seen
him for four years and had forgotten what an extremely nice and intelligent man he is. After a very short time we resumed the intimacy of
heretofore. We share the same interests. He has a quiet manner of speaking with little inflexion in the voice, and a whimsical turn of phrase. We
went to tea at his old aunt's, the Honourable Alexandrina Peckover – I
like the roll of the prefix and names – at Bank House on the North Brink
of the Nene. We discussed with the old lady, who is eighty-six, the advantage to her of handing over the property to the National Trust now. I

[209] Alexander Penrose (1896–1950) of Bradenham Hall, Norfolk.

found her rather pathetic, for she is stately and proud, and yet was clearly incapable of understanding what we were driving at. I remarked afterwards to Alec that so often old ladies must be cheated by unscrupulous lawyers and business tricksters. Miss Peckover is a strict Quaker. When her father died she inherited a fabulous cellar of vintage port and wine. Before Alec had time to stop her, she and her maid had poured the contents of every single bottle on to the roots of her vines in the greenhouse.

Saturday, 20th November

I had tea at Dame Una's and fetched the tweed James has given me for a new suit. The fog was so dense that on my way home I had to stop at Geoffrey Houghton Brown's and dine with him. On leaving him the fog, which I thought had lifted a little, became worse by the river so that, even with my torch I walked by mistake across Albert Bridge to find myself in Battersea.

Monday, 22nd November

At Brooks's I talked with Simon Harcourt-Smith about Anarchism, for he too believes it may be the only political creed that holds out a hope for peace and justice. He said that his wife, Rosamund who is about to become a Papist, was a confirmed Anarchist. The Farm Street Jesuits told her that far from being incompatible, Catholicism and Anarchism were reconcilable, and she could embrace both. Simon knows no Anarchist except Herbert Read, whom he greatly admires and to whom he will introduce me. I tried to press him for light on the positive side of the creed. I admitted that I shared the dislikes, but was a little bewildered by the negative likes, and apparent lack of constructive policy. Simon was not able to enlighten me. He said Anarchism was a state of mind, presenting a goal to be kept in the mind's eye, however distant and unattainable. When I told Carol Dugdale at luncheon that Simon was the only anarchist I knew, she said: 'Thank you very much. I don't need to know any more to be put off Anarchism for ever.'

Simon Harcourt-Smith also imparted that Tom Jones[210] of the Pilgrim Trust told him if Winston Churchill had been born ten years later he would, in the 1930s, have made England a fascist state, ranged with the other fascist powers; but that he was too old a man with roots too firmly planted in the Victorian aristocratic traditions to adopt so alien a philosophy.

---

[210] Thomas Jones (1870–1955), civil servant, administrator, diarist and private secretary to Lloyd George, Bonar Law and Stanley Baldwin.

Tuesday, 23rd November

Went to Kenneth Clark's second lecture at the National Gallery, and sat in the front row with Clarissa. As he came in K. Clark said to me, 'You are being sacrificed.' I dumbly said, 'To what?' He said, 'My lectures.' Again this one was beautiful, scholarly and shaped like a work of art, rather like a Walter Pater essay. The subject was romantic landscape painters related to romantic poets, Girtin and Wordsworth, Turner and Byron. To my disappointment and shame I had to leave before the end to accompany Clarissa to *The Ideal Husband*. Martita Hunt in the principal rôle; décor by Rex Whistler. James and Bridget Paget were of the party. Clarissa had a hired car to take her to and from the theatre, which for a girl of twenty-three struck me as rather nonsense.

Wednesday, 24th November

This afternoon Madame de Polignac rang me up and asked me to dine tonight. At first I said 'no', because I was on fire-watching duty, then succumbed to the temptation when she said I might leave early after dinner.

I arrived at 55 Park Lane earlier than I should have done. Only Alvilde Chaplin there. She told me before my hostess came in how worried she was about the princess's health. She has angina and lately has been having as many as twenty attacks a day, and the drugs she takes seem to have less and less effect. The attacks are worse at nights. Then she came into the room wearing a green dress and nothing on her thick grey hair. She moved slowly and sedately. Her remarkable face, like some mountainous crag, was sunset pink. I talked to her before dinner and, almost exclusively, during dinner. All the other guests were French, including her niece, Madame de Vogüé. The dinner was more delicious than words can express, and ended with a succulent mince pie, followed by an egg savoury flavoured with garlic. Algerian wine to drink. I told my hostess about Kenneth Clark's lecture and she said she would write and ask him to let her read the script, since she supposed the series of lectures would be subsequently published. She too has an immense regard for K.

She recommended me to read all the books by E. M. Forster I could get hold of. She said Proust's limited knowledge of England came through Ruskin; and that one of the first things he wrote was a preface to a French translation of Ruskin. The last time she saw Proust was at a dinner party given for him in Paris. He attended pale and ill, wearing a long seal-skin dressing-gown down to his ankles. The Duke of Marlborough, who was at the dinner party, was indignant at the informality of his clothes. The duke had no idea who Proust was when he was explained to him. The princess again told me she never liked Proust. He was always hopelessly, but platonically in love with someone who did not requite his love. And this was wearisome for his friends.

I left early for firewatching in my office.

Thursday, 25th November

I caught the 10.15 for Stockport, where I was met and driven to Lyme Park. As we climbed the long drive there was snow lying on the ground. This vast seat is 800 feet above sea level. The park gates are at the entrance to the suburbs of Stockport. In other words Lyme forms a bulwark against Manchester and its satellite horrors. The greater part of the 3,000-acre property stretches in the opposite direction, towards the Peak. All morning while I was in the train the sun was shining. At Lyme it was snowing from a leaden sky. A butler met me at the front door and conducted me through the central courtyard, up some stone steps and into the hall on the *piano nobile*. Lord Newton lives and eats in the great library with a huge fire burning, and two equally huge dogs lying at his feet. Lyme is one of England's greatest houses. The exterior is practically all Leoni's work. The south side is a little too severe to be beautiful. Lewis Wyatt's chunky, square tower over the pediment is ponderous, like the central imposition on Buckingham Palace. A corridor runs the whole way round the first floor (from which staterooms open), with windows looking into the courtyard (which is architecturally the most satisfying composition at Lyme). The contents of the staterooms are magnificent, notably the Chippendale chairs, the Charles II beds and the Mortlake tapestries. There is a fascinating Byronic portrait over the staircase of Thomas Legh in Greek costume standing by a horse. My bedroom on the west side of the first floor had two Sargent portraits, one of Lord Newton's mother and the other of his mother-in-law.

Lord Newton is hopeless. The world is too much for him, and no wonder. He does not know what he can do, ought to do or wants to do. He just throws up his hands in despair. The only thing he is sure about is that his descendants will never want to live at Lyme after an unbroken residence of 600 years. I am already sure that he will not see out his ownership.

There were forty evacuated children in the house, but they have now gone. The park is cut to pieces by thousands and thousands of R.A.F. lorries, for it is at present a lorry depot.

Friday, 26th November

A rather dreadful thing happened. I had providentially brought with me my electric pad, for the cold at Lyme was intense. When we went to bed I dived around the skirting to look for a plug hole, attached the electric cord to it and turned on the switch. Instantly there was a loud sizzling sound and a blue flash ran round the cornice of the room. Simultaneously the dressing-table light went out, but not the reading lamp by the bed, or indeed the pad. It remained deliciously hot all night, and after reading peacefully I turned out the lamp. This morning I stumbled down darkened passages to the library for breakfast. No light in the library. The plate warmer not even working. Lord Newton was pacing up and down the room in a frenzy. He said, 'A most extraordinary thing! Every single light in the house went out last night soon after we went to bed. I can't understand it. Such a catastrophe has never happened before. I have had to send to Stockport for an electrician. I had a dreadful night for I was unable to look for candles, and I can't sleep without reading first. How did you manage?' 'Oh, fine!' I said, 'I read all right. My lamp worked perfectly.' I felt a fearful cad.

On my return I dined with Stuart at White's. I was very distressed by his greeting me with the news that the Princesse de Polignac died suddenly last night. She told me on Wednesday that she was dining with Sibyl Colefax the following night. She did so and sat next to Bogey Harris. Jamesey talked to her after dinner. She left at 11, was unwell in the taxi and sat, with Ronald Storrs, downstairs in her block of flats until she felt better, then went upstairs to bed. At 2 a.m. she died of a bad heart attack in the presence of poor Alvilde Chaplin and a doctor. She was a very remarkable woman indeed, and I am glad that at the end of her life I had the privilege of meeting her. I shall revere her memory.

Saturday, 27th November

At 12 o'clock Bogey Harris and I went to 4 Cheyne Walk to see the painted ceiling and staircase walls. They are evidently mid-eighteenth century and possibly Italian. The painting is directly on the walls, not on canvas. It is a beautiful house. George Eliot died in it. Bogey Harris then took me to No. 23 which he has bought. It is a dear little house, but with rather dark flowered wallpapers. Nancy Rodd lunched with me. She was as amazed as I was at Stuart paying a call on Alvilde Chaplin yesterday morning at 10 o'clock, to find her in tears only a few hours after the princess's death in the next room. An extraordinary thing to have done, considering how little he knows either. Oh well, customs differ on the opposite sides of the Atlantic! Nancy told me that Tim Bailey [her cousin] has become a Papist in a German prisoner-of-war camp, and this has distressed and aged his parents more than the death in action of their two other sons, Anthony and Chris. Her mother has told her that Tom Mosley, who was very ill and thought to be dying, is already improved in health since leaving prison; and that Diana is radiantly happy to be out and with her children again. Nancy's aunt at Olney gave her news of Diana Worthington's pathetic behaviour before her death. Diana was practically out of her mind and had taken it into her head that the village people were against her. Of course the very opposite was the case, for everyone loved her.

Keith Miller Jones introduced me to Oswald Normanby,[211] another hero. He is shockingly bald but handsome, with charming manners. He said he would not give his house to the National Trust for anything in the world. May he never have occasion to. He said that in his German prison the inmates were provided with a newspaper in English entitled *Camp*, edited he supposed by some pro-Nazi Englishman, as well as German newspapers. Anthony Beaumont with whom I dined said that Robin Campbell,[212] an exchanged prisoner, enraged Mr. Churchill at Chequers by telling him how well the Germans had treated him, and how nice they were. Churchill replied, 'It is a pity they did not take off your head as well as your leg.'

Tuesday, 30th November

I lunched with Eddy at Brooks's. He has just recovered from influenza. His nose bled continuously throughout luncheon. He complained that his broadcast of the *Odyssey* in conjunction with Benjamin Britten last week had not been well received by the press, and that congratulations from his friends meant nothing to him in consequence.

I went to a shop in Kensington Church Street to look at a small oil painting, a religious subject by Christina Rossetti. The owner of the shop, an eccentric man called Wilson, spoke of his hatred of the Government. I took him to be a brother Anarchist. When I asked him if he was, he said he had never been so insulted in his life. He said he was an arch conservative. I said I was too. I think he took me for a lunatic.

I dined with Ivy C.-B. and Margaret J. Basil Marsden-Smedley[213] who was there spoke vehemently against the Jews in this country. He told us how his Ministry of Economic Warfare intercepted code messages through the mail between neutral countries. By this means he had Ribbentrop's brother-in-law arrested in America.

Wednesday, 1st December

The Princesse de Polignac's Requiem Mass at Farm Street was a very solemn and dignified affair. Peter Pears sang Bach, Mozart and Fauré

---

[211] The present Marquis of Normanby, severely wounded, taken prisoner and repatriated. Parliamentary Secretary to Secretary of State for Dominion Affairs 1944–5.
[212] Robin Campbell, D.S.O., Director of Art, Arts Council.
[213] Basil Marsden-Smedley (1901–64), barrister, member of L.C.C. and Mayor of Chelsea 1957–9.

most movingly. When the Mass was over James, who had joined me in
my pew, and I walked to Heywood Hill's shop. We watched Nancy
returning to it ahead of us. She was running down South Audley Street
to get warm. She made a strange spectacle, very thin and upright, her
arms folded over her chest, and her long legs jerking to left and right of
her like a marionette's. I really believe she finds it easier to run than to
walk.

I have been wanting to see Harold since his return from Sweden. He
asked me to dine tonight. To my disappointment he was not alone. There
were Godfrey Nicholson, M.P., Guy Burgess and a Dr. Dietmar. The last
is a tall, fair young man now teaching in a secondary school at Raynes
Park. Harold got him out of an internment camp a few months ago. He
is immensely grateful to Harold, earnest and rather a bore. Guy actually
left us before dinner and rejoined us immediately after. Harold gave us
champagne. I ought to have been firewatching in my office, and when
the siren went during dinner rose to go. Harold quite rightly was
shocked, for he has never once shirked firewatching duty in the House.
However, the all-clear sounded almost immediately, so I sat down again,
chastened. Talk was about lying. Harold said he never lied except over sex
matters. Then he and Guy became engrossed in political shop which I
found very tedious. I am interested in politics *per se,* but long anecdotes
on how Mr. Bevan snubbed Lady Astor, who got her own back by insulting Mr. Attlee strike me as childish and contemptible. I also think that
when M.P.s treat politics like a game for scoring off one another they are
behaving dishonestly towards their constituents, who have not voted
them into the House of Commons for that purpose. Guy is obsessed with
this aspect of the beastly business.

I walked to Victoria and my office with Godfrey Nicholson who I
would say is an honourable, conscientious but not a brilliant man, aged
about forty. He told me he was passionately in love with his wife, and
deplored the fact that Vita was not a more womanly wife to Harold
whom he considers deserving the greatest matrimonial happiness. I did
not feel inclined to discuss Harold and Vita's relations, merely remarking
that I thought they were a blissfully happy couple. Nicholson said the
House of Commons held Harold in poor esteem; and his brain counted
for little with them. More fools they, is my opinion. I have always supposed Harold's great abilities to be wasted in that ridiculous place.

Thursday, 2nd December

Went by train to Bath for luncheon. Lunched with Major Strutt and
Henshaw, and talked about St. Catherine's Court. Strutt is unwilling to
make over as much endowment as the Trust asks for. I returned in time

to dine with the [Peter] Heskeths, having had a brief talk in Brooks's with Simon Harcourt-Smith and Lord Donegall.[214] Both said Rommel and von Keitel had flown to Cairo with peace terms, which Roosevelt and Stalin were favouring, but Winston Churchill was not.

Friday, 3rd December

A foggy morning. I collected the National Trust car from Moon's garage, picked up Jamesey at his flat, and drove through the East End to Ipswich where we lunched. We browsed in a secondhand bookshop and bought a few books. In pouring rain we drove to Helmingham Hall. We first of all looked at the flint church, which was filled with monuments to the Tollemache family. One should always visit the parish church before the big house in order to learn the history of the land-owning families from the memorials. We walked through the churchyard and across the park. The object of this expedition was to see as much as possible of the outside of the house. The Trust has been left £20,000 in reversion for the Hall's preservation. The present holder of the barony is disputing the will, and won't allow the Trust to inspect the place or go inside the house. From what we could see without approaching too close, the Hall with its moat and drawbridge was gabled and romantic. On our return we had tea at Colchester and a drink at Ingatestone. The whole long, joyous day we gossiped and rocked with laughter. Our talk was scandalous, unedifying and highly constructive. James said, 'Being with you is like being by myself, only nicer.' I said, 'I am glad it is nicer. Surely when you are by yourself you don't talk and laugh quite so much.' 'Yes, I do,' he said, 'inwardly. And I say to myself things I would not dare say to anyone else, except you.'

Sunday, 5th December

At Mass in Cheyne Row I felt devout again. My devoutness is more readily maintained by having my rosary and telling beads. It is when I am distracted from my devotions – I can't honestly say, prayers – by trying to make sense of the liturgy, or indeed listening to the sermon, that everything goes wrong. The moment reason takes over faith flies out of the door. But concentrating on my rosary to a background of symbolic acts, punctuated and not interrupted by rising for the Gospel, kneeling for the sanctus bell and elevation, and crossing myself on approaching certain well-known and loved landmarks, then I can often be devout. Then I can feel I am making contact. I wonder if other Papists feel as I do. God

---

[214] Marquess of Donegall, Hereditary Lord High Admiral of Lough Neagh, journalist and British war correspondent 1939–45.

preserve us from too much illumination. What I need is a twilight atmosphere relieved by myriads of twinkling candles from crystal chandeliers, a plethora of gold, jewels, rich raiment, silver vessels, clouds of incense, and the tinkling and tolling of innumerable bells. Beauty in fact, not austerity, is what I crave in order to be religious.

Bridget Parsons lunched at the Ritz Grill. Afterwards we walked all round Hyde Park in the cold sunshine. Although Bridget was not looking her best in an old teddy bear coat and a Russian hat of frayed astrakhan, her hair as it were suspended from it like leather straps, nevertheless she was mysterious. (Stuart complains how badly she dresses, just as he complains how badly I dress, whereas his clothes hang on him like sacks.) Bridget talked politics. She is terrified of American influence upon our way of life. She despises Americans for being children, as many English people do. She also fears their desire to get out of the war at any price, and is certain that were it not for Roosevelt, they would kick off. On this account she is in favour of a speedy negotiated peace, not 'at any price' she explained, that not being necessary now we have the upper hand. For the sake of arguing I disagreed. I do honestly believe that the Brits would have every justification in stringing up Churchill and our war-mongering politicians if at the end of the war they discovered nothing had been achieved by the whole ghastly business.

I dined with Emerald. Only Jamesey and Enid Paget, aged 19, whom he is now mad about, were present. Emerald said Sibyl Colefax had telephoned that Cecil [Beaton] was back in England, his plane having burst into flames on rising. He and all the passengers escaped, but his luggage was destroyed. Cecil is badly shocked and in bed. No wonder!

Talk ranged over love and the drama. Emerald explained very succinctly why Oscar Wilde's *Ideal Husband* displayed utter cynicism. For not only does the hero get away with his outrageous fraud, but is rewarded by the fulfilment of his grossly material ambitions; and the audience is made to sympathize with and wholeheartedly approve his behaviour.

Monday, 6th December

Cyril has told Stuart that Cecil's strongest passion is spite. So I have told Stuart to ask Cecil what Cyril's strongest passion is.

I stayed at home this evening and began editing the S.P.A.B.'s memorandum on Bath and new uses for Georgian town houses after the war.

Tuesday, 7th December

Everyone is talking of the imminence of the Germans' rocket shells. The Germans themselves announced over the wireless on Saturday that these shells would shortly rain upon London and totally destroy it. The War

Office takes them very seriously, and soldiers are commanded to carry steel helmets again.

Wednesday, 8th December

I went to the Charing Cross Hotel at 1 o'clock. In a private room was a large table to seat some twenty members of the Cocked Hat Club, an inner circle of the Society of Antiquaries. There was an old cocked hat in the middle of the table, and a flag bearing each member's coat of arms in front of his seat. One other person and I were guests. James Mann,[215] my host, introduced me to several distinguished antiquarians whom I knew already, like Lord Ilchester (the Chairman), Sir Charles Peers, Rob Holland-Martin and Professor Richardson, and some I didn't know, like Dr. Mortimer Wheeler, now a brigadier and just back from Italy. I got slightly nervous as we sat down and asked Mann whether there were to be speeches. 'Only rather informal ones,' he said, 'and you will be asked to say a few words.' Now I cannot speak even two words in public, and this news dismayed me just as I was beginning to enjoy myself. I had only sipped a glass of sherry before luncheon, so I ate very little and drank just as much hock as I could get down. Oh God, the dreadful humiliation! I would far rather go over the top into a nest of German commandos, armed with hand grenades and bayonets, any day, than rise and say, 'My lords and gentlemen, it is a great privilege to be received in this august company.' Oh Lord! oh lords, the fatuity too!

I dined with Johnny Dashwood at the Travellers'. The British consul in Lisbon was there. He is what is called a rough diamond, shrewd, self-pushed up, with dozens of amusing stories – a sympathetic man. He told me that Gulbenkian, now living in Lisbon, was being slighted by the British Embassy and society because although a British subject, he was evading income tax. Consequently Gulbenkian had hinted to the consul that he might after all not leave his pictures and collections, now in England, to this country. Did I know Kenneth Clark? And would I do something? I have written to K. Clark about this.

Thursday, 9th December

I went to Sittingbourne to see the Court House, Milton Regis. I found it but could not get in. It was locked, and the owner, a retired postman, had been called upon to resume his duties today, and so was away on his rounds. However, without seeing the inside I estimated that it was not a suitable property for us. It is a fifteenth-century, half-timbered building

---

[215] Sir James Mann (*d.* 1963), Director of Wallace Collection and Master of the Armouries, Tower of London.

with overhangs, in a shocking state of decay. I was disappointed not to meet the postman in order to find out why he was the owner.

Friday, 10th December

Lying in the bath this evening, with the hot tap gently running and the water making throaty noises down the waste-pipe – a thing one is strictly enjoined not to allow in war-time – I thought how maddening it is that the worst sins are the most enjoyable. I wondered could it possibly be that these sins would recoil upon me in my old age. For at present they don't seem to do my soul much harm. And the lusts of the flesh, instead of alienating me from God, seem to draw me closer to him in a perverse way. He on the other hand may not be drawn to me. Yet I feel he ought to know how to shake me off if he wants to. Can it be that he is too polite, as I am when Clifford Smith button-holes me at a party, and I am longing to escape? How oddly one's body behaves in the bath as though it did not belong to one. Admiring my slender limbs through the clear water I thought, what a pity they aren't somebody else's.

Saturday, 11th December

I woke at 7 and left the house in pitch dark for Paddington. There I met Paul Methuen on the platform. Having with difficulty engaged two seats in a first-class compartment I went to a telephone box. Rang up K. Kennet just to say good morning and goodbye and Jamesey who, thank God, did not propose to Enid Paget last night, as he had told me he was going to do. When he asked for my advice I warned him not to. He said it was not my advice (I bet it was) but his better judgment which dissuaded him.

Paul Methuen is very difficult to communicate with. I like him immensely and I admire him because he has so many interests besides painting, of which he is a professional. But his mind works in a curious, laborious way. One thinks he does not hear because he may completely ignore what one is saying to him. Ten minutes later, when one has either moved on to another topic of conversation or forgotten the previous one, he will reply, or make an oblique reference to what one was saying. His mind is far away from mundane matters, and he is not the least interested in gossip or the behaviour of his friends; he is only interested in their ideas. If they have no ideas, he is not interested in them at all. We were met at Chippenham by his sister-in-law, Mrs. Anthony Methuen, who motored us to Ivy House where she and her husband live. The brother is a stiff man, and looks years older than Paul. Up to now he has opposed Corsham, which is entailed upon his son, being made over to the National Trust. The cold in the A. Methuen's house was Siberian.

Wednesday, 15th December

I left London early by car for Lacock [Wiltshire]. It is exhilarating to motor long distances again. Driving alone I feel happy and carefree. Every expedition is an adventure. I gave a lift to an R.A.F. sergeant instructor as far as Marlborough. He told me that our new bombers did not need to see their targets, and aimed by mathematical, or navigational precision. I asked if the results could possibly be accurate. He said they bombed from a height of four miles and guaranteed to drop their load within ten yards of the target. He said that girls were much more accurate in plotting than men. He spoke highly of the W.A.A.F.s. He said 'morality' – and this word always makes me smile – was far greater among girls in the forces than girls in the factories; and venereal disease was less rife because every girl in the W.A.A.F.s was examined once a week, whether she wanted to be or not.

I reached Lacock Abbey at 2. Miss Talbot[216] was bustling about the great Sanderson Miller hall as I entered. A large log fire was burning, and the room was filled with smoke which has blackened the walls and ceiling. It was warm and smelled sweet and cosy. Miss Talbot said, 'I hate fresh air. It is the cause of most of our ills in England.' She is a dear, selfless woman, and extremely high-minded. She has the most unbending sense of duty towards her tenants and the estate to the extent that she allows herself only a few hundreds a year on which to live. She spends hardly a farthing on herself, and lives like an anchorite. She wants to hand over Lacock now, abbey and village. I believe we shall acquire this splendid property quite soon. Her old agent, Mr. Foley, took me round the house again. It certainly could well be adapted to institutional purposes.

Thursday, 16th December

In the morning I motored to Sutton Court. Lord Strachie showed me round. The house, which has historical associations with John Locke, has been in the Strachey family for centuries. It is built of a cold grey stone. The outstanding features are a crenellated curtain wall, and a central square pele tower with circular stair turret, dating from Edward II's reign. Bess of Hardwick, one of whose husbands was a Strachey, added the north wing. But the whole house was horribly restored in 1858, so that I doubt its acceptability. There are many interesting family portraits, and one by Dance of Clive of India to whom the first Strachey baronet was

---

[216] Miss Matilda Talbot (1871–1958) succeeded her uncle in 1916 and assumed the name Talbot in lieu of Gilchrist-Clark. Lacock was inherited by the Talbots by marriage with the Sharington heiress in the sixteenth century. Miss Talbot gave the abbey, most of the village and 320 acres to the National Trust in 1944.

private secretary. The estate of 500 acres covers a pretty but not spectacular landscape.

I lunched in Bath, looked at the Assembly Rooms and was surprised that all the outer walls were intact. Bought two Rockingham china pen trays at Angells shop. Saw Henshaw about St. Catherine's Court and went to Great Chalfield Manor,[217] where a children's Christmas Tree party was in progress. The old Fullers are always friendly. He explained where he intends hanging the tapestries which he is buying for the great hall. I approved.

Saturday, 18th December

Bridget and I went to welcome Hamish Erskine who has returned. His mother [Lady Rosslyn] and brother David were there when we arrived, both jubilant. Hamish is much thinner in the face, but has a good colour. After Tobruk he was in hospital and prison in Italy. He escaped and walked all the way down to our lines. Lady Rosslyn produced from a cardboard box and tissue paper the trousers, old black tail coat and hat he had lived and slept in for nine weeks. You would not clothe a scarecrow in them.

Wednesday, 22nd December

James dined at Brooks's. He was on night duty and I was to firewatch in my office. I gave him for Christmas one of the Rockingham pen trays with which he was delighted. We were both dull this evening, presumably because we had no money even to pay for one glass of wine. He was much distressed by Father Burdett's death. I accompanied him to the War Office. In the Mall we agreed that, no matter how much we might kick against the pricks and no matter how disloyal we were to the Church, Catholic principles were for us the only right and true ones; that we were both temperamentally and fundamentally Catholic; and that we were both bitterly opposed to the prosecution of this war and to the government's uncompromising determination to smash Germany to smithereens.

Thursday, 23rd December

Today the announcement of the National Trust's acquisition of West Wycombe Park appeared in the press: at last, after protracted negotiations since 1938.

I lunched with Lord and Lady Newton at their flat in Park Street. They were pleased with the suggestion that Manchester University might rent

---

[217] Given to the Trust in 1943 by Major R. Fuller.

Lyme Park from the Trust. Lady Newton must once have been handsome. She is tall; and she is thin like everyone else these days. But she is
languid and as hopeless as her husband. Both said they would never be
able to reconcile themselves to the new order after the war. They admitted that their day was done, and life as they had known it was gone for
ever. How right they are, poor people.

Friday, 24th December

At Brooks's I saw Eddy and a guest lunching the other side of the room.
They beckoned me over to their table. The guest was William Plomer, a
thick-set man with small moustache, aged about forty. His face was unre-
markable until I looked into it. His manner was quiet, but when he spoke
he spoke forcibly. Rather a winning smile. They had practically finished
eating when I joined them, and soon left.

Then a large man of about sixty with a rough, smiling face and
rather coarse features, with a bald top to his head and white hair at the
sides, sat down opposite me. He said, 'Good morning' with much genial-
ity. I had no idea who he was. He had a north-country voice. I recommended the treacle tart I was eating. He observed that the club food
was very good. I said it had improved lately, but that food generally
was pretty indifferent nowadays. I wondered how the poor managed on
their limited rations. It was all right for us who could go to restaurants.
He said the British Restaurants had been started to help the poor man.
I said how good most of them were, and I hoped they might continue
when the war was over. He said, 'They will. My name is Woolton.'[218] He
told me he visited the British Restaurants all over the country and
spoke to the people in them. He always asked for their opinions. He
received an average of 200 letters a day from strangers, making recom-
mendations or complaints. We talked of Speke Hall, which at one time
he thought of renting; but his wife said it was too inconveniently
planned.

Saturday, 25th December

Christmas Day. I met Stuart at the Brompton Oratory for High Mass.
Children's beautiful voices singing. We walked to the Hyde Park Hotel,
where we sat and talked rather sadly. I left him for Dame Una's Christmas
luncheon in Ladbroke Grove. John, Jamesey and Nancy Rodd were
there. We exchanged little gifts. I gave them each a piece of soap shaped
like a lemon. Dame Una gave me a honeycomb, and Nancy one of her
hen's eggs and an ounce of real farm butter, golden yellow. A huge turkey

---

[218] 1st Earl of Woolton, at the time Minister of Food.

was carved, and we had an excellent plum pudding. The boys soon left for their respective offices. The Dame, Nancy and I talked about Italy, the looting by British troops, and the Italians' dislike of us. The Dame said Montgomery hated the Catholic Church and was determined to destroy Rome. Even Nancy was aghast at this and wished our bombing were not so relentless.

I bussed and walked with Nancy to her house in Blomfield Road. We looked at the terraces round Paddington Station and the Canal basin, and the house Browning lived in at Little Venice.[219] It is now shabby and bombed, but so romantic. I left Nancy in the Harrow Road on her way to deliver a leather tea cosy for her charwoman who is in hospital. She is sweetly kind in this way. I went to tea with Emerald Cunard, who was alone. She gave me a book for Christmas. At first she was absent-minded. Then she warmed up and was enchanting. She talked of Chips Channon and the Stuart row. 'Do you really think, dear, he made up to him?' Of Hore-Belisha, who designed the battledress, she said: 'He is not a man of taste.' She talked of the Knighthood of the Garter, mandragora, Shakespeare, Galsworthy 'who looked a gentleman and may have been one', of a friend of hers who loved a man with £3,000,000, of the lack of culture among Americans and the English middle-classes. 'Do they really not care for the arts? How extraordinary of them!' I stayed till 7 o'clock.

Tuesday, 28th December

Margaret Rénéville, Clare Sheridan's daughter, is not as handsome as her mother. There is little love between them. Margaret says Clare is mad these days and thinks herself the reincarnation of Queen Emma. This may well be so, but Clare is not the least bit boring.

Friday, 31st December

Having dined with Geoffrey I walked home and went early to bed. I read, but the Battersea church bells started pealing across the river, contrary as I thought to the regulations. It was more than I could bear, so I went downstairs to put cotton wool in my ears. Still I heard them. At midnight I stuffed my fingers into my ears in order not to listen to the striking of the little tortoise-shell and silver clock at my bedside. The loneliness of this moment, wholly artificial though it be, harrows me. When it had passed I went on reading. At 12.30 the telephone rang. I threw the sheets back and leapt out of bed. Book, paper and pencil clattered to the floor. It must, I thought, be the voice I longed for. It would be contrite,

---

[219] Ultimately destroyed, not by Hitler, but by the L.C.C

solicitous, loving. No such thing. It was that bore Dr. Dietmar to wish me a Happy New Year, as though 1944 could augur anything but the direst misery of our lives. Only a German could be so obtuse. I was not very friendly, and pretended that he had woken me up.

1944

I had tea in Jamesey Pope-Hennessy's flat. He was discussing with Miss Eve Kirk a posthumous portrait he wants her to do for him of Father Burdett. Dame Una who joined us after tea said Miss Kirk was a convert of Father Burdett, and had at one time supposedly been in love with her own brother. The Dame asked me if I kept my diary for posterity. 'Perhaps,' I answered, 'but it won't be read until fifty years after my death.' 'Since we can't possibly die,' Jamesey said, 'that means never. Just as well.' The Dame looked wise and said nothing.

Bridget Parsons lunched with me, or rather, since we went shares, we lunched together. The arrangement, however necessary, seems all wrong. We agreed that the Ritz is no more expensive than anywhere else these days, and far more agreeable.

Sir Edwin Lutyens has died. He was the best architect of our time. Robert Byron always maintained this. Lutyens had the manner of a genius. I only once met him while staying at Batsford with the Dulvertons. He came over with some friends, and after tea took me aside in order to regale me with puns and obscene witticisms. Very funny too. I remember Victoria Dulverton saying afterwards how nervous she was lest he might say things that would embarrass her. He was leonine, breezy, untidy, flamboyant and inspired.

At dinner Wyndham Goodden told me that his wife had left him with two babies on his hands. I have never seen a man so unhappy. I tried to cheer him by pointing out to him his blessings – doubtless a fatuous thing to do at such a time. But what else could I do? Besides he does have blessings. As I left his door the siren went, and I walked home during a raid over the Thames estuary. It was a beautiful, clear moonlit night under a violet starry sky. I saw the shells bursting in the east like innumerable stars twinkling, but heard not a sound. Orange flares were reflected in the Serpentine as I crossed the Park. On my return at 12.45 the telephone rang, and my heart leapt. It was Oliver Messel inviting me to a party in the Norwich Assembly Rooms next Wednesday. Very sweet of him, but quite impossible.

At 6 went to a meeting to wind up the Federal Union Club at the Squires' flat. Only the Squires, Keith Miller-Jones, Sainsbury and

Miss Ward present, a sad little gathering. I thought of poor Robert Byron, our President, and Derek Rawnsley, the fair, fanatical young man who also was killed. Keith and I walked to Brooks's and dined there. He recommended my reading Festing Jones's life of Samuel Butler. When young, Keith knew Festing Jones, who told him many anecdotes of Butler. The third unpublished sonnet of Butler to Miss Savage began, 'Had I the desires of a common sailor after three weeks' abstinence,' or words to that effect. Butler had a woman upon whom he vented his appetite, often, according to Festing Jones, without troubling to unbutton his trousers.

Tuesday, 4th January

John Betjeman lunched with me at Brooks's, the first time since the war. He seemed to enjoy himself, jumping up and down in his chair and snapping his fingers, in laughter. He is sweeter and funnier than anyone on earth. He never changes, is totally unselfconscious, eccentric, untidy and green-faced. He works at the Ministry of Information and simply hates it, returning every Saturday till Monday to Uffington. In his *Daily Herald* articles he surreptitiously damns the war and progress, and the left wing. Talked about the slave state in which we are already living. Said he loved Ireland but not the Irish middle class. Only liked the country eccentrics like Penelope's distant relations, the Chetwode-Ailkens. When they claimed to be cousins Penelope retorted, 'No, you can't be. Your branch was extinct fifty years ago.' When the Betjemans left Ireland de Valera sent for them. Penelope said to him, 'My husband knows nothing of politics; or of journalism. He knows nothing at all.' She offered to plan an equestrian tour for de Valera, and her last words to him were, 'I hope you won't let the Irish roads deteriorate. I mean I hope you won't have them metalled and tarmacked.'

After luncheon we talked of architecture and the Greek Revival. John said that there had been no book on this style yet, and that K. Clark's *Gothic Revival* ignored Morris and the serious purpose of mid-nineteenth-century Gothic. He said there was an architect, by name May, still living in Sussex, who had been articled to Decimus Burton. May told John how in 1879 he took his prospective wife to see Burton, whose single comment was, 'Approved.' We walked down Jermyn Street and he pointed out two buildings by Morphew that had singular merit. Any surviving Georgian building provoked him to say, 'They ought to have that down. That's too good.' I showed him the Athenian Stuart façade in St. James's Square, which to my surprise he did not know. He is a committed High Churchman, and wishes to edit a church magazine after the war. Suffers much from guilt complexes over his youth, which must surely have been more innocent than most people's - 'but the flesh hasn't been so provoking during the past fortnight'.

As we passed the site of Pennethorne's old Geological Museum he reminded me of our visits years ago during luncheon breaks. There was never a soul, either an attendant or visitor. We used to insert into the dusty glass cases old chestnuts and pebbles which we labelled with long names in Latin, invented by us amidst peals of laughter. They remained where we put them until the building was pulled down.

Wednesday, 5th January

George Scherhof ('Sarcophagus' Betjeman calls him) gave me luncheon at Brown's Hotel. He has returned from Algiers with a broken arm and shoulder blade, badly mended, and is in great discomfort. He is a captain in the army. He told me his father and mother were both Prussians, 'the worst sort,' he said. But he loves his mother. He was born in England. What a hideous accident birth is. It is a toss-up whether one is fighting with or against one's nearest and dearest, and indicates the folly of the whole damn thing.

Friday, 7th January

I had meant to dine at home but Eardley Knollys induced me to have a drink in order to show me the Samuel Palmer etchings he has just bought. The land of faery they lead one to. Heavenly things, but what does one do with them? Framed and hung on a wall they are lost. And in a portfolio they are equally lost.

Saturday, 8th January

I lunched at Rick Stewart-Jones's Café and sat next to Ethel Walker who talked about twentieth-century painting. She railed against Emerald Cunard for being taken in by Marie Laurencin. She heartily dislikes Emerald, as I would expect her to. Throughout the meal she fed her dirty old white dog on its chain. It was difficult to understand what she was saying because of mouth trouble. I guessed by the unyielding shape of her jaw that her teeth were false, quite apart from their unnatural white-ness. And so they proved to be, false to their poor owner - for she had hardly spoken with a little too much throwing back of the head and wide opening of the lips, as though to flaunt these glorious new appendages when they fell, or rather spurted out in one piece. Dexterously she caught them in her right hand. I behaved with absolute correctness, merely turning my eyes with deep solicitude upon the revolting dog. She went on to explain, quite undeterred by the incident, that she paints as well today as she has ever done. I marvelled, when I looked at those filmy blue eyes, that this could be so. She said she learnt at the Slade with John, who was a god, handsome, gifted and desired by all, till seduced by drink. Wilson Steer was the worst teacher in the world. He never instructed his pupils, but in a melancholy voice would say slowly and sleepily, 'If I were you I would make the nose longer, the arms fatter; give more light to the hair,' and so on. She hated George Moore, whom she called a cad and a lecher. He told her that the first time he met Emerald Cunard was at an exhibition; and that Emerald went up to him and asked him to kiss her on the lips. I don't believe this story.

Sunday, 9th January

I went to tea with Dame Ethel. She lives at 127 Cheyne Walk, further west than my house. Her Victorian apartment is undecorated, drab and grubby. I should have gone at 4 and was too late to see her pictures properly, for it was a dark day. The room was stacked with pictures. We sat on two broken-down armchairs by a coal fire. At last the kettle boiled on the hob. I was given a mouse-nibbled Digestive biscuit to eat. When I left at 5.30 she said, 'Perhaps one day you will let me paint you?' 'I should love to sit to you,' I said. She asked 'When?' I said, 'Next Saturday morning.' She fixed the time and said, 'Don't let's think of money.'

At 6.30 I went to Viva King's house in Thurloe Square. She is pretty, fair-skinned, silver-haired, plump, well-dressed and very intelligent without being blue-stocking. Norman Douglas was present. I was surprised to find an old man, nearly 80 I should say, sitting on a low sofa, rather hunched up, unrecognizing, with a regular-featured but red face, and beautifully brushed white hair parted in the middle, drinking whisky. He had just come in before me and was not yet lit up, for he has to drink a great deal, lives in rooms near by, is lonely and, I am told, disreputable. We talked about *Home Life with Herbert Spencer* by two old ladies, with whom Spencer lived out his remaining years. He was eccentric and selfish to a degree unparalleled. Norman Douglas laughed a lot in an unregistering way, and spoke very little. Viva rather cross with him.

Monday, 10th January

Meeting day. Matheson is leaving on 1st March for six months. I wrote him a note, which he showed Esher and Zetland, that I did not want to become secretary if it entailed abandoning my historic buildings work, and that I could not anyway cope with the secretarial routine. I feel very unwell nearly all the time.

Went to Lady Crewe's party. It was hell. Not much to drink, hardly anyone I knew, and the atmosphere far from relaxed. Lady Crewe is awkward and shy. I talked a bit with Hamish Erskine about Rosslyn

Chapel, which he wants the Scottish National Trust to take over. He says he is so blind in the dark that this evening he found himself cocking a leg over the bonnet of a bus, supposing it to be the way in. I watched Mrs. Keppel hobbling round the room and smoking from a long holder. She is rather shapeless, with hunched shoulders, a long white powdered face. She was gazing with mournful eyes as though in search of something. Colonel Keppel, with big moustache, is very much a Brigade of Guards officer of the old school.

Wednesday, 12th January

Went to Pierre Lansel again for injections. I have not the courage to tell him that I simply cannot continue with them, and would prefer to be bayoneted any day.

Dined at Sibyl Colefax's Ordinary and sat next Baroness Budberg and Olga Lynn, who asked to have me as neighbour. Both of them hugely fat, plain and delightful. The Baroness talked to me about Catholicism and the Greek Church, to which she belongs. She said she much disliked the Roman faith and could not swallow the Pope or Infallibility. Oggy Lynn discussed the war, saying she predicted in 1939 that it would end in the spring of 1945, and that the soundest man about the war was General Aspinall–Oglander. After dinner I talked to Mrs. Oglander about Nunwell, their home in the Isle of Wight, and then to the General, who is compiling a history of the place and the Oglanders. The earliest family letters date from the fourteenth century. I enjoyed this evening, and returned at 10.30.

Friday, 14th January

Motored to Loose Wool House, Kent, that detestable little half-timbered atrocity. There I went over the furniture that is ours. The tenants offer to buy it for over £100, and good riddance to bad rubbish. Very friendly, very *quelconque* people who have evidently made money. They kindly gave me luncheon which they called dinner, and we drank tea afterwards. On leaving I was presented with four eggs, of which two were ducks'. At Stoneacre the old woman took me round. The house is still in good trim, the tenant not returned from Canada yet. Then to Bradbourne, and had a brief survey of this wonderful house which the horticultural people maintain jolly well on the whole. The director has good taste, and is a splendid man with all the right ideas. A crisp, sunny day which deluded me into thinking that life still held forth promise and fulfilment. Continued to Sole Street where the contours of God's orchards are homely. Met Daphne Baker on the road. She gave me tea at the Tudor Yeoman's House. Three unimportant little National Trust properties I

have seen today, and one superb house, which is not ours and only protected by covenants.

Saturday, 15th January

I went to the office early. Then shopped. No books, no shoes, in fact
nothing bought – and a thick fog. Went to the Leicester Galleries to see
the Michael Sadler collection now on show, before dispersal. Probably
the best collection of modern paintings we shall see for a long time, certainly have seen since the war. Horrible Picasso self-portrait, all in angles,
but Mark Gertler's mother and Henry Lamb's death of a peasant among
the best. Oh, the Renoir lady in blue too, but I coveted a hundred others.
I understand that several have already been bought by K. Clark,
Raymond Mortimer and Harold Nicolson.

Lunched at the café, and General Kennedy, D.M.O., beckoned me to
him. Catherine is in waiting. He has two days off and is bored stiff. I asked
him how he whiled the time away. He said by painting kingfishers over
and over again, poor man. He is courteous, gentle and appealing. All afternoon I worked like a demon, then prepared tea for Ethel Walker who did
not come. At 5.30 she rang the bell, having failed the first time to push
open the iron gate. She and the dog ate two cakes. She closely studied
the Peter Scott drawing of me and asked to see a photograph of me. None
could be found. She said the least beautiful part of the female anatomy
for drawing was the breast. I refrained from saying I could think of a less
beautiful part.

At 6 in the fog I reached Hyde Park Gardens for Sir Ian Hamilton's
92nd birthday party. He was standing in the hall, dressed in a white waistcoat and a red carnation, being flashlight-photographed, with some
Highland pipers. A crowded party, lots of Americans and Highlanders in
kilts.

At 7.15 to Emerald's. She was speaking on the telephone on business
as I came in, so I read the evening paper. She said Jamesey was dining
with her and pressed me to stay. Then the siren went, and I consented.
There was a great to-do about ordering a third cover, and Emerald lost
her temper on the telephone, and stormed. She said the chef was a liar,
she would speak to the Minister of Food, she would come downstairs
and make a 'scandal' in the hall by screaming at the telephonist, that the
waiters were all Nazis or Bolsheviks, she did not know which, the
Dorchester was like a commercial traveller's doss house, the place
Bedlam, a charity institution in a Dickens novel, like Dotheboys Hall, and
so forth. Luckily James arrived in the middle of all this and I was not left
alone to feel uncomfortable. Afterwards dinner upstairs passed happily
enough. We lamented that the younger generation, never having been to

the continent, only thought of European cities, which their fathers had revered as seats of culture, as targets to be bombed. We were allowing the continental seats of learning to be wiped out, and making little boys from the suburbs into heroes for committing these acts of barbarism. J. and E. talked Balzac. Emerald said we must live after the war in Paris, where the trees are all 'fluorescent' because there is no smoke in the atmosphere, and the women are beautiful and dress in silks and satins to match the horse carriages in which they drive, because there are no motors.

Sunday, 16th January

Today I really was intending to go to Cumberland Lodge, for Stuart Preston had pledged himself to accompany me. Magdalen FitzAlan-Howard rings me up at least once a week and I make a succession of excuses. But this morning she telephoned to say the fog was very thick. Indeed it was so bad here that I had to postpone. Stuart and I lunched instead very happily at the Travellers'. The fog got thicker and thicker, and gorgeously yellow. When we stepped into Pall Mall it was like a blanket. How I love it. We somehow managed to reach Cheyne Walk by bus. S. spent the rest of the day sprawling over his books on the floor, sprawling over the armchair, sprawling over everything.

Tuesday, 18th January

We had a Country Houses Committee this afternoon, which passed all right. Eardley's scheme for making Montacute into a furnished house was accepted.

Wednesday, 19th January

I walked away from the Georgian Group meeting with Gerry Wellington, who talked about the future of Apsley House. In the afternoon Mortimer Wheeler addressed the S.P.A.B. committee on the work done, or rather not done, so far by the British authorities in North Africa and Italy. He gave a depressing and infuriating picture. The apathetic, ignorant and casual attitude shocked even me, who never cease to deplore British philistinism. It appears that up to date only three British experts have been sent to Italy to join twelve American experts, already there. They have no authority to act, and so their presence is merely an encumbrance to the Americans. Nothing is done to protect historic monuments when British troops withdraw from operations, except to billet more troops in them, and so render them more ruinous than they were during the fighting.

This evening I dined at Claridges with Alfred and Clementine Beit. Arrived at 8 and waited in the hall. Espied Gerry likewise sitting waiting

He said, 'Shall we have a drink?' I said, 'A good idea.' 'We will not have cocktails. They are too expensive,' he said in that well-known way. Actually I sympathize with him. So we each paid for a small glass of sherry at 4/-, which was preposterous. He told me that his gross income today was £40,000. After income and super tax there was £4,000 left over. Out of this he has to pay schedule A on Stratfield Saye and Apsley House, which leaves him barely enough for wages and food. I asked whether he had any servants at Apsley House. He said, 'Oh yes, I have the chamberlain's wife and the house carpenter.' He said he did not pay death duties on either of these two houses, or the lands attached, because they don't belong to him, but to Parliament. He is applying to Parliament to take back Apsley House - with the gift of the valuable contents which are his - on condition that they will make it into a museum under his guidance, and allow him to live in a corner of it. It is, he says, a perfect museum, not having been altered in any particular since the Great Duke's death in 1852.

Joan Moore joined us. At 8.30 it occurred to us that the Beits might have taken a private dining-room, which is what they had done. Joan and I talked of passionate, desperate, hopeless love. General conversation after dinner. Most enjoyable it was too. I walked in the rain to Hyde Park Corner with Gerry, who feigned to be nervous, cautious and old-mannish, as though it became his new ducal status. He kept saying it was a terribly long way to go. I think a person's age can be measured by his reaction to the blackout. Gerry was, however, charming, as he always is to me. He says that being a duke and inheriting two houses is like having a glittering present every day.

Thursday, 20th January

Johnnie Dashwood and Clifford Smith lunched with me at Brooks's to discuss West Wycombe affairs. I sensed they disliked each other.

Hamish dined alone with me at Brooks's. A boozy evening. I had three whiskies and soda before dinner. We had a bottle of burgundy at dinner, and two glasses of port each after dinner. Hamish told me all about his bravery, for which he got the M.C., treating it all as a great joke. His gun was shot to atoms and he received wounds all down the left side. His sergeant dragged him to safety. He denied that he was courageous. There was no alternative to what he had to do. A few times only he had a sense of personal fear when at close quarters to the enemy. The German soldiers were kind to prisoners. The Italian were only interested in their money. They have no respect for us and deadly fear of the Germans, who say, 'If you do so and so, we shoot,' and do shoot. Whereas we say the same, and don't shoot. He recounted his escape and hiding in a ditch, while hearing Germans shout, '*Fritz, wo ist er?*' I said, 'I suppose if they had found you, they would have bayoneted you on the spot?' He looked surprised and said, 'Not at all. They would have clapped me on the shoulder and said, "Bad luck! Now we must lock you up again."' But he was anxious then. 'I had my rosary and was racing round it faster than you could have gone round the inner circle.' I said, 'When the Germans left and you realized you were safe, what did you say to Our Lady?' 'Whoopee, Virge!' We went back to his mews and drank beer till 2.30. He prepared a bed for me and said before he went to the bathroom, 'I hope you will be comfortable, but if you can't sleep you will have to come to mine,' which was a great double bed. When he came back I said, 'You were quite right in saying the sheets on my bed would only reach to my navel.' So Hamish said, 'Well, you'd better come to my bed, though I have wasted a clean pair on yours for nothing.'

Sunday, 23rd January

At 10.30 Stuart met me at Paddington Station. While waiting for him I watched a woman passenger have a row with an officious woman ticket collector at the barrier. The first threw the other's ticket puncher to the ground. The second threw the first's handbag to the ground, took off her own coat, and flew at her opponent. They punched and scratched and finally became interlocked, each grasping the other's hair which came away in handfuls. I felt quite sick and intervened. Then they both hit me. I roared for help, and two policemen dragged the combatants apart. The other passengers, mostly soldiers, merely looked on.

From Windsor station we made for the Park and down the Long Walk, the far end of which is felled, the elm trunks being quite rotten. Fine day with a biting wind. I had my filthy old mackintosh on which always puts me in the wrong frame of mind. It's curious how the clothes one is wearing dictate one's mood. Stuart kept saying, 'I do hope there is a good luncheon, and lots to eat.' I had misgivings.

There were only us and the family. Lord FitzAlan is past conversation now, having become very old and deaf. Magdalen has no conversation anyway, but is not deaf. Alathea looked sad and cold, no wonder. Stuart tried to be bright. I felt ill at ease, and suddenly realized I would have been able to make more effort if alone, without S. As we went into the dining-room Magdalen said, 'I hope there will be enough for you to eat. There is only soup.' It was too true. S. took some Scotch broth, and Alathea said, 'I should put some potato into it if I were you.' I overheard S. exclaim, 'What! potato in the soup? No thanks.' He soon did, however, on discovering that this really was the only dish. We got up rattling. S. was very forgiving on the way back. In Windsor we had a filthy tea at the Nell Gwynne café, to make up for the non-luncheon.

Tuesday, 25th January

Kathleen Kennet went to the National Gallery early and took a seat for me, good soul, and bought sandwiches. Myra Hess fed our two starved souls with delicious Mozart.

I behaved badly tonight by cutting Sibyl Colefax's Ordinary, which annoyed her, and cutting the boring Dr. Dietmar's dinner too. Harold Nicolson asked me to go to a play with him. It was *There Shall Be No Night*, a propaganda play, but excellent, with Lynn Fontanne and Alfred Lunt. She is a woman I could love and marry, I told Harold. At King's Bench Walk afterwards Harold discussed his political perplexities. He has been offered by Eden a seat in the Lords, which Harold toys with, because of the independence it promises. On the other hand if there is a chance of his getting back into the Commons at the next election, he will refuse. He thinks there is little chance. He cannot stand as National Labour again, and will not stand as Tory or straight Labour. Would like to stand as Liberal but the Liberals have opposed him in his constituency. I said, 'Damn the lot, and be a lord.' Harold looked shocked, and maintained that the problem was of the greatest consequence.

Thursday, 27th January

Curious how much I dislike going away, and three days' absence from London seems like exile. I had a very comfortable first-class sleeper to Plymouth, yet the knowledge that I would be called at 5.30 a.m. kept me from sleeping. Actually the train was two hours late and I was not called till 6. Why couldn't it have been at 7.30? Arrived Falmouth very late. Had breakfast at 9.30 with the town librarian who is very worried about the fate of Arwenack Manor. To him, poor old man, the salvation of this house is his life's purpose. We went there, and it is not of architectural importance. In Elizabethan times it was a large mansion, and there are remains of a banqueting hall, one outer wall to be exact. The place was held by the Killigrews and burnt out in the Civil Wars. What is left of the house is now tenements. Today the R.A.F. occupy part of it. The young officer in command who took us round made intelligent suggestions. But blotted his copybook in the librarian's eyes by suggesting that a guest house was the most fitting use, come peace-time. I agreed, but the librarian was greatly pained. I had to tell him that it was not the N.T.'s concern, but I would recommend that Falmouth corporation should save it from demolition and the surrounding land from development.

I left Falmouth by a 12.40 train, having been given an enormous

Cornish pasty by the dear old librarian. It was his own luncheon. I did not get to Sherborne till 8.30. A honeymoon couple in my carriage were douched with confetti as the train drew out, and I was covered. The stuff even got down my neck. What can be the origin of this barbaric custom?

Friday, 28th January

Today was devoted to Sherborne Castle. At 10 the solicitor, who was also staying at the Digby Arms, took me to Rawlence, the agent's office, and the three of us motored to the Castle grounds bordering the town. We walked through the large walled gardens and the large stable yard. Then motored past the house towards the Palladian bridge, uphill to see the deer, but not as far as the unsightly American hospital buildings. Walked round the park and returned to the entrance. At first glance the outside of the house is disappointing. The cement rendering makes it gloomy. The plate-glass windows give it a blind, eyeless look. Yet the house reminds me of Westwood Park in that it too has a central late-Elizabethan block (built as a hunting lodge by Sir Walter Raleigh) to which four arms were added in Restoration times. The dressings are of Ham stone. Fine entrance gates at the south and north sides, forming two open courts. Like Westwood the house is terribly confusing inside, for it is very tall, with many floor levels. There is little inside to take the breath away, but much that is good, notably the great marble chimneypieces of Jacobean date and, above all, the two interior porches in the downstairs dining-room. The great saloon is oddly shaped with two broken arms at the ends because of Raleigh's hexagonal towers, into which on all floors one constantly seems to be walking. At present the furniture is stored away, for American troops have requisitioned the castle. There are cavernous basements.

So far the lordly owner has not appeared, and we three of low degree lunch at the hotel. Twice Rawlence is called away to be advised by the Colonel's butler at what time we are to appear for coffee, port and cigars. The Wingfield Digbys are in Raleigh's lodge for the 'duration'. The Colonel is a stooping M.F.H., with the manner of one. Very autocratic, very conscious of his not inconsiderable dignity. He addresses Rawlence as Major Rawlence, in spite of the latter's father and grandfather also having been agents to the family, and Rawlence being every inch a gent. Rawlence addresses him as Colonel, and often as Sir. An awkward interview takes place. I explain as best I can what the transaction would involve. But they are not the sort of people to welcome public access.

After the interview we sallied forth to the pleasance. The Colonel and Mrs. W. D. took us over the old ruined castle and through the very beautiful wooded walks round the lake. Here we came upon Raleigh's Seat, where the servant is said to have thrown the water over his master while he was smoking; and Pope's Seat, where the poet wrote letters to Martha Blount. The Colonel showed little interest in these fascinating associations. When, on the second Seat being pointed out, I responded excitedly, the Colonel snorted, 'Pope indeed. I've no idea which pope it could have been.'

The Wingfield Digbys, finding that I was to dine alone, very kindly bade me dine with them. They showed me some rare miniatures - of Arabella Stuart, Kenelm Digby and Venetia Digby; also a jewel given to Ambassador Digby by the court of Spain. I liked the W. D.s although Anne Rosse had previously warned that they might not like me. And there was one awkward moment when, a propos of nothing, the Colonel exclaimed, 'I can't stick Roman Catholics. One can smell 'em a mile off,' or words to that effect. Mrs. Wingfield Digby, who, although her sentiments were clearly the same as her husband's, wished to appear open-minded, then said, 'But, Freddy, they do have a right to their own point of view,' adding after a pregnant pause, 'Of course one can't trust them one yard.' I thought it best to remain mum.

Anne had also told me a hair-raising story of the Colonel's behaviour during a severe frost. The lake at Sherborne froze, and people from near and far assembled to skate, as they do on these occasions, without by your leave. So 'Cousin Freddy' climbed up one of the Castle towers, and with a rifle peppered the ice to make it crack.

Saturday, 29th January

Up early and while it was not properly light went to the Abbey. A fine fan-vaulted ceiling to the nave. The chief ornament is a monster marble monument to a Digby Earl of Bristol signed by John Nost about 1698. Pope in a letter written from Sherborne commented favourably upon it. I looked at the old Hospital chapel next door, walked through the Close and the School to Sherborne House, now a girls' school, to see the Thornhill staircase walls and ceiling. This house belongs to the Digby estate. The Thornhill paintings are flaking through having been varnished over with coach varnish by a Digby predecessor. The stair rail turns into a gnarled, knuckled fist over the bottom newel.

Caught an 11 o'clock train to Semley station where I parked my bag and, with the aid of my map, walked to Pythouse, up a hill with the finest imaginable view across the Nadder valley towards Wardour. Sang (wildly out of tune, of course) all the way at the top of my voice. Pythouse is the prototype of nearby Dinton and the owner Colonel Stanford-Benett had asked me to pay him a visit. House built about 1800 with great Ionic portico. The side elevations are attached to wings by rounded angles, not very pretty. But what a setting, backed by trees! The old man is stone deaf. The house full of paying guests. Nothing remarkable about the interior, but a curiously narrow, long staircase. The first Benett was secretary to Prince Rupert, and they have a number of Charles I's letters and his death mask. The Stanford-Benetts are so old that by the time luncheon was over they were worn out. At 2.30 I rose to go. Wandered round the place by myself before setting of for Semley station. Got to Waterloo at 7 and gave Bridget Parsons dinner. She at her most beautiful. I firewatched in the office, rushing there at top speed when I heard the siren at 10.30. There was much gunfire. Lovel, the office caretaker, told me shrapnel fell on his steel helmet, and a large jagged bit just missed his shoulder.

Sunday, 30th January

That wretched old Ethel Walker and her dirty old dog came to tea. She talked of religion and the spheres of heaven having recently been cleansed. How it benefits the world at this nadir of spatial circumnavigations I fail to appreciate.

Thursday, 3rd February

I gave a luncheon party at the Ritz – Sibyl Colefax, Honey Harris and Cyril Connolly. The Ritz was crowded and there was much noise. I did not hear one word Sibyl uttered, and not for one instant did she draw breath. I asked Cyril whether he had heard anything, and he said nothing at all. The party was not therefore a rollicking success as far as the host was concerned.

At 6 I met Alvilde Chaplin at Mrs. Gordon Woodhouse's flat. Mrs. Woodhouse is old and little, but agile and rapid. Full of conversation. She was seated at a clavichord when I entered. After Alvilde joined us she turned to another clavichord made by Tom Goff. She played a Bach prelude, and I thought how lovely. After some more I decided that the instrument was too thin. I needed more volume to be satisfied. When I remarked that I could not claim to be really musical, she stopped. She talked about her house, Nether Lypiatt, and called in Lord Barrington who showed me his sepia drawings of the house. He is a sweet, friendly, simple creature, and I would suppose not up to her exacting intellectual level. Went on to dine with Bridget in Mount Street. B. had bad toothache, and was wearing a turban and dressing gown with no buttons down the front. It was a diaphanous garment. 'Did she expose that blue varicose vein?' Anne asked me later. B. rattled off a host of questions, which is her present conversational technique, as though eagerly seeking information. Poor B., she is infinitely pathetic, for all her beauty and fastidiousness, which does not extend to her dress.

Friday, 4th February

Started off at 10.30 this morning for Norfolk, taking Geoffrey Houghton-Brown with me. Now he *is* a relaxed companion.

After the mugginess of the past few days the sudden cold and fierce north wind has come as a shock. But from inside the fairly warm car the wide landscape of East Anglia, which the storm clouds and fitful sunbeams were chasing, was very dramatic. Having gone out of the way to look at Wimpole from the end of the great elm avenue, we first stopped in Cambridge, bought books and drank coffee. On to Ely, stopping outside the town to eat sandwiches and feast on the distant cathedral. Admired the satisfactory marriage of the mid-Victorian barrel roof, painted by, I believe, a Le Strange of Hunstanton, with the Norman nave. Drove on to Norfolk and looked at the outside of Ryston Hall, built in the 1650s by Sir Roger Pratt. Ryston is still owned by a Roger Pratt. The Inigo Jones-like central portion can be detected under the Soane alterations. Stopped at Stoke Ferry Hall. It was empty. We pushed open a window at the back and walked into the deserted house. The soldiery have just vacated, so the condition is deplorable. Not by any means a remarkable house. High, plain, red-brick façade to the street, dated 1788 – the category of doctor's or solicitor's house. Spacious and well proportioned within. Spacious, many-walled garden. Everything I like, yet this pleasant old house is not worthy of the Trust, I fear. The conditions attached to the offer are not attractive; and besides, who would wish to live here? We continued past romantic Oxburgh Hall which we looked at from the road, and peered at the fine Bedingfeld terracotta monuments through the church windows. On to Swanton Morley. Tried in vain to find the vicar or anyone who might know where exactly was the site of Abraham Lincoln's forebears' cottage. No one of the four inhabitants we asked could tell. No one seemed to care. Nor did Geoffrey or I for that matter.

Just as it was growing dark the car konked out at the end of the lime walk at Blickling. In a downpour we pushed it to Miss O'Sullivan's door. Geoffrey stayed at the inn, I in Miss O'Sullivan's flat.

Saturday, 5th February

In the morning we went round the house looking at the furniture salvaged by me from the R.A.F.'s quarters. After a stroll in the garden, we drove on to Cromer, a mechanic from Aylsham having mended the car. The points needed adjusting. Found an hotel for G. in Cromer. It was the only one open in the whole town, a dingy, dirty building on the sea front. I arrived at Felbrigg in time for luncheon with Wyndham

Ketton-Cremer in his great hall, barely warmed by one small stove. Otherwise no heating and no electric light. Only oil lamps at night.

In the afternoon he and I motored to Beeston Hall, the property of his late brother, whose presumed death in action was announced in the press this week to Wyndham's infinite distress. A bomb has lately fallen in front of the house. In any case the house, altered Georgian, has not much merit. We proceeded to Beeston Priory and Farm, both owned by Mrs. Reynolds, a rich farmer's widow. The Priory ruins, scheduled by the Ministry of Works, are extensive. Ivy-clad nave walls and some Early English pointed window heads. Mrs. Reynolds is of that splendid, sturdy yeoman stock, like the Miss Smyths of Earlswood Moat House. She is integrity personified, quick-witted, direct and talkative to boot. With the Priory she enjoys some curious rights of pasturage over the surrounding lands, not her own. These she jealously cherishes, and accordingly prevents building development over much of the coast here. At tea she gave us such a spread as I have not enjoyed for years. Farm bread and butter with apple jelly, and a rich rum cake, the best I have ever eaten. She made me take some away with me.

I was very tired after Wyndham's excellent dinner, and slept in front of the stove in spite of the cold. We talked about his book, *Norfolk Portraits*. He is a delightful, cultivated man; a most conscientious landowner. Perhaps a little too good to be true, a little too old for his age.

Sunday, 6th February

Left Wyndham at 10. A glorious still, sunny morning, the pattering of raindrops on crisp, curled leaves and the sucking up of puddles in the rutted drive clearly audible. Picked up Geoffrey in Cromer. At Gunton we got out, and walked to the edge of the lake, looking across at the house which some years ago was gutted by fire. In Norwich G. wanted to attend Mass in an ugly but well-built Catholic church. I was struck by the drabness of the packed congregation compared to what it would have been in 1939. In the cathedral three old women and one American formed the congregation. Looked at Sweet Vi, the late Bishop's girl friend in marble, kneeling in the ambulatory, very smug and Edwardian. In Wymondham Abbey we admired Comper's gilt reredos.

Tuesday, 8th February

A large deputation of the Liverpool City Council came to see me this morning about the Speke Hall lease and the heirlooms, all of which, ghastly fakes for the most part, they want. Horne, playing the part of the tough lawyer, supported me, taking the part of the generous fool. The combination worked well.

Wednesday, 9th February

A young member of the Trust called for me at the office and at 11.30 we set off in the car for Hitchin. He is a nice, earnest black-coated worker, called Teagle, madly keen on archaeological remains, birds and nature. He hikes every weekend in the summer in the Home Counties with his wife, and stays in youth hostels. I took him to a British Restaurant in Hitchin where we had a tolerable meal of thick soup, roast mutton and baked potatoes. This was quickly over and we went to an area of land which he has found and wants us to save. We got out and walked for an hour. A small river valley bounded by a straight stretch of the Icknield Way. In this sunswept, windswept landscape our noses ran. He wiped his nose with the back of his hand. I had one handkerchief and debated with myself whether to share it. Decided against. I motored him as far as Ayot St. Lawrence where we looked at the old ruined church and the new. At the gate of Bernard Shaw's house I parted with him.

Shaw's Corner is a very ugly, dark red-brick villa, built in 1902. I rang the bell and a small maid in uniform led me across the hall to a drawing-room, with open views on to the garden and the country beyond, for the house is at the end of the village. There was a fire burning in the pinched little grate. Walls distempered, the distemper flaking badly in patches. The quality of the contents of the room was on a par with that of the villa. Indifferent water colours of the Roman Campagna, trout pools, etc. in cheap gilt frames. One rather good veneered Queen Anne bureau (for which G.B.S. said he had given £80) and one fake lacquer bureau. In the window a statuette of himself by Paul Troubetskoy. On the mantelpiece a late Staffordshire figure of Shakespeare (for which he paid 10/-), a china house, the lid of which forms a box. Only a few conventionally bound classics, plus Osbert Sitwell's latest publication prominently displayed on a table. Two stiff armchairs before the fire and brass fender. A shoddy three-ply screen attached to the fireplace to shelter from draughts anyone sitting between the fire and doorway.

I waited five minutes and looked around, at a chronometer and the serried row of Shakespeare plays in soft leather bindings. Presently the door opened and in came the great man. I was instantly struck by the snow-white head and beard, the blue eyes and the blue nose, with a small ripe spot over the left nostril. He was not so tall as I imagined, for he stoops slightly. He was dressed in a pepper-and-salt knickerbocker suit. A loose, yellow tie from a pink collar over a thick woollen vest rather than shirt. Several waistcoats. Mittens over blue hands. He evidently feels the cold for there were electric fires in every room and the passage. He shook hands and I forget what he first said. Nothing special anyway. Asked me to sit down, and put questions to me straight off, such as, could he make over the property now and retain a right of user. His friend, Lord Astor (Arstor), had done so. I had not expected the strong Irish brogue. This peasant origin makes him all the more impressive. It put me in mind of Thomas Carlyle, of whom, curiously enough, he spoke. I said I preferred Mrs. to Mr. Carlyle. He said Carlyle was out of fashion because of the prevailing anti-German prejudice; that there had been worse husbands than he. G.B.S. said he wished to impose no conditions on the hand-over, but he did not wish the house to become a dead museum. Hoped it would be a living shrine. He wanted to settle matters now, for since his wife's death he was bound to re-make his will, and in three years' time he might be quite dotty, if he was alive at all. He is 88, and very agile. He showed me his statuette, which he likes, and bust (copy) by Rodin which he does not care for. Took me into his study where he works at an untidy writing table. In this room is another Queen Anne bureau. The wall facing it is covered with reference books, and all the bound proofs of his own books, corrected by him. These, I said, ought to remain here. There are no pictures or photographs of his wife to be seen. The dining-room is far from beautiful. It contains some fumed oak furniture and a portrait of him done in 1913. He ran upstairs, pointing admiringly to the enlarged bird etchings on the stair wall. He showed me his wife's room and his bedroom, and the one spare room. He has lived in this house since 1908.

When he smiles his face softens and becomes engaging. He is not at all deaf, but comes close up to one to talk, breathing into one's face. His breath is remarkably sweet for an old man's. Having looked upstairs we descended. He tripped going down, and I was afraid he was going to fall headlong. He then said, 'We will go out and have a look at the curtilage' – rolling the 'r' of this unusual word. It was fearfully cold by now, and raining heavily. He put on a long, snow-white mackintosh and chose a stick. From the hall hat-rack, hung with a variety of curious headgear, he took an archaic rough felt hat, of a buff colour, high in crown and wide of brim. In this garb he resembled Carlyle, and was the very picture of the sage, striding forth, a little wobbly and bent perhaps, pointing out the extent of the 'curtilage' and the line of the hedge which he had de-rooted with his own hands so as to lengthen the garden. The boundary trees of spruce were planted by him. 'Trees grow like mushrooms in these parts,' he said. We came to a little asbestos-roofed summer house that revolves on its own axis. Here he also writes and works. There is a little table covered with writing material, and a couch. The summer house was pad-locked. I said, 'Do you sit out here in the winter then?' 'I have an elec-tric stove,' and he pointed to a thick cable attached to the summer house from an iron pylon behind it. 'This will be an attraction to the *birthplace*, if it survives,' he said. We passed piles of logs, which he told me he had chopped himself He showed me his and his wife's initials carved on the coach-house door and engraved on a glass pane of the greenhouse. Took me into the coach-house where there are three cars under dust sheets, one a Rolls-Royce. 'When I want to use this,' he said, 'I become very decrepit, and the authorities allow me coupons.' We continued down the road.

A collie puppy dog met us in the road and jumped up at the old man who paid it much attention. He led me to Revett's curious church. He explained at length that the reigning squire began demolishing the old church because he considered it 'an aesthetic disgrace' and 'barbarous Gothic'. The Bishop stopped it entirely disappearing, but not the erection of Revett's church in the 'fashionable Palladian'. G.B.S. walked up the steps and with reverence took off his hat. We walked inside. The interior is certainly cold and unspiritual. 'But it has good proportions,' Shaw allowed. The worst mistake is the ugly coloured glass in the windows. Classical churches are always spoilt by coloured glass. The organ case is contemporary. When we left he tapped with his stick a scrolled tombstone and made me read the inscription. It was to some woman who had died in the 1890s, aged 76, and below were inscribed the words, 'Cut off ere her prime,' or words to such effect. 'That,' G.B.S. said, 'is what persuaded me to come and live in the parish thirty-six years ago, for I assumed I stood some chance of at least reaching my ninetieth year.' We continued past the house and across the field, to the old church. He explained that although he never worshipped in the church he had spent £100 on its preservation. He remarked that the font had been overturned at some time. Took me outside to see the grave of Queen Victoria's tallest army officer, and admire the tracery moulding on a doorway, now blocked, at the west end. He wishes to buy the little corner cottage in order to destroy it, because it hides a view of the church from his own house. By the time we got back to the house I was wet through.

Tea was brought on a tray to the drawing-room. A glass of milk only for him; but tea and cakes for me. I was given a mug to drink out of. We talked of Esher's letter to The Times, of which he heartily approved. Decried the madness of the times, and the war. He said wars cease to be wars when chivalry is altogether excluded, as now, and become mass murder. That we had yet to witness the day when conscientious objection would be organized on such a universal scale that wars just could not happen. Up to now conscientious objection had failed, but one day it would succeed. It would be interesting to see how it would work if ever this country declared war on Soviet Russia. The present war was due, not to man's wickedness, but to his ignorance. In the last war he wrote a letter to *The Times* urging that air-raid shelters be provided for children. *The Times* refused to publish it because the editor was shocked by the implied suggestion that the enemy could, or would bomb school-children. The *News Chronicle* refused likewise. I asked, 'What would you do if you were given Winston Churchill's powers and position today?' He said wisely enough, 'All action depends upon actual circumstance, but I would endeavour to bring fighting to an instant conclusion.' I said, 'I doubt whether the Germans would follow suit.' He condemned the folly of insisting upon unconditional surrender. There can be no such thing. The Government ought to tell the Germans what conditions we would accept and what terms we should impose. He mocked at the press's pretence that Winston Churchill and Stalin were in agreement. Their aims were becoming more and more widely divergent. He was nauseated by the lies disseminated by the press. At the same time he laughed at the Left Wing for supposing that today they could achieve their aims by general strikes, for 'You do not do well to starve on the enemy's doorstep.'

We talked about Hardy's Max Gate. 'Pull it down,' he said. He advised the National Trust to hold his house alienably, so that, supposing in twenty years' time we found that his name was forgotten, we could reap the benefit of selling it. He liked the idea of our holding T. E. Lawrence's Cloud's Hill, for 'it is good for nothing else'. Talked a lot about Lawrence. Said people would not grasp that T.E.L. was physically under-developed and never grew up, scarcely shaved, and also was mentally adolescent. He used to tell Lawrence that he knew no one who kept his anonymity so much in the limelight. He and his wife corrected the proofs of *The Seven Pillars*. The published version was scarcely recognizable. The Shaws cut out so much that was sheer guilt complex. Lawrence was tormented by the recollection of the lives he had personally 'terminated'. Lawrence's great discovery had been that the surest way of directing affairs of any department was by enlisting at the bottom and remaining there. His was the lowest rank of aircraftsman and he had to pretend to be illiterate in order to avoid promotion. Shaw tried to persuade Baldwin, 'that pure humbug', to give T.E.L. a pension. Lawrence refused to consider one although he confessed to Shaw that sometimes to get a square meal he would hang around the Duke of York's steps until a friend took him off to luncheon.

At 5.15 G.B.S. jumped up, saying it was getting dark and he had kept me a quarter of an hour too long. Thanked me for coming. I said I had enjoyed the afternoon immensely. He said he had too. Before I left however he talked about his will again; said he would not leave any money to his relations for he did not wish them to grow up in idleness and luxury. He wanted to leave his money for the sole purpose of inaugurating a new alphabet of something like 140 letters instead of the 26. He had calculated that the saving of expense in print and paper within one generation would be enough to finance three more world wars. And if that didn't appeal to this government, what would? He came on to the road without hat or coat and stood until I drove off. In the mirror I watched him still standing on the road.

Thursday, 10th February

Dined at Sibyl Colefax's Ordinary in the Dorchester and sat between Emerald and Christabel Aberconway. The latter blinks her eyelids at one and acts the clown, whereas she is shrewd, shrewd. She threw a knife and fork at Professor Joad while dining at Emerald's, which is good marks for her. After dinner talked with Cyril and Rosemary Hinchingbrooke about religions. Cyril is all for them as purveyors of a moral standard so long as they are not heaven inspired. I said the trouble about religions was that they purveyed not one, but several conflicting moral standards.

Saturday, 12th February

Oh, such a ridiculous ceremony! At noon to the American Embassy. In an ugly back room like a schoolroom a contingent of black, or rather dark yellow American troops, Angus Malcolm, the Bonham-Carters, myself and the press waited. Soon Thurtle of the M.O.I., Lord Zetland, Colonel Jack Leslie and the American Ambassador entered and sat under two flags of the U.K. and U.S.A. Speeches ensued and Colonel Leslie handed the deeds of the site of Abraham Lincoln's ancestors' cottage at Swanton Morley to Lord Zetland. Zetland spoke well, succinctly, and not dully. The Ambassador, who is a handsome, dark man, with low brow and jet eyes, read a well composed speech on Lincoln's democratic ideals, but so haltingly and shyly that I felt embarrassed for him. It is strange that he should be so painfully shy.

Talked to Professor Richardson at Brooks's. He is determined the Georgian Group shall extend its functions so as to become the arbiter of taste in modern architecture, a dangerous step for a preservation society in my opinion. Accompanied him to the Courtauld Institute for the Georgian Group reception. Left as soon as decently possible with Dame Una and James. Over tea the Dame very censorious of the new Archbishop for encouraging Catholics to agitate over the Education Bill. She strongly deprecates Catholics concerning themselves with political issues, as they do in Ireland. I don't think I agree any more than I agreed with the Professor this afternoon. The truth is I can't come to snap decisions, but like to have time to think matters over. My mind works slowly and creakily.

Sunday, 13th February

Lunched at Kathleen Kennet's house. He ill in bed. K. and I walked across the Park to the Albert Hall to a Beethoven concert. On the way she told me she had written a letter to *The Times* (which they have not published) to the effect that she would gladly sacrifice Rome for the life of her two sons. (So likely that she will be given the choice!) This silly argument angered me. She was cross and threatened not to see me again and to have me reported to the police for holding subversive views. I replied that I was quite indifferent to these threats. A coolness ensued.

To tea with Emerald. How funny she was. I recall Gerald Berners's definition of Sibyl Colefax's and Emerald's parties. The first was a party of lunatics presided over by an efficient, trained hospital nurse; the second a party of lunatics presided over by a lunatic. It is impossible to recollect or record accurately Emerald's particular funninesses. She told us how Count So-and-So shocked her correct husband, Sir Bache, by bringing to Nevill Holt where they lived his Austrian mistress for a week's hunting. 'My dear, she was an Abbess' - by which she meant a chanoinesse, a hereditary dignity.

Monday, 14th February

Matheson made Martineau take the Finance Committee today and me the Executive. Martineau was so nervous that he called every committee member 'Sir' between each word, and even members of the staff. My heart bled for him. Esher said to me, 'I have never seen a fellow in such a stew. You seemed to do all right,' which, strictly speaking, was not the case, for I knew nothing of half the items on the agenda, Matheson having dealt with them exclusively. I am too charitable to suspect that he was gloating over our discomfiture.

Wednesday, 16th February

News has come of the bombing of Monte Cassino monastery. This is comparable with the German shelling of Rheims cathedral in the last war. No war-mindedness can possibly justify it.

Thursday, 17th February

James Mann of the Wallace Collection lunched with me. He agreed that we had far better lose the war than destroy Rome. He came to discuss the future of Sir Edward Barry's house, Ockwells. Sir E. has made him an executor. He has advised Sir E. to sell the property now, but at a reasonable figure, and not to stick out for a fancy price. I wrote again to Captain John Hill suggesting Mr. Cook as a purchaser.

Friday, 18th February

I dined at Emerald's and sat next to Joan Moore and Lady Russell, wife of Sir Claud, retired ambassador to Portugal. She is half-Greek. Aubrey Moody, a new friend of Emerald's, present. He sends her flowers all the week, according to Joan. Emerald persistent in calling upon me to talk about my visit to Bernard Shaw, which I was loth to do, because I could see that the Ambassador did not want to listen. Emerald likes every guest to play a part. She is like a prompter in the theatre, or a conductor at the opera. Having failed over G.B.S. - fortunately - she made me read aloud a letter which Daisy Fellowes had just received, beginning, 'Divine Creature, I have been chaste since 1st January, which I find uncomfortable . . . I am faithful to you and White's Club only. I adore you.' We agreed that it was not a serious love letter.

On my return at 12.30 Joan telephoned, and we talked for half an hour. The instant she put down the receiver the sirens went, and the worst raid for years occurred. The noise of guns was deafening. Miss Paterson and I went downstairs and ate buns in the kitchen, trembling with fear. When the all-clear sounded, there were fires to be seen in all directions. The result is, we brought down five raiders only, and four of them over France.

Sunday, 20th February

By the evening I was very tired for I slept badly last night. On returning home was obliged to shelter in South Kensington tube during another severe and noisy raid. A lot more fires and a bomb dropped on the Treasury buildings. The Carmelite church in Kensington destroyed.

Monday, 21st February

Dining with the Moores in Ladbroke Grove, Garrett said, 'Look at Jim's nose!', and indeed I felt it burning red from the sudden heat after the intense cold outside. Emerald said that a certain duke - she would not disclose which - remarked about his wife, whom E. had been praising, 'Yes, but you don't have to sleep with her.' 'Now, dear,' E. remarked, 'isn't that what you call caddish?' There was only one answer. Joan said that recently a visiting Polish general sat next to a handsome English general who spoke in a deep voice about strategy. Suddenly the English general took out a powder puff, then a lipstick. It was the Duchess of Marlborough.

Alfred Beit talked to me about the parliamentary amenities group and the bombing of monuments versus lives argument. Said the Bishop of Chichester was responsible for raising this unnecessary and irrelevant matter in the Lords by suggesting that all German cultural centres should be spared. Alfred said the only hope of doing our cause good was by keeping calm, not writing emotional letters to the press, but sending to the ministers concerned a deputation of the most respected M.P.s from the Amenity Group. The Beits motored me to Chelsea across the Park. The gates were closed, so I got out and opened them.

Tuesday, 22nd February

Alec Penrose and Eddy Sackville-West lunched today, for Alec said he wished to meet him again. Alec began by being inscrutable and delusively diffident. That is what I like about his plain, dour face and manner. After a bit he blossoms into the sensitive, poetical man he is. His poem he sent me for Christmas is proof enough. Eddy in a *voix blanche* mood. The windows of the west front of Knole have been blown out by a bomb in the park. The heraldic beasts on the gable finials turned round on their plinths and presented their backs to the outrage committed. What proud and noble behaviour!

At midnight a very bad raid. Miss P. and I sat on the stairs in our fur coats, cowering. It was the noisiest raid I have ever heard. It lasted an hour. For a stretch of five minutes the gunfire was so continuous that it was like prolonged thunder rolls. The little house shook. Did not hear whistling of bombs, but frequent concussions. There were no fires visible from our windows.

Wednesday, 23rd February

Ate at the delicious Churchill Club canteen for 2/6. At 7.30 Kenneth Clark lectured on 'How to Look at Pictures', and showed slides. I was deeply impressed by the felicity of his choice of words, the rhythm of his sentences, the total lack of apparent contrivance. It was a scholarly talk, yet not above the audience's heads. And they a society lot.

I returned to my office at 9.15. Christopher Gibbs on firewatching duty with me. We talked until 10.30 when the sirens went. We donned our steel helmets and joined the other firewatchers from our block. We were both astonished by the unashamed way in which most of them, including the men, admitted that they were not going to take risks in putting out incendiary bombs, or rescuing people. I said in surprise, 'But I thought that was what we were here for!' Several close crumps shook the building so that one and all ducked to the ground. One – I speak for myself – feels foolish on rising again. Christopher and I went out several times between the bursts of gunfire to look around. A clear, starry night. It was beautiful but shameful to enjoy the glow of fires, the red bursts of distant shells and the criss-cross of searchlights. I suppose that Nero derived a similar thrill from watching the Christians used as human torches, and did not feel ashamed. Then we saw the slow descent of what looked like a lump of cotton wool. Our leader lost his head, shouting, 'It's a German parachute! We must run. It's coming down here,' etc. In fact it was far away. I rather wickedly said, 'On the contrary I think it may be a land mine,' which sent him off in terror. Christopher Gibbs, who has been a colonel in the war, was furious with the man. I could not help ragging him in very bad taste, for it seemed so funny. I am far better in raids when I have something to do, especially when others lose their heads. Fear then seems driven away by farce.

Thursday, 24th February

There is no doubt our nerves are beginning to be frayed. Frank telephoned this morning. I could tell by his voice he was upset. He said he was going to leave the Paddington area and thought Chelsea or Belgravia would be safer. I said I doubted whether the Germans discriminated to that extent. This evening I went to see a crater in the road, now railed off, in front of St. James's Palace, at the junction of Pall Mall with St. James's Street. The Palace front sadly knocked about, the clock awry, the windows gaping, and shrapnel marks on the walls. A twisted car in the middle of the road. Geoffrey's Pall Mall flat devastated, and the Lelys from Castle Howard he has just bought presumed lost. The staircase to the flat quite gone. A colonel who lived above him has entirely disappeared, only two buttons of his tunic and a part of his cap have been retrieved. In King Street Willis's Rooms finally destroyed, one half having gone in the raid of 1941 when I was sheltering in the Piccadilly Hotel. Poor Frank Partridge's shop devastated, and presumably Leonard Knight's. Drowns, the picture restorers, where I took the two Greville primitives, gone altogether. This is an ill-fated area. The London Library received a hit. Whereas fewer bombs are dropped than formerly, they must be of larger calibre, for the damage they do is greater. A huge bomb fell last night at the World's End killing many people. Miss P., alone in Cheyne Walk, was buffeted by blast. Poor little Mrs. Beckwith's house in Battersea bombed, and she didn't come to work today, but sent her daughter to tell us before we left for the office. During the luncheon hour Miss P. and I cleared up some of the grit and dust that had collected in the house. So far no windows broken here.

This evening at 9.45 another raid of an hour. The weather is cold, the air clear, the moonless sky starry. Lovely weather for bombing. There was one ugly moment when a big bomb dropped near. It provoked a deafening cannonade of guns in retaliation.

Friday, 25th February

After work I went to Hamish's for a drink. How could one exist without a drink these days? Or two drinks? Jennifer Heber-Percy there. She said she once laughed so uncontrollably in the High Street, St. Albans, that she did herself a mischief, as my Aunt Dorothy expresses it. People noticed, yet she could not help herself. It happened outside an inn. When she looked up she saw the name of the inn was The Waterspout. She was so convulsed that she started all over again.

Saturday, 26th February

Jamesey lunched at Brooks's. His mother has been ill with double pneumonia and consequently J. has been in a great state. He said we must meet more often. We went to the London Library for five minutes and met John [Pope-Hennessy] in the art room, which has caved in. All the books are scattered but unharmed. Most of them have already been removed from this exposed room to safety. All the glass, and skylights smashed. I promised to go tomorrow and help salvage. The rest of the afternoon spent at home drafting the Annual Report and finishing Virginia Woolf's *A Haunted House*.

Sunday, 27th February

Made my breakfast, washed up, did the minimum of dusting, and, packing a small suitcase with a tidy suit, went off to Mass in the Sardinian chapel. Found there was no Mass, and was furious, cursing outwardly which put me in a worse state of grace than ever. So, read the papers in Brooks's and walked to the London Library in my corduroy trousers and an old golfing jacket. Joined the volunteers for two exhausting hours in salvaging damaged books from the new wing which sustained a direct hit on Wednesday night. They think about 20,000 books are lost. It is a tragic sight. Theology (which one can best do without) practically wiped out, and biography (which one can't) partially. The books lying torn and coverless, scattered under debris and in a pitiable state, enough to make one weep. The dust overwhelming. I looked like a snowman by the end. One had to select from the mess books that seemed usable again, rejecting others, chucking the good from hand to hand in a chain, in order to get them under cover. For one hour I was perched precariously on a projecting girder over an abyss, trying not to look downwards but to catch what my neighbour threw to me. If it rains thousands more will be destroyed, for they are exposed to the sky. It is interesting how the modern girder-constructed buildings withstand the bombs, for those parts not directly hit, but adjacent to hit parts, twist but resist the concussion to a surprising extent. For instance, the stairs and floors of metal are perfectly firm even when projecting into space. You can walk to the very edge of the abyss.

To lunch with Stuart at the Travellers' where I washed and changed although my hair remained glutinous with dirt. Hamish joined us. When the two went off to play bridge with Nancy, I returned to the London Library for another hour and a half. Again was a link in a human chain passing bucket-loads of shattered books from hand to hand. It was very exhilarating and very exhausting.

Monday, 28th February

Miss P. went at luncheon time to see our bombed charwoman in Battersea. She was shocked by the condition of her house. No ceilings, or rather no plaster left to them, no glass, no light, and dirt and dust indescribable. No doors fitting, and woodwork torn off. Mrs. Beckwith dares not leave the house for fear of looters. Miss P. said she did not understand how humans could live in such conditions. And the Borough says it can do nothing for Mrs. B. because she is lucky enough to have a roof over her head. We must do something.

I dined with Harold Nicolson at Boulestin's, to meet Robin Maugham who failed to turn up. There was a young man called Myles Hildyard. Fair-haired, tough, nice. Oddly enough he is the person whose diary of an escape from the Germans in Crete I was lent by Woodbine Parish, and which I so much admired.

Harold told us several stories about literary celebrities. In 1919 he dined with Proust, who made H. tell him all he had done that day. He did not let him omit one detail, and made him describe events from the beginning. Who called him in the morning? Was the bath water run for him? What razor did he shave with? Did he use lotion? And what was it called? Why this? How that? Virginia Woolf had a similar appetite for little things. Her curiosity was insatiable. She wanted to know what pen nibs office clerks used, and how often they changed their blotting paper. Harold feels sure that posterity will always read her for her observation of detail if for no other reason. Sociologically she is important, as well as literarily. Harold is clearly fascinated by Virginia Woolf. She had no memory. I told him that Logan Pearsall Smith said 'The Mark on the Wall' in her last book, *A Haunted House*, was a direct crib from Thackeray. Harold maintained that all great artists plagiarized, and he told the story I have heard before of her being threatened with a libel action for taking a live lady novelist's name for a tombstone inscription in *The Voyage Out*.

H. said that Henry James hated George Moore. Mrs. Hunter, determined to bring them together, invited them both to stay for the same weekend, or, more correctly, Saturday to Monday, as she would have termed it. On Sunday morning she sent them off for a walk together. They returned. George Moore without a word went upstairs. James sat down on a sofa. 'Well,' said Mrs. Hunter, 'and how did you get on?' Henry James replied, 'Of all the literary figures I have met in a long life, I have never met one more absolutely, more persistently, more irredeemably - *dull*, dear lady.'

Wednesday, 1st March

Roger Senhouse told me at the Travellers' that Kenneth Clark's library in Hampstead has been burnt out, not in an air raid, but the moment after an electrician left the house. Roger showed me a book of Flaxman's drawings in original boards for which only two guineas is asked.

Friday, 3rd March

Said good-bye to Rick Stewart-Jones, who has at last got a commission, but in the Pioneer Corps. This army unit is always referred to with contempt, but I daresay fulfils just as necessary and honourable work as the crack regiments.

I lunched with Nancy and Bridget at Gunter's. Speaking of Alice Harding whose husband has returned to her and is all solicitous affection, Bridget said 'But I thought they were ruptured?' 'No, they are un-ruptured now,' said Nancy. 'In fact they are trussed.'

Saturday, 4th March

Finished reading *Mansfield Park*, which more than ever convinces me that Jane Austen is trivial, facetious and commonplace.

Sunday, 5th March

Hamish, Stuart and I dined together in Sloane Square. Hamish spoke of the vulgarity of the Edwardians, in particular his three aunts, Sutherland, Warwick and Westmorland, and how contemptible their behaviour was, but with little true conviction. S. and I told him that he was essentially an Edwardian sibling. S. said, 'You are like a highly bred, high stepping little pony.' 'Yes,' I added, 'with highly polished brass coronets on your blinkers, as you paw the air in front of your mistress's front door, highly curbed, highly glossy and highly arrogant.' H. was delighted. 'Go on,' he said. Then he said he intended to get Lady Angela Forbes, another aunt, to dictate to him some inside Edwardian gossip, such as her experience of hiding under the low bedstead in which her half-sister Lady Warwick was lying with King Edward VII, and of getting covered with bruises

from head to foot in consequence. With all his absurdities Hamish has a
keep-your-distance attitude, which Stuart says he respects.

Monday, 6th March

Went to Partridge's Bruton Street shop to look at the Blickling pictures
which have suffered severely from two foot of water rushing into the
strong-room in King Street during the raid. Partridge's lost a third of their
own things. The Holbein of Henry VIII, Zucchero of Queen Elizabeth
and Samuel Scott of the Thames, all from Blickling; very bad indeed. All
the varnish off and what to my eye seemed much of the paint too, the
bare canvas showing. But the restorer wiped the surfaces with a rag and
some methylated spirit and the pictures miraculously reappeared for an
instant, then faded away. If treated at once they can be saved, he maintains.

Dined at Alvilde's in the Princesse de Polignac's old flat. Exquisite
dinner, a rich curry with plenty of onion, and a pudding of bananas and
much beside. Eddy, his friend Mrs. Richards, and the Strathallans there.
A jolly evening discussing food ad nauseam, regurgitation and wind -
favourite subjects of Eddy's.

Tuesday, 7th March

The National Trust has held an open competition for a group of cottages
and a village hall at West Wycombe. Two hundred and forty competitors.
All today the three judges, Edward Maufe, Darcy Braddell and William
Weir, were unpacking and rejecting designs. By 6 o'clock they had only
got halfway through, leaving some twenty for reconsideration. I was
amazed at the dullness of most of the designs. Very few were positively
modernistic, and very few neo-Georgian. The vast majority were commonplace and rubbishy.

Went to a National Gallery concert to hear Irene Scharrer. She is an
unintellectual, or do I mean an un-architectural pianist. It took me an
hour to get home from dining with Tony Beaumont and Brinsley Ford
(Captain in Army Intelligence). I read in the bus Vita's book on Knole
into which she has poured her heart, and soul.

Wednesday, 8th March

I am extremely busy at the N.T. now that Matheson is away. There seem
to be endless committees to prepare agendas, minutes, and reports for,
and have them all circulated. The post of acting secretary has its draw-
backs.

This evening I went to the Dorchester for one of Sibyl's Ordinaries in
a hideous, linenfold-panelled room upstairs. Sibyl ill with a cold and

could not come. I sat next to Harold and Nancy. Emerald Cunard joined
the dinner late as usual. I was rather sorry she came at all for her personality is so strong that she monopolizes. We were seated round a large
round table, and from the moment she entered the room Emerald took
over the conversation. She made repeated bad shots, but by dint of inex-
haustible efforts like a hurdy-gurdy player she occasionally hit upon a
good tune, and was quite funny. She told a story of Lord Curzon sending
her two notes, one an invitation to dinner and another, obviously
intended for somebody else and put into a wrong envelope. It began: 'My
beautiful white swan, I long to press you to my heart.' Harold gave an
instance of Curzon's blatant rudeness. He once summoned Sir George
Clerk to see him in his room in the Foreign Office. He kept him standing, while he wrote out invitation cards in his own hand. He turned to
Clerk and said, 'I suppose you too occasionally entertain in your small
way.' Harold reminded Lord Curzon of this story. Curzon indignantly
rebutted it, saying, 'It can't be true. It can't be.' Then, 'I believe I did. I
believe I did,' and his shoulders shook with laughter. Harold told Curzon
that his staff were frightened of him. Curzon was distressed by this information. He was sensitive about people's opinion of him, just as Lloyd
George is. Underneath the imperious façade was a kind-hearted man,
more human than his contemporaries Asquith, Balfour and Bonar Law.
Emerald emphasized the important part women played in politics behind
the scenes in those days. For instance, Lady Curzon sent Lord Crewe to
Paris and she, Emerald, sent Lord D'Abernon to Berlin. Emerald said
Lady Randolph Churchill had the loveliest mouth of any woman, and
admirers stole photographs of her from other admirers. Her grandmother, said Emerald, was a Red Indian, called Sitting Bull; and her sister,
Mrs. Moreton Frewen, was the mistress of King Milan of Serbia. I walked
away with Nancy who said that at times Emerald seemed practically
gugga. 'Gug', said Nancy, who always abbreviates. I rather took against
Emerald tonight.

Friday, 10th March

A strange luncheon at Claridges with the Secretary of the Royal Medical
Society who wants to rent a N.T. country house for his society. A very
affected old gentleman. He revealed that he was married to the Lord
Chancellor's daughter and had a son who was a Papist convert.

Dined with Geoffrey Houghton-Brown to meet John Fowler, Sibyl
Colefax's working partner. A very sympathetic man. He has a large upper
lip which makes him look like the duchess in *Alice in Wonderland*. Also a
very handsome young man with steel-blue eyes, called Ian McCallum.
He works on the Architectural Press.

Saturday, 11th March

Angus Acworth lunched to discuss the future of the Georgian Group. He wants to get the Duke of Wellington to resume chairmanship. He fears that if the Group relaxes into being just another preservation body it had better die altogether. I agreed that we must bear in mind Robert Byron's objective, which was that it should be a ginger group. To achieve this purpose it was to resort to any and every weapon, mockery, vituperation, scurrility, pillorying if needs be prime ministers and archbishops, with gloves off. Our methods were what distinguished us from the S.P.A.B. and the old societies, established before the flood. Acworth thinks the Georgians should now co-ordinate with the other societies to the extent of setting up under one roof. The idea occurred to me that when the N.T. deputation to Morrison takes place we might ask for the Government's financial assistance to forward this end.

I dined with Grandy Jersey at the Hyde Park Hotel. I have not seen him since 1939 when he was beautiful, wan and pale like some rare hot-house lily. He is still pale but has grown a sandy moustache. He is just as suspicious and cautious as ever. Virginia unfortunately was not present. After dinner, back in his flat in Chesham House, he launched upon the purpose of our meeting. First he produced a plan of the Osterley estate. Then he disclosed that he wanted the Trust to take it over. For six years this is what I have been hoping might happen. At 11 I went to the office to firewatch. Lovell told me they had made a mistake in the rota and I was down for tomorrow. Since it was so late I stayed the night on the spare office camp bed.

Sunday, 12th March

Caught a Waterloo train this morning for Weybridge, there joining Geoffrey Houghton-Brown, John Fowler, young Ian McCallum and Hardy Amies. From the station we walked to Oatlands Park and lunched in the hotel. Spent the afternoon in the sun looking at the grounds and then the grotto. The present house is a huge, ugly shapeless pile, chiefly of 1860 though incorporating earlier work. There is a square Osborne-like tower at one corner. The grounds laid out by Kent between 1740 and 1748 have a long, steep terrace down to a serpentine lake. There are many Palladian urns along the terrace and two stone gate-piers at the drive entrance, not very fine in design and somewhat top heavy. The grotto however is fascinating. It must have been constructed about 1795 by a Duke of Newcastle. It is extremely elaborate. Unfortunately it is fast deteriorating, being at the mercy of children who pick the shells off the walls. The outside is made of decayed lava stone, encrusted with large fossils and sea urchins. It contains an upstairs room in bad condition, the walls inlaid with fluorspar and Vauxhall looking-glass plates, the ceiling hung with great stalactites of felspar. Below are wonderful passages and a subterranean hall dripping with stalactites. The walls are decorated in rude chevrons of glittering red and blue stones, and lit by specially constructed windows once filled with stained glass, judging from the few bits that remain. There is a tiled bathroom, its walls and ceilings decorated with whorls of mussel shells, and great conches. Of its kind this is far the best grotto I have ever seen, a superb plaything of variety and imagination. John Fowler was greatly impressed. He thinks it must have taken at least five years to make, and was probably done, not by amateur members of the family but by trained Italian grottoists. From the lead pipes everywhere in evidence it is apparent that the walls were made to drip and cascade with water, when the rare stones glistened. There are niches for flambeaux. Chandeliers may have hung from some of the stalactites. In front of the grotto is a deep depression which was at one time a pool for swans and ducks. The hermitage nearby was pulled down just before the war. I took three photographs of the outside of the grotto, but the light was bad and my lens too narrow to take the interior, unfortunately.

Tuesday, 14th March

I lunched with G. M. Trevelyan at the Goring Hotel before the Estates Committee meeting, at which I felt uncomfortable. Try as I did I could not master the intricacies of the Government's white paper on sheep farming.

Wednesday, 15th March

These are days of feverish activity in the office. Besides, I am desperately preparing my lecture for tomorrow at the Raynes Park County School. Yesterday too there was another hideous air raid. Two high explosives in Anderson Street and Cliveden Place, Chelsea, one near Heinz Dietmar's lodgings so that all his windows were blown out. In our office, as a consequence of this raid, there were no gas fires and no telephone. We all sat in overcoats shivering with cold today.

Friday, 17th March

Took the 9.10 to Shrewsbury, arriving after 1 o'clock. Walked to the Lion and lunched there. Looked at the ballroom built on to the back of the hotel. It is a sort of Assembly Room of Adam date and style well proportioned, with plaster walls and marble chimneypieces with lions' heads carved on them. A gallery, and doors with classical dancing figures painted à la Angelica Kauffmann. Delightful and provincial.

Hired a car for £1 to take me to Pitchford Hall. A most glorious day, though keen and sharp. The black-and-white of this house is a bit too much of a good thing. The house is supposed to be late fifteenth or early sixteenth century, but I suspect it to be much later. The clock-tower porch is obviously Jacobean. The north wing extension of 1880 was well done, but over-contributes to the black-and-white. However today the place looked highly romantic amid the buds of spring, flowering crocuses and primroses. Met Forsyth, the architect, in the drive who told me Sir Charles Grant was waiting for me. Was conducted upstairs to a small, shapeless end room in the west wing, where he sprawled, listening to the European news in that way country people do most of the livelong day. He is well over 60, still handsome, and rather mischievous. Indeed a sweet man who must once have been very attractive. He is an old friend of that fellow General, Lord Sackville. Eddy told me that he remembers him staying at Knole years ago. The two men were discussing something rather excitedly. Lord Sackville said, 'What you can't understand, Charlie darl- ', and stopped dead. Too late, Eddy's mother, who was present, rose from her chair and stalked out of the room, head in air.

Now Sir Charles vegetates, and talks volubly and a little irrelevantly about his ancestors, his friends and acquaintances. He galloped me through the house, pointing out the contents which he thought he would give with it. But so rapid was our progress that I could not take in individual things. I don't think there is much that is very good. The rooms have an oddly incongruous early Victorian air, which is sad and romantic. All the rooms are low and dark in spite of the sun shining outside, the birds singing and the water falling over the stones. He dearly loves the place. His proposals are vague however, and he does not intend to transfer any land over and above what the house stands on, even omitting the orangery and walled garden. While he was talking to me on the lawn Lady Sybil approached. Out of the corner of one eye I saw a fat, dumpy figure waddling and supporting herself with a tall stick. She wore a long, blue coat down to her calves. One foot had on a stocking, the other was bare. On her head was an orange bonnet, draped with an orange scarf which floated down to her ankles. She had orange hair kept in place by a wide-meshed blue net. She took great care to shield her extraordinary face, extraordinary because, although the skin is beautiful, the shape is absolutely round and the lips are the vividest orange I have ever beheld. She looks like a clairvoyante preserved in ectoplasm. As a special favour she took me to the orangery where she lives all the time, for she hates the house. She says it is haunted. She cannot sleep on the east side for the noise of the water or on the north because of the grave-yard. She and Sir Charles send messages to each other throughout the day and night, and meet for coffee on the lawn when the weather permits. She would not allow Forsyth to come near the orangery, which is her sanctum, converted by her into one large living-room with a wood fire, and one bedroom. She talked incessantly for an hour, complaining how the aeroplanes swooped so low that she lost her voice and was obliged to move into a caravan in a ploughed field to escape from them. Said that her French maid 'never revealed that she was mad', when she came to her, and stole all her, Lady S.'s clothes. The only way she recovered them was by sending the maid to confession. The abbess made her give them all back. Her gruff laugh and her low, sepulchral voice and disjointed phrases reminded me of Lady Crewe, her sister. She had sprained her ankle – hence the one bare leg – and made me pour a solution of Ponds Extract over it out of a heavy lead Marie Antoinette watering can.

Forsyth motored me to Attingham where I stayed the night. I walked into the deer park looking for Lord Berwick. Found him exercising his little dog, Muffet. He talks to me far more confidently than he used to. I think he is one of the most endearing men I have ever met in my life – feckless, helpless and courteous. We had a good dinner of four courses, including chicken and burgundy. Lady Sybil Grant said of him, 'Poor Tom, he should not have lived in this age. He cannot drive a car, ride a bicycle, fish or shoot. He would have stepped in and out of a sedan chair so beautifully.'

Saturday, 18th March

Forsyth came soon after breakfast which I had in my bedroom. Lord Berwick met him and showed him round the house. Forsyth was greatly impressed. Indeed I am more and more impressed by the beauty of the house, the rich-toned Pompeian walls and the crimson damask and the gilt furniture. We drove to Pitchford. Sir Charles was out fishing and Lady Sybil either enshrined in her orangery or seated in the delicious tree house, which is of half-timber with a rococo plaster ceiling and walls. I visited the church to look at the fine thirteenth century Crusader effigy carved in oak, the effigy and Gothic table all of a piece. I walked round the policies and arrived at the tree house. Climbed up to it and, not finding Lady Sybil, went inside. Forsyth took me into the roof of the house to show me how poor its condition was. When the nineteenth-century extensions were built the main part was re-roofed. Terrible amputations of the main beams had been perpetrated, and flimsy struts of deal substituted for stout oak purlins and rafters.

We drove back to St. Albans. Stopped on the way at Wall to look at our Roman remains and the dreary little museum full of broken pottery displayed in cardboard boxes. The stone foundations are split by successive frosts and need covering with sheds, though how anyone who has seen Roman temples above ground can be bothered with these miserable subterranean fragments is beyond my comprehension. The property is poor, down-at-heel and neglected. At Towcester we stopped for a hurried tea in a tiny cheap café. Coming out after paying the bill I ran into Georgia Sitwell in her policewoman's uniform. Forsyth said to me afterwards in his Uriah Heep-like manner, 'What beautiful ladies you do know, Mr. Lees-Milne.' 'Yes, don't I,' I answered.

On my return to London telephoned Bridget who dined with me at the Ritz. Across the dining-room we spied Nancy dining with Peter Rodd who had walked into her shop this morning, having come straight from an Italian beachhead after three years' absence. They sent a note across to us and joined us for beer after their dinner. Peter, looking bronzed, tough and well, was slightly drunk, and grinned and laughed a good deal. Even so, Bridget and I expected he might lash out at poor Nancy at a moment's notice, and on the slightest provocation. She at once turned into a different Nancy, apprehensive, solicitous, and adoring. We plied Peter with questions, but he never answered any. Instead he talked incessantly in his boring manner without appearing to listen to one word we said. We gathered from the exaggerated things he did say in disparagement of the Americans, much to Nancy's relish, that they were disliked by the English troops. There is much resentment over their being in command of our armies. Peter said that quite 60 per cent of the American troops had venereal diseases and so were incapacitated from fighting; that they pitched our crack troops into impossible positions and the Brigade of Guards was cut to pieces in consequence. Also that Simon Combe, my company commander, when captured and led off by Germans, seized a tommy-gun, slew five of them, and escaped. He will get a decoration for this. Peter had been in charge of Italian refugees in the Anzio area, and said he had great difficulty in preventing American troops from jumping on to the relief ships taking the refugees to Naples. The Italians have no liking for the English, but think favourably of the Americans because of the money they can extract from them. The sad truth is that one should believe only a quarter of what Peter says.

I accompanied B. to her flat and stayed the night at Brooks's.

Monday, 20th March

A.W. Lawrence lunched with me at the Grosvenor Hotel. He is a brother of Lawrence of Arabia. I had expected an older man. Instead he looks barely 40. He resembles Raymond Mortimer in build and has the same thick, dark, unruly hair, which, unlike R.'s, is unbrushed. He has a slightly contemptuous, slightly mocking smile. He answers abruptly, deliberately, as though to assert his disrespect for people and authority. Not good-looking; a lean face, clear skin, but dark and swarthy. Not like his brother in appearance. He stares at you with penetration while he speaks. I had invited him in order to ask if he would contribute to the appeal the N.T. is issuing for money for Seathwaite farm in Borrowdale, out of the Seven Pillars of Wisdom Fund, of which he is a trustee. He seems prepared to help.

Tuesday, 21st March

Went to see Dame Una after work. She is up and better, but looks thin and white. Complains that now restrictions are imposed upon the sea coast, there is nowhere she can go to recuperate. Talked about her monumental *Life of Dickens*, which is finished. Dickens, she said, had the power of hypnotizing his audiences. His sex life was very odd, and she deals with this at length. She said Jamesey had been asked by Batsford to write a book about the House of Commons, all material found, but J. may decline because he so much hates politics. John is writing a book on Domenichino. He came down to talk likewise. Dame Una lent me her book on Russia in which there are two chapters about Tsarkoe Selo and Pavlovsk, the palaces built by the Scottish architect, Charles Cameron. She says the raids we have now are more terrifying than the old ones, but James is courageous, consolatory and efficient during them.

Tonight at 1 a.m. there was another raid. The sirens woke me from a sound sleep. I hoped there might be no guns, but they soon started. I got out of bed and Miss P. handed me my fur-lined coat. Together we crouched on the stairs in our chosen corner. The windows rattled with the thunder of guns. We quailed and did not speak. When the gunfire subsided I put on my gumboots and walked to Battersea Bridge. Actually the raiders tonight had kept to the south-east. I saw distant fires across the water making the sky red, but none near at hand.

Thursday, 23rd March

The three assessors finally awarded first prize to the winner of the West Wycombe Cottage Competition this morning. It is not to my mind a very beautiful elevation, and has two pointed gables which I think feeble and reactionary. However – they find the planning so much better than the second winner's, whose elevation to my eye was preferable. Maufe had to leave early, but Darcy Braddell and William Weir lunched with me at Overton's off crab. The wonderful William Weir is a little deaf and on the verge of senility. Braddell was rather short with him and inclined to leave him out of the talk. Braddell is a sweet man, but what sort of architect I cannot tell. He said he was Ernest George's last pupil. George would draw every detail of his designs for a room or building for his faithful carver to reproduce. He would lie full length on the floor, rapidly and accurately sketching. When commissioned to design a building, he would ask what style was required - Gothic? Queen Anne? Jacobean? Not a thing done today fortunately. Braddell said that the more cultivated and academically educated an architect the worse he was, and the less creative. *Vide* George, Blomfield, Baker. Both he and Weir agreed that Lutyens was the greatest architect since the late Georgians of the early nineteenth century. And of these Decimus Burton was the most brilliant.

Ian McCallum dined with me at Brooks's. He is an enthusiast. He regards as deplorable reactionaries Richardson, Rendel and Braddell. Rendel he hates; and says that when he was President of the Architectural Association the students turned him out. Ian is a pacifist and conscientious objector who has twice been to prison, once with hard labour, for his convictions. He says prison atrophies the sensibilities so that life becomes grey and the prospect of ultimate release cannot evoke a spark of happy anticipation. There was a raid at midnight, but nothing serious.

Friday, 24th March

Stuart told me what he considers the worst thing ever said of anyone: John Betjeman's description of Charles Fry as 'a phallus with a business sense'.

After dinner the sirens went. The guns sounded very distant, so borrowing Stuart's American steel helmet I decided to walk home from Tyburnia. While in Hyde Park and before I reached the Serpentine, the guns beside me opened up cruelly. I put on the steel helmet and cowered under a tree, with the trunk between me and the tarmac road. As there was no building to shelter in I decided it was safer to stay under the tree branches, which might break the fall of the shrapnel raining down like hailstones. I heard it crackling through the leaves and thudding on the grass. On the road it struck sparks as it fell. The noise of the Hyde Park guns was deafening, and the rocket shells were specially frightening. One gun close to me blew out the tails of my overcoat with blast at every shot. I was lonely and felt as though I were in no man's land. The gunfire seemed horizontal with the ground. There was a continuous thunder for three-quarters of an hour. They say this was the noisiest London raid of the war. Occasionally I heard German planes diving. But there were no fires, and I heard no bombs.

Sunday, 26th March

Breakfasted at Brooks's and rang up Clementine Beit who said, 'Yes, do bring the Sergeant,' thinking I meant any old sergeant, a driver perhaps, and asked, 'Does he eat at our end of the house, or the other?' I told Stuart this, and he was not amused. Today has been wonderful. Bright, warm sun; the earth dry and brown for there has been no rain. This augurs ill for the summer, perhaps well for this horrifying impending invasion. I drove Stuart to Hughenden. Mrs. Langley-Taylor received us in the new wing built forty years ago by Coningsby Disraeli, Dizzy's nephew and heir. I recall being brought here in about 1930 from Oxford, and being received by Coningsby Disraeli in the library. He was wearing a dusty velvet skull cap and, if I remember right, a blue velvet jacket and string bow tie. The main part of the house is at present used by the R.A.F. for target-spotting, and cannot be entered. Mrs. Langley-Taylor told me that after the war nearly every room will be furnished for show, and that Major Abbey, when he bought the property also bought the Disraeli contents. Hughenden will make a splendid and interesting National Trust property for three reasons – its historic association, its mid-Victorian architecture and furnishing, and its amenity land on the outskirts of horrid High Wycombe. The park is beautiful and well maintained. Some fine trees and the garden laid out in Victorian parterres with plenty of terracotta urns and insipid statuary of cherubs and angels, now put away, which Queen Mary called 'sugar babies' when she visited the place. I was delighted with Hughenden. It is deliciously hideous. Disraeli stripped it of its white stucco, revealed the red brick, and added the ugly window surrounds and crenellations. Mrs. Langley-Taylor showed us Disraeli's bedroom, which is now her own. She said Lady Desborough remembers being patted on the head by Disraeli here, and being repelled by his greasy black curls.

After luncheon we all lay in the sun in a field and talked. The Sergeant was a great success with the Beits.

Tuesday, 28th March

Anthony Wagner lunched with me and was optimistic about future planning legislation. He now works at the Ministry of Planning under Lord Woolton. In normal times he is a herald. Nice, quiet, dark, reserved, taciturn man. This evening I dined at Rules' with Acworth, Keeling, M.P., Oliver Messel and John Summerson to discuss our policy at the forthcoming meeting of the Georgian Group next Saturday. We decided to press for the appointment of a small subcommittee to consider particular questions of policy, a new secretary, the enlisting of local authorities' support, and a post-war getting together of all the amenity societies.

Wednesday, 29th March

After a morning at Cliveden, making notes for my guidebook, and Stoke Poges, where Hubert Smith, the Trust's new agent, agreed with me that we should not allow part of our field to be taken for additional burial space for what are no longer 'rude forefathers of the hamlet', but the genteel residents of suburbia - to Osterley.

What a decline since 1939! Now total disorder and disarray. Bombs have fallen in the park, blowing out many windows; the Adam orangery has been burnt out, and the garden beds are totally overgrown. We did not go round the house which is taken over by Glyn Mills bank, but round the confines of the estate. There are still 600 acres as yet unsold. Smith and I both deprecated the breezy way in which the Osterley agent advocated further slices to the south-east of the house being sold for building development, in order to raise an endowment It is going to be a difficult problem how to estimate figures where so much is so problematical, viz. the outgoings associated with the museum, the number of visitors and the potential building value of the land itself.

I am quite sure that of the inside of Cliveden the public need only see the hall, drawing-room, and the 'Louis Quinze' dining-room. Apart from a few Reynoldses and the Blenheim tapestries there is nothing much in the furniture line.

Thursday, 30th March

Started off in the N.T. car at 10 o'clock for Gloucestershire and drove without a break to Nether Lypiatt Manor, near Stroud, to lunch at this wonderful little house with Mrs. Gordon Woodhouse. There were Mr. Woodhouse, a little, dull old man with a flabby hand, genial Lord Barrington with hairs growing out of his cheeks and ears, and homespun Miss Walker, daughter of Sir Emery, the friend of William Morris. The house is perched high on a hill, overlooking a built-up village. It is compact and tall, with two flanking wings, one new so as to balance the other old one. It is unspoilt late seventeenth century, and perfect in every way. In fact an ideal, if not *the* ideal small country house. It retains all its wainscoting, doors with high brass handles and locks, one lovely chimneypiece in the hall, of white stone against a ground of blue slate. The rich staircase has three twisted balusters to each tread. There is much good furniture, including several Barrington family portraits. The forecourt enclosure with stone piers and balls, the contemporary wrought-iron gates, and the Cotswold stable block complete the dependencies.

Mrs. Woodhouse was wearing a kind of black satin bonnet, not becoming, and a black knitted dress. Luncheon consisted of one egg in a jacketed potato. The boiler having just burst the household was in a state of perturbation. There is one servant. It is a curious colony. Mrs. Woodhouse talked a lot about houses and Ted Lister, whose irascibility amuses her.

After luncheon she and Lord Barrington took me round the house, and he took me round the garden, which is enchanting, with modern yew walks and a flourishing young lime avenue, the trees planted closely together. There is an obelisk to the horse of the builder of the house who 'served his master good and true, and died at the age of forty-two'.

I went on to Woodchester Priory, arriving at tea time. But no tea because my host, bluff ex-naval commander Bruce Metcalfe, was conducting a unit of American soldiers, lecturing them good humouredly but bombastically, and boasting of English customs in a manner which I found condescending and embarrassing; but not they, it seemed. I did not take to him at first – and did later, as usual. I wondered how I was going to stick this visit until the following morning. The Commander and his wife live in this by no means small house with absolutely no servants at all. It is an H-shaped Tudor building with pointed gables, and was spoilt in the last century by the insertion of plate glass, and the addition of a French-style tower. The Commander showed me the site of the Roman Villa which is uncovered every ten years. Thank God it is covered now. We had dinner in the kitchen. Mrs. M. benignant, jolly, and friendly.

I find that I take an hour or two to adjust myself to different sorts of people. Going as I do from the sophisticated to the simple, the rich to the poor, the clever to the stupid. I get bewildered. But in the end I usually manage to adapt myself. Which means of course that I am a chameleon, with little or no personality of my own. I assume the qualities of others. I am a mirror of other people's moods, opinions and prejudices. But I am pernickety, and would not doss down in anybody's bed just for a crust or a new pair of shoes.

Sunday, 2nd April

Bridget and I lunched together in the Ritz Grill. As she sat down she said querulously that Emerald and Sir Robert Abdy were joining us. This they did at 2 o'clock. Bridget rather surly with Emerald for coming but I was glad to see her for she is usually bright and gay. Sir R. was totally different from the picture of him I had formed in my mind. That was of a little black old dormouse, somewhat like Gerald Berners. But not at all. Abdy is youthful, tall, fair, with light horn-rimmed spectacles; and very charming and unaffected. I was obliged to build up an entirely different personality behind the exterior I had so grievously misrepresented to myself. Emerald began in true form by grumbling to the waiters about the food. She ought to know that in the fifth year of the war choice of food for luncheon after 2 o'clock on a Sunday is limited. After saying that she would eat nothing, she ate everything. She said Kenneth Clark made the mistake of depreciating his own scholarship. This surprised me. 'Yes,' she repeated, 'I have advised him not to be so diffident, or people will cease to respect him.' She said, 'Supreme self-confidence is the essential quality if one is to achieve anything; and one must be an expert on at least one subject, or another.' I said, 'You may be right there; but surely K. has already achieved everything. I would have thought he was not the least bit self-depreciatory.'

Wednesday, 5th April

Walking past Buckingham Palace I looked at it critically for the first time. What a heavy, uninspired, lumpish elevation! The Corinthian pilasters are too small for the heavy entablature; the columns in the centrepiece ought to be disengaged. As for the circular basin of the Victoria Memorial, it is not too bad, and the bas-reliefs are good. But the black Michelangelesque figures are far too large and out of scale with the monument.

Good Friday, 7th April

At 8.45 a car ordered by Michael Rosse came to take me and Bridget, whom I picked up in Mount Street, to King's Cross. We were in such good time that we were on the platform by 9.20 and discovered in front of us an earlier train to Doncaster than the 10.30 which we had meant to catch. There then ensued one of those scatter-brained hesitations, indecisions and muddles. I said we must stick to the later train, for we would merely have to wait at Doncaster, if we arrived earlier than expected. B. said we might just as well wait at Doncaster as at King's Cross. I said King's Cross was preferable – besides, secretly I wanted to telephone someone. For nearly ten minutes we argued about which station was preferable, B. obdurately sticking out for Doncaster. Anyway she settled the matter by hurling her luggage into a carriage just as the 9.30 was leaving. I had to shove her from behind and then throw my luggage and haul myself through the door, followed by execrations from the guard. On arrival at Doncaster we were obliged to wait in the cold. B. complained that it was a loathsome station. While waiting for the car we munched a slice of stale cake which I managed to buy in the station hotel.

We reached Womersley at 2.30. Michael was there for the day only and had to depart before midnight, because all leave had been cancelled. We did not see him again. But with Anne Rosse I am always happy. She giggles, makes the most wicked innuendoes, and giggles again. The noise she makes is like an extremely lyrical burn rushing over pebbles, and her witticisms have to be caught on the wing. Her merriment is infectious, and it is laced with just a dash of arsenic.

Monday, 10th April

As usual I have eaten too much, drunk too much, and I feel lethargic. I should never stay away longer than two nights. The truth is that like a cart horse I must be working, regularly, with only the shortest of breaks in between. I have however read *Edwin Drood*, and finished the hateful *Cousin Pons*.

Thursday, 13th April

At midnight Emerald rang up. She talked of Tintern Abbey, of Bertie Abdy who is unwell, of the Invasion (she says all the Americans are leaving London – which signifies something is afoot), of Dickens and of Balzac. After half an hour's discussion of *Cousin Pons* she rang off abruptly, without warning.

I caught the 1.15 to Reading where Gerry Wellington met me at the station in his small car, for he gets twenty gallons a month for being a duke. Drove me straight to the Reading museum where he showed me the Roman relics from Silchester, on loan from his family. I was most interested in the small, homely objects like door keys and hinges. It is so strange that Roman things differ so little from our own. Arriving at the entrance to Stratfield Saye park we stopped at the first duke's great polished granite pillar, with his image by Marochetti standing on the top. It is carefully executed, and the huge blocks of granite are finely cut. Stopped again to look at the house from the east clairvoyée, down a straight vista across the park. The house is not particularly striking from this distance; an indistinguishable huddle of buildings. Stopped again at the 1750 church, of Greek cruciform. A spectacular monument inside to the Pitt builder of the house signed by Christmas and dated 1640. It is rare for so early a monument to be signed. A Wellington monument by Flaxman, and another by Boehm. The great galleried family pew in which the Iron Duke worshipped was swept away by an ignorant vicar just before Gerry succeeded, greatly to his annoyance, chagrin and disappointment, for while abroad he had been looking forward to worshipping in it. In its place a hideous substitute, with a monster linenfold door of fumed oak, has recently been erected. Close to it is a mural tablet of Donne period to an incumbent who 'for forty years was a most painful preacher'.

The western view of Stratfield Saye house clearly shows it to date from Charles I's reign. The original red brick was covered with a dull compo rendering in the eighteenth century, which is a pity. The house reminds Gerry of West Horsley, the Crewes' house in Surrey, with its Kew Palace-like pedimented gables. Odd pilasters resting on nothing appear upon the first storey in typical Charles I non-style. The stable and coach-house blocks, axial with the house, are of the same date. The house is low-lying, unpretentious, having been built, as an early guide book describes it, 'for convenience rather than for parade', by the Rivers family. They made alterations in the 1740s and added a wing in the 1790s. Benjamin Wyatt carried out work for the first duke, and added the porch and conservatory. The east front is not so regular as the west, and the terraces are deformed by messy Edwardian flower beds. Gerry, who hates flowers, will soon have them away. The pleasure grounds contain fine specimens of every tree, hard wood and soft. There is a rustic garden-house made of wood, *circa* 1840, with *trompe-l'oeil* inlaid walls, like the sides of a Nonesuch box. Under a tree is Copenhagen's gravestone. The heavy gilded state coach in the coach-house is in splendid condition.

Having eaten little luncheon I was famished, but tea consisted of only a few of the thinnest slices of bread and butter imaginable. After tea we did a tour of the inside of the house, beginning with the hall. When my stomach started to rumble with hunger Gerry looked at it with a reproachful air, and said nothing. It went on making the most awful noise like a horse's. The hall has a gallery along the wall opposite the entrance. The open balusters were boxed in so as to prevent the servants being seen from below by the visitors. Gerry's mother used to say that nothing of them was visible save their behinds, as they crouched and bobbed across the gallery. There are some pictures so huge that they can only hang sloping. In the flagged floor are inset two large mosaic pavements from Silchester. The whole hall is painted nineteenth-century brown and the walls are hung with very faded red flock paper. Against the columns of the gallery are plinths supporting white marble busts of Pitt, the Russian Czars, Walter Scott and the Great Duke, etc.

The Gallery is long and low – 'matey' Gerry calls it – the walls covered with prints pasted upon a ground of gold leaf. Rather attractive, but G. wishes to cover these walls with damask, without however injuring the prints but so as to allow room for family portraits, for elsewhere there is singularly little space. At either end of the Gallery are brown painted columns, forming screens. The ceilings are covered with Edwardian lodging-house lincrusta. To the north is a small room with niches. The walls are hung with a delightful, flowery, 1850 gold and cream paper. In front of the fireplace is a special device of the Great Duke, namely a curious brass rail, with rings for curtains, to keep off excessive heat. The drawing-room has a rococo ceiling, and the same wallpaper as in the previous room. In it are some Boule cabinets and commodes by Levasseur and pictures acquired by the first duke. The dining-room is shut up, all the Apsley House pictures being stored there for the war, and valued at a million pounds, so G. says. The library is of Lord Burlington date. In it are the Duke's library chairs as seen in the conversation piece by Thorburn of this room, hanging in the Small Cabinet Room. Beyond it a billiard table and Regency lights for colza oil, very pretty, and beyond again the Great Duke's private rooms and his original bath. These rooms G. is going to make his own. The bath is very deep and satisfactory. A curious feature in this house is the water closets in each room, put there by the Great Duke inside great 1840-ish cupboards of maplewood.

After tea Gerry took a rod, and fished in the lake for perch with a minnow, but caught nothing. He cast with much ease and abandon. When I tried I found it difficult, and made rather a fool of myself. After dinner, at which there were no drinks except beer, he showed me his grandfather's collection of gems and intaglios, mounted on long, gold chains. When held against the oil lights some of the stones were very beautiful. A few are ancient, some Renaissance. G. is fussy over his key bunches, everything being carefully locked up. He has a butler, cook and two housemaids, and a secretary, Miss Jones. The last has meals with him during the week, and nearly drives him mad with her archness. 'Aren't you naughty today?' she says. She is unable to type, so when he wishes to despatch a letter not written by himself, he types it and gives it to her to sign.

Sunday, 16th April

Called at 7.30. Gerry motored me, the cook and a housemaid to Mass at Heckfield Park chapel. He called for us after Mass. Very good of him, for he went to his own church at 11. After church we unpacked in the attics brown paper parcels tied with string by fingers of the Great Duke's time, and not hitherto opened. This was very exciting. We blew away the dust and undid the knots of string, never cutting. Regency wall sconces emerged.

After luncheon we motored to Silchester and looked at the Roman walls which the Ministry of Works began repairing before the war, or rather taking down stone by stone, and re-building with new mortar. In other words the walls are no longer Roman fourth century but English twentieth century. G. is a most companionable and delightful person to be with, full of enthusiasms, abounding in historic anecdotes, and often very funny.

After tea we finished the tour of the house, upstairs. Everywhere brown paint is peeling off woodwork, where the door panels have not been scratched to glory by Duchess Maud's dogs. She can have had no house pride at all. Baths have been put into bedrooms, with naked pipes clambering up walls into the ceilings; and steam has made the wallpaper hang in tatters. The upstairs is really very grubby. The prints in nearly every bedroom and landing become a bore, but since most of them were stuck on by the Great Duke's own hands, G. thinks it would be an act of impiety to remove them.

Monday, 17th April

Gerry motored me to Reading in his little car which takes hours to start up. At Bristol station Eardley Knollys met me, and we drove to Westbury College, a poor sort of property which the Trust would not accept today. It consists of an old square gatehouse with fifteenth-century vaulting in the tower, and a large tumble-down white Georgian block adjacent. Then to Blaise hamlet of nine cottages, called Vine Cottage, Circular Cottage, Rose Cottage, etc. We compared their present condition with the early nineteenth-century lithographs of each, which we brought with us. After lunching in Bristol at the Mauretania restaurant, in a room which was once an old ship's dining-room of 1907 – Edwardian classical, black and gold – we motored past Sutton Court. Scouted round the outside and decided that the house, which I had seen before, was not good enough to accept. At Wells walked over our Tor Hill, and at Glastonbury up our Tor Hill to examine the fifteenth-century tower. Drove to West Pennard barn. It is not of outstanding importance, though a decent little building. I did not like the tiles the S.P.A.B. have used instead of stone slates; and their roof timbers looked flimsy and unconvincing. We visited Glastonbury barn, which is far finer, with its double tier of Gothic purlins and braces. To Bridgwater and stayed comfortably at the Royal Clarence.

Tuesday, 18th April

Today – Bridgwater Church; Coleridge's cottage at Nether Stowey; Holford village. Given luncheon by a Mr. Mantle, eccentric tenant, looking like an Italian organ-grinder (but without monkey), very friendly; Dunster Castle; Minehead, tea with Mr. Gunn, genteel and no less friendly, one of our architectural advisers; Holnicote House; Exmoor; Lynmouth, staying comfortably at the Lyndale Hotel. Had an abortive interview with a ghastly business man who owns some land we covet and won't consider an offer we have made. I don't altogether blame him.

Wednesday, 19th April

A gorgeous morning. E. and I walked up the valley to Watersmeet. Into the bottom of this precipitous gorge the sun seldom penetrates even in mid summer. Today the sky seen through the green canopy of trees was brightest blue, far brighter than when seen from the top of the gorge. Curious. At 11 we were back at Lynmouth. Motored up the hill and down again to Woolacombe, where we lunched with the American Army in a one-time hotel. Delicious American food. Only the Adjutant, in his shirt sleeves, entertained us. We felt rather a nuisance and unwanted. However we gorged. Bearded the Rev. Allfield in his filthy dog kennel of a villa. In the rain proceeded to Baggy Point. Talked to our farmer who complained of the damage done by the American troops who use it as a range for every sort of explosive. Barnstaple; no tea, only cake in the car. Walked up Kipling Tors, another poorish property. It was pelting with rain so we had no view. East Titchberry Farm which is really remote and wild. E. is most conscientious with his farmers, and on the best of terms with them. Soaked, we dined at the Hoop Inn sparingly, for there was little food. Nevertheless they produced a bottle of very good claret to warm the cockles. Stayed the night at Bideford, my room overlooking the river and old bridge. I sat in my Regency bow window before going to sleep, and pondered upon the vanity of sublunary appetites and torments.

Thursday, 20th April

Hatherleigh; Lydford Gorge; Tavistock. Drove over Dartmoor which is very desolate and full of terror, and to me not very appealing. Widecombe Moor Church House - bad plate glass in the windows. The good features, the stout ceiling beams of the lower rooms, and the sparkling granite of which the whole thing is built. One wants to suck it like barley sugar. The church has a low oak screen to the chancel, with painted panels of saints. Fifteenth century I suppose. One peculiar panel of Abraham sacrificing Isaac with reprehensible detachment and complacency. En route to Exeter we got stuck in a very long military convoy moving towards us. We thought the Invasion had surely begun. But we are always thinking this nowadays.

Saturday, 22nd April

Nancy Mitford lunched with me at the Ritz, and we sat at a table by the door. We were chatting very happily when at 2 o'clock Emerald came in with Bertie Abdy, who having had an operation has gone grey from the intense pain within one week. Emerald told us how Nancy's grandfather, Lord Redesdale, behaved. 'My dear, he used to accompany King Edward to Paris, where they went wenching together.' At 2.30 I left for the R.I.B.A. Library, for I am contemplating an article on Decimus Burton. Then caught the 4.45 for Oxford to stay with the Harrods.

Walked from Oxford station to the Harrods' house in St. Aldate's. Dear Billa rushed down the stairs and we embraced on the doorstep. She said

I had not seen her since 1938. I cannot think why not, and this visit has reminded me how very devoted to her I am. We started with a large glass of sherry. Then Roy joined us. He is quiet, and has attentive good manners. If I knew him better I might like him very much. He soon left for some college function, and Billa and I dined alone, deliciously, with the candles lit, though it was full daylight and the sun shining. We gossiped in great content.

Sunday, 23rd April

After breakfast in bed I went to Mass next door, in Bishop King's Palace where Ronnie Knox used to be priest, but now Father Vernon Johnson, who today was ill. As it is the first Sunday of term, the chapel was packed. After Mass we walked to Christ Church garden. The garden was a dream, and we sat on a seat like an elderly married couple, while the two Harrod children played. The elder boy is handsome, with jet black hair like Billa's, and the longest black eyelashes I have seen. His features resemble Roy's. The younger boy has a squint, and wears an eye shade. At luncheon we ate enormously, with the result that I felt languid for the remainder of the afternoon. We walked round the university, looking first at the naked Shelley memorial, to which Billa is devoted. The base of the sarcophagus is typically Victorian, and the glistening figure rendered beautiful with the submarine light from the dome striking it. I think the walls, instead of being boring 'Elizabethan' panels, should be painted with sea urchins, fishes and jellyfish, to give an enhanced submarine effect. On re-thinking, I am not sure that Shelley ought to be commemorated with a great body and that drooping penis, for one does not associate the too ethereal poet with the gross flesh. And this beautiful figure, although far from gross, is physically alluring. Then we strolled through my old college, Magdalen, where the quadrangular cloisters have been renewed, stone by stone, and did the round of Addison's Walk. The meadows were covered with fritillaries.

At 7 Roy took me to dine in Christ Church hall, at the high table. By the time we sat down most of the undergraduates had finished their dinner and gone. Roy says that today they all eat in hall, are all serious, and impecunious. There is none of the plutocratic gaiety of the old days. He thinks there never will be again, for the state subsidizes undergraduates now. I sat next to Roy and the Dean, and opposite Dundas. We had a very full and heavy dinner, with strong red wine, so that afterwards I felt worse than ever. When dinner was over, the Dean rose. We all followed him, carrying our napkins according to custom, down a circular staircase, to the Common Room where the port was freely circulated round the table. I sat next to David Cecil. It is difficult to reconcile his

Dresden china appearance with his ever accelerating loquacity, twinkling of eyes, twisting of long fingers, and loose limbed jerkiness. Rather disconcerting. I felt like a slow-witted bull beside him. He talked of Hatfield and the state kept there when he was a child; also of the terrifying intellectual level of the conversation, and the devotional atmosphere. I imagine there was something a bit forced about both. Roy complained about the declining population – 'Now the rot has spread to the lower classes,' he said. Now he is talking rot, I thought to myself, but did not say so.

Billa very funny when we got back. She said that breeding was hell, and Roy must not suppose that she was going to do any more. Talking of pederasty, Roy said that the late King George V when told of Lord Beauchamp's trouble, exclaimed, 'Why, I thought people like that always shot themselves.' 'Heavens,' said Billa, 'I do hope the poor darlings won't start doing that. It would be like living through a permanent air raid.' I caught a 10 o'clock train to London which did not reach Paddington till midnight. The last tube had gone, so, carrying my bag, I walked home to Chelsea.

Tuesday, 25th April

Eardley and I walked to the Belgrave Square canteen to lunch with Sibyl Colefax, who when she is not animated – and this is seldom – is an old woman, rather bent. She does not often allow this evidence of her age to be revealed. At 4 I met the Eshers and Hubert Smith at Osterley Park gates. It was a ravishing day and Esher commented on the beauty of the shrubs and blossom in the suburban gardens. We motored round the park, and Esher's view was that it did not matter whether one could see building development from the house, if the house was to become a museum and never be inhabited again. Smith and I dissented from this pronouncement.

Wednesday, 26th April

At 10 started off in the car for Oxford. Gave two soldiers a lift there. Called for Billa at 12.15. She produced a glass of red wine which after a slight hangover from last night I was not really in need of. We drove to Faringdon. It was a day of unexcelled loveliness, the apex of spring-tide, warm sun and no wind. We had the roof of the car open, B.'s raven tresses swirling above her head and practically lassoing my neck. At Faringdon House Jennifer Heber-Percy was sitting in the sun, on a swing seat, against the curved retaining wall. There were small chickens running around. This frightened Billa for she hates birds. We talked until 1.45 when we lunched off chicken (she doesn't mind eating them) and rice.

Lord Berners, wearing a green knitted skull cap and yellow bow tie, was positively cordial. He is a considerate host. Robert [Heber-Percy] came in to lunch from driving a tractor on the farm. He was wearing a pair of battledress trousers and a yellow aertex shirt open at the neck. Very bronzed by the sun, youthful and handsome. He is the *enfant terrible*, all right. What a curious family they were, sitting round this large round table. But they know how to live. I thought how enviable their ménage.

After luncheon I picked up Mr. Leigh Wyatt, the Pleydell-Bouverie agent, and motored him to Coleshill. The Army is in partial occupation of the house, and has through an explosion destroyed one of the gate piers and part of the wall at the office entrance. The elder Miss Pleydell-Bouverie, who is kindly, shy and stooping, looks as old as her mother seemed to be in 1936. The younger, also unmarried sister lives in a cottage in the park, and is a potter. They told me how desperately anxious they were for the N.T. to own the place, but that because of their father's settlement, they could not give any part of it away. The 5,000 acres of the estate cover a beautiful area of England. Since the Bouverie family have always been conscientious landowners the estate is in good condition, although the sisters are very poor.

I left at 4, motoring past Great Coxwell barn, which must be the finest barn in England. I thought if this estate can be acquired, then I ought to try and get the Buscot and Faringdon estates protected by covenants. The three would form a wonderful block.

At Faringdon found Berners alone, Billa and Jennifer having gone for a walk. He showed me round the downstairs of the house, for the Army is in occupation of the bedroom floor. Whereas the stone flags of the hall floor are worn down by generations of feet, the hard black marble ribs are not. Lord B. thinks some of the seemingly late eighteenth-century doorheads are in fact nineteenth-century and should be removed; but I am not so sure. The house is attractively untidy in an Irish way, with beds, but beautiful ones, scattered in the downstairs rooms. Much confusion and comfort combined. Jennifer's baby Victoria playing on the floor like a kitten. Lord B. said that this afternoon one of the Negro soldiers – and the place is stiff with them – accosted him in the garden with the request, 'Massa, may I pick just a little bunch of flowers for our colonel?'

After tea I motored Jennifer and Billa to Kelmscott Manor. Since we didn't have an appointment the tenant would not let us in. In dudgeon we walked round the garden, Billa being frightfully caustic and urging us to pick the flowers. She kept saying, 'These flowers are madly Pre-Raph. Do you suppose William planted these? Did Rossetti really sit on this seat?' I pointed to a garden house and said, 'That's where Queen Elizabeth went to the loo when she came to tea with the William Morrises.' 'And

Queen Victoria stood outside, keeping *cave*,' Billa said. We drove to the church and found the Morrises' tombstone. The little church is the prettiest imaginable. Robert accompanied me in the car back to London, eating a chicken leg in his fingers, and wearing a dark blue pullover. Then he had indigestion, and consumed quantities of soda mints.

Thursday, 27th April

Took the 10.10 from St. Pancras, arriving Stockport at 2.30. It was a balmy day when I started, and cold on arrival, with a cutting wind. An alderman met me in his car and motored me to Dukinfield. There I was shown round the town hall, a hideous building entirely lined inside with shiny yellow, lavatory brick, and windows of opaque stained glass in tulip patterns. We then inspected Dukinfield Old Hall. It stands in dreary surroundings, on one side an ungainly factory, and on the other a canal, filled with detritus, and tall chimneys. The ancient hall is of brick and timber construction, for long in decay and now divided into four tenement dwellings. I went inside them all. Apart from a few stout beams and a fleurs-de-lys plaster ceiling in one dwelling, there was nothing remarkable. The house is worth saving because of the scarcity of old buildings in these industrial parts, and I think that if the Corporation will do it up under our supervision, the Trust should hold it, provided we are involved in no expense.

The alderman took me back to his bungalow for tea. To my surprise his daughter was carving a ham, but although I do not care for sweet ham and had already eaten adequately in the train, I simply had to say 'yes'. These local worthies are all the same. They attach the wrong values to old houses, such as Domesday origin and absentee ownership by some medieval baron, which have little or no consequence whatever in relation to the architecture.

At 5 o'clock I met Mr. Hobson, my host of the forthcoming night. He called for me at the town hall in a large brown Ford car and whisked me away from this gloomy district into the recesses of the Pennine Chain, as far as Hayfield, where his house, Park Hall, is. Here I stayed. Mr. Hobson is a massive, florid man of about 60 from Belfast, with a strong Irish brogue, completely self-made. He told me he came to England with £5 in his pocket to seek his fortune – just like my great-grandfather, Sir Joseph Bailey, who walked from Yorkshire to South Wales barefoot in 1790. This, I must confess, was the only thing about him I liked. His wife, English, grey haired and very sweet and kind, spoke with the strongest cockney accent. The house, built *c.* 1770, is of no interest or distinction outside. The inside has been reconstructed by the Hobsons in the most appalling style. He has wainscoted all the walls with unvarnished walnut in giant linenfold pattern. There are deep friezes of lincrusta, painted a sort of clown yellow; door surrounds inlaid with mother-of-pearl. The front door has had a V-shaped window inserted, with 'Please ring' engraved in gold. The 'lounge', as they call it, is furnished with several base French pieces and 'easy chairs' in Tottenham Court Road leather, complete with bronze ashtrays attached to tails of grey suede filled with lead, daintily displayed over the arms. The walls covered with 1880 Royal Academy conversation pieces, though in my bedroom I found a Copley Fielding. There were Carrara busts on marble pedestals of insipid girls with forefingers coyly pointed at their lips, and on their heads lace caps crocheted by Mrs. Hobson.

The site of the house is very fine. The valley in the middle of the property of seventy acres is so precipitous that you imagine the property is far larger than it is. The Lantern Pike looms on one side. Eccles Pike can be seen from the house to the left. Behind the house are the moors. The estate is densely wooded, which is unusual, for there are few trees in these parts. The crescent-shaped stable block must once have been rather interesting, but Mr. Hobson has made it into four or five separate dwellings. In fact in a mild way he is a bit of a speculator, for he has also built five cottages which he lets to Manchester business folk. The house too contains flats. He has built a heated swimming pool to which thousands resort in the summer, paying an entrance fee and buying teas. I found it difficult to decide whether the Trust ought to accept this property on account of the land.

Friday, 28th April

It is bitterly cold up here. I was called early. Breakfast at 8.15. We began with sweet grapefruit from a tin, eggs and bacon and the lot. These sort of people always press one to eat more than one wants - a tiresome conventional politeness - so that one has almost to snap to be allowed any respite. After toast I was offered custard trifle in a glass.

Saturday, 29th April

Went to the Dorchester at 5.45 and found Emerald about to step into a taxi. We drove to the theatre, Emlyn Williams's *Druid's Rest*, an enjoyable Welsh play, the small boy acting quite unselfconsciously as only children can. In the stalls a friend of Emerald's was sitting behind us, Jim Thomas, a Cabinet minister of some sort, Welsh, about 40, personable. He came back to the Dorchester and dined with us. The three of us sat round a small table till 12.20 when I rose to go. They gossiped about political friends which rather bored me. Thomas is an intimate friend of Eden. He says the Prime Minister depends on Eden to such an extent that he consults him over every issue, and Eden is worn out by this strain on top of all his own duties. J. Thomas motored me to Victoria for I was to firewatch in the office.

Sunday, 30th April

I filled the car with the Polesden pictures I had collected yesterday from the National Gallery. Drove to the Oratory, and then fetched Nancy and Milly her pug. At Polesden we ate sandwiches on the south verandah. Nancy even sunbathed in the afternoon. When I had finished my work we wandered in the fields, picking cowslips (nearly over already). N. at her sweetest and happiest. A heavenly day.

Tuesday, 2nd May

Caught an early train to Guildford where Hubert Smith met me in the car. We drove past the N.T. cottages in Ockford Road, Godalming - not very interesting - of timber construction upon a raised causeway. Stopped at Eashing Bridges, built supposedly in King John's reign. Tanks have been over the bridges, but this has now been stopped. The arches have the look of incredible antiquity. The plain wooden rails in place of parapet are becoming loose, the military traffic having run into them. We passed Witley Common, which Hubert says can never be reinstated - it has been turned into a parade ground with tarmac roadways and brick barracks - to Tennyson's Lane and Boarden Door. Ravishingly paintable they looked today, these Surrey trees and faint misty blue downs. We motored on to Black Down, newly acquired, with distant, seemingly infinite views, for it is over 900 ft. high in parts. Then to Slindon, near Arundel, where we ate our sandwiches in the agent's house.

This property belongs to Mr. Isaacson, an old man of 88, who offers it with 4,000 acres. We motored all round the estate. The park with semi-circle of beech trees and carpets of bluebells was a dream of beauty. We drove to the Downs at the north extremity of the estate, with a view towards Bignor. Then to the house, which is a travesty. Originally Elizabethan brick with flint courses, it underwent extensive Georgian alterations outside and in. The present owner mistakenly removed nearly all of these after the last war, inserting bogus ceilings with plasterine ribs. The main façade is practically re-built with 'Jacobethan' bays where none existed before, and windows of plate glass in lieu of sash. The only good features left are the seventeenth-century screen in the hall, and the over-doors, the pretty eighteenth-century wrought-iron balustrade of the staircase and rococo plaster ceiling above it. The other main staircase was partially boarded up, but I think the framework is modern, with Charles II panels inserted. Of their genuineness I am not sure. There is a little

Regency temple with Trafalgar balcony around it, which the soldiery
have burnt out. The big house has troops in it, and is sadly knocked about.
The dirt and the dreariness of the surroundings are what one has come
to expect in these circumstances.

Wednesday, 3rd May

Went at 12 to see a Mr. Hunter at his office in the Strand. He is, I believe,
chairman of some newspaper firm, very business-like, steel-grey hair,
brown suit, well groomed, the Roderick Jones type, only nice. He began
by criticizing the N.T. for its slapdash methods. This surprised me; then he
disclosed that the secretary had made three appointments and failed to
keep any. Since he is a benefactor and gave me therewith a cheque for
£1,750 my predicament was to pacify him without seeming disloyal to the
secretary. A tangled web again. However, we made friends, and he is asking
me to luncheon to meet his architect, whom he wants to erect a tower on
Black Down in memory of his wife. I am not sure about the tower.

An American officer lunched with me at Brooks's. He criticized his
superior officer, for which I piously rebuked him, and expressed a terror
I have seldom seen across the face of any man, lest he might be dropped
as a parachutist in the forthcoming invasion. I sympathized deeply, imag-
ining my terror if I were faced with the command, but again piously
begged him to keep such apprehensions to himself, lest other people, not
so charitable as me, might interpret them as cowardice.

Thursday, 4th May

Martineau and I lunched at the Park Lane Hotel with Lord Braybrooke
who has recently succeeded two cousins (killed on active service), inheriting the title and Audley End. He is a bald, common-sensical, very nice
business man of 45, embarrassed by his inheritance. At his wits' end what
to do with Audley End. Who wouldn't be? We discussed how the N.T.
might take the house over. It was arranged that Martineau and I would
visit the house with him in June. It is requisitioned by the Army and used
for highly secret purposes, so that even he is not allowed into the rooms
except in the company of a senior officer. Consequently he hardly knows
the way round his own house. Two lots of death duties have had to be paid
on the estate. When the present lord was only 21 he was heir presump-
tive. Since then however he never expected to be in the running again.

Friday, 5th May

During the luncheon hour, to the National Gallery. A lecture on
Beethoven by Ivor James, the cellist of the Menges Quartet, which afterwards played Beethoven.

Jamesey met me at Brooks's, and we dined excellently at the White Tower - soup, coquille St. Jacques, and veal. I was sure these two courses were illegal, and felt guilty. James in addition had asparagus, and both of us had pudding. We drank Algerian wine. J. was extremely tired. He is over-worked. His War Office hours are 8.50 to 7 p.m. every day in the week, but one. He is in love with no one; and, worse still, no one is in love with him. Truly he is in a bad way.

Saturday, 6th May

Lunched with Eddy, who was in spanking form. He spied across the room a young officer, tanned darkest brown and wearing a kilt. He was sitting opposite me. Eddy made me change places before I realized his intention. Having reseated himself he said, 'You had better put your spectacles on.' I said, 'That's a bit late in the day in view of your extraordinary behaviour.' He talked of his lack of heart, yet not lack of feeling. He also said that whereas he considered disqualifications in himself to be a crime, he would consider the same in others to be merely a pity. James joined us at the end to judge the Blickling 'Holbein' of Henry VIII which I had in the car, outside. John Pope-Hennessy, whom I had invited, did not turn up.

Geoffrey Houghton-Brown called at 2.30 and we walked in Regent's Park. The walk was spoilt by the bitter cold and my new shoes, which cost me £6.10.0. and are agony. We searched for Decimus Burton buildings. Clarence Terrace, Cornwall Terrace and Holme Villa are his. These terraces have suffered grievously from the raids. Large pieces of plaster have flaked off and the shoddiness of Nash's methods is revealed. I said to Geoffrey I often wondered if an objective person like the Pope thought the English deserved to win this war; and I was pretty certain that, since it had dragged on so long, it would not matter in fifty years' time who had won it. Geoffrey said that Bobbie Harris, who has just returned from Italy, told him the Italians so hate us that they walk out of buildings when the British enter. Bobbie said the only people who may like us after the war are the Germans.

Nancy at dinner wore a little Queen Alexandra hat, with feathers on the brim, pulled down over her eyes, and was looking very pretty and debonair.

Wednesday, 10th May

After a meeting of the Polesden Lacey executors I went to the Kennets'. They arrived at 6, for he had been delivering a speech in the House of Lords. K. gave me tulips and lilies of the valley, her olive branch. This was our first meeting since the row in February outside the Albert Hall. Adorable woman.

Thursday, 11th May

Captain Hill came to see me in the morning to suggest the N.T. buying 4,000 acres of the Clumber estate from the Duke of Newcastle, to whom he now acts as agent. The area covers the park lands alone, the house having been totally destroyed. When I was last there, the house still stood, though gutted.

At about 4 I left in the car for Warwickshire. The sun was brilliant and with the roof of the car open I was drenched in sunshine. I shall soon become as brown as Eddy's officer, and then where shall I be? Admiring myself in the looking-glass, with my spectacles on? Stopped at St. Albans Cathedral. Its over-restoration is a disaster. It was one of the cases which brought the S.P.A.B. into being during the 1870s. The Early English style was actually substituted by the criminal Lord Grimthorpe for the Norman. Gilbert Scott never committed an offence like this. There was a service in progress as I tripped down one aisle, my brown shoes squeaking most horribly and shamefully. It must be the way I walk that makes all my shoes do this after a time. I arrived at Packwood House at 8 precisely, and there was Baron Ash on the drive awaiting me.

Friday, 12th May

Baron kept me up till 1 a.m. with woes, but I was down for breakfast at 8.30. During the morning we walked round the garden and down the avenue as far as it extends, the continuation of it having lately been given to the N.T. by Baron's brother-in-law. Baron is very distressed by the condition of the yews which have not been clipped or tied back for two years. He is right in stressing that the Commonwealth yew garden is of prime historic importance. With one gardener and two land girls it is impossible to look after the yews properly. Besides, if the land girls worked at them the Ministry of Labour would promptly take them, the land girls, away.

At 12 I left. Looked at the Children's Field, Knowle, a miserable little property - merely a flat field. There is nothing more to be said about it. On my way I passed Grimshaw Hall, that horrid, little, over-restored house. Stopped to eat some stale sandwiches in the porch of Castle Bromwich church.

At 2, according to plan, I reached Bloxwich, a suburb of Walsall, and went to the office of Messrs. Wiggin & Co. Old Mr. Wiggin received me and told me he was chairman of a family business of stainless steel, founded by his father. He was immensely proud of it. Showed me brochures of hideously designed coffee pots, thermos flasks, etc. A fortnight ago he bought Moseley Old Hall from the colliery company which has owned it, and is touchingly pleased. His life's ambition has been to own this house. He does not want to live in it, or to make it into a show place, but to restore it with the best expert advice, keep it as a place to take his firm's distinguished guests to, and in short, to gloat over it. I suggested covenants with the National Trust. He was delighted with this idea. One by one he summoned his two sons and two brothers, to each of whom in turn I had to explain the meaning of covenants. The old man was slow of speech. He appealed to his family to approve his motives and intentions point by point, delivering himself of a sort of inspired sermon. He reminded me of some Old Testament prophet addressing a tribe. It was a curious party and I was struck by the earnestness and sincerity and public spirit of this very worthy family, clustered round the revered autocrat, the patriarch. Then a brother and a son motored me to Moseley. To my pleasant surprise the old Hall is still in remote country, surrounded by and approached through lanes. Unhappily there are several fields of colliery pit heads and pylons in the near distance. The curious purple brick case stuck on to the outside in the 1870s is rather appealing. Of course I should prefer to see the half-timbering revealed, if it were at all possible, which I doubt. The Hall is a farmhouse which is nice. The interior has scarcely altered since the time when Charles II took refuge in it after the Battle of Worcester. It is a pity that the secret hides have lost their secrecy, their door slides having become hinged and handled. But they survive. The attic chapel, Father Huddleston's chamber, the King's little square black hole in which he crouched, are intact. The place is redolent of papistry, monarchy and sanctity.

I left at 3.30 for Boscobel, which is similarly farm-housey and unspoilt. It belongs to Lord Bradford. The oak tree, the garden mound are there, and the hide which Father Owen constructed as ingeniously as he did the ones at Moseley. The woman who showed me round explained that the pointed lancet and latticed windows painted on the chimney breast were Papist signs that here priests could find sanctuary. Hitherto I had deplored what I took to be bogus attempts to feign the real things.

Arrived at Weston Park at 5 precisely, hoping to look cool, the heat being terrific. I was given no opportunity to wash. Having rung the bell I was conducted by a young nephew straight into a room on the right of the hall where Lady Bradford was standing before a tea-kettle. She did not hear me enter, for she is deaf. She looked like a French *châteleine*. Lord Bradford very territorial and patrician. Both charming, with wonderful manners towards the stranger. After tea I begged to be allowed to see the pink French tapestries in the drawing-room. They are in superb condition. Lady Bradford walked me through the tunnel where, she told me, Queen Mary knocked her hat right off, to the Temple of Diana built by

Paine. It has a superb plaster ceiling like the Osterley temples, and a circular room at the rear with painted Etruscan ceiling panels. The central ceiling of the China Room has just collapsed, smashing all the china. There are Chinese Chippendale chairs made for the room. We continued round the lake. A temple has been built on the verge of it by Gerry Wellington. Lady B. said The Cottage was also built by Paine. To me it looked later.

Saturday, 13th May

Slept very soundly, and up early. Went to the office, put away the car and caught the 10 a.m. from Liverpool Street, having foolishly gone to King's Cross by mistake. Arrived Ipswich at 12.15 where Marshall Sisson met me and drove me to Swanton Morley. We stopped at the White Hart Inn at Scole for a drink. Sisson says there is no finer inn in the country. Caroline Flemish gables of red brick. We ate sandwiches in the car and reached Swanton Morley a little after 2.30. Found Colonel Jack Leslie with old Mr. Bullard, a brewer, the local rector and others. The purpose of this visit is very strange. Colonel Leslie had given a plot of land in the village, on which it was supposed once stood the cottage lived in by the ancestors of Abraham Lincoln, and demolished fifty years ago. With great ceremony Lord Zetland received the deeds from Ambassador Winant in February. Several plans were considered for a memorial on the site, one of which was a replica of the demolished cottage. With all this sentiment I disagreed, too strongly according to Matheson, from the first. Sisson, who was sent on our behalf to investigate the site soon after the gift was declared inalienable, suspected that it was the wrong one. By comparing a seventeenth-century map recording Lincoln land with an up-to-date twenty-five-inch ordinance, his suspicions were confirmed. Finally Leslie and the other local enthusiasts admitted that a mistake had in all innocence been made. It transpires that two-thirds of the old Lincoln house does indisputably exist in the present Angel inn, belonging to Bullard. There is even a small sketch of it on the old map. Bullard is prepared to give us a strip of freehold at the back of the inn. It is very important that eventually we should acquire the inn itself, which he won't surrender. Why should he? It retains a magnificent central cluster of octagonal brick chimneys and several beams with original moulds and stops. All the Lincoln fields marked on the seventeenth-century map survive today, with the same demarcations and hedge boundaries; even the lanes and ponds are the same. The Trust is left with a useless plot of land, an old chicken run of no beauty and less historic interest which it can never get rid of except by special Act of Parliament.

Sisson motored me back to Ipswich and I reached London at 10.30.

Monday, 15th May

Dined with Alvilde Chaplin at 55 Park Lane. Left rather early for fire-watching in the office, where I slept beautifully on my camp bed without sheets. Such a deprivation does not worry me in the least. Alvilde had been to see Ethel Smyth three days before she died. She was living in great discomfort, almost in squalor, and lay on an iron bedstead, looking like Wagner.

Tuesday, 16th May

Lunched at the Savoy with Mr. Hunter, the donor of Black Down, and was exactly on time. It was just as well for he remarked upon it. He is an autocratic tycoon. He had his architect to meet me, a man with, I suspect, no taste at all. We discussed the tower Mr. Hunter wishes to erect on the Down in memory of his wife. He wishes it to be higher than the Leith Hill tower, and to be made of such durable material that the trippers cannot disfigure it by cutting their names.

Wednesday, 17th May

The three Pope-Hennessys have great family pride and are very united. Dame Una said to me, 'Can't you write a book and join us?' I thought, even if I could write a book I wouldn't be permitted to join them, however much I might want to. Speaking of Lord Hartington's marriage they all declared it was a mistake to marry out of one's station, that people like us should not marry dukes and dukes' daughters, it was shocking. The Dame said, 'The Kennedy girl will never be able to take her place.' I could see that Jamesey was amused.

Thursday, 18th May

Took the 4 o'clock train to Lincolnshire and reached Gunby Hall in time for dinner. The old Field-Marshal gave me a warm welcome. He loves to talk about Gunby, its history and problems. He and Lady Massingberd are true county squirearchy, with a high sense of public duty towards the estate and the neighbourhood. They live in easy austerity, no wine, but good, solid food, and enough of it. They have a butler, his wife the cook, a pantry boy, two housemaids, a chauffeur, and lead a feudal existence on a modest scale.

Friday, 19th May

This morning I motored in a hired car to Harrington Hall, seven miles away. It is two miles from Somersby, just off the wolds, and very remote. Belongs to some people called Holiday Hartley. In 1927 the house was to be sold in lots by auction. In the morning a Major Rawnsley bought it, but so late that the auction had to take place just the same. The staircase had already been sold, and Rawnsley had to buy it back. He could not buy the sundial over the porch, and so had to have a copy made. Rawnsley sold Harrington to the Hartleys for £1,500, on condition that if they parted with it they would give an option to purchase either to the Rawnsley family or the National Trust. It is beautiful, romantic, and finely situated. Originally early Tudor, with a high brick Henry VIII central porch. The rest is Charles II. The oak staircase is better than the Gunby one, yet similar, with arcaded, fan-lighted doorways leading to it. There is a walled garden immediately behind the house, and behind that a wood with the remains of an oblong canal, longer than the Gunby one, and a lime avenue. A remarkable feature is the raised terrace garden, 'the high hall garden' of Tennyson's *Maud*, which was written with Harrington in mind. Maud's 'little oak room', alas, has had the early Renaissance and linenfold wainscoting removed. The Hartleys offer the house and fifty acres of park to the N.T. but without endowment.

In the afternoon I walked round part of Gunby estate with the Field-Marshal. After dinner he talked about Churchill. Said that he must have learnt much from his study of Marlborough, for Marlborough also had remarkable contacts with crowned heads, and leaders of countries when he dashed around Europe. The Field-Marshal said that he and Weygand and Pétain were the sole survivors of the Council of the Allies held in 1918 when the fortunes of the allies were at their lowest ebb. Churchill, then Minister of Munitions, came over to France and asked what he could most usefully do to help. The Field-Marshal said 'Keep an eye on Pétain. I suspect that he may let us down.' The Field-Marshal greatly admires Montgomery, who is no relation, and Alexander even more. He says Alexander has never put a foot wrong.

Sunday, 21st May

Nancy asked me to lunch. I willingly accepted, but I should have stayed at home and worked. She has just bought for £40 a huge Dresden china clock which she thinks lovely. It is not eighteenth century, more likely 1840s, and the face even later. Alas, it won't go, and we pushed the pendulum, shook the clock and propped it on paper wedges, to no avail. She walked Milly and me round St. John's Wood, looking at houses. How charming some of these streets are. I left at 3.30 and worked at an article on my return.

At 7.30 to Harold Acton's flat in Chesterfield Court, where Norman Douglas was. We drank whisky till 9.45 and dined at the Ritz Grill. Norman Douglas said he was 21 in 1890, so he is well over 70. He has straight white hair, is thin, has a mottled face, slightly beaky features. I would not say a particularly striking face on first meeting. He laughs intermittently, explosively, and talks a lot of bawdy. He told us he had written about the destruction of London buildings in a recent number of *Life and Letters*. Until this war he had not been in London or England indeed, since 1916. Hates it, and the cold of it, and the restraint, the bad food and the puritanism. Is delighted to be able to talk to the Italian waiters in the Ritz Grill in their own language. Has no idea what has happened to his house and belongings in Florence. I accompanied him in the tube to Gloucester Road, for he is afraid of having fainting fits, to which he is prone. He asked me what they did with the earth they dug out in excavating the tubes. I had no idea, but Eardley tells me a lot was sent to Mill Hill. Douglas said that in Florence he cultivated the reputation of being a bear in order to avoid social persecution by the wrong people. We shook hands warmly at Gloucester Road. He said he would ask Viva King to bring us together again.

Monday, 22nd May

To the George Inn, Southwark, at tea-time, and met Forsyth and the painter to consider some light cream Forsyth was trying out on the gallery balusters. I emphatically disapproved of this colour, and voted for retention of the existing chocolate brown as enhancing the Dickensian gloom of the in. Voted for the walls behind the galleries to be painted the same yellow as the distemper on the adjoining range of buildings, of which the Inn forms part, the woodwork of this range to be painted chocolate likewise, so as to preserve the uniformity. Was pleased that both Eardley and Forsyth agreed in the end, and so this decision was carried.

Tuesday, 23rd May

At 9.30 Eardley and I set off to look at Lord Hambleden's estate over which he has given the Trust covenants, entirely through Eardley's efforts. We looked over Culham Court, now used as a nursery school. It is a compact, small house, very well planned. Neat entrance hall. All the vaulting of the passage ceilings is delightful. Two drawing-rooms preserve circular relief panels over the chimneypieces. The eastern drawing-room is green with gilded gesso panels, pretty and apparently contemporary, though E. thinks they may be by Lenygon.[1] If so, they are well well done. Some bolection-mould mantelpieces have been inserted. They of course are wrong and make me suspicious of the rest. The house might have been built by Sir Robert Taylor. The outside is a very pretty pink brick.

---

[1] A fashionable decorating firm in the 1920s.

It is a pity that the trees have been allowed to grow so thickly along the reach of the river, and that there are too many conifers round the house.

We motored in and out of the drive of Greenlands. Walked down the azalea ride of Great Wood. Were shown over Hambleden Manor by the tenant, a lady who drives round the garden in a swift, silent electric chair. This house was built in 1604 with three pointed gables of knapped flint on each elevation. In 1814 an additional wing with elliptical bay formed a Regency ballroom. More recently a bad billiard-room has appeared. The house has been over-restored by rich people. Walked across to Kenricks, which, formerly the parsonage house, is of red brick, *circa* 1720. The outside rendering having been removed, leaves the brick rather blotchy. A little stiff and dull inside.

Wednesday, 24th May

After a Georgian Group meeting Puss Milnes-Gaskell lunched with me. She was looking sad. She said that Fitzroy Maclean was to have travelled in the same aeroplane as her son, Charles, which crashed, but that circumstances made him too late, and he had to take the next. I asked her whether Queen Mary would accept the Presidentship, if asked, and she seemed to think she might, and would not be too adversely influenced by Lord Harewood. So I have written to Lord Zetland. I would like Queen Mary to become President of the National Trust, because she is the only member of the royal family interested in such things. Puss told me she was in Partridge's shop with the Queen. Partridge showed them a bed cover of seventeenth-century crewel work, telling them he had already sold the hangings of the same stuff. Puss recognized it as having come from her old home. Mr. Partridge pressed her to accept the bed cover as a present. Puss resolutely protested until Queen Mary turned on her, and said, 'Constance, never refuse a firm offer. I never do.' Thereupon Puss had to accept.

After luncheon we walked to Prunier's where David Lloyd, his wife and mother were lunching. The two Ladies Lloyd were arguing amicably about the lot of poor women having to look after their children. The younger was saying, 'I think our class do not realize what hell it is having to look after children all day and every day.' Blanche replied, 'But then our class are not accustomed to it, my dear.'

I dined at Emerald's, and sat next to Lady Juliet Duff and Mrs. McEwen, a sweet, gentle woman. Her husband was there, one of the Government Whips, a high Tory; Rory Cameron, in the U.S. army, a new friend of Emerald's; Daisy Fellowes, wearing a mantilla and looking remarkably, deceptively demure, and beautiful. She is a sparkling conversationalist, with a distinctive, corn-crakey voice, and French intonation.

It was an enjoyable dinner. Lord Sherwood came in afterwards. He is supposed to have great success with women, but looks a runt with a large nose. He talked republicanism, is against kings, etc., and yet has accepted a peerage, which is an inconsistency. Drawing-room politics ensued. Emerald was not at her best, and kept harping upon Chips Channon, saying, 'I think Chips longs to have a grand passion, and doesn't know how to. The trouble is he hates women. Now Jim, what do you think?' as though I had any views on the subject. She said a few funny things, such as, 'Robert Byron's father used to poke his daughters with a sadistic fork,' and, 'Women today are so unromantic, so - un-succulent.' She surprised us by saying she had once been asked to stand for Parliament for Mells, apparently meaning Stroud.

Thursday, 25th May

I went off in the car at 4.30 and arrived at Wickhamford at 7.45. Mama looks much older, is very thin and very lined. I hate this, and I hate to see her on her hands and knees dusting the floor and polishing the boards. It is moreover quite unnecessary.

Friday, 26th May

This morning Mama talked to me about her will. She has made several odd codicils. She wishes to be buried a day after her death; there are to be no wreaths at all on her grave; there is to be no lead lining to her coffin because it is unfair on the bearers; she is to be buried in her best nightdress, and not in a winding sheet tied up at the head like a bonnet, as old Mrs. Someone-or-other was in the village, fit to make you split with laughter. These clauses in her own inimitable layman's wording were very funny, as she solemnly read them out to me.

I motored to Overbury, picked up Thurstan Holland-Martin and drove him to Tewkesbury. He showed me the cottages and buildings round the Abbey which his Trust intends to buy if we will provide some money from our Cathedral Amenities Fund. I do not absolutely share his ideas for I see he is a vista-maker. But I do think his Trust should be helped to acquire the dwellings lest a chain store purchases them in order to put up something beastly. Thurstan wants to pull down some Georgian dwellings of little intrinsic worth, and to reconstitute some medieval overhangs and fronts.

I returned to Overbury Court and lunched there. Mrs. Holland-Martin has become very old, small and bent. She still has that deep, capable voice which I remember from early childhood days, a voice which frightened me to death during tennis tournaments, when she umpired. Woe betide whoever partnered a son of hers, and let him down in a boys' double, which I invariably did. For this reason I simply dreaded being paired with Thurstan. Sitting on a stepladder Mrs. Holland-Martin would boom out, 'Pull up your socks, young Lees-Milne.' Oh, the agony and dread. And Mama told me this morning how at the beginning of the war she and other Worcestershire ladies were being drilled by Mrs. H.-M. I said, 'Are you sure you were drilled?' 'Yes, of course,' she said, 'and I went on parade with my shooting stick, and while we were forming fours, it got entangled in Josey Duncombe's shoe-laces and brought her crashing to the ground. And you know she is over 80. And Nell gave me the most terrible dressing down in front of the whole platoon.'

Today Mrs. Holland-Martin was absolutely docile and friendly.

Saturday, 27th May

All morning in the Polytechnic with Miss Paterson and old William Weir, arranging 260 designs by competitors for the West Wycombe village hall. This lasted till 2.30. We took Weir back to Cheyne Walk and gave him an odd meal of tea and eggs. Weir reminded me that he had been a pupil of Philip Webb, who had been a pupil of Edmund Street. He has a great regard for Webb for having dissociated himself from Street when the latter embarked upon the Law Courts. But I admire the Law Courts.

Sunday, 28th May

I crept into Westminster Abbey through the west door during a service. After the oven-like heat of outside the charnel cool of the inside was refreshing. There was a procession of dean and canons in beautiful copes, and choirboys in Elizabethan ruffs, singing a hymn. On my way from the cloisters to Dean's Yard I noticed for the first time a high marble monument to an Admiral Cornwall, *circa* 1750, a cliff-like structure hung with reliefs, and encrusted with shells, sea urchins and rocaille ornaments. It is jet-black with dirt, and would look wonderful if cleaned.

Monday, 29th May

The hottest day I remember. With my four windows wide open, and in my shirt sleeves I dripped, while compiling a memorandum for the National Trust. I nearly died of the combination of heat and work. Thus occupied all day until dinner at the St. James's Club with Charles Fry. Batsford's are going to produce the official book in celebration of the N.T.'s fiftieth birthday.

Tuesday, 30th May

Had a great shock this morning, for the Gas Company telephoned to say my cheque to them had bounced. I rang up the bank at Evesham who were sorry and said I was £200 overdrawn. I am terrified lest other cheques may be returned. I wrote to my father in desperation and shame. Now he has always implied, like King George V about buggers, that men shoot themselves for such a disgrace. As for the other offence I dread to think what he supposes they should do, slowly roast themselves to death on a spit, I daresay. Oh Lord, he will be furious.

Visited Pierre Lansel, who in Piccadilly the other day begged me to see him. He said it was madness not to continue my treatment a little longer, and in proof of his wisdom showed me a graph of my blood behaviour, nodding in a knowing way. It meant nothing to me, and I was too alarmed to ask for a detailed explanation. Besides I can't possibly afford the treatment, and daren't risk a cheque bouncing off him.

Dined at Emerald's. Nancy, Joan Moore and a don called Denis Rickett, terrifyingly incisive, intellectual and All Soulsish. Emerald was in sparkling form. Venetia Montagu came in at 11.30. She is a very clever, well-informed woman, with a masculine and independent mind. Denis Rickett told Emerald that she had an astounding knowledge of the classics. It is true. Talk was of George Eliot and English novelists. There seems to be no novel that Emerald hasn't read, and, what's more, remembered.

Wednesday, 31st May

This morning I tubed to Totteridge to see a house called Darlands and 100 acres, making a real island of country in a horribly built up area. The house, dating from 1930, is built by Guy Dawber in decent red brick, with a sloping tiled roof. A well laid out garden. I thought it one of the best houses of this period. It does not quite verge on the arty, which the best houses of 1910 tend to do. The bailiff took me round the property which Mrs. Kemp, a biscuit manufacturer's widow, wishes to leave to the Trust. I favour covenants, for I don't think the place would be of much use to the public.

Returned in time to lunch with Nancy at Gunter's. Alvilde Chaplin and Hamish there. Alan Pryce-Jones joined us for coffee. Nancy said that last Sunday *Reynolds' News* reproduced a Spanish caricature of King George and Queen Elizabeth in bed. The Queen was saying to the King, 'George, why do you look so low this morning?' and the King was replying, 'Because I have it on the best authority that Winston means to swap me for an old destroyer.'

Dr. Vaughan-Williams came into the office this afternoon. I did not realize until after he left that he was the composer. He came to announce that his brother of Leith Hill Place had died this morning, leaving the property to him, and that he wished to give it to the National Trust. He was not wasting much time. He is an elderly, stout man, handsome and distinguished, not at all practical. He was wrapped in thought and had a distracted manner. He kept rubbing his hand through his untidy white hair. In shaking his hand I noticed how soft and resistant it was, as though he were frightened of injuring it.

Thursday, 1st June

Lady Cohen asked me to luncheon at the Greek Club to meet Lady Luke. I supposed she must be the Bovril Lord Luke's wife, until she said, 'I am afraid I am only a common knight's wife.' I liked her for this.

At 6 I called for Loelia Westminster and took her to Wilton's, where we met Anne and Esmond Rothermere, and ate dressed crab and drank sherry and white wine, as a preliminary to a charity film, *This Happy Breed* by Noël Coward, a kind of continuation of *Cavalcade*. It was in colour, and quite horribly and insidiously sentimental, so that I had constant lumps in the throat and wanted to cry, while realizing all the time that my lowest emotions were being played upon. Loelia had paid I don't know how many guineas for each seat. At Ciro's afterwards they were talking of a party the other night which cost £75, and how disgraceful it was of someone or other only to have contributed £10. So I quickly thought I would not even make a gesture of contributing to this entertainment, for had I proffered £5 it would have been accepted as though it were 5d. Nonetheless I felt rather uncomfortable. But they are all so vastly rich, and I am so rat poor.

Lord Rothermere is very tall, with a mouth like a cupid's. He seems to think the Invasion will be a walk-over, 'for the Germans cannot stand much more of a licking'. He talked of the embarrassment caused by Mrs. Roosevelt's public statement that Churchill was sixty years out of date. I said I supposed we would hear nothing of it owing to the strict censorship of the British papers. He said the censorship was too rigid; so much was bottled up that when a news item was released it often made more noise than its importance justified.

Friday, 2nd June

Trained to Hatch End, arriving punctually at 10. Lord and Lady Braybrooke waiting in their car, and Anthony Martineau already arrived. They motored us to Audley End.

Audley End is at present used as a military college. The principal state-rooms are closed to the soldiers and stacked high with furniture. The rooms lately in use have been most carefully protected by the Ministry of Works, even the stair treads being boarded over. It is a very secret place and only with difficulty was permission granted us to see round. We went all over, through the back regions, into practically every room and on the great lead roof, which looked in good order. It is of course a huge house, although three-quarters of it was demolished 200 years ago. It is certainly extremely important, being on a par with Blickling and Hatfield. The hall screen was once painted white, and I wish it were again. Vanbrugh constructed the grand staircase at the other end of the hall. I was fascinated by the Walpolian Gothick chapel. The eighteenth-century rooms on the south side, painted and decorated by Rebecca, are of poor quality and mean size. It is interesting that successive alterations in the eighteenth and nineteenth centuries were done with much care to reproduce the Jacobean style, notably in the design of windows and bays, and ceiling plasterwork, much of which is indistinguishable from the original. The Great Hall and the Fish Saloon are very impressive. There is an early nineteenth-century flavour in the paintwork of the rooms. The portrait copies in the Saloon are atrocious. Some Adam suites of furniture are good of their kind, but there is a deal of indifferent stuff in the rooms which makes Audley End a true English country house, and not a museum.

We drove across the road to the circular Robert Adam temple where we had an excellent picnic luncheon. A noble view of the house from up here. The beautiful, undulating park is by Capability Brown, and could never be mistaken for nature's accident. The stable block is supposedly late sixteenth century, but looks early sixteenth to me, although there are no depressed arches discernible. An Elysian Temple, Lady Portsmouth's column and Brettingham's Temple of Concord complete the park features. Lord Braybrooke can barely find his way about. He is very keen to preserve his inheritance by means of the National Trust. He is willing for Mrs. Van der Elst to rent from the Trust, but he will not sell to her. We looked at Abbey Farm, and the almshouses which the Royal Historical Commission ranks high.

I returned by train to dine with Margaret Jourdain. The train was crammed, and I stood in the guard's van, almost dead with fatigue, my legs aching. Margaret was alone. She read me extracts of the William Kent letters she has found and is publishing. We discussed the possibility of a joint book on Kent, and also of editing the Bennet Langton papers, now at Gunby. She is a wickedly entertaining woman, and can be cruel about people less well informed than herself, notably poor old Clifford Smith, whose ignorance she never tires of exposing. She says Ivy [Compton-Burnett] will not come back to London, she is so afraid of bombs. We talked a lot about Ivy's books and the unreality of the characters. Margaret says Ivy lives in the past, and nothing after 1914 has any reality for her.

Saturday, 3rd June

Went to Dickie Girouard's nuptial Mass at Spanish Place. It was solemn and moving, and lasted one hour and a quarter. Billa Harrod was sitting in front of me. We went together to the Dorchester reception given by the bride's mother. We found Nancy there and the three of us tucked into chicken mousse and tongue, washed down with cider cup. Then chocolate and cocktails, which we had not been offered before. Billa could not restrain her greed, and ate and ate. Nancy says Peter Rodd tells her the invading troops are penned up like prisoners in barbed wire enclosures awaiting the signal; that Peter actually knows which beaches they are to land on. He keeps appearing and disappearing, stressing how frightened he is because he has already participated in two invasions, saying goodbye for ever and warning Nancy that a widow's pension is very small.

Sunday, 4th June

Dined with James and Constantia Rumbold at the Allies' Club. Talked of poverty and overdrafts, and of the impending invasion. Both of them knew beforehand the date of the North African invasion, but denied they knew anything about the forthcoming one.

Tuesday, 6th June

Miss P. woke me early at 7.30 and we breakfasted soon after 8. Consequently she missed the 8 o'clock news in her bedroom to which she usually listens. I left for the 9.30 at King's Cross, bought a paper and read of the capture of Rome without destruction, which was cheering. Hubert Smith met me at Grantham at 11.55. It was bitterly cold. He asked me if I knew anything about the Invasion. I said I knew nothing. Had it begun? He said the 8 o'clock news intimated that it had. I was filled with mingled emotions, apprehension over the outcome, anxiety for my friends, regret and guilt that I was not participating, relief that I was not. Hubert Smith drove me to Grantham House, where we were received by the two Miss Sedgwicks, old women of the churchy, godly sort. They are very north country, abrupt and spinsterish. They expected me to stay the night, and seemed cross when I said I must leave in the afternoon. In actual fact there was nothing for me to do, and my visit was a waste of time. Their wireless would not work, the battery having perished, so we heard no news at 1 o'clock. Had a rhubarby luncheon, rather nasty. Miss Marion left for a funeral, and Miss Winifred took us to look at the property the other side of the river. It rained and was depressing. Never before have I been so conscious of the fatuity of my work, fiddling while Rome burns - though, thank God, the actual Rome is spared. After tea and a rock cake at 3 we left.

A long, straight drive of a mile brought us to Harlaxton Manor. The butler at the lodge said he dared not show us the house without a written letter from Mrs. Van der Elst. I hadn't got one, I explained, but the agent said I might see over. The butler accompanied us to the back premises and telephoned to London. Meanwhile Hubert and I looked at the outside. The date 1837 is carved on the parapet of the porch. The stone of which the house is built is a beautiful bronze yellow, almost like Stanway's. The design is meant to put one in mind of Burghley. The pavilions and gate piers of the forecourt are as baroque as Vanbrugh. Mrs. Van der Elst has made ghastly, insipid white marble statues peer from bushes and sit on pinnacles. The butler was away so long that Hugh and I went to look for him. We walked for miles in a rabbit warren of back passages. Mrs. Van der Elst has suggested that we should sell Harlaxton for her, and with the proceeds endow Audley End, which she will rent. The butler finally reappeared, having spoken to Mrs. Van der Elst. She refused categorically to allow us to set foot inside the premises. I was made extremely angry by this treatment.

Hubert motored me to Oxford. I ate a sandwich at the Randolph. Just before Oxford we saw about 100 aeroplanes towing gliders, evidently returning from France. All day I have felt excited and longed to have news. On Didcot station waiting for a train I met Willy Teeling, now M.P. for Brighton, and travelled to Paddington with him. He said he must get to his constituency since his constituents felt safe if he were there. No harm in this, but he is yet another example of a man whose head the 'House' has turned. He told me Lord Vansittart complained to him at Denham that since the P.M. took office he had never consulted him or addressed a word to him, but systematically cut him.

Wednesday, 7th June

National Buildings Record photographic exhibition at the National Gallery. Those provided by the Warburg Institute of the detailed bosses, tombs and effigies in Westminster Abbey are superb. The heads of the early Plantagenet kings and queens must be portraits, they have such character. Equally revealing are the Warburg photographs of St. Paul's, taken of views one never can see oneself, such as the drum of the dome from above, the window heads of the turrets.

Had tea with old Mr. Rhys-Williams of Merthyr, a strange, unappetizing old man who told me he hated his eldest son, whose mother had turned him against his father, and when they lived under the same roof treated him as though he were an idiot. But he hounded them both out of the house all right, and will never speak to them again. I asked him if he had other sons. He said, 'Yes, but my second son is not mine really. It's sad in a way.'

I trained to Rochester in the afternoon to look at the Old Hall. From the gate of this rambling old place, close to the Cathedral and opposite the Castle, the owner, Miss Shinkwin (Dickensian name), came bustling forth, accompanied by several cats and pekingeses. Elderly, dumpy, she was wearing a too light summer frock, silver ear-rings and finger rings. She had dusty dyed hair and stockingless legs. I was disposed to dislike this Pomeranian lady, but she was so good-hearted, enthusiastic and kind that I soon took to her. She spoke in a curious, high, exaggerated drawl. The Old Hall is a muddle of wings and gables, and basically early Tudor. The inside suggests a second-rate antique shop with its pickled walnut 'chiffoniers', 'davenports', 'chesterfields', Knole settees and lampshades made of parchment deeds. Miss Shinkwin has within ten years unveiled square yards of very perished wall stencilling and one complete room of mid-Tudor painted panelling, of a conventionalized flower device which is in fair condition. But there is so much revealed timbering, which never ought to have been revealed, that my enthusiasm quickly flagged. Even so, Miss Shinkwin is beginning upon two more rooms, scraping away to disclose more painted, or stencilled wainscot. Above one chimneypiece she has brought to light two allegorical figures of Justice and Truth in pre-Tudor dress, reminiscent, she declares, of Sienese primitive paintings.

Harold Nicolson dined at the White Tower. Stuart and his friend Robin Brewster, just come from America, joined us. We were in a very noisy upstairs room and I could barely hear one word Harold uttered. He was, I think, tired and trying his utmost, as he always does, to entertain us. Not a highly enjoyable evening. Brewster is a set, earnest young man with fanatical, sunk eyes. Stuart says he is the 'last Puritan', as well as immensely rich. He is buying from Agnew's a Watteau for £5,000. He hardly spoke, and looked cross and difficult. He left us after dinner, and Stuart and I accompanied Harold to King's Bench Walk. Harold was intrigued by Brewster's reticence, and asked about his private life. Stuart knows nothing of it, although he is one of his oldest friends.

This morning I trained to Leatherhead with Christopher Gibbs and his wife Peggy. They have grown to look exactly like one another – an infallible indication of a happy marriage. We lunched at Christopher's parents' house, Goddards, one of Lutyens's earliest domestic buildings, full of oak timbers and ingle nooks. Although I can see how well designed, and well executed every detail is, nevertheless I do not care for a contrived 'olde worlde' flavour. Christopher motored me to Leith Hill. We picked up Roland Vaughan-Williams and passed Tanhurst, his house on the edge of the Leith Hill slope, with splendid views. The house is square, early Georgian. We continued to Leith Hill Place, likewise on the slope, a short distance away. His cousin the composer, Ralph Vaughan-Williams, was waiting for us. This house is likewise fairly small, and was built about 1730 for a General Folliot. It has two flanking wings with pedimented gables, very wide and rather Kent-like. The south side is faced with Portland stone. The windows have nice period surrounds with pulvinated friezes. Inside there is not much decoration, apart from a decent feature or two. The composer remembers his father removing the exterior roof balustrade and inserting the dormer windows. He showed us what had been his nursery and his bedroom when he was a boy. He wants the house to be used as an institution, which is a pity, for it is just the sort of house that would let privately. There is a large walled garden, with trees, shrubs and an azalea walk, which is lovely. Unfortunately the whole property is destitute. It is offered without endowment.

The composer is a very sweet man, with a most impressive appearance. He is big and broad and has a large head with sharply defined features, and eyes that look far into the distance. He has shaggy white hair that is not long. Slender hands and fingers with square-ended, or rather bitten nails. He is very courteous and when it began to rain in the garden, offered to go into the house to fetch my burberry. I had some difficulty in preventing him. He is longing to disembarrass himself of his responsibility for the estate. When asked by Christopher to resolve some estate matter, he replied, 'We will let things continue as before, for the present.' In the car he told me that when young musicians came to him for advice he always discouraged them, for he said that those who seriously intended to make music their career would always do so willy-nilly. He has a quiet, dry humour which expresses itself in very few words. He laughs in a low key.

Sunday, 11th June

All day I read, and slept, for I feel worn out. Dinner at Alvilde Chaplin's promised to be, and was, fun, for Nancy, Emerald, Harold Acton and Palewski, General de Gaulle's *chef de cabinet*, a bright, cheerful man, were there. Emerald asked a lot of inadvertent questions, such as how many French troops there were in France now. Palewski is staunchly loyal about de Gaulle, says he is charming but shy, and does not wish for power. We have heard that so often. There was much criticism of Americans and Roosevelt for their non-recognition of de Gaulle, and pusillanimous reasons given, namely their wanting to wait and see which way the cat jumped before committing themselves to his support. I said to Palewski, surely the reason is that Americans think de Gaulle stands for authoritarian power, or what in their democratic eyes is authoritarian power. If de Gaulle no longer favours the old *laissez faire* democracy which brought France to perdition in 1940, then I was all for him. A good deal of talk about French literature between Harold and Palewski, who is a cultivated man. Few fireworks from Emerald. She did say, 'What is the use of handsome husbands? They soon become less handsome, and in the end they are nothing but an incubus.'

Wednesday, 14th June

Lunched with Sibyl Colefax and Mrs. Gladwyn Jebb at the Canteen. Sibyl said Lord Bruntisfield told her the aeroplane brought down on Monday night near Liverpool Street station was a pilotless one, a kind of rocket. For the present the Government are not releasing the news. She said no one in authority expected the war to be over for a very long time. I walked away with her, and we took a bus as far as Bond Street. In the open she appears very tiny, round shouldered, old and pathetic.

Stuart told me that in his office the American soldiers speak with surprise about the familiarity of English girls, none of whom decline to sleep with them. They are convinced that all English women are tarts, and despise them accordingly, just as English soldiers despised the French girls during the last war.

Thursday, 15th June

To the Courtauld Institute for Kenneth Clark's lecture on Cézanne. A great crowd. It was a brilliant lecture, delivered with that purring ease which I admire in him so much, yet with haste, and packed with meat. Slides of Cézanne in black and white are not wholly satisfactory. John Fowler dined at Brooks's. He told me some horrifying stories of how American troops behave after dark. One night this week John and two friends were walking home at midnight through the Green Park. One friend stopped to pee behind a tree, while the other two walked on. He took a long time so they retraced their steps. They found him on the ground, pouring with blood, having been assaulted, knocked down and stamped upon by two drunk G.I.s. The rest of our conversation was about art in our time, and how general depreciation of quality as well as lack of time for rumination drove us to being preservationists, and thus uncreative.

While I was in bed, very tired, the siren went. There was severe intermittent gunfire throughout the night until, indeed, 9.45 a.m. when the all–clear sounded. This is unprecedented since the early raids. I heard one aeroplane roar overhead extremely low.

Friday, 16th June

I lunched with Philip Frere, who is working at the Ministry of Aircraft Production. He told me that last night 140 pilotless planes came over. They are guided by radio and when they land their bomb load of 2,000 lbs. explodes. This is like an H. G. Wells story. It is almost inconceivable. Some of these things have landed in Surrey, some around and in London, doing great mischief. Morrison in the House of Commons has disclosed this information today. Frere talked of Lord Lloyd, and how he first met him. Lloyd told him before his death that Darlan gave him a signed pledge that he would not surrender the French fleet to the Germans. After G. Ll.'s death they looked everywhere for this document, but it has not yet been found.

L.H. brought her son to see me. He has just returned from South Africa. She has always gone on and on about his exceptional good looks and wonderful intelligence. He appeared extremely sallow, with no back to his head, a long cadaverous face and a Hitlerian black moustache. To all my enquiries about South Africa he was unable, or unwilling to stammer one word. How mothers deceive themselves. I trust mine does not sing my praises to strangers. Somehow I think not.

At midnight the sirens went. I was very tired, and did not get to sleep till 5. Intermittent gunfire extremely noisy. Shrapnel clattered on to the road, and the looking glass in the kitchen fell off the wall, breaking into a thousand fragments.

Saturday, 17th June

Worn out all day, but recovered marvellously in the evening. Worked in the R.I.B.A. Library this morning, and Brooks's library in the afternoon. I am always happy in Brooks's stuffy, dingy, Victorian library in which silence is accentuated by the relentless tick of the old, stuffy clock. I love the old, stuffy books on the stuffy brown shelves, books which nobody reads, except Eddie Marsh, and he falls fast asleep over them. The very atmosphere is calculated to send one asleep, but into the gentlest, most happy, nostalgic dreams of nineteenth–century stability, self-satisfaction, and promise of an eternity of heavenly stuffiness, world without end. How much I adore this library, and club, nobody knows. May it survive Hitler, Stalin and all the beastliness which besets us.

I had to return to prepare tea for Nancy in Cheyne Walk. When we had begun Stuart walked in. Talk was of little else but the pilotless planes. They came over again all evening. We kept rushing to the window to look for them, but were always disappointed. I have only seen plumes of smoke across the river where they have landed. I believe they are hardly ever shot on the wing either by our fighters or by anti-aircraft guns. Nancy cracked very bad taste jokes about them, implying that she welcomed them as a hilarious diversion during these dull days. She said Palewski, who accompanied de Gaulle to France this week, was deeply impressed by the quiet, reverential way in which the General was everywhere received. Montgomery, he said, was tactful, and on greeting him apologized for being too busy to escort him, and so let him be on his own, which he, Monty, knew was what he wanted.

Nancy agreed to dine with James and me. When she and I were outside Bridget's flat in Mount Street, suddenly Michael Rosse in battledress, and wearing a beret and thick, fleece-lined waterproof, approached us round a corner. He had unexpectedly come up from Wanstead with his brigadier for an hour and a half. The whole Guards division is there, and have not yet gone to France. They wait like caged swans, for the north wind to drop before they can sail. We accompanied him into Bridget's flat. I talked to him while he had a bath. He said that in a few days' time a huge offensive would be launched, but that unless things went very wrong, his company would not be in it. He wants Bridget to tell Anne this, for he dares not do so on the telephone, and letters are censored. He warned us that all trunk calls are listened in to. He was very cheerful, and yet looked sad. I felt extremely sad. He was so matter of fact and unsentimental that I was much moved. Nancy and I said good-bye to him in Mount Street.

We met James outside Rules' restaurant, which was shut. So we dined at Simpson's, Nancy dashing to the window whenever we heard a rocket. She made us laugh a lot. Told a story about the tart in Curzon Street who, when asked how the war was treating her, replied that for a reserved occupation, £700 a week tax free, plus emoluments from the Government for reporting the indiscretions of soldier clients, was so satisfactory she only wished she could open a second front. After dinner we walked along the embankment. We watched two boys, who had clambered on to the subsidiary bridge at Westminster, throw large planks from it into the Thames until a policeman chased them away. This amused Nancy. James and I put her into a bus at Victoria and wandered round Pimlico until I went to the office for firewatching. We held a conference in the warden's post and agreed that those of us who could sleep should do so, and those who could not, should from time to time patrol the streets after gunfire. I of course am one of the non-sleepers. This night turned out to be worse than the previous ones. Nevertheless I felt far safer downstairs in Eardley's company than at home, and slept better than on Thursday and Friday nights.

Sunday, 18th June

At Mass at 11 there was a great noise of gunfire and a rocket. In the after-noon Stuart walked in and said that a rocket had landed on the Guards' Chapel during service this morning, totally demolishing it and killing enormous numbers of Guards officers and men. Now this news did shake me. After dining at the Churchill Club we walked through Queen Anne's Gate, where a lot of windows with the old crinkly blown glass panes have been broken. In St. James's Park crowds of people were looking at the Guards' Chapel across Birdcage Walk, now roped off. I could see nothing but gaunt walls standing, and gaping windows. No roof at all. While I watched four stretcher bearers carry a body under a blanket, the siren went, and everyone scattered. I felt suddenly sick. Then a rage of fury against the war welled inside me. For sheer damnable devilry what could be worse than this awful instrument? We heard another go very close over our heads, and explode. I left Stuart in St. James's Park underground, and walked to Victoria. On getting out of the bus in Beaufort Street I heard and saw my first rocket. It was rushing overhead at great speed north-wards. Half an hour ago, while writing this, I heard another, and saw one out of my west window, like a dagger with a flaming beacon at its tail. Then the engine cut off, and I watched it dive over the World's End. In a second the windows rattled, and a thin plume of smoke rose to the sky. There was a faint, distant sound of wailing. Dame Una tells me that today they have destroyed Tyburn Convent and the Charing Cross bridge.

Tuesday, 20th June

I lunched with Lord Esher at Brooks's and discussed a number of N.T. problems with him, including M.'s feud with Mr. H. Esher said it was utterly useless his arbitrating in specific disputes where the trouble was irreconcilable incompatibility of temperament. There was nothing any man could do.

Another fearful night. Nothing dropped in Chelsea that I know of but before midnight one just across the river made a hideous clatter, and the house shook like a jelly. The guns have ceased firing now because they merely bring the rockets down – when they hit them – to explode in the streets, just as they do if they fall of their own accord, which is sometimes in open country. In fact, for the same reason the balloons have been removed to open country outside London, as well as the guns, where the barrage to the south of the city must be terrific. Whereas previously I cursed the guns for the ceaseless noise they made throughout the night, now I find that without them I am more frightened. Quite irrationally I feel let down. The lack of guns strikes me as an admission of failure in defence. Instead I lie awake for hours and hours, my ears waiting for the sound of rocket planes. Here in Cheyne Walk we have distant trams, trains, motor vehicles and river traffic which one mistakes at first for a plane. There are also the factories across the river, where a horrid ghostly warble is released every single time a plane is approaching. It warns the workers before the sirens blow. This too is distracting. During the past week the sirens have ceaselessly blown, and there is a raid quite as often as there is an all clear. This night I was awake until 5. Miss P. is very good but nervous, and whenever she hears a plane will get up and sit on the stairs. I put on my gumboots and in my dressing-gown walk about the road, watching the fingers of the searchlights prodding the planes and catching them in their beams. Tonight I talked to an old man in a bowler hat who is night watchman on the boat moored on the embankment immediately below this house. He took me into his cabin, which had a blazing fire in the grate. One or two others, wardens and so on, congregated there. We all talked about the bombs and the war. It was very cosy and intimate, like being inside Peggotty's upturned boat on Yarmouth sands. I feel I need never be lonely with these nice people so close.

Thursday, 22nd June

Jamesey rang me up this evening, and I went round to his flat. We moved to the garden of the inn next door, which he has only just discovered. We sat on the terrace drinking cider and gin till we were quite tipsy. Then, rather fearfully, staggered up the hill to dine with Dame Una, who hates drink, especially if it is 'brought home to her', as J. puts it. She has rocket bombs on the brain and can talk of nothing but first-hand atrocity stories of the appalling things that have happened to people. James can hardly bear it any longer. He and I walked away and upset ourselves very much by studying in a morbid manner the dreadful chaos at the sharp angle of Kensington Church Street, where a rocket has fallen. Widespread devastation has been caused to several houses. Gaping holes reveal people's pathetic little pictures still clinging to walls over an abyss.

Friday, 23rd June

Very tired and gugga this morning after a bad night. At 10.15 to a sub-committee of the Georgian Group in Keeling's house. After Keeling and Alfred Beit left, Dame Una and Acworth and I stayed on talking. I proposed there and then that we should urge the House of Commons Amenity Group to invite the chairmen of the C.P.R.E., the N.T., the S.P.A.B. and the Georgian Group to attend a meeting. The Amenity

Group should stress its concern about the lack of co-ordination among these bodies, and persuade them to get together and eventually amalgamate. Acworth and the Dame agreed. We shall prepare a statement to be sent to Keeling for him, Strauss and the other M.P.s to digest in the hope that they will convene a meeting of Abercrombie, Zetland, Esher and Wellington.

Tonight after 11 o'clock, against a velvet purple sky, a rocket plane sailed over Lots Power station, a huge red flame issuing from its tail, and a dimmer light gleaming at the fore. There was a flash over Hammersmith way, and a second or two later an explosion which shook my windows. After dinner Miss P. and I fixed up a bed for her downstairs in the disused dining-room, where she certainly feels safer and cosier.

Saturday, 24th June

A very fine day, and free from fly bombs. I went to Emerald's at 5.45. She and I waited downstairs for Mrs. Corrigan, who bowled up in a small car. Bogey Harris joined us and we four motored to the Saville Theatre to see *The Gipsy Princess*, an old-fashioned, newly hashed-up musical comedy. I thought what a strange party we were, these three old Edwardians and me. I sat next to Emerald who praised the singers without stint, and talked rather loudly of sex. She said she did not, could not understand the need for it, and asked why people did it, dear? If one loved someone one did not think of sex, which was quite incidental. I could hardly subscribe to this argument. Then she asked me in what way animals behaved differently. She knew very little about them. Horses, she supposed, had to be severely controlled, it was very terrifying.

We dined in Mrs. Corrigan's suite in Claridges. She is a young 60, on first sight well preserved. But everything about her appearance may be false. Certainly her chestnut hair seems unnatural. Her smooth face is rather mask-like. She wears two of the largest pearls on one ring I have ever beheld. She is very rich and very generous. Everything she does is in great style. Everyone is lavishly tipped. We had a delicious dinner, and a white wine like nectar. There were pats of butter like cricket balls, and peaches. She dispensed the food and wine and would not suffer any assistance. If one offered to help she got quite cross. Emerald kept whispering to me, 'I don't suppose you will like her. She is not cultivated.' But I did. She seems to have eminent good sense and is outspoken. But she is incorrigibly social, and a great malaprop. She said of Lord Londonderry, 'Charlie has three balls on his cuisse.' She is a little disingenuous, and angles for compliments by telling stories to her own credit. Apart from that venial failing her manifest virtues appealed to me.

Monday, 26th June

Today was meeting day. I did not get home from the office till 10.30, and then wrote letters. At midnight the siren went, and I put on my boots and watched the fly bombs from the embankment. Because of clouds the beacons from their tails lit up the sky in a weird, uncanny manner. A number came over. I went to bed soon after 1 a.m., and fell asleep. At 2.30 I was woken abruptly by a terrific concussion, sat up in bed, and heard a cascade of glass, plaster and broken woodwork. But the house stood up. I was intensely alarmed, and went down to Miss P., now sleeping in the disused dining-room. I did not know whether I should find her alive or dead, since not a sound came from her direction. She had been awake, heard the plane approaching and covered her head with a pillow, which with the rest of the bed was strewn with fragments of powdered glass. A tiny muffled voice came from under the bedclothes. I said, 'Don't move an inch until I can see what's happened.' My feet were crunching glass on the floor. I found the torch. Her bed looked as if buried under a snow drift. I removed the glass as carefully as I could and disinterred her. She was not even scratched. Neither of us was hurt a bit. The bomb had fallen in the river opposite Turner's house, which has already been blitzed, and 100 yards from us. We walked into the kitchen, and even in the dim light could see the air filled with clouds of dust. A cupboard had burst open and disclosed a chimney belching a heap of soot. The only window in the house not broken was my bedroom one. My big room was inundated with glass fragments, which had shot across the room through the blinds and curtains, which were cut to ribbons. Nothing of furniture or objects was broken. All rugs inundated with soot and muck. The back door was blown across the passage. Window casements and wooden surrounds torn out, and the poor little house terribly shaken. Oddly enough this bomb killed no one.

Tuesday, 27th June

We made some tea and went back to bed. In the morning surveyed the damage. We did not go to the office, but put all our furniture in the middle of the room, packed away china and covered the lot with the torn curtains. There is nothing else we can do until the Borough send men to render first-aid. Meanwhile there is a howling gale driving rain through the open windows. The house is quite uninhabitable, but I did have a bath this afternoon, oblivious of the fact - of which I was informed later - that, since the bathroom windows were out and part of the wall was down, an admiring crowd watched my naked form drying itself. Good Eardley took pity on me and is having me down to the Bothy for two nights. Raymond Mortimer there too, and very kind and solicitous. The only encouraging factor is the excellence of the news in France, Italy and Russia. Raymond jubilant over it.

Thursday, 29th June

Lunched at the Ivy with Acworth and Dame Una to discuss Acworth's admirable draft letter to be sent by the three of us to Keeling, M.P., for him and the other Amenity Groupers in both Houses to address to the chairmen of the principal societies. The siren went during luncheon, and Dame Una made stately preparations to dive under the table at the first sound of a robot plane. I repeated Nancy's hairdresser's remark while indulging in an orgy of bomb experiences, 'And I came into her room, and what did I see? A spongey mass of blood and feathers.'

I dined at Sibyl Colefax's Ordinary. Met Chips Channon in the Dorchester beforehand, and had a drink. He said New York was quite pre-war, but Washington rather bustling. Everyone there thought the pilotless plane a fiction. It was too terrible to be true.

Emerald came in very late and tapped me on the shoulder, saying I had been a success with Mrs. Corrigan. Apologizing and having a word with everyone, she caused her usual consternation. She walked down Park Lane with Chips and me. She has absolutely no fear of bombs and will not leave her rooms on the top of the Dorchester.

Friday, 30th June

Rick Stewart-Jones has been very kind getting the Borough men to work on my house. They were plumbers with the most rudimentary ideas of carpentry. I tipped them £1, so they plastered over the holes in my ceiling, a thing they are not allowed to do. The filth of the house is indescribable, and only my bedroom is a refuge. A bomb in Battersea this evening blew out the makeshift windows they put in this morning.

Saturday, 1st July

All afternoon, planes came over. For the first time I am feeling despondent and dispirited. Miss P., having tidied the house up a bit, left for the country. I am glad for her poor old sake. The workmen are still in the house, and the head workman was almost as drunk as I was last night. I induced him to go home. What a life this is! How wasteful too, for I cannot read or write, having nowhere to do either.

At 6 I met James at King's Bench Walk, and we tubed to East Aldgate. We walked down the Commercial Road to the river. God, the squalor, the desolation and the dreariness of the East End! Poor inhabitants. We passed one beautiful church, burnt out, which I said must be by

Vanbrugh. J. identified it from his pocket guide-book as St. George's-in-the-East, by Hawksmoor. The pinnacled square towers like those of All Souls gave the clue.

We were smartly dressed underneath, but wore over our suits dirty old burberries buttoned up to the chin. Went into a pub for a drink and a robot came over, nearer and nearer, exploding a few yards away. The pub keeper turned us out and shut the door, saying he had had enough for one day. We wished him good luck. 'All the best,' he said. We wandered through Wapping, to Wapping Old Stairs where Judge Jeffreys was captured trying to escape to France dressed as a sailor. Then to the Prospect of Whitby on the water, with its rickety galleries built over the river on piles. Found Philip Toynbee there with a pretty little girl, a Communist. We sat together on the gallery drinking beer and eating sandwiches, watching large boats struggle up the river, pirouette in front of us, and retreat into the docks. From here Jamesey saw his first robot. It scurried through the clouds at a great rate, and seemed to be circling and not going straight. By 9.30 the inn was full, and a piano and a clarinet were playing hot music. Women sang into a harsh microphone, sailors stamped, and peroxide blondes and the worst characters of London danced like dervishes, sang and swilled gallons of beer. It was a strange, gay, operatic scene. J., who was looking forward to meeting his romance of two nights ago, was bitterly put out when the romance turned his back on him and was frankly rude. Philip said he did not know life yet, for the masses were incorrigibly fickle and perfidious. Philip has much charm, affability and the novelist's enquiring, curious, humorous mind. He is 28, dark with what are, I think, called pronounced features. I guess he will become a great writer.

Slept in John Fowler's Anderson shelter on the top bunk, which was very luxurious, although there were as many as five of us in the shelter. A noisy night, but quieter at dawn. Incessant jokes and hoots of laughter non-stop. In fact we laughed ourselves to sleep. Nobody woke before 10.15.

Sunday, 2nd July

Tonight for the first time I slept in the basement of 93 Cheyne Walk, Mrs. Gaskell's birthplace, where this morning with John Russell's help I moved my bed. John Russell and another young man sleeping in the same room. Not very comfortable because there is no light to read by, and I cannot go to the loo in the middle of the night. There isn't one downstairs, and the girls sleep in the passageway immediately outside our room. It was a very bad night indeed. Every ten minutes the factory warning warbled across the river, and two or three planes came over at a time. There were many loud crumps. I hardly slept a wink.

Monday, 3rd July

Raby, the permanent head of the Ancient Monuments Department of the Ministry of Works, lunched with me. He is a dry old medievalist, and not easy to talk to. Firewatching in the office tonight, and my hour of vigilance in the street was 5 to 6. Eardley called me. It was the best night we have had, and I am mightily refreshed.

Tuesday, 4th July

I went to Chawton, near Alton. Travelled from Waterloo in the same carriage as Sir Edgar Bonham-Carter. What a wise and yet diffident man he is. Owing to a robot having fallen on the line near Wimbledon the train was one and a half hours late. I lunched quite well at the Swan in Alton, and walked to Chawton House. The village of Chawton is long, straggly and attractive. At the Winchester road bifurcation is the house Jane Austen lived in. It is now divided into three workers' tenements. Chawton House is approached by a straight drive, with the church rebuilt in the 1870s and full of older Knight monuments on the right, the attractive stables on the left. The house, not very large, is irregular, with a tall porch of white clunch and flint. It is mainly Elizabethan, having been built by a Knight and altered in the mid-seventeenth century. The south front is rosy red brick, the rest flint and brick. The windows are lately restored. The situation on rising ground is salubrious. The lime avenue to the south was planted under Jane Austen's direction, so Mrs. Knight told me. She is small and pretty with gold red hair, and has a beautiful little boy. She took me over the house, which is full of old wainscoting, and has two Caroline staircases. There are some good Mortlake tapestries, framed in the panelling, and one sixteenth-century panel which must be very rare indeed. It is a pleasant, happy old house, in which Jane Austen spent much time, particularly in one large oak-panelled room on the first floor, which she constantly referred to in her letters. The place belongs to Mrs. Knight's husband, who is serving in India. She is merely playing with the idea of the N.T., and there is no indication that her husband will do anything. He is descended from Jane Austen's brother who was adopted by the last Knights of Chawton. They took a great fancy to him, his father and mother having settled in the village. At present Barnardo children occupy three-quarters of the house. Mrs. Knight says they are very undisciplined and destructive.

Wednesday, 5th July

Had a rather curious luncheon with a man called Campbell Stuart, editor of the *Sunday Pictorial*, with whom I have lately been having acrimonious correspondence about a gross mis-statement his paper made on our

announcement of the Gunby Hall acquisition. He is a young
middle-aged, rather brash, extremely affable, nimble-witted man. His
sandy hair is parted in the centre too exactly to look natural. I liked his
friendliness and abrupt plunge into the issue in hand. I explained to him
the Trust's motives in the preservation of beautiful houses and estates. He
expressed much ignorance about the Trust and aesthetic matters generally. Thought Blenheim too ugly for words and was surprised that the
Trust should want to own any eighteenth-century buildings. I boldly told
him that I thought his paper had behaved scurvily. He ended in asking
me to write an article for the *Pictorial* about the Trust.

We talked of other matters. He despairs over the future for, he says, no
plans are being worked out by the Government. Except as a fighter,
Churchill is a disaster. He lives for war and killing Germans, as though
they were pigeons. He is a man of no ideals, no principles; is an opportunist surrounded by yes-men, most of them insincere and of little
integrity. Aneurin Bevan he thinks one of the few men in the Commons
of undoubted integrity, and he is too temperamental. Eden is a flabby,
middle-aged man, unhappy with the Prime Minister. He thinks that only
men representing the professions and trades ought to sit in the
Commons; that there should be no 'professional' M.P.s on the other
hand; that the House of Lords should consist of life peers only. He says
no naval battle takes place that is not directed by the Prime Minister personally from the Admiralty, whither he rushes the moment there is an
engagement. I said, 'Churchill may not be a good man, but surely he is a
great man?' He said, 'Not a great man in the way Lloyd George was; but
undeniably a great personality, which is another matter.' Lloyd George
cared passionately for good causes, but, alas, today, he is becoming senile
and he forgets things.

C. Stuart said he often has to attend press conferences in Downing
Street, and these invariably end in a flaming row. Churchill loses his
temper and dismisses the press, who no longer can resist the temptation
of baiting him. They taunt him by inferring that he cares nothing about
the future, and enjoys the war like a game of chess. He fears Churchill
will certainly try to remain Prime Minister when the war is over and the
country will re-elect him. He does not foresee a swing over to Socialism
after the war, but a tempered form of dictatorship. All Churchill's closest
associates are unscrupulous, opportunist, fascist, crooked or vicious men;
and he went through the list.

Campbell Stuart thinks Frank Pakenham the ablest of the younger
aspirants towards rule. He thinks that possibly a new radical party
may merge from the Liberals, who must first of all drop their Whig
element.

Friday, 7th July

I got to King's Cross punctually at 9.30. The train for Peterborough was not scheduled to leave until 10.30. Even so, only through a Ist class reserved seat becoming de-reserved, did I manage to get a seat. The corridors were crammed. On my return I had to stand all the way from Peterborough, having just squeezed through a door. At Peterborough I caught a bus which did not take me as far as Cotterstock. Started to walk, and was picked up by Lady Ethelreda Wickham, who had driven to meet me.

She is 80. Her father, she told me, was born in 1792, the same year as Shelley. She is very upright and active, though a little shaky on her feet. She drives a high-powered car and smokes innumerable cigarettes. She is very broadminded when one discounts the fact that she hates all foreigners. She is wonderfully well bred, and says good-bye in that dismissive, indifferent manner of the upper classes of the old school.

Cotterstock is a compact, small manor house in the village, dated 1658, thus built during the Commonwealth. It has a large scrolly gable behind and above the porch. It is set in an ocean of lush, low-lying meadows, with Fotheringay in the distance. The inside has nothing very remarkable. On the top floor is an oak-lined room with slanting ceilings where Dryden wrote much of his verse. The house was at that time, I think, Vane property. Lady Ethel motored me back to Peterborough and I walked through the Cathedral. Struck by the Gothic iron stoves with little doors of ogee shape; and of course by the great beauty of the fan vaulting of the ambulatory.

Saturday, 8th July

I drove Stuart to his rooms where he packed his books and various clothing into a big, blue kit-bag for me to store in Cheyne Walk during his absence.

I had tea with Nancy in her garden, which is a wilderness of rank grass and chickens. She talked about Skittles, the Victorian tart kept by the present Duke of Devonshire's great uncle, to whom the present Duke paid £2,000 a year until her recent death when, so he told Nancy, he discovered that Lord Coventry had settled a like sum upon her. Nancy boasts that she is not the least frightened of the fly bombs. In bed at night she beckons to them, 'Come on, come on,' and then waves them away with, 'Go on, go on. And they always do, my dear.'

Sunday, 9th July

I left in the car soon after 10 in pouring rain. I arrived at B. House precisely at 1.30 in time for luncheon. When I told Stuart where I was going, he laughed and said, 'Lord — has the worst reputation in the world. His taste is Lascars.' Well, I thought, then I am all right. He is a natty, foxy little man with blue eyes and a boyish figure and boyish hair cut, though well over 60. A young American with a baby face was staying. He disappeared after luncheon. Lord — took me round the grounds and then round the house which has thirty-six bedrooms. In one we came upon baby face fast asleep in an enormous bed, just a turned-up nose projecting over the top sheet. In every room a delicious smell of rose water, or furniture polish, I was not sure which, mixed with that sweet mustiness of calf-bound books. Lord — inherited B. from his mother who lived here until her death. She had no commerce with her children, and would not see a soul. She never left the house. She slept all day, and prowled around the house all night. I was bound to tell my host that I much doubted the Trust being able to help him. He was very nice about it. I left before tea.

Thursday, 13th July

After dining alone I walked in St. James's Park in the rain and the sunshine, then doubled back to the Travellers'. Found Harold Nicolson who had also been dining alone. He wanted to know if I was frightened of the buzz bombs. I said, 'Quite honestly I am when I hear them near me. But not when I see them. And the moment they are gone I do not give them another thought.' Harold says we shall be in Paris in three weeks, and on the Rhine in mid-September. How can clever people be so stupid? Soon Harold left for firewatching at the House of Commons. When there is a raid he sits on the top of the Victoria Tower pressing bells. He says it is immensely exciting.

Friday, 14th July

So many of my friends have already gone, or are about to go overseas that I feel extremely restless and dissatisfied with my sheltered life. Went this afternoon to the Red Cross Society and spoke to the secretary about a possible job in France. Felt idiotically shy and secretive, not wanting the other people in the interview room to hear. To my surprise he said that if I could pass my medical test, and could get the sanction of the Ministry of Labour, I might go as an officer with a unit in three weeks' time. Alas, I could not possibly leave before 1st September when Matheson returns. And could I pass the medical? Nevertheless was quite pleased when the secretary said other units were bound to be going later.

I dined at Emerald's. Gladwyn Jebb was there, and Lady Kenmare, very beautiful, with sweet melting blue eyes. She has lost four husbands, all by death. Also Lady Kitty Lambton, magnificent, eccentric with dark glowing eyes, very wild, and a tumble of grey hair. She was gay and teasing. When she left Emerald complained, 'She is not sequential in her conversation. She does not make sense. She is a descendant of Nell Gwynne,' as though that explained everything. Emerald not in her best form, and abusive of the waiters again, which is agony. She said it made her angry when her friends praised the food at the Dorchester. She said American food used to be so good and is now atrocious. 'It is all so distracted and dejected, you cannot enjoy it.' I thought she was somewhat distracted and dejected tonight.

Saturday, 15th July

Got back from Buckinghamshire in time for a late dinner at Brooks's with John Fowler. At 9.30 Stuart walked in. He said, 'Well, I do go tomorrow. I have come to say good-bye. It was in this room that we met m 1938.' There was little to say, and what I did say was fatuous, 'Yes, I was sitting in that chair by the door.' 'No,' he said, 'you were standing against the fireplace,' which was scarcely more pointful.

Sunday, 16th July

Found a message from Nancy asking me to lunch with her. We ate in her funny little garden, or non-garden as she rightly calls it. She told me that her upbringing had taught her never to show to others what she felt. I thought how lamentably my upbringing had failed in this respect, and how too perfectly in her case, for there is a vein of callousness in her which almost amounts to cruelty. All Mitfords seem to have it, even Tom, who has never directed it at me, though I have seen him turn it upon others. And I have blanched at the spectacle.

Monday, 17th July

Had another interview with the Red Cross who raised further difficulties as to my chances of going overseas, in that the Ministry of Labour, even if they released me from the N.T., might re-draft me into the Army. I know this to be impossible. A great pity I can't go with the first unit in three weeks' time.

Tuesday, 18th July

We had the Country Houses Committee in the afternoon. Every time I thought I heard a buzz bomb I warned Esher, who is slightly deaf, and without shame he threw his papers before him and dashed to the door and the staircase; then laughed at himself. After the meeting Lord Carlisle said he wanted to see me and talk about Naworth, and I must go there.

On walking past the Ritz I heard Nancy give a cry; and there she was with Tom, back from the Mediterranean after two and a half years' absence. He almost embraced me in the street, saying, 'My dear old friend, my very oldest and dearest friend,' which was most affecting. He looks younger than his age, is rather thin, and still extremely handsome. We went up to his suite in the Ritz – how civilized and pretty after the Dorchester and modern jazz hotels. There he telephoned Harold Acton and Bridget, bidding them to dine this evening. Rather cross with me because I simply would not cut the Girouards' dinner party.

Wednesday, 19th July

Before firewatching I dined with Bridget in her flat. She has not slept properly for six nights. She began by not minding the bombs: now they have got on her nerves. Besides, she has a new job at the Foreign Office, eight hours a day, six days a week, and nothing to do. She sits mending stockings and reading novels, and the dragging of time nearly kills her. When I left she went to Claridges where she has taken a room for the nights, since Lord Newburgh, in whose cupboard downstairs she has lately been sleeping for safety, has returned to his flat. It is true that her bedroom in Mount Street has a huge plate-glass window immediately opposite the bed.

Thursday, 20th July

Called at James's flat at 7 and we drank gin and lime in the pub garden. How I hate the taste of gin. Unquestionably J. and I are no longer the confidants we used to be. I do not care for his arrogance and vanity. In order to take him down a peg I foolishly told him that the Kenneth Clarks disliked him and me – I included myself. I was sorry too late, for J. harped on this. Moreover I have broken an elementary rule of social conduct by repeating what a third person has told me.

A very noisy and frightening night. Buzz bombs, three at a time, coming over, and incessant explosions on all sides. Sirens never cease blowing, and they get on the nerves more than the bombs.

Friday, 21st July

Cold east wind, and sunless as usual. Bombs very bad. One at breakfast blew out the linen windows in Miss P.'s bedroom. Everyone much excited by the abortive attempt on Hitler's life and inclined to attach too much significance to the revolt, calling it civil war.

Monday, 24th July

Arrived Paddington at midday and met Mr. Parker of Bewdley. We lunched with Geoffrey Sturt. Our endeavours to protect the banks of the Severn between Bewdley and Stourport make little progress, alas.

I dined at Emerald's in the Dorchester. The party consisted of Freya Stark, the heroine of the party, Nancy Mitford, Lord and Lady Londonderry, Oliver Stanley and the Duke of Devonshire. I sat next to Emerald and Lady Londonderry, who is very tall and masculine, dressed as a brigadier in khaki. She told me that this evening's flying bomb made for Londonderry House, but on seeing it it swerved to the left over the Park, and exploded near the Serpentine. Lord Londonderry told Nancy the same story three times over. He is very handsome and patrician. He told me how he snubbed Sir Charles Trevelyan once, and was so amused by his story that I thought he was never going to stop laughing.

The Duke of Devonshire is ferociously anti-Catholic. He said, 'I am a black Protestant, and I am proud of it,' and told several anti-papal stories. His ancestor Lord Richard Cavendish, whose portrait by Landseer hangs over his bed here in London, was cut off by his family and sent to India as Bishop of Madras because he stayed at Hatfield, a Tory High Church household. This Duke's own father looked askance at his son's marriage with a daughter of Lord Salisbury for the same reason. When this Duke left Eton his father, very embarrassed, felt he must give him a pi-jaw. He said, 'Don't take to strong alcohol. Don't take to women. Some men may think they need women before they marry. It isn't true. And above all, don't ever go inside the Carlton Club.' He said he had just received an indignant letter of remonstrance from Gerry Wellington because Debo Cavendish, his daughter-in-law, has given her son at his christening the name Morny, a diminutive of one of the Wellesley titles, Mornington. 'How would you like it,' Gerry wrote, 'if I christened my grandson Harty or Burlington?' Nancy said, 'But Debo christened him after her favourite jockey. She has never even heard of the Duke of Wellington.' Emerald expostulated, 'You should have put this duke of only a hundred years creation in his proper place. You must have courage, Eddie.' Lord Londonderry interpolated, 'I too am only a peer of mushroom growth.'

Emerald said Tom [Mitford] was very rude the other night to the Chilean Paz Subercaseaux about Papists, calling them aliens, and saying it was quite out of the question his ever marrying one. Paz, slightly nettled, with two eligible papist daughters of her own, asked, 'But if you were staying at Arundel, would you consider the Duke of Norfolk an alien?' 'Certainly,' Tom replied. The Duke of Devonshire then said, 'Quite right. Papists owe a divided allegiance. They put God before their country.'

Tuesday, 25th July

Talked to Mr. Batsford about the Trust's Jubilee book. Conversation soon turned to the flying bombs, how they were getting people down, and how terrible living conditions were in parts of London. Streatham, Wandsworth and Battersea are the worst hit. It is thought that less is done to relieve people living in Tory districts than in red ones, like Battersea.

Took the train to Henley and Eardley motored me to the Bothy. After dinner we sat on a table by the river, watching stream after stream of heavy bombers, with lights at the tips of their wings fly southwestwards. The roar was like that of Niagara waterfall. We could barely hear each other speak. Hundreds passed.

Wednesday, 26th July

We motored to Somerset. A showery but not un-beautiful day. Climbed to the top of Lardon Chase and admired the view across the Thames. At Figsbury Ring we walked along the outer rampart of this curious pre-historic site. It is remote, with a distant view of the tip of Salisbury spire. But the remoteness is spoilt by some hideous half-timber villas along the main road, which never should have been allowed. We had difficulty in passing a long convoy of tanks on heavy lorries, bound for the coast. They were flying the Croix de Lorraine, and so must have been Free French troops.

After lunching in Salisbury we drove to Trafalgar. This great red-brick house lies beyond Longford, in the same valley, on the same river, sur-rounded by beech trees. It was built in 1733 by John Wood, with a Grecian portico added by Revett in 1760, as were the two connecting pavilions. A niece with a distinctly off-centre accent welcomed us. Presently there was a hurried puffing sound, and in bustled Lord Nelson. He is 87, the great-nephew of 'the Admiral' as he refers to his forebear, as small as Nelson, with white flowing hair and a large mouth. His spare build, peculiar shape of head and features are identical to the Admiral's. With a little mutilation, an eye out here, an arm off there, he would be the very incarnation. He was most hospitable and genial; in full posses-sion of faculties; but eccentric. He has a trick of picking at one's coat as he talks. We liked him immensely. He showed us round. There is a picture by Rigaud of Nelson aged 22. There are several miniatures and relics, and some furniture from the *Victory*. He has not however got so good a Nelson collection as Nelson Ward and others. There is much fine French furniture. The interior of the house is splendid. I particularly admired the ingenious oval staircase, the central hall which is a cube with plaster ceiling and a fireplace carrying a bust of Inigo Jones. The old man walked us round the outside. He almost cried when he asked why the world was indulging in an orgy of cruelty. He said the best trait in the Admiral's character was his capacity for affection.

We gave him a lift to the main road and left him waiting for a bus. If we had not done this he would have walked the three miles to the nearest bus stop for Salisbury.

Eardley and I proceeded to Montacute where we had tea with the Yateses in the King's Arms. At 7 Lord Aberconway motored over to make suggestions for improvement to the gardens. He advocated turning the north garden into a formal kitchen garden. E. liked this idea. I not so keen. There are 600 Negro troops at Montacute. They smile and say, 'Hello' in an engaging manner.

Thursday, 27th July

In the morning we went over the house. Then drove to Muchelney to look at the Priest's House, which is a good little property. The church has a barrel nave roof with painted panels of *décolletés* angels with pendulous bosoms, of the time of Charles I. I returned to London by train, in time for a scratch meal at home before firewatching in the office.

Friday, 28th July

Rose from my camp bed at 6. Breakfasted at the Great Eastern Hotel and caught the 8 o'clock train for Colchester. Here Sisson met me and motored me to Caister. We ate sandwiches, sitting on the grass-covered outer wall of the Roman city, Venta Icenorum. He shares my disquiet about the future. He says it is fruitless caring for good buildings, for wars will continue, and there will be underground architecture only. We looked at the site of the Anglo-Saxon cemetery over which we are offered covenants. It is a detached spinney on a hill, from which all finds have been exhumed. It was a hot day and I felt tired. Got back in time to dine with Harold Acton and Roger Spence.

I went to bed soon after 11 in our cellar. At 12.15 a bomb fell with great noise. The basement was filled with fumes, so I guessed the bomb had been pretty close. Got out of bed, put on gumboots and burberry, and walked into the road. Even in the clear light of the moon I could see a cloud of explosive steaming from the river in front of me. This fly bomb had cut out its engine, and recovered twice before finally falling. As I watched I heard people in the street shout, 'Look out, another's coming!' and they rushed down to their shelter. I was left transfixed, and knew there was no time to descend into my basement, down the rickety area steps. So I looked at the light of the bomb coming straight at me. Then the engine stopped, and I knew we were in for it. I lay flat on my face on the pavement, as close as could be to the embankment wall. I heard the bomb swish through the air. It too fell in the river, only closer than the last, and sent a spray of water over me. At dawn I met a policeman

picking up a fragment of the bomb from the road. It was over a foot long.
It must have hurtled over my head. I could see that all my windows and
the window frames at no. 104 were out again. I saw poor Kiki Cruft at
the gate of no. 97. She had been alone in the house and was rather start-
led. I talked to her before returning to my basement. This time I had
experienced the familiar phenomenon of not registering the actual
explosion of the bomb, because it was only a few yards away. I attribute
it to my preparedness and the automatic instinct of tautening the
whole body, including ears, to resist it. I remember hoping that my out-
stretched legs, which seemed so far from my cowering head, would not
be cut off.

Saturday, 29th July

Left home early this morning for Paddington, and caught the 9.10 to
Leamington. There was a vast crowd waiting for the train to draw in; and
a still vaster crowd the other side of the platform waiting for the
Plymouth train which, when it came, caused an astonishing spectacle of
women, children and old men fighting with their fists to cram themselves
into the apertures at the end of each coach. When our train approached
I was amused by our crowd ducking down to pick up their bags and
eagerly rising again, all in one rhythmic movement, as though they were
a trained chorus in a pantomime. It was like wind rippling over a stream.
I tried not to belong to the crowd.

At Leamington Hubert Smith met me and motored me to Bewdley,
complaining of the awful manners of the accountant who is 'evacuated
upon' him at Polesden Lacey. We lunched with the Parkers at Tickenhill.
She is a dear little brown body, like a clever dormouse. In the afternoon
motored round the Ribbesford estate, and was distressed that my uncle
had sold it in lots after the last war.

Hubert dropped me at the Sandys Arms, Wickhamford. I talked to
Maggie at her kitchen window. She had soapsuds up to the elbow. I was
fascinated by the way they dried on her bare arms, first they gently burst
one by one, and then they left little broken rings of dry grey scurf. Parents
delighted to see me, and my father very gentle and kind.

Tuesday, 1st August

Called upon the Labour Exchange who encouraged me to suppose they
would not obstruct my efforts to rejoin the Red Cross. I asked James to
meet me at Brooks's at 7. On arrival I ran into Tom, and drank with
him. When James was announced I told Tom he must be polite, for I
understood he hated him. He was polite, but I saw it went against the
grain.

Wednesday, 2nd August

An S.P.A.B. meeting, and many items of great interest to me. Went to Brooks's at 6 to talk to Tom. He said he must marry and asked my advice which of his girls he should choose. I said, 'Let me know which are in the running?' So he began, ticking them off one by one on his fingers. He told me, with that engaging frankness with which he always confides in me, the names of those he had already slept with, and how often, those he rather loved and those he merely liked, until I stopped him with, 'But all this sounds most unromantic to me. If I were one of those girls and knew how you were discussing me, I wouldn't dream of marrying you.' 'Oh, but they don't know,' he said, and roared and roared with laughter.

Tom also told me that Professor Lindemann (Lord Cherwell) was in disgrace with the P.M. for having made light of the flying bombs before they actually arrived. He saw Winston Churchill when he was in Libya, and the P.M. gave him news of his sister Decca, now married again and living in America. When in America the P.M. sent for Decca, and told her he felt sure she would be glad to know that her sister Diana was now much happier in prison because she was reunited with Tom [Oswald] Mosley. Decca said very abruptly, 'I don't want to hear her name mentioned.' He then offered to get her a job on Lord Halifax's staff. Decca answered, 'I wouldn't touch him with a barge pole.' The P.M. felt very snubbed. She is as fanatically Communist as ever.

Thursday, 3rd August

This morning I went to the Red Cross who told me they might be having a meeting of the selection board, to be followed by a medical examination next Wednesday.

Grandy Jersey, who called at the office, is very busy dealing with the flying bombs. He assured me that more than half those launched are destroyed by us; but that they will definitely continue until the war is over. The Germans are able to establish new bases within a few days.

Saturday, 5th August

Went to an indifferent revue. Standing in the street after the first act I was accosted by a familiar voice. It came from Patrick O'Donovan in battle-dress, back from Normandy three days ago. I barely recognized him, for he was wounded in the face. It was caused by his standing up in his tank, and being practically decapitated by a wire stretched across a village street. He broke the upper part of his jaw. He was sensitive about his appearance, and kept his hand over his mouth when speaking, for his teeth were painted gold in hospital for some reason. We went off to eat together. During dinner he said he was wretched not being in

Normandy, which he loved. He said that every night he used to sleep under his tank in a slit trench; that German tanks were better than ours; and that German prisoners were very demoralized. He was sure the war would be over in two months. The most offensive things on a battlefield were dead cows, which swelled to enormous proportions, and burst. The stench was appalling. He was seldom frightened. In burying the dead the troops found it very difficult not to break down, so services were made as short and informal as possible. No hymns and no bugles. He was constantly weeping over dead friends.

Sunday, 6th August

My birthday, and the less I think about it the better. Only members of the family remember; for I suppose they are the only people to whom one's existence does matter just a little.

Went to Mass in Warwick Street and lit candles for friends. Candles may help. At least they can't hinder. Caught an afternoon train to Kelvedon, and walked two miles in great heat to Felix Hall. Since I was last here before the war, the centre block has been gutted by fire and the two late eighteenth-century pavilions have been demolished by Geoffrey Houghton-Brown. He now lives in one large room reconstructed out of old bits and pieces. It gives the impression of Crowther's shop. In the room where I slept, the walls were panelled with early wallpaper brocatelle, dated 1812, which Geoffrey salvaged from one of the demolished pavilions.

Monday, 7th August

This morning Geoffrey, one of the guests and I bicycled six miles to Layer Marney church. In addition to the famous terracotta Renaissance monuments, a superbly beautiful mural painting of St. Christopher on the north wall arrested my attention. The wavelets of the water and the little fishes were meticulously linear. The gravity of the saint's head, turned to one side, was most moving. The house was empty, so we walked up to it and pressed our noses against the windows. There have been horrible recent additions to the tower, a bad adaptation of the barn and a contemptible garden layout. If the place were mine I would pull down practically everything, leaving the great, perpendicular tower standing in a naked meadow.

Wednesday, 9th August

Lunched with Anne Rosse in Bridget's flat. Bridget, Dmitri of R. and Harold Acton there. Anne provided vodka, a ham with cloves stuck in it, hock, peaches and cream. And she called it a picnic. I went back at 4 to talk to Anne alone for an hour. I told her I might be going to France and she seemed genuinely sad, which touched me. She writes to Michael and he to her every single day. She is tremendously proud of him, and if anything happened to him, it would, I firmly believe, kill her.

I had a letter from Esher this morning – rather a chill and formal one – merely saying that the Committee could hardly oppose my going, if (underlined) I should pass my medical test.

Rick called at 1.30 at night when I was fast asleep. I was woken by a loud peal of the bell. He stayed till 3.30, and we ate cake in the kitchen. He leaves for the Middle East on Monday, and gave me all sorts of directions what to do, if he did not come back. They are all going.

Friday, 11th August

Mr. Hobson of Sotheby's lunched with me in order to talk over his ideas about museums. He is writing a book on the subject, and wants restrictions on the export of works of art to be lifted. He claims that it does not matter in which country works of art are kept, so long as they are properly cared for; that there are too many in this country; and that those which remain will eventually be mummified in a museum. He believes that a museum curator should be, not a stuffy expert, but a Reinhardt with a dramatic sense. In many respects I agree with him, but by no means in all. There are very many English works of art, for instance, which I would hate to see leave this country. Hobson is a big, burly man, deaf with an efficient apparatus.

I had a long talk with Eddy in Brooks's. He is suffering from a cist on his lip and large blemishes on his forehead. 'It is my anaemia,' he says. He has learnt to despise the buzz bombs. 'They are just incredibly silly.' Yet he feels worn out. I suppose even we civilians are suffering from war weariness to some extent.

Saturday, 12th August

Bought *The Golden Bowl* at Heywood Hill's shop on my way to lunch with Osbert Lancaster at the Holborn Restaurant, a marvellous 1870 building of every known expensive marble. We drank Algerian wine although it was too hot a day. Osbert bubbling with gossip. He explained Nancy's indifference to bombs as being a consequence of steeling herself to an indifference to Peter's misbehaviour.

I finished *The Hotel* in Brooks's – not a good novel, although Eddy recommends it. I found Ralph Jarvis at dinner, and ate with him. He is just back from Rome, which he says is not at all knocked about. Naples is no more damaged than London; rather less so. Frascati has gone; and every village on the road from Naples to Rome gone. Damnation. He spoke favourably of the Vatican. It was fascinating, he said, watching its cautious reaction to Stalin's feelers towards the Church in Russia. The Vatican wouldn't commit itself, suspecting that Stalin's intentions might be purely expedient. 'Of course they must be,' I couldn't help saying.

Sunday, 13th August

To Mass in Cheyne Row. Was wonderfully devout and well disposed to the world in general; gave my seat to an old man, and stood myself. I took Bridget to Polesden. While I sorted things she lay on the grass in the sun. Like others she was enraptured with Mrs. Greville's visitors' book. It is odd how people can be fascinated by lists of signatures and dates, and nothing else. We had a picnic luncheon and tea on the terrace.

Drove back in time to dine with the Rodds, at Claridges. Peter ordered drinks and left me to pay for them. This I did, but was determined not to be similarly stung with the expense of the dinner. If Peter had not been present it would have been more enjoyable. As it was, he interrupted every time one of us tried to speak. He made irrelevant remarks which were nonsense. He is a hopeless character. He puts Nancy on edge, and makes her pathetically anxious not to displease him. Now why should a husband put a wife under such an obligation? I walked home with Bridget.

Monday, 14th August

Eardley and I motored to Bristol. We lunched in Marlborough, having had a puncture and changed the wheel ourselves, getting covered in oil and dust in the process. Picked up an architect and drove to Thornbury. Sir Algar Howard took us over the castle. I was cross with Eardley for hating the place and saying that the Trust should reject it on the grounds that it was badly restored and hideous. I agreed that the mid-Victorian interior was deplorable – the only decent things being the green Morris wallpapers. But the outer walls are genuine and the side facing the church has the glamour of stage scenery. Besides, the twisted brick chimneys and the clover leaf windows of Henry VIII's reign are of the highest importance. Pugin greatly admired and drew them. The garden the Howards have made is simple, orchardy and Pre-Raphaelite. Admittedly no one could possibly want to live in the gloomy, ill-conceived warren, which Salvin made out of the ruin. The castle ought in my opinion to be made back into a ruin.

It was an extremely hot and sultry day. At 5.30 we had high tea, which portended nothing more to eat till breakfast next day, a depressing prospect. Eardley and the architect drove away, and I was left to stay the night. Sir Algar and I walked in the garden. He told me that new peers and knights and even commoners sought grants of arms now in wartime as much as they ever did. All the College of Heralds' books of reference are stored in the castle.

With eagerness we – the Howards and I – listened to the news at 9, anxious to learn whether the German Army had been enveloped and annihilated in the pocket near Falaise.

Tuesday, 15th August

Eardley called for me at 10.30 and we motored to Lacock. We lunched off delicious goose in the Abbey. I think Miss Talbot is one of the noblest and most exemplary benefactors we have had to deal with. She has a number of lonely, white-haired octogenarian ladies lodging with her. While we were in the village with the agent, an old shopkeeper said that at noon a special announcement told of a fresh invasion on the Riviera. We rushed to the Abbey and made the old ladies turn on the wireless. Somehow this news falls rather flat after D-day. One cannot be keyed up all the time.

The pictures in the Abbey are in a deplorable condition; so is the furniture, stacked together without dust sheets. The English have become an untidy, as well as a grubby people. And still they maintain an overweening and quite unjustifiable sense of superiority over all other nations, firmly believing that foreigners never wash.

Wednesday, 16th August

Stayed last night with Eardley at the Bothy. En route near Devizes we were slowed up by a troop of German prisoners. We felt ghoulish staring at them. They stared at us just as hard, but with impassive, expressionless faces. They showed no sign of either chagrin or relief, poor brutes. First came the officers, then the men, all hatless. They were a fine looking lot, bronzed and with only a day's growth of beard, and had presumably been captured some twenty-four hours before. Among them were a few very young boys, and some quite old men. They marched well and made an impressive spectacle. A few feeble looking American soldiers, physically infinitely their inferiors, were in charge of them, holding rifles with their fingers on the trigger.

Thursday, 17th August

Depressed by receiving a letter from the Red Cross that after all they will not accept me.

At 11 I had an interview with W. S. Morrison, the Minister of Planning. An upstanding, grey-haired, middle-aged man, handsome and efficient. A strong Scotch accent. He advised against the N.T. pressing for the insertion of a clause in the new Bill, to protect its inalienable properties from possible acquisition by local authorities He said Parliamentary Counsel assured him that the Trust's powers were already adequately protected by our Acts of Parliament, and that a general clause would arouse the hostility of several government departments. He spoke sympathetically of the Trust's work, and said Parliament generally favoured us. This was gratifying, but not wholly satisfactory. Morrison's face is arresting. His mouth is chiselled like that of an Alfred Stevens model.

Saturday, 20th August

James and I accompanied Dame Una - to whom I gave all my eggs - to Peckham by bus. The objective was to look for the house where Dickens kept his mistress and where he began writing *Edwin Drood*. She says, were it not for income tax amounting to 75 per cent, she would undoubtedly make a fortune from sales in the United States and here.

Our expedition was a failure. It rained hard, we lost our way, and were confused by the bus routes. The Dame's earnest enquiries of local inhabitants for the house of Dickens's mistress evoked astonishment and made J. and me giggle uncontrollably. His amused, placatory indulgence of her as though she were a child put her in a bad humour. We never found the house which he and I believe was either demolished before the war, or even disappeared in the recent raids. We were horrified by the devastation of this part of London by flying bombs. I think, without exaggerating, that two-thirds of the buildings in Peckham and Camberwell have been destroyed or irredeemably ruined.

Sunday, 21st August

A terrible morning, dark with torrential rain, like a non-stop stage storm scene, and constant sirens and flying bombs coming over very low and noisily. I stayed half lying in bed, half running to the shelter on the stairs, and half (this makes one and a half) telephoning to Bridget and the Pope-Hennessys to ask for news of those bombs I heard flying over me. Bridget said the windows of the shops opposite her flat in Mount Street had all gone, and seven ambulances were passing as she spoke. Dame Una said what an infuriating bore it would be to be killed now that the Americans are actually in Paris, and the bombs must cease in a few days' time. This is inspiriting.

At 4.30 I went to Bridget's flat where Tom was. Together we went to Nancy's for tea. Then we walked to look at the damage caused by a flying bomb which settled this morning on the roof of Lansdowne House flats, at the corner of Berkeley Street. In the neighbouring streets all windows were blown out. Shop windows have strewn their contents on the pavements.

Tuesday, 22nd August

At 6.45 I went to see Alan Lennox-Boyd. He was in his bath and I sat with him while he washed and washed, I have seldom seen anything like it. It makes me suppose I must be very dirty. Alan said he had no news of Francis (his youngest brother) who has been missing since D-day. Alan was with him from 6-7 on the eve of D-day, for both knew that afternoon what was about to happen. It appears that Francis was among the first to leave soon after midnight. The trap of his aeroplane failed to open the first time they were over the target. Upon returning again over the target the trap opened unexpectedly, and Francis fell through a little while before the other paratroops. He has not been heard of since, and it is supposed he fell behind the enemy lines. Alan still believes he may either be a prisoner or in hiding, but it seems unlikely to me. Francis was one of the most sensitive, fastidious, delicate men I have ever known. A. is a spontaneous and generous man. He poured figs and peaches into my hands on parting.

Alan said that the percentage of fly bombs brought down over England out of the total number launched, was actually forty-four, not counting those brought down over the Channel. That the production of seven fly bombs corresponded in cost and time with that of one Spitfire. That a straightforward kind of German rocket may start at any moment. One school of thought estimates that the weight of each may indeed be less than that of the old fly bomb, which contains one ton of explosive; the other school predicts that it may contain seven tons of explosive.

Sunday, 27th August

Tom and I dined at Brooks's. I asked him pointblank if he still sympathized with the Nazis. He emphatically said Yes. That all the best Germans were Nazis. That if he were a German he would be one. That he was an imperialist. He considered that life without power and without might with which to strike fear into every other nation would not be worth living for an Englishman. I absolutely contradicted him. Told him I was unrepentantly pacifist, and would prefer to live in a country of tenth rate power, provided there were peace and freedom of action and speech. The sweet side of Tom is that he never minds how much an old friend disagrees with him. But woe betide an acquaintance.

At luncheon I practically had a row with Eddy over the Vatican and his indictment of the Pope. Now here are two friends I love, and profoundly disagree with.

After the S.P.A.B. meeting I picked up Marshall Sisson and motored him to Dedham. At Colchester we digressed to visit Bourne Mill, a charming old property of the N.T., only spoilt by the ugly villas built along the road since we acquired it. The strange little conceit, built in 1591, was doubtless intended for a fishing lodge. Its extravagant curved gables and Flemish finials are appealing. In the early nineteenth century it was converted into a mill, when the hoist was added. For long now it has been derelict, but the admirable Sisson showed me his plans for its conversion into a dwelling, without any alteration to the elevations. The mill machinery may have to go, which will be a pity.

I like the Sissons immensely. He belongs to the same type as Alec Penrose - has very good taste and sound views; is quiet, anti-social, dry-humorous, scholarly and contemplative. He is a liberal-intellectual, or intellectual-liberal. His chief passion is architecture. He is besides an incurable pessimist and an avowed anti-philistine. She is positively no-nonsensical, enlightened, well-read, willing to be amused and clever. She is an invalid who walks with a rubber-tipped stick. They are childless and devoted, each the complement of the other, I would think. Obviously no troubles are allowed to detract from the harmony of their easy-going, cultured, marital life. Shermans, their house in Dedham High Street, opposite the church, is a gem. It is a red brick, 1730–40 doll's house, perfectly symmetrical, with a sun-dial on the front. The inside is set curiously askew on the axis, so as to fit into an awkward site. Everything has been sacrificed to the remarkable little text-book façade. Plain wainscoted rooms, appropriately furnished. For dinner we had duck and hock. Sisson is a pacifist. He deplores tyranny, slavery, and is sceptical about the outcome of this war and the future peace. He is a Spenglerian too. Excellent and delightful couple.

During the night - and I slept ill - there was a distant siren. I heard several flying bombs. Five of them exploded fairly close. The last was very close and made the house rattle like a dice box so that I thought windows must have broken. For a minute my heart beat faster. Then I recalled that I was in the country, away from London, and felt, quite irrationally, that I was safe. It was odd to hear these sounds away from London.

This morning I motored Sisson to Blickling. A glorious day in a world of ripening corn, with harvest sheaves stacked under a blue sky spangled with fluffy white clouds. We lunched at the inn with Birkbeck, the agent, and in the afternoon went round the house and garden. I had to indulge in rather too much consoling and jollying of Miss O'Sullivan and Miss James. The latter wishes to leave, and I must take no steps to prevent her.

Sisson is convinced that the Blickling garden layout dates from about 1700, a thing I always thought might be the case, but was not sure about.

Friday, 1st September

A crisp, chilly morning, with that whiff of melancholy in the air. Autumn is well on the way. I would not mind if only I felt well, clear-headed and un-drugged. Sisson took me to Flatford Mill which the N.T. has acquired. I love Constable, but I do not love this place. It has been made a travesty of the totally unpretentious, rural, domestic scene of one of England's greatest painters. Today the manor house is too picture post-cardy for words. Willy Lott's Cottage is abominably whimsy inside. Sisson favours whitewashing or white painting all interior beams, I am glad to say. I concur with nearly all his ideas. The Mill itself is still relatively unspoilt, and the island garden, with fat box hedges and old apple trees is full of charm. We drove to Thorington Hall. It has a rather neglected look, and the furniture inside - well! The house has had evacuees, and not been inhabited as a private house since the war, which explains much. I left the Sissons after luncheon and drove to Paycocke's, that hideously over-restored house in Coggeshall. The tenants' bogus French furniture most inappropriate. Sisson and I would like to whitewash all the harsh new brick nogging on the street elevation. Back in London in time to take Bridget out to dinner. Sweet tonight like a lioness on her off day, and just as provocative as that beautiful dangerous creature.

Saturday, 2nd September

Pouring wet day, so I read the *Chartreuse de Parme*, and revelled in it. After tea I packed and went to Send for the weekend with Loelia. I do like her immensely, although her world is not mine. During Mass the Pope's letter to Londoners was read by the officiating priest. There has been too much criticism of the Pope lately. Why can't Protestant England understand the dilemma he is in? Why does it suppose that he should only care for the souls of two million British Catholics, and cast into utter darkness those of twenty million German and Italian Catholics? Why are we so arrogant, so obtuse a race?

Monday, 4th September

Matheson is back. At 11.30 we drank coffee at the Grosvenor Hotel, and then lunched. We talked for hours about the Trust and what had hap-pened in his absence. He was almost touchingly appreciative. Yet our talk was unprogressive and went round in circles. I cannot fathom his mind.

After dinner I called on the Kennedys. The General had last week been flying over France and tearing round France in a jeep with Montgomery, whom he and Catherine hero-worship. General says the devastation of the towns and villages and farms in the battle zone is truly appalling. He thinks there will be no armistice with Germany; that the Nazis will never negotiate, and that guerrilla warfare will proceed indefinitely in Germany. He says that our destruction of the flying bombs averages 90 per cent of those launched (I don't believe it), for by mathematical calculation and precision we have mastered them; and that no more can be launched, now the Pas de Calais is captured. Holland is too far away for launching, he says.

Tuesday, 5th September

Met Loelia and Lady Diana Cooper in the Ritz. Lady D., as she shook hands, looked at and through me with those legendary blue eyes which petrify. She does not know me and those goddess eyes were presumably assessing the strange worm which had dared rise on its tail from the mock Savonnerie carpet. Her beauty is rather divine than human. Not a line visible. Her hair, celestially golden (again mythological) all curled and thick, had, she said, just been permanently waved in Algiers by a child of nine. Loelia lunched with me alone. She told me some particulars of her marriage. In the 1930s the Duke lived like a prince. Eaton was more like a town than a house. She had acted mistakenly in not leaving it as it was, a period piece of the 1870s. Instead she endeavoured to bring it up to date by making it less ugly and more liveable, in fact spoiling it. She thinks she will go down to posterity as a vandal. But she was very young, which excuses her. The first dinner party she presided over numbered seventy-five guests. Eaton could house 100 guests, each with a servant, and still there was room for more. Red carpets were put down each time she and her husband left the house, and red carpets were put down at the station. When they got off the channel boat, other passengers were made to stand aside. Since she loved flowers the Duke marshalled an army of gardeners to bring them into her rooms in barrow loads. A botanical institute was provided for her. She had two maids. The Westminsters seldom stayed more than two nights anywhere. Life was spent in planning where to go next. The Duke always intended to stay for ever, but never did, for the moment he arrived anywhere, something annoyed him and he had to move on. Since Loelia suffers from sickness in aeroplanes and on boats she was perpetually ill. Whenever she admired a piece of jewellery or a motor-car belonging to another person, a duplicate would be given to her. Yet jealousy and bad temper made her life a misery.

Loelia's married life is a definition of unadulterated hell. Two yachts, three houses in Scotland, one in London, two in France, one in Venice, besides Eaton and goodness knows how many more in the English country, contribute to it, without the spoilt and good-for-nothing lord and master. Loelia said, 'Of course, when I married him I was a poor girl who made all her own clothes.'

As we left the Ritz the porter told us that the Germans had surrendered. We were greatly excited. The news was in the *Evening Standard* But is not confirmed. The canard was started by the Belgians.

Friday, 8th September

Perishingly cold east wind, and sunny between showers. I can't think why I record such information which will be of no possible interest to a single soul tomorrow, or the day after. I motored to West Wycombe and met Lord Esher. He extends his hand in a studiedly polite, keep your distance way, which I appreciate. We walked down to the village and were conducted by Captain Hill to the proposed site for the Village Hall. Hill was quite truculent, for he loathes Esher, Helen Dashwood and me. Yet he kept taking me aside in order to mock their (and, presumably, my) undemocratic, antiquated ideas. I was constrained to tell him that I shared their ideas unreservedly. He made a noise like what I imagine the word 'pshaw' in Ouida's novels is meant to sound like, and cast such a look of malevolent contempt upon me that I took a step backwards. Esher of course grasped the situation at once, and in his quick way teased Hill madly by associating him with the most outrageously revolutionary opinions. Instead of feigning amusement Hill, silly ass, went purple, and earnestly, and gravely rebutted each charge. I do love Esher.

Sunday, 10th September

Bridget accompanied me to Sussex. We stopped at a pub and drank ginger beer and ate sandwiches. At Bateman's the hospitable Parishes gave us coffee, port and figs. Most of their windows were blown out and some upstairs ceilings brought down by the buzz bomb which fell thirty yards away. Mr. Parish, who was expecting me to bring an agent, was delighted with Bridget who indeed made every effort to please. We drove on to Brede. Clare Sheridan was dressed in green with a coloured bandeau floating above her head like a halo. We had tea in her little wooden house. She showed us her new carvings, one pine figure of Mary the Immaculate, a young woman with child, and another of Queen Emma, looking remarkably like Clare, who believes herself to be the reincarnation of that remote sovereign. Clare is anxious to give Brede Place to the National Trust if she can thereby forgo Schedule A tax and all rates. Her wish is to caretake and live in a small part, using the greater part as a gallery for her sculpture. I thought Clare was more magnificent, eccentric and enchanting than ever. On parting she said to B., 'You are very beautiful.'

Monday, 11th September

Grandy Jersey told me that his department was warned last Christmas Eve to expect 1,000 flying bombs to be launched by the Germans in one day. The day to be chosen would be a foggy, dark one in mid-winter. London would have had no warning. The terror and chaos would have been without precedent. It was entirely due to the R.A.F. strafing the bombing sites that this little scheme came to nothing.

Tuesday, 12th September

At about 6 a.m. I with thousands of others in London was woken up by an explosion like an earthquake, followed by a prolonged rumble, which at first I mistook for thunder. The explosion was followed by a second. Both, I learnt later, were caused by V2 rockets which other people have heard before. I am told that quite thirty have so far been dropped on different parts of the country. This morning's are said to have fallen at Chiswick. They have greater penetrative but less lateral destructive power than the V1s. They are very exciting and not frightening at all, for when you hear them you know you are all right.

Wednesday, 13th September

This morning Lord Londonderry called at the office to discuss Londonderry House, of which he owns the freehold, and its entire collections – it contains six Lawrences at least. He was very charming, friendly and diffident, saying, 'No, no, it cannot claim to be a great London house,' which I suppose is true. On the other hand so many of the greatest have already gone, and their collections are dispersed.

Johnny Philipps lunched at Brooks's to meet Professor Richardson. Johnny delighted with him, told him all about Picton Castle and asked him to help restore it after the war. The Professor recounted quips and jokes he made with George V when building the Jockey Club for the King at Newmarket.

People in the street stop one to discuss the V2, which thrills us all. James gave me further confirmation of its authenticity this evening, while we were drinking at Simpson's. He said the press are not allowed to release news of it, so that the Germans may not learn where it has fallen. The rockets are released from mobile emplacements along the main roads, inside Germany. James has met a French girl cousin, witty, intellectual, beautiful, with whom he has fallen madly – he thinks – in love.

Thursday, 14th September

Met Eardley with the car at the canteen, where we lunched with Nancy and Bridget. Then we motored through Maidenhead to Shottesbrooke Park. It belongs to Miss Smith, a descendant of the Vansittarts who owned the place. She lives in a cottage under the shadow of the church spire. The house is used as a hospital for Free Czechoslovakian wounded soldiers. It is a Jacobean house of red brick, altered inside in George I's reign, and outside in the early nineteenth century. The prevailing flavour is of the later period. Inside there is a good deal of George I work left, oak staircase, panelled rooms, cornices, and rococo plaster-work. The park is flat and uneventful. I would not recommend it for a property, but the lady offers covenants. Neither of us liked her much. She is a charmless horsey lady, with down on her jowl. She has some good pictures, one of the Medici family that came from Horace Walpole's collection.

Sunday, 17th September

I am staying with my Aunt Doreen Cuninghame in Stow-on-the Wold. After tea, or rather after several cups of coffee and slices of cake at the kitchen table, I went for a walk. I started down the hill to Broadwell, a secluded little village. I noticed sadly how the grey stone tiles of the barns and farm buildings are falling, and breaking. They will not be replaced. Just beside the old church is an enchanting house, Broadwell Manor, of yellow Cotswold stone. It has a classical façade of late seventeenth-century date. A notice by the gate invited entry at a charge of 2d. for the Red Cross, so I walked into the garden. I soon found that this ideal house faced due north, the south and back side having an ugly, sloping roof, and no windows. It thereupon ceased to be my ideal house. A pretty, simple garden full of yellow autumn flowers, and a stream purling somewhere out of sight. Through the front door I spied a Georgian oak staircase and other elegancies. The church contained mural tablets to the Leigh family (of Adlestrop), then as now lords of the manor. I found Anthony Bailey's grave under a rough headstone. Proceeded across fields and past hedges of massed brambles to Maugersbury. Was told which was the Baileys' house and found Mrs. Bailey sitting in a garden hut, looking the same as she did twenty-five years ago when I first met her, and wearing a thick black velvet band round her throat. She and the Colonel seemed pleased to see me. They talked of Chris, and told me how he was shot through the lungs in North Africa. His colonel sent a messenger with a white flag to Benghazi to beg the Germans for medical assistance. They captured the messenger and sent no assistance. The parents presume Chris died of his wounds. This was two years ago.

Anthony was killed flying, owing to a fighter plane cutting in just as he was landing his bomber.

Monday, 18th September

Bussed to Cheltenham; changed into another bus to Gloucester. Bought photographs of Wickhamford church from Sydney Pitcher, who has an amazing collection. Walked round the Cathedral and marvelled again at the lavish beauty of the Perpendicular cloisters, surely the best in Britain. Met Eardley at the New Inn where we lunched. We motored to Monmouth. Here we climbed up the Kymin hill on foot. The Trust owns the summit, including the Round House, built by a Duke of Beaufort as a folly, where Nelson lunched at a small mahogany table, now the Trust's property and used by the old couple who inhabit the house, with rain-water pouring through the roof. There is a quaint temple close by, erected to the memory of Nelson's admirals, with tablets commemorating them, now painted white but formerly the respective colour of each admiral, with his name in gold lettering. There are distant views from the temple in all directions. E. and I visited the Nelson Museum in the town, the collection bequeathed by Lady Llangattock. It is one of the largest collections of relics of a single historic individual I have ever beheld. The room itself is ugly, and the contents are not attractively arranged, or well maintained.

We drove on to Llanwern, Lady Rhondda's house, which was occupied by troops in 1939. It is now empty, spoilt and desolate. It is a George II house, rectangular, with an unsightly well in the centre. It is built of grim red brick and stone dressings, but has no pediment, parapet, or ornamentation of any kind outside. Indeed it is a plain, forbidding house, of unsympathetic texture. Within, however, there are much good early Georgian wainscote, rococo plaster ceilings and bold rusticated doorways with ogival heads. Structurally the house is still sound, although pipes have burst and water has been allowed to seep on to the floors and lie in pools. Unless the house is given immediate attention, it will quickly disintegrate. The garden is in desperate plight. So too are the park and trees. The surrounding country is beautiful, but Newport is stepping perilously near.

Tuesday, 19th September

Eardley and I stayed last night in Cardiff, not an agreeable city. At 11 I went to the Castle and was shown round by Lord Bute's housekeeper. It is astonishing that in these days one great nobleman can own a vast dwelling house and hundreds of acres of carefully kept gardens and park right in the middle of the capital of a principality. Lord Bute rarely comes to Cardiff more than once in two years. In peacetime the Castle ruins are open to the public, but not the grounds. The Norman keep is on a high mound. Surrounding the whole castle enclave is an earth rampart, under which a Roman wall has recently been discovered. It is this wall that Sir Cyril Fox raves about. The present Lord Bute has constructed a crenellated wall on the outside of the rampart. The Castle proper is, inside and out, the most hideous building I have ever seen. The core may be early medieval. It was made Nash-like and pretty about 1800. Its present appearance dates from the 1870s. William Burges was the architect who entirely reconstructed it. There are Arab rooms and rooms wainscoted in pitch pine, inlaid with looking-glass between the crenellations of the dados. There are a few pieces of furniture and several family portraits of interest. There is a private chapel of unparalleled hideousness – encaustic tiles, embattled chimneypieces, coffered gilt ceilings. The old housekeeper, a Papist like all who serve this family, was very proud of the Castle, which she keeps spotless and polished.

I met Eardley in the National Museum. Sir Cyril was in London. We admired the way he displays the exhibits. We had tea in Tenby, an enchanting Regency town, perched above a sickle of golden sands. We watched the duck swimming in and out of the waves with enviable abandon. The N.T. has a boring little property up a back street, called the Old Tudor Merchant's House. It has a monstrously large chimney, some Gothic windows and fireplaces of the rudest kind. The thick cob walls, painted and stencilled, are now covered with hoarding to protect them from the evacuees who use the house as a clearing centre. I bought a tea pot for 10/- because the knob of the lid was off, and E. a picture frame and Bristol vase at an antique shop. Spent the night at the Ivy Bush in Carmarthen. Good solid food.

Wednesday, 20th September

Was made very cross this morning. I telephoned Picton Castle to make sure that John Philipps was expecting us, to be told by the housekeeper that he was still in London and was expecting us to stay next week. So instead we booked rooms in Tenby and drove off to Dolaucothi. Lloyd-Johnes was away, but we found his factotum, an old estate workman, whom E. familiarly calls David. He is a charming character with perfect manners. In these remote parts the Welsh are very hospitable. For instance, when this morning we called at a cottage up the valley to fetch a key to see over a neighbouring house for sale, the cottage woman, who could hardly speak English, invited us to luncheon. Dolaucothi House is not a show place, but a sunny, cheerful, early nineteenth-century house, of moderate size, made symmetrical by the addition of two square, blank walls, to complete the main façade. The result is fairly satisfactory when viewed from the front, but slightly absurd from the side. There are two projecting bays at either end. The whole is painted a cheerful yellow. But the situation is low and oppressive. The estate is in a poor way, and the land overgrown with thistles and bracken.

We lunched at the Dolaucothi Arms off fried eggs and thick slabs of home-cured bacon. I drank tea; Eardley beer. The meal was given us by the landlady who would not allow us to pay a penny. The Dolaucothi valley is renowned, but I thought the lower part where the house and Pumpsaint village stand, was too enclosed. When we drove up the valley, it broadened and became singularly lovely like a Scotch lowland glen, with sheep grazing on the horizon of the hills.

We stayed the night at Tenby, in a little old-fashioned Inn on the front. There was nowhere to sit after dinner, so I went to bed at 8.30. Alas, there was no reading lamp.

Sursday, 21st September

E. and I very cross with each other this morning. He could not get the car to start. I pushed him in it down the hill. He said I ought to have continued pushing while he put the car in gear. I did, but it wouldn't move. I said, it was all very fine for him sitting pretty at the wheel while I sweated my guts out. He said he was trying with might and main. 'It is I who am struggling, and suffering,' I said querulously. Finally we got off. I read the half-inch map wrong and directed him in the opposite direction to the right one. But E. is never cross for more than five minutes, if that. At Manorbier there is a disfiguring aerodrome with huts. We could not enter the castle which is closed. The outside is very overgrown with ivy. We drove past Carew Castle, and down a long, bad drive to Slebech, a cardboard Walpole castle on a mere, romantic, but empty and dilapidated. It belongs to John Philipps's brother-in-law. We called at Picton Castle for letters. The house is now a military hospital.

In a field overlooking St. Bride's Bay and the blue sea beyond we and the agent of the Trust's Pembrokeshire properties ate our luncheon of a loaf of bread, margarine, honey and tomatoes. Walked to the Deer Park at the tip of the cape opposite Skomer Island. We watched seaplanes practise bombing in ehc bay. Interminable discussion between E. and the agent whether or not we would erect a water ram for Farmer Codd. His wife, in eager expectation that we would, gave us a great tea of luscious bread and butter in their parlour. On this hot day they had a roaring fire, and we nearly died of the heat, and the flies. Nice, friendly people.

Motored towards the setting sun, visiting more N.T. properties and protected coast line. We stayed at a farmhouse, called Lleithy, under the dark hulk of two mountains, near St. David's Head, which Graham Sutherland paints. Given lovely fresh farm food. Slept in a large feather bed. One sinks and sinks until one is drowned in prickly, stifling asthma-inducing plumage.

Friday, 22nd September

To our chagrin the weather has completely broken. All day it poured. St. David's Cathedral was completely empty, and for an hour we were the only visitors. It is built on a slope so that to walk from the west to east end one climbs a hill. Gilbert Scott restored it well. The interior is uncongested and austere. The bones of St. David are preserved in a casket behind a grille, and would of course be venerated if this were a Catholic cathedral. The Ministry of Works have taken over Cilgerran Castle from us and installed a uniformed official with a peaked cap. He says he is lucky if he has one visitor a day. Reached Dolgelly and stayed at the Golden Lion.

Saturday, 23rd September

Motored in the rain to Dolmelynllyn, a spectacular property on one side of a valley. The house perfectly hideous, with a gable of carved wood, fashioned out of an Indian bed. We walked up to the waterfall, Rhaiadr Ddu. Lunched excellently off lamb, apple pie and cream at the Tyn-y-Groes Inn, and drove through mountain valleys to Conway. Aberconwy is greatly improved by loans from the National Museum of Wales. Arrived Bodnant at tea-time.

The house is large, Victorian and not distinguished, but the gardens are world-renowned, and superbly sited, with a view across the Conway tidal river towards the mountains – Snowdon behind the range in front of us. Lord Aberconway walked us round the gardens after tea. Milner, the Victorian landscapist, actually began them for Aberconway's grandfather. There are terraces and two large pools on two levels, the lower bounded at one end by a yew stage with wings, and at the opposite end by a Kent-like edifice, moved here in 1939 from Gloucestershire. It is called Pin Mill. It is hung with French seventeenth-century arabesque Poitiers tapestries. An upstairs room retains its contemporary wainscoting, and the parquetry floor comes from a demolished house in Whitehall Gardens.

Sunday, 24th September

Lord Aberconway, our host, is solicitous and affable. He is a man of much versatility and shrewdness. A great gardener, he has wide business interests, steel, ships and aeroplanes. This afternoon he conducted us for two hours round the remainder of the garden. We walked slowly through the

Dell, a steep narrow valley with a stream, lined with rare conifers to which he is much attached – macrocarpa, sequoia, Atlantic cedar, and firs of all sorts. He particularly likes *Pinus insignis*. There are too many conifers for my taste. I like them to be interspersed with hardwoods as at Stourhead. We returned through a stretch of rare gentians, now in bloom, with little water sprays laid on to each batch. There is a long, tunnelled pergola of laburnum. The glasshouses contain cactuses, some very exotic tropical shrubs, and plants with giant spotted leaves.

After tea he took us over the house. The best things are the carpets. An expert comes once every two months to mend them. There are portraits of his grandfather with scientific instruments by Ouless, his mother by Tissot, and paintings by Cranach – and conversation pieces by Rankin. He has bought and inserted many early and late Georgian chimney-pieces. The architect of the house was Ould, who built Wightwick Manor and Hill Bark, Cheshire. I could not have liked Lord A. more for his kindness, politeness and intelligence.

Monday, 24th September

The beginnings of what I know will be a bad cold. E. and I were up early and left by 9. At breakfast Lord Aberconway was as polite as ever. But he had the businessman's Monday morning face on, and was I could see anxious to dismiss us and get down to answering letters.

Today, after trying twenty times unsuccessfully to buy razor blades, I procured one at the twenty-first shop.

We motored across Telford's Menai Bridge and inspected the N.T. field, by name Cae-glan-y-Mhor. Then to Beaumaris, for I wished to see the outside of Baron's Hill, built by the architect of Attingham. It is spoilt by an addition on the west side. We drove right across Anglesey to another N.T. cliff field at the extreme northern point, Dinas Gynfor. It is an unimportant patch of a large unspoilt area. After a puncture we crossed to the mainland and reached Vaynol at 1.30.

Michael Duff, extremely friendly, welcomed us. He is taller than me and as thin, and carries himself straight and proud. A very handsome man with melting eyes like a dog's. He gave us an excellent luncheon somewhere in the back regions of this house, which is a military hospital. Michael speaks Welsh and makes his local speeches in Welsh, which is a great credit to him. I have been astonished during this tour how universally Welsh is still spoken by the middle classes as well as the peasants, but seldom if ever (except in Michael's case) by the upper classes.

We left at 4 for Segontium the Roman fort. Museum well kept, but the site overgrown with nettles. No one to cut them, and no money to pay if there were someone. Continued down the projecting arm of

Caernarvon to look at a dreary bit of land offered us on the coast. My cold getting worse. We stayed in Harlech.

Tuesday, 26th September

I slept badly, my cold much developed in chest and throat. Eardley came into my room ashen grey to announce that he too felt awful. We agreed to cut short our tour and return home, or rather to his Bothy.

Wednesday, 27th September

Lay in bed all morning. E. has invited me to stay tonight and the following night. Saintly of him, in the, I should say in my, circumstances. In the afternoon we went to see old Mr. Mackenzie of Fawley Court, who may give us restrictive covenants over his property, which lies between the Greenlands estate and Henley-on-Thames. With the greatest effort and by sheer willpower I prevented myself from sneezing and spluttering over this ancient man. But when the effort is no longer called for the bottled up rheum explodes worse than ever.

Thursday, 28th September

E. and I motored to London early. He dropped me at Cheyne Walk. I immediately had my hair cut and washed. The washing may have been a great error. Miss P. gave me luncheon at home and I caught the 2.10 from Paddington for Much Wenlock.

Carried my bags across the fields to the Abbey. Mary Motley greeted me. She lives in this large house with four children, all boys, a nurse and an old general servant. Several women and girls come in at odd hours of the day. Loo, her husband, is as yet away. By dinner-time I was not feeling at all well.

Friday, 29th September

Got up late for breakfast but felt so awful that Mary took my temperature which was over 100 and sent me straight back to bed, where I remained, dozing and reading - Trevelyan's *Social History*, just out, Fynes Moryson's *Itinerary*, Harrison's *Elizabethan Times*, and Sir John Reresby's *Memoirs* - until

Sunday, 1st October

when I got up for dinner with a temperature of nearly 100. Met Loo for the first time in years. I had never been at all on his beam, and considered him a philistine. He doubtless considered me a cissy. But by midnight I really liked him. When we first met this evening he neither addressed a word to me, nor smiled. I was determined slowly and cautiously to break down this animal suspicion. And I believe I succeeded. He talked of rockets and aeroplanes. He is manufacturing rockets at this moment. He so impressed me with his ability to reckon speeds and revolutions with mathematical precision that I thought to myself, 'The man is perhaps one of the geniuses of our time. He is certainly wonderfully in line with scientific inventions. Unlike the stuffy, escapist intellectuals among my friends he is positively contributing to an ultimately better world, for he intends to turn his dreadful instruments of destruction, the moment the war is over, into instruments of benevolence and succour.' We drank a lot, and after dinner were on the best of terms. He complained bitterly of the restrictions upon big employers, and inveighed against the Government for their ignorant interference with business, and pandering to the voters. He abused the workers for responding only to harsh treatment and rejecting offers to participate with management.

Mary told me this morning that Loo began with nothing. He borrowed £200 and set up his inventions with that capital. Now he has a turnover of £750,000 a year, and yet his actual spendable net income is £800.

Loo says that the German rocket, V2, goes eighty miles into the air, and descends forty feet into the earth, where it explodes. It does less damage than the V1 on the whole. Its range is longer than the V1s. It is launched in Holland.

Tuesday, 3rd October

Yesterday morning the Motleys left, and I have had two glorious days entirely to myself. I cannot express my gratitude to these good Samaritans for their kind treatment. I only wish I could stay here for ever. I must go somewhere else, and don't want to return to London before my month is up. I rang up Pitchford last night. Sir Charles Grant was away, and Lady Sybil answered. I understand her now - she is like a little girl with a mind as sharp as a razor's edge, and quite unaccountable. She said, 'Yes, I know who you are. You wrote afterwards to Charles and never asked after my leg, which I thought rather beastly of you.' I apologized and said I was sure it had quite recovered by now. 'It hasn't, as a matter of fact,' she said.

I could not make up my mind whether or not I was still ill. After luncheon I took my temperature. It was just under 100. I decided that I was still ill, and had nowhere to go to be ill in, except my kind Aunt Deenie's. So in despair I put through a trunk call to her at Stow-on-the-Wold. There was no answer. I thought again, and took my temperature again. It was sub-normal. This, I decided, was absurd, and to take it out of myself, I would bicycle to Attingham. This I did, ten miles there, up and down precipitous hills, in a piercing east wind. I felt very much better for it. Lady Berwick was alone and gave me tea. She was charming to me. Told me that, after all the cancellations, the Shropshire Education Committee were re-considering Attingham for their adult educational college.

Wednesday, 4th October

Left Wenlock by an 8.30 train to Shrewsbury. There I had to wait. I looked very closely at St. Chad's church by George Steuart. It is built on an oval plan. It has two narthexes, one with a delicate curved stairway and mahogany handrail leading to the gallery. The pews, beautifully shaped to conform to the oval, are preserved. A hideous reredos presented as a war memorial. I changed again at Crewe and reached Glasgow at 7. Could get into no hotel and motored round the town looking for a room. Finally found one miles down Sauchiehall Street near the Museum. It had a double bed and the landlady expressed surprise that I should want it all to myself. Horrible smells of yesterday's cooking, and the sheets of that coarse variety which cause one to fear what may lie underneath them.

Thursday, 5th October

To the Art Gallery where no pictures are hanging, and there is nothing to see but a few bits of machinery. I took the 12.15 to Oban where I was met by Aunt Dorothy and driven by her to Ardachy.

Tuesday, 10th October

I am left much to my own devices, but this enables me to make progress with the chapter for my National Trust book. I am enjoying this visit even more than I did two years ago. One day I bicycled to Bonawe up Loch Etive where the road comes to an end, and a track follows the loch past the quarries, sharply to the north.

On Sunday I bicycled to Connel Ferry to Mass in Dunstaffnage's wooden chapel, which is exactly like a hen house, under the bridge by the edge of the loch. Another day we motored to Oban. Seated in the ring on wooden steps covered with spittle and manure from farmers' boots, we watched Highland cattle being auctioned. The highest price a heifer fetched was £82. I also went to a meeting at which Tom Johnston, the Secretary of State for Scotland, spoke to the farmers. He is a distinguished elderly man whom the local Conservative M.P. praises as the best Minister, though Labour, that Scotland has ever had.

Wednesday, 11th October

Today we went for a hundred-mile drive round Argyllshire, pursuing land girls, of which army Aunt D. is chairman of a large section in the county.

We started over Connel bridge, up the river Awe to Loch Awe. There we left the Glasgow road and struck left up Glen Orchy. The river Orchy, a galloping, chestnut-backed river. Past the Falls of Glen Orchy to the bridge of that name, and Loch Tulla. Through Glencoe which is weird, cruel and haunted, emerging upon Loch Leven. Along the east bank of Loch Linnhe, through Appin and back again to our Loch Etive. Lovely indeed it was, although visibility was bad. There is more romance in Scotch hills than in Welsh. In Wales you do not sense the eternal presence of Celtic deities. There is not the same terrifying passion in the way the clouds envelop the bare brown mountain tops. Yet as I watched the silver water tumble in lively ribbons from these bleak mountains, their tops wreathed in black cotton-wool-soaked clouds, I wanted to be away from them, and back in the friendly south. I can well understand how eighteenth-century travellers from England found them 'horrid', with nothing beautiful about them. Only an aggressive sublimity.

Thursday, 12th October

Left Connel at midday. I reached Glasgow at 4.30 and again could get no room in an hotel, so finally stayed in an apartment next to the house of ill fame of my previous visit. Was bored and had nothing to do. I waited for the London train, hoping that Geoffrey Houghton-Brown might be on it; but there was no Geoffrey and by that time it was too late for a cinema. Besides, it was dark and raining. I found a cheap restaurant where I ate and read my book. As I was finishing, a man two tables away got into conversation. He came across to my table and offered me a drink. We drank beer, which I hate. For an hour and a half he told me his life story, beginning at the age of 2 when he claimed he first remembered falling in love with his mother. 'Rather early?' I suggested. 'Not a bit,' he said; 'from that instant I knew that women were to be my line. I never looked back. And now I will tell you how my first adventures began.' I groaned. He took no notice, and proceeded. His first love affair was at the age of 5 with his pillow. His second at the age of 8 with his sister. His third at 12 with God knows whom. I rose from my seat. He pulled me down, ordered more beer and went on to the next infinitely boring adventure. After several more glasses he had only reached the age of 20 – he must now be 60 years old at the least I calculated. I could bear it no longer and pleaded that my bladder needed relieving. 'Good God,' he exclaimed, 'fancy that. It's on the left there, and when you return I will tell you what I did with that photograph.' Mercifully he did not see me bolt through the door into the street, and run as fast as my legs would carry me. Now why do strangers have to persecute harmless individuals like me in this way?

Tuesday, 17th October

Today we had our monthly meeting and also the annual meeting. Lord Zetland announced the gift of the two Queen Anne Street houses, which we may make into our offices. As regards situation they would be very suitable.

During my long absence from London nothing has been done to my house. But today, twelve hours after my return, an army of builders have begun putting in glass to the windows, mending frames, the bathroom ceiling, doorlocks, etc. Thank goodness, but the mess is once again appalling.

To my intense surprise and delight the Committee have given me a bonus of £200 for my work during Matheson's absence.

Saturday, 21st October

Looked over 17 Alexander Place, which Geoffrey Houghton-Brown has just bought with a view to my fitting myself into it too. A nice little house but I don't see how it can easily be divided up.

Caught a train to Bradford-on-Avon and stayed the night with Mrs. Moulton at the Dower House. Had a long talk after dinner, when his mother had gone to bed, with Alex Moulton about the future, which promises apparently to be less black for his generation – he is about 24 – than for mine. In actual fact I don't think this applies to me particularly because I have never known riches and pre-war luxury, unlike most of my contemporaries from Eton. I am not gloomy about the future for myself. He is a rather appealing young man in that he is very earnest, intelligent and already successful, with a fine grasp of business. The youngest of three children, he is the one who loves The Hall, and is about to return to work in his family business, Spencer-Moulton, at the bottom of The Hall garden. The works are screened by trees. He is determined to and undoubtedly will make money. He will be a conscientious manager, for he has enlightened views about the conditions of his workers, who number 700 Bradfordians. He is very proud of the proximity of the factory to The Hall, and rejoices in it. He is also determined to do his duty by The Hall. He is now going to live in the stables, which he is about to convert into bachelor lodgings, and eventually move into The Hall when he has made enough money. We went all round the house, which was heavily restored by his great-grandfather in the 1840s. The furniture which I saw the last time I was here has been sold since. The house has distinct academic interest.

On Sunday afternoon I drove over to Westwood Manor and stayed the night with Ted Lister. I enjoyed it but Ted will not go to bed till the early hours and thinks one offensive if one slips away before 3 a.m. John Leslie and Sir Orme Sargent dined. The latter is a tall man with a sloping fore-head, nose and chin: all slopes. An agreeable evening with much Edwardian gossip and laughter. These three elderly gentlemen are given to story-telling. Have you heard this one? The hotel commissionaire saying confusedly to the lift boy, 'Take this lady up to P. I mean to letter P. I mean to letter P on the door' - and others of this calibre.

Tuesday, 24th October

Lunched at the Travellers' with Johnnie Dashwood, who calls all the wait-resses, 'My dear,' and cracks jokes with them. They love him in conse-quence. Indeed he is the most good natured, jolly man imaginable. He is very cross with the Trust for suggesting that the West Wycombe account is overdrawn; says that our accountant and Hill both have tortuous minds, and that together their tortuosity is invincible. He has been in Rome, which is clean and gay; food obtained by the rich through the black market, and by the poor through excellent soup kitchens, so no one starves. All sections of the British, officials down to the common soldiers, hold the Italians in greatest contempt for having treated our prisoners so badly. The Romans pay no heed to the Pope, who, he considers, has not played fair, by them or by us.

Johnnie repeated the statement which I have heard before, that the Pontiff blessed the Italian troops at the outset of their Abyssinian cam-paign, but never blessed our troops on their entry to Rome to relieve the Romans of the Germans. Anyway he thinks the Curia a farce with its preponderancy of Italian cardinals. With this sentiment I heartily agree, and have always considered it the one irrefutable indictment of the Vatican set-up.

Had tea with Lord and Lady Esher at the Dorchester. At 5.30 Lord E. and I walked to Londonderry House. Lord Londonderry's secretary showed us round. Troops occupy all the state-rooms, which in their present condition are tawdry and unimpressive. The grand staircase is indeed grand, but from what I could see the architecture of the house is so-so. Of course with the return of all the furniture which belongs, it would look entirely different. It was odd to see at the end of the great gallery where the famous *Miranda* hung, an exhibition of worn motor lorry tyres. We went over the Londonderrys' reserved part where they now live, and which they call 'a flat', but which we calculated could be divided into five and possibly six expensive Park Lane flats. Lord Esher asked how many servants the Londonderrys employed before this war. The answer was, 'Twenty-eight in the kitchen, and sixteen in the steward's room.'

Lord E. and I agreed that Londonderry House should not be reserved as a museum exclusively; but that we should ask the Government if they would rent it from us for official entertainments. He thinks Benjamin Wyatt a mightily indifferent architect.

Wednesday, 25th October

I lunched with Lord Carlisle in the House of Lords. Found him in the library, which was dark as pitch. Several other peers emerged from the half light. I thought what a seedy, drab collection of old crocks, and above all how out of date. Lord C. on the contrary is very spry. He has spent three years in Turkey; his wife is an A.T.S. General in India; his son is fighting in Italy. He may be sent on a mission to Yugoslavia in a few weeks' time. He talked of Naworth, which is, he believes, the king of all castles. His son loves it too. He may never live in it again, and wants the N.T. to have it. He suggests a school renting it. Asked me to come and stay there in a fortnight's time, which I shall enjoy doing. After luncheon the House sat, and I stood behind the Bar for a few minutes in the Chamber, which is now the Robing Room, smaller, cosier and more intimate than the old Chamber. There were the Lord Chancellor in his wig, the bishops in their lawn sleeves, and the stately attendants in boiled shirt-fronts and tail coats, with medals hanging round their necks on chains, which clattered against the starch. The peers, mostly decrepit, looked gaga in the dim yellow light, and remarkably nineteenth century. This is the best place in which to recapture nineteenth-century atmosphere. I love it, and would not have it any different.

Thursday, 26th October

Went to Mrs. Ionides's house in Twickenham at 9.30. Very foggy and so could not see much of the riverside scenery. Mrs. Ionides owns the grounds of old Orleans House, now pulled down, and Gibbs's beautiful Octagon, which she showed me. It is well preserved. She offers to leave it and eight acres, which adjoin Marble Hill, including a building which contains two derelict flats. She hates the local council, who wanted to pull down the Octagon, and who cheered when told that Radnor House had been demolished by a bomb. Before I left she offered to include her pictures of Twickenham, including a Zuccarelli, which K. Clark wants for the National Gallery. The offer is certainly a worthy one. She is a highly intelligent old woman, a sister of Lord Bearsted, and talks of 'ceows'. I liked her.

I rushed back to Brooks's and talked to G. M. Young about his contribution to the N.T. book, and read his chapter in manuscript. We talked of Robert Byron. He said Mrs. Byron was going through all his diaries and letters. He did not know if any monograph about Robert was to be published.

Met Major and Mrs. Fuller, their daughter Mrs. Boyle, recently widowed, and all trained to Uxbridge. We ate sandwiches in the tube. In a warehouse we looked at a set of four Flemish tapestries of biblical scenes, *circa* 1680, the colours extremely strong. Major Fuller had contemplated buying them for Great Chalfield Manor, but was disappointed with them. He thought the figures too large and too classical. But I feel sure they are good tapestries.

At 5.30 to tea with Emerald. Lord Berners gave us a white powder to sniff, which he said was cocaine. It smelled of menthol, and I liked it, but Emerald did not, complaining that it burned the membrane of her nose. She talked of trees, and asked, 'Are you intimate with trees? I know a man who is. He tells me that when they transplant them, they have to be given an anaesthetic for they feel the pain so badly.'

Friday, 27th October

Sir Cyril Fox, director of the Museum of Wales, lunched with me at Brooks's. He offers to give the Trust help and advice on our archaeological properties, and wants to do a tour of them with me after the war. We had a long, useful talk about the Trust's post-war problems, and about Cardiff Castle. To my surprise he admires it very much, particularly the Victorian work by Burges. Said Lord Bute is quite impossible, and will not make up his mind; nor will Lord Tredegar about Tredegar Park. In fact he said rather wistfully, 'The aristocracy are all the same. They keep to themselves, and are afraid of outside contacts. I do not expect them to fraternize with a mere ordinary citizen like myself, but they might discuss cultural matters with me on a common level.' I said that they were probably frightened of cultivated, highbrow people like himself - although no one could be more charming or less frightening than Sir Cyril - and they were deeply suspicious of city councillors, government officials and the Inland Revenue. He ought to understand that.

I took the train to Sevenoaks, and had tea with Lord Sackville and Mason (the agent) at Knole. Lord S. is always charming, and exquisitely dressed. Mason is down to earth and sensible. Lord S. agreed, as I thought he would, not to press for a 100-year lease, but to abide by whatever term of years the Court of Chancery decides upon. He said no one after Eddy would be able to live in Knole. I broached the park problem, about which Davidge the town planner spoke to me this morning, asking me if I would ascertain privately what Lord Sackville would accept in compensation. Would he accept £100 per acre, amounting in all to £100,000, a sum he believed the local authorities would provide? I did not need to put this question, for Lord S. advanced the view, which came as a surprise to me, but sensible, that if he accepted this sum, then he would benefit after income tax by £300 a year only, and Eddy would have to pay additional death duties of 40 per cent. Whereas by not doing so and keeping the parkland, which is unproductive, Eddy would pay only nominal death duties as he, Lord S. had done on succeeding his brother, and he would be able to threaten to sell parts if occasion arose, and thus bargain with the local authorities. If they then wished to preserve it from development, as they do now, they could purchase it from Eddy for an open space. After tea we walked in the garden, which is well maintained in spite of the war, and looked at the outside of the house. I had no idea how much glass was lost when the landmine fell in the park in the spring. Most of it has already been replaced with excellent new panes, and the injured mullions have been well restored. Incidentally £1,500 has been spent on the damaged roof, out of the war damage fund, at no expense to the estate.

Dined with Puss Milnes-Gaskell, who had Sir Hughe Knatchbull-Hugessen, just appointed Ambassador to Belgium, and Lady. He shrewd, she abrupt. He said that lunching at Buckingham Palace yesterday the Queen pointed out to him that they still had no glass in their windows, only cellophane.

Sunday, 29th October

Lunched at home, and worked at my chapter. Tea with Logan Pearsall Smith, who is getting very old, and breathless. Nevertheless he talks like a river. He is devoted to Stuart and read me some extracts of a letter from him, with which he is well pleased. He gave me his book of Aphorisms, in which he wrote my name. Afterwards I remembered he had given me one already. He said Sibyl Colefax was a genuine friend, kind and painstaking; that Emerald's ingenuous remarks about love were a pose. Nevertheless she was a brilliant talker, *the* most brilliant. Next time we met, he said we must have a 'serpent-talk' instead of a 'dove-talk' .

Monday, 30th October

Trained to Luton and walked to the offices of a rather seedy, be-pince-nezed solicitor. He took me across the street to tea in a bun shop, and told me he had a collection of Bernard Shaw books, press cuttings, theatre programmes and photographs which he wished to leave by will to Shaw's Corner. He is 42. Shaw is his absorbing hobby, and has been ever since at the age of 15 he read an article by Shaw against the last war in 1915, having overheard his father warn his mother not to let the boy see it. After school he left Birmingham, where his parents lived, and set

up in Luton in order to be near Ayot St. Lawrence where Shaw lived.
At the time he was so poor he could not afford to buy the newspapers
in which articles about Shaw were published. So he copied them out in
his own hand in the public library. He now knows Shaw, and constantly
goes to his house. He also knows Lowenstein, who with his help is compiling a Shaw bibliography. He even learnt German in order to read a
biography of Shaw in that language.

Got back from Luton just in time to pick up Jamesey at his flat, and
walk to dine with the Moores. I sat next to Joan and Diane Abdy who is
so defenceless one wants to hug her. She said she bought a lavatory this
afternoon in a smart shop. The sales manager in a frock coat pulled,
tweaked bits of paper, threw them into the pan, and flushed with absurdly
exaggerated, genteel gestures. Joan played Mozart and Bach after dinner,
exquisitely, poignantly. Drank too much. Damn.

Tuesday, 31st October

Several loud crumps from rockets during the night, which woke me up.
Several more today. They are becoming worse, and will doubtless continue for the rest of the war. They say they come from inside Germany,
even from the Tyrol. Nancy Mitford saw one descend in a ball of fire, like
the setting sun. Even she had a cold sweat, and was riveted to the ground.

At 9.30 I accompanied Mike Peto to Mark Turner's office. Turner proposed that the Pilgrim Trust should buy Audley End; the Trust should let
to Lord Braybrooke, and he in turn re-let to the Fyffes for their girls'
school. I doubt if this will work out. Matheson disturbed me by saying
that Mr. Hobson of Park Hall thought I did not know what I was about.
The truth is I knew only too well, but I could not tell him.

Dr. Tom Jones lunched with me at Brooks's. Very Welsh. A little old
man with white hair, a pointed intelligent face. He knows everyone. His
manners are abrupt. He seized the food himself and plumped the fish on
to my plate. Now I would not dare do that if I were lunching with him.
I liked him all the same. We talked of the N.T. and the Pilgrim Trust,
which has tremendous power, of course wielded by himself. His shrewdness is by no means to be disregarded. He was, I think, secretary to
Baldwin's Cabinet, and is a kind of perpetual power behind thrones.

Wednesday, 1st November

All Saints' Day does not mean so much to me as All Souls', for one day
I shall be one of the latter, and never one of the former. Went at 12.30 to
old Reginald Blunt's memorial service (for he died last week) in St.
Luke's beautiful church, Chelsea. During the service I thought about the
dentist; and at the dentist's this evening I thought about Reginald Blunt.

I thought of his lifetime love of Chelsea, which in spite of his efforts the Chelsea Council persists in spoiling, while the Mayor draped in chains piously attends his service as a mourner. An odd world.

Mann of the Wallace Collection lunched with me and was more informative, and less bottled up than previously. I understand why he is a power in the museum world, for he is very positive and go-ahead. He thinks owners should be paid by the state to live in their ancestral houses. He disapproves of the institutional age ahead of us, and the inevitable lack of individualism that will accompany it. He thinks Raby a stick-in-the-mud. G. M. Young came to the office to look through files about N.T. manor houses. I went to Harold in King's Bench Walk. He talked with pride of Nigel's cleverness; and said he would stand for Parliament in a Highland constituency. Then I dined with Bridget.

Friday, 3rd November

I lunched at the Reform Club with Peter Watson, who said he would publish my architectural article in *Horizon*, if I amplified it a little.

Went to no. 40 Queen Anne's Gate, which with no. 42 has been given us by Mrs. Murray Smith, and is to be made into our new offices. No. 40 suffered a good deal when the Guards' Chapel was hit by a flying bomb. All windows are out; parts of inner walls down, doors wrenched off, and ceilings down. We expect to move into no. 42 next spring. The old lady was there, fumbling through old letters, and infinitely pathetic. I had been asked to choose from the furniture any pieces we might want, but she had changed her mind and would not look at furniture today. So the visit was rather wasted. However I saw over the house. No. 42 is charming. I think we should have the outside plaster removed; it would be an improvement. Matheson and I went to Twickenham to see the Octagon and Mrs. Ionides's land. Matheson wondered how we could afford to look after it. He is right, it will need capital outlay. I made a plea on behalf of Miss Paterson that she is grossly overworked. I hope he has taken this in.

Monday, 6th November

Received a letter from my mother that she has rheumatoid arthritis in her hands, which has made me extremely sad. Mothers wring the heart.

I dined at the Travellers' with Harold Nicolson to meet a young poet and playwright, by name Michael Clayton-Hutton, aged 23. I took an instant dislike to him, for he is rather off-hand and hideously pleased with himself. Shaftesbury Avenue looks, moreover. Harold talked politics over port wine. He said Hitler told a friend of his, the Swiss Governor of Danzig, that Hitler lamented there was no prominent English statesman to whom he could speak freely in his or our tongue. The Danzig Governor asked what he would say to the Englishman. Hitler replied: 'Supposing it were Lord Halifax I would say – I offer your country the ports of Antwerp, Dunkirk, Le Havre, etc., absolutely, on the understanding that I take Poland and the Balkans without interference.' Harold said that when the Germans walked into Slovakia, he was with Winston Churchill and Lord Cecil. After serious discussion Lord Cecil left, saying, 'Well, Winston, I must go. Things are desperate. I feel twenty years older.' Churchill replied equally seriously, 'Yes, Bob, things are desperate. I feel twenty years younger,' and these words convinced Harold there and then that Churchill was a great man. It convinces me that Churchill enjoys war.

Tuesday, 7th November

Took the train to Portsmouth with Sir Humphrey Prideaux-Brune. We crossed the Sound in a launch to Gosport, and taxied to Rowner, where Sir Humphrey's family owned property from the fourteenth century until the 1920s. This Sir H. has bought back five acres round the old church and wants to hand them over to the National Trust. He was so nice, so enthusiastic, and has so great a sentimental attachment to the place that I had not the heart to tell him I thought it not important enough. With no endowment it would be an uneconomic property. Besides it has no national interest whatever. Sir Humphrey has spent thirty years in China. His wife who was ill in Switzerland in 1939 was caught there, and has not got away. He has not seen her all these years.

After dinner with the Darwins Esther Darlington drank tea with me, and persuaded me reluctantly to become Hon. Secretary of the Chelsea Society until the end of the war and Rick's return. Because of my admiration of Mr. Blunt and friendship for Rick I consented, but I shall have little enough time to be active.

Wednesday, 8th November

Nancy rang up to say that her father had a diamond necklace which all the West End jewellers valued at £1,000, but a pawnbroker gave him £2,500 for it. I took mine to Spinks this morning and they only offered me £400. Now I shall try Nancy's pawnbroker.

Thursday, 9th November

Took the morning train from Euston to Carlisle, arriving at 4.30. Read *Phineas Redux* all the way. At Carlisle took a bus to Brampton, and another to Naworth, reaching the drive gate in the dark and frost. Walked downhill to the Gatehouse, just above the Castle; and Lord Carlisle was there to greet me. This little house, formerly the estate office, is let to a Miss Mounsey Heysham, an old lady, and a Miss Chance, with whom Lord Carlisle stays when he is here. Since the war began the Castle has been first a school, Rossall, and then a military headquarters. Now the military have gone from the Castle and merely occupy a few huts in the park. Bitterly cold, and had it not been for my electric pad, I should have been frozen in the night.

Lord Carlisle is young middle-aged, stout, smiling, entertaining, and a very nice host indeed. This morning was clear bright, there having been a hard frost. We went all over the Castle. The surrounding country is idyllic. Scotch hills in the distance and few scattered farmhouses. The Castle is perched above two deep glens which unite at the foot of the 1881 wing. There is a square walled garden made by Belted Will about 1600. There are two detached, rugged buildings, the Gatehouse proper and the Bote House. The Castle walls are of beautiful gold and red stone, and date from the fourteenth century. Fairly discreetly added to one end is the Stanley wing, by Salvin according to Carlisle, but I should say by a later hand.[2] It makes the house enormous. The Castle is a rabbit warren of rooms, and uneven floors, and endless corridors. There is only one room that is actually old, namely Lord William's Library in his tower, where the stout fourteenth-century ceiling is preserved. It is of massive beams, with Gothic panels and fat bosses between. All the other rooms and the gallery are of Salvin's time, for there was a disastrous fire in 1840. The Great Hall is new likewise, the walls covered with very fine early Gobelin tapestries that belonged to Henry of Navarre, with his monogram and a crown in the cresting. Lord C. was offered £100,000 for them by the French Government in 1914. The war came and the offer was never repeated. Otherwise the Castle is completely empty, the furniture being stacked in the stables. The Army have treated the building well. It is undamaged, clean and kept heated. All the rooms, like those of most castles, lack shape and proportion, and are inelegant, with poky windows in deep embrasures. The open courtyard is certainly beautiful, with steps leading to the Great Hall. Lord C. loves the place and thinks it the best castle in the United Kingdom. Yet he is determined not to live in it again, and offers it without grounds, and without endowment.

In the afternoon Carlisle and Miss Heysham, aged 75, very crumpled, dotty and angelic, went after pheasants. A Mrs. Hamer and I, with a perambulator and baby, walked down to Lanercost Abbey, which embraces the parish church and the ruins given to the Office of Works. The

---

[2] Actually by James Fergusson.

Howards are buried in the ruined east end, which makes a romantic mausoleum.

Saturday, 11th November

I walked by myself round the Castle and into the gardens, and along the ravine in the morning. After luncheon, was motored by Lord Carlisle to catch the 3.30 train. Last night we had a long talk about the war. Lord C. said he was convinced that wars had nothing but a demoralizing effect upon troops and civilians alike. I agreed. I got home at midnight and drank quantities of tea and ate apples.

Sunday, 12th November

Had a glass of sherry at Brooks's with Tom, who walked in. He tells me he is soon off to Burma at his own request, for he does not wish to go to Germany killing German civilians, whom he likes. He prefers to kill Japanese whom he does not like. Tom makes me sad because he looks so sad, and because I am so deeply devoted to him.

Monday, 13th November

Meeting day. Esher asked Smith and me to lunch with him at the Grosvenor Hotel, in order to talk about his property, Watlington, which though delightful is not exactly a national monument, in spite of its one fine ceiling by Abraham Swan. The Finance Committee have in their good, considerate way, agreed to let me have the £200 they gave me, in kind instead of in cash, on which I would have to pay tax. So I may have £200 worth of the secondary Polesden furniture they lent me, not at probate value but market value.

Dining with Pam Chichester I met G. B. Stern. She was very talkative and cordial. She is a hugely fat Jewess, bulging everywhere. She has straight, cropped grey hair à la Gwen Farrar, a curious sight. She discussed schoolgirl books, but I am not well read in that branch of literature.

Tuesday, 14th November

Nancy's pawnbroker in the Strand has given me £525 for my necklace. Consequently I feel extremely rich.

Looked over Miss Noel-Hill's little house in Graham Street. It is tiny, with extremely tiny rooms. I could have had it there and then and would have been tempted were it not for the Underground, which passes above ground just behind her garden wall.

Johnnie Churchill followed me into Brooks's. He said Midge Tweeddale died of galloping cancer of the lung which attacked and finished her off within a week. I liked her so much. He said that Mary his

wife was a fanatical Protestant and was going to bring up Cornelia as one.
I said I disapproved.

Thursday, 16th November

Attended a lecture at the Courtauld Institute by Anthony Blunt, on
Castiglione. He delivered it extremely well, with no notes of any kind.
K. Clark present and looked benignly approving, which is the greatest
compliment a man can receive.

Saturday, 13th November

B. lunched with me, and for the first time was wearing a small black beret
on one side of her head, which suited her. She talked rather pathetically
about her future. Said she had never yet been in love with anyone who
loved her. I asked if it irritated her having someone in love with her. She
denied this. She said that her first affair was with X who wanted to leave
his wife for her. Now she was glad he had not done so. He would have
got on her nerves. Y was another suitor, but he was too noisy and boisterous. She would like to marry someone with a small country seat, so as
to have a garden, dogs and birds. She would marry Z if he showed any
inclination. I observed that Z had neither seat, garden, dogs nor birds.
     Listened to Delius in the Albert Hall. Aimless and soporific, without
beginning and without end.

Monday, 20th November

My train to Newton Abbot was one and a half hours late owing to floods
across the line. A taxi drove me eight miles down narrow lanes to Little
Hempston Manor, seemingly miles from anywhere. It belongs to the
Dundases. He is a first cousin of Lord Zetland. Being with this cosy,
modest and by no means affluent couple, made me ponder on the near
accidents of birth, and the advantages and disadvantages of primogeniture.

Tuesday, 21st November

They kept me talking till after midnight. I was very exhausted this
morning. Little Hempston is a tiny, medieval manor house with forecourt. It is built round a minute central court. It has some six rooms in
all on the ground floor, and six bed and dressing-rooms upstairs. The
outside is of the simplest character. No one knows whether it is actually
a manor house, or a parsonage. It has its original, very coarse screens, and
screens' passage. A great hall with half-timber partition over the screens.
The walls are of plaster, pink-washed. Over the far wall is a fresco of
the Resurrection, date about 1450. The house itself is supposed to be
fourteenth century. Most of the windows have been restored not too well

by the late owners, who found it derelict and bought it from the Church. Though its general disposition is practically untouched, some details have been altered with circumspection and even improvement. Yet the flanking barns of the forecourt still retain unsightly corrugated roofs. Little Hempston is situated at the bottom of a steep ravine, and the river Dart is just visible from the house. Dartington Hall is on the other side of the river. We went there this afternoon. It is a frightful mess. The great hall with its pointed windows is magnificent outside, but the new roof is too flimsy and the new screen of unvarnished oak inexact.

I felt really sorry for the poor Dundases. She told me she has not been away one single night since the war began, but has slaved in the house all these years single-handed, cooking, housemaiding and caring for a boy aged 8, and girl aged 2½. Endless chatter about the house, of which she is intensely proud, being very medieval-minded. I liked him even better: a tall, youthful 45, very blind with thick spectacle lenses and a Roman nose like Lord Zetland's. But poles away from Lord Z.'s. exclusive, vice-regal, patrician ambience. These two people have sacrificed their money and their health for this house, which is not a hereditary possession.

Wednesday, 22nd November

On arrival at Paddington station I watched a porter drive an electric trolley over the edge of the platform on to the railway line. The machine having tilted over, pinned him against one line. Yet he went on smoking, never moved and never called out. Instantly soldiers and other porters jumped down, and within three minutes had lifted the trolley off his legs and freed him. Then he collapsed. I went to the restaurant, ordered some tea, and felt sick. Yet I had done nothing to help. I am amazed and deeply impressed by the porter's stoical courage, and the quick, concerted action of the bystanders.

Ian McCallum dined at Brooks's and talked about the new House of Commons to be built by Gilbert Scott. He had with him the White Paper and plans, and thinks the neo-Neogothic designs fairly competent. He doubts whether the *Architectural Review* will attack it.

Miss P. told me that last night at 11 a rocket fell in Battersea. The noise was the loudest and most terrible she had ever heard. It fell one and a half miles away, yet several window panes in our house were broken, and the ceiling in my large room is cracked worse than before, and sagging rather perilously.

Friday, 24th November

Had a postcard this morning from Father Francis Moncrieff, written from Hambleton, saying that old Mrs. Astley Cooper died last Sunday after three weeks' illness. Mrs. Cooper was very good to me when I was in disgrace with my family ten years ago, and gave me my missal. She was a remarkable old woman with a first-class brain, a man's attitude to life and its problems. She hated pettinesses, and had no patience with small irritations or small points of view. Accordingly few women liked her. She had a sad life, in losing her favourite children and quarrelling violently with the others and her relations. But she had a magnificently embracing sense of humour, was a realist and a cynic, and could never be taken in or deceived. She discovered Noël Coward as a boy, was an intimate friend of Malcolm Sargent and of Scott Moncrieff, whom she helped translate Proust's novels at Hambleton and who dedicated the series to her in the moving poem published in *Swann's Way*. She was a convert, who loved and revered the Church, respecting it for its intellectual, rational and ruthless approach to life. Although she frequently rebelled, she always returned to it. People were frightened by her direct manner, her immediate circumvention of all conventional and social façades. I have had many a meal with her, she sitting, groaning and shaking with mirth at some foolish person's expense, a massive, shapeless lump of a woman, over the most delicious English food. Fred, the tall, respectful, stately, P. G. Wodehouse butler, was always in the background. Rarely can two people have had a more profound affection and admiration for one another. Unfortunately Mrs. Cooper became more and more self-adulatory in a sly way, and her constant, roundabout fishing for praise exasperated me. I had not seen her for some three or four years. I shall always respect and love her, for she contributed a lot to my life. There was absolutely no nonsense about her. Her trouble was that she was a woman with a brain, born into English upper-class county circles.

James telephoned just before midnight that tomorrow evening he is at last to sleep with his first woman. Everything has been arranged. He dreads it and is terrified, and will telephone first thing on Sunday morning to let me know how it proceeded. Asked me to think of him and pray for him tomorrow evening.

Saturday, 25th November

Went to tea with Logan who told me the same stories over again, but one new - to me - saga about the wickedness of Lady Ottoline Morrell who succeeded in breaking up happy relationships, and tried to separate Ethel Sands and Nan Hudson. Lady O. was constantly throwing herself upon men. Logan asked me if I liked foul-mouthed men who otherwise led blameless lives. I said, No, I preferred clean-mouthed people who gave physical expression to their lusts. He seemed shocked. Why? For two hours he criticized everyone, asking me if I did not agree. Since half the people criticized were unknown to me, I was unable to agree. This disappointed him. When I suggested that a mutual acquaintance was malicious, and another a pompous prig, he flatly contradicted me. Tom Mitford at Brooks's said he would like to be taken to tea with Logan, 'for I am a keen etymologist'.

At the Ritz bar Guy Burgess called to me. I dined with him and Charles Fletcher-Cooke at the Gargoyle. Drank too much beer and gin mixed, and talked a great deal about politics and sex, disagreeing with Guy over both. He does and says the most dangerous and indiscreet things. However we laughed a lot. Mary Churchill who was there, joined us. I do not know her. She is prettier than her sister Diana and looks like her mother. She talked all the time about her father whom she adores unreservedly. I walked home from the Gargoyle in the moonlight. It took an hour. In bed at 2.

Sunday, 26th November

James telephoned this morning, and said tersely, 'I am still alive. It was quite easy, but was not riotous.'

I fear that in this diary I disclose the nastier, the more frivolous side of myself. I sincerely believe and fervently hope that I am not as nasty as I may appear. It is difficult to be entirely honest about oneself, because one does not necessarily know oneself. One thinks one knows. The consequence of being as honest as I try to be, must surely be that readers of these lines would pronounce me worse than many of my contemporaries who do not keep frank records of themselves. Frank? Not entirely, because I withhold things.

Monday, 27th November

Michael Peto lunched at Brooks's. Lord Braybrooke was to have done so, but when he learnt that Mark Turner could not come, he decided not to. Mike and I agreed that an impasse has been reached over Audley End. On returning to the office on foot just in front of Victoria Station I was, with the minimum of warning, stricken with a blackout. A passing cab drove me home.

Tuesday, 28th November

Kathleen Kennet, Eddy and Nancy lunched with me. Nancy had long wanted to meet her. I began by saying to K., 'Nancy is simply mad about Captain Scott.' 'So am I,' she replied. Nancy told me she had discovered how they peed – into a tin inside their bags. K. said Captain Scott hated any unkindness to animals. It was torture to him when they suffered on his account. Nancy says she wants to go to the Pole after the war.

Wednesday, 29th November

Lunched at Eaton Terrace, Anne's little house. We picnicked off soup and lobster salad, the last brought in a brown paper parcel by John Sutro. Sachie Sitwell there. When he laughs his face breaks into a thousand tiny fragments, and reassembles. I have never seen anything more endearing.

Mrs. Ionides came to the office, and agreed to leave Riverside House to the N.T. in addition to the Octagon and the Orleans House grounds. Now we shall not be hard up for funds to maintain the Octagon.

Eardley and I walked from the office this evening to Sibyl's. Talked to Elizabeth Bowen and John Lehmann about our morbid dislike of revisiting houses we had lived in during our adulthood, as opposed to childhood. Knickerbocker, the American journalist, came in later, and told us how he drove into Paris at the head of the American army in a jeep. The welcome was something he can never forget. Sibyl left before her guests with Stephen Tennant, who to my eye does not look particularly young. He has long fair hair, and the mannerisms of an Edwardian hostess. T. S. Eliot came in and went out again before I knew who he was - a dark, sharp-featured man, with hair brushed smoothly down each side of his head.

Thursday, 30th November

Hubert Smith and I attended a conference at the Middlesex County Council offices with representatives of that Council and of Heston, to discuss Osterley. Much to our surprise both Councils appeared ready to make up the annual deficit, even offering to increase rather than decrease the deficit figure.

Called for Anne Rosse at Bridget's flat and walked to the Dorchester. Dined with Emerald. Two stars present were very witty, but so spiky, pulling everyone to pieces, that I hated them both and the whole evening. I was dumb and unable to contribute a word. One of the stars said, 'Sibyl Colefax is getting too big for her boots,' to which the other replied, 'You mean she is getting too big for her hump.'

Friday, 1st December

Joan Moore lunched with me at Wilton's. She brought a huge sack which the waiters filled with oyster-shells for her hens. It was so heavy that we had to wait for a taxi to pull up at the door.

It was with much reluctance that I dined with Emerald again tonight, but I had promised to do so earlier in the week. I had a hot bath and set forth in the worst form, taking three books for her to read. Met Peter Quennell downstairs in the Dorchester. We drank whisky and soda together and went up. As so often happens when one least expects it, the dinner was hugely enjoyable. There were the two Chaplins, Alice Harding and Peter. Anthony Chaplin told us what it felt like in the rear of a bomber with a gun. He said the cold was quite appalling. You were numb all the time, and sick. But the spirit of camaraderie and loyalty among the crew was such that it could only be described as pure love. He said that in 1940 many of our planes were destroyed by bombs dropped from above by our own planes.

We talked of George Moore. Emerald showed us a letter from him to her, beginning 'Dearest Maud', comparing her to Christ and Sophocles, and acclaiming her genius. She was very modest about it. Then she brought from her bedroom a large cardboard box, shook it and said, 'These are all letters to me from George Moore. I cannot tell you what they are about.' Peter tried to persuade her to let him go through them with her, but she was reluctant, not wanting them published. Then she talked of Paris before 1914 and the affectation of Robert de Montesquiou – who Peter said was the prototype of Charlus – and how he loved to be pressed to recite his own poems, leaning against a marble pedestalled bust in an absurd posture. While she was telling this story I realized wherein her genius lay, for she has a prodigious memory, and a wonderful gift of narrative, spiced with a frivolity and humour which are unique, and totally irresistible. It was an enjoyable evening because conversation was not a denigration of contemporary socialites whom I did not know, but about the recent historic past.

Saturday, 2nd December

Just caught the 11.50 for Cambridge by jumping into the train as it was moving along the platform. Stood all the way which gave me sciatica. Met Michael and Frances Peto on arrival and went to a play in Cambridge about the Brontës which I enjoyed very much. Drove to Longstowe Hall and stayed the night with the Fyffes in their girls' school. It was fun dancing polkas, lancers, Highland flings with the girls, all of whom looked pretty and some bewitching in their long dresses, swirling around the great hall. I liked Fyffe, a very shrewd, matter of fact, Scotch architect. When the girls had gone to bed we discussed Audley End; but I fear the project will come to nought.

Sunday, 3rd December

I left soon after breakfast. The train connections extremely bad so that I did not get to Euston till late in the afternoon. Impossible to cross Piccadilly because of the Home Guard procession to the Palace. All day I read and finished Rosamond Lehmann's novel, *The Ballad and the Source*.

which Logan P.-S. thinks the best novel since Henry James. I daresay he
is right, and I am immensely impressed. My only criticisms are that the
story is told in dialogue, and I do not think it altogether convincing that
a child of 10 to 14 should be the channel through which a terrible drama
is unfolded. Nevertheless, what a story!

Tuesday, 5th December

Magdalen FitzAlan Howard lunched at the Queen's restaurant, poor old
thing. She is so gentle, and so pitiable. Why? Because she is a middle-aged
spinster? I don't think so. But because of her slightly faded, lost air of one
stranded by cruel time, and cruel love. Anyway she enjoys a harmless little
gossip, and like all fervent Catholics is interested in the marital predicaments of other Catholics.

I went to a late tea at Emerald's to meet Madame Carcano, the
Argentine Ambassadress, again. She wants advice upon the enlargement
of her country villa in the Argentine. A little difficult for me to give satisfaction in this matter. But she is an agreeable lady. Lady Kemsley came,
and talked about Dropmore and the lamentable deterioration of the
house owing to its requisition by the army. She said it was a fine house,
now utterly ruined. I promised to get in touch with the Ministry of
Works about it. It was difficult to concentrate on what Mme Carcano
was saying while Emerald in loud whispers was explaining to Lady
Kemsley who I was. Lady (Claud) Russell came in. Her beautiful name
is Atenais, and she is a Greek. Emerald addressed her in her inconse-
quential way, 'We were just saying that Greece must become a British
colony in order that all this shooting may stop.'

Wednesday, 6th December

Grandy Jersey lunched, and brought me a musquash fur lining in a brown
paper parcel, which he said had belonged to his grandfather and he feared
was too old to be of any use. Nonetheless I am grateful and delighted. I
took it to John Walls who plucked at it, and the tips of the fur came away
in their fingers. They are sending it to their experts to see if they can stop
it moulting.

Friday, 8th December

Lunched with John Philipps at the St. James's Club. He told me that
when I first met him at the beginning of the war he was odious - which
I had sensed for myself - and drunken. Now he was reformed, and was
only happy at home in Pembrokeshire. This candour I find endearing.

I left Diane Abdy's flat with Joan Moore. We agreed that cocktail
parties were absolutely unrewarding and soul-destroying, and wondered

why we ever went to them. She asked me, 'Will you ever go to another?'
I sighed and said, 'I fear I shall.' I walked to Albany to meet Lord Wilton
at Johnny Philipps's. He is about 23, tall, fair, handsome, and very shy. He
is passionately interested in architecture and wants to buy a large country
house, but cannot find one large enough. I intend to find one for him.

Emerald described how she dined last night at a large party of earnest
women who asked her questions like these: 'Lady Cunard, what do you
think about the state of morality among south-eastern Europeans?'
Answer, 'Not enough immorality.' 'What do you think then about the
lack of education in the industrial north?' Answer, 'Too much of it. There
should be less,' and so on.

Saturday, 9th December

Matheson being taken suddenly ill, I had to go through the Executive
Committee agenda with Lord Zetland in the office. He was remarkably
friendly, and to my amazement some item amused him, and he began
giggling. Then pulled himself together with a jerk. But it was too late. He
had betrayed the fact that he was a human being. I shall no longer be in
awe of him.

Sunday, 10th December

I am so pleased I decided not to go away for the weekend. Instead I have
worked hard at home, and been very happy. Alvilde lunched out with
me, after which I went straight home again. John Fowler telephoned and
persuaded me to leave off work and dine with him. The moment I put
down the receiver I regretted it. When I got there he was so friendly and
amusing that I was glad I went. He brought up dinner on two trays which
we ate in front of the fire. Told me horrifying stories of acquaintances
being blown to fragments in the streets and in their houses because they
would not have Anderson shelters.

Monday, 11th December

John Walls report that the fur Grandy has given me is ginette, a kind that
always moults a little; but that after beating and combing this one, which
once had moth, it ought to be all right. The texture is so silky and opulent
that I have decided to have an overcoat built to fit it.

Went to Harold at K.B.W. at 6.30. He told me he thought Clayton-
Hutton was a little mad, bad and dangerous to know, but was un-
doubtedly a poetic genius. He has not heard anything of him since.
Harold thinks he might well commit suicide [he did].

Tuesday, 12th December

Bought for four guineas a so-called Constable oil sketch which I saw in a shop window in Warwick Street. Went to the Wildenstein gallery to see the exhibition there. Robin Darwin asked me what I was carrying. He gave the sketch one look and roared with oafish laughter, saying that not by one in a million chances could it be a Constable, and asked how much I paid for it. I was so shaken that I lied, and said 10/-. After I had seen the high quality of the Constables exhibited I realized what a fool I had made of myself

Met Jamesey in Sloane Square for a drink. He very affectionate and sad about departing, and leaving me and others, so that I do believe he cares for me a little. But I do resent his egocentric and tyrannical ways.

After dining with Bertie Abdy we went to the Bearsteds' suite in the Dorchester and drank brandy, which is death to me. B. Abdy has very definite views. He repeated that he lived for art, pleasure and himself. Not enough, thought I. I advocated the exhibition of surplus works of art, now stored in museum basements, in tube stations where thousands could admire them while waiting for the trains. He was very shocked, which I think foolish. He hates and despises even the best quality English eighteenth century furniture. I was shocked.

Wednesday, 13th December

At 5 o'clock I took Tom Mitford to tea with Logan. I think Tom, whose manners can be abrupt, was bored, and certainly Logan was rather boring, for he would read from his own books and from the *Dictionary of National Biography* about all the Mitfords that had ever been. But he is a dear old man, and when he got up, all bent, and fumbled in his shelves I rather loved him. When Tom and I left it was pitch dark, the fog having thickened. It was almost impossible to see a thing. By tapping with my stick against the kerb, he clinging to my left arm, we reached the King's Road. After a fond farewell, and Tom's farewells are so fond they always touch me, we separated. Slowly and cautiously I followed in the wake of motor lights and walkers' torches, presuming that I was on my way to the Chelsea Hospital road. After half an hour, not knowing where I was, and almost desperate I bumped violently into someone. I apologized. The victim apologized. It was Tom. Peals of laughter ensued. We clove to one another, and agreed not to separate again. We staggered to his flat, and abandoned our different projects for that evening. Instead we ate scrambled eggs and drank red wine. Once I am indoors I love pea-soupers, the cosiness, the isolation, the calm broken by distant squeals of taxis and thuds of wary footfalls, the tapping of sticks against area railings, and the blessed expansion of confidence between two friends.

Saturday, 16th December

Stopped to look at the ruins of Donnington Castle which Macgregor tells me are fourteenth century. All that remains is a central gatehouse with two round turrets of red brick and flint. I continued to Roche Old Court, one mile off the Andover-Salisbury road, close to the Pheasant Inn. The little manor house, fourteen rooms in all, is of red brick with stone dressings. Chettle says the date is *circa* 1620 because the brick is in English bond. In front of it are an old brick wall and several old farm-buildings, including a tithe barn of timber post construction, *circa* 1400. The house inside has much early plain wainscoting, and stairs of William and Mary period. The owner, Major Trevor Cox, M.P., was at Eton with me. Was at Hill's house. Says he remembers me. I vaguely remember him. Eton is an unfailing bond between those who were educated there, and an irritation to those who were not. He is not going bald like me, but grey about the whiskers.

I arrived at the Vyne at 5.30. Mrs. Chute, grey-haired, once doubtless a pretty woman, now like a superannuated schoolgirl, received me. As schoolgirls pick shyly at their pinafores, so she picked at her skirt. We had tea in the Henry VIII linenfold panelled parlour. He, Charles Chute, a brother of Jackie Chute, came in later. He is tall and better looking than his brother, and lacks any charm whatever. Highly educated, a scholar at Eton, winner of several firsts, he is pedagogic although not a schoolmaster. Rather abrupt, contradictory and snubbing. I did not care for either – much. He hates Horace Walpole, and has little use for his own forebear, John Chute, Horace's friend. Thinks them both, and me too I have little doubt, 'scugs'.

Sunday, 17th December

During the night it poured with rain. Water dripped through my bedroom ceiling, so I put my sponge bowl to catch the drips. Before breakfast, at 8.45 precisely, a sort of school bell rang, and we all trooped into the chapel for prayers, that is to say, the Chutes, I, the headmaster and mistresses of the school billeted here – the boys are now on holiday - the matron, followed by five servant girls in uniform. Mr. Chute read the prayers, and the schoolmaster alone read the responses in so loud and aggressive a voice that I guessed he hated him. A sort of sparring match ensued. However it was all over in ten minutes. I liked it, but it is the first time I have ever attended Protestant prayers in a country house. The schoolmaster, rather sulky and surly, and the mistresses, singularly dreary, attend every meal. The mistresses exhale a forced, bumbling bonhomie. There is one perky little Irish woman at whose lamentable jests it is customary to roar. I joined in the chorus out of politeness.

The Vyne is a very wonderful house. Yet I was a trifle disappointed. The rooms are awfully dark. The John Chute staircase, though a tour-de-force, is too narrow to be magnificent. The early Renaissance panelling is of great historical importance, yet ugly. The Webb fireplaces look out of place, and the Webb portico is top-heavy. It does not belong to the façade, upon which it has been stuck like a postage stamp upon a piece of string. Mr. Chute conducted me through practically every room. The Chapel is superb, with traces of early Renaissance in the friezes of the stall canopies, stained glass and coloured tiles.

When I left, worn down by the Chutes, I decided I hated country houses and never wished to see another. I drove at 4.15 to Bramley Church and looked at the fine Banks monument there, which is almost as good as the superb Chaloner Chute one at the Vyne. Yes, I think the Chutes were Parliamentarians which accounts for their puritanism today. Then to Stratfield Saye. Found Gerry and his very handsome son and daughter-in-law (to whom I was introduced, titles and all mentioned by Gerry) cutting branches and clearing the shrubbery at the conservatory side of the house. A vast improvement has already been made. I can think of no house needing improvements that has fallen into better hands. We had tea in the dining-room, a beautiful room with a ceiling taken from Wood's book on Palmyra. From the window the landscape with water is just like the Vyne's. Gerry has already begun to clear away the fussy beds beyond the terrace. The Douros left and I settled down to talk to Gerry about Tuesday's agenda and the Vyne, when the Douros returned. Their car would not start nor would it start when I pushed it round and round the sweep with mine. All that happened was that my bumper got jammed in theirs and could only be extricated by a jack. All I received for my pains was a scolding from Gerry for being maladroit. After this interruption it was time for me to leave. Gerry did not press me to dine.

Monday, 18th December

Lunched with Derek Hill at the Reform. Filthy food – smelts, well named, and rice pudding. The rogue in porcelain, somebody has called him. He is certainly attractive, but was rather distrait and inattentive today. I daresay I bore him. He spoke with much affection of Jamesey and sorrow over his impending departure. I attended a very interesting conference at the C.P.R.E. office concerning the list of historic buildings which the Ministry of Planning is to compile under the new Act. I thought we were a good representative collection of people, Keeling in the chair, Abercrombie next to me, John Macgregor of the S.P.A.B., and James Mann from the Wallace, etc.

Worked late in the office and from there walked to Brooks's. Got drinking with John Walter.

Tuesday, 19th December

At Brooks's Lord Braybrooke lunched with me; also Esher and Mark Turner. We talked about Audley End, without reaching any conclusion, other than that the Fyffes' school was 'out'. In the afternoon a meeting of the Country Houses Committee. Very small attendance. Gerry did not come, but Harold Nicolson came for the first time. The Committee agreed to my proposal that the Trust should ask the Government for funds for country houses, not inhabited by the families of their donors.

John Preston came to see me. He is greatly improved, and I found him sympathetic. He told me he was present at a recent press conference in France which was addressed by Eisenhower. The General inspired tremendous confidence and convinced the troops that by hook or by crook he would not allow the field to stagnate during the winter months. John thereby deduces that the recent break-through by von Runstedt may not be altogether unwelcome.

Tony Gandarillos drove me away from Sibyl's Ordinary, via the St. James's Club where he drank two whiskies and soda before facing the fog. At the best of times he is an alarming driver, but tonight he was terrifying. We were constantly on the pavement. I laughed so much that I thought I should have died. He is like a teddy bear. He told me he had twice been married. Also that at dinner at Emerald's some weeks ago Peter Rodd insisted upon talking to her about Nancy Cunard, her daughter, which all Emerald's friends recognize to be a forbidden subject. Nancy [Rodd] miserably embarrassed, but could not stop him. Emerald finally said, 'Mr. Rodd, Nancy does not like me. It is a very painful subject.' The consequence is that Emerald does not speak very kindly about poor Nancy Rodd, who is utterly blameless.

Wednesday, 20th December

Met Goodhart-Rendel at the Travellers' to talk about Hatchlands, and lunched with him. He has glassy, fish-like eyes, rather protuberant, which dart around. They give him a sinister appearance. Anyone who did not know what a clever and learned man he is, might consider him unbalanced.

I dined with James in the fog. There were orange flares today at Hyde Park Corner. The fog confines one within a small world. Beyond the enveloping Dickensian gloom is the vast, illimitable unknown. James was in his best mood. We drank rum and dined at the Gargoyle. We visited pubs down the Strand. I do not enjoy these visitations, because I find it difficult to swallow half a pint of beer, and I never know what to say to strangers. J. told me that yesterday Clarissa had been with Mrs. Churchill, who was practically in tears over the news. Dame Una thinks the war will be prolonged another three years. I cannot bring myself to recognize such a thing.

Tuesday, 21st December

The shortest day. Eardley and I went to Morden Hall by tube. The house is nothing, a comfortable Victorian mansion. It is the park and grounds in this horrid suburban area that count. There are some 120 acres. It will be useful to the local people, and I think on the whole the N.T. are right to hold it, although its aesthetic value is slight.

Harold dined with me at Brooks's. He was very upset because Ben has been knocked down by a lorry in Italy and is in hospital with concussion. An officer friend of Ben's in England had been informed by letter, and reported the accident to Harold. I told Harold that if it were serious he would have been informed by cable, and he should not worry. After dinner he took me to Pratt's which is next door. He is going to second me, and Tom propose me for membership. The subscription is only £5 a year. One can get food there till midnight, a distinct advantage. Tonight Bill Astor, A. P. Herbert and others were assembled, and Harold delivered himself of a lecture against American criticism of British imperialism, and nothing would stop him. There were two Americans present, but he would not let them get a word in edgeways. I was a little embarrassed.

Friday, 22nd December

I gave Miss P. all the furniture in her bedroom as a Christmas present. Her delight and gratitude were touching. Eardley and I gave luncheon to Sir Geoffrey Hippisley Cox at the Basque Restaurant. We discussed the scheme for making Montacute into a furnished museum, or rather country house. He is very enthusiastic, and will be chairman of a small sub-committee. He is intelligent, with the right ideas, not a highbrow, and not - for once - a peer. I drove straight to Hampstead, to Fenton House, which belongs to Lady Binning, an elderly, delicate, hot-housey lady. Fenton House was built in 1693 of beautiful red brick and has wrought-iron gates of the period. It is large for London, and has a large walled garden. Much of the pine wainscoting has been stripped by Lady Binning. She intends to leave her excellent furniture, and wishes the house to be a museum, but I feel it ought to be put to some use. Her porcelain collection is first-rate and at present bequeathed to the V & A, but she is prepared to alter her will.

She gave me tea, and we liked each other, I fancy. At the end of tea she disclosed that she was anti-democratic, very pro-German and pro-Nazi. She denied that the Germans had committed atrocities, and declared that the Jews were the root of all evil. Oh dear ! She ought to meet Tom.

John Preston came to say good-bye to me at Brooks's. He leaves for the States tomorrow. Friends come and go, for short, for long periods, and one takes it as a matter of course. Only I remain stuck, which, to use an Irishism, is unsettling.

Saturday, 23rd December

Motored Tom to Swinbrook and lunched in Lady Redesdale's cottage. Bobo was there. She has become rather plain and fat, and says she weighs 13½ stone. Her mind is that of a sophisticated child, and she is still very amusing in that Mitford manner, whlch is not everyone's taste, but is certainly mine. She talked a little about the Führer, as though she still admired him, and was very disapproving of the zest with which the British press records the bombing of German cities. Being with her made me sad, for I love this family, and I see no future for Bobo but a gradually dissolving fantasy existence.

I continued to Gloucester, picking up on the way a drunk and dissatisfied tramp. Along the wilder road above Cheltenham I felt a little frightened of him. I turned him out in Gloucester and gave him half a crown. Called on the Dean and inspected the Old Raven Tavern, a miserable, dilapidated, half-timbered building, once the home of the Hoare family, some of whom migrated thence to the U.S.A. in the Mayflower. The N.T. has prematurely consented to accept this inn, but I query the propriety of doing so. I attended a 4 o'clock service in the Cathedral and the distribution of children's presents from a Christmas tree at the west end, a moving ceremony. Then had tea with the Dean and Mrs. Costley-White, who have left the Deanery for a smaller, Georgian house in the Close.

Wednesday, 27th December

All this Christmastide my father has been perfectly charming, and companionable. I believe that by taking the initiative and showing a sympathy for his not inconsiderable difficulties, which I ought to have done years ago, I may at last have broken down his suspicion and reserve. At least I hope so.

I left Wickhamford after breakfast and reached Swinbrook at 10.30. Lady Redesdale gave us sherry and cake. Bobo made Tom laugh a great deal. He is perfectly sweet and patient with her. Indeed with those of whom he is fond his manner is irresistible. He said good-bye to his mother, who was brave and good about his departure, which he told me might be for three years. An extremely frosty morning, the air glacial, and all living things arrested. The sun came out once and made the trees, swathed in hoar frost, glitter like fairy godmothers in the pantomime. At Oxford I stopped to look at some seventeenth-century lacquer furniture which Mrs. Price offers us, together with some early needlework hangings. We lunched off bread and butter and cake, en route. Tom such a good companion. He is my oldest friend, whom I first met in 1919, and have loved from that moment onwards.

Friday, 29th December

Peter Watson lunched at Brooks's. He said Cyril Connolly's book was too subjective to be first-rate, although Cyril considers it quite objective. It is the brilliant production of a disappointed, uncreative critic, approaching 40, who is frightfully ugly.

Sunday, 31st December

Lunched with Keith Miller-Jones and Tom. Tom never addressed one word to Keith who thought him morose and rude. Tom kept repeating, as though to himself, but I suppose they were addressed to me, Hermione Baddeley's not very funny jokes in the pantomime we went to yesterday afternoon. Nevertheless he wanted to pay for the three of us, saying that he must get rid of his money for on active service there is absolutely no way of spending it. But we would not allow this. Keith was resolute, which is not surprising.

At 7.30 according to plan I went to Lady Moray's house where Tom was. He was anxious for me to meet her; and I am glad I have met her. She is well dressed, very pretty, with a creamy complexion and golden ringlets of hair through which she runs her fingers. She has the slightly croaky and caressing voice of the cosmopolitan American woman. She evidently brings the best out of Tom. He accompanied me downstairs, and I said good-bye to him on the doorstep of Hans Place.

Dined at the Chaplins'. Lady Kenmare, James and Derek Hill there. Anthony talked marvellous uproarious nonsense for two hours about a bogus Constable he had bought, purporting to be of Willy Lott's, Tilly Losch's cottage he called it. James and I left at 11.20. We walked in the moonlight. At Hyde Park Corner we heard a crash, followed by the roar of a rocket that made our hearts beat. Then we laughed. Just before midnight I left him at Sloane Square station and continued homewards. Crowds were singing in the square like zanies. There were sounds of merriment from lighted windows. They seemed forced to me. There were no church bells, and for the first time I did not feel left out, nostalgic or particularly sad. Merely indifferent to it all.

1945

The year has opened in a melancholy way. Tom has gone to Burma and James to Washington. The V2 rockets have begun again to some tune. One fell on Tuesday morning with a terrific explosion and roar on the eastern wing of Wren's Chelsea Hospital, completely wrecking it and breaking windows for miles around. In the afternoon I walked down St. Leonard's Terrace and asked after Logan. He was in bed, but he and the servants were unhurt. All his windows on both sides of the house were smashed, doors wrenched off, both outer and inner; and partitions and ceilings down. Much of his furniture was destroyed. Yesterday rockets fell like autumn leaves, and between dinner and midnight there were six near our house. Miss P. and I were terrified. I put every china ornament away in cupboards. The V2 has become far more alarming than the V1, quite contrary to what I thought at first, because it gives no warning sound. One finds oneself waiting for it, and jumps out of one's skin at the slightest bang or unexpected noise like a car backfire or even a door slam.

Jamesey sailed yesterday. On Wednesday we drank whisky at the Allies Club and with much affection pledged a renewal of friendship and confidences. We agreed that during last year there had been a coolness.

Last Saturday Major Benton Fletcher died suddenly at no. 3 Cheyne Walk. He was found fully clothed on his bed on Sunday morning. I was called. He was evidently in process of cooking something in a saucepan on an electric ring. The saucepan had burnt into an unrecognizable tangle of metal, but did not set the room on fire. Benton Fletcher was lying hunched up, as if frozen stiff. Indeed I believe he may have died of the cold, for he would not spend a penny on heating. The neighbour said to me it would be only decent for us to lay him flat. I did not like the grisly prospect. We tried. It was impossible to bend the limbs and straighten him. All the while there were those glazed and staring eyes. I felt sick, and said to myself, 'Give me V2s every minute rather than a repetition of this experience.'

At first it was thought there might have to be an inquest. As there was absolutely nobody to take matters in hand I had to arrange about the post mortem, the funeral, and caretaking of the house. I went through all his papers. He had hardly any personal belongings and only very few clothes. He lived entirely alone, with no one even to clean for him, in great dirt and squalor. This sort of death is a bourgeois business. I only hope I die in splendour. I want my body to be burned immediately on a pyre, not at

Golders Green, preferably at Wickhamford, close to the church, and my ashes to be scattered there. Then an enormous marble monument, two, three storeys in height, to be erected in the nave above our pew, with a lengthy epitaph in complicated Latin, so that the stranger reading it will not make head or tail of whom it commemorates, or what it means. It must be beautiful.

Saturday, 6th January

The rockets keep on falling, chiefly round the river, which I am told is their guide. There is little doubt, so the Chelsea people maintain, that they are getting their eye in. But they have no eye, and surely no mind either, being launched hundreds of miles away. Certainly they are increasing. They make my windows rattle in a horrible sort of concussion, which is disturbing. No anti-aircraft device can stop, or arrest them. Therefore, if the war continues through this year I do not see how, considering their number and wide range, they can fail to get most of us in the end. They are perpetual swords of Damocles over the head.

At 7.30 Lieutenant George Dix U.S.A. Navy came for a drink. Nice. At 10 o'clock John Sutro took me to a film drinking party. It was hellish; thick smoke, stifling heat and everyone talking at cross purposes at top speed. Noël Coward there, red in the face, assertive, middle-aged and middle-class. I left at 11.

Sunday, 7th January

I picked up John Wilton and drove him to Audley End. I like his quiet intelligence and his taste in things and people, which concurs with mine. Lord Braybrooke met us at Audley End which was perishingly cold. We had a sandwich luncheon in the lodge over a fire which was not hot enough. The troops are out of the house which has barely suffered from them, and is quite clean. John liked it very much, but in Lord B.'s presence was shy and never once spoke of what was in his mind. I felt that Lord B. was nonplussed. However, on the way home J.W. opened up and suggested buying the house, endowing it and living in it. It would be too wonderful to be true. He stayed to dinner and talked till 11 when I went firewatching.

Tuesday, 7th January

At 11.30 Matheson and I drove to Brompton Cemetery to pay our last respects to Major Benton Fletcher's remains. Deep snow lying, and intense cold. I wore a thick pair of snow boots over my shoes, and thus clad braved the snow and slush. But feet so unnaturally gigantic that I kept tripping up over my toes, and once dangerously near the grave's edge. At the chapel no

one but ourselves, a nephew by marriage, and Roger Quilter the composer, his only friend, who appeared grief-stricken. We watched the old
man, who had had so many acquaintances, lowered lonely into his grave.
We promptly turned and left him to his own devices. Oh, the cruelty of it
all. The nephew told me that before 1914 Benton Fletcher's name was to
be seen at the end of every list of dinner parties, and balls, in *The Times*.
He quarrelled with nearly everyone but me, and died unloved, neglected,
and mourned by Mr. Quilter.

Wednesday, 10th January

A girl came to see me in the office this afternoon ostensibly to talk about
Manoeline architecture, and to seek my advice on a thesis she is writing at
the Polytechnic. She walked into the room, dressed to kill, draped in gold
chains and bangles, her fingers covered with flashy rings, smoking from a
long, gold cigarette holder (a thing I have not seen before), and was
wearing rimless pince-nez. She knew nothing about the Manoeline, or
even the subject she is writing about, which apparently is not architecture
at all. None of these vacuities would have mattered, had it not been for the
pince-nez. It was with difficulty that I got rid of her.

Thursday, 11th January

The cold persists. It is appalling, and I have run out of anthracite. I only
have two bucketfuls of coal left. I ordered 10 cwt. of anthracite, my first
order since March of last year, in November. It has not been delivered yet.
I was to have gone to Kiplin in Yorkshire today. Thank goodness the visit
was put off by Miss [Bridget] Talbot who has a chill.

John Philipps lunched. He says he is mad on farming his own land and
studies the cow sheets night and morning. The war has made him as interested in cows as he used to be in William Kent. We went and bought beautiful leather waistcoats in Turnbull & Asser's.

Had tea at Emerald's, after the office shut. Mr. Partridge was brought in.
E. tried, I like to think, to put him at his ease, but her thin manner over-
laid an inclination to show him the social differences. She introduced him
to us all in turn: 'Princess Kallimachi, who lives at the Ritz: Lady Kemsley,
whose husband owns all the newspapers: Mr. Peter Hesketh, who owns a
whole town: and Mr. L.-M., head of the National Trust, who looks after
all the public houses.'

Saturday, 13th January

Yesterday I resolved not to be disagreeable and cross, or rude, or to show
pique, envy, and malice. The day went fairly well, for I was at home most
of it, though I was not too pleasant to poor Miss P., who has a cold, and

will sniff. But this morning in the office I was distinctly unpleasant to Matheson in complaining that the agents never came into the office on Saturdays.

Lunched at the Argentine Embassy in Belgrave Square. The Ambassador is charming and cultivated, and Madame Cárcano no less so. Peter Quennell was there and Jakey Astor, who has just married Chikita Cárcano. I had been asked to help them find a house, but they were so vague as to what kind and date of house they wanted, and where it was to be, not seeming to know whether it was to be large or small, in Scotland or in England, that I gave up.

The Education Officer of the Cambridgeshire County Council called this morning about Audley End, and is convening a meeting of representatives of other East Anglian county councils, which he wants me to attend. His interest seems unfeigned. This may spur John Wilton to make up his mind. He dined at Brooks's. He is complaisant and will agree to eat what one suggests, drink what one suggests, and do what one suggests. Yet I feel there is a will of iron underneath, which if one struck it would send out sparks and dent the offending instrument. His is one of the most curious minds I have come across. It resembles the Princesse de Polignac's - questioning, cautious, non-committal, tentative, then - crash! out comes a devastating bomb, but muffled, for he seldom raises his voice; nor did she. Nothing escapes him, and his memory is alarming. He is acutely observant like Cecil Beaton. Every blemish of others is recorded on that photographic retina. If he could write he would be a great novelist in the George Sand manner. Or is he just a Disraelian young duke, Byronically moody and damned? He seems determined to take Audley End, and has steeped himself in the history of the Nevilles. We drank at Brooks's till midnight, then went to Cheyne Walk in spite of my warnings that there was no fire, the anthracite not having arrived, and only a handful of coal dust left. We lit the coal dust with difficulty and drank tea. At 2 there was a siren and four flying bombs shook my windows. At 3 John Wilton left in a hired car.

Sunday, 14th January

Slept till 10 and breakfasted at 11. Nancy lunched at the Ritz. She was distressed by Simon Elwes's sudden illness. He returned on Friday after three years in India. Spent Saturday playing very happily with his children. At dinner felt sick and went to bed. At 2 his wife rang up Nancy to say he had had a stroke and was dying. This morning not expected to live. Peter astonished Nancy by being quite indifferent. He said he had never admired his character and that his wife, Peter's sister, would be provided for. Peter is a horror.

A wonderful concert in the Albert Hall, B.B.C. orchestra, Boult conducting. The Rachmaninoff concerto with Moiseiwitch at the piano. Brahms symphony inspiriting. Lady Kenmare was in Emerald's box, wearing a little hat of strawberry feathers, as it were entwined in her grey hair. She looked too beautiful for words.

Michael Rosse came back this evening on leave from Holland. At 6 I went to Bridget's flat. Anne was in a great state and fluster, awaiting him. Soon Michael telephoned that he was on the way, so the assembled party mostly dispersed, I among them. At midnight Anne and Michael rang me up to say I should have stayed, but I thought I had done the discreet thing. I dined at Brooks's because it was too cold to stay at home without fuel of any sort.

Thursday, 18th January

Grandy Jersey lunched with me. He wishes to hold up the Osterley negotiations until the County Council have consented to purchase the land belonging to his trustees. But this they have said they will not do. However, he has met Pepler at the Ministry through me, and will follow his advice. He took me to Müntzer in Albemarle Street, a decorating firm he has bought and is now running. He wishes, he says, to make money. It seems to me a sure way of losing it. I like Grandy. He is inscrutable, but well-intentioned.

Friday, 19th January

Heywood Hill lunched with me. He is so shy that, because I was not in the club precisely at 12.50 and because he is a corporal in uniform, rather than wait he went away. Eddy, whom I met in a bus lunched with us too, for Heywood returned later. Heywood is rather like John Wilton in that he appears to lack self-confidence, and is exceedingly gentle in manner, but has underneath a will of iron. He and I went to the Wildenstein Gallery to see Derek Hill's pictures.

Saturday, 20th January

It is so appallingly cold – snowing again and freezing – that I cannot, without anthracite, face my room in Cheyne Walk. Went to Brooks's and there worked before the fire, interrupted at times by Sir Warren Fisher's chat about the superiority of Brooks's to all other clubs. At 3.45 I set out to walk in the snow. In Westminster Abbey I found Robert Adam's grave slab in the south transept. It is simple and worn by the feet which have trampled over it these 150 years. There is no other memorial or monument to him, whereas there are tablets to Wyatt and Taylor, who are less distinguished architects. I looked at many monuments. How dirty they

are. How wonderful though. They are history. The Abbey enshrines
England's history. It is a volume of a thousand pages. England's most
precious sanctum. How cumbersome Charles James Fox's oversize monument is, and how baroque are some of Gibbs's to unknown persons.
Roubiliac's to the Duke of Argyll is the noblest, with the most panache of
them all.

I had a drink with John Philipps. He showed me Beatrix Potter's
drawing of 'Johnnie the town mouse' and said, 'That's me to the life. I am
just like that. I saw a woman in the street the other day, just like that too.
So I went up to her and said, "You are a mouse. You ought to have married
me."' Whenever I see one of these delicious drawings I find it hard to reconcile the Mrs. Heelis I met with the Beatrix Potter who conceived and
produced them. For Mrs. Heelis was an unbending, masculine, stalwart
woman, with an acute business sense. She was rather tart with her dim
husband and adored her sheep, not for sentimental Beatrix Potter reasons
but for hard cash Heelis ones. She drove bargains with farmers at sales and
the National Trust over her benefactions.

Sunday, 21st January

At the Albert Hall concert I roughed out some notes for the letter John
Wilton is to send to me at the National Trust. At tea in Brooks's he took
pen and paper, and made me dictate word for word his letter to me, which
he copied down. From nothing did he dissent. This almost embarrassed me
as though, I told him, I were a Jewish moneylender making him sign away
his birthright.

Tuesday, 23rd January

Madame Massigli is very beguiling with her Roman nose and profile. She
dresses beautifully, with true French chic. The Ambassador is tall and jet
black. It always amuses me how ambassadors at dinner parties will agree in
heartfelt tones with our views on the world situation; then can go home
and straightway declare war upon us. The Massiglis motored me in their
luxurious car as far as Sloane Street. We parted with expressions of the most
fervent mutual esteem, and promises to meet continually. Shall I ever see
them again? I walked home.

Wednesday, 24th January

A terrible day. Arctic cold. I caught the 9.40 a.m. from King's Cross, reaching Darlington at 4. Changed for Scorton, arriving at 4.45. Already getting
dark, and a leaden, snow-filled sky of the most ominous description, the
silence promising the blackest frost. There was no car to meet me at the
station, somewhat to my surprise. Consequently I walked two miles from

the station to the village, carrying my bags. My hands were numb with cold. On reaching a garage and thawing them before a fire, they hurt so badly I feared they were frostbitten. A taxi drove me to Kiplin Hall, put me down and drove away. There was no Miss Talbot who had asked me to stay. I trudged round the empty house, in which not a glimmer of light was to be seen, and could not get inside. What I did see in the twilight was enough to convince me that this house was not acceptable. The centre part, the brickwork and the eccentric towers, almost French Renaissance in plan, were interesting. But there was too much nineteenth-century alteration and addition.

I chased round the village enquiring for Miss Talbot. Finally a friend of hers told me she had telegraphed that she was not coming down from London after all. I was furious, and returned to Darlington. Since I could get no room in any hotel, I decided to catch the 7.50 p.m. back to London. In the train there was no heating, and I reached King's Cross at 3.35 a.m. frozen to the very marrow. There were no taxis at that hour, and there was no alternative to walking with my bags to the far end of Cheyne Walk. Got home, in my wet and clammy clothes at 5.30. As I tried to force a comb through my hair, which was stiff with hoar frost, I cursed that wretched Miss Talbot.

Friday, 26th January

I believe this to be the coldest spell England has experienced for fifty years. Everything is frozen stiff. People are suffering tortures from cold, without enough fuel. Last night at home, squatting under layers of coats and rugs I could not get warm enough to work, so went to bed in my clothes.

Today I went to a late tea with Emerald. The Dorchester was beautifully heated, yet Emerald was throwing wads of newspaper into an empty grate, setting matches to them and murmuring that London was as deprived as Paris, and we were heroes. She may say this with some justice by next winter.

Saturday, 27th January

Walked to the Adelphi to see what, if anything, remained of Adam's work there. Nothing to speak of. Just the butt-ends of some buildings with the familiar wide pilaster bands of terracotta, disporting huge honeysuckle emblems. What a monstrous abomination of a building the new Adelphi block is. Utterly and absolutely without merit. While I was at Charing Cross there was a terrific V2 explosion. It sounded right in my ear. I learned afterwards that many people in widely scattered parts of London thought the same thing.

Dined at the Étoile. Cyril Connolly sat at the next table. He said he came back from Paris two hours ago; that in Paris you felt the French were living, whereas in London you knew the English were dead. Poor English!

Sunday, 28th January

The appalling cold and frost persisting, I live and work, when not in the office, in Brooks's, only returning to Cheyne Walk to sleep. I dined excellently with Colin Agnew, a dear little, tiny man, who lives for pictures and nothing else, except his friends, of whom he has many.

Monday, 29th January

Never read the diaries or impressions of men who have written in the fear of death, for their records cannot be honest.

The thaw having set in, our pipes burst, and we are without water, if we disregard the condensation pouring from the walls. For the past fortnight the pipes have been frozen and out of action. Which predicament is the worse? At any rate we are warmer now, thank God.

Wednesday, 31st January

Dr. Wittkower of the Warburg Institute lunched at Brooks's. He is so hesitant, and so burbling in that irritating German accent that I can barely listen to what he says. Yet he is a great scholar. Within that huge head one senses, almost sees, cavern after cavern crammed with documents in German, French, Italian and English, and rolled parchments covered in the dust and must of ages. He told me a lot about the Institute and his own book about Lord Burlington. He offers any amount of help, and will put numerous books of reference at my disposal at Denham, where the Institute staff is living during the war. A kind and generous man, ready to impart information from his great store. This is by no means always the case with scholars. In return, I have helped him a little by introducing him to Lord Spencer and persuading that difficult nobleman to put the Althorp papers at his disposal.

At 2.30 to Batsford's where, with Mr. Harry Batsford and Charles Fry I made a final selection of illustrations. Mr. B. is the dirtiest, yet the sweetest old person I ever saw. He smokes, and coughs, and shakes incessantly, while the cigarette ash spills down his front, and not only ash. Saliva also. His eccentricities are Dickensian. He adores cats, and fills his coat pockets with the heads, tails and entrails of fish. As he stumbles down the pavements he distributes these remnants to the congregating cats. The scene is like the Pied Piper of Hamlin. The smell of his clothes is overpowering. Charles is devoted to him.

Saturday, 3rd February

This morning in the office I typed out a memorandum I composed in the train yesterday with much care and thought, suggesting that the museum aspect – for lack of a better phrase – of the Trust's work should be recognized to be as important as the agents', solicitors' and accountants' departments now are; suggesting that, instead of Country Houses Secretary, a foolish title, there should be a chief curator or some such officer, responsible to a new Committee of Taste. I feel very strongly on the subject, and pretty confident that Esher, who is my consistent ally, will agree.

I joined Rory's party for a farce, called *Three's a Family*, American nonsense about babies, nappies and a stooge aunt. Quite funny. English comedians make the mistake of laughing at their own and each other's jokes, to show the dense audience when they ought to be amused. It is like putting too many apostrophes after facetious sentences in a letter. We dined at Rory's house.

Monday, 5th February

Trained to Chippenham and motored to Lacock where I joined Eardley and Mr. Gordon Hake, the architect. He has long white hair and wears a cape and sombrero. A polite man, with, I think, good taste and ideas. On the way back I got into conversation with a radiant young Air Force officer on the platform at Chippenham. He was a dentist, and told me that you never pulled a tooth out; you pushed it down on either side, and it popped out. I was too late for Sibyl's Ordinary.

Tuesday, 6th February

Went to see Harold after 6. He was very upset by the death of his great friend, Robert Bernays, M.P., in an aeroplane crash. He said there had been another aeroplane crash in which the Prime Minister's staff en route to the meeting of the Big Three, were involved. They cannot release the news yet. Harold told me that Ben is better but still in hospital in Italy. His spine is affected by his motor accident and he is encased up to the chin in plaster of Paris. His beard causes him much discomfort.

Wednesday, 7th February

At a meeting of the Montacute Committee Bertie Abdy stunned the members by denouncing the purposes for which we were met. He said, 'We can't possibly let the public inside a house with valuable works of art. They smell.' With much tact the chairman, Sir Geoffrey Cox, disregarded this observation, as though it had not been made, and proceeded with the next item on the agenda.

Pauly Sudley dined with me. He is very odd indeed. He said his whole life was tormented by guilt over not liking what he ought to like. I said, 'But there should be no such thing as "ought" in your case.' Then he said he could not travel by train, or cross the Channel, two complexes he was unable to overcome.

Thursday, 8th February

Had a late tea with Logan, who was less rambling and more lucid. Yet some of his remarks were quite irrational. He said all the aristocracy took bribes and commissions in selling their possessions to each other; that one of the national museum directors had bought some illuminated manuscripts from a bishop's wife, ostensibly for his museum, and sold them elsewhere at great profit to himself. He could prove it, he stoutly maintained.

Friday, 9th February

By train to Bramber to look at the Castle, which the Trust is urged to buy. All that remains is a high piece of Norman gatehouse, and some flint ramparts. I took a bus to Brighton and looked at Single Speech Hamilton's house by Adam on the Steyne. It has an apsidal library with vaulted ceiling, and a rather pretty little octagonal boudoir behind a square, coved hall.

I dined with the Moores. Bewitching Mrs. Fellowes arranged that I should take her to Coleshill next Saturday week, which will doubtless involve us in troubles all round. The Argentine Ambassador said that none of us knows in the least what the Russians intend to do – ever; that when de Gaulle went to conclude the Franco-Russian treaty, and everything was tied up and settled for signature, Stalin suddenly announced, pen in hand, 'You must of course agree to recognize the Lublin government, or I shall not sign.' De Gaulle objected that such a condition had never been part of the bargain. Thereupon they parted, and the treaty was not signed. Twenty-four hours later Stalin asked for de Gaulle, and signed then and there. No reference to Lublin was even made by him. Alan Lennox-Boyd was saying last night that the Allies don't know the strength of the Russian Air Force, or if they even have any civil planes in existence. They know nothing about Russia at all. What amazes me is how the Allies can ever have imagined they would be treated like civilized persons by these bloody barbarians. How I wish to God we were fighting against them, and not with them.

Sunday, 11th February

I dined last night and lunched again today with Desmond Shawe-Taylor and Eddy Sackville-West at Brooks's. The latter wishes to be buried in the Sackville vault at Withyham, amongst the velvet palls and silver coroneted coffins of his eighteenth-century ancestors. He went there the other day – 'just for fun' – with his father. His uncle lies there on a trestle.

I was taken last night to a *louche* club. What we saw going on was disturbing in general and disgusting in particular. There is something horribly genteel about brothels and their equivalents. Male and female harlots talk politely about the weather, and their talk, for they have no conversation, is laced with prurient innuendoes and punctuated with adolescent giggles. Why the hell don't they get down to business straight away, and hold out their hands for the notes? Instead they perch like suburban housewives on the edge of their stools, prolonging the ghastly farce as though to make believe they are respectable dowagers on gilt chairs in a Mayfair ballroom. I walked home alone, sickened and unsatisfied.

Monday, 12th February

Meeting day. Lord Esher told me how much he agreed with my memo about the aesthetic aspect of the Trust's work, and did not agree with the Secretary's proposal that my department should be subordinate to the agents'.

Tuesday, 13th February

Joan Moore lunched with me. She read me extracts of a letter from Jamesey. We both agreed he was one of the very best letter-writers – I said the best of our age. She is devoted to him, yet far too clever to be taken in by his wicked little blandishments.

To a lecture at the R.I.B.A. given by Goodhart-Rendel on Lutyens. Very good indeed, in spite of his speaking too fast, and lisping. He convinced his audience that Lutyens was an architect of the highest calibre, *vide* his Viceroy's House at Delhi, and designs for Liverpool Cathedral, with its medley of piers in the nave and huge space under the dome. Anstey said that Lutyens would take his place among the immortal dome builders, Michelangelo and Wren. Gerry Wellington proposed a neat vote of thanks in a very charming, ducal manner. Eddie Marsh accompanied me back to Brooks's and afterwards to the Dorchester for Sibyl's Ordinary. At my table were five men, all members of Brooks's. I sat next to Olga Lynn and Lord Gage. Enjoyable dinner. Olga Lynn told me she suffered from diabetes and took an injection every morning at 8; that two generous friends in this room gave her large sums of money every Christmas, and there was no feeling of obligation. We agreed that the very rich never derived the same joys as the rather poor, like ourselves. Lord Gage talked of schoolmasters and their inhumanity. Lady Aberconway said the Parisian poor were fishing for starving cats from tenement blocks with a line, and a hook at the end attached to a bit of fish. They hoisted up the cats and ate them.

Wednesday, 14th February

I set my alarum for 7 o'clock, and the inevitable consequence was that I slept very badly, waiting for the damned thing to go off. Lord Braybrooke met me at Saffron Walden station, his humble little Ford car sitting under the grand 1840 portico, erected for the benefit of his forebears' carriage and pair. With rude spluttering sounds as of an amplified sewing-machine, the Ford lurched from the portico under the supercilious gaze of one ancient porter, lolling against the wall. We drove to Audley End. After a talk, Sisson joined us. We walked and motored round the boundary which Lord B. proposes selling to J. Wilton. I said I thought the land across the road, including the Adam round temple, ought to be included. We had a picnic luncheon in the lodge. Sisson, the steward and I went over the house. This time so much of it struck me as of poor quality: the gloomy rooms in the North wing; all the 1825 'Jacobean' state-rooms in the South wing, including the 1785 state bedrooms by Rebecca.

I was home soon after 6. At 7 the doorbell rang, and there was my father who had called unannounced in a taxi. We welcomed him and Miss P. gave us dinner in the kitchen. He told me how my grandfather, on inheriting Crompton Hall, sent every single piece of eighteenth-century furniture to Druce's to be refashioned, as well as the priceless oak beds. All of them were ruined by Druce. The oak four-posters, which had been in the Crompton family for generations untouched, were made into buffets, pedestals for aspidistras and ferns, and overmantels for Ribbesford. My grandfather 'improved' Crompton itself in the most ghastly way. My father was delightful, because totally relaxed. When it was time for him to go no taxi was obtainable. I walked with him to the bus stop, for I don't think he has ever been in a bus in his life. Immediately the bus drew up there was a flash, and the terrific explosion of a rocket.

Friday, 16th February

George Dix is a well-bred, well-mannered, civilized American; and he is direct. He has a craze for papier mâché, having bought several good early trays, an inkstand by Clay, a maker in Covent Garden, and a number of chairs, which I don't find very pretty; also two rare vases, positively ugly. He has a number of Edward Lear water-colour sketches, all dated 1854 with the time of day, viz. '8 a.m.' and faint descriptions, 'Rocks', 'Pale lemon sky' pencilled in. We dined at the Reform Club not too badly, and talked for hours. I walked home, arriving at 3.20 a.m.

Saturday, 17th February

In talking to Garrett Moore I made a hideous gaffe by reading to him part of a letter from James in which he wrote that Garrett was the reincarnation of Lord Fawn. When I got home I made two discoveries, one – that Lord Fawn was a foolish, pompous ass, and two – that Jamesey had written that Garrett was the antithesis of Lord Fawn. Now should I, or shouldn't I telephone to explain? Decided that I might make matters worse by doing so. James would be furious with me, because he is devoted to the Moores. Moral – never read to friends parts of a letter about them from a mutual friend. Read either the whole thing or nothing. Nothing is better.

After lunching I went to Lansdowne House. I need make no comment on the mess made of the exterior. The interior is worse. Of poor Adam's work, what has been allowed to remain, is now a travesty. The façade has been pushed back one room's width, so that the glorious entrance hall and the ante-room no longer exist. The bow room is left, but the niches have been ruthlessly cut into disproportionate openings. The room-for-company-before-dinner seems to survive, although I suspect that the apsidal end of the ante-room has been stuck haphazard on to the east end of this room. The two rotundas at the end of Smirke's picture gallery have been hacked about, and galleries introduced. The whole maelstrom is a deplorable instance of thirtyish decadence – total lack of respect for great architecture of the past, and total lack of confidence in that of the present. The result a shamefully hideous mess and muddle.

Sunday, 18th February

The singing in the Oratory this morning moved me to noble aspirations. This is, I suppose, the motive of the Roman liturgy, as it is the essence of the Christian teaching. I took the underground to Richmond, and walked across the desolate green, made less green than it should be by the concrete shelters, to the Old Palace where the Jerseys now live. After luncheon Grandy took me to Syon.

The Duke of Northumberland was away and his nice housekeeper showed us round. The Doric double cube hall is a masterpiece of vigour. The twisted columns of the lower windows upon fat, writhing console scrolls, the brawny ceiling ribs, and above all the curvature of end apses and steps make this monumental room alive. A large chunk of plaster has just fallen from the ceiling. The Vestibule is as lovely as I imagined, with its incredibly vivid colours, yellow, red and blue. Two of the gold figures from the entablature have fallen and smashed to pieces, and there are cracks in the scagliola floor. Every window in the house has been smashed by bombs. The buzz bombs last summer did the worst damage. The famous verde antique columns of this room are swathed in bandages to protect them, and so cannot be seen at all. Next comes the Eating Room, the chimneypieces all boarded up. Apses and screens again here. The Cipriani *chiaroscuros* are thin and feeble; the ceiling early Adam. The Red Drawing

Room must be magnificent. The gorgeous rose damask walls are covered in sheets; the pier glasses boxed up. The housekeeper showed us a circular painted rosette of Angelica Kauffmann that has fallen from the ceiling owing to an upstairs bath overflowing. It is painted on parchment. On the underside are the remains of a white paste which stuck it to the ceiling. The rosette looked atrociously executed, when held in the hand. A child could have painted it.

The long Gallery is of course a *tour de force*. If one may criticize, it is too fussy. Adam was very clever in accentuating the gallery's width, which is a mere fourteen feet, by his ceiling design, contrived to appear as though part only of a continuous larger design. In the square closet the glass panels and canvases have been removed for safety. The birdcage from the round closet has also been put away. Several canvases from the Gallery panels have been blown out. They are of very indifferent workmanship. Patches of damp have appeared on the looking-glasses, for there is no central heating at all. But there is electric light. We climbed on to the lead roof where Grandy photographed me under the Percy lion. As far as the eyes can see there are trees, and Kew Gardens across the river. Syon is more parklike than Osterley. We saw the vaulted crypt, now full of pictures from Albury, and Fowler's charming conservatory with glass dome, still intact. It was a beautiful, sunny spring afternoon, and the sun on the lead roof positively radiated warmth – the first warm day since last May.

We returned to Richmond for tea, having looked at the outside of Asgill House and of Trumpeter's House, which Grandy is about to rent. Virginia is very gentle and appealing. She is extremely shortsighted and has to wear spectacles, which is a pity. She has lovely fair skin, white teeth and a neat figure.

After tea I called, by pre-arrangement upon Aunt Katie, my grand-father's sister, the sole survivor of that large family. My grandfather, born in 1847, was a second son, so Aunt Katie must be about 90. She is very blind and quiet, but distinguished and sedate. She hardly uttered, and derived no pleasure from my visit. She was somewhat out of humour and growled at her companion for knocking against her chair. 'For the last time I must ask you not to do that,' she barked. She did however tell me she was brought up at Clarksfield Lees, and the view across the valley, though magnificent in her day, looked upon distant factory chimneys.

Monday, 19th February

Today I bought a pair of gunmetal and ormolu Regency candlesticks and a pair of Copenhagen fruitstands of the same date, in gold and blue, very pretty – all for £21.

Tuesday, 20th February

Charles Fry and I went to High Wycombe by train. He is not a congenial travelling companion. Like Mr. Harry Batsford, he chain-smokes, splutters and coughs at every breath. He stops for gin or whisky at every step. He loses his temper with waitresses at luncheon and in the tobacconist's shop. He rushed through High Wycombe church, not stopping to admire the Carlini monument. At West Wycombe he rushed round the house. Poor Mrs. Eaton, whom I am very fond of, was rushed off her poor old legs. The house has been shaken by the flying bomb which fell at Hughenden last summer. The sun was shining. How beautiful it was on the colonnade. Charles conceded that the house was the theatrical creation of an amateur with good taste. He would not stay to tea because he wanted to go to George Dix's cocktail party. We returned hurriedly to London. The great draw at this party was the Duchess of Richmond, a very sweet, simple, old lady. She talked affably to Charles and me about West Wycombe, then about tripe, animals' intestines, and haggis. I really think Charles is Satan. He makes me say the most outrageous things, and even makes a dear old duchess talk about brutish indelicacies.

Wednesday, 21st February

George Dix took me into no. 9 Clifford Street. It was once a great town house, called Clarendon House. It is now divided into tailors' shops. An extraordinary discovery, a huge staircase hall of late seventeenth-century date, a double flight staircase with Ionic columns and thick balusters of acanthus leaves. A ribbed plaster ceiling over all, and pedimented door-cases, like Coleshill in miniature.

I took the train to Richmond and walked to Ham House. Sir Lyonel is now aged 91; young Lyonel is 60. The old man is courteous and charming, rather deaf, but very sprightly and straight. He wears an old-fashioned black cravat. Lady Tollemache looks younger, but they were married in 1881. This time conversation took a more positive turn. As at Osterley, so here we must ask the Government or the London County Council for help. Ham is superb, but far more impracticable than most great houses. Quite impossible as a private residence these days, and not suited to any institutional use. The first floor is all state-rooms; the second all intercommunicating rooms. The attic floor not fit for animals, far less for modern servants, when obtainable. The basement vast, dark and rambling. All the best pictures and furniture are away in the country. I had tea with the family and then walked round the garden with young Lyonel. Rather touching, but oh what an unhappy man. All of them seem hopelessly defeatist, anti-Government, anti-people, and anti-world. More so than me really. Of course their difficulties are formidable, but unlike the French aristocracy the English usually manage to adapt themselves to current trends, and play a leading rôle in the end, if only to survive.

Thursday, 22nd February

I went to see Dame Una, in bed with a slight fever. She looked very ill and pale, her poor face thin and her grey hair springing from cadaverous temples. I am so frightened that she may not live long; for this would devastate Jamesey. She was full of chatter and gossip notwithstanding, and much amused by the naïveté of the American young. Her bedroom was very severe, like a hospital ward. A hard modern bed, with no yield about it.

Friday, 23rd February

Took an early train to Bookham, arriving 9.30. I walked to Polesden which is beginning to look shabby. Mlle. Liron, Mrs. Greville's old maid, was evidently pleased to see me. With her I am a success. She says I am the only friend she has from whom she can ask for things. Professor Richardson's gravestone to Mrs. G. is up. It looks like the top of an old-fashioned servant's trunk, half buried in the grass. It has two ribs protruding from it, resembling those wooden supporting struts which the lids of such trunks used to have.

Sunday, 25th February

I dined at Emerald's. Gladwyn Jebb had been at the Yalta Conference. He said the food, and above all the wine, were superb: that Roosevelt seemed as though he were dying; that Stalin wore a fantastic uniform with a red star on the breast and monstrous epaulettes, and a thick red stripe down his trouser legs. He looked like a bear dressed up. While talking he fidgets, and when particularly emotional, walks round his desk-stand like a bear on a leash. He is very quick in all his retorts, cracks jokes and has charm, which I don't like to hear.

The dinner began badly, and I was preoccupied in trying to remember the Latin collect I learnt by heart this morning. Then Gladwyn Jebb insinuated that Emerald had made a misstatement. Emerald jumped upon him. 'You have got it wrong. Just mind your words.' She said she admired Sir Orme Sargent and pumped Jebb about him. Had he been in love? 'Good gracious, no, never.' 'Oh then, is he a homosexualist?' 'Certainly not. He is nothing of the kind.' Tony Gandarillos drove me home and said that Nancy Cunard had been to say good-bye to him. She was off to Paris. She asked if her mother looked much older. When Tony said No, she said, 'What a pity.' She said Emerald was 69, for she, aged 50, was born when Emerald was 19.

Monday, 26th February

I had tea with Lady Binning in Fenton House. She is perfectly agreeable to our keeping the house as a semi-museum, if we cannot get anyone to live in it. She said emphatically that she could not like Lord Esher, no matter how much I expostulated, because he was a Jew!

Tuesday, 27th February

Went to Emerald at 6. John Lehmann was alone with her. Presently others came in, including the Duff Coopers. Lady Diana was wearing a hat like a Tudor head-dress, square, with a veil of spots. Emerald said to Desmond MacCarthy, 'Do tell Diana how much we admire her hat.' He replied, 'I can't very well, for I have just told her how much I dislike it.' Daisy Fellowes walked in wearing a yellow satin turban, wound round the head into a twist at the top, and a jewel in it. Even she failed to look un-self-conscious. A horrid, uneasy gathering, being chivvied from the edge of one seat to another.

Wednesday, 28th February

In talking to me in the bar of the St. James's club, Charles Fry spat all over me. Like an absolute gentleman I merely laughed. He said, 'Good God!', took out his handkerchief and wiped my face. I passed it off but could have been sick. Coming home, for no reason I fell flat on my face on the Piccadilly pavement, bruised my hip and was shaken. A kind old man who was passing by, said, as he ran to help, 'Dear me, I am sorry,' tripped, and fell flat on his face likewise. I was unable to run towards him, but lay laughing, and crying with the pain, and laughing. He did not laugh.

Thursday, 1st March

I went to Brighton and lunched with Goodhart-Rendel in his flat. In talking to, or rather lecturing one, he paces up and down the room. He is very informative about architecture, rather dogmatic, and yet not very inspiring. He owns all the gardens and foreshore terraces of Sussex Gardens at Kemp Town, built by an architect called Charles Busby for Kemp in the 1830s. It is an ambitious and splendid layout, perhaps unique of its kind, although no individual house is of high account. It would be a new departure for the Trust to hold these lands.

Friday, 2nd March

Went by car to Oxford. Arrived at Lady Margaret Hall with some trepidation. Was ushered upstairs to the flat of the Principal, a plain elderly, smiling dame, Miss Greir. When she had swathed herself in an old rabbit fur coat, full of moth, we drove off together. A little beyond Chipping

Norton we ate our luncheon in the car, and discussed what it was that acti-
vated live wires within feeble constitutions. She gave instances of teachers,
philosophers and statesmen; I of architects, painters and poets. We arrived
at Cornwell, and wandered round the hamlet, lately tarted up – tastefully,
let there be no mistake – by Clough Williams-Ellis, if self-consciously. The
manor house we could not enter, for we had no permission, and it is an
A.T.S. convalescent home. I had omitted to get permission beforehand. It
is a pretty house, with a gay Georgian façade, urns (modern) on the
parapet. It faces a valley in which are canals and a pool, and beyond, a
beech-lined road. The remarkable thing about the façade is the flat
string courses, which, on reaching the windows, dip downwards, so as to
form sills, and sweep up again. A very ugly yellow-varnished front door.
A picturesque Cotswold back to the manor. We made a circuit of the
outside, having good views from each quarter. It is expensively maintained. There is much to be said for Clough's theatrical sense in this drab
age.

At 3 o'clock we drove to Daylesford, but could not see the house from
the road. It, like Adlestrop opposite, contains a huge camp of American
troops. We drove to Chastleton which is open to the public. Walked up the
drive to the front door where we pealed a great dinner bell. On payment
of 1/- each the old butler conducted us round. We were shortly joined by
a party of American officers, looking like Thomas Patch cartoons. They
smoked as they shuffled round. Only the hall and white painted oak
drawing-room were visible. There is nothing very good in the way of furniture. Bishop Juxon's chair is, I think, made up. But Charles I's bible, given
to the bishop, and the Jones family portraits are evocative relics of this
ancient home. The texture of the stone outside is very beautiful. The
famous box topiary work is weird, and rather ugly.

I left Miss Greir at Moreton-in-Marsh station and continued to
Bourton House, and had tea with Miss Bligh and her old sister, both very
sweet and both wearing red wigs. Together we prepared scones in the
kitchen which we ate in the dining-room, the old ladies running to and
fro. They refused my request that we should eat in the kitchen. Miss Bligh
showed me Major Benton Fletcher's musical instruments, which she has
stored. So did Mrs. Murray, who has another consignment at the Rectory.
She is the alarming hunting wife of the Archdeacon. She clips her 'g's and
hammers her sentences hard as though on an anvil. I got to Wickhamford
for supper.

Saturday, 3rd March

Midi and I set out on a fine and frosty morning to Pershore station. We
picked up Mr. Harry Batsford and drove to Pirton Church, which has a

fifteenth-century tower; and on to Croome. There is now an aerodrome close to the park. I disagree with James and Charles Fry who find Croome a tawdry house. The hall has the familiar Adam Doric screen, but is otherwise rococo. I noticed two very classical tables with Doric entablatures which I suppose were designed for the room. The Gallery has a Roman coffered ceiling, and some of the wall panels, meant to be in stucco, were never completed and were left in grisaille. The saloon cannot be by Adam. It is rather coarse George II work, as one can tell from the gilt picture frames. The mahogany library bookshelves with honeysuckle finials are superb.

After lunching at the Angel in Pershore we returned to Croome. Mr. Harry took photographs inside the church with an enormous box Brownie, which he propped on a tower of heavy bibles and prayer books taken from the Coventry pew. The postures of the defunct noblemen with coronets perched precariously on their marble heads are rather funny. This Gothic church, so pretty in photographs, is somewhat thin in reality. We walked down to the beautiful orangery, of which the sash frames have all been smashed. The vase and swags of fruit in the tympanum of the pediment are finely carved in high relief.

We drove to Strensham, past the castle folly (surely by Sanderson Miller, for it resembles the Hagley one). At the end of a grass-grown drive we came upon a lonely little church and pretty vicarage, perched on the edge of a steep bank above the Avon. The front door of the vicarage was opened by a witch-like housekeeper. The dilapidation and dirt of the inside were truly frightening. In an inner room Mr. Davenport, the little old vicar, with long wavy white hair, was bent over a water-colour drawing of Oxford, hand-printing a verse which he had composed, to record the scene. He said he had not been to Oxford for 22 years, or left Strensham during that time. He made an extraordinary spectacle, like a Phiz illustration of some Dickensian curiosity shop proprietor in the 1820s. The church is as dilapidated and neglected as the vicarage. But it is remarkable. It contains several monuments to the Russells, of which one, possibly by Scheemakers, is a work of art. The nave barrel ceiling is supported by tie beams, one with a huge central boss of an angel holding an open bible. There are painted panels of saints on the gallery front. The church is dark, eerie and mysterious. Mr. Harry conducted us over Strensham Court, piled high with tea chests. It is an 1840 classical house with portico, now falling to ruin. After a large tea in a pub in Ripple we put Mr. Harry into the train at Ripple station.

I interviewed Lady Margaret Sackville, a charming woman, who wants to become curator of Knole. She is a poet and has only £100 a year to live on. I foresee family embarrassments.

Sunday, 4th March

I drove Mama to Harvington Hall. She brought her two pekingeses, to which she talked dog language incessantly. Inspected four or five pieces of furniture offered to the collection. Thence to Charlecote. My mother is the most extraordinary travelling companion, for she makes friends everywhere. In asking the way at Droitwich of a man sweeping his doorstep, she got from him his life history, how much rent he was paying and how many children he had. Finally he called his wife, and the two of them sat on the step of the car stroking the dogs. At Harvington the caretaker, unsolicited, brought us tea, discussed her ailments, her son's love life and her religious beliefs.

Tuesday, 6th March

The Distillers own no. 20 St. James's Square. It has suffered badly from bombs. An oil bomb fell at the rear, burning out the Adam rooms there. The other rooms have suffered more or less; ceilings down, looking-glasses smashed. The wonderful coved room upstairs is not badly damaged.

Thursday, 8th March

I was motored by an agent from Yeovil to Trent, five miles away, where we ate sandwiches in the pub. In the afternoon we looked at the 1,200-acre estate which Mr. Cook has bought. I think there is little point in the Trust holding it because it is no more remarkable than the surrounding country in these parts. The manor house is very disappointing. It was horribly spoilt about 1912. Charles II's hiding place still survives but little else. The King spent nineteen days here after Worcester. I took the 4 o'clock train from Yeovil and got home at 10.45, very tired.

Friday, 9th March

Eardley and I walked to King's Bench Walk to a party Harold and Vita gave together, a very exceptional occasion. Harold in a gay and frolicsome mood; Vita very beautiful, regal, tall and thin, wearing a wide-brimmed hat over her eyes and smoking from a long cigarette holder. She is never frolicsome.

At Brooks's Lord Spencer told me that Professor Richardson made an excellent speech for him in Northampton, but said that all Americans were vulgar, and gave too long a dissertation on Georgian water closets. He had to keep these embellishments out of the newspaper.

Dinner at Emerald's. She showed me a portrait by Steer of a coster-monger, done in 1880. Mrs. Snow, the American, to whom she showed it, kept repeating 'My dear, what a wonderful likeness.' Emerald made me pick up a heavy marble bust of a Venus, which she stroked while saying to Cecil Beaton and me, 'You know the uniformity of these Greek sculptures is the secret of their beauty. This might be the body of a man. Just take them away [pointing at the breasts]. No, leave them. Some men have breasts like these, so they tell me. Is that true, Cecil? You ought to know. No, now don't laugh,' and so on.

Stephen Spender at Harold's party talked to me about anarchism, and said it did not work; that syndicalism could no more run a nation than a concatenation of parish councils.

Saturday, 10th March

A sunny, balmy day. I walked without an overcoat to lunch with Alice Harding at the Basque Restaurant. The Sachie Sitwells, their son Reresby and George Dix there. Sachie has old-fashioned good manners. Anecdotes fly from his lips like little birds from an open cage.

Dined with Rory and Lady Kenmare. A large party. When the women left the dining-room Beverley Baxter and Lord Margesson, formerly chief Whip and Minister for War, started talking about the recent debate on Yalta. They said it was perhaps a pity the Prime Minister claimed the Polish settlement, which they agreed was the only possible solution, to be a wise and beneficent one. Quite suddenly I became furious, and, red in the face, exclaimed, 'Beneficent, my foot! Expedient doubtless. It is a disgrace and an indictment of Parliament that only twenty-one Members had the courage of their convictions to vote against you. The Poles have every reason to feel betrayed. Our country has openly and brazenly betrayed them.' I was somewhat surprised at myself. Lord Margesson became indignant, and said, 'Look here! We must have your reasons for this allegation, etc. What would you have the Government do?' I said rather truculently, 'The allegation is borne out by the deed. What the Government ought to do is something honourable. It's not for me to dictate. I'm not a professional politician,' which was a bit lame. He said more angrily than before that politicians were just as other men. I checked myself saying what I thought of him and most of them. In the course of the argument that ensued I said the Russians were less to be trusted than the Germans, and were far more dangerous. We had got our enemies wrong, since it was peoples not systems that we were evidently fighting against. And I defended the Pope and bishops against the charge of condoning Fascism. I told them that the Pope had to put ideals before countries, and that all Christians ought to put the Church before their own country. Lord M. and the other men present were, I could see, shocked and annoyed. Not an enjoyable evening.

Monday, 12th March

In between the two meetings today I lunched with Esher, who was very outspoken in his objection to the agents' encroachment upon the aesthetes' work. He laughed mischievously and said, 'After all, L.-M., you must remember, they are only plumbers.' At this morning's meeting it was decided to extend the function of the Country Houses Committee, henceforth to be called the Historic Buildings Committee.

Thursday, 15th March

This morning and this evening we had two very close and noisy rocket explosions. There had been several during the night. The damage they are said to do is terrific. Three hundred people were killed by one in the City last week. This evening's one made a prolonged, echoing roar like a roll of thunder.

Friday, 16th March

This morning I walked from Wooton Farm up the lane to Friday Street, where Christopher Gibbs met me, and motored me to Severell's Copse. When unspoilt, Surrey landscape is rich and luxuriant like those tight, condensed water colours by Linnell. After walking through the Copse with the timber control officer, we continued to Leith Hill Place. Dr. Vaughan-Williams was there. He is rather old and muddly, but disarming and very generous. He seems only too anxious to divest himself of all mundane trappings. We walked round the house, making a list of those contents he would like to remain in the house. They consisted mostly of Wedgwood and Darwin prints and miniatures. Two great black figures on plinths, signed and dated Coade 1797. Lunched with the Gibbs family at Goddards. Good olde English down-to-earthe foode.

    Dined at the Argentine Embassy. Jacqueline Killearn, whom I haven't seen since I was 18, told me that her father, Sir Aldo Castellani, is incarcerated in the Quirinal with the Prince of Piedmont, and that all parties have treated him abominably. He is not the least interested in politics, only in his medicine and his friends. She has not seen him for six years. She has not been home to England for six years. Lord Margesson was polite to me in spite of our difference the other evening, and said I was the first person to have explained to him George Lloyd's complex character. There was one row at dinner, when Chips foolishly belittled the K.C.s, saying they were not in society and were bourgeois. At this I spoke up. I said I hardly knew the C.s, but he was undoubtedly one of the most brilliant and distinguished men of our generation. Emerald said to Chips, 'You are as much an upstart as K.C., and so am I. We are both from across the Atlantic. As for you [to Lord Margesson], you know nothing about the arts or the intellect. You are only fit for politics and love. You know nothing of anything else.' Chips then said that Mrs. Corrigan was in the best society, and that anyone in Paris who was not received by her was 'beneath consideration'. Jacqueline and I agreed that talk about 'society' was outside our understanding. To her such talk was unintelligible, and parvenu.

Saturday, 17th March

To the office this morning, with a hangover. How ill drink makes me, and what a bad effect on my temper. To Denham by train. Walked from the station to the Wittkowers' house. A coldish wind but all the blackthorn out. Yesterday there were Lent lilies at Leith Hill Place. Dr. Wittkower was away and I looked through several eighteenth-century tomes. I was given a good vegetarian luncheon in the kitchen, with five odd German Jewess blue-stockings, all down to bedrock (or do I mean rock bottom?), serious and friendly.

Monday 19thMarch

I travelled to Yeovil with Bertie Abdy. He holds the most unorthodox views about art. Deprecates every artifact that happens to be English, which makes me want to ask him why he consented to join the Montacute Committee. A horrid day, it poured with rain and Eardley failed to turn up. I thought the Committee most tiresome for, apart from Christopher Hussey, none of them has the faintest idea how the house ought to be arranged.

Thursday, 22nd March

G. M. Trevelyan came to the office early, with the proofs of the National Trust book. He thinks not enough reference has been made to specific N.T. properties and too much has been said about the various aspects, archaeological, entomological, etc. of the Trust's work. He showed me the first half of his Introduction, and asked what he should say in the last half. I said, please stress the Trust's opposition to museumization, and its wish to preserve the face of England as it was under private ownership.

Friday, 23rd March

I dined with John Fowler. I arrived at 8.30 because he always eats late; even so we did not sit down till 9.45. Geoffrey Houghton-Brown was there and Captain (Billy) Henderson, who arrived at 8 o'clock this evening with the Viceroy from India. He breakfasted this morning in Sicily, having dined last night in Cairo. He said the aeroplane was very comfortable, with good food and beds to lie down on. India was a continent of enchantment - the beauty of the peasant women, all wearing silks and silver bracelets and anklets. He said there are 360 servants in the Palace at Delhi; the building is very ugly, the dome raised on stilts; and many of the rooms face internal wells. The sandstone of the building gets so hot that in summer you cannot bear your hand on it at midnight. The best architecture is Sir Herbert Baker's Secretariat.

Saturday, 24th March

This morning I called for Mrs. Fellowes at the Dorchester and motored her to Faringdon, where we lunched with Berners and Robert Heber-Percy. At 3 we called at Coleshill. The Miss Pleydell-Bouveries took us over the house, but Mrs. F. was not as pleased with it as I had hoped. She did not think it well equipped, for it only has three bathrooms. We went on to the roof. The cupola with its golden ball is swathed in rugs to prevent it being a landmark to German aeroplanes by moonlight. From here the beautiful, stalwart chimneys can be seen to advantage. Mrs. F. had vertigo looking over the parapet. I noticed in the large saloon how finely carved the Chippendale armchairs are. A curious thing I observed in the elevation was that the lines of the cornice are curved and the roof dormers are set, not at right angles to the roof, but slightly splayed outwards. Presumably this arrangement was intended to minimize the severity and marked tightness of the design and to create 'movement', in the way that the stylobate of the Parthenon was deliberately laid out of the true. We had tea off a large table, covered with a thick old linen cloth. Mrs. F. much liked the elder sister with her twinkling eye. She is like a little hedgehog.

We got to Compton Beauchamp at 5.30, exactly the same moment as Chips Channon and Terence Rattigan.

For so sophisticated a woman, Daisy – this is what Mrs. Fellowes tells me to call her – has simple country tastes. Yet I cannot help seeing her as Reynolds's Mrs. Graham, the society lady masquerading as a housemaid with a broom. She keeps a cow which she likes to milk herself, when she is here. She asked someone the other day if the cow would mind her going to Paris for a long weekend without being milked during her absence.

Compton Beauchamp combines so many qualities that are desirable in a country house. It is completely surrounded by a moat, for romance. It has a pleasant, central square courtyard, for shelter. The approach is by a symmetrical forecourt with two detached flanking stable wings, retaining wall, stone piers and magnificent iron gates, for grandeur. The principal façade is classical Queen Anne of rustic simplicity, for cosiness and dignity. The other façades are medieval and Jacobean, for historic continuity. There is an extremely pretty garden at the back with contemporary raised terraces. A box garden behind that; another magnificent iron gate between piers, cut and set askew to the wall. It is a small paradise in a fold of the downs, with tinkling fountains in the forecourt and courtyard. A dream country house in which I could gladly be incarcerated for the rest of my life, and which I would never be tempted to leave.

Tuesday, 27th March

To St. Leonard's-on-Sea to inspect some furniture which a Mr. Tate wants to leave to the Trust. While I was under a table running my fingers in a professional manner up and down the legs, like a horsecoper examining fetlocks at a sale, I realized how ignorant I was, with no pretensions to judge what is genuine and what fake in furniture. I rely upon instinct, sharpened by years of experience, rather than upon imbibed knowledge from textbooks.

Wednesday, 28th March

This evening I went to Tony Gandarillos's house. After three glasses of whisky and soda I realized in a flash that I must be careful. At the moment of enlightenment Poulenc and a companion arrived. How crazy and ugly French men can be. This enormous man, ungainly as an elephant, strode into the room while talking at the top of his voice, and gesticulating like a fury. With a good deal of the traditional *ou-là-là* he threw himself into an armchair, imprecating and shouting in French, as though I did not exist. Had I not been a little drunk I would have hated this middle-aged Frog, eminent though he be.

Easter Sunday, 1st April

I am staying at Monk Hopton near Bridgnorth for Easter. The house of red brick is not beautiful or interesting. Lady de Vesci, *grande dame*, handsome, slim and upright, works hard at her garden all day. It is too full of conifers for my taste. The surrounding country, lush with deciduous trees, is on the other hand superb. Poor Bridget has injured her eye with a twig.

I was called rather early this morning, and lent a bicycle. Pedalled three miles to Mass at Aldenham Park. The house stands well on an eminence at the end of a long, straight avenue, approached through wrought-iron gates, with a clairvoyée. Expectation of coming upon a worthwhile building dwindles as the bicycle nears the goal. The Georgian house must have been encased in stone and given plate-glass windows in the nineteenth century. By the historian Lord Acton? I did not go inside. A nuns' school occupies it at present. There are red brick stable buildings. The detached chapel, about 1870, is on the terrace. It is a rather nice, classical structure. The chapel was filled with nuns in white hoods. I sat behind them in the small congregation, mostly children, the Actons' presumably, because like all Catholics they have dozens. Ronnie Knox said Mass in that unmistakable Oxford accent. I got back to breakfast at 11.

Monday, 2nd April

Bridget returned to London this evening. Lord and Lady de Vesci and I went for a long walk across fields and through woods to Upton Cresset, now a farmhouse. It is a red brick Elizabethan house, with two vast, twisted chimneystacks, and a detached gatehouse of two round towers. We entered this. It has remains of some elaborate plasterwork in overmantel and ceiling; and a newel staircase.

Wednesday, 4th April

My much anticipated-with-apprehension-but-pleasurable dinner with Daisy Fellowes. There she was, splendid in black lace and a black mantilla over her hair, with violets in it for my benefit, so she said. A limousine took us to the Basque Restaurant in Dover Street. There was no wine, so we had to be contented with two glasses of sherry each, nothing more. The bill came to £4.10.0 with tip, which was monstrous. There was no actual breakdown in conversation, yet there were awkward pauses. I felt mesmerized like a rabbit by a stoat, and frightened to death until, come the pudding, I pulled myself together with 'Fool!' and pinched myself, with 'To hell!' and proceeded to enjoy the rest of the evening mightily. Anyway I am to go to the theatre with her next week.

When I got home I read in the evening paper that poor Ava [Lord Dufferin] had been killed. Ava was with Tom the friend I most admired at my private school, and at Eton, where the three of us edited magazines together. I saw little of him at Oxford, and rarely met him afterwards. He had the best brain of my generation, and was at school a brilliant scholar, winning prizes after doing the minimum amount of work, always at the last moment. As a boy he was an eccentric in that, during intense concentration, he would literally eat his handkerchief and suck ink from the end of a pen without realizing what he was doing. I think he was ruined for life by the late Lord Birkenhead, who at Oxford taught him and others of his group to drink. Consequently he became a sad physical wreck before he was thirty.

Thursday, 5th April

This morning's *Times* has an appreciation of Ava by Frank Pakenham. All day I have thought of him, and lamented that the opportunity never came to bridge the break in our friendship. On the very few occasions when we did meet the affection was still there

Took the 9 o'clock train to Salisbury. Eardley met me and motored me to Boyton. This is David Herbert's house, which he has inherited from an uncle and wants to sell. We looked at it for Cook. It is a beautiful square Cotswoldy house with pointed gables, about 1610, and projecting porch. Built of stone, covered with a harl in dappled wash. Much Jacobean and William and Mary wainscoting, and one long parlour on the first floor facing east, with ordinary ribbed plaster ceiling. Troops have been in it, but treated it well. There is a mown terraced lawn, and a long vista of curving woodlands and a meadow.

Returning to Salisbury we called at Dinton. The American camp immediately in front of Hyde's House is a real desecration. I have never seen anything so disagreeable – concrete roads, tin huts with smoking chimneys, in short a hideous shanty town in what was a beautiful park. The original concave glass panes of Dinton House glinted in the sunshine.

Sunday, 8th April

And now what I so long foreboded and dreaded has happened. I was at home working all day. At 6.30, when just about to leave for Bridget's to take her out to dinner, Nancy rang me up to say Tom had been killed in Burma. They heard yesterday. He was wounded in the stomach, and died on Good Friday. Whether he was with Ava they don't know. I could barely finish speaking to Nancy, who was very composed. She says her parents are shattered. Beloved, handsome Tom, who should have been married and had hosts of beautiful children; Tom, caviar to the general possibly, but to me the most loyal and affectionate of friends. It is hell. Luckily Bridget was dining with me. She was wonderful, calm and sympathetic, and wretched too. I loved her for it.

Tuesday, 10th April

Asked Nancy to lunch at Gunter's to show her the Appreciation, about which I had cold feet lest she might be embarrassed. But she seemed to like it. I was greatly cheered and took it to *The Times*. Nancy was very brave, laughing and making jokes, but said she was still stunned. When Bobo was told she said, 'I do envy Tom having such fascinating arguments with Dr. Johnson now,' and to the vicar's wife, 'How lucky Tom was to die on Good Friday,' which amused Nancy very much and would have amused Tom. Lady Redesdale has come up to London, and to N.'s surprise is braver than any of them, and almost cheerful. There has been a gathering of the sisters. Diana unexpectedly walked into the Mews where they were all assembled, not having seen her father for seven years, he declining to set eyes on her ever since her marriage to Tom [Sir Oswald] Mosley. Nancy said she sailed in unabashed, and at once, like the old Diana, held the stage and became the centre of them all. To their amazement Lord Redesdale greeted her affectionately. Diana had motored up in a Daimler with two policemen in attendance. Lord R. in his old-fashioned way insisted on sending out cups of hot, sweet tea, which he said was what policemen always liked best. Diana whispered in some trepidation that Tom Mosley was waiting in the car, and warned Nancy to keep her father away. But he insisted on taking Diana downstairs when she left in spite of Diana's

remonstrances, saying that he would accompany her to the car. Finally she
had to explain, 'Farve, the Man Mosley [Lord R. always refers to him as
such] is waiting in the motor for me.' Lord Redesdale laughed and let her
go. Infinitely poignant I think.

At 6 I called for Daisy Fellowes at the Dorchester. She was in her suite
drinking champagne with her husband, who sat in an armchair looking as
though in the last stages. Daisy treats him with much solicitude and sweetness. He has had one leg amputated, for he suffers from clotting blood.
In her car we fetched Compton Mackenzie. He is out-going,
forward-looking, communicative, friendly. We drove to the Chancellor of
the Exchequer's house in Lord North Street and picked up Lady
Anderson. One policeman on duty outside the house. Drove to the theatre
for an Agatha Christie play. Returned to the Dorchester and had a delicious supper with more white wine. Lady Anderson told me she was
anxious to form a committee of Gerry Wellington and me to advise on
the decoration and furnishing of 11 Downing Street. She is anxious that
the house should be dealt with in such a way that succeeding Chancellors
of the Exchequer cannot scrap their predecessors' alterations and make
their own. The same danger faces no. 10. She said she dreaded to think
what hash Ernest Bevin might make if he ever inhabited one or the other.

Compton Mackenzie, rather like a child, produced a birthday book and
made us all sign our names against our dates of birth. He has a sharp
pointed beard and wears a cape.

Thursday, 12th April

Yesterday I came by train to Haverfordwest. I am staying at Picton Castle.
This afternoon Johnnie Philipps motored me across the Priscilly Hills to
Llangwair, the Bowens' place. They have let the house to the Salvation
Army for the war. It is filled with old women bombed out of the East End.
The Bowens picnic in a caravan and a tent, winter and summer. Llangwair
is a medium-sized house, the outside roughcast, the inside wainscoted with
William and Mary panels. Situation over a rushing river, facing the hills
above Newport. Picturesque. A Welsh stranded gentry set-up. Johnnie was
a great help in assessing the merits and demerits, for he knows his country
well. We were given tea in the caravan and on the grass, for we could not
all get inside the caravan.

Friday, 13th April

We rise very late here; and how one sleeps and yawns. Relaxation does not
suit me. Johnnie and I walked over the fields to Slebech, his widowed sister
Sheila de Rutzen's house, her daughter Victoria riding her pony beside us.
It was a cloudless day. The banks were thick with primroses and the woods
with bluebells in bud. From a hillock between the two houses we had

distant views over the creek of the river. Slebech is actually on the creek, and more romantically situated than Picton. We went over this delightful house. A fresh unit of troops was trying to clean up the appalling mess left by the last. Since January water has been allowed to seep from burst pipes through the ceilings and down the walls. Most of the stair balusters have disappeared. Mahogany doors have been kicked to pieces. Floor boards are ripped up. All rooms mottled with and stinking of damp. I imagine dry rot has set in everywhere. We walked back above the river through the woods. It became so extremely hot that I took off all but my shirt.

After tea we did a tour of this castle. The thick ribbed thirteenth-century undercroft is archaeologically important. A pity it is so disfigured by a criss-cross of hot-water pipes and wires. The great hall is decent provincial Palladian. The small, low drawing-room is rococo. Some good pre-Adam chimneypieces of marble. The chapel is of Wren date, with rough contemporary pews. The walls have been stencilled with Victorian texts and darkened by two very poor stained-glass windows in memory of an aunt.

Sunday, 15th April

At tonight's dinner party, which I attended at a round table in a resonant room, everyone talked across at one another. It was like trying to speak to someone on the telephone when other peoples' lines have crossed one's own.

Wednesday, 18th April

I went with Bridget and Anne to Ava's memorial service in St. Margaret's, Westminster. Archbishop Lang of Canterbury conducted the service and gave an address. He referred to Basil's unusual gifts and – what I thought was correct but brave – the temptations that had beset and nearly overcome him, but which he had so resolutely resisted. The Last Post was played from behind the aisle, not made less poignant by the roar of traffic during the silent pauses. I thought how sublime this would have sounded in the Abbey, the prolonged notes receding from the larger waste of Gothic piers, and echoing down the distant cloisters.

Saturday, 21st April

Dined with Daisy for the Cavendish ball in the Dorchester. I danced mostly with Bridget, and we walked away arm in arm, discoursing. Both of us remarked that the older men become, the more they stick their behinds out when dancing. Why is this?

Wednesday, 25th April

Came home at 7 to find that a bomb had fallen near by and my water tank had in consequence burst. All my best books are saturated, which makes me very unhappy. I spent a melancholy evening mopping up. There was an inch of water in the big room.

Thursday, 26th April

Angst is the strangest, most unpredictable enemy. It assails one for no apparent reason in the most unlikely places. Today in Manchester walking from the station to the Midland Hotel I was so overwhelmed with a sense of my own futility that I was terrified lest someone might speak to me. It was most unlikely that someone would, for I know nobody and nobody knows me down here. But I skulked close to the wall on the side of the street away from the sun so as to be as inconspicuous as possible. I have noticed that April is always the worst month for this kind of non-sense.

Friday, 27th April

A bitter east wind, in fact the Protestant wind, so named by James II when he feared the beastly Orange's armada. I called myself at 7 and caught a train for Mow Cop. Yesterday (apart from the skulking episode) and today have been blissful because I have been totally alone. From Mow Cop station I climbed the steep hill to the ridiculous castle folly which belongs to the N. Trust. It blew so hard at the top that I could scarcely breathe. Having inspected this monument associated with the Primitive Methodists, I descended across the fields to Little Moreton Hall. A truly picturesque scene, with the cows lying – it is going to rain – before the moat. The house looked more grotesque than ever; the gallery is so uneven and undulating that it must topple over into the moat. The chapel end subsides in an acute angle. And yet it stands like the Tower of Pisa. How, I wonder?

I love the old-fashioned farmyard atmosphere, the heavy, polished Victorian furniture in the great hall, the brown teapot, the scones and marmalade and eggs for luncheon. Charming farmeresses waiting on me, and gossiping with each other, and me, and for ever polishing. The caretaker, Mrs. Bailey, was away in hospital. She is the daughter of my great friend, Mrs. Dale, the farmer's wife, descended from the Dale 'carpeder' who left his name on the compass windows, having made them 'by the grac of God' in 1559. One of the ladies confided in me that this daughter was temperamental, odd and, she whispered very loudly, a shop-lifter.

On my return I called on Bridget. Mark Ogilvie-Grant was with her. He is just back from a German prison camp after four years' absence and, he assured me, was disappointingly sane and 'unpsychological'. He was released three weeks ago. For the last six months all he was given for breakfast was ersatz coffee, for luncheon three or four small potatoes, and for dinner vegetable soup with, twice a week, some scraps of meat in it. He is thinner.

The account of that brute Mussolini's summary execution and the indignities inflicted upon his corpse by the hands of the partisans does not make edifying reading. But how typical of present-day political morality. No one party, no one nation seems to behave better than another. Doubtless the summary execution was a better way of despatching Mussolini than by a long-drawn-out trial, which would have exasperated the people and have led to a lynching, like Caruso's death. In fact it is obvious that you cannot try civilian captives, who will excuse their past conduct before the law with the plea that they were acting according to the instructions of their superiors, or the constitution of their country. But the fate of Mussolini ought to be a salutary deterrent to aspiring dictators of the future. It won't be of course.

This afternoon Mr. Sedgwick motored me to see his house, South End House, at the end of Montpelier Row, Twickenham, facing the Marble Hill estate. It is a fine 1720 building with projecting closets from ground floor to roof in the Owletts manner. One large room was built on in Strawberry Hill style, with a magnificent chimneypiece like a Westminster Abbey tomb, flanked by Gothic piers and capped by pineapples. The Sedgwicks dislike it and want to take it down. I tried to dissuade them. He and his wife gave me a delicious tea. The house is divided into four flats – lovely they are – Walter de la Mare and Professor Reilly occupying two. In the garden is a splendid plane tree of enormous girth, contemporary with the house.

At 4 o'clock to the Bank of England. Ruby Holland-Martin gave me permission to be shown round by an official. To my surprise there is absolutely nothing left of Sampson, Taylor or Soane's work inside, and outside only Soane's outer wall. And that has been mutilated by Sir Herbert Baker. I was disgusted by the re-erection of the Taylor court room, which Baker tampered with to suit his own devices. Had he demolished the whole building and built anew from the foundations I should have respected him more, but he has compromised by reproducing Taylor vaulting and Soane motifs in the basement. Yet Baker is a distinctive architect and craftsman. His clocks, for example, are truly noble artifacts not to be despised. His lapses into Kraal detail are undignified in classical work.

I worked and dined alone in Brooks's. At 10.30 a member rushed into the morning room announcing that Hitler's death had just come through on the tape. We all ran to read about it. Somehow, I fancy, none of us was very excited. We have waited, and suffered too long. Three years ago we would have been out of our minds with jubilation and excitement – and with prognostications of a happy issue out of all our afflictions.

Wednesday, 2nd May

Had a drink this evening with Lady Berwick at the Ladies' Carlton Club. Victor Cunard brought an earnest young Italian from the Embassy. He was fanatically anti-Fascist. He thought Mussolini's death the best way out, but I was glad that he hoped there would be no further reprisals, and that Donna Rachele and her children were being protected by the partisans. He, a northerner, has the greatest contempt for the southern Italians. Lady Berwick spoke brilliantly about the Italian character, which she knows well.

Saturday, 5th May

I really love Blickling and feel happy here. I spent the morning in the Long Gallery, at the large table in the window overlooking the garden. The sun cast square blobs of yellow joy upon the floor, but did not reach the book-shelves. I looked through the old architectural books, while Miss O'Sullivan worked away at her catalogue of the 12,000 volumes. I seriously consider spending part of my holiday here. After luncheon I left for King's Lynn. Stayed the night at the Globe with Penrose, whose company ele-vates me. He has become an Anglo-Catholic, and is convinced that Christianity alone can save the world. He is an optimist. He is standing as Liberal candidate for Lynn.

Sunday, 6th May

Went to Mass at 10 and was devout, the result of Alec's uplifting society. Sisson came for luncheon and we spent the afternoon in St. George's Hall, which Alec has bought to save. At present it is in a deplorable state, and full of junk. It is supposed to be the largest British guildhall surviving. Alec and Sisson think more of it than I do. True, the shell is intact, and so are most of the roof timbers. Nevertheless only one of the intricate curved tiebeams is intact. The building dates from the late fourteenth century. From the sixteenth to the nineteenth it was used as a theatre. Shakespeare's company is known to have acted in it. Behind it long medieval warehouses trail down to the river. Included in the property is a stone-fronted Queen Anne town house, which to me is more attractive than this rather dreary hall. We wandered round the town which has a doomed, anachronistic, unwanted look. King Street and Queen Street are, I think, the finest old streets anywhere in England.

Monday, 7th May

Grandy Jersey lunched at Brooks's. I have asked his firm to make an estimate of the repairs needed to the stuffs in the state-rooms at Blickling.

Grandy overheard two shopgirls in the street this morning say they did not feel like 'jubilating', and would be happier going to the shop as usual. All day there has been a feeling in the air of expectancy, hysteria and uncertainty. The papers tell us that the Germans have capitulated, yet make no announcement about the ridiculous VE day. Aimlessly I walk to Bridget's flat and have a drink with her and Anne [Rosse], then back to Brooks's. Aeroplanes keep flying low over London, nobody knows why. People say peace negotiations have broken down, and we have declared war on the Russians. Passionately longing for peace though I am, I know in my inmost being that this is what we ought to do. Lanning Roper turned up in naval uniform. He is handsome, and serious.

All this evening people have roamed the streets in an uncertain sort of way, jubilating very half-heartedly. When Roper and I left Brooks's to walk down Bond Street there were not many jubilators in Piccadilly. In fact there was little shouting and gaiety.

Tuesday, 8th May

This is V day at last. I got home at 9.30, had a bath and changed. At midday went to Bridget's flat, and with her and Anne to lunch with John Sutro at Driver's. We were joined by Oliver Messel and a quiet, mystery man of about 50. We ate oysters and lobsters and drank sweet champagne. Then returned to hear Churchill's speech at 3 o'clock. It was merely a short announcement that peace had been declared. We were all rather disappointed, and wondered what was the necessity for telling us what we already knew.

I went to John Sutro's house at 7 and found Bridget there. Had it not been for the mystery man arriving uninvited at 8 o'clock and staying with us, the evening would have been unalloyed fun. The three of us being such old friends were perfectly contented with our own company. Bridget was more beautiful and alluring than ever I remember her. John and I kept remarking upon this to each other over and over again. We drank muscat wine, and listened to the King's speech at 9. It was perfect, well phrased, well delivered in his rich, resonant voice, expressed with true feeling and tinged with an appropriate emotion for the occasion. Bridget and I cooked the dinner, she scrambling eggs, I frying bacon in great quantity. This was all we had, but it was delicious. We drank a bottle of excellent white wine and some very old brandy, sitting till 11.45 at the table. All the while the sad mystery man sat speechless. John played Chopin on the piano. At midnight I insisted on our joining the revels. It was a very warm night.

Thousands of searchlights swept the sky. Otherwise there were few illu-minations and no street lights at all. Claridges and the Ritz were lit up. We walked down Bond Street passing small groups singing, not boisterously. Piccadilly was however full of swarming people and littered with paper.

We walked arm in arm into the middle of Piccadilly Circus which was brilliantly illuminated by arc lamps. Here the crowds were singing, and yelling and laughing. They were orderly and good humoured. All the English virtues were on the surface. We watched individuals climb the lamp posts, and plant flags on the top amidst tumultuous applause from bystanders. We walked down Piccadilly towards the Ritz. In the Green Park there was a huge bonfire under the trees, and too near one poor tree which caught fire. Bridget made us push through the crowd collected on the pavement to a ring of people round the bonfire. They were very funny, bringing huge posts from nowhere and hurling them on to the fire. Six or seven people were struggling under barricades of wood and whole door-ways from air raid shelters which they dragged on to the fire. The fire's reflection upon thousands of faces, packed on the pavement, squatting on the grass and cramming the windows of the Piccadilly houses reminded me for some reason of a Harrison Ainsworth illustration of the crowds wit-nessing Charles I's execution. One extraordinary figure, a bearded, naval titan, organized an absurd nonsense game, by calling out the Navy and making them tear round the bonfire carrying the Union Jack; then the R.A.F.; then the Army; then the Land Army, represented by three girls only; then the Americans; then the civilians. If we had been a little drunker we would have joined in. As it was Bridget took a flying leap over the pyre in sheer exuberance of spirits. The scene was more Elizabethan than neo-Georgian, a spontaneous peasant game, a dance round the maypole, almost Bruegelian, infinitely bucolic. No one was bullied into joining who didn't want to, and the spectators enjoyed it as much as the participants. I thought, if we could have a V night once a month, and invite the Poles, Germans, even Russians to do what we were doing now, there might never be another war.

We left B. at Mount Street. John and I went to his house where I slept the night. This was about 3 a.m.

Wednesday, 9th May

Woke rather bedraggled at 10.30, but pulled myself together enough to prepare a scratch breakfast. John is hopelessly disorganized in the absence of his wife, but the best company in the world on such an occasion. He, Bridget and I had planned to motor to the country, but the back tyre was punctured, and that was that. This VE business is getting me down with fatigue. I was rather pleased to stay at home instead. I went to tea with

Dame Una, who read me long and excellent letters from James. Then to Alvilde, and found crowds of people. Paul Sudley told me Tom Goff was complaining that I had diddled him out of Holt Court, his inheritance, by persuading his father, whom I knew to be out of his mind, to give it to the Trust, while he, Tom was overseas. Raymond Mortimer, whether or not to tease me I don't know, said that Tom Goff had a real grievance, and if he went to law the N.T.'s position would look very ugly. Derek Hill, who misses nothing, took all this in, and repeated it word for word to Eardley later. I feel sensitive about this unjust charge. Lady Cecilie, Tom's mother, was present throughout all our discussions about Holt Court and never said a word or made a sign of dissent.

Dined at Lady Kenmare's to meet the Italian Ambassador and wife. He is delightful, she intense. Emerald said to me, 'You are a very perspicacious man, Jim, oh yes,' when all I had said was that Mr. Churchill was devoted to his brother Jack, now dying in hospital, because he was 'the repository of his confidences'. Emerald recounted her row with Noël Coward last night. He greeted her with, 'Emerald darling!' She replied, 'Why do you call me "darling". I don't know you very well.' Then she said, 'I have never liked you.' And again later, 'You are a very common man.' Tony Gandarillos practically had to separate them.

Friday, 11th May

This morning to a meeting at Horne's office with Brian Fairfax-Lucy and his solicitor, where we discussed the transfer of Charlecote to the Trust. Brian wishes us to pay for maintenance as from the date of acceptance, which was last month. He is such a generous person that I hope the Trust won't haggle. He also wants us to buy the First Folio and the gold cup given by Charles II to his ancestor.

An enjoyable dinner at Emerald's tonight. Lord Margesson is quick-witted and teases Emerald deliciously. He is a good talker when he gets on to beastly politics, as Emerald remarked, and has a beautiful timbre to his soft voice, which he never raises even when roused; on the contrary he lowers it. I suppose the House of Commons teaches a man to control his emotions. Emerald was tonight quicker with her repartee than I ever remember. I was amazed by her brilliant, incisive mind. Conversation flitted from nonsense to seriousness. Lord Gage said, 'Once in Berlin a painted young creature said to me, "Darling, don't be county now." Imagine such a thing, to me, who literally am the county of Sussex.' Emerald said the Minister for Food invited her to sit on his knee. Lord Margesson spoke well about the Bolshevik situation. He said Churchill was terribly depressed by their stubborn non-co-operation, and the blackout they have lowered over their side of the German front. They will allow no one to penetrate it, and no one to enter Vienna. It is thought they are putting all Germans to the sword, with the exception of those thousands they are deporting as slaves to Russia. This a most terrible and sickening thing. Clarissa [Churchill] said one must not mind. But I do. All agreed that we are powerless with the Bolsheviks. It remains to be seen whether they march further west, or remain content with what they have already got; whether they are motivated by imperialism, or are merely taking steps to forestall Great Britain one day turning a democratized Germany upon them.

Saturday, 12th May

A notice to quit this house [no. 104 Cheyne Walk] has already reached me. June 11th is the day I must leave. What is to happen to poor Miss P.?

I stay the weekend with the Somerset de Chairs at Chilham. The approach to the Castle is through two lodges built by Sir Herbert Baker traditionally and decently. A narrow lime avenue to the entrance. Sir Herbert did a great deal to the house for the late Sir Edmund Davis, wisely and modestly I think. Nearly every window mullion had to be renewed; also the glazing. Much grey panelling has been inserted and faked up. The best interior feature is the arcaded staircase of 1616. In two bedrooms are chimneypieces of beautiful Bethesden marble. Two bedrooms have original plaster ceilings. Otherwise there is little left. Somerset is quite certain Inigo Jones was the architect because the watermark on the early plan corresponds with the watermark on some other paper used by Inigo, a German paper.

Sunday, 13th May

After luncheon we walked across the fields to Godmersham. The situation of this house, though only two miles from Chilham, is quite different. Whereas Chilham with its wonderful descending brick terraces is situated on a hill overlooking a valley and the Downs, Godmersham, which is early Georgian with flanking wings, lies in a broad and unconfined basin. From the house, which springs out of the green park meadowland, the sides of the basin gently rise from all sides. From every window are visible quietly curving lines and contours. The Trittons have spent thousands on altering and improving. She is the widow and heiress of Sir Bernard Baron, who was fabulously rich. The consequence is the house is a little too perfect. The furniture is superb. Good pictures are few; some Devises and Zoffanys. The garden side was entirely rebuilt by Walter Sarrell. The Orangery is by Felix Harbord. I question whether it is entirely successful. The early Georgian entrance hall is untouched, a magnificent Burlingtonian speci- men, with heavy enrichments, apses with shell soffits, and plaques in high relief. Mr. Tritton attributes the house to Colin Campbell, but on what authority I don't know. He took us round with great pride.

Tuesday, 15th May

I was told by someone who accompanied them that the two Princesses insisted on walking round the town incognito, on VE night. They walked at such tremendous speed that their companions had the greatest difficulty in keeping pace. The public never recognized them until, on returning to Buckingham Palace, they started shouting for the King and Queen.

Wednesday, 16th May

Philip James, Art Director of C.E.M.A., lunched. He wants to take a National Trust house, close to some provincial town, as an art centre. I said I heartily approved the idea, but had been disillusioned by the number of similar suggestions, all of which had come to nothing. At 6 o'clock I met Geoffrey Houghton-Brown at 17 Alexander Place, off Thurloe Square. He has offered me the first floor and one spare room upstairs. It is good of him. I like the idea.

At Sibyl's Ordinary tonight I sat next to Lady Birkenhead, Freddy's mother. She adored Ava who, she said, constantly stayed with her. She used to find her best books floating in the bath after he left, and the floor a swamp. Freddy and Randolph Churchill shared a room in Czechoslovakia, and Randolph was quite intolerable. Freddy threw a book at Randolph, who got out of bed, and a fight ensued. Once at a party Randolph gave Lady Birkenhead a violent blow, aimed at Lord Castlerosse. I left with Harold for Pratt's where we drank a glass of port. The Duke of Devonshire joined us. His funny old-fashioned starched collar had come detached from the front stud and twisted round his neck in a very extraordinary manner. I did not know him well enough to tell him, and Harold was so busy talking he never noticed.

Thursday, 17th May

I have avoided the office yesterday and today, for the move from 7 Buckingham Palace Gardens to 42 Queen Anne's Gate is proceeding. The new house is smaller than the old and in a state of near ruin, for it is close to the Guards' Chapel which was destroyed by a flying bomb last year. At 10 I went to Peterborough, standing in the corridor, with a first-class ticket. From there took a train to Oundle, arriving at 1 o'clock. Was met and driven to Cotterstock by Lady Ethel Wickham, who is delightful and absolutely on the ball. She has quite made up her mind to leave the property to the Trust in memory of her husband. We talked and smoked all afternoon, having despatched our business during luncheon.

Clough Williams-Ellis called at the office at 4.30 to discuss his book on the N.T. and stayed till 7.15. He is an man of fantasy, with long whiskers, and today was wearing a deep blue shirt and stock. He is cranky, hearty, arty and disarming.

John Wilton, who had telephoned at breakfast time to announce his return from Paris, dined at Brooks's. He was very communicative and stayed till midnight, when I walked home. We telephoned Lord Braybrooke and arranged for John to visit Audley End on Thursday. He wanted me to accompany him but I declined to do this. He seems quite determined to proceed with the purchase.

He told me that he went to Belsen camp during the hot weather. The stench was so overpowering that he and others were physically sick. Then they became accustomed to it. The atrocities committed there were worse than the press disclosed. He saw several corpses with deep cuts across the small of the back. Starving fellow-prisoners had done this in the attempt to extract human liver and kidney to assuage their hunger. Other corpses had their private parts torn off. He himself saw a wooden shield, the sort on which we mount a fox's mask, with a man's chest impaled upon it, the nipples and hair intact. He saw a torture chamber with stone bench, troughs and channels for the blood to run into. He looked at the Beast of Belsen behind his cage. He was later shot. He said that our troops watched him and the German S.S. guards under arrest in dead calm and with horror-struck dignity. But some American and British troops did walk a few S.S. men out of the wards and shoot them.

Wednesday, 23rd May

Matheson and I talked to Pepler of the Ministry of Planning. He asked me to prepare a list of not more than fifty of the greatest country houses which, if offered, we should ask the Government for funds to maintain.

Having failed to get on to the 4.15 from Paddington owing to the crowds, I caught the 6.30 for Chippenham. Paul Methuen, in battledress and a beret, drove me to Corsham. Just returned from Belgium, and always absent minded, he started driving on the right side of the road to our peril. I stayed the night in his brother's house in the village, because their agent, Captain Turner, was staying in the Court. He is also agent for the Cirencester estate, and we discussed this in relation to the N.T. The Methuens live in Nash's Gothic library where they have all their meals. A military hospital occupies the rest of the house. Paul gave me to read his reports on historic monuments in Calvados. They are very good and beautifully illustrated by him.

I watched the hospital orderlies banging the furniture of the staterooms, with the backs of their brooms. Mercifully the settees are put away.

Paul is strictly vegetarian, because he dislikes the idea of flesh. In consequence his complexion is fresh, clean and youthful. He is a good man, though opinionated; and so floating in the clouds that it is hard to pull him down to face facts. She is dignified and sweet in manner. She is however sharp, and does not suffer fools gladly. They are a liberal-minded couple, and very devoted.

At 6.30 we drove to Great Chalfield Manor to see the Flemish tapestries, which after all Major Fuller bought in Uxbridge. They are now hanging in the great hall where they look well enough.

After dinner we talked about laying spirits. Paul and Norah believe implicitly in them, and commune with spirits 'over the other side'.

Friday, 25th May

Daisy Fellowes has just returned from Paris, her hair cut and curled, which is far more attractive than when recently scooped up from the back, with a tumble of matted fringe over the forehead. She says you can get anything done in Paris through bribery. De Gaulle is very unpopular, for he concerns himself only with France's prestige in the eyes of Europe, and does nothing to improve the milk-round or stop the cynical corruption of rich and poor alike. She says the Prime Minister has made a mistake in driving the Socialists to insist upon a general election, not because they think a coalition Government should terminate, but because they are fed up with his autocratic ways in matters not exclusively concerned with the war.

Saturday, 26th May

I caught a midday train to Derby, where it was very cold again. Found a taxi and drove to Kedleston. Down the long drive there suddenly bursts upon the vision the great house, best seen from the Adam bridge. It is very grand, very large and symmetrical from this side, the north. The two pavilions are plastered and coloured ruddy brown. The centre block is of severe, dark Derbyshire stone. Lord Curzon, with his just sense of the magnificent, erected the screen of Adamesque railings, the great gates and overthrows to form the forecourt, now overgrown with grass. At the entrance to these gates is a series of army huts with a little suburban garden in front of each. Again, all over the park are unsightly poles and wires, something to do with radio location. The two north pavilions, designed by Brettingham and built by Paine, are in themselves quite large houses, at least large enough to command a respectable park for themselves. The south side is disappointing, for poor Adam has again been roughly treated here. His two additional pavilions were never carried out. His beautiful centre block and dome, so full of movement and grace, is not given a fair chance, with the tiresome poplars in front of the east pavilion, and the west hidden by scrubby little trees. Also the parish church should not have been left where it is, enveloped by the house like a rat by a boa constrictor. It does not enhance the group like, say, the church at Dyrham, which, the most perfect example I know of "sharawadgi", is a beautiful Gothic foil to the classical house, indeed dominating without oppressing the group, and lovely in being of the same radiant Bath stone.

Lord Scarsdale's mother greeted me at the door of the east pavilion where the family live. The Army are occupying the west pavilion. The centre block is unoccupied, and under dust sheets. Whereas Lord Curzon thought he was pigging it with only thirty indoor servants, today they have one woman for three hours each morning. The mother is living here with a granddaughter, Mrs. Willson, a young Grenadier officer's lethargic wife, and her baby; also Mrs. Willson's sister, Julie, aged 16, very bright and well informed. On my arrival they conducted me round the outside of the house, and after tea round the inside. In the church is a monument which Adam designed for a Curzon, with background pyramid. It is dull and uninspired. Lord Curzon's own monument to himself and his first wife is splendid. His marble effigy was put in place during his lifetime.

Structurally the house is fairly sound, but superficially tattered – the dust sheets don't look as though put on by a trained housemaid – and minor dilapidations are evident. The bluejohn inlay of the Music Room chimneypiece is flaking off. I think only Syon can be compared to Kedleston for splendour. The monolith alabaster columns of the hall are of a startling green which no photograph even faintly indicates. The marble floor is springy, and I wonder if it is very safe. The acoustics are appalling. One thing worries me about this wonderful room. On entry you are confronted with a three-foot narthex before the hall proper begins with a screen of columns. The hall ends in engaged columns. I can't see why Robert Adam had to do this. There may be good reason for a narthex in a church or public assembly room, but not in a private house. But then Dr. Johnson criticized this room for looking like a town hall. Again the oval screen compartment of the Boudoir is, I think, a mistake. In the Saloon I have nothing to criticize. Americans have unscrewed and stolen the centre of the door handles for souvenirs, the brutes.

Sunday, 27th May

All morning I toured the house by myself, taking notes as I went. The Dining-room alcove end is spoilt by the large doorhead impinging upon

the wall. The Library contains a number of good architectural and topo-
graphical books. The bedrooms are pretty with coved ceilings. The
Orangery is suffering badly from damp. The Bath House is falling to ruin.
So is the Boat House. But then what can these unfortunate people do?
Theirs is a tragic predicament. I notice that the portico has lost swags and
wreaths. When the sun comes out the sharp shadows give the south front
the movement Adam intended. This visit has made me sad. I am convinced
that this wonderful house is a doomed anachronism.

Monday, 28th May

A very full day. Interview with the Principal of Trinity College of Music.
He is taken with the idea of the Benton Fletcher Cheyne Walk house
becoming a centre of early keyboard music study. I lunched at Wilton's
with John Wilton and Sisson, who liked each other and discussed the
Audley End project. Took John to Drown's, where Christopher Norris
demonstrated how the Polesden pictures should be cleaned. Interviewed
Mrs. Gates about her inventory of the Ellen Terry Museum contents. Had
tea with Hinchingbrooke, and examined his small panel of tapestry for
Montacute.

Tuesday, 29th May

Forsyth and I trained to Shrewsbury. We reached Attingham in time for
luncheon and spent the whole day going over the house, examining and
criticizmg the County Council's proposed alterations to suit their college.
Attingham is far more Regency than Adam, and shows the influence of
Holland. All its proportions – portico, pilasters, rooms – are exaggeratedly
attenuated. I would not have them otherwise.

Forsyth is doubtless a most worthy man. But he is a frightful bore. His
Victorian manners give one the jitters, whereas good manners ought to
put one at ease. He will never go through a doorway before another man
of whatever age. He hesitates, bows, retreats, apologizes and looks bashful.
In a person of over 70 and his distinction this is absurd. He is terrified too
of committing himself to an opinion, even when one looks to him for it.
Yet he is untrustworthy as regards carrying out instructions. I hate obse-
quiousness. I could shake him.

Wednesday, 30th May

Lady Berwick motored me to the station this morning. She stood on the
platform talking, and when I begged her not to catch cold, said it was such
a pleasure just to talk to somebody. Poor woman, she has not much com-
panionship with Lord B. I got to Evesham in the afternoon, took a bus to
Badsey, and walked across the fields to Wickhamford.

Thursday, 31st May

Motored to Charlecote, picking up Clifford Smith at Leamington Spa station. Brian [Fairfax-Lucy] was his smiling and helpful self, but the agent an obstructive ass. Clifford's hesitant enthusiasms were constantly unleashed at the wrong moment, and so delayed progress in the outdoor consultations. I had to chivvy him indoors where he properly belongs. Today we examined the Brewery, with its vats and implements, all of which can be revived; and the harness room with rows of brightly kept bridles and bits, and the coachhouses stuffed with Victorian buggies, spiders and barouches. I urged the family to save and leave these things, for they will make a fascinating exhibit to future generations who will not have known the world in which they played a prominent everyday part.

Clifford and I discovered in the gatehouse, the stables and disused servants' hall, several ancient pieces of furniture, notably the hall table of great length, another Elizabethan table and a Queen Anne walnut veneered table, which must have been thrown out during the last century. We are going to have them brought back. The house was too drastically altered in the 1850s. The strange thing is that Mrs. George Lucy, who perpetrated the abominations, was the one member of the family who most loved Charlecote and revered its Shakespearian associations. Yet she over-restored the house out of all recognition, and introduced furniture and fabrics, like napkins, which she pretended Shakespeare and Queen Elizabeth saw and used. The ability of righteous people to deceive themselves always amazes me.

The Gatehouse, forecourt garden and stables form an extremely picturesque group. The park, with deer and sheep, the Avon below the library window, the flat meadows on the far bank, the long lime avenue, make Charlecote a dream of slumbering beauty.

Friday, 1st June

The lengths to which I have gone, the depths which I have plumbed, the concessions which I have (once most reluctantly) granted to acquire properties for the National Trust, will not all be known by that august and ungrateful body. It might be shocked by the extreme zeal of its servant, if it did. Yet I like to think that the interest of the property, or building, rather than the Trust has been my objective. I have to guard against the collector's acquisitiveness. It isn't always to the advantage of a property to be swallowed by our capacious, if benevolent maw. These pious reflections came to me in the bath this morning.

Early after luncheon Midi motored me to Hagley in her new (old) car, I providing coupons for three gallons. From the outside, Hagley is just like

Croome, only its *piano nobile* is raised higher so that the basement floor provides decent sized rooms, of which one, a sort of passage way, is a grotto of shells and spars. Lady Cobham is very fat and spread, but has dignity. Lord C. was at Eton with my father, and is handsome, austere and unsmiling. He has an involved mind which works slowly, methodically, and seemingly backwards. He has profound knowledge of Hagley, and is very proud of it, rightly. He took Midi and me round the house till we were nearly dropping with fatigue. In the Vandyke Room are some good pictures, particularly one of Lord Carlisle, and the famous Quentin Matsys of the misers. Three-quarters of the house was burnt out in 1925, but reconstituted by Lord Cobham with exemplary discretion. He even employed Italian *stuccatori* faithfully to copy from photographs the intricate designs of walls and ceilings, of which the former partially survived. Thus the big military trophy swags in the Saloon are, apart from a few lost pieces, the originals tidied up. The chimneypieces, all being of stone, were spared. Only Lord Cobham can tell what is old, and what new. Yet when he pointed out the new stucco it did look to me a little thinner than the original. Notwithstanding the renewal, the Saloon walls are about as fine as any I have seen. The tapestries and most of the pictures were saved. The Gallery was not destroyed, and the carving of picture frames, chimneypiece and furniture is attributed to Chippendale. Oddly enough it is in the natural wood, never having been gilded or painted. Lord C.'s uncles played cricket in this splendid room, and in consequence the furniture and delicate woodwork suffered greatly. He said that his grandfather, although a scholar, allowed this. The Chippendale torchères and candelabra, which are in the most delicate Chinese, or rocaille style, are sadly knocked about. The same uncles were allowed to play a jumping game of their own invention on the rare volumes in the library.

At tea time a daughter came into the library from the farm, wearing trousers, her hair touselled and spattered with dung. Lord Cobham told us that an American officer, on being shown the Vandyke *Descent from the Cross*, pointed to the figure of Our Lord and asked, 'Who was that guy that looked sick?'

I got to Paddington at midnight, and walked to Chelsea, carrying my two bags and walking-stick.

Saturday, 2nd June

The new office is chaotic still, the house falling to bits, and no windows.

Charles Fry dined with me to discuss the National Trust book. He arrived very drunk indeed. He was maudlin, self-pitying and self-concerned. It is quite impossible to associate with him in this condition. What bores drunks are!

Monday, 4th June

I bought Evelyn Waugh's new novel today. The reviews say it is as good as can be. I lunched with Leigh Ashton who said that his Museum would co-operate with us in maintaining and cataloguing the contents of our houses. This is a splendid thing. He said Charles Fry was obstreperously drunk in the St. James's Club all yesterday, even after my experience with him the night before. I had an interview with the National Council of Social Services at 2.30. They are now eager to establish the committee for mutual help, they thus receiving accommodation in, and we a use for, some of our houses.

Tuesday, 5th June

At 17 Alexander Place I bribed the sailor painting there to do several things for me, including fixing up bookshelves. I gave him £1 in a gauche way. I hope he and his wife are honest. She is going to look after my two rooms.

Went to Billericay to lunch with a Mrs. Cater. The house no good at all. Just the end of a Tudor Essex farmhouse, the other part being modern. She, poor woman, showed me her pictures, which were of no account. I told her as politely as I could that the Trust could not accept. Before I had set foot in the front door I knew the place was no good.

Wednesday, 6th June

Met R. in the bus and lunched with her in Cheyne Walk. She affects to be mightily concerned about the election. She still hankers after a *ménage à deux*, but can't find the second person. 'Don't we all?' I said rather brutally, lest there might be grounds for any misunderstanding.

I hired a car and took some of my more precious things to Alexander Place. Then to Claridges to meet Lady Muriel Barclay-Harvey, who wants to lend her family portraits to Montacute while she rebuilds her own house, Uffington near Stamford. Anne dined with me. Her advice tonight was, 'Laugh, and the world laughs with you; weep, and you sleep alone.'

Thursday, 7th June

Today Miss P. and I did not go to the office, for we moved from no. 104. The van came in the morning early, and the men were helpful and kind, but terribly rough. I had a moment of sadness while peeing in the *cabinet* for the last time, but have few serious regrets at leaving this dilapidated little hovel. Only the river and my splendid Whistlerian view I regret. No. 17 is wonderfully clean, but the bath is not fixed up and there is no telephone yet. It was lonely here tonight without Miss P. or a telephone.

At 6 I went to see Lord Newton, who talked of Lyme again. My impression is that with adroitness and tact he can be helped to do what he and we want, and that he looks upon me as an ally, who sympathizes with his predicaments.

Friday, 8th June

Went to Brooks's at 7.30 a.m., and had a bath and breakfast. Then took the train from Blackfriars station to Eynsford, spending the morning with Mr. Major, a dear old boy who wishes to leave four acres and a colony of wooden shacks, called *Robsacks*, in which he lives. The place has good views of Lullingstone Castle and a valley the other side of the ridge on which it is perched, but nothing else to recommend it. After dinner with Desmond at Brooks's I put my books more or less in order on the ramshackle bookcase which Geoffrey has lent me. Previously I had a drink with Anne, whom I love as much as any of my friends. I count her among my first five women friends. At least I think there are as many.

Saturday, 9th June

In the train to Swindon I brought my diary up to date. A woman sitting opposite me was bewildered by seeing someone covering sheets of paper in shorthand. I suppose people seldom write in shorthand unless they are dictated to.

Wednesday, 13th June

After a meeting in the office Brian Fairfax-Lucy lunched with me at Brooks's and I found myself speaking too frankly about his odious father. When I excused myself, he agreed with what I said, and elaborated to some tune. He said that all Sir Henry's children were terrified of him, and the lives of all of them had been ruined by him. The inhibitions of some of them were due to his treatment. After luncheon [Professor] Richardson introduced me to Lord Crawford who was absolutely charming. One must beware of charmers.

I went round Chandos House this evening. It is vast inside but by no means interesting, save the staircase, another Adam achievement within a narrow compass. Mrs. Hawker invited me to meet her son Lord Scarsdale at Claridges. I accepted only because I understood he wanted to discuss Kedleston in relation to the National Trust. He kept us waiting three-quarters of an hour, and when he came never mentioned the subject.

Thursday, 14th June

To Gunby for the night. The Field-Marshal extremely pleased to see me. The old man has become rather more ponderous and slow. He has bought several more portraits of Massingberds.

Friday, 15th June

This morning I walked with him round the estate, visiting employees, paying their wages and collecting savings funds from them. This estate is extraordinarily feudal, and has an air of wellbeing and content. The cottages are all very spick and span and the inmates on the best of terms with the Field-Marshal. He has a habit of stopping and turning to me whenever he has something to say, which delays progress, and makes walking with him in the winter extremely cold. He is very concerned about the election. I have never since a child seen such huge and succulent strawberries as the Gunby ones. We ate them with honey, far better than sugar, and cream. Although the war is over there is no alcohol in this house.

Saturday, 16th June

This morning the telephone man came to Alexander Place to say he would install my telephone on Monday. My bureau is to arrive that day. My bookshelves and curtain rods are to be put up next week. So things are moving. The bath however is still unattached to the pipes. The house painter and I picnic together. I leave the house each morning at 7.30 to bathe and shave at Brooks's, where I virtually live. Sometimes I breakfast with Professor Richardson, sometimes with Walter Ogilvie.

In Heywood's shop I met Diana Mosley and Evelyn Waugh with Nancy. I kissed Diana who said the last time we met was when I stayed the night at Wootton Lodge, and we both wept when Edward VIII made his abdication broadcast. I remember it well, and Diana speaking in eggy-peggy to Tom Mosley over the telephone so as not to be overheard. Diana looks as radiant as ever. She was the most divine adolescent I have ever beheld. Divine is the word, for she was a goddess, more immaculate, more perfect, more celestial than Botticelli's seaborne Venus. We all lunched at Gunter's and Harold Acton joined us. It was the first occasion on which he and Evelyn had seen Diana since her marriage to Tom. Her two Guinness boys from Eton also joined us: Jonathan, a little cross and supercilious, Desmond good-looking like his father. He, aged 13, said to me about his father, 'I wish Bryan would not go on having more children, for the money won't go round at this rate.' Diana said she had ordered a taxi-cab; she supposed it would come. 'The driver, I think and hope, is a fifth columnist.' She is funny. Evelyn said his book is already sold out – 14,000 copies.

Kathleen Kennet, who took me to the theatre, said Peter Scott's new book on battle boats has 24,000 copies printed. The play, *The Skin of our Teeth*, was hell. We could not be bothered to understand what it was all about. I had tea with the Kennets at Leinster Corner. K. and I are the best of friends again. Indeed I love her dearly.

I dined with Simon Harcourt-Smith, who said that in my Adam book I ought to discuss Adam's relationship with Chippendale, his importance compared with Gabriel and contemporary foreign architects, and the Roman-Greek controversy. At 10 I left Brooks's for home and ran into a friend in Piccadilly. 'Where are you hurrying?' I asked. 'To the Music Box,' he said, 'come too.' There Sandy Baird, whom I have not spoken to since Eton days, introduced himself to me, and me to a *louche* little sailor. The sailor called me Jimmie, and while Sandy was getting us drinks, said 'Give me your address.' 'Ask Sandy for it,' I replied. He hissed in a whisper, 'God, no, I can't ask him.' So much for fidelity, I thought. He also said to me 'I don't want money; only friendship.' I was flattered, but would not accompany them to another club. I hate these places. They disinter one's dead adolescence, and point to the pathetic loneliness of middle age.

Sunday, 17th June

In Warwick Street church I looked about me, because Evelyn had said the Belgian priest there proposes to dismantle the walls encrusted with silver hearts and thank-offerings and erect a new chapel along the north aisle.

Monday, 18th June

National Trust meeting day. The new secretary, Mallaby, appointed. I walked to Brooks's with Esher, and we lunched together. I suggested that all future minor staff candidates ought to be vetted by the committee before appointment, and not left to the Secretary's sole choice.

Had a drink with Mary and Auberon Herbert, who is now a captain in the Polish Army. He told harrowing tales of Russian atrocities committed upon the Poles. He saw thirty Polish women raped by a regiment of Bolsheviks who had 'liberated' a town in which he was. The soldiers ripped open the women's clothes with their bayonets, and four other soldiers held down a limb each. He says the Poles consider the Russians a far worse menace than the Germans. Then I dined with Pauly Sudley, who spoke not one single word throughout the meal – not one word. I left at 9 o'clock.

Thursday, 21st June

Mama made me drive her to Broadway to see the Sidneys' Flemish primitives and Tudor family portraits which, I gathered, they had just discovered in their Northumberland house, Cowpen Hall. Colonel Sidney is one of my father's favourite cronies and one of the stupidest men in all England, which is saying something. Among the portraits was a small one of Sir Philip Sidney with reddish hair. When I extolled Sidney's literary merits, the Colonel gave an impatient wave of the hand, saying, 'Yes, yes, a fine soldier, a fine soldier.' 'A humane as well as heroic man,' I ventured. 'A fine soldier, fine soldier,' he repeated.

I drove alone to Charlecote and lunched with the Fairfax-Lucys, meeting Brian's wife, Alice, for the first time. Attractive, quizzical and intelligent. Not John Buchan's daughter for nothing. They were very forbearing in letting Clifford Smith and me go round the rooms and make a selection of things from the list she had prepared the previous day.

On my way back to London I motored up the drive of Compton Verney. The beautiful park is a mature specimen of Capability Brown's work. Alas, all the balustrading of the lovely Adam bridge has been knocked down by the soldiers. When I got home at 11 my opposite neighbour called, which I thought a distinct bore. He made me have a drink in his house. The ground floor has been baronialized and given a vast cocktail bar.

Friday, 22nd June

Went by train to Horsmonden. Was met by Mr. Courthope and driven to Sprivers. He lives here with his sister. It is a red-brick house, built in 1756, small, pretty and unspoilt. An enormous bushy wistaria completely envelops the Georgian front, greatly to its detriment. The garden is waist-high in grass and weeds, and the gravel drive indistinguishable from the lawns. Altogether rather a mess. The house has a central hall with rococo cartouches on the walls, enclosing heraldic escutcheons of the Courthope family who built it. Otherwise, apart from the chestnut doorcases, two staircases of very rustic Chinese Chippendale design, and some rococo chimneypieces, there is nothing much inside for the public to enjoy. I got back at 7 and John Wyndham dined with me. He is Lord Leconfield's nephew and eventual heir. He is anxious for his uncle to hand over Petworth now. We decided to stress upon the feudal, reactionary Lord L. that (1) during his lifetime he will not be disturbed in any particular, (2) he may be better off financially, (3) he may retain the contents (for the best will be exempted on J.W.'s succession) and (4) by transferring now he will establish the only assurance that his successors can live at Petworth. John Wyndham is dark, bespectacled, like a wise young owl; not demonstrative, but cynical and extremely bright. He seemed quite, but not very pleased with the outcome of our meeting.

Saturday, 23rd June

With all my luggage, pens, papers, notes and books I reached Blickling by 8.

Sunday, 24th June

I am blissfully happy this afternoon. I write this at my table on the raised platform at the south-east end of the Gallery, as I had for so long pictured myself doing, surrounded by 12,000 calf-bound books looking on to the beautiful but unkempt, unmown garden. There is still quite a lot of colour in the formal beds now rank in long grass. Ivory's temple at the far end of the vista is in a straight line with me. Here I intend to work for a fortnight, and pray to God that no distractions will prevent me. But my character is weak, and I bow before temptation. I sleep and breakfast in Miss O'Sullivan's flat in the wing; I take all other meals at the inn, where the landlady Mrs. O'Donoghue is my friend. It is a warm sunny day. The air smells of roses and pinks. The tranquillity accentuates the extreme remoteness of Blickling, this beautiful house which I love.

Monday, 25th June

And here is temptation literally at the door, and again at the end of the telephone. At midday Wyndham Ketton-Cremer called on me as I was working in the library. He plans to come over next Tuesday week (another temptation) and take me to Wolterton. After he left I was told that Lord Wilton was on the line. By the time I reached the telephone, he had gone. After work I walked to Aylsham, hired a bicycle and rode to Oxnead. Looked at the old church where the latest Paston memorial is to Dame Katharine Paston, dated 1636, with a very fine bust of that lady, wearing choker pearls round an open neck like Henrietta Maria. It is a work of art. I wonder who the sculptor was.[3] I wandered in front of the house, of which only one wing is now left. It has three large chimney stacks and stone mullioned windows. At right angles to it is a long barn-like building, all of brick. In the grounds are remains of substructions and terraces, punctuated by widely spreading Irish yews. There are fragments of gadrooned stone urns resembling some of those now at Blickling, whither Lord Buckinghamshire removed them in the eighteenth century. There is an isolated brick screen with three open colonnades of Jacobean date in the field by the canal. It has two apses in the end openings, and buttresses behind them, as though once they held statues. What it means I could not ascertain. Standing at the front gate I learned from a roadman that Mr. Mosley lived there; and then I remembered Aunt Dorothy saying that Johnnie Mosley had bought a house in these parts. Oxnead has the air of a deserted, neglected home of an extinct family.

John Wilton put through a personal call from the Savoy at 9 p.m. He

---

[3] It was Nicholas Stone.

seemed anxious to see me, so I suggested his coming for the weekend, and he has accepted. Temptation always wins every encounter.

Tuesday, 26th June

A telegram from Müntzers the decorators, annoumcing their arrival at midday. Damn! This is not temptation, it is worse – duty. Miss O'Sullivan is much put out because she had prepared to do her week's baking today. Also a cinema company is due to film a scene here, the day of their arrival depending upon the weather. Mercifully it is raining. Müntzer's men arrived, but not Grandy Jersey. I gave them luncheon and brought them to the Hall. They made several useful suggestions and will submit a written report to me. They said the tapestries must be repaired and cleaned; and the panelling in the dining-room vinegared urgently. I suggested their tinting the snow-white ceiling in the Peter the Great room.

In spite of Müntzer's men (they left at 3.45) today's work was rather successful. At 9.15 I went for a glorious bicycle ride round the estate by Itteringham.

Wednesday, 27th June

This morning the R.A.F. sergeant gave me the key of the garden door in the north-east turret, so that I need not go all through the back regions of the house to reach the library. Instead I can slip unobserved through the garden. The Gainsborough film people were taking shots this afternoon, whenever it stopped raining. All morning it poured. I wrote the entire day, save after tea when I bicycled to Cawston. The hammerbeam angel roof of the church is superb. Along a frieze, over the clerestory, are angel masks with wings spread from their cheeks. They look like great bats. This roof apparently dates from 1380.

Rode past Reepham to Salle church, the finest of the lot. It is of later date than Cawston, about 1450, is symmetrical with projecting wings and angle turrets at the west end; corresponding north and south porches and transepts. The symmetry is exact and almost classical. The interior is very spacious and the clear windows with square panes are so vast that I wonder the walls sustain the roof. God is light, they seem to declare. The rood screen, not as fine as Cawston's, has original white priming on the woodwork. Three-decker pulpit, the sounding board Jacobean. The font cover, a skeleton without flesh, but still immensely impressive, is very slim and tall, shaped like an elongated candle-extinguisher, suspended from an original crane. An Ivory mural tablet to Miss Evans, dated 1798.

Thursday, 28th June

Conducted the film producer round the state rooms. To my surprise he was well informed. He said, 'You must not remove the nineteenth-century library shelves, for they have a period interest and show how the house has grown over the centuries.' He might have been me speaking. Birkbeck, the agent, appeared in the afternoon and motored me round parts of the estate. He showed me his nursery of young oaks and Douglases; also his new plantation opposite Hercules Wood, with which he is exceedingly pleased. We talked with Salmon the carpenter and Atto the woodman. Walked to the mausoleum and Lady's Cottage, thatched and almost drowned in an ocean of bracken. The troops have broken into this romantic little building and knocked it about too.

Friday, 29th June

I wonder if cart horses are as satisfied as I am after a full day's work. After a cup of tea I bicycled northwards for a change. Visited Itteringham church, just on the estate. Nothing of interest, bar some retreating perspective panelling, probably brought from a private house. On to Little Barningham church. Thought there was nothing here when, on leaving, my eye caught a small wooden effigy of Death, perched upon a pew-end, sickle in one hand, hour-glass in the other. Beyond the pew door were the following lines, dated 1640:

'All you that shall pass this place by
Remember that you soon must dye.
Even as you are, so once was I.
As I am now, you soon shall be.
Prepare therefore to follow me.'

Instead, I continued to Barningham Park, and without being stopped, bicyded down the drive through rows of Nissen huts. A dull evening; the place and park flat and dreary. Had a good look at the outside of the house. It is tall and top-heavy, of Tudor red brick, with central projecting porch and slim, octagonal angles; great chimneystacks and pedimented windows; crow-stepped gables, typically Norfolk. The wide window-panes and overbalanced dormers give this house a Victorian air. I peered through a window to the right of the porch and saw a big Jacobean stone fireplace. The ruined church beyond contains monuments to the Mott family. Came home by Calthorpe. Church here aisleless, wide, empty and barrel vaulted, with holes in the roof. The font cover is gaudily painted, and so is other woodwork. The emptiness and colour remind me of a French parish church. Too exhausted to visit Ingworth church on the way back to supper.

Saturday, 30th June

Humphry Repton's tombstone on the south wall outside Aylsham church has the following, appropriate quotation under his epitaph:

'Not like Egyptian tyrants consecrate
Unmixed with others shall my dust remain,
But moldring, blending, melting into earth
Mine shall give form and colour to the rose,
And while its vivid colours chear mankind
Its perfumed odours shall ascend to heaven.'

'Form and colour to the rose.' The sentence is borne out by a long, leggy briar, with one tiny bud, clambering up the wall from roots among that distinguished dust.

I worked the entire day until 6.45 and am well away with the Roman-Greek controversy. Walked to the station at Aylsham and met John Wilton. From the moment I greeted him at the station it has poured with rain. He is staying at the inn, where we dined. We walked round the lake, talking.

Sunday, 1st July

Today a whole holiday from work. Unfortunately a beastly day and raining constantly. John back from Europe says the British troops hate the French, and like the Germans. The American troops do the same. Nothing the politicians may say prevents it. We walked after luncheon to the mausoleum. While we were there it flashed lightning, and we feared the great iron doors might be struck, so hid in one of the empty embrasures. The thunder was deafening as it rolled and echoed round the reverberating dome of the mausoleum. We agreed that nothing could be more dramatic or eerie. The Buckinghamshire coffins remained motionless on their shelves.

Monday, 2nd July

Worked all day till dinner, John sitting around the state rooms reading and apparently content. Stuart telephoned this evening from London. He is back from the continent. I can see further temptation looming.

Tuesday, 3rd July

Wyndham Ketton-Cremer spent the morning with me in the library which, he says, contains the finest collection of seventeenth-century tracts he has come across. We lunched at the inn, and he agreed to take John on our tour. We called at Heydon first. The large house is let by the Bulwers to Lady Playfair, an old woman. It is a pretty house, centre part 1580, with Reptonish additions in the same style. Mrs. Bulwer is a widow, charming, living in a dower house. She showed us her collection of teapots, hundreds of them, all English, mostly porcelain, some pottery, and a few very eccentric. Her house is overcrowded with treasures. There is a Queen Anne dolls' house, inherited by her husband from a direct ancestor. The outside is dull, but the contents are fascinating, particularly a chandelier enclosed in a glass bubble for protection, ivory forks and knives in a shagreen case, the servants and the owner and his wife with their names inscribed. Among other extra dolls' house treasures were a pair of velvet shoes which belonged to Charles I.

Then to Wolterton. Lady Walpole showed us round and gave us tea. The house of beautiful, coursed brickwork. A heraldic achievement in the pediment finely carved. One wing has been added which is a pity. The porch on the north front is unfortunate, and should go. The *piano nobile* is raised high, and the rooms on the ground, or basement floor, are quite habitable and cosy for the cold winters they get in Norfolk. The state rooms are splendid, though at present in a mess, for until lately Lady Walpole had officers billeted on her throughout the war, Lord Walpole still being in the army. Ripley may have been a second-rate architect, but the quality of his craftsmanship is far from shoddy. The carving of the doors is on the other hand coarse. Chimneypieces of a variety of marbles. Wolterton could be made a wonderful place in spite of the flat terrain. The troops are still in Nissen huts along the drive under the trees.

The wrought-iron stair balusters have a wide handrail of inlaid amboyna. Stairwell worth examining at the top, being beautifully lit. All the subsidiary landings solidly vaulted. Lady Walpole provided a good nursery tea on the ground floor. Her little boy was rude and spoilt. John and I walked back to Blickling from the house. I showed him the staircase with carved hunting scenes on the ends of the risers in Itteringham farmhouse. The farmer complained about the Trust not painting his front door.

Wednesday, 4th July

John left at midday. I worked in the Gallery all morning, afternoon and evening, finishing a chapter.

Thursday, 5th July

Polling day but not for me. I simply cannot make up my mind how to vote. My dislike of socialism is almost equalled by my dislike of what Mr. Churchill stands for. Ever since the war in Europe has ended I have ruminated upon the outcome. What has it brought us? Perhaps the answer is that it has brought us nothing positively good, but has saved us from something infinitely bad. But to that answer I would retort that it has brought us something else infinitely bad, if not worse, namely Russian occupation of eastern Europe. Moreover this damnable occupation of Christian countries which form part of our civilization, will spread like a disease, and we, being too tired and feeble to resist, will complacently defer, in our typically phlegmatic British way, resisting this disease until it is too late. No, politically speaking, I am miserable. Nevertheless, my joy at the ghastly fighting having stopped, is great. This relief makes me so complacent that if asked tomorrow whether I would be prepared to resume fighting Communists instead of Nazis, I would hesitate – I hope not for long. But a short respite is needed. It must only be a respite.

At 2 o'clock met Birkbeck and the painter at Aylsham Old Hall. The army have de-requisitioned it, and given us £450 for dilapidations, out of which we are allowed to spend £100 if the work is undertaken before August 1st. After that date only £10 p.a. is allowed, which means that no one can possibly inhabit large houses after troops have been billeted in them for six years. It would be quite acceptable if the army, on clearing out, were allowed to reinstate what they had spoilt. As it stands the regulation is unfair and absurd. The Old Hall is a delightful house of about 1700; red brick, with large rooms of William and Mary wainscoting. There is a contemporary overmantel picture of the house itself and the barn beside it, almost as they are now. A pity the roof is of slate. One day we must put back the Norfolk pantiles. I bicycled over to Rippon and dined with the Birkbecks.

Friday, 6th July

A glorious day of full sun. I worked and walked in my shirt sleeves. The R.A.F. were bathing in the lake and lying in the sun. After dinner I bicycled to Erpingham where the N.T. owns a small detached parcel of the Blickling estate. I looked through the windows of Ingworth church, shut at this hour, and noticed a rood screen that seemed to be Jacobean. On the way back a delicious evening smell of amber hay. Bats flitting across the pale lemon sky.

Last night I had a dream about Tom. He was reading and sucking his pipe in the morning-room in Brooks's. I rushed up to him and he threw his arms round me. I said, 'Tom, they told me you were dead, and here I see and know that you are alive.' He laughed and said most convincingly, 'Yes, it was all a mistake.' Then I woke up.

Saturday, 7th July

I bicycled to Aylsham, surrendered my machine at the shop I hired it from, and walked to the station. Train punctual, and there on the platform was Stuart, smiling with pleasure. He was in his sergeant's uniform, unchanged in figure and face, though a little red like a porcupine without quills – the suns of Normandy. We went straight to the inn where he had an enormous meal at 3.30 of eggs and tea. It was as though there had been no break in our relations. Indeed there had been none. We went to the house and looked at the state rooms, then walked round the lake, and reclined under the trees in an Elizabethan fashion, chins hand-cupped. He had a bath in the bathroom next to the Chinese bedroom before we dined. The Sissons having arrived to stay at the inn for a fortnight, ate with us. I don't think either party liked the other much. Incompatibility of interests; lack of common acquaintances; and that instantaneous, suspicious antipathy of strangers. I am always naively surprised when my friends do not immediately click. After dinner Stuart and I left the Sissons and strolled round the lake, pausing at the remote end to take in the view of the house. Across the placid water it looked like a palace in a dream, insubstantial, and as the darkness crept between us, it melted like a palace in a dream. Returned to the inn where we smoked and talked. It was past midnight when I left. The front door being barred and bolted, and no key anywhere visible, I let myself out of a window into a bed of nasturtiums and ran home. Luckily Miss O'Sullivan does not lock her front door.

Sunday, 8th July

We left after luncheon for London. In Alexander Place the bath is installed, but no hot water connected. The house still occupied by the painter, and in a filthy mess.

Monday, 9th July

This morning a meeting at the Middlesex Guildhall with the Middlesex County Council, the Heston Council, and Grandy Jersey. They agreed to purchase Grandy's trustees' additional land. The meeting was a success. Had my hair cut at Trumper's, and in the evening went to Richmond to stay the night at Grandy's. After dinner he invited the Mayor of Richmond and six other worthies to meet me and discuss Ham House. This too a success, for they finally agreed they would recommend contribution of the whole endowment sum we need for that house. After dinner I said to Grandy gaily, 'And where is Virginia? I suppose she has gone out to avoid the mayoral meeting.' Grandy said very solemnly, 'No. We have separated.' All I could say was I was sorry. There are moments in life when all words are superfluous.

Tuesday, 10th July

Luncheon at the White Tower. Ben Nicolson, John Russell and an American called Louis Auchincloss, who spoke so softly that I could not hear one word he said, and was obliged to turn away. Ben said that at Windsor the other day the King was looking at his pictures with him. John Piper was present. The King closely scrutinized Piper's pictures of the Castle, turned to him and remarked, 'You seem to have very bad luck with your weather, Mr. Piper.'

At 3 a meeting with Farrer, Lord Leconfield's solicitor, and Balfour, the Petworth estate's solicitor. They both informed me that Lord Leconfield, with the blood of the 'proud' Duke of Somerset in his veins, was the most arrogant man in England. They warned me when I met him, not to mention Lady Leconfield's name. At 5 I had tea with Lord and Lady Newton. They are in a great fluster about Lyme and their furniture. I agreed to ask Margaret Jourdain to help them with the furniture, although I don't in the least know what exactly they want her to do. Nor do they, it seems. Not an examination, not a valuation, for these have already been done. However Margaret, to whom I have spoken, has agreed to go if they ask her.

Wednesday, 11th July

Dora Prescott, that incorrigible woman, telephoned. I asked her how she liked Paris. She answered, 'It was wonderful. I ate and drank the most marvellous food every day. With people starving in the streets, it gave me such a cosy feeling, a sort of *après moi le déluge* feeling.' Really, how dare she say such a thing, even if she feels it. I hope the deluge quickly immerses her.

Thursday, 12th July

At Slatter's exhibition of Dutch seventeenth-century pictures there are two N.T. pictures, lent by us, the Pieter de Hooch of those beastly, whimsy children with golf clubs, and a Cornelis de Mann which, now cleaned, looks fine. Went to see some furniture offered by old Mrs. Maclachlan. No earthly good. Was to have dined with George Dix, but met Alvilde in the street, and she asked us both to dine with her. Just ourselves.

Saturday, 14th July

This morning I met Margaret Jourdain at the V & A library, to which she introduced me. Lunched at Boodle's with Alastair Forbes. The devil gets into me when I am with M.P.s or political aspirants, and I find myself saying outrageous things which I do not always mean. Thus such people consider me wicked, mad or stupid, possibly all three. Possibly they don't think anything about me at all.

In the train I read the life of Matthew Boulton and James's indifferent little book on the Houses of Parliament. Very poor illustrations and it costs 15/-. Gerry Wellington met me at Mortimer station and motored me to Stratfield Saye for a late tea. The Eshers and Eddie Marsh are staying. The Eshers are very sweet to each other. They tease each other. Gerry is growing a paunch. Eddie is growing old. Gerry is extremely fussy. Eddie broke a miniature and had to own up. Gerry said it didn't matter in a tone of voice which indicated how desperately he thought it did. In handing round the Great Duke's 'George', he said to me who was sitting next to Eddie, 'Don't let Eddie hold it. He breaks works of art.' Before we went to bed he gave Eddie a whisky and soda, exhorting him not to exceed his ration of one bottle for a week's visit.

Sunday, 15th July

Gerry let me drive myself in his car down the Wellingtonia avenue to Heckfield Park for Mass. I like privately owned chapels, and the women trailing in straight from the bedroom, while they adjust their mantillas. When I returned the others had finished breakfast, Gerry having had his alone before they were down, as is his custom.

The Eshers are great ones for sitting around and chatting. They sat in the drawing-room after luncheon and talked non-stop till dinner time. They began upon Jane Austen – Gerry and Eddie strong partisans – whereas Lady E. and I upheld Trollope. Then politics and Russia. Esher is pro-Russia, for he believes they hold the germ of an idea. Some germ. Although most contradictory in his opinions, he is a fundamental Liberal, but no National Liberal. He disagrees with all Gerry's views, even on houses, for he believes Charlecote to be very important on account of the Shakespeare associations. Gerry most emphatically does not. After dinner I left, Gerry motoring me to Mortimer. The train late, arriving Paddington 12.20. I walked in the rain to Alexander Place. Found the house upside down. My room is having the floor boards darkened, and the bed is an island in the middle, with nothing else near it. I slept in this huddle.

Monday, 16th July

I left at 7.30 for breakfast with Eardley. He in his good-natured way is having me to stay in his flat. The office is likewise in a state of chaos, for the workmen are now hammering in the agents' rooms.

Eardley and I travelled by train to Bangor to stay with Michael Duff at Vaynol. I have a window overlooking the lake and Snowdon, a sublime view – meadows, water, woods, mountains and – why is it? – so much sky. Only Juliet, Michael's mother, is staying.

Tuesday, 17th July

This morning Michael motored us through Llanberis, up the pass to the little hotel at the far end, whence tourists begin their climb of Snowdon, which from here we could not see, for it was round the corner. Snowdon belongs to Michael, who wishes to protect it and the whole Llanberis Pass by covenants. He told me he owns 60,000 acres in Wales. We returned by Caernarvon Castle. Walked into the central court which leaves me cold. Only the picturesque exterior moves me.

After luncheon to see Michael's quarries, huge terraces cut into the mountain-side, looking like a John Martin landscape – Belshazzer's Feast. I motored to Plas Newydd on Anglesey. Found Lord and Lady Anglesey at the bottom of the stairs, sitting on the floor sorting objects for a local fête sale. And wonderful things they were too, which they were pricing at only a few shillings. Lady Anglesey with very white hair, slight and well made, and well dressed in a tartan skirt, smelling of upper-class scent and cigarettes. She has a little wizened face like a marmoset's, and is extremely attractive. Pretty looks compared to Lady Diana's beautiful looks. Lord Anglesey is very handsome, with much affability and charm. I explained to him what the National Trust was. I suspected that his enquiries were not very serious.

Plas Newydd was built about 1780, then altered by James Wyatt. Lord Anglesey has again done a good deal of altering, and adding a large wing where Wyatt's unconsecrated chapel stood. There is still a Gothic saloon left like the Birr one, and the staircase is classical with shallow apses and columns, somehow unmistakably Wyatt. There are many family portraits and relics of the 1st Marquess, 'One leg', Lady Anglesey calls him. There is an extremely long room with a huge canvas facing the windows, of a pastiche scene by Rex Whistler, who was a close family friend. The best thing about Plas Newydd is the situation, which is unsurpassed – the straits below, the Snowdon range, the tubular bridge and the monument to the first Marquess. The Angleseys plan to pull down half the house which will be an improvement. They complain that there is no one on the island to talk to.

Thursday, 19th July

After cursing the caretaker at Polesden for neglecting his duties, and taking away two silver teapots bequeathed to Sir John Bailey, I arrived at Petworth at 3.30. I stopped at the street entrance, walked through a long, gloomy passage, crossed a drive, passed under a *porte cochère* into a hall, and was ushered into Lord Leconfield's presence. He gave me a hurried handshake without a smile, and told the housekeeper to show me round the inside. This she did, bewailing the damage caused to ceilings and walls by Saturday's storm. She and one housemaid look after this vast palace. All the state rooms being shut up and the furniture under dustsheets, I had difficulty, with most of the shutters fastened, in seeing. I liked the housekeeper. She keeps the house spotless and polished. Then I was handed back to Lord Leconfield.

My first impression was of a pompous old ass, with a blue face and fish eyes. He seemed deliberately to misunderstand what the National Trust was all about. He was highly suspicious. He looked up and said,

'Understand, this visit commits me to nothing. I much doubt whether the National Trust can help me.' He complained, understandably enough, of surtax, and would not grasp the fact that the Trust was exempt from taxation. He implied that we would turn him out of the house the moment we took over. He walked me very slowly round the park. He told me that neither his father nor grandfather would allow the name of his great-grandfather, Lord Egremont, to be mentioned, although his grandfather was the son (illegitimate) of that excellent patron of artists. He said that the Victorian architect Salvin, when summoned by his father, stood on the mound in the park, and pointing to the house said, 'My Lord, there is only one thing to be done. Pull the whole house down and re-build it.' His father replied, 'You had better see the inside first.'

At 5.45 Lord Leconfield, tired out, led me to the street door where he dismissed me. Pointing to a tea house with an enormous notice CLOSED hanging in the window, he said, 'You will get a very good tea in there. Put it down to me. Goodbye.' Had I not been forewarned I would have concluded that my visit was a distinct failure.

Friday, 20th July

Dined with Margaret Jourdain and Ivy Compton-Burnett, both delighted to be back in London. Ivy rather repetitive, but funny as usual in her abrupt, clipped manner. She talked of the days before motor cars. She told how it was common practice for a barefooted man to run from a country station two or three miles behind one's carriage in the hope of being allowed to take the luggage upstairs, and so to receive a 6d. tip, if lucky. Usually he wasn't lucky, for the servants of the house where one was staying would shoo the man away, which meant a plod back to the station, unrewarded. Can this have been true in her lifetime?

Sunday, 22nd July

Mass at Warwick Street. I found myself sitting next to Evelyn Waugh and did not speak to him. Had no luncheon, but put my rooms in order, hanging pictures till tea, which I had with Dame Una. Bishop Mathew, who was present, talked to me about Wardour Castle. He had advised Dame Una not to join the Montacute Committee, because it would be a waste of her time. This made me cross. The Bishop laughs like a schoolgirl in a shrill falsetto. I saw him off, waddling with his breviary under his arm. The Dame says he is sure to be a cardinal, one of the new thirty. I hope so. He is just back from Abyssinia and has a high regard for the Lion of Judah's culture. No one else in that country can even talk sense, only gibberish. The nobility are very feudal, but like savages; the ordinary people like wild animals.

Wednesday, 25th July

This afternoon to the Law Courts, and for two hours I listened to the
Coughton Court case in Chambers. Four barristers, one a woman, in their
attractive curled wigs, each with two little grey pigtails. I wish all men could
wear wigs as in the eighteenth century. Our counsel, King, was very dictatorial to Horne and me, and I did not like him. Sir Robert Throckmorton
attended for half an hour. I was not at all bored, although the Judge, Vaisey,
dealt with the most intricate technical points. I greatly admired his authority in dealing with counsels, his consummate mastery of the case, and his
dry humour. He was delightful, and reminded me of Roger Fulford.

Thursday, 26th July

Up early and breakfasted at the Paddington Hotel before catching the 9.10
to Leamington. Arrived Charlecote at 11.30 in pouring rain. Found
Clifford Smith and Mrs. Fairfax-Lucy in something of a state. No progress
has been made since our last visit. No one will come to remove the billiard table and the other furniture we want to get rid of. She is a sweet
woman. Cliffy says there is nothing wrong about her, and everything she
says is right. She likes him very much, but begged me the next time I came
down not to bring him, for we shall get on quicker without him.

I laughed so much with Alice Fairfax-Lucy while we were staggering
under the weight of a bust of a Lucy, in fear that we would drop it, that I
almost did myself a mischief, damned nearly. Clifford made two very old
retainers carry a pair of marble busts from the great hall into the library,
and then back again to their original places. The groans of the retainers
were heart-rending.

Friday, 27th July

Clifford rang up to say the silver cup he found at Charlecote and brought
to the V & A is exceedingly rare. Its date is 1524 and it is the fourth earliest wine cup in existence, the Danny cup being the earliest.

Saturday, 28th July

I set out to stay with Ted Lister at Westwood, but on approaching
Paddington at 9 found a queue stretching from the Bayswater Road,
almost from the Park. Taxis were being directed by mounted policemen to
the end of the queue. I gave up, and didn't make any further attempt.

Tuesday, 31st July

Matheson left the office today, and we are in chaos.

I had luncheon with Eddy who goes this week to live with Eardley and
Desmond Shawe-Taylor at Long Crichel in Dorset. I had a drink this
evening with Jock Murray in Albemarle Street. Peter Quennell was present

and, speaking of Brendan Bracken, said, 'I always distrust men with pubic hair on their heads.'

Thursday, 2nd August

Motored to Faringdon and lunched at the hotel. Read through my National Trust book which is now out. It looks rather thin and cheap. Called upon Mr. Furley, aged 90, at Kencot Manor, a very simple type of farmhouse, of little importance. I can't think why we hold it. He is a dear old man. He complained of his age and said questioningly, 'I shall never be able to do my carpentering again' in such a tone that I suspected he hoped I would contradict him, but I thought it better not to. Although so old, he walked me all over the house and round the garden; then gave me tea. He is a retired Winchester master. We discussed politics and Stafford Cripps, his neighbour and one time school pupil. He thinks him a man of the strictest integrity, who is carried away by fervour to make regrettable utterances. I left him soon after tea and drove to Lechlade, where I telephoned to Mama, then sat in the churchyard in the declining sun and read.

Stayed this night at Cirencester Park with Lady Apsley, who is an active-minded woman, of common sense. She has just been defeated in the election, but spoke with no bitterness of the socialists, having implicit confidence in the future; why, I don't quite understand. She told me that a friend of hers had returned this week from Rome, having had an audience of the Pope. The Pope said the result of our election would be misunderstood throughout Europe; the continent would assume that England had gone red. The sequel would be revolutions in Denmark, France, Italy, Spain and Greece. This would be one disastrous outcome of the election.

Lady Apsley sits in a chair in which she pushes herself from one room to another, for she is paralysed from the waist downwards, her poor legs stiffly splayed outwards. I found myself wanting to stare at them. Her father-in-law and husband both died within a year of each other, and her son has had to pay two lots of death duties. She wishes to covenant with the N.T. or else make them sole trustees, and thus get off death duties on the park, which is open to the public all the year round. The inside and outside of the house have been spoilt, but the outside not irreparably, because the plate-glass windows could be replaced with sashes, and the creeper removed; so could the Victorian flower beds. The inside could be improved, although it can never have been a very good one. Several family portraits, Romneys and Lawrences, and two Knellers in grisaille given by Pope to the 1st Earl Bathurst.

Friday, 3rd August

This morning the agent, Captain Turner, motored me round the property. The whole estate covers 14,000 acres, the park about 4,000. There is an avenue five miles long and a central junction, called Ten Ride Point, a most impressive feature. Several temples, one hexagonal, and Pope's Seat, some mid-eighteenth-century follies, cardboard castellated lodges, and so forth. Though the layout dating from the 1st Earl's time is on an astonishing scale, there are few natural contours, and the park is flat. There is a tall column with an effigy of Queen Anne on the summit in a direct line from the house. Otherwise the rides are made axial with the church, presumably because the tower is so high that it can be seen from a greater distance than the house.

Saturday, 4th August

I motored Geoffrey Houghton-Brown to Felix Hall where I deposited him. An extremely hot, burning day, the car emitting strong fumes of oil and dense smoke. On the way we visited Thorndon, near Brentwood. To my great surprise the house remains, the centre block having been gutted by fire in the 1880s, but the walls perfect. The bricks, beautifully jointed, stone dressings and tabernacle framed windows still in excellent repair. The two pavilions not so good. A golf club is housed in one, to which they have made unsightly additions. The other has soldiers in it, and looks bad. The site is an eminence with rural views towards Brentwood and other directions. The two-mile avenue to Brentwood has now gone. What amazed us was the lime trees planted immediately beneath the north front of the main block, just as though the owners had something to be ashamed of. I believe the Petre family sold the place before the war, and the club intend to demolish it as soon as they can. Only an hour or so earlier Geoffrey and I remarked that the screen of trees round St. Clement Danes was just where no trees were needed. Good architecture needs no shrouding.

I arrived for the weekend at Shermans, Dedham, to stay with the Sissons.

This morning I sat in the back garden roasting myself in the sun and reading Fiske Kimball's Rococo book. Being a civilized man Sisson knows how to leave one alone of a morning – a splendid but little understood virtue in a host. Perhaps I make it too apparent that I like to be left alone. In the afternoon storm-clouds gathered. Sisson and I walked to Flatford Mill, where we watched the milling crowds bathing, running, jumping and enjoying themselves.

Tuesday, 7th August

Doreen Baynes having telephoned, I went to see her at Brown's Hotel at 6, our first meeting since 1939. She has not altered much, and still looks very frail. We both professed inordinate pleasure and deep affection. Nevertheless I sensed that our protestations were a tiny bit forced, simply owing to the time lag. Affection has to be nourished on constant communication, either direct or indirect, by meeting or correspondence – the latter the better I opine.

Wednesday, 8th August

John Wilton telephoned that his trustees refuse categorically to sanction his buying Audley End. I am very disappointed but not the least surprised by this. Helen Dashwood lunched with me at the Bagatelle wearing a vast magenta felt hat with pheasant's plume, bought in Paris. I met John Wilton at the Connaught, proud and splendid. Disappointed though I am, I cannot be angry with him.

All day I have been made to feel despairing, careless and numb by the atom bomb. Nothing has a purpose any more, with these awful clouds of desolation hovering over us. I am shocked, shocked, shocked by our use of this appalling bomb, a tiny instrument the size of a golf ball, dropped on the Japanese and devastating four square miles. It is horrifying, and utterly damnable.

Thursday, 9th August

At last I have found an electrician. He came to the house at 9 this morning. He was so delightful, fatherly and reassuring that I could have embraced him. Such kindness as he showed is more than one dares expect.

A very full attendance at my Historic Buildings Committee. Michael Rosse was present for the first time. Too much flippancy and exclusiveness today. Esher asked me to lunch with him at Brooks's. We discussed various matters, including this. No agents will work for the Trust unless salaries are raised. Raise them is the answer. Money is always there when needed.

Friday, 10th August

Oh the onslaught of age! I met Lord Redesdale in Heywood's shop. Nancy said, 'You know Farve,' and there, leaning on a stick was a bent figure with a shrunken, twisted face, wearing round, thick spectacles, looking like a piano tuner. Last time I saw him he was upstanding and one of the best-looking men of his generation. I suppose Tom's death has helped hasten this terrible declension. I melted with compassion.

I had to lunch with Charles Fry my publisher at the Park Lane Hotel. He was late, having just got up after some orgy *à trois* with whips, etc. He is terribly depraved and related every detail, not questioning whether I wished to listen. In the middle of the narration I simply said, 'Stop! Stop!' At the same table an officer was eating, and imbibing every word. I thought he gave me a crooked look for having spoilt his fun.

My delight in Churchill's defeat, disapproval of the Socialists' victory, detestation of the atom bomb and disgust with the Allies' treatment of Germany are about equal. Muddle.

Saturday, 11th August

This afternoon I endeavoured to select furniture with old Mrs. Murray Smith in 40 Queen Anne's Gate; but she is in her second childhood, and we made no progress at all. She is bent almost double, her poor old head torn down to her chest. Her house is in an indescribable mess and looks as if it has not been cleaned since she came to live here fifty years ago. It is dreadful that no one looks after this pathetic old lady.

Monday, 13th August

This afternoon with Christopher Gibbs to inspect the Cedar House at Cobham. It has a pretty, irregular Georgian front of red brick, good railings and gate piers bearing stone pineapples. The view, over the road, and into the low-lying meadow is bucolic. The faked up medieval hall, with bogus long window and gallery is horrid. Some oak quatrefoils in the roof spandrels may be original.

Wednesday, 15th August

Miss Ballachey telephoned at 8 to say the war was over, and today and tomorrow were public holidays. I am strangely unmoved by this announcement. The world is left a victim of chaos, great uncertainty and heinous turpitude. Apparently the news was given on the midnight bulletin which I, having no wireless set, did not hear. I did hear at 2 a.m. distant sounds of hilarity. This morning no buses are running, and everything is very tiresome, including the drizzle. I breakfasted at Brooks's since the milkman left me no milk and the charwoman no bread yesterday. Nevertheless I went to the office and drafted letters. Worked all afternoon.

I dined at the Ordinary and didn't enjoy it a bit, although several friends were present, including the Nicolson boys. Nigel was looking wonderfully healthy and handsome. He astonished me and embarrassed Ben by saying loudly, as we sat on a sofa together, 'I do wish men would make up their faces.' I can think of several who might improve themselves in this way, although Nigel has no need to do it. He made wry references to James's behaviour as though he were surprised and pained by it. I left with Desmond Shawe-Taylor, and we walked against a stream of people coming away from Buckingham Palace. We stood for three-quarters of an hour on the Victoria Monument gazing expectantly at the crimson and gold hangings over the balcony. Floodlit the façade looked splendid, but the minute royal standard was out of scale. Desmond could not bear waiting, being an impatient man, but I was determined to wait. Besides I easily get into a sort of cabbage condition and can't be bothered to uproot myself. The crowd showed some excitement, calling, 'We want the King,' 'We want the Queen,' but not uproariously. At last, just after midnight, the French window opened a crack, then wider, and out came the King and Queen. They were tiny. I could barely distinguish her little figure swathed in a fur, and something sparkling in her hair. The gold buttons of his Admiral's uniform glistened. Both waved in a slightly self-conscious fashion and stood for three minutes Then they retreated. The crowd waved with great applause, and all walked quietly home.

I was mightily flattered by Cyril telling me this evening that my *Horizon* article was one of the best, whatever that precisely means.

Thursday, 16th August

In combing through chapter 2 of *Adam* I realize how badly it is written. It reads choppily and disjointedly. It is heavy, dull and unrelieved by picturesque and humorous allusions. Jamesey would enliven what he wrote so as to make his prose flow and curve, caracole and purl.

I lunched at the Argentine Ambassadress's. Sir Ronald Storrs had Lady Abingdon on one side and me on the other. She had an enormous straw hat with black ribbon round the crown, sloping off one side of her head. This side was next to him. The effect was that of a Picasso portrait of a lady with face tilted awry. The consequence was that he could neither catch a glimpse of her face nor a word she spoke, and so turned to me. I was delighted. He agreed that the Tories in the last Government had badly let us down by condoning all the iniquities of the Bolsheviks in Eastern Europe. For instance, they (Bolsheviks, not Tories) crucified three Lithuanian bishops on hot iron. This was deliberately kept out of the British press. But, he said, Bevin was standing up to Stalin. He opened proceedings at Potsdam by saying, as he thrust his hands into his braces, 'Mr. Stalin, I am a Yorkshireman, and I tells you straight, I don't sign no documents what I doesn't understand, do you see?' The Russians are disappointed with the change of government because they fear the Labour leaders will be more outspoken than were Churchill and Eden, who were over-anxious not to offend susceptibilities in view of their known pre-war antagonism to the Soviet.

Saturday, 18th August

I asked John Fowler to meet Margaret Jourdain for luncheon at the Normandie, and so fulfilled for him a long cherished desire. We went back to her flat and drank coffee with her and Ivy. John was amazed by the bareness and austerity of their flat, the uniform stark apple-green decoration and the floor linoleum against which their few nice Georgian pieces of furniture look islanded and insignificant. He returned and drank tea with me here.

This evening I changed into a dinner jacket, the first time since the war, and dined with Aubrey Moody on King's Guard at St. James's Palace. Enjoyed it immensely. We ate well, off an expensive snow-white tablecloth and with brightly polished silver. Delicious wines. I sat next a young sub-altern who had broken, like me, a vertebra of his spine but, unlike me, from landing on a parachute. Hector Bolitho also a guest. He talks in riddles. He has a round, quizzical face and the manner of a schoolmaster. Nice man, and no highbrow.

Monday, 20th August

Lunched with Hector Bolitho at the Connaught Hotel, till 3.15. He told me that he was born a New Zealander, and first came to London aged 21. He discovered for himself the allure of old buildings, and art generally. The first thing he looked at was the Charles I statue at Charing Cross. This opened his eyes. Hitherto he had never come upon a work of art of any sort.

Then to Batsford's. Charles Fry wants the National Trust to apply for more paper for Batsford to print another 10,000 copies of my N.T. book, which is selling over and beyond their expectations. The 7,500 copies they printed have gone already in under a week.

Tuesday, 21st August

Went by train to Ampthill. Got a taxi, picked up Professor Richardson at Avenue House, he hobbling uneasily with a broken ankle, and drove to Ampthill House. We lunched with Sir Anthony Wingfield, a delightful, intelligent old man in his 90th year. He is very active, only a little deaf and blind. During luncheon we discussed executions, of Monmouth and Mary Queen of Scots. The Professor is the most enlivening companion, bubbling with anecdotes and jokes. Sir Anthony showed me a watch given to his great-uncle at Harrow in 1806 and a letter from Byron. The letter was addressed, 'Dearest John' and stressed that their friendship was based on no 'ordinary affection'. He has silver spoons and forks which belonged to the Prince Regent at the Pavilion, heavily embossed with mask heads and tro-phies. Sir Anthony's butler, called Cooper, wrote a few years ago a book on his service with the aristocracy which Sir A. has lent me. We walked to look at his house in the street which he wishes to leave to the N.T. It is a fine 1740 house of harsh brick with stone dressings and a projecting porch, but much knocked about by troops. I accompanied the Professor to Avenue House, built by Holland. It is chock-a-block with treasures. The Professor looks like a Rowlandson figure among so much Georgian elegance.

Thursday, 23rd August

Dined and drank far too much with Michael Rosse on King's Guard. I walked, how I don't know, back with Oliver [Messel] peering into antique shops in the Brompton Road. We went all round his new house in Pelham Crescent, next door to Alexander Place. It is huge, being two houses knocked into one, and was pitch dark because no lights were working. We could only feel our way around by dint of a muslin moon. Consequently my gush was slightly tempered by the invisibility. Found myself swaying, and once had to clutch the back of Oliver's neck.

Friday, 24th August

Jasper Holdsworth lunched with me (having invited himself) at the Café Royal, which was so depressing that it put me in a filthy mood. Jasper never helps one out, and is a sort of nature's vampire. He takes but does not give, and his schemes, professedly to one's, and I will admit, to his own advantage, seldom materialize. It was getting late. His car, he assured me, would arrive in a minute and would motor me back to the office. Of course it never came, and I had to walk.

Saturday, 25th August

This has been a very long day. I woke at 5.45, and at 6.45 the car ordered by Michael Rosse called for me. It picked him up in Mount Street and drove us to Euston for the 8.15 to Holyhead. Travelled in comfort and ease. I read several books during the journey, Michael much amused because I read standing in queues on the boat. I always do this, for what is the point of letting the minutes roll by in vacancy?

At Holyhead Anne's two Armstrong-Jones children joined us. After a smooth crossing we reached Kingstown at 7.30. I was at once struck by the old-fashioned air of everything: horse-cabs at the quay, cobbled streets with delicious horse-droppings on them. Met by a taxi cab come all the way from Birr, costing £8. Letter of greeting from Anne to Michael. Vodka for Michael and me in the car. We drove straight to Birr. Even through the closed windows of the car I caught the sweet smell of peat in the air. Curious scenes, ragged children on horses drawing old carts along country lanes. Our driver sounded his horn loudly through Birr, that piercing, pretty foreign horn. The gates of the castle shot open as if by magic. A group of people were clustered outside the gate. We swept up the drive. All the castle windows were alight, and there on the sweep was a large crowd of employees and tenants gathered to welcome Michael back from the war. Anne, the two Parsons boys, and Mr. Garvie the agent on the steps. Behind them Leavy the butler, the footman, housekeeper, and six or seven maids. A fire blazing in the library and everywhere immense vases of flowers. We heard Michael make a short speech from the steps, followed by cheers and 'For he's a jolly good fellow', a song which always makes me go hot and cold, mostly hot. The crowd then trooped off to a beano and drinks, while we sat down to a huge champagne supper at 11 o'clock.

Sunday, 26th August

I rose late this morning, just in time for Mass in the town 'with the natives'. The church very full and crowded, and somehow horribly sectarian and un-Roman; but clean and polished. Indeed there is an air of well-being and contentment in Ireland, and almost of prosperity after England. The house-fronts in the town are painted and the inhabitants well clothed, whereas before the war I remember them as squalid and poverty-stricken. This shows how English standards and conditions must have deteriorated during the war years. The streets in Birr are swept. There is as little traffic as before the war. The smell of horse-dung everywhere is very refreshing after the petrol fumes.

Tuesday, 28th August

Bridget came from Abbey Leix yesterday, and today Lord X. He is an agreeable, plump, intelligent Irishman, a Catholic from Galway. He says the priests arc so bigoted and politically minded that he fears there will be a strong reaction from Catholicism in Ireland within the next generation. Most of the priests are peasants' sons, with no true vocation. They become priests because it gives them social status. He blames Maynooth College. A generation ago the neophytes went to Rome. Now they are totally nationalistic and provincial in outlook. The Cardinal is positively chauvinistic. Lord X. blames the Vatican for not taking the Irish hierarchy in hand. The people are kept in great ignorance as in Spain.

We went for a walk this afternoon with the children, in the bog, leaping from tuft to tuft. The wide, flat expanse of bog with purple heather growing upon it, and the purple hills, always just in sight, very nostalgic. I find the climate extremely relaxing. I eat a lot, am sleepy, and wake up feeling doped. The food is rich after England, and the cooking full of butter and cream.

Thursday, 30th August

We motored up the mountain, got out and walked over the heather in the sun. The heather smells acrid. It is curious how quite high up you come upon soggy patches of bog where the turf has been sliced away. Oh yes, the climate of Ireland is far too relaxing. There is something dead about the country and the people. It is like living on a luxuriant moon. I dislike the way individuals remain for hours on end standing and staring into space. We passed this morning one woman sitting on a stile, with the face of a zany, staring, not at the view, but at her toes. When we returned this evening, she was still there in exactly the same idiotic posture, and still staring at her toes. This gives me the creeps.

Friday, 31st August

Michael and I motored thirty miles to Abbey Leix to fetch his mother, Lady de Vesci. I was last here at Easter 1936 staying with Desmond Parsons. I had forgotten the extraordinary beauty of the park and trees. The vivid fresh green of Ireland in August after the aridity of England is startling. The house was built about 1780 and is Adam-like. A beautiful hall with columned screen, delicate frieze, and the whitest statuary marble chimneypiece. Two drawing-rooms both with thin decorated ceilings, and one with deep sky-blue Morris wallpaper which, though wrong, is very attractive with the gold mirrors and frames. The library has pink scagliola columns, green walls, mud-coloured bookcases and Siena doorways, all dating from about 1850 and very charming: facing full south. The exterior has been too Victorianized, balustrades added, window-surrounds altered, and some plate glass inserted.

At Roscrea, on our return to Birr, a large brown dog walked under the car which drove right over its body. Lady de Vesci made the driver pull up. She said he ought just to apologize. He got out and we all sat still. I saw the poor dog kicking in the road, but by the time the driver reached it, it was dead and being dragged to the verge. I felt rather sick. This is the first time such a thing has happened to me, though I expected this driver would kill a dog sooner or later. In Ireland the dogs are not well trained to avoid motor cars, as they seem to be in England. Michael and his mother were quite unmoved, and so it seemed were the owners of the dog. What a contrast to my mother's behaviour. If she had been present she would have created the most embarrassing scene, tearing out the driver's hair in rage, hugging the corpse and emptying her purse into the lap of the owner.

Saturday, 1st September

Before leaving Birr for Dublin I spent the afternoon with Anne alone, the others having gone for a walk in the woods. She conducted me round the castle, showing me all the portraits and little things belonging to Parsons ancestors that mean so much to her. She is a proud chatelaine and looks after her possessions with tender care. I have the greatest admiration for her efficiency, her vitality, her keen wit and good nature. She always has the ready answer.

The train to Dublin was packed with folk going up to the Games. There is only one train each weekday, and none on Sundays. At Dublin I spent three-quarters of an hour in an appalling jam trying to extricate my bag, which unfortunately the chauffeur had put in the van because he thought I should not get a seat and would have no room for it in the corridor. A typical Irish scene of muddle and confusion. Before we got to the train it left the platform, to our dismay. Eventually it returned, whereupon porters and passengers screamed and scrambled over each other, the passengers complaining vociferously at the inadequacy of the system which, they maintained, could only be experienced in Ireland. Had a foreigner agreed with them, they would doubtless have set upon him. In Dublin I was pushed into a four-wheeler with two other passengers, and we bowled over the cobbles to the Hibernian Hotel. Here I found Geoffrey Houghton-Brown and we dined after 10. No difficulty getting a meal at this hour and plenty of waiters.

Sunday, 2nd September

Walked this morning to the Municipal Museum. Quite a good collection of modern pictures: Lavery, Jack Yeats, and the Hugh Lane collection – coresponding to our Tate Gallery. All the churches so crowded we could hardly enter one. The devotion of the men and women is not so much exemplary as alarming, for the Irish are not a spiritual people.

You see no platinum blondes, no tarts in Dublin streets. There is absolutely no evidence of vice on the surface. Yet the squalor of the slums is formidable. We walked into several doorways in Henrietta Street. Splendid mid-Georgian grand houses, now tenements in neglect, dirt and disrepair. But what a wonderful town. Streets of flat façaded houses, dull maybe, but of long unbroken elevation and layout. The atmosphere created by the four-wheelers, the side-cars, the smell of ammonia from horses and the stale straw from mews is of the 1890s. The bouquets of ferns and geraniums tied round lampposts conjure up 'art nouveau' poster designs. We looked at the Custom House, the Four Courts, the Castle, Trinity College and several churches. We bought sweets and ate them in the street. The view across the river, which reminded me of the Arno, of the magnificent elevation of the Four Courts is spoilt by mean little trees.

Tuesday, 4th September

Badk in London. At 4, Anthony Martineau and I had a painful meeting about Ham House at the Richmond town hall with the town councillors and the Tollemache family: old Sir Lyonel aged 93 and his son. The town clerk and councillors were gushing and deferential; the Tollemaches proud and patronizing. When the Tollemaches left we stayed behind and the town councillors became outspoken in their derision and dislike. I was horribly and uncomfortably aware of the hostility between the two classes.

This evening I had a glass of sherry, South African and rather hot, with Doreen Baynes, once again in her drawing-room in 18 Ovington Square, with the alcove, the peach satin sofa, the satinwood Sheraton furniture on spindly legs, the fragile Chelsea shepherdesses, and the very same wax magnolias not even dusted since 1939. It was a more satisfactory meeting than our last in Brown's Hotel. We both poured out confidential chat. She told me she goes through such agonies over reviews of her books that she often retires to bed for a week, with blinds drawn, silently weeping. We agreed that we were both over-sensitive, infantine, only fairly intelligent and not intellectual; that Dame Una and Eddy were too intellectual for us, and made us gauche, awkward and rather idiotic; and that far from having too much vanity we had too much humility.

Thursday, 6th September

This morning Anthony Martineau and I attended another local authority meeting, this time with the Middlesex County Council and the Heston Council in the Guildhall. Grandy Jersey was not present but if he had been, there would have been no Lady Catherine de Burgh attitude, such as was evinced the other day. Anthony said I handled them perfectly. This was not quite true, but I certainly tried to treat them as sensible human creatures, without scolding, without high-hatting, and I pulled their legs and my own.

Sunday, 9th September

Hinch talked to me in Brooks's about Hinchingbrooke, which he wants to convert into a Cromwellian museum, he living in a part only after pulling down an ugly Victorian wing. He says we must expect no reduction in taxation from this Government, but probably allowances will be increased for the benefit of the small salary earner. That's me, hurrah!

I spoke to Dame Una on the telephone. I find that families who are too closely knit incline to indulge in self-adulation. Her Dickens book is having poor reviews, which she attributes to the ignorance of the reviewers. She complains that they have all failed to detect her new discoveries about her subject. I hazard the guess that she biographizes better than she analyses. Nevertheless the Dame says she will go into a third edition by Christmas and her publishers would like to print 100,000 copies. All this was delivered in a clipped, slightly self-satisfied, superior tone, which does not endear her to some people. But she has long ago endeared herself to me, and will not be de-endeared.

Monday, 10th September

Dined with Mark Ogilvie-Grant this evening. Princess Aspasia of Greece called for me at 7.15. She drove a large, black, glossy car, bringing with her

Lady Patsy Ward, whom I like because she is so outspoken. Princess Aspasia is tall and dark, and what is called very well preserved. She is easy and gay and seems intelligent. She was morganatically married to the King of Greece who died of a monkey bite, I believe, and her daughter is the present Queen of Yugoslavia. After dinner conversation got on to rabies – this was none of my initiating – and the fatal bites of mad dogs and other animals. We talked of anarchism, communism and fascism. She said she made no distinction between them. When King Peter, her son-in-law, went to see Bevin the other day, the latter admitted that he disliked the communists, and Tito, who, he declared, had gone back on his word. Balkan royalties must be optimists, otherwise they would cease to work for a return to their miserable thrones. Anyway there is nothing else in the world they can, or are allowed to do.

Tuesday, 11th September

Took the 1.10 train to Cheshire, and was driven from Chelford to stay two nights at Tabley Hall with the Leicester-Warrens, a charming couple, he a little older than my father and married the same year. Both very simple and sweet; she full of prejudices and conventions; he rather less so, but I guess has had a stroke. Their son and heir is the rabbit-faced, chin-less boy, who was at Eton with me. He was mercilessly teased, poor thing, which was beastly. Although I was not one of the bullies, being more of a bullyee, I look back upon his torments with sadness, for he was, and I understand still is, as good as gold. I must say I remember no bullying at Eton among the older boys, only among the 12- and 13-year-olds.

Tabley is of similar size and disposition to Kedleston, consisting of a centre block and two projecting pavilions to the north. There is the sweeping perron on the south side; and, to make the resemblance closer, the Charles II chapel from the island has been re-erected and connected to the north-west pavilion. But it is far coarser and heavier, this Carr house, than the Adam one. The exterior is really uninspiring, and from the distance lumpish, although the material is a pleasant hard, red brick, nicely jointed. The place has the same crumbling look as Kedleston; and is equally doomed. The neglected rooms have the same bloom of mould over them. They contain an unkempt jumble of furniture, not properly dust-sheeted, through lack of servants. The interesting thing about Tabley is that although it was begun in 1762 it is absolutely pre-Adam in detail. Walls and ceilings are very black because it is only fifteen miles from Manchester, and close to Knutsford, still a pretty town. The park is flat and dull. The Old Hall cannot be seen from the house because of the undergrowth on the island. It is also unapproachable because the bridge to it is unsafe. The Brunner-Mond mining for salt brine has caused the Old Hall's collapse.

So all its furniture has been removed and the fine Jacobean chimneypiece taken down and re-inserted in the connecting corridor to the chapel.

The picture gallery of about 1805 is not in itself handsome, but it has several interesting pictures, all badly in need of cleaning: some by Turner, whom the 1st Lord de Tabley patronized, one of Tabley from across the lake: a series of Devises of Tabley, so faint it is diffcult to distinguish the views. The two Romneys of Emma have been sold, but there are paintings by Ward, Cotes, Northcote, all protégés of Lord de Tabley. I did not notice much good furniture, apart from some Chippendale serpentine chests and bedroom stuff, some Regency chairs, a settee from Romney's house in Hampstead. The stairs have a gentle ascent and the brackets are beautifully carved by Shillito. There are good George III chimneypieces and three excellent rococo overmantel glasses. The stable block is plain. There are too many bushes – rhododendrons and shaggy spruce trees – close to the house. The poor Leicester-Warrens don't in the least know what to do with the place, and are too old to adapt themselves to a new form of life in it. A younger generation might find it quite feasible to live in one of the wings, or to let the two wings and ground floor of the centre block for an institution, reserving the *piano nobile* either for use (which I would do) or for show. The *piano nobile* is full of interesting things to see. If Tabley is not on the whole a very refined building, it is nevertheless a great house.

The Leicester-Warrens have a butler and some four indoor servants of sorts. Yet all the wallpapers are torn, the walls damp, and the woodwork in need of paint. What should they do?

Thursday, 13th September

Arrived in London after luncheon. Saw the Coke solicitor who talked of Holkham, and at 6 met Mr. Bradley-Birt, a laughably snobbish, pretentious old gent, who talked about Birtsmorton Court.

Friday, 14th September

National Trust meeting day. Lord Crawford took the chair at the Executive Committee for the first time. He did it well in an easy and engaging manner. He is shy in conversation, yet is a man of stout determination, I would guess. Harold Nicolson and Chorley were elected to the Finance Committee, and Leigh Ashton to the Historic Buildings Committee. I lunched with Esher who told me about his tour. He said Charlecote must be let as a hostel, and only the gatehouse be shown to the public.

Dined at Brooks's with Ben Nicolson, and then taxied to King's Cross where I took the night train to Edinburgh, sitting up in a 1st class, non-smoking compartment.

Arrived 8.30. Breakfasted and established myself in the Railway Hotel. Had a full and successful day. First I visited Adam's Register House and was shown round by a dour Scot, the curator of the public records. Was rather disappointed with this building. Then to the National Library and looked at two manuscript letters of R. Adam. Then to St. Giles's Cathedral, which did not please me greatly. Adam's University however I thought very fine indeed, in particular the street elevation and Playfair's inner court. After luncheon I climbed Carlton Hill, which is Edinburgh's acropolis, with its temple of Lysicrates, etc., and crossing the road, looked at Adam's tomb for David Hume. The city is splendid from this site. A strong, warm wind was chopping the distant sea below the Forth Bridge. Arthur's Seat a prominent feature from here. In the afternoon I walked an unconscionable amount, admiring the architecture of the New Town, George Street, Adam's Charlotte Square. Was duly edified by Steel's memorial to the Prince Consort with sentimental groups at the corners of aristocrats, bureaucrats, peasants and artisans, paying ridiculous homage to him. The iron railings and lamp standards in this square survive intact. There are some truly majestic Squares and Crescents with palatial houses, like those in Moray Place, on a grander scale than Dublin's, Bath's or Brighton's. Edinburgh is a very black city due, I suppose, to the railway line, which really should not be allowed to run in the great valley. After looking at numerous Adam houses I caught an evening train to Berwick.

From Berwick I was driven to Beale foreshore, where I changed into a ramshackle, rusty old car which drove me in the dark across the sands to Holy Island, quite three miles away. Although the tide was out we splashed through water on parts of the causeway, for the sands are never thoroughly dry. Sometimes when the tide is out a horse and cart have to be used, and when the tide is up, a motor boat. There are two lines of posts to guide vehicles, for off the track the sands are treacherous. A weird, open, grey expanse of mudflat with millions of worm-casts, flights of duck over one's head, and pencilled hills in the distance. The car mounts the bank of the island shore, and bumbles along a tolerable road through the little village of Lindisfarne. Beyond the village is Lindisfarne Castle, perched high on an abrupt rock. The car bumps over the grass and stops. Mr. de Stein and a friend were there to greet me. We walked up a cobbled path to the portcullis, and then further steps. A family of islanders looks after the Castle, and serves de Stein whenever he comes here. Jack, known as the uncrowned king, a splendid old man of 77, strong and healthy, with twinkling blue eyes, his wife the cook, their daughter the maid, their son and his wife, and the grandchildren – all live in the castle.

De Stein is a peppery, fussy, schoolmasterish little man, with whom I should hate to have a row. He has not got a good manner. After dinner we had a long talk about mysticism. He recommended a book by William James on the subject. The friend staying is about my age, fair-haired, stocky, an expert botanist who has worked in East Africa, attached in some way to Kew Gardens, and now in the army. Rather nice. I liked him. I can't quite make de Stein out. He is prudish and disapproving, yet he puts his arm round one's waist and makes rapid, sly remarks which I think it best to leave unheeded.

Sunday, 16th September

After breakfast we went sailing in a cockleshell, moored just below the Castle. De Stein began by being rather dictatorial, shouting directions at the islanders, who I sensed knew their business better than he did, and nagging at us. Now I loathe all boats, large and small. I thought the best plan was for me to make a joke of my lack of expertise. It succeeded. He soon laughed when I was caught up in those damned ropes, and getting in everyone's way. The sail began badly for there was a dead calm. Suddenly the wind rose, and we had to reef in a great hurry. There was a good deal of luffing, and getting one's head bashed by the boom, or whatever the piece of swivelling wood is called. We fairly scudded through the water, the keel dashing itself against the advancing waves, almost to breaking point. The warm sun made the oilskin smell deliciously of fish and seaweed. Up and down we tacked alongside St. Cuthbert's little island, looking at wild duck and geese. If it hadn't been for the anxiety of being lassoed by those ropes and dragged under the keel, if it hadn't been for that slight accompaniment of nausea, and if it hadn't been for the fear of making an unutterable fool of myself, I might have enjoyed this expedition. It was a great relief to be on dry land again.

Before luncheon we walked round the Castle. All the furniture was bought from Edward Hudson, and so is good of its sort, the bulk of the sort being oak. De Stein has given the contents to the Trust with the Castle. It is a charming little castle, all stone steps and passageways with low vaulted ceilings. The interior is totally Lutyens. The walls are so thick that winter and summer a fire of logs washed up from wrecks, flotsam and jetsam, has to be kept burning. There is no electric light, but dozens of candles are kept alight even by day. In the afternoon we motored to Bamburgh Castle, and in the rain walked round, but not inside it. It is very large and very much restored. The eleventh-century keep is square like Rochester Castle's. We went into Grace Darling's museum, which is rather touching, containing old hats, jugs and bric-à-brac which she used. She was only in her twenties when she died of consumption. On our return to the shore the car broke down, so we took off our shoes and stockings and walked across the sands between the posts marking the old monks' route, along which the Catholic pilgrims still process behind the priests and bishops, chanting a way to the Priory. Lovely, almost erotic feel of worm-casts under the bare, curling toes.

After dinner de Stein, who is a financier, talked politics. He is pleased that Labour is in, but terribly depressed by the fact that the Trade Unions discourage men from working. For example, they will only allow brick-layers to lay 450 bricks a day, yet they must still work seven hours. This means that good bricklayers have to slack whether they want to or not, and are bored. And who benefits? No one.

Tuesday, 18th September

Travelled to London all yesterday, only having to stand from Berwick to Newcastle, where by dint of bribing the car attendant 2/- I got a seat. Tonight I dined with Colonel Mallaby, the secretary-elect of the N.T. On the whole a sympathetic man. Wondered if he has a strong personality: and decided that one would not perhaps take liberties with him. At least he is human. He gave me a good dinner at the Rag and a lot to drink. I prob-ably talked too much. I liked him, and sensed that he liked me, but I may well be mistaken.

He gave me a few side-lines about the present Cabinet, for he attends all their meetings and takes their minutes. Attlee, he says, is undoubtedly not forceful, yet a man of unimpeachable integrity. At times he can become waspish, and asserts himself. Bevin is, he thinks, made in a big mould, is a true imperialist and may be considered the greatest Foreign Secretary since Palmerston. Most of the Cabinet are men of little calibre, and will soon be superseded by younger men. For instance, Pethick Lawrence sleeps throughout every Cabinet meeting. After Churchill of course Attlee is a flea.

Wednesday, 18th September

Harold dined with me at Brooks's. As Esher said the other day the fiction that Harold is still 'a young man' cannot be substantiated by his jaunty walk and the carnation he wears in his buttonhole. He must be 60, and is such an angelic man that I try not to think of his ever getting old, or dying. He told me in strict confidence this evening that the Government want to make him a peer, and Attlee has spoken to him about it. H. does not want to, and indeed will not be beholden to the Labour Government, yet he would warmly welcome a seat in Parliament. He is keen to remain in pol-itics, and make speeches on the subjects he feels deeply and knows much about, without being subject to any party whip. He wants to be quite independent, and said he could only return to the House of Commons if elected to a University seat. Nigel has been invited to contest his old Leicester seat. Harold said Attlee was undoubtedly a nice man, honest as the day. He thinks highly of Bevin. All good people seem to. H. talked of the N. Trust and will join the Finance Committee, but feels that members of the committees should personally visit any doubtful property before making a pronouncement on its merits or demerits. He takes the view that if he serves he must be prepared to answer any question which might be put to him by a Royal Commission of Enquiry.

Thursday, 20th September

A long day. Trained to Swindon where Eardley met me. We drove to inspect thirty acres at Blunsdon St. Andrews which have been offered to the Trust. They consist of a deserted garden and the ruin of a house in the Gothic style, built of stone in about 1850, and burnt out in 1904. The ruin is romantic, being overgrown with ivy. It has trees pushing a way out of the dining-room windows. But no funds are offered, and we could not hold a garden and woodlands and leave them totally neglected for ever. Then we looked at another doubtful case in Woolstone village at the foot of the White Horse. The cottages offered were nothing out of the ordinary, just white stone with thatched roofs. If the Trust doesn't take them and spend money on them, they will be condemned.

On the way to Clouds Hill in Dorset, E. told me that Wiltshire farmers found the German prisoners would not stop working. They are the best workers they have ever known, far better than the British. He repeated a story told him by someone who was present at Himmler's death. Himmler evidently bit a phial of poison which he was holding in his cheek. After his suicide he was lying on the floor, naked but for a khaki shirt. His face was green and twisted to one side, and he had an enormous erection which persisted for twelve hours after his death. The British troops were so angry with Himmler for having had a quick and apparently pleasant death that they kicked him in the balls.

Clouds Hill, T. E. Lawrence's cottage, is in the middle of Bovington Heath, which is a blasted waste of desolation, churned feet-deep in mud by a thousand army tanks. The cottage is embowered in rhododendrons. It is a pathetic little shoddy place. The visitors have stolen all they could lay their hands on, including the screw of the porthole window in Lawrence's bedroom, and the hasps of the other windows. The bunk gives an idea of his asceticism. Pat Knowles, his batman, is back from abroad. He and his wife, Mrs. Knowles, a pretty, gazelle-like woman, live in another cottage across the way where Lawrence fed with them. They conduct visitors over Clouds Hill, and dare not let them out of their sight for a minute.

Knowles is a high-minded, cultivated proletarian, a youngish 45 with ves-
tiges of gold hair. Bespectacled face now a little puffy, but must once have
been handsome.

Saturday, 22nd September

Lord and Lady Bradford met and conducted me round Castle Bromwich
Hall. It is a fine red-brick house of Elizabethan date with several late-sev-
enteenth-century ceilings of the compartmented, baywreath type,
Wren-ish, deeply undercut and in high relief. Much early and much
William and Mary panelling. The painted ceiling over the staircase by
Laguerre. The house is empty, having been vacated by the troops, and in
consequence is in a filthy mess. Every window, and these were casemented
and quarried, broken by several bombs dropped in the garden. All the
heraldic glass has been destroyed in this way. Yet in other respects surprisingly little structural damage incurred. The most alarming threat to the
building is the dry-rot which is rampant, particularly around the door
behind the hall screen. The garden, now very neglected, is contained
within a brick wall. It has descending terraces, a contemporary maze and
holly hedges in the formal style. I would say it is an important and complete garden of *circa* 1700.

Lord Bradford is a very courteous man, the epitome of good breeding.
Lady B., whom I like, kept snubbing him. He accepted her rebukes
without once answering back. She told him he ought to give the place to
the Trust without any further thought. What was the good, she said, in
letting it to unsatisfactory business firms who had no idea how to look
after it. The family would never want to live in it again. This I think is
incontrovertible. She pointed out that he had let the stable block to some
depot for £100 p.a., out of which he receives, after paying tax, £2.10.0. I
suggested that perhaps Birmingham might have some use for this marvellous old house, still so tranquil, so well sited on its hill and yet now so close
to the city.

On my way to Wickhamford I stopped at our property, Chadwich
Manor, a little 1700 house with walls of red stretchers and purple headers,
and a splendid oak staircase going right to the top attic. The tenants very
friendly and welcoming, he in plumber's overall, smelling like a plumber.
Hideous things in the house.

Monday, 24th September

I met Heywood Hill at Leamington Spa station and drove him to
Charlecote. He spent two days going through the library books, searching for rare volumes, while Brian and Alice and I arranged the rooms. It

must be beastly for them having me and hosts of London officials browsing through and meddling with their brother's possessions. They are so
good about it.

Wednesday, 26th September

Heywood is convinced that Charlecote is eminently worthy, being a
house full of interesting objects, and a collection of portraits displaying the
family's ancient association with the place, a house set in a park of exceptional beauty. Miss Fairfax-Lucy amused him very much by describing the
weird behaviour of her brother, Sir Montgomery, when he stayed with her
for three months. He is so accustomed to solitude and the service of his
black servants in Africa that he cannot reconcile himself to company and
English war-time restrictions. He refused to let her address a word to him
after 6 o'clock, and scolded her for saying 'Good night' because it implied
that he might not have a good night. Brian told us that when at Eton he
was the only boy not allowed home for long leave, his father, Sir Henry,
either disapproving of the unnecessary three-day holiday, or considering
the train fare a waste of money. As children he, his brothers and sisters
were practically starved. They used to walk into Stratford-on-Avon and
flatten their faces against the window panes of the cake shops.

Heywood and I stayed at the King's Head, Wellesbourne, he for one
night, I for two.

At 12 I arrived at Stoneleigh Abbey. Lord Leigh, whom I remember at
Eton, is short, stocky, grey, with pale blue eyes and red veins on his cheeks.
He looks less astute than he certainly is. He has definite and sound ideas
about Stoneleigh, having already divided the house into three flats. He is
going to show the state rooms to the public next year. These state rooms
are comprised in the 1720 Francis Smith block, which is superb. All the
rooms on the *piano nobile* are wainscoted in large oak fielded panels
between robust pilasters with Corinthian capitals. The central saloon has a
heavy ceiling, a little later in date, *circa* 1750 I would guess, just pre-Adam.
Lord Leigh assured me several times that the plasterwork was by Cipriani,
which I find hard to believe unless there was an earlier stuccoist of the
same name as the well-known painter. The chairs, contemporary with the
house, are upholstered either in velvet or petit-point. Many portraits of
Leighs. The bedroom floor suite redecorated in 1850 for Queen
Victoria in white and gold is very pretty. The French furniture and
even the Chippendale chairs were likewise decorated in this manner.
The house is built round a courtyard on Lacock Abbey lines, three sides
of it being Jacobean over twelfth-century undercrofts. The Smith block
is very rich and impressive, though built of porous and friable red sandstone.

Thursday, 27th September

Lunched alone with Kathleen (Kennet) who is more rugged than ever –
her iron grey hair very closely cropped – and more lovable than ever.

After dinner with the Subercaseaux I talked with Paz and the Italian
Ambassador for an hour about conditions in Italy, which he says are
appalling. Firewood costs thousands of lire, and 99 per cent of the inhabitants freeze in the winter. He is a great admirer of the Pope who sits with
a little fur over his knees and hands, because he will not have a fire while
the people are without fuel. The Ambassador told the Pope during his last
audience that the Australians were dissatisfied with not having a Cardinal.
He spoke of the Russian Ambassador here, who will meet no one.
Entering the Soviet Embassy is like being directed into the commonest,
lowest schoolhouse in the East End.

Friday, 28th September

Jamesey is in a gentle, complaisant mood which indicates that he is rather
bored with me. He spends his days in Argyll House going through Lord
Houghton's papers for his biography. He says Lord Houghton's commonplace book contains some revealing low-downs about his early contemporaries – a note that Byron always carried a contraceptive in his waistcoat
pocket – that Bishop Heber was detected 'handling' a peer's son in the
gallery of the House of Lords – that Lord Courtenay paid a butcher boy
£250 for the privilege of kissing his arse – and that Lord John Russell once
woke up in a hotel bedroom to feel the weight of a large woman on top
of him, 'helping herself'.

Saturday, 29th September

I lunched at the Royal Empire Society with Major Ney, who wants me to
sit on a committee for his imperial youth movement. He assures me he is
very interested in Naworth Castle and talks gaily of raising £100,000 to
endow the place, as though it were chicken feed.

Went to tea at Emerald's. Violet Trefusis was there – a large, clumsy, plain
woman wearing a top-heavy hat, and sitting in such a way that one could
see a naked expanse of thigh. Young Giles Romilly was also there. He is
distant and distraught. He told me he had not yet recovered from being a
prisoner of war; that being out of prison has no savour, no matter how
relieved he knows he ought to feel at being free again. It is like wanting to
smoke after a cold. The cigarette tastes of nothing. He is a communist,
which I don't find endearing, but an interesting young man. Although he
can't be more than 25 he has grey streaks in his black hair. He said he hated
society women, the sort that were know-alls, were in the know, in the
swim, had to be 'in with' everything, and were merely pretentious,

pseudo-intellectuals. I asked him why then he mixed with them. He said he only did so to glean material for the novels he hoped to write. I said I too detested the sort of women he described, but all rich and grand women were not like that, nodding at Emerald, whom I never think of as a 'society woman', that hateful term.

When the guests left I stayed talking to Emerald about the world's great novels, about the discontent of the rich and the still greater discontent of the poor. 'It's less sad to be rich,' Emerald concluded. When Emerald gets talking about literature and music, about which she knows so much and which she loves so passionately, I realize that, for all her faults, she is a woman out of the common run. She is almost a phenomenon, and a rare and inspired talker. When she is with company her nonsense can be funnier than any nonsense I have ever enjoyed.

Esher was for once wrong when he criticized her yesterday. She shocked him by telling him how she took off her shoes to show her beautiful feet to a young man. 'Just fancy an old woman of eighty-two doing a thing like that,' he said. I said I thought it was enchanting of Emerald, for her feet are still beautiful, and her spontaneity is beautiful. Lady E. on this occasion asked if she might call me James, since everyone else seemed to do so. I said I was delighted with the concession, for James was well on the way to Jim, which my friends called me. Lord E. chuckled, for out of policy he steadfastly calls me Mr. L.-M. 'If we were on Christian name terms,' he said, 'it would be very awkward if I had to sack you.'

Sunday, 30th September

Malcolm [Bullock] dined at Brooks's. He told me he had just seen Sibyl Colefax, who asked him how he was. He replied that he was quite well, apart from his varicose veins. When she asked him why he had varicose veins, he said they were caused by his having to stand whenever he came to see me. Sibyl did not cotton on to the allusion, that her firm has not yet delivered my sofa, which it has been re-upholstering for months and months.

Monday, 1st October

This morning I went – oh never mind where. It is not interesting. Besides, my old typewriter has broken down, and I have cut the index finger of my right hand. Besides too, the war is over to all intents and purposes, so this diary ought to have an end. Its background was the war. Its only point was the war.

And the war is over now – to all intents and purposes – isn't it?

Index